Religion in America

ADVISORY EDITOR

Edwin S. Gaustad

THE HISTORY

OF THE

SOCIETY OF FRIENDS

IN

AMERICA

By JAMES BOWDEN

Volumes I and II

ARNO PRESS

A NEW YORK TIMES COMPANY

New York • 1972

Reprint Edition 1972 by Arno Press Inc.

Reprinted from a copy in
The State Historical Society of Wisconsin Library

RELIGION IN AMERICA - Series II
ISBN for complete set: 0-405-04050-4
See last pages of this volume for titles.

Manufactured in the United States of America

Library of Congress Cataloging in Publication Data

Bowden, James, b. 1811.
    The history of the Society of Friends in America.

    (Religion in America, series II)
    Reprint of the 1850-54 ed.
    1. Friends, Society of--History. I. Title.
BX7635.B6 1972   289.6'73   73-38440
ISBN 0-405-04061-X

THE HISTORY

OF THE

SOCIETY OF FRIENDS

IN

AMERICA.

LONDON :
RICHARD BARRETT, PRINTER,
MARK LANE.

THE HISTORY

OF THE

SOCIETY OF FRIENDS

IN

AMERICA.

By JAMES BOWDEN.

" Whatsoever is born of God overcometh the world : and this is the victory that overcometh the world, even our faith.

" Who is he that overcometh the world, but he that believeth that Jesus is the Son of God ?"—1 JOHN v. 4, 5.

VOL. I.

LONDON:

CHARLES GILPIN, 5, BISHOPSGATE STREET WITHOUT.

1850.

LONDON:
RICHARD BARRETT, PRINTER,
MARK LANE.

PREFACE.

To investigate the rise and to trace the progress of a particular section of the religious community is an interesting object, and when it has reference to a people such as the Society of Friends, whose principles and practices so prominently distinguish them among others of the Christian name, the interest of such a pursuit becomes greatly enhanced. The design of the following sheets is to record the history of this people in America,—a country in which they experienced the extremes of entire freedom of conscience on the one hand, and cruel religious persecution on the other.

There exist at the present time on the North American continent nearly six hundred distinct religious assemblies of the Society of Friends, scattered over the region extending from Canada and Maine in the north, to the Carolinas and Tennessee in the South, and from its cities and ports on the Atlantic, to the countries lying west of the Mississippi. These compose in all seven separate and independent Yearly Meetings, and form in the aggregate four-fifths of the whole number of this people in the world. The consideration of this fact is calculated therefore to excite an inquiry such as that to which this work is devoted.

It is true, that no inconsiderable portions of the valuable histories both of Sewel and Gough, have reference to the proceedings of Friends in America. The details, however, which these furnish are confined principally to the sufferings of some of their early members or ministers in New England, and to transactions of the Society within the limits of Pennsylvania and the Jerseys. The present work embraces a much wider field, and aims to exhibit a distinct history of each individual Yearly Meeting of Friends in America from its rise down to a period comparatively recent.

The new and unpublished materials relating to the Society of Friends in the western world, which, under many favourable circumstances the writer has been enabled to collect from various sources on both sides of the Atlantic, together with an easy access to numerous printed works of ancient date and of great scarcity, have placed within his reach the means of effecting the object to a much larger extent than he could have anticipated. And here he desires to acknowledge the kind and valuable assistance which he has derived both from meetings and individuals, in the readiness with which they have allowed him access to MSS., including some thousands of letters of early Friends; with other important historical documents of more recent date.

In studying the history of the Society of Friends, it has appeared to the author important, rightly to understand the religious character and condition of the population amongst which our early Friends arose. With this view the chapter on the discovery and colonization of North America has been introduced, and though somewhat extended, it is hoped that its details will not be considered inappropriate.

It had been intended also to accompany this work with an

introductory essay on the various dispensations of Divine Providence to man, and to notice the remarkable series of events, by which way was gradually prepared for the introduction into the world of the religion of our Lord and Saviour Jesus Christ, as well as to give a brief view of the history of the Christian church down to the time of George Fox; but, as observations of this kind appear to be more suited to a general history of Friends, they have not been introduced into this more restricted work. Before passing from this subject, however, it may be remarked, that a prominent object in penning the essay in question, was to show that the Protestant Reformation and the subsequent rise of the Puritan professors of Christianity, were circumstances in the overruling providences of the Divine Hand, calculated to prepare the hearts of many for the reception of those spiritual and primitive doctrines of the Christian religion, which George Fox and his associates enunciated and revived, after the long and dark night of the Romish apostacy. In tracing the history of Christianity, the reflective mind cannot fail, we think, to be impressed with the gradually progressive nature of the Divine dispensations. It might be expected that in treating upon the history of a particular section of the Christian church, some systematic account would appear of the religious views by which it is distinguished; but for the reasons just advanced, in the present instance it has not been attempted.

In reading this history there may be those who in reference to some of its early chapters, may think that the cruel and anti-christian conduct exhibited by some of the religious bodies in America towards Friends might have been revived with less prominence, in deference to the feelings of those,

who, although professing the same religious opinions, now
entertain views far different.from those of their predecessors,
as to the toleration of individual sentiment in religion.   But
the historian, to be faithful to his trust, cannot with justice
listen to such pleadings, however congenial they may be to his
own feelings.   It is his duty to lay before the reader the
transactions of the times, without considerations of this sort.
If such an objection were admitted, it would apply not only
to all ecclesiastical history, but to general history also, and
it will at once be seen that the practical carrying out of the
principle alluded to, would render histories extremely partial
and unsatisfactory.

Others again in perusing these pages, may be inclined to
censure as stubborn and self-willed, the conduct of those
who exhibited on many occasions, their inflexible adherence
to conscientious conviction.   It was observed of Friends in
the time of George Fox, that they were *as stiff as trees.*
Their refusal to pay tithes, to perform military service, to take
oaths, &c., in the sure prospect of sufferings, gave rise to this
remark.   This particular trait in the character of Friends,
has been maintained from their rise, with greater or smaller
exception, down to the present day.   Clarkson, in noticing
this uncompromising characteristic, thus speaks, " It has been
an established rule with them, from the formation of the
Society, not to temporize, or violate their conscience ; or, in
other words, not to do that which, as a body of Christians,
they believe to be wrong, though the usages of the world, or
the government of the country under which they live, should
require it; but rather to submit to the frowns and indignation of the one, and the legal penalties annexed to their
disobedience by the other." After alluding to the testimony

which Friends bear against what they believe to be wrong, he proceeds, " this noble practice of *bearing testimony*, by which a few individuals attempt to stem the torrent of immorality, by opposing themselves to its stream; and which may be considered as a living martyrdom, does, in a moral point of view, a great deal of good to those who conscientiously adopt it. It recalls first principles to their minds. It keeps in their remembrance the religious rights of man. It teaches them to reason upon principle, and to make their estimates by a moral standard. It is productive both of patience and of courage. It occasions them to be kind, and attentive, and merciful to those who are persecuted and oppressed. It throws them into the presence of Divinity, when they are persecuted themselves. In short, it warms their moral feelings, and elevates their religious thoughts. Like oil it keeps them from rusting. Like a whet-stone, it gives them a new edge. Take away this practice from the constitution of the members of this Society, and you pull down a considerable support of their moral character." " It is a great pity," he continues, " that, as professing Christians, we should not more of us incorporate this noble principle individually into our religion. We concur unquestionably in customs, through the fear of being reputed singular, of which our hearts do not always approve; though nothing is more true, than that a Christian is expected to be singular, with respect to the corruptions of the world. What an immensity of good would be done, if cases of persons, choosing rather to suffer than to temporize, were so numerous as to attract the general notice of men! Would not every case of suffering, operate as one of the most forcible lessons that could be given, to those who should see it? And how long would that infamous system have to live, which makes a distinction between political expediency and moral right ?"*

In the course of this history the reader will meet with many biographical sketches of the lives of those who were prominently and devotedly engaged in promoting the Redeemer's kingdom in the western world, by the public advocacy of the simple and spiritual views of this Society. The Christian constancy, the inflexible perseverance, the meekness, the patience, and the holy resignation exhibited by them, under a variety of trying circumstances, and many of them under a most cruel and barbarous persecution, and in some cases even to the taking away of their lives, offer to the world an undeniable testimony to the unfailing support of the faithful in the everlasting power of Jehovah, and to the consolations and joys experienced by the true believers in Christ.

With a view the more distinctly to point out the geographical situation of meetings and places, and to enable the reader the more readily to trace the course of those who travelled in gospel labours in America, maps and plans will be occasionally introduced. Fac-similes of original documents and of letters of early Friends, will also be given.

In conclusion, the writer would observe, that if in the following pages he has been successful in furnishing his friends with reading from which they may derive instruction, and of inducing among them, more especially the younger classes of the Society, an increased interest in the history of their own people, he will have the pleasing reflection that his labours have not been in vain.

London, Ninth Month, 1850.

* Portraiture of Quakerism, vol. iii. p. 198.

A MAP
of the
ENGLISH COLONIES
in
North America,
IN 1656.

THE HISTORY

OF THE

SOCIETY OF FRIENDS IN AMERICA

CHAPTER I.

America unknown to the Ancients—Icelandic MS. accounts of Northmen—The discovery of America by Columbus and Cabot—The expedition of Cortereal, a PORTUGUESE, to North America—He kidnaps
the Indians for slaves—The FRENCH attempt to form colonies under
Verazzani and Cartier—The emigration of the French Huguenots and
Romanists—The SPANIARDS endeavour to plant settlements in Florida,
under Ponce de Leon, Narvaez, Fernando de Soto, and Don Pedro
Melendez—The ENGLISH, under Gilbert and Raleigh, attempt to establish colonies in Carolina—The settlement of Virginia—The character
of the settlers—Disastrous conflict with the Indians—The introduction of Negro Slavery—The persecution of the Puritans in England—
James I. grants them a charter for a province in New England—
They settle at Plymouth—The Massachusetts Company—The religious
intolerance of the Puritans in America—Their character—Their
persecutions in Massachusetts—Roger Williams is exiled, and forms
a settlement at Providence—Anne Hutchinson and the Antinomians
are banished, and establish a colony on Rhode Island—The persecution and banishment of the Baptists by the Puritans—The colonization of New Hampshire and Connecticut—The Dutch settle at
New York—The Swedish colony of Delaware—Maryland colonized by
Papists and others, under Lord Baltimore—Carolina and its government under Locke's "Constitutions;" its success under John Archdale, a Friend—Recapitulation—Concluding remarks.

THE geography of Europe, Asia, and Africa, appears to have
been well understood by the ancients, but they entertained not
the remotest idea of the existence of the vast continent of

America. Who were the first discoverers of the western world, still remains doubtful. "The Royal Society of Northern Antiquaries," at Copenhagen, a few years since, published a work to prove that Northmen, in the tenth century, were its original discoverers. The work is compiled chiefly from Icelandic historical manuscripts. Much doubt has been thrown on the authenticity of these ancient documents, yet no sufficient reason has been shown, for altogether rejecting the conclusion that the North American continent was visited by Northmen, although great uncertainty exists as to the portion of the coast on which they may have landed. No desire, however, of inquiring into the secrets of the Atlantic, arose, until suggested towards the close of the fifteenth century by the surpassing genius of Christopher Columbus, a native of Genoa.

Columbus, under the auspices of Isabella of Spain, set sail in the Sixth Month of 1492, on the maritime enterprise, which has so remarkably signalized his name. He conceived the idea that it was practicable to reach the distant and unknown shores of eastern Asia, by crossing the Atlantic, but without any expectation that this attempt would lead to the discovery of a new continent. After a sail of two months, he descried one of the Bahama Islands, and subsequently discovered Cuba and Hayti ; but returned without touching the continent of America. In the Ninth Month of the following year, this enterprising navigator left the shores of Spain on a second western expedition ; but his voyage extended no further than two of the Caribbee Islands, Puerto Rico, and Jamaica. A third expedition followed, and early in 1498, he touched that part of the continent of South America, near which the Orinoco pours its vast stream into the Mexican Gulf.

The achievements of Columbus appear to have kindled in the hearts of the emulous, a desire for renown similar to that which characterized his name, and in the year 1496, John Cabot obtained from Henry VII., for himself and three sons, a patent for discovery and conquest of unknown lands. John Cabot was a Venetian merchant, who resided occasionally in Bristol. Little is known of his history further than that he was wealthy, intelligent, and fond of maritime discovery. Sebastian his son, was born in Bristol in 1477. With his son Sebastian he set sail from Bristol, and in the Fourth Month of the same year came in sight of the cliffs of Labrador. No account of this voyage has been preserved, further than the statement of this discovery; it is supposed, however, that the navigators returned pretty directly to England, an opinion which is corroborated by the following entry in the privy purse expenses of Henry VII.— " 10th August, 1497. To hym that found the New Isle £10." If we reject the claims of the Danish antiquarians for the Northmen of the tenth century, to the Cabots must be attributed the first discovery of the western continent, being fourteen months before Columbus, on his third voyage, touched the shore of that part now termed Columbia, and almost two years before the coasts of South America were explored by Amerigo Vespucci; from whom, under the supposition that he was the earliest discoverer of the New World, the name of America is derived.

A second western voyage was undertaken by Sebastian Cabot in the spring of 1498, but with reference to commerce more than to discovery. In this enterprise Henry VII. was a partner. Cabot again reached the coast of Labrador, and turning southward, proceeded along the shores of the Continent about as far as Albemarle Sound in North Carolina.

As it is not within the design of the present work to particularise all the enterprises of those, who, from different motives, soon made their way to the newly discovered continent; but merely, by way of introduction, to sketch an outline of the discovery and colonization of North America, it will be sufficient for this purpose briefly to allude to some of the most striking of these adventures.

Following the second expedition of the Cabots, the next important discovery was made in 1500, by Gaspar Cortereal, a Portuguese. Having reached Newfoundland, he sailed northward until he came to a long range of coast; to which, in reference to the ability of the natives for labour, he gave the name of Labrador. It is stated, that he found the country covered with timber, and that its Indian inhabitants were a robust and hardy race.

Cortereal seeing that they were well fitted for labour, captured fifty-three of them, whom he sold as slaves on his return to Portugal. Trafficking in the bodies of men was an enormity, with which the Portuguese had, for more than half a century, made themselves familiar ; and to that nation must be attributed the lasting disgrace of having been the first to connect the abominations of the Slave-trade with the American continent. It is said that this navigator perished in an affray with the Indians, in a second voyage which he undertook for the purpose of kidnapping more of them. These voyages of Gaspar Cortereal are all that history records of PORTUGUESE expeditions to North America.

The FRENCH, though less of a maritime nation than either the Spanish or Portuguese, were desirous of participating in the advantages, which territorial conquest might afford them in the new world. With this view, Francis I. employed Juan Verazzani, a skilful Florentine navigator, to sail for its distant shores. Passing by way of Madeira, and having encountered a severe tempest, Verazzani, in the Eleventh Month 1523, came in sight of the coast of North Carolina, and sailing northward, he entered the inlets which afterwards became the harbours of New York and Newport. The land which he passed, being covered with gentle and finely wooded hills, reminded him of Rhodes, and from hence may be traced the derivation of Rhode Island. The expedition continuing its course northward, proceeded as far as Nova Scotia. While the natives of Carolina welcomed the strangers to their shores, those of the northern region were hostile and suspicious. The visits of the Portuguese to the latter, for the nefarious object of procuring slaves, are sufficient to explain this difference.

The voyage of Verazzani which extended along seven hundred miles of coast, including a large portion of the present United States, and most of British North America, gave to the French some claim to a considerable extent of territory, on the assumption of discovery ; and with the desire of exploring still further and of settling colonies in those parts, an expedition for these purposes was formed under Cartier in 1534, and another in 1541. These and several other subsequent attempts of the French nation to plant colonies in North America, entirely failed, until the settlement at Port Royal, now Annapolis, in 1605, under De Monts, a Calvinist. He obtained from the French king permission for the free exercise of religion, for himself, and for those Huguenot emigrants who accompanied him. The French Catholics, whose attention was directed to the new settlement, became anxious to proselyte the Indians to their religion, and the arrival of Jesuits with this express object, quickly followed. Biart and De Beincourt of this order, went to reside among the Indians of the Algonquin race, and were successful in inducing the Penobscot and other native tribes of Maine, to embrace the Popish religion, which to this day is professed by the New England Indians. Under Champlain, monks from France also found their way to Canada, but the presence of these proselyting Romanists led to dissensions between them and the Calvinists, which impeded the success of the colony. The French, during their settlement in Canada, having quarrelled with the English, were driven from their possessions, but they were reinstated by treaty in 1632. The extension of American colonization was now undertaken by the French with increased vigour, and under the direction of Champlain in 1642, a chain of settlements was formed, extending from Quebec to Montreal, and in a few years after as far west as the shores of Lake Ontario.

Whilst the French were endeavouring to extend their territories on this vast continent, the SPANIARDS, encouraged by their successes in the South, strove also for territorial acquisitions in North America. In 1512, on the day called Palm Sunday, or in Spanish, " Pasqua Florida," Ponce de Leon, an enterprising Spaniard, discovered an extensive range of country crowned with magnificent forest, and to this, in honour of the day on which he discovered it, he gave the name of Florida. Returning to Spain, he obtained authority from the king to lead an expedition to the country he had discovered. This object however he did not live to accomplish, but died on his passage thither. Notwithstanding the death of Ponce de Leon, the expedition proceeded, and soon found its way to Florida, but no attempt at colonization appears to have been made by the adventurers, and little is known of the result of this and some other expeditions of the Spaniards, except that they followed the example of their neighbours the Portuguese, in the iniquitous practice of kidnapping the unsuspecting Indians for slaves. The idea of planting a colony in Florida, was a favourite one with the Spaniards, and in 1528, they made another attempt, on a considerable scale ; no less than six hundred men in five vessels, having embarked for the object under Narvaez, a distinguished adventurer of the time. The people in this expedition, being regarded by the natives as invaders of their country, were met on their landing by signs of much opposition, but fear of European power soon caused the Indians to retreat into the depths of their unknown forests. Under the impression that golden treasures existed in the country, Narvaez determined to explore the interior. To their dismay, however, they found their hopes of wealth, a perfect chimera, and, after traversing a rugged and mountainous country, interspersed with extensive lagoons and marshes, and maintaining frequent conflicts with the exasperated Indians, a remnant only of the inland party returned to relate their sad adventures.

The calamitous issue of the attempt of Narvaez, so far from extinguishing the desire for colonial enterprise in the new country, seems to have led to more determined efforts for its prosecution. In 1539, Fernando de Soto, who had accompanied Pizarro in his Peruvian invasion, formed the bold idea of settling a kingdom in Florida, with himself for its supreme head, and with this view he sailed from Spain with nine hundred adventurers. Aware of the disasters which had befallen those who had preceded him, in consequence of the hostility of the natives, Soto was anxious to avoid a similar danger by endeavouring to conciliate them. The hatred of the Indians towards their heartless invaders, was, however too deep to be effaced by professions of Spanish friendship, and the attempts to reconcile them entirely failed. " If they were honest," replied the natives, " they would stay at home and cultivate their own soil, instead of coming to distant climates to expose themselves by their robberies, to the execration of mankind." After a long and disastrous attempt to find mineral wealth in North America, Soto died in Florida, and his party, having concluded to abandon the country, made their way to Mexico.

Notwithstanding that the Spaniards made many efforts to plant colonies in North America, not a single permanent settlement had been formed by them until 1565, when Don Pedro Melendez received a commission from Philip II. to make another trial, and also to extirpate as heretics, some Huguenots who had landed in Florida. Melendez sailed, and crossing the Atlantic, took up his position on the river (St.) Augustine, and founded the town now known by that name. Excepting those on the Mexican isthmus, (St.) Augustine therefore may be considered as the oldest European settlement on the continent of North America. The Spaniards kept possession of Florida for two centuries from this date, but with scarcely any extension of their settlement, and as late as 1830 this country, containing an area somewhat greater than all England, had a population of only about 19,000 free persons. The love of this people for gold, which they had so easily and so abundantly obtained in Peru and Mexico, unfitted them for colonizing those countries in which agricultural labour only was available, and to this cause may be attributed the failure of the Spanish to extend their settlements in North America.

The ENGLISH, though the discoverers of America, were evidently less earnest than either the French or Spaniards to form settlements in that country. This may be partly accounted for by the circumstance, that the public mind was much occupied on the subject of the Protestant Reformation, and some other topics of an engrossing character; it would be difficult otherwise to understand why nearly a century should have passed away before any considerable effort was made by them to plant a colony in the newly discovered world. Sir Humphrey Gilbert, a man of distinguished rank, was the first to form a plan for settling an English colony in North America, an enterprise in which he was much encouraged and assisted by Sir Walter Raleigh. He put to sea in 1583, with five vessels, containing in all two hundred and sixty persons, " skilled in every faculty;" of whom carpenters, masons, and more particularly those skilled in working and refining metals, formed a considerable part. In about three months the expedition reached the banks of Newfoundland, where Gilbert found no less than thirty-six vessels busily engaged in the fishery ; over these he assumed an absolute control, and by virtue of the patent granted to him by Elizabeth, he claimed a territory extending two hundred miles from the harbour of (St.) John's, where he then happened to be. In pursuance of the more immediate object of his voyage, he quitted Newfoundland, and bent his course for the south, but from this time he encountered a series of disasters, which prevented him from landing on the coast, and after witnessing the wreck of one of his vessels, and the departure of two others for England on account of sickness, Gilbert prudently determined to return home. On the passage they were overtaken by a hurricane, in which Gilbert's vessel suddenly disappeared, leaving but a small one reduced almost to a wreck, which returned alone.

The disastrous result of Sir Humphrey Gilbert's expedition did not discourage the English from making another attempt to gain a footing in the New World. Raleigh, who was a man of distinguished genius and enterprise, undertook at his sole expense a grand scheme for the purpose. His first step was to send out two small vessels to explore the coasts ; and these, favoured with a successful voyage, reached the shores of North Carolina in safety. The natives, who were described as " handsome men, and very courteous in their demeanour," soon flocked to the vessels, and were treated with much kindness. After coasting a little further along North Carolina, the exploring party returned, and reported that " the soil was the most plentiful, sweet, fruitful and wholesome of all the world," and that the natives were " most gentle, loving and faithful, void of all guile and treason." Raleigh was delighted with the favourable account, and the nation looked forward with high expectations to the undeveloped treasures of the new continent. Queen Elizabeth, gratified with the prospect of thus extending her dominions, accepted the honour of giving a name to the promising country, and as a memorial of her single state of life, it was named VIRGINIA.

Raleigh now lost no time in preparing another expedition, and at the expense of nearly all his fortune, (for Elizabeth was too cautious and penurious to expend the public money in this way) he equipped, in 1585, a fleet of seven vessels, containing one hundred and eight colonists, placing them under the command of Greenville, a man of considerable ability. The vessels reached Virginia in safety, and after exploring the coast for more than two hundred miles, the emigrants landed at Roanoke. "We have discovered the main," remarks one of them, "to be the goodliest soil under the cope of heaven. It is the goodliest and most pleasing territory of the world ; for the soil is of a huge unknown greatnesse, and very well peopled and towned, though savagely."* The English had not long occupied Roanoke ere they unhappily commenced a hostile course towards the natives. In their early conflicts with these sons of the forest, they were enabled by the use of fire-arms to drive them into the woods, but they soon found to their dismay that they had made a dangerous and terrible foe of the North American Indian. The tribes of Carolina rightly estimating the strength of their new enemy, united for the purpose of driving the English from their country, and had not Drake arrived with a fleet in which the colonists were conveyed home, the result would doubtless have been fatal to them all.

Raleigh, thoughtful of his Virginian enterprise, had dispatched a vessel laden with stores for the colonists, but ere the ship arrived, Roanoke had been deserted. In another fortnight Greenville came with three ships and about fifty new settlers, but great was his disappointment on finding the settlement entirely unpeopled ; unwilling, however, that the English should forfeit their right to the country, he left fifteen of his men to keep possession of Roanoke, and returned to England. These were dispiriting circumstances to Raleigh, but he was not dismayed by them. His opinion of the importance and value of founding a colony in the New World was decided, and he determined to use every endeavour to accomplish it. The fame of

---

* Lane, in Hakluyt, iii. p. 311.

the country made it easy to procure emigrants, and a new expedition was accordingly planned, to which Raleigh granted a charter of incorporation, and in the summer of 1587, it reached Roanoke. Here the new adventurers searched in vain for the men left by Greenville, but the human bones scattered around left no doubt that they had perished by the hands of the natives. The new emigrants, consisting of eighty-nine men and seventeen women, fondly anticipating that they were settling a State in the new world, began the foundation of a city, which they named Raleigh. The settlers, however, soon began to entertain gloomy apprehensions for the future, and their governor was sent to England to use his persuasion for fresh reinforcements and supplies. More than a year passed away before he returned, and then to his astonishment he found the island of Roanoke a second time deserted, and the city of Raleigh without a single European. What became of the settlers still remains a mystery, but it is conjectured that, being reduced to extreme distress, they were hospitably adopted into the tribe of Hatteras Indians. The later physical character of the tribe, and a tradition existing among its descendants are adduced in confirmation of this supposition.

The colonization of America by the English after Raleigh's disasters lay dormant for many years, but the additional accounts which were furnished by navigators, of its fertility and beauty, gave at length a new impulse to the adventurous to seek a home in the new world. In 1606, a patent was granted to some wealthy Londoners for planting a colony in Virginia, and another to some enterprising noblemen in the west of England. The patent of the London company comprehended the present territory of Maryland, Virginia, and Carolina ; and the other, called the Plymouth adventurers, the country north of Maryland. The attempts of the Plymouth company proved a failure until the Puritans undertook it in 1620, but the London, or more properly the Virginian company, were more successful. In 1606, preparations were made by the latter on a larger scale than in any preceding effort of the English for such an object. Three ships were fitted out, and in the early part of 1607 anchored safely in Chesapeake Bay. From thence the emigrants ascended a river, and founded a town on its banks, to which, in honour of the reigning sovereign, they gave the name of James's Town. For several years the colony proceeded but slowly, and with much difficulty, arising partly from constant collisions with the irritated natives, and partly from the class of persons who had emigrated, whom the governor described as " poor gentlemen, tradesmen, serving-men, libertines, and such like, ten times more fit to spoil a commonwealth, than either to begin or maintain one." Proceeding as many of these people did, with extravagant hopes of accumulating wealth, they paid but little attention to those pursuits which were necessary to draw subsistence even from the fertile soil of Virginia. The transportation of criminals to the settlement was another source of evil, tending to lower the moral tone of the colony, and to these unfavourable circumstances may be added the political strife by which the province was distracted in the time of Charles I. and the Commonwealth. The restoration of the monarchy was, however, the commencement of a more auspicious era for the colony, many persons preferring to leave England, and proving to be useful settlers. In 1660, being more than half a century from its foundation, it had only 10,000 inhabitants, but ten years later it could number 40,000.

In the early settlement of Virginia, it had been specially enacted, that the religion of the colony, should be according to the doctrines and rites of the Church of England. Subsequently, however, Puritans from New England, attracted by the fertility of the land, found their way to the country, and so much religious liberty was permitted, that large numbers were preparing to follow them : but English intolerance interfered ; and in 1643, under the administration of Sir W. Berkley, it was enacted that no minister should preach or teach, publicly or privately, except in conformity to the English Church.* The passing of this measure was soon followed by the banishment of Nonconformists. Yet the settlers, though mostly Episcopalians, and favourable to the cause of the Royalists, were glad to avail themselves of the increase of political liberty, under the Protectorate ; a new order

* Act 64. Heming, i. p. 277.

of things, in regard to religious freedom, followed as a consequence of this change, and, but for an act in 1658, by which Friends were banished, and their return was deemed to be felony,* religious toleration would have been nearly complete in Virginia.

The right of the Indians to their native soil was a principle never recognised by the Virginians, the claims of justice were overlooked and trampled on, and the tribes of that territory, being alarmed for the safety of their hunting grounds, conceived the horrible idea of exterminating their invaders. The plan was contrived, and kept in great secrecy, and in the Third Month, 1618, the irritated and revengeful Algonquin, fell upon the unsuspecting settlers, and in one hour, destroyed 347 of those located on the banks of James's river. Providentially, a converted Indian had revealed the plot to the inhabitants of James's Town the night before, otherwise it is probable that the whole colony would have perished. The effect of this sudden carnage was most disastrous to the rising colony. At the time of the massacre it had more than 4000 English, but within a year, they were reduced to nearly one-half that number. The feelings of alarm which prompted the settlers to abandon their new homes, on this outbreak of the angry natives, soon gave way to those of revenge, and in return, a war of extermination being commenced against the Indians, drove them into the fastnesses of the interior. But, notwithstanding this, the natives in 1644, made another sudden attack, and killed three hundred of the colonists.

Before concluding the sketch of this first permanent settlement of the English in America, we must not omit to notice the introduction of negro slavery. In 1620, a Dutch ship of war entered James's river, and offered twenty negroes for sale. The settlers unhappily bought them ; and thus commenced in America an iniquitous system, the baneful effects of which on the temporal and religious interests of the colony, it is impossible to estimate. To what extent negro slavery in America has been the means of retarding the spread of vital religion in the earth,

* Norwood in Bancroft, i. p. 532.

is known only to Him who is omniscient, but we may be well assured that it has been great, and, that the responsibility of introducing and upholding such a cruel outrage on humanity, and which so violates the rights of man, must be tremendous.   To Virginia then, attaches the indelible stain of being the first to promote on the North American continent, the sin of negro slavery.   In tracing the future history of the American colonies, it is not difficult to perceive that the rod of divine displeasure has signally rested on this guilty state, furnishing to mankind another teaching lesson, that the surest guarantee for the ultimate success and prosperity of a people, is an uncompromising adherence to the law of universal righteousness.

For more than a century after the discovery of the Western World, the English had landed on its shores, comparatively speaking, but a mere handful of people.   After repeated failures, the colonization of Virginia, under the management of the London company, led to great expectations ; but it was reserved for the Puritans to give the greatest impulse to the tide of emigration to the new country.

The Reformation in England had never been accompanied by a full toleration of individual sentiment in matters of religion, and hence may be dated the establishment of the colonies in NEW ENGLAND.   The Nonconformist emigrants to that region, were individuals, who contended for a more thorough reformation in religion, than that recognized by Queen Elizabeth.   They were dissatisfied with the pompous display of the Anglican Church, and regarded it as a remnant of the Romish apostacy.   The use of organs and other instruments of music in the time of public worship, the prohibition of extemporaneous prayer, the bowing at the name of Jesus, the use of the surplice and other priestly vestments, together with the liturgy and the various distinctions of rank among the ministers of religion, were among the leading grounds of dissent held by this class of English Reformers.   The Protestants of England thus became divided into two parties, the one pleading for greater purity and simplicity in the church, and the other for entire conformity to the reformed religion as recognized by law.   The latter being the more powerful of the two, soon had recourse to the civil power in the enforcement of their views. In 1554 an "Act of Conformity" was passed, and at the instigation of Elizabeth in 1593, another act of greater severity followed, including provisions for penalties and imprisonments, and even for capital punishment, against those who refused to conform to the usages of the church established by law.

The enactments for enforcing conformity to the Anglican church, drove the Puritan party to speak openly of secession, and at last in 1572, they formed a separate congregation. The laws against nonconformists were now cruelly enforced, numbers were banished the country, and two were even hanged at Tyburn. The persecuted Puritans finding that Holland afforded them a refuge, fled thither, and a congregation of them was formed at Amsterdam ; but the intermarriages of their members with Dutch families decreased their numbers, and this, with some other considerations, led most of the younger part of their church to resolve on a removal to America. An application for a grant of land was accordingly obtained, and was sanctioned by King James ; but he refused to enter into any stipulation for the free exercise of their religion ; saying, that "if they demeaned themselves quietly, no inquiry would be made." In the summer of 1620, one hundred persons, having about £2,400 in goods and provisions, embarked as exiles, seeking a new home on the western shores of the Atlantic. After a voyage of two months, they arrived in the harbour of Cape Cod, in sight of the most barren part of Massachusetts. The country on which they landed, had, a few years before, been rendered a lonely desert by a pestilence which had swept over it. Wigwams were found, but their tenants had disappeared ; the rising smoke in the distance, however, indicated that the Indian was not far off,—a fact which was soon confirmed by the sound of the war-whoop, for the natives knew the European only as the kidnapper of their race. After exploring the country, the emigrants chose a spot, as the most inviting on which to form a settlement, and to this they gave the name of Plymouth. The winter was passed in endurance of extreme privation, and ere another summer's sun had beamed upon the little company, one-half of their number had closed their earthly career. In imitation of the primitive Chris-

was repugnant to the spirit of true religion. Roger Williams of Salem, " a young minister godly and zealous," was one of this class, and one who did not hesitate boldly to declare, that " the doctrine of persecution for cause of conscience, is most evidently and lamentably contrary to the doctrine of Christ." The presence of every man at public worship in New England was insisted upon, but this, Roger Williams contended, was an invasion of the natural rights of the subject. Doctrines thus openly professed and promulgated, were viewed as treason by the ministers of Massachusetts, and at length, in 1635, the magistrates resolved to banish Williams, as a disturber of the order of church and state. Exiled from his friends, Roger Williams sought shelter among the Indians of Narragansett Bay. They received him gladly. " The ravens," he remarked, "fed me in the wilderness." He determined upon founding a new colony, and acknowledging the rights of the native inhabitant to the soil; he purchased a territory, and established a new colony. Roger Williams thus became the founder of an American plantation, and pursuing an enlightened and Christian course, he founded it on the principles of absolute religious freedom. A spot having been selected for a settlement, he began to build, and in commemoration of the mereies of the Most High, he called it Providence, desiring that it might be " a shelter for persons of distressed conscience."* The liberal policy of the founder of this settlement was duly appreciated, and he soon had the satisfaction of welcoming to the wilds of Narragansett, " godly people from England, who apprehended a special hand of Providence in raising this plantation, and whose hearts were stirred to come over." Its English population consequently increased rapidly.

Scarcely had the first dwellings in Providence been tenanted by the exiles from Massachusetts, ere that intolerant colony was subjected to a new schism. A Calvinistic sect, entertaining the notion that the Puritans of New England placed a dangerous reliance on the strictness and severity of their lives for salvation, and that the doctrine of justification by faith alone, constituted the true ground of the Christian's hope, gave rise to this division.

* Backus, i. p. 94, in Bancroft.

Anne Hutchinson, a woman of great eloquence and ability was the leader of these Antinomians, and Harry Vane, then governor of the province, and who afterwards became so conspicuous in England, identified himself with their cause. A furious controversy between the ministers and the Hutchinsonians took place. The former convened a synod, which, after declaring the orthodoxy of the New England church, proceeded to denounce Anne Hutchinson and her party, " as unfit for society," and to exile them from the province. The larger portion of the new sect, headed by William Coddington, in 1637 proceeded southward, and with the assistance of Roger Williams, succeeded in purchasing of the Narragansett Indians the picturesque little territory of Rhode Island. Another colony was thus founded, and Coddington was chosen as its governor. The broad principle of liberty of conscience was fully recognized in its constitution ; it being agreed "that none be accounted a delinquent for doctrine."

The colonies of Providence and Rhode Island had not been secured a political existence by a charter from the mother country, and consequently were excluded from the colonial union of New England. The settlers, feeling that their existence as a separate province, depended on the protection of a charter, appointed Roger Williams in 1643, to proceed to England for the purpose of obtaining one. Sir Harry Vane, then an influential member of the Parliament, favoured the application, and through his exertions, a charter was obtained, incorporating the two colonies under the title of " RHODE ISLAND." The inhabitants of the new province now happily experienced the blessings of liberty of conscience. "We have not felt," they said in 1654, in an address to their patron Sir H. Vane, "the iron yoke of wolvish bishops, or the new chains of the Presbyterian tyrants, nor, in this colony, have we been consumed by the over-zealous fire of the (so called) godly Christian magistrate. We have not known what an excise means—we have almost forgotten what tithes are." Such was the happy experience of the early inhabitants of Rhode Island.

Returning again to the colonies of Massachusetts, we find, that in a few years after the Antinomians had been cast out,

Anabaptism sprang up, and disturbed the intolerant Puritan. The denying of infant baptism, and the holding of separate meetings, was called, " setting up an altar of their own against God's altar." " God forbid," said Dudley in his old age, " that we should tolerate errors." " To say that men ought to have liberty of conscience, is impious ignorance," said another." " Religion," responded the notorious priest, Norton, " admits of no eccentric notions." The conscientious Anabaptist shared no quarter, and fines, whippings, and finally, banishments, cleared Massachusetts of its Baptist population. How then can we wonder that in Puritanic New England, Quakerism should draw down a severer persecution ?

The territory of NEW HAMPSHIRE was formed into a colony in 1622 ; its progress, however, was slow. The inhabitants were chiefly Puritans from Massachusetts, which claimed the right of jurisdiction over the district ; and in 1642, it was annexed to that colony ; but in 1679 it received a distinct charter, and became another province.

The valley of the Connecticut, by its alluvial fertility, early attracted settlers from Massachusetts. In 1635, a company of sixty of the Pilgrims emigrated in a body through the forests to this country, and in the following year, when still larger numbers found their way to it, the government of CONNECTICUT was established under the auspices of Winthrop. The fur trade, also, attracted many to settle on the banks of its noble river ; these were chiefly Dutch from New Amsterdam. In 1662, the colony obtained a charter from Charles II. Soon after emigration to Connecticut had begun, a colony sprung up at New Haven, under Puritan auspices ; it never, however, obtained a charter, but became incorporated with the former under one government.

The country comprehending the province of NEW YORK, appears to have been first visited by Henry Hudson in 1609, whilst in the employ of the Dutch. This enterprise led the Dutch nation to claim the country contiguous to the river which bears the name of this navigator ; and, in the following year, some Amsterdam merchants traded with the Indians on the shores of Long Island Sound ; and a few years later, some Dutch fur traders took up their abode on the island of Manhattan. In 1621, the Dutch West India Company obtained a charter to plant colonies in America, and four years later, several dwellings of persons who came to prosecute the fur trade, were erected on the site of the present city of New York. Subsequently, all the country extending from Maryland to New England, was claimed by the Dutch. In colonizing this country, then called New Netherlands, the Dutch West India Company recognized religious toleration. " Let every peaceful citizen," wrote the directors from Amsterdam, " enjoy freedom of conscience; this maxim has made our city the asylum for fugitives from every land; tread in its steps and you shall be blessed."* The liberty thus allowed, attracted persons from different parts of Europe, and the Dutch colony soon became a home, not only for English, French, and Belgians, but also for Germans, Bohemians, Swiss, and Italians. The French protestants came in such numbers, that official documents were sometimes issued in their language, as well as in Dutch and English.† The enlightened legislation of New Netherlands, forms a bright spot in the colonization of America, and, but for the conduct of the Calvinistic Stuyvesant, its governor, in persecuting some Lutherans and Friends, religious toleration would have been complete within its limits. The duration of Dutch power in America, was, however, but short. In a war with the English in 1664, it was lost, and a dismemberment of New Netherlands followed the conquest. New York fell into the hands of James, the brother of Charles II., and the country east of the Delaware, was assigned to Lord Berkeley and Sir George Carteret, both proprietors in Carolina; and which now received the name of NEW JERSEY.

The colonization of DELAWARE begun in 1631, when about thirty Dutch people formed a settlement near Lewistown, and it became a separate colony. Before Europeans had planted themselves on the soil of Delaware, Gustavus Adolphus, King of Sweden, had planned an enterprise for settling a colony of his people in the new world, and at his instance, a company was incor-

---

* Albany Records.   † Ibid.

porated for the purpose. It was not, however, until 1638, that the Scandinavians found their way to the territory of Delaware. Their numbers, though small at first, gradually increased ; and in 1654, they amounted to about seven hundred settlers. At this date they were conquered by the Dutch, and the colony came under the control of that people. The Swedish emigrants were protestants of considerable piety : they took much pains to educate their children, and lived on terms of peace with the aborigines. The country attracted a few English from New England, for the enlightened Gustavus desired that it should be open to " all oppressed Christendom."

The favourable accounts which the early settlers in Virginia gave of the fertility and resources of the western continent, increased the enthusiasm of the English for American plantations ; and Sir George Calvert, afterwards Lord Baltimore, a member of the Virginian company, and a man of ability and enterprise, shared largely in the feeling. He became a convert to Papacy, and, avowing his opinions, resigned his office of Secretary of State. Baltimore, on embracing the Romish faith, entertained the idea of emigrating to America, but the laws of Virginia excluded Papists from its territory. The country lying northward of the Potomac, being, however, yet untenanted by the English, in 1632 he applied for and obtained from Charles I. a grant of land, which he called MARYLAND, in honour of Henrietta Maria, the consort of the King. In framing the laws of the province, Lord Baltimore determined that no preference should be given to any sect. It became an asylum for Papists, but equality in religious rights, and civil freedom, were assured to all. Religious liberty was the basis adopted by the governor of Maryland. " I will not," said he in his oath, " by myself or any other, directly or indirectly, molest any person professing to believe in Jesus Christ, for or in respect of religion." The liberal institutions of the new colony, together with the fertility of the soil, attracted many adventurers ; the lonely forests were soon converted into prosperous plantations, and both Protestants from Europe, and Puritans from New England, flocked in considerable numbers to the province. The troubles in the mother country between Charles I.

and the Parliament, were watched with much interest by the Papists of Maryland ; and, fearing lest the ascendency of the latter, might endanger the religious privileges of the colony, they concluded in 1649, to pass an act, to protect freedom of conscience in matters of religion. Unhappily for Maryland, a dispute arose between Lord Baltimore and Clayborne, a resolute and enterprising man, who claimed a right to the province, on the plea of a grant from the Virginian company in 1631, and in which he was supported by many of the colonists. The conflicting claims of the two parties greatly divided the population, and sectarianism had no small influence in the controversy. The Puritans, who had been welcomed by the governor, and to whose liberal policy they were indebted for a home in the colony, threw their influence into the scale of the Clayborne party, and made it preponderate. The change which took place in the government of Maryland was followed by religious intolerance, and in a new assembly held in 1654, the Puritans, under the auspices of Clayborne, supported the passing of an act, which refused religious liberty to those who professed "popery or prelacy ;" but the ungrateful enactment was never countenanced by Cromwell. Lord Baltimore, when he heard of these proceedings, became indignant, and resolved to vindicate his supremacy. The Puritans and Claybornites, however, took to arms, and repelling the forces of the governor, maintained their power until the restoration of the monarchy ; when the authority of Baltimore was again recognized. The prosperity of Maryland was progressive ; it had become famed as an asylum for the persecuted of every class and country, and emigrants from France, from Germany, from Holland, from Sweden, from Piedmont, and from Bohemia, sought its unsectarian soil. In that province, remarks a modern historian,* " the empire of justice and humanity had been complete, but for the sufferings of the people called Quakers."

Except the disastrous attempt on the Roanoke in 1587, under the auspices of the disappointed Raleigh, and the settlement in 1650 of some Virginian planters, and also a few years after them, of some New England men in the vicinity of Cape Fear, no

---

* Bancroft's United States.

attempts at colonization in CAROLINA appear to have been made by the English, until the year 1667.

But although the tide of emigration had been checked in this direction, by the failure of the early expeditions, the fertility of the southern lands of North America was still remembered ; and Carolina was constituted a province by a grant of Charles II. to some of his most influential courtiers. The great philosopher John Locke, who was intimately acquainted with the Earl of Shaftesbury, one of the proprietaries, undertook, at his solicitation, to frame a constitution for the new colony.

In laying down the form of its government, Locke evidently desired that aristocratic influence should be maintained in its councils, but he nevertheless supported religious toleration. An express clause in the charter opened the way for its recognition ; and religious freedom to " Jews, heathens, and other dissenters," to " men of any religion," was allowed to settlers in Carolina. The unsectarian constitution of the province was appreciated, and together with the fertility of the country, it attracted, not only English and Irish, but Dutch from New York and Holland ; persecuted Huguenots from France, and exiled Covenanters from Scotland.

The recognition of negro slavery in Locke's " constitutions" for the southern settlement, was, however, a deep blot upon his system, and promising and fruitful as the country appeared to be, the colony advanced slowly, and with difficulty. In North Carolina the settlers soon became uneasy under the political restraints of the government, and in 1680, the " constitutions" were abandoned, as inapplicable to men who sought a more popular government.

The colonists of South Carolina began also to feel that their rights were restricted by the legislation of Locke, and the proprietors seeing the futility of attempting to enforce it, entirely laid aside the scheme of the great philosopher. This was in the year 1693, the year preceding the election by the proprietors, of John Archdale, a Friend of Chipping Wycombe in Buckinghamshire, as governor of South Carolina. Under the management of " the peaceful Archdale," as he is termed, " the mediator between factions," the province began to thrive, and the fame of Carolina, as "the American Canaan that flowed with milk and honey," increased. The colony, says its enlightened Quaker governor, " stood circumstanced with the honour of a true English government, zealous for the increase of virtue, as well as outward trade and business." The representatives of the freemen of the settlement, sensible of the cause of this happy change, declared that John Archdale " by his wisdom, and labour, had laid a firm foundation for a most glorious superstructure,"* and voted him an address of thanks.

Having now included in our introductory pages, a condensed narrative of the discovery of the North American continent, and of the settlement of its several European colonies, down to nearly the end of the seventeenth century, it may not be amiss, before retiring from the subject, briefly to recapitulate the leading points of the history. We have seen that the attempts of the PORTUGUESE and of the SPANISH nations for territorial acquisitions in this portion of the western world, were failures ; that the FRENCH, more successful in their endeavours, had formed settlements of considerable extent in the region now known as Canada ; that the enterprising DUTCH had planted themselves in considerable numbers on the banks of the Hudson, and that protestant SWEDES, encouraged by Gustavus, their king, occupied both the right and left banks of the Delaware ; but, we have also seen that to the enterprising exertions of the ENGLISH nation, the colonisation of this vast country is mainly attributable.

One of the chief objects in penning this introductory relation is to exhibit the moral and religious character of the several provinces at the time referred to, and also the degree of religious toleration which they individually recognised. VIRGINIA the earliest permanent settlement of the English, founded in 1607, was colonised by a class of men mostly of the high Anglican church, who proceeded to the new country with extravagant hopes of wealth. For the first half century they refused to allow the exercise of any religion other than Episcopacy ; but, from the

* Assembly's Address in Archdale's Carolina, p. 18.

time of the Commonwealth, their views regarding religious toleration were modified, and excepting the law of 1658, for banishing Friends, which was enforced, in a few cases only, religious freedom prevailed in the colony. Next in succession followed the settlement of the Pilgrim Fathers in MASSACHUSETTS. Professing to be the uncompromising opponents to Romish declension, and as such, to the pompous display and prelacy of the Anglican Church, they refused the introduction of Papacy and Episcopacy into their jurisdiction, and also every kind of religion, excepting Puritanism ; and in their zeal to uphold these views, they were led into great excesses of persecution. These remarks respecting the Puritans in Massachusetts will apply to those of CONNECTICUT, where the exclusive principle was also upheld and enforced. The colony of MARYLAND, the very antipodes of Puritanic New England as respects religious liberty, was commenced in 1633, under the auspices of Lord Baltimore, a leading papist ; but, contrary to the practices of his own church, and to both Episcopal Virginia and the Pilgrim Fathers, he allowed complete liberty of conscience. The result of his liberal policy was the influx of settlers of all shades of religious opinions. The intolerance of the Pilgrims of Massachusetts gave rise, in 1636, to the settlement on RHODE ISLAND. The occupiers of this delightful locality were men of enlightened minds. They had been persecuted and banished for their religion, and evinced their condemnation of these unchristian practices, by granting in their own jurisdiction entire religious freedom. Thirty years later, the same principle was still further extended in the new world, in the settlement of the CAROLINAS. The crowning example of religious freedom, and of enlightened Christian legislation in America, and indeed in the world at large, was, however, in the settlement of Pennsylvania, and the Jerseys, under the directing hand of William Penn. This interesting subject will be more appropriately treated upon in the future pages of this work, as it occurs in the order of time.

We see then, that, excepting Massachusetts and Connecticut, North America offered an asylum for the persecuted of every class, and for the people of every clime ; we cannot therefore wonder that its unsectarian soil became the resort, not only of English, and

Irish, and Scotch, but also of emigrants from almost every nation in Europe.

In studying the history of the Society of Friends, the observant reader, cannot, we think, fail to notice, that it was only in countries where the darkness of popery had been much dispelled, that its spiritual and enlightened views found steady acceptance. Although our early Friends were engaged in gospel labours in several of the Roman Catholic countries of Europe, we do not find that they were successful in the establishment of a single meeting, or except in a few cases, in obtaining an individual conversion to their principles ; whilst on the other hand, in almost every Protestant nation in which they preached, communities were gathered, who professed and promulgated their doctrines.   The Reformation, therefore, was instrumental in preparing the way for the introduction of Quakerism into Christendom.   But enfranchised, as most of the settlers of the western world were, from the shackles of popery, and to a large extent from prelacy also ; and consisting, as they did of considerable numbers of pious individuals, who had been driven from their respective countries for the cause of religion, the colonies of America presented a sphere peculiarly adapted for the reception of those high and enlightened views of christianity, which the Society of Friends were called to uphold, and to advocate among their fellow-men.   Of the labours of their gospel messengers, and of the manner in which their principles were received in the new world, it will be the object of our future pages to treat.

CHAPTER II.

The rise of the Society of Friends—George Fox's brief narrative respecting it—Mary Fisher and Anne Austin visit Barbadoes and New England—Fac-simile of a letter from Mary Fisher to George Fox—The prejudice of the Puritans against Friends—Mary Fisher and Anne Austin reach Boston—Their trunks are searched for Quaker books—A special council of the magistrates of Boston convened—They issue an order for the imprisonment and banishment of the two Friends—Their books are burnt—They are searched as witches—Are banished, and sent to Barbadoes—Letter of Henry Fell to Margaret Fell, from Barbadoes—Sketch of the life of Mary Fisher and Anne Austin.

THE rise of the religious Society of Friends appears from the most authentic data to have taken place in 1644; the year in which some piously-disposed persons, residing in Leicestershire, one of the midland counties of England, first associated themselves in religious profession with George Fox. For about seven years from this period, the Society had not extended much beyond a few of the neighbouring counties, including Yorkshire. In a brief account given by George Fox of "the spreading of truth," he thus notices the early progress of the Society. " The truth sprang up first to us, so as to be a people to the Lord, in Leicestershire in 1644, in Warwickshire in 1645, in Nottinghamshire in 1646, in Derbyshire in 1647, and in the adjacent counties in 1648, 1649, and 1650; in Yorkshire in 1651."* The year 1652 was marked by a very considerable enlargement of the Society, and many individuals, who became eminent instruments in the hand of the Lord for the promotion of his holy cause, united with the new association. At this date it numbered

* Journal of George Fox, Leeds Ed., vol. ii. p. 465.

twenty-five ministers, by whom, remarks George Fox, "multitudes were convinced." The ministry of these gospel labourers, during this and the subsequent year, was principally confined to the northern and midland portions of the kingdom ; but in 1654, we find Quaker ministers travelling in nearly all the counties of England and Wales, and in parts of Scotland and Ireland, whilst the establishment of meetings had taken place in most parts of the nation. There were now no fewer than sixty engaged in the work of the ministry, and their labours were followed with signal success ; a convincing power attended them in these engagements, which impressed awful considerations, and awakened the slumbering consciences of their audiences to an earnest desire for the salvation of their souls. "Their preaching," says an historian, "was in the demonstration of the Spirit and with power ; multitudes flocked to hear them, and many embraced their doctrines."*

Deeply sensible, as were the early Friends, of the spirituality and importance of the views which they had embraced, and of their entire accordance with the doctrines and precepts of Christ, they longed for their universal reception ; and, under the influence of the Holy Spirit, their hearts were warmed in gospel love to their fellow-men every where. Having themselves felt the efficacy of the free teaching of Christ, they were drawn to invite others to the same blessed experience, and "come, taste and see that the Lord is good," was the emphatic language of their souls. Enlightened by the Sun of Righteousness, they were given to see, that great darkness and deadness in religion had overspread professing Christendom. They deeply lamented the departure from the primitive purity and simplicity of the true church, which so generally prevailed, and under an apprehension of a call from on high, many, at a very early period of the Society's progress, travelled in distant lands to preach the glad tidings of peace and salvation, through Jesus Christ, and him crucified. Under these impressions, we find that in 1655, some had passed over to the European continent, while Mary Fisher and Anne Austin, feeling

* Gough's History of Friends, vol. i. p. 143.

My Deare father

— Lett me not be forgotton of thee but lett that promisse be for me that I may contenue faithfull to the end if any of our frendes be pleasd to com ouer you may be serviseabell heere is many contrineed & many desire to know the way so I rest

from the Barbados the 30 day
of the month called January

Mary ffisher

for Gorgo ffoxe

His Seruant

their minds drawn to visit the western world, proceeded to the
island of Barbadoes ; and from thence in the spring of 1656, to
New England. " In 1655," says George Fox, " many went
beyond sea, where truth also sprang up ; and in 1656, it broke
forth in America."*

Soon after the arrival of Mary Fisher and Anne Austin at
Barbadoes, the former addressed a letter to George Fox. The
original is still in existence, and we insert the following extract
from it, as of historical interest at this early date :—

MARY FISHER TO GEORGE FOX.

MY DEAR FATHER,

—— Let me not be forgotten of thee, but let thy prayers be for
me that I may continue faithful to the end. If any of our Friends
be free to come over, they may be serviceable ; here are many
convinced, and many desire to know the way, so I rest.

*From the Barbadoes the 30th day of the
month called January, [Eleventh
Month, O. S.] 1655.*

Mary Fisher

It has been observed, in the preceding chapter, that there
existed in some parts of New England, more especially in the
state of Massachusetts, a spirit of great intolerance and persecution. Confident in the notion of their own righteousness and in
that profession of religion which subjected their ancestors to so
much cruelty in the mother country, and which ultimately drove
the Pilgrim Fathers to seek a refuge in the American wilderness,
the Puritans of New England unhappily cherished a disposition
inimical to religious freedom. They contended for the right of
judging in spiritual things, and bore their testimony against
prelacy and whatever else they deemed to be error, but all dissent
from their own doctrines they held to be heresy. Very early
after the rise of Friends in Great Britain, many of them had to
undergo much suffering and oppression from both priests and

---

* Journal of George Fox, Leeds Ed., vol. ii. p. 465.

rulers. Episcopacy was at that time no longer the acknowledged religion of the state. The pulpits were occupied both by Presbyterians and Independents. Between the civil and ecclesiastical powers at home therefore, and those of New England, there was at this period, a great identity of feeling, and that desire for the establishment of uniformity in religion, which prompted the Presbyterians to endeavour to set up a consistory in every parish throughout England,* found its ample response in the bosoms of the bigoted rulers of Massachusetts.

Striking, as the principles of the Society of Friends do, at the very foundation of hierarchical systems, and all distinctions between laity and clergy, they met with vehement opposition from almost every class of religious professors, and both Royalist and Parliamentarian joined in common cause to oppress them. Their enemies, not content with persecuting this despised people for sentiments which they really held and preached, endeavoured, by an enormous amount of misrepresentation, to raise a prejudice against them in the minds of those who had not an opportunity of judging for themselves. The distorted accounts† which were industriously circulated respecting them, had, at a very early period of their history, reached the remotest settlements of the British empire ; and, as it regards the American colonists, had produced among them not only a settled prejudice against Friends, but also a deep-rooted repugnance to the spiritual views which they advocated. The manner in which this feeling was manifested in Puritan New England, will be shewn in the subsequent pages.

It was in the early part of the Fifth Month, 1656, that Mary Fisher and Anne Austin arrived at Boston, and their approach appears to have caused no inconsiderable degree of consternation to the authorities of Massachusetts Bay. The news of the arrival of the two strangers had no sooner reached the ears of Bellingham, the deputy governor, the governor himself being absent, than, in his zeal to avert the dreaded introduction of

* Neal's History of the Puritans, vol. iii. p. 24, Ed. 1795.

† See " Heretical Quakers deluded by the Devil," in " A Mirror or Looking Glass," by Samuel Clark ; Edition of 1656.

heretical doctrines into the colony, he forthwith ordered that the two Friends should be detained on board the ship in which they came, and that their trunks should be searched for any printed works which they might have brought. These orders were strictly carried out; they were kept closely confined in the vessel, and about one hundred books were taken from them, and committed to the custody of the officers. On this " extraordinary occasion," as the historian Neal terms it,* the magistrates of Boston took the alarm; and, as if the town were threatened with some imminent danger, by the arrival of two quiet and harmless English women, a special council was convened, whose deliberations terminated in the issue of the following order :—

" *At a council held at Boston*, 11*th July*, 1656,—

" Whereas, there are several laws long since made and published in this jurisdiction, bearing testimony against heretics and erroneous persons; yet, notwithstanding, Simon Kempthorn of Charlestown, master of the ship *Swallow* of Boston, hath brought into this jurisdiction, from the island of Barbadoes, two women, who name themselves Anne, the wife of one Austin, and Mary Fisher, being of that sort of people commonly known by the name of Quakers, who, upon examination are found not only to be transgressors of the former laws, but to hold very dangerous, heretical, and blasphemous opinions; and they do also acknowledge that they came here purposely to propagate their said errors and heresies, bringing with them and spreading here sundry books, wherein are contained most corrupt, heretical, and blasphemous doctrines, contrary to the truth of the gospel here professed amongst us. The council therefore, tendering the preservation of the peace and truth, enjoyed and professed among the churches of Christ in this country, do hereby order :

" *First*. That all such corrupt books as shall be found upon search to be brought in and spread by the aforesaid persons, be forthwith burned and destroyed by the common executioner.

" *Secondly*. That the said Anne and Mary be kept in close

---

* Neal's History of New England, vol. i. p. 292.

prison, and none admitted communication with them without leave from the governor, deputy governor, or two magistrates, to prevent the spreading their corrupt opinions, until such time as they be delivered aboard of some vessel, to be transported out of the country.

" *Thirdly.* The said Simon Kempthorn is hereby enjoined, speedily and directly, to transport or cause to be transported, the said persons from hence to Barbadoes, from whence they came, he defraying all the charges of their imprisonment ; and for the effectual performance hereof, he is to give security in a bond of £100. sterling, and on his refusal to give such security, he is to be committed to prison till he do it."

In the extraordinary proceedings of the council of Boston in passing this order, we see the first deliberate act of the rulers of New England in their corporate capacity, towards Friends. The instructions thus issued were not only rigorously, but even barbarously enforced. Mary Fisher and Anne Austin were brought on shore and confined in the dismal gaol of Boston, whilst their books were committed to the flames by the hands of the executioner. " Oh, learned and malicious cruelty ! " remarks one who was soon after a prisoner in Boston for his Quaker's principles,* " as if another man had not been sufficient to burn a few harmless books, which, like their masters, can neither fight, strike, nor quarrel." The authorities, in their determination to prevent the " heretical doctrines" from spreading among the settlers, threatened to inflict a penalty of £5. on any one who should even attempt to converse with the Friends through the window of their prison ; subsequently they had it boarded up as an additional security, and not deeming these precautionary measures sufficient, they next deprived the prisoners of their writing materials.

The order of the council was severe, but the revolting treatment to which these harmless women were afterwards exposed, was a still greater outrage upon humanity. For some years pre-

* Humphrey Norton.

ceding, a delusion of a most extraordinary and alarming character, in reference to the subject of witches, had unhappily taken
hold on the minds of the colonists of New England, and several
persons had already been put to death under the charge of witchcraft.   Two had been executed at Boston, one in 1648, and
another, Bellingham's own sister-in-law, but a few months before
the arrival of the two strangers.   Whether the persecutors of
Mary Fisher and Anne Austin, were really designing the death
of the victims of their bigotry, and in effecting it were endeavouring to avoid offering violence to the feelings of the community, we know not, but the cry of witchcraft was now raised
against them.   They were accordingly subjected to a close examination, but no overt act in substantiation of the malignant
charge, could be adduced.   The authorities, thus foiled in their
wicked purpose, next subjected them to an indecent and cruel
examination of their persons, to see if some marks of witchcraft
were not upon them, under the popular superstitious notion, that
some distinctive sign would be found on the bodies of those who
had thus sold themselves to Satan.   It would have been a fearful
thing had any mark or mole of a peculiar kind been apparent,
but nothing of the sort was to be found, and they thus escaped
an ignominious death.

The magistrates, baffled in their wicked design, now refused
to furnish their prisoners with provisions, or even to allow the
citizens of Boston to do so ; but He who fed Elijah in the
wilderness, and who careth for His saints under every variety of
circumstance, was near to help.   An aged inhabitant of the
city, touched with compassion for their sufferings, bribed the
gaoler, by giving him five shillings a week, to allow him privately
to administer to their wants.

After an imprisonment of nearly five weeks, and the loss of
their beds and their bible, which the gaoler took for his fees,
Mary Fisher and Anne Austin, were sent on board the vessel in
which they came, and which was now about to sail to Barbadoes,
the captain being bound, under a penalty of one hundred pounds,
to carry them to that island, and to prevent their either landing
in New England, or in any way communicating with its people.

The date of their banishment from Boston, was the 5th of the Sixth Month, 1656. Kempthorn, the captain, submitted to the arbitrary requisition of the council ; and, it is supposed, paid for the returning passage of the two Friends to Barbadoes. Whilst these proceedings were going forward, Endicot, the governor, was in another part of the colony ; and to his absence from Boston may be attributed the escape of Mary Fisher, and her companion, from a cruelty of another kind. " If I had been present," said this persecuting Puritan, on hearing the course adopted towards them, " I would have had them well whipped." This was that Endicot who afterwards made himself so conspicuous in the New England persecutions. The following unpublished letter in the Swarthmore collection of manuscripts, written by Henry Fell, who visited Barbadoes about this time, contains an account of the arrival of the banished Friends at that island, and will probably be read with interest.

HENRY FELL TO MARGARET FELL.

Barbadoes, *the 3rd day of ye Ninth Month,* (56).

MY DEARLY BELOVED,

In the Lord Jesus Christ, my dear love salutes thee.—
I landed here upon the Barbadoes the 7th day of the Eighth Month, in the afternoon, and that night went to a Friend's house in the country, six miles off, (a widow woman), where I was gladly received. She told me that Peter Head, John Rous, and Mary Fisher, were gone from the island the day before, (for any thing she knew) ; but it proved otherwise, for the next morning I went to Indian-Bridge, where they were to have taken shipping for the Leeward Islands, namely Nevis and Antego, about eighty or ninety leagues from their place ; but I found them not gone, for the shipping that should have carried them had deceived them. And truly I was much refreshed and strengthened by finding of them there. They continued here about fourteen days after I came hither, before they got shipping from hence, in which time we had several meetings amongst Friends, and so they passed away. I know nothing of their return hither

again, for they could say little of it, or which way they should be disposed of. Mary Fisher, (and one Anne Austin, who is lately come from England,) had been here before, and went from hence to New England, where they were put in prison, and very cruelly used and searched as witches, and their books taken from them and burnt, and none suffered to come to speak to them, while they were in prison : for there was a fine of five pounds laid upon any one that should come to see them in prison, or should conceal any of their books. Notwithstanding, there was one man came to the prison, and proffered to pay the fine that he might speak with them, but could not be admitted ; so, afterwards, they were sent aboard again, and not suffered any liberty at all ashore, and so were brought again to Barbadoes, from whence they came by order from the Governor of New England. Truly Mary Fisher is a precious heart, and hath been very serviceable here ; so likewise have John Rous and Peter Head, and the Lord hath given a blessing to their labours, for the fruits thereof appear, for here are many people convinced of the truth, (among whom the Lord is placing his name), who meet together in silence, in three several places in the island ; and the Lord is adding more, such as shall be saved.

Glen: Fell: *

As it will be interesting to know something further of the history of Mary Fisher, and Anne Austin, being the first who landed on the American continent to promulgate the doctrines of

---

* Henry Fell was an eminent minister in the Society. In 1656, he proceeded on a visit to some of the West India Islands, and again in 1658. During the first visit, he was absent from home about one year. From 1659 to 1662, he was mostly engaged in gospel labours in England, and from this period we lose all trace of him. He is mentioned in Whiting's Catalogue as having died in America ; but in what part, or at what time, we are uninformed. His home was in Lancashire, and there is reason to believe that he was a near relative of Judge Fell. He appears to have received an education considerably above most of his day.

Friends, the present chapter will conclude with a brief sketch of their lives, as far as historical materials permit.

MARY FISHER was born in the north of England about the year 1623, and at a very early period of the Society's progress in that part, joined in profession with it, but of the precise date and circumstance of her convincement we have no record. She was one who possessed talents much above the average of her sex, and " whose intellectual faculties," observes an early writer, " were greatly adorned by the gravity of her deportment."* Her residence at the time of her convincement it is believed was at Pontefract in Yorkshire. She came forth as a minister of the gospel in 1652, and in the same year we find her imprisoned within York Castle, for addressing an assembly at the close of public worship at Selby ; an imprisonment which lasted sixteen months.† Almost immediately on her release from this long confinement, she proceeded on a gospel mission to the south-eastern parts of England, in company with Elizabeth Williams, a fellow-labourer in the ministry. Two females thus travelling from county to county, publicly preaching the doctrines of the new Society in parts where hitherto its name had scarcely been known, must have excited no small surprise in the people amongst whom they came. They passed, however, without molestation through the country, until the Tenth Month, 1653, when they arrived at Cambridge. To the students at this seat of learning, the presence of itinerant preachers appeared an absurdity, but that Quaker women should attempt to preach in Cambridge, was, in their estimation, a still greater presumption. Mary Fisher and her friend, faithful to their call, " discoursed about the things of God" with the young students, and "preached at Sidney College gate" to the inmates of that establishment. But the doctrine of the freedom of gospel ministry, and the disuse of all ceremonial observances in religion, appeared to the letter-learned collegians mere jargon, and they began to mock and deride the two strangers as religious fanatics, whilst the mayor of the town, eager to support the orthodoxy of his church, ordered them to be taken to the

---

* Gerard Croese's History of the Quakers. Book second, p. 124.

† Besse's Sufferings of the People called Quakers. Vol. ii. p. 89.

market cross, and whipped, "until the blood ran down their bodies;"* a sentence which was executed with much barbarity. Before they had been tied to the whipping-post, in presence of the gazing multitude, these innocent women, at the footstool of divine mercy, sought forgiveness for their persecutors. The scene was altogether new and strange to the spectators, and they were astonished on beholding the Christian patience and constancy which characterized the conduct of the sufferers, and more especially when they heard them pray that their persecutors might be pardoned. The first imprisonment of a Friend, was that of George Fox, at Nottingham, in 1649. He had also, with several others of his fellow professors, borne much personal abuse: but it was not until Mary Fisher and her companion visited Cambridge, that any were publicly scourged. On this occasion Mary Fisher, under a presentiment of the troubles that awaited Friends, was heard to say, "this is but the beginning of the sufferings of the people of God."†

Towards the close of 1653, she felt called to "declare the truth in the steeple-house" at Pontefract, an act of dedication for which she was immured six months within the walls of York Castle. In the following year, she was subjected, by the Mayor of Pontefract, to three months additional confinement in this fortress, because she was "unrepentant" for addressing the assembly at Pontefract, "and for refusing to give sureties for her good behaviour." In 1655, we find her travelling in the ministry in Buckinghamshire, where she again for some months became the inmate of a prison, for "giving Christian exhortations to the priest and people."‡ It was also during 1655, that Mary Fisher felt a religious call to leave the shores of her native country, for the West India Islands, and North America. The date of her return from the western world was probably in the early part of 1657. During the same year she again visited the West Indies. In 1658, we trace her at Nevis. § In 1660, under an impression of religious duty to visit Sultan Mahomet IV., she performed a long and arduous journey to the continent of Asia. After

* Besse's Sufferings, vol. i. p. 85.   † Ibid, vol. ii. p. 85.
‡ MS. Sufferings of Friends.   § Besse's Sufferings, vol. ii. p. 352.

visiting Italy, Zante, Corinth, and Smyrna, she at last reached
Adrianople ; where the Sultan was encamped with his army.
Her interview with this great Asiatic monarch, and the courteous
manner in which she was received by him, are circumstances so
well known, as to render it unnecessary for us to refer more
particularly to them. On leaving the court of this Mahommedan
potentate, she proceeded to Constantinople, from whence she took
her departure for England.

Soon after Mary Fisher had returned from the east, she was
united in marriage with William Bayley of Poole, in Dorsetshire,
an eminent minister in the Society. The marriage took place in
the early part of 1662. William Bayley was by occupation a
mariner, and occasionally made voyages to the West Indies, but
he died when at sea, in the Fourth Month, 1675. Of the issue
of this marriage we have no record ; we find, however, that Sophia
Hume, a ministering Friend of extraordinary character, was the
grand-daughter of William and Mary Bayley.* In the Seventh
Month, 1678, Mary Bayley was united in marriage with John
Cross of London.†

How long John Cross and his wife resided in London after
their union, does not appear, but, following the example of many
other Friends of that day, they emigrated to America. In 1697,
we find Mary a second time a widow, residing at Charlestown in
South Carolina. Robert Barrow, after his providential escape
from shipwreck on the coast of Florida, whilst travelling in the
ministry, was conveyed by the Spaniards of St. Augustine, to
Charlestown, where he became her welcome guest. Writing to his
wife from this place, after mentioning the severe illness he had
endured, arising from his privations, he thus speaks of his kind
hostess : " At length we arrived at Ashley River, and it pleased
God, I had the great fortune to have a good nurse, one whose
name you have heard of, a Yorkshire woman, born within two
miles of York ; her maiden name was Mary Fisher, she that
spake to the great Turk ; afterwards William Bayley's wife. She

* Yearly Meeting of London MS. Testimonies concerning deceased
ministers.
† Minutes of the " Two Weeks' Meeting" of London, vol. i. p. 118.

is now my landlady and nurse. She is a widow of a second husband, her name is now Mary Cross.*

At the date of Robert Barrow's letter, the age of Mary Cross could not have been much under seventy years. Since she left the shores of Britain for New England, forty-one years had elapsed. She doubtless finished her earthly course at Charlestown, but we regret that hitherto we have been unable to meet with any particulars of the close of her eventful life, or of the date when it took place. We may, however, reverently believe, that she was not unprepared for the solemn summons ; and that she has entered into that rest, and enjoys that crown of righteousness, which the Lord the righteous Judge giveth unto all those that love his appearing.

Respecting ANNE AUSTIN we have but few particulars to narrate. At the time of her visit to New England, she was mentioned as one "stricken in years,"† and as being the mother of five children. Her residence it appears was in the city of London. Expelled from Boston, she was carried with her companion Mary Fisher, to Barbadoes. Her stay on that island was not a prolonged one ; as we find the expenses of her returning passage to England, included in the accounts of the Society for 1656-7. Continuing faithful in her high calling as a minister of Christ, Anne Austin, on her return to her native land, had to feel the persecuting hands of ungodly men ; and thus one of the filthy gaols of London in 1659, became her abode, for exercising her gift in the assemblies of her own Society. From the time of her imprisonment at this date, to that of her decease, no incident is recorded of this dedicated woman. Her death occurred during the awful visitation of 1665, by which 100,000 of the inhabitants of London were called from time to eternity. The burial register of the Society states, that she died in the Sixth Month, 1665, of the plague, and was interred at Bunhill-fields ; and we doubt not but that she was called to receive that reward, which is the sure inheritance of all the faithful in Christ.

---

* MS. Letter of R. Barrow to his wife, dated Twelfth Month, 1696-7.
† Gerard Croese's History of the Quakers, book ii. p. 124.

CHAPTER III.

Eight Ministers of the Society arrive at Boston from London—Their trunks are searched—They are committed to prison and sentenced to banishment—The captain who brought them, bound over to take them back to England—The magistrates take measures to legalize their persecuting proceedings—A law is enacted for banishing Friends from the colony of Boston—Nicholas Upshal testifies against the law —He is arrested, fined, imprisoned, and banished—He seeks refuge within the colony of Plymouth, and winters there—Is banished thence, and proceeds to Rhode Island.

In the expulsion of Friends from New England, the rulers of Boston had evidently much underrated the task which they had unhappily imposed upon themselves ; and well would it have been for their country had their actions responded to the advice given by Gamaliel, in reference to the preaching of the Apostles at Jerusalem, when the Jews sought to slay them : " Refrain from these men, and let them alone, for if this counsel or this work be of men, it will come to nought ; but if it be of God, ye cannot overthrow it."* Scarcely had the ship, which bore the two messengers of the gospel from the shores of Massachusetts, bent her course towards the Carribbean sea, when another vessel from London, having on board eight other Friends, arrived in Boston Bay. These were Christopher Holder, John Copeland, Thomas Thurston, William Brend, Mary Prince, Sarah Gibbons, Mary Weatherhead, and Dorothy Waugh.† The date of their

* Acts v. 38.

† In a letter of John Audland's to Margaret Fell, written during 1655, from Bristol, we find the following remark in reference to some of these. "Many are raised up and moved for several parts ; there are four from hereaway moved to go for New England, two men and two women ; some are gone for France, and some for Holland." The cir-

arrival was the 7th of the Sixth Month, 1656, being only two days after the departure of Mary Fisher and Anne Austin. "They had been brought here," they said, "in the will of God, having been made sensible of the cries and groans of his seed, which was crying unto him for help and deliverance under cruel bondage."*

The master of the vessel, almost immediately on his arrival, furnished the governor with a list of his passengers, and when it was known that eight of them were Quakers from England, with Richard Smith an inhabitant of Long Island, who professed with them, officers were forthwith sent on board with a warrant, commanding them "to search the boxes, chests, and trunks of the Quakers, for erroneous books and hellish pamphlets,"† and also to bring the Friends before the court then sitting at Boston. The orders being promptly executed, the Friends were subjected to a long and frivolous examination, mostly in reference to their belief in the nature of the Divine Being, and concerning the Scriptures. Respecting the latter, one of the priests contended, on the authority of the passage in the second epistle of Peter, i. 19, which alludes to "the more sure word of prophecy," that the Scriptures were the only rule and guide of life. The priest during the discussion, finding it difficult to maintain his position, began to admit more than was in accordance with the views of some of the magistrates, on which much dissension arose among them to the no small alarm and consternation of the priest. Long as the examination had been, the court was nevertheless desirous to resume it on the following day; the Friends were therefore committed to prison for the night, and brought up again on the following morning. The subjects upon which the prisoners were now interrogated, being those which they had

---

cumstance is also thus alluded to in a letter of Francis Howgill's, written a few months later. "Four from London and four from Bristol, are gone towards New England; pretty hearts; the blessing of the Lord is with them, and his dread goes before them."—*Caton's Collection of MSS.*

* Humphrey Norton's New England's Ensign, p. 7.   † Ibid, p. 8.

discussed on the previous day, they declined replying, except by referring the magistrates to their former answers, which had been all carefully taken down. They then demanded to know why they had been arrested, and deprived of their liberty. Endicot, who had returned from the country, evading an answer to the question, replied, " Take heed ye break not *our ecclesiastical laws*, for then ye are sure to stretch by a halter."*

Notwithstanding the intolerant course pursued by the priests and magistrates on this occasion, it must not be supposed that the proceedings met with the sanction of the inhabitants generally ; and it is only proper to add that the language of their governor gave rise to very intelligible marks of dissatisfaction. At the close of the examination, a sentence of banishment was pronounced upon the prisoners, instructions being issued for the close confinement of the eight English Friends, until the ship in which they came should be ready to return. Richard Smith, the Friend of Long Island, they determined should be sent home by sea, rather than by the shorter and more convenient way by land ; these bigoted rulers considering it needful to use all precautionary means to prevent the " Quaker heretics" from even passing through their country.

The authorities having taken so summary a course against the Friends, now sent for the master of the vessel in which they came, in order to make him give bond in the sum of £500.† for conveying them to England at his own cost. The honest seaman, feeling that he had violated no law of his country, in having brought her free-born inhabitants to this part of her dominions, refused to comply with the arbitrary requisition. His opposition, however, proved unavailing ; an imprisonment of four days sufficed to overcome his feelings of independence, and to reduce him to submission.

The authorities of Boston, anxious in their zeal to adopt every mode to secure the colony from the influence of Quakerism, issued the following order to the keeper of the prison :—

" You are, by virtue hereof, to keep the Quakers formerly

* New England Judged, by George Bishop, p. 10.
† Hutchinson's Hist. of Massachusetts, vol. i. p. 197.

committed to your custody as dangerous persons, industrious to improve all their abilities to seduce the people of this jurisdiction, both by words and letters, to the abominable tenets of the Quakers, and to keep them close prisoners, not suffering them to speak or confer with any person, nor permitting them to have paper or ink.

"EDWARD RAWSON, *Secretary.*"

August the 18th, 1656.

Subsequently, the gaoler was also ordered "to search, as often as he saw meet, the boxes, chests and things of the Quakers formerly committed to his custody, for pen, ink and paper, papers and books, and to take them from them."*

The extraordinary course, which the rulers of Massachusetts had taken in the prosecution of Friends, was not only in opposition to the laws of the mother country, but also without sanction from any of those of the colony. The authorities of Boston, eager as they were in the work of persecution, were not blind to their position in this respect; and hence we find them anxiously endeavouring to promote measures for legalizing their wicked proceedings. On the 2nd of the Seventh Month, 1656, the governor and magistrates of the Boston patent assembled, and prepared a letter addressed to "The Commissioners of the United Provinces," who were about to meet at Plymouth; in which they recommended, "That some generall rules may bee comended to each Generall Court, to prevent the coming in amongst us from foraigne places such notorious heretiques, as Quakers, Ranters, &c." The subject having been thus brought before the commissioners, the sanction of that body was obtained for framing a law, to justify the course which the rulers at Boston had pursued, and to legalize future intolerance. They agreed to "propose to the several Generall Courts, that all Quakers, Ranters, and other notorious heretiques bee prohibited coming into the United Colonies; and if any shall hereafter come or arise amongst us, that they bee forthwith cecured or removed out of all the jurisdictions."

* Besse, vol. ii. p. 179.

Encouraged by the recommendation of the Commissioners, the authorities at Boston soon passed a law for the banishment of Friends from their territory. This persecuting enactment was the first in America specially directed against the Society. It is as follows : —

" At a General Court held at Boston the 14th of October, 1656.

" Whereas, there is a cursed sect of *heretics* lately risen up in the world, which are commonly called Quakers, who take upon them to be immediately sent of God, and infallibly assisted by the Spirit, to speak and write blasphemous opinions, despising government, and the order of God in the church and commonwealth, speaking evil of dignities, reproaching and reviling magistrates and ministers, seeking to turn the people from the faith, and gain proselytes to their pernicious ways. This court, taking into consideration the premises, and to prevent the like mischief, as by their means is wrought in our land, doth hereby order, and by authority of this court, be it ordered and enacted, that what master, or commander of any ship, bark, pink, or ketch, shall henceforth bring into any harbour, creek or cove, within this jurisdiction, any Quaker or Quakers, or other blasphemous heretics, shall pay or cause to be paid, the fine of one hundred pounds to the treasurer of the country, except it appear he want true knowledge or information of their being such, and in that case he hath liberty to clear himself by his oath, when sufficient proof to the contrary is wanting : and for default of good payment, or good security for it, shall be cast into prison, and there to continue till the said sum be satisfied to the Treasurer as aforesaid. And the commander of any ketch, ship or vessel, being legally convicted, shall give in sufficient security to the governor, or any one or more of the magistrates, who have power to determine the same, to carry them back to the place whence he brought them, and on his refusal so to do, the governor, or one or more of the magistrates, are hereby empowered to issue out his or their warrants, to commit such master or commander to prison, there to continue till he give in sufficient security to the content of the governor, or any of the magistrates aforesaid. And it is hereby further ordered and enacted, That what Quaker soever shall arrive in this country from foreign parts, or shall come into this jurisdiction from any parts adjacent, shall be forthwith committed to the house of correction, and, at their entrance, to be severely whipped, and by the master thereof to be kept constantly to work, and none suffered to converse or speak with them during the time of their imprisonment, which shall be no longer than necessity requires. And it is ordered, If any person shall knowingly import into any harbour of this jurisdiction any Quaker books, or writings concerning their devilish opinions, shall pay for such book or writing, being legally proved against him or them, the sum of five pounds ; and whosoever shall disperse or conceal any such book, or writing, and it be found with him or her, or in his or her house, and shall not immediately deliver the same to the next magistrate, shall forfeit or pay five pounds for the dispersing or concealing of every such book or writing. And it is hereby further enacted, That if any person within this colony shall take upon them to defend the heretical opinions of the Quakers, or any of their books or papers as aforesaid, if legally proved, shall be fined for the first time forty shillings ; if they shall persist in the same, and shall again defend it the second time, four pounds ; if notwithstanding they shall again defend and maintain the said Quakers' heretical opinions, they shall be committed to the house of correction till there be convenient passage to send them out of the land, being sentenced by the court of assistants to banishment. Lastly, it is hereby ordered, That what person or persons soever shall revile the persons of magistrates or ministers, as is usual with the Quakers, such person or persons shall be severely whipped, or pay the sum of five pounds.

" This is a true copy of the court's order, as attests

" EDWARD RAWSON, *Secretary.*"

The passing of the foregoing law in the usual way, together with its official recognition on the statute books of the colony, was, in the estimation of its advocates, too quiet a mode of disposing of the measure. It was important in their view that the settlers of Massachusetts should be thoroughly impressed with

the fearful character of the " cursed sect," and the dangerous
consequences to which they would be exposed, if such " blasphemous heretics" were permitted to come amongst them. With
beat of drum, therefore, in order to arouse the attention of the
inhabitants, the law in question, was in a few days publicly proclaimed in the streets of Boston, producing a degree of excitement and commotion, to which the city had hitherto been much
a stranger.

Turning again to the imprisoned Friends, we find as the time
for their embarkation approached, that the officers under the provisions of another warrant, made a distraint on the goods of the
prisoners for the payment of the gaoler's fees, in pursuance of
which all their bedding was taken. In this state, unprepared for
a voyage across the wide Atlantic, the sufferers were inhumanly
thrust on board the vessel now about to sail, and had not their
goods been kindly redeemed by some of the inhabitants, who
were touched with sympathy for them in their distress—they
would have been forced away, thus unprovided, from the shores of
America. After an imprisonment of about eleven weeks, and in
the Eighth Month, 1656, the Friends were borne off from
Boston, and after crossing the ocean in safety, they landed at
London. Thus ended the second attempt of members of the
Society to preach the gospel on the continent of the western
world.

The preceding details of Puritan persecution in New England,
relate to the treatment of those, who came as strangers to that
country. Our attention will now be directed to cruelties practised
towards colonists, who had been convinced that the principles of
the banished Friends, harmonized with the doctrines and precepts
of Christ. In the relation of the treatment which Mary Fisher
and Anne Austin received at Boston, allusion is made to the
christian conduct of an aged inhabitant of the place, in supplying those persecuted women with provisions during their imprisonment. This individual was Nicholas Upshal, whose sufferings
we have now to record, under the conscientious testimony which
he bore, against the wicked and arbitrary proceedings of his
countrymen. He had " long been an inhabitant and freeman of

Boston," was a zealous and faithful christian, and one, who, from his earlier years, had been held in much esteem, as a man of "sober and unblameable conversation." He had been a Puritan in religious profession, and in the prosperity of the particular congregation to which he belonged, he had been deeply interested for a long series of years. But the forms and cere-monies of his church had for some time past been burdensome to him. He had felt their insufficiency to satisfy the soul in its longing and thirsting after God; and he was prepared to receive more spiritual views of religious truth. When therefore, he found on inquiry, that the views of the persecuted strangers, who renounced all outward observances in religion, pointed emphati-cally to the inward appearance of Christ, as the consolation and strength of the Christian, and as the leader and guide of his people everywhere, they met with a response in his bosom, and "he was much refreshed."*

The cruel law enacted in New England against Friends, and which had been ostentatiously announced to the citizens of Boston by beat of drum, deeply affected the mind of this good man. Being "grieved at the heart," therefore, under the im-pression that these unrighteous actions would be followed by the just judgments of the Most High, when the proclamation of the law was made before his own door, he felt constrained to raise his voice in public disapprobation of the act. He was anxious that his fellow-citizens might know that he disclaimed any participa-tion in proceedings utterly at variance with the character of true religion. The conscientious course pursued by the venerable colonist, was viewed by the self-righteous rulers as a grave offence against their authority, and one which required the marked severity of the court. On the following morning, therefore, he was cited to appear before them, to answer the charge preferred against him, "for having expressed his disapprobation of the law against Quakers." Thus arraigned, Nicholas Upshal, "in much tenderness and love," pleaded with his fellow-citizens on the iniquitous course they were pursuing, and warned them "to take heed lest they should be found fighting against God."† The

* Norton's Ensign, p. 12.   † Ibid, p. 13.

magistrates were untouched by his appeal, and in their determination to crush any questioning of their acts, fined, imprisoned, and banished him from the colony. The fine was twenty pounds, and the time allowed him to prepare for his expatriation was only thirty days, four of which he passed in prison. He was also subjected to an additional fine of three pounds, for not attending the usual place of worship, while under sentence of banishment.

The time had arrived when Nicholas Upshal was to bid a final farewell to a city, memorable to himself, and others of the older inhabitants, as a place of refuge, which, through many trials and difficulties, they had sought in the wilds of the western world, from "persecution at home." The weak and "aged" colonist, leaving his wife and children, towards the close of the Tenth Month, proceeded southward in the hope of finding a shelter at Sandwich, within the colony of Plymouth. The governor of this colony, had it appears, been apprised of his intention, and, desiring to assist in driving Quakers from Massachusetts, had issued a warrant, forbidding any of the people of Sandwich to entertain him. The inhabitants of the town, however, were not disposed to close their doors on the distressed, many of them had too much regard for the precepts of Christianity, to abandon the houseless and aged stranger to the inclemencies of a wintry season; and Nicholas Upshal found a ready home amongst them. But the hospitality of the kind-hearted people of Sandwich, displeased their governor, who, desirous of having this victim of priestly intolerance more immediately within his grasp, issued a special warrant for his appearance before him at Plymouth. The coldness of the winter, together with the precarious state of Nicholas Upshal's health, would, he believed, endanger his life, if he attempted to obey the summons. He, therefore, wisely concluded not to comply, and informed the governor by letter, that if the warrant should be enforced, and he perished, his blood would be required at his hands. His resolution not to remove from Sandwich is supposed to have received encouragement from the townsmen, by whom also it appears the constabulary were restrained from enforcing the warrant, and to the same course some of the more moderate of the magistrates inclined. In the early part of the following spring, however, the authorities of Sandwich at the unremitting solicitation of the governor, resolved that the banished man should find a home elsewhere. On the intimation of this resolution, the attention of the exile was directed to Rhode Island, as a place of safety. He knew that its liberal-minded settlers would allow him a home amongst them ; could he be favoured to reach their free soil. This he attempted, and, " through many difficulties and dangers," at last landed at Newport, its principal town. Here his banishment became the general theme of conversation. The untutored Indians, who still lingered about the dwellings of the white man, heard the tale with emotions of sorrow ; and one, who was touched with the hardness of his lot, offered him a home among his tribe ; and promised that, " if he would come and live with him, he would make him a good warm house."* Another chief, whose contemplative mind led him to reflect on the character of that religion, which could prompt its followers to such acts of inhumanity, was heard to exclaim, " What a God have the English, who deal so with one another about their God !"†

The tyranny which had marked the conduct of the rulers of Massachusetts began to open the eyes of many of the settlers, to the incongruity of the spirit, which prompted to such deeds, with that of the benign religion of Jesus Christ. Notwithstanding the earnest endeavours of the priests and rulers, by the stringent clauses of their act against Quakers, to prevent the introduction of their tenets, a desire was excited in the minds of not a few, to acquaint themselves more intimately with the doctrines and practices of a sect, whose presence it was even deemed improper to allow among them ; and, thus, very soon, a knowledge of Quaker doctrines was more or less spread abroad in all the New England colonies. Among these, as in the mother country, there were found piously disposed individuals, who were, to a great extent, prepared to receive the simple and spiritual views of Christianity, as professed by Friends, and some, at a very early period became united in religious fellowship with them. Further remarks on this interesting point will be given in a future chapter.

---

* Norton's Ensign, p. 14. † Sewel's History of Friends, p. 161.

CHAPTER IV.

For a few months after the banishment of Nicholas Upshal, the colony of Boston appeared to be clear of " Quaker heretics." The law which had been passed for their exclusion, the Puritan rulers and ecclesiastics fondly hoped would prove effectual for its intended purpose ; and thus ended the year 1656. But this eventful period in the history of Friends in America had scarcely closed, ere others of the Society were directing their course to the forbidden land of Massachusetts, and as early probably as the First Month of 1657, Mary Dyer and Ann Burden reached the bay of that colony.

Mary Dyer was an inhabitant of Rhode Island, and had been on a visit to Great Britain, but for what purpose it is not clear. Whilst in England, she became convinced of the principles of Friends, and had received a gift in the ministry. Ann Burden, it appears, at this period was not a minister. She had formerly lived in New England, having been an inhabitant of Boston or its vicinity for sixteen years; but her husband had removed his family to England and died there. She therefore now came to Boston, for the purpose of collecting some debts due to his estate. Both had been Antinomian exiles of Massachusetts; * Mary Dyer and her husband on their banishment, had sought refuge in the free colony of Rhode Island, whilst Ann Burden and her husband returned to their native land, to enjoy that religious freedom which the Puritans found under the Commonwealth.

Almost immediately on the arrival of M. Dyer and A. Burden off Boston, under the provisions of the Act against Quakers, they were seized by order of the magistrates, and placed under close confinement, in order " that none might come at them."† On their examination, Ann Burden pleaded the lawfulness of her business in the colony, but the only reply given to her reasoning was, that " she was a plain Quaker, and must abide their law.‡ After an imprisonment of three months, during which she suffered from indisposition, she was placed on shipboard for banishment.

The object of Ann Burden's voyage from England being thus frustrated by the unrelenting rulers, the sympathy of the kind-hearted people of the town was excited on her behalf : some of them exerted themselves in favour of the persecuted widow, and her fatherless children, and collected a portion of her debts, in goods, to the value of about forty pounds. But the goods being of a description unsuited for the English market, they interceded with the magistracy that she might be allowed to take them to Barbadoes, where they would find a ready sale. This humane and reasonable request was, however, unavailing. The master of the ship was " compelled to carry her to England ;§ and on inquiring from whom he was to receive payment for her returning passage, he was advised to seize a sufficient quantity of her goods to meet the charge ; but with the remark that it was without her consent that she became his passenger, he declined to act upon the recommendation. The moral sensibilities of the magistrates blunted by sectarian bigotry, not being so nice on the question of

---

* See Introduction, p. 20.　　† New England Judged, p. 38.
‡ New England Judged, p. 38.　　§ Ibid, p. 39.

right or wrong in the matter, as that which the sea captain had evinced, they immediately ordered a distraint upon the goods of the prisoner, to the amount of six pounds and ten shillings, for payment of the passage money ; and, not deeming this a sufficient infliction on the distressed widow for professing Quakerism in their territory, they subsequently directed that none of the remaining portion of her goods should be shipped ; so that, she received no part of the goods collected for her ; and, excepting the small sum of six shillings, sent by an honest debtor, she obtained no portion of the amount due to her husband's estate.

How long Mary Dyer was imprisoned is not stated, but her husband, who was not in religious profession with Friends, on hearing of his wife's imprisonment, came from Rhode Island to fetch her. So much, however, did the priests and rulers of Boston dread Quaker influence, that they would not allow him to take her to his home, "until he became bound in a great penalty not to lodge her in any town of the colony, nor permit any to have speech with her on her journey."*

The following extract from a letter addressed by Henry Fell to Margaret Fell, contains some additional facts relative to the visit of Mary Dyer and Ann Burden.

HENRY FELL TO MARGARET FELL.

Barbadoes, 19*th of Twelfth Month*, 1656.

MY DEARLY BELOVED, in the Lord Jesus Christ,—

I was expecting to come away with the next ship, seeing freedom to come away from this place, and knowing no other then but for England. But truly at present the Lord hath ordered it otherwise, and, though it was contrary to my own will, yet by his eternal power, I was made willing to give up all to Him who hath laid down his life for me. Upon the 9th day of the Eleventh Month, the word of the Lord came to me that I should go to New England, there to be a witness for Him ; so I was made willing to offer up my life and all, in obedience to the Lord ;

* New England Judged, p. 39.

for his word was as a fire, and a hammer in me ; though then in outward appearance there was no likelihood of getting passage thither, by reason of a cruel law which they have made against any Friends coming thither, (the copy whereof is here enclosed) but yet I was made confident, and bid [of the Lord] to wait till there was way made for me, and so about fourteen days after, a ship came in hither, which was going to New England, and was upon that coast, but the storms were so violent that they were forced to come hither, while the winter there was nearly over. In this ship are two Friends, Ann Burden of Bristol, and one Mary Dyer from London ; both lived in New England formerly, and were members cast out of their churches. Mary goes to her husband who lives upon Rhode Island, (which they [the Puritans] call the island of error ;) where they do banish those to, that dissent from them in judgment ; and its likely Ann Burden hath some outward business there. In this ship the master hath permitted me passage, whom the Lord hath made pretty willing to carry me, and, he saith he will endeavour to put me ashore upon some part of New England, out of their power and jurisdiction, who have made that law. In the jurisdiction of Plymouth patent, where there is a people not so rigid as the other at Boston, are great desires among them after the truth ; some there are, as I hear, convinced, who meet in silence at a place called Salem. Oh ! truly great is the desire of my soul to be amongst them for the Seed's sake, which groans for deliverance from under that Egyptian bondage. I cannot express the desire of my soul towards them, and the love that flows out after them daily ; for I see in the eternal light, the Lord hath a great work to do in that nation ; and the time is hastening, and coming on apace, wherein He will exalt his own name and his power over all the heathen that know Him not."*

Hen: Fell.

---

* It does not appear that Henry Fell was enabled to reach New England on this occasion.

The ship which conveyed Ann Burden to the shores of Britain, had scarcely weighed anchor for her passage across the Atlantic, before six of the eight Friends, who had been expelled from Boston in the preceding year, believed themselves required to attempt another voyage to New England, "being firmly persuaded that the Lord had called them to bear testimony to his truth in these parts, and having a full assurance of faith, that He would support them through whatsoever exercises He should be pleased to suffer them to be tried with." These were, William Brend, Christopher Holder, John Copeland, Sarah Gibbons, Mary Wetherhead and Dorothy Waugh.* About the same time a similar impression of religious duty was felt by five others, viz., Robert Hodgson, Humphrey Norton, Richard Doudney, William Robinson and Mary Clark.

The persecuting enactment of the court of Boston, which imposed serious penalties on the master of any ship who should venture to land Quakers within the limits of its jurisdiction, had

* The remaining two of the eight were Thomas Thurston and Mary Prince. The former again visited America, and to whom we shall hereafter refer ; but the latter does not appear to have had any further call in her divine Master's service to that land. As it is our intention to give brief notices of the lives of those who visited the new continent in the work of the gospel, before we turn from the subject of the visit of Mary Prince and her companions, we shall give a few particulars concerning her.

Mary Prince was an inhabitant of Bristol, and was one of those who were convinced through the powerful and baptizing ministry of John Camm and John Audland, on their visit to that city in 1654. Soon after her convincement she was called to labour in word and doctrine, we have, however, no particulars of her services as a gospel minister, until her visit to Boston in 1656. In 1660, she travelled extensively on the continent of Europe with Mary Fisher. During the years 1663 and 1664, this devoted Friend, in common with most of her fellow-professors in Bristol, suffered severely for her religion. Within these two years she was three times committed to prison in that city. Her daughter Hannah, about this period, was united in marriage with Charles Marshall, a physician of Bristol, who had also been convinced, and, who in a few years after also came forth in the ministry. Mary Prince died in the Tenth Month 1679 : in the burial record she is described as a widow of Castle Precincts, Bristol.

now become known in England, and a reluctance was naturally felt by the owners of vessels to take them as passengers. There appeared, therefore, no very early prospect that these devoted individuals would be able to obtain a passage to New England. But He, who is wonderful in working, and excellent in counsel, and who is often pleased to manifest his wisdom and power, at a time and in a way least expected by short-sighted man, was providing a means by which his servants might be enabled to go forward in the work to which He had called them. Robert Fowler, a ministering Friend of Burlington, in Yorkshire, a mariner by occupation, had about this time, completed the building of a small vessel ; and whilst it was in the course of construction, he was impressed with the belief, that he should have to devote it to some purpose in furtherance of the cause of Truth. He first sailed in his new ship to London ; and whilst at this port thought it right to state the feelings which had impressed him to Gerard Roberts, a merchant of Watling Street. Gerard, who was one of the most active members of the Society in making the needful arrangements for the visits of its ministers to foreign parts, was not slow to discover that a providential hand had led to their interview. To all human appearance the vessel was far too small to venture with safety on the mighty billows of the Atlantic ; but Gerard Roberts and his brethren, not questioning that this was the mode provided for conveying the party to New England, engaged it for that purpose.*

The fact, that eleven Friends in the ministry were about to leave their native land for the shores of New England, and under circumstances so peculiar, did not fail, as it may be readily supposed, to produce an unusual degree of interest in the Society ;

---

* The expenses incurred by several of these early missions were considerable, but the services having been undertaken with the full concurrence of the Society, the charges were paid from a fund raised for the purpose, in a manner similar to the practice of the Society in the present day. In the year following that in which Robert Fowler sailed with the little company for America, the first Yearly Meeting of the Society was held. It took place at Scalehouse, about three miles from Skipton, in Yorkshire. At this meeting the subject of the visits of Friends " beyond

and a deep solicitude was felt, that He who holdeth the waters as in the hollow of his hand, might go with them, and prosper them in that whereunto they were sent. On the 1st

sea " claimed much attention, and it was agreed to recommend a general collection in aid of these gospel missions. In pursuance of this conclusion the following epistle was issued :—

At a meeting of Friends out of the Northern Counties of York, Lincoln, Lancaster, Chester, Nottingham, Derby, Westmoreland, Cumberland, Durham, and Northumberland, at Scalehouse, the 24th of the Fourth Month, 1658.

Having heard of great things done by the mighty power of God, in many nations beyond the seas, whither He hath called forth many of our dear brethren and sisters, to preach the everlasting Gospel ; by whom He hath revealed the mystery of His truth, which hath been hid from ages and generations, who are now in strange lands, in great straits and hardships, and in the daily hazard of their lives :—our bowels yearn for them, and our hearts are filled with tender love to those precious ones of God, who so freely have given up for the Seed's sake, their friends, their near relations, their country and worldly estates, yea, and their own lives also ; and in the feeling we are [have] of their trials, necessities and sufferings, we do therefore in the unity of the Spirit and bond of truth, cheerfully agree, in the Lord's name and power, to move and stir up the hearts of Friends in these counties, (whom God hath called and gathered out of the world,) with one consent, freely and liberally, to offer up unto God of their earthly substance, according as God hath blessed every one,—to be speedily sent up to London, as a free-will offering for the Seed's sake ; that the hands of those that are beyond the seas in the Lord's work may be strengthened, and their bowels refreshed, from the love of their brethren. And we commit it to the care of our dear brethren of London, Amos Stoddart, Gerrard Roberts, John Boulton, Thomas Hart, and Richard Davis, to order and dispose of what shall be from us sent unto them, for the supply of such as are already gone forth, or such as shall be moved of the Lord to go forth, into any other nation, of whose care and faithfulness we are well assured. And such Friends as are here present, are to be diligent in their several counties and places, that the work may be hastened with all convenient speed.

[Signed by many Friends.]

From the Original.

The appeal thus made was liberally responded to, and, considering the relative value of money at that period, a large amount was raised. Respecting this collection, and the manner in which it was expended, a

of the Fourth Month, 1657, Robert Fowler sailed with the party
from London, and on the following day reached the Downs. Here,

curious and interesting account, hitherto unpublished, has been found in
the Swarthmore collection of MSS., which is inserted :—

ACCOMPTS OF MONIES RECEIVED FOR THE SERVICE OF TRUTH.	£	s.	d.	MONIES DISBURSED FOR THE SERVICE OF TRUTH.	£	s.	d.
Yorkshire - -	30	0	0	For Friends diet returning			
Berkshire - -	46	11	4	from New England -	12	0	0
Essex - - -	48	10	5	John Stubbs, to Holland	4	13	0
Buckinghamshire	9	0	4	For clothes and other things	5	7	9
Kingston - -	2	15	0	To take with him -	3	10	2
Wellingborough -	5	13	0	Paid in Holland for him,			
Kent - - -	14	1	0	and other Friends there	19	18	0
Sussex - -	24	16	4	Will. Caton, to Holland	2	10	0
Camb. and Hunting-				Geo. Bayley, to France -	4	5	0
don - - -	19	12	9	Will. Shaw, a suit -	2	4	0
Cheshire - -	19	5	0	Books to France and Jersey	4	10	0
Shrewsbury - -	1	14	4				
Durham - -	21	0	0	To NEW ENGLAND.			
Guildford - -	19	17	9	For provision for their voyage	29	10	0
Lincolnshire -	12	0	0	Paid to the master for part			
Norfolk - - -	38	0	0	of his freight - -	30	0	0
Worcestershire -	10	13	1	For bedding and other things	12	8	0
Newport - -	6	8	8	And in money - -	35	4	4
Tibbalds - -	4	6	6	More to William Brend	1	10	8
Leicestershire -	4	18	6	Do. M. Weatherhead	2	0	0
Southampton -	8	18	8	Do. Sarah Gibbons	4	10	0
Cornwall - -	14	0	0	To TURKEY.			
Radnorshire. -	2	9	0				
Suffolk - - -	30	4	11	For passage, to Cpt. Marshall	25	0	0
Dorsetshire -	3	12	0	For their diet - -	10	0	0
Bedfordshire - -	2	7	0	For bedding, and other ne-			
Jacob-street -	4	4	0	cessaries - - -	7	16	0
Rutlandshire - -	4	16	4	Paid in money to them	46	19	11
Oxford - -	3	0	0	Paid by bill of exchange for			
Gloucestershire -	2	2	6	them in Turkey -	60	0	0
Somersetshire -	17	11	8	Again, by bill for John			
Banbury - -	10	13	4	Perrot in Turkey - -	20	0	0
				Again for their use in money			
The total,	443	3	5	and other things -	7	9	8
				Over,	341	6	6

William Dewsbury, who was engaged in gospel labours in Kent, went on board to visit them, and was enabled to hand them a

	£	s.	d.
Brought over,	443	3	5

	£	s.	d.
Brought over,	341	6	6
For Geo. Rofe, to Holland	2	10	0
For Ann Austin's passage back from Barbadoes -	8	6	0
For part of M. Fisher's passage back from Barbadoes	2	4	6
For letters out of France	0	17	0
To Hester Biddle -	1	10	0
To Geo. Bayley, in France	5	0	0
For Books to Virginia -	2	5	0
John Hall, to Holland	10	12	8
For two Friends that returned from Hamburgh	1	10	0
For necessaries for John Hall - - -	4	15	11
To Sam. Fisher - -	12	4	6
More to Sam. Fisher -	1	7	6
For the Friends that went to Venice - -	47	1	0
For one Friend to Jamaica, for her passage - -	6	0	0
For necessaries - -	8	5	6
To the other Friends that went to Jamaica -	12	4	8
More for Friends beyond sea	1	0	0
To Hen. Fell, clothes and necessaries - -	4	0	8
For clothes for Ann Austin, when she went to keep Sam. Fisher's house	3	1	0
To John Harwood, when he came out of France -	4	10	0

Brought over,	443	3	5

The total sum,	480	12	5

At the General or Yearly Meeting held at Skipton, the 25th day of the Second Month, 1660, an epistle was issued containing a recommendation for a similar collection. It commences thus :—

" DEAR FRIENDS AND BRETHREN,

" We having certain information from some Friends of London, of

word of encouragement. Writing to Margaret Fell about that time, he thus notices going on board :—

WILLIAM DEWSBURY TO MARGARET FELL.*

Kent, *the 5th of Fourth Month,* 1657.

DEAR SISTER,

—— Friends that go to New England I was aboard with in the Downs, the third day of this month. They were, in their measure, bold in the power of God : the life did arise in them. When I came off, they did go on in the name and power of the Lord our God. His everlasting presence keep them in the unity, in the life, and prosper them in his work : for many dear children shall come forth in the power of God in those countries where they desire to go.

In the power of the Lord God, farewell.

[signature: William Dewsbury]

As they passed down the English Channel the wind blew roughly, and it was deemed advisable to put in at Portsmouth. Whilst at this place, William Robinson, one of the eleven, addressed the following letter to Margaret Fell :—

the great work and service of the Lord beyond the seas, in several parts and regions, as Germany, America, and many other islands and places, as Florence, Mantua, Palatine, Tuscany, Italy, Rome, Turkey, Jerusalem, France, Geneva, Norway, Barbadoes, Bermuda, Antigua, Jamaica, Surinam, Newfoundland ; through all which, Friends have passed in the service of the Lord, and divers other countries, places, islands, and nations ; and among many nations of the Indians, in which they have had service for the Lord, and through great travails have published His name, and declared the everlasting gospel of peace unto them that have been afar off, that they might be brought nigh unto God," &c.

A collection is then recommended in every particular meeting, to be sent " as formerly, to London, for the service and use aforesaid."

* Caton Collection of MSS., being an ancient volume of letters of Early Friends copied by William Caton.

WILLIAM ROBINSON TO MARGARET FELL.

Southampton, *the 6th of the Fourth Month*, 1657.

M. F.,

Dear Sister, my dear love salutes thee in that which thinks not ill, which was before words were, in which I stand faithful to him who hath called us, and doth arm us against the fiery darts of the enemy, even in the fear and dread of the Almighty. I know thee and have union with thee, though absent from thee. I thought it meet to let thee know, that the ship that carries Friends to New England is now riding in Portsmouth harbour. We only stay for a fair wind. The two Friends, the man and his wife, which thou told me of when I was with thee at Swarthmore, I hear nothing of their coming to London as yet; so I thought good to let thee know the names of them that do go, which are ten in number, in the work of the ministry; Humphrey Norton, Robert Hodshon, Dorithy Waugh, Christo. Holder, William Brend, John Copeland, Rich. Doudney, Mary Weatherhead, Sarah Gibbons, Mary Clarke. The master of the ship, his name is Robert Fowler, a Friend; so in that which changes not, I remain,

William Robinson

Robert Hodshon is with me at this place, for we came hither this afternoon to have a meeting, seeing the wind is at present contrary; but we intend, if the Lord permit, to return back again to the ship to-morrow. Robert remembers his dear love to thee, and to the rest of Friends, with mine also.—W. R.

They sailed from Portsmouth on the 11th of the Fourth Month, and after once more touching English ground, the little bark was fairly launched on the mighty ocean. During the passage, several incidents of an interesting character occurred, which are detailed in a descriptive account penned by Robert Fowler himself; a manuscript copy of which, endorsed by George Fox, is still preserved among the archives of the Society in London. The narrative, though lengthy, is too interesting to be omitted in these pages. It is as follows:—

M: F

Southampton ye 6. of ye 4: mth 1657.

Deare Sister, my deare Love saluts thee; it ye wth hope in ye ....

...

William Robinson

Robert Bothum, who is wth mee at this place, ...

W: R

A TRUE RELATION OF THE VOYAGE UNDERTAKEN BY ME ROBERT
FOWLER, WITH MY SMALL VESSEL CALLED THE "WOODHOUSE;"
BUT PERFORMED BY THE LORD, LIKE AS HE DID NOAH'S ARK,
WHEREIN HE SHUT UP A FEW RIGHTEOUS PERSONS AND LANDED
THEM SAFE, EVEN AT THE HILL ARARAT.

The true discourse taken as followeth. This vessel was appointed for this service from the beginning, as I have often had
it manifested unto me ; that it was said within me several times,
" Thou hast her not for nothing ;" and also New England presented before me. Also, when she was finished and freighted,
and made to sea, contrary to my will, was brought to London,
where, speaking touching this matter to Gerard Roberts and
others, they confirmed the matter in behalf of the Lord, that it
must be so. Yet entering into reasoning, and letting in temptations and hardships, and the loss of my life, wife, and children,
with the enjoyment of all earthly things, it brought me as low as
the grave, and laid me as one dead as to the things of God. But
by his instrument George Fox, was I refreshed and raised up
again, which before was much contrary to myself, that I could as
willingly have died as have gone ; but by the strength of God I
was [now] made willing to do his will ; yea, the customs and
fashions of the custom-house could not stop me. Still was I
assaulted with the enemy, who pressed from me my servants ;*
so that for this long voyage we were but two men and three boys,
besides myself.

Upon the 1st day of the Fourth Month, called June, received
I the Lord's servants aboard, who came with a mighty hand and
an outstretched arm with them ; so that with courage we set
sail, and came to the Downs the 2nd day, where our dearly
beloved William Dewsbury, with Mich. Thompson came aboard,
and in them we were much refreshed ; and, after recommending
us to the grace of God, we launched forth.

* England had about this time fitted out a fleet for the Baltic, in
order, as was alleged, to stop the aggressions of the Swedish monarch
towards Denmark.

Again reason entered upon me, and thoughts rose in me to have gone to the Admiral, and have made complaint for the want of my servants, and for a convoy, from which thing I was withholden by that Hand which was my helper. Shortly after the south wind blew a little hard, so that it caused us to put in at Portsmouth, where I was furnished with choice of men, according to one of the captains words to me, that I might have enough for money ; but he said my vessel was so small, he would not go the voyage for her.

Certain days we lay there, wherein the ministers of Christ were not idle, but went forth and gathered sticks, and kindled a fire, and left it burning ; also several Friends came on board and visited us, in which we were refreshed. Again we launched forth from thence about the 11th day of the Fourth Month, and were put back again into South Yarmouth, where we went ashore, and there in some measure did the like. Also we met with three pretty large ships which were for the Newfoundland, who did accompany us about fifty leagues, but might have done 300, if they had not feared the men-of-war ; but for escaping them they took to the northward, and left us without hope of help as to the outward ; though before our parting it was showed to Humphrey Norton early in the morning, that they were nigh unto us that sought our lives, and he called unto me and told me ; but said, " Thus saith the Lord, ye shall be carried away as in a mist ;" and presently we espied a great ship making up towards us, and the three great ships were much afraid, and tacked about with what speed they could ; in the very interim the Lord God fulfilled his promise, and struck our enemies in the face with a contrary wind, wonderfully to our refreshment. Then upon our parting from these three ships we were brought to ask counsel of the Lord, and the word was from Him, " Cut through and steer your straightest course, and mind nothing but me ;" unto which thing He much provoked us, and caused us to meet together every day, and He himself met with us, and manifested himself largely unto us, so that by storms we were not prevented [from meeting] above three times in all our voyage. The sea was my figure, for if anything got up within, the sea without rose up against me, and then the floods clapped their hands, of which in time I took notice, and told Humphrey Norton. Again, in a vision of the night, I saw some anchors swimming about the water, and something also of a ship which crossed our way, which in our meeting I saw fulfilled, for I myself, with others, had lost ours, so that for a little season the vessel run loose in a manner ; which afterwards, by the wisdom of God, was recovered into a better condition than before.

Also upon the 25th day of the same month, in the morning, we saw another great ship making up towards us, which did appear, far off, to be a frigate, and made her sign for us to come to them, which unto me was a great cross, we being to windward of them ; and it was said, " Go speak him, the cross is sure ; did I ever fail thee therein ?" And unto others there appeared no danger in it, so that we did ; and it proved a tradesman of London, by whom we writ back. Also it is very remarkable, when we had been five weeks at sea in a bark, wherein the powers of darkness appeared in the greatest strength against us, having sailed but about 300 leagues, Humphrey Norton falling into communion with God, told me that he had received a comfortable answer ; and also that about such a day we should land in America, which was even so fulfilled. Also thus it was all the voyage with the faithful, who were carried far above storms and tempests, that when the ship went either to the right hand or to the left, their hands joined all as one, and did direct her way ; so that we have seen and said, we see the Lord leading our vessel even as it were a man leading a horse by the head ; we regarding neither latitude nor longitude, but kept to our Line, which was and is our Leader, Guide, and Rule, but they that did failed.

Upon the last day of the Fifth Month, 1657, we made land. It was part of Long Island, far contrary to the expectations of the pilot ; furthermore, our drawing had been all the passage to keep to the southwards, until the evening before we made land, and then the word was, " There is a lion in the way ;" unto which we gave obedience, and said, " Let them steer northwards until the day following ;" and soon after the middle of the day

there was a drawing to meet together before our usual time, and
it was said, that we may look abroad in the evening ; and as we
sat waiting upon the Lord they discovered the land, and our
mouths were opened in prayer and thanksgiving ; and as way
was made, we made towards it, and espying a creek, our advice
was to enter there, but the will of man [in the pilot] resisted ;
but in that state we had learned to be content, and told him both
sides were safe, but going that way would be more trouble to
him ; also he saw after he had laid by all the night, the thing
fulfilled.

Now to lay before you, in short, the largeness of the wisdom,
will, and power of God ! thus, this creek led us in between the
Dutch Plantation and Long Island, where the movings of some
Friends were unto, which otherwise had been very difficult
for them to have gotten to : also the Lord God that moved them
brought them to the place appointed, and led us into our way,
according to the word which came unto Christopher Holder,
" You are in the road to Rhode Island." In that creek came a
shallop to meet us, taking us to be strangers, we making our way
with our boat, and they spoke English, and informed us, and also
guided us along. The power of the Lord fell much upon us, and
an irresistible word came unto us, That the seed in America
shall be as the sand of the sea ; it was published in the ears of
the brethren, which caused tears to break forth with fulness of
joy ; so that presently for these places some prepared themselves,
who were Robert Hodgson, Richard Doudney, Sarah Gibbons,
Mary Weatherhead, and Dorothy Waugh, who the next day were
put safely ashore into the Dutch plantation, called New Amsterdam.* We came, and it being the First-day of the week several
came aboard to us, and we began our work. I was caused to go
to the Governor, and Robert Hodgson with me—he was moderate
both in words and actions.

Robert and I had several days before seen in a vision the
vessel in great danger ; the day following this, it was fulfilled, there

* Upon the acquisition of New Netherlands, the English changed the
name of New Amsterdam to New York, in honour of the Duke of York,
afterwards James II.

being a passage betwixt two lands, which is called by the name
of Hell-gate; we lay very conveniently for a pilot, and into that
place we came, and into it were forced, and over it were carried,
which I never heard of any before that were ; [there were] rocks
many on both sides, so that I believe one yard's length would
have endangered loss of both vessel and goods. Also there was
a shoal of fish which pursued our vessel, and followed her
strangely, and along close by our rudder ; and in our meeting
it was shewn me, these fish are to thee a figure. Thus doth the
prayers of the churches proceed to the Lord for thee and the
rest. Surely in our meeting did the thing run through me as
oil, and bid me much rejoice.

Robart Fowler

Endorsed by George Fox,
" *R. Fowler's Voyage,* 1657."

It has been already stated, that of the eleven Friends who
crossed the Atlantic in the " Woodhouse," five, viz. Robert
Hodgson, Richard Doudney, Sarah Gibbons, Mary Weatherhead,
and Dorothy Waugh, landed at New Amsterdam on the 1st of
the Sixth Month, 1657, being two months from the time of
their leaving London.

The rest of this little band of gospel labourers left New Amsterdam in Robert Fowler's vessel on the 3rd of the Sixth Month,
and passing through Long Island Sound, reached Rhode Island
in safety. Whilst here, John Copeland addressed the following
letter to his parents in England :—

Rhode Island, *the 12th of the Sixth Month,* 1657.

Dear Father and Mother,

My love salutes you and all the faithful in Christ Jesus, who
is my joy, and in whom I do rejoice at present. This is to let
you all know that I am at Rhode Island and in health, where we
are received with much joy of heart ; but now I and Christopher
Holder are going to Martha's Vineyard, in obedience to the will
of our God, whose will is our joy.

Humphrey Norton is at present at Rhode Island ; Mary Clark waiting to go towards Boston ; William Brend is towards Providence. The Lord God of Hosts is with us, the shout of a King is amongst us, the people fear our God, for his goodness is large and great, and reaches to the ends of the earth ; his power has led us all along, and I have seen his glory, and am overcome with his love. Take no thought for me, for my trust is in the Lord ; only be valiant for the truth upon earth. The Lord's power hath overshadowed me, and man I do not fear ; for my trust is in the Lord, who is become our shield and buckler, and exceeding great reward.

The enclosed is the voyage as Robert Fowler did give it, which you may read as you can. Salute me dearly to my dear friends, with whom my life is, and the Lord's power overshadow you ; so may you be preserved to his glory. Amen, amen. Stand fast in the Lord. We are about to sail to the Vineyard, and having this opportunity, I was free to let you know, by the Barbadoes, how we are. Farewell. I am your servant for the Lord's sake,

JOHN COPELAND.

CHAPTER V.

SEVERAL gospel ministers having now landed in New England, it will be interesting to trace the directions they severally took, in the prosecution of their religious labours. William Robinson appears to have been engaged for some time within the limits of Rhode Island ; he then travelled southward as far as Maryland and Virginia ; and, after an absence of two years, returned to New England. We shall hereafter have to speak of his engagements in this part of America.

Mary Clark, to whom John Copeland refers in his letter, as being at Rhode Island, " waiting to go towards Boston," arrived at that town in the latter part of the Sixth Month. The magistrates having soon been informed of the arrival of Mary Clark, immediately issued a warrant for her arrest, and on committing her to prison ordered her to be severely whipped. This punishment was executed with great barbarity, twenty strokes with a heavy three-corded whip, "laid on with fury," being inflicted upon her. For three months she was detained a prisoner in Boston gaol, during which time she suffered much from cold.

John Copeland and Christopher Holder, very early after landing on Rhode Island, felt it required of them to visit the island of Martha's Vineyard, which lay a few leagues from the main land, where they landed on the 16th of the Sixth Month. The principal portion of its inhabitants at this period consisted of Indians of the Algonquin race, among whom the Puritans had established a mission for their conversion to Christianity. At the head of this was the son of the governor of the island. The class to whom the religious labours of the two Friends were more immediately directed, being the English settlers of the island, they thought it right to attend their place of worship. Here, after waiting quietly until Mayhew, the priest, had concluded, one of them spoke a few words to the company. The liberty thus taken gave great offence, and the Friends were forthwith "thrust out of doors," by the constable. This rough treatment did not discourage them from making another attempt, and in the afternoon they again assembled with the congregation. On this occasion, "they had some dispute" on doctrinal points, and were allowed quietly to withdraw. The governor, however, participating in the prejudices against Friends, determined to rid Martha's Vineyard of them ; and accordingly, on the following morning, taking a constable with him, he called on the two strangers, and ordered them forthwith to leave the island. But John Copeland and Christopher Holder, who came as they believed in obedience to a divine call, and not in their own will, replied, that "in the will of God they stood as He made way." "It is the will of God," rejoined the governor, "that you should go to-day ;" and having hired an Indian to convey them to the mainland, ordered the Friends to pay for the passage themselves. But not being willing to facilitate their own banishment, and not feeling that it was their divine Master's will for them to leave the island, they declined to go, or to pay the Indian who was hired to take them.

The refusal was unexpected to the governor, and after directing the constable forcibly to obtain the requisite sum from the strangers, he gave peremptory orders to the natives to take them away in their canoes. The Algonquins, however, not being in any great haste to execute the bidding of the governor contrary to the will of the Friends, and at a time too when the weather was stormy, entertained them for three days with marked kindness and hospitality. A change in the weather then taking place, and the banished ones feeling that it was no longer required of them to stay on the island, the Indians, at their own request, prepared to take them across. Before leaving the island, the Friends offered to remunerate the natives for their kindness, but these poor people, from the generous impulses of their hearts, acting more in unison with the spirit of Christianity than those who were wont to be their teachers, declined to receive any reward; " You are strangers," they replied, " and Jehovah hath taught us to love strangers."* Such simple and feeling language from the lips of a North American Indian, was a striking rebuke to the bigotry and intolerance which marked the conduct of their highly professing teachers.

John Copeland and Christopher Holder landed on the coast of Massachusetts on the 20th of the Sixth Month, 1657, and proceeded to the town of Sandwich. Their arrival at this place was hailed with feelings of satisfaction by many who were sincere seekers after heavenly riches, but who had long been burthened with a lifeless ministry and dead forms in religion. To these, in the authority and life of the gospel, the two Friends were enabled to offer the word of consolation and encouragement. But the town of Sandwich had its advocates of religious intolerance, and no small commotion ensued, when it was generally known that two English Quakers had arrived amongst them. " Great was the stir and noise of the tumultuous town," they remark, " yea, all in an uproar, hearing that we, who were called by such a name as Quakers, were come into those parts. A great fire was kindled, and the hearts of many did burn within them, so that in the heat thereof some said one thing, and some another; but the most part knew not what was the matter."†

* Norton's Ensign, p. 22.　　　　　　† Ibid. p. 22.

The stay of John Copeland and Christopher Holder at Sandwich was but short, and from thence they proceeded to Plymouth. Here, as at Sandwich, their presence seems to have caused much consternation, especially among the rulers and ecclesiastics of the place. Whilst " at the ordinary there," some who desired to ascertain the fact that Quaker ministers had really arrived, came and had a " long dispute " with them ; and, finding that they were of the heretical sect, told them that they could not be permitted to remain within the limits of that colony. The Friends, however, feeling that it was required of them to return to Sandwich, frankly told the magistrates that they could not leave the colony, until they had again visited that town. They returned that night unmolested to their lodgings, but on the following morning they were arrested and taken before the magistrates. On their examination many questions were put to them, but as there was no ground for their committal to prison, they were discharged, with express orders from the bench, " to be gone out of their colony." On the following morning they left for Sandwich, but had not proceeded far before they were overtaken and arrested by a constable, who, having orders to prevent their travelling in that direction, conveyed them six miles towards Rhode Island, and then left them. This interruption of their course did not, however, deter them from attempting to reach Sandwich. The priests there, alarmed at the return of the Friends, prevailed on the local magistracy, after a few days, to have them arrested and taken back to Plymouth, where they were again examined in the presence of the governor. No infraction of the law was proved against them, they were nevertheless " required to depart " from the colony. Feeling that the service required of them in that part of New England was not accomplished, they intimated to the governor that they could not accede to his request, and that it was their intention to return to Sandwich. It appears that their gospel ministry had been instrumental in convincing many at this place of the principles of Friends, a circumstance which increased the alarm of the priests, who now exerted their utmost influence to procure their banishment. The urgent appeal was effective, and the governor to satisfy them, issued a warrant for

the arrest of the Friends, " as extravagant persons and vagabonds," to be brought before him at Plymouth. A copy of the
warrant under which they were thus deprived of their liberty
being asked for and refused, William Newland, at whose house
the meetings of the newly convinced had been held, insisted that
it was illegal thus to commit the strangers without acceding to
their demand. A severe rebuke, and a fine of ten shillings, was
the result of his exertions on behalf of the prisoners. The
prisoners again arraigned before the court at Plymouth, were told
by the magistrates, who were urged on by the priests, that there
was a law forbidding them to remain in that jurisdiction. The
Friends replied, that they could not promise to leave. The following warrant for their expulsion was then issued, accompanied
with a threat from the bench, that if they returned they should
be whipped as vagabonds :

" To the Under-Marshal of the Jurisdiction of Plymouth,

" Whereas, there hath been two extravagant persons, professing themselves to be Quakers, at the town of Plymouth, who,
according to order, may not be permitted to abide within the liberty
of this jurisdiction. These are therefore in the name of his highness, the Lord Protector of England, Scotland, and Ireland, to
will and command you forthwith, on receipt hereof, to convey the
said persons, viz. Christopher Holder and John Copeland, unto
the utmost bounds of our jurisdiction. Whereof fail not at your
peril."*

" Dated at Plymouth, the 31st of August, 1657.

The under-marshal, in fulfilment of his charge, conveyed
them fifty miles in the direction of Rhode Island, and then set
them at liberty ; and the Friends soon reached that asylum for
the persecuted.

In the course of this history, and especially in the New England division of it, several instances of Friends having entered
the public places of worship will be met with. One has already

* Norton's Ensign, p. 24.

been mentioned in the foregoing account of the religious services of C. Holder and J. Copeland.   Much censure has been undeservedly cast upon our early Friends, by some modern writers, for these acts of devotedness ; we say undeservedly, because the practice of individuals addressing the congregation after the minister had concluded his sermon, was not unfrequent during the Commonwealth, nor at all peculiar to Friends.   The subject is one of much interest, as affecting the character of many of the prominent members of the Society, during its rise, both in this country and America ; and, in the hope that they may tend to remove the censure which has been unjustly entertained in this respect, the following remarks are offered.

It is generally admitted, that the Christian church in apostolic days recognised no one individual as the appointed minister of their religious congregations, but that all present, who felt a divine call to address the assembly, were at liberty to do so.   " Ye may all prophesy," said Paul to the Corinthian church, " one by one, that all may learn, and all may be comforted ;"*—" wherefore brethren," he continues, " covet to prophesy."   The original practice of the Christian church in this respect, agreed with the usages of the Jewish Synagogues, in which it was the custom for persons holding no office or appointment, to address the assembly. Thus we find, that Paul and Barnabas preached to the Jews in their synagogue at Salamis,† and that Paul, both at Corinth and Ephesus, " entered into the synagogue and reasoned with them."‡ As the Christian church departed from its primitive purity and simplicity, this individual liberty was discontinued, but at what particular period of its history the restriction took place, it is not easy to ascertain.   Several allusions are made to these administrations in the writings of the Fathers of the first century, and we also find them noticed during the latter part of the second century.   Justin Martyr in his dialogue with Trypho the Jew, A.D. 133, mentions that the gifts of prophecy were exercised both by men and women ; they are also referred to by Ireneus, bishop of Lyons, A.D. 178.   " We hear many brethren in the church,"

* 1 Cor. xiv. 31.   † Acts xiii. 5.   ‡ Acts xviii. 4-19.

he remarks, who are endued with prophetic gifts ; who speak by the Spirit in all kinds of languages ; who bring to light the secrets of men for good purposes, and who declare divine mysteries."*

During the long night of apostacy which followed, the freedom of gospel ministry was superseded by human ordination and intervention, and it does not appear that Luther and his reforming contemporaries, were enlightened on this manifest departure from Christian principle. Amongst the dissenting bodies, however, that arose soon after the Reformation, the liberty for any individual member of the church who felt himself divinely called to address the congregation, was again admitted. The Baptist and Independent churches of Great Britain, and also the Pilgrim Fathers of New England, recognised the primitive example. In a work, entitled " The True Constitution of a particular visible church," published in 1642, by John Cotton, Puritan pastor of Boston, in Massachusetts, he thus describes the degree of liberty then allowed :—" Where there be more prophets as pastors and teachers, they may prophesy two or three, and if the time permit, the elders may call any other of the brethren, whether of the same church, or any, to speak a word of exhortation to the people, and for the better edifying of a man's self, or others, it may be lawful for any (young or old,) save only for women, to ask questions at the mouth of the prophets." The Baptists in 1643, thus express themselves on the subject : " Although it is incumbent on the pastors and teachers of the churches to be instant in preaching the word, by way of office ; yet the work of preaching the word is not so peculiarly confined to them, but that others also gifted and fitted by the Holy Ghost for it, and approved, being by lawful ways and means, in the providence of God called thereto, may publickly, ordinarily, and constantly perform it, so that they give themselves up thereto."† " The English Independents," remarks Robert Barclay, " also go so far as to affirm, that any gifted brother, as they call them, if he find himself qualified

* Modern translation from Adv. Hæres, lib. v. cap. 6.

† A declaration of the faith and order of the (Baptists) congregational churches in England. Ed. 1658.

thereto, may instruct, exhort, and preach in the church."* During
the civil wars in the time of Charles I., it was no uncommon
practice for the laity, and even for soldiers, to preach in the
public places of worship, and with the sanction of the civil power.
Sir John Cheke, when High Sheriff of Oxfordshire, preached at
the University at Oxford dressed in his sheriff's robe and gold
chain of office. The rigid Presbyterians of Scotland, however,
never admitted the liberty ; and during Cromwell's victorious
campaign in that country in 1650, the Scotch ministers expressed
their dissatisfaction with him for "opening the pulpit doors to
all intruders ;" to which he returned this memorable reply; "We
look on ministers as helpers of, not lords over, the faith of God's
people. I appeal to their consciences, whether any, denying their
doctrines or dissenting from them, will not incur the censure of a
sectary. And what is this but to deny Christians their liberty,
and assume the infallible chair ? Where do you find in Scripture that preaching is exclusively your functions ? Though an
approbation from men has order in it, and may be well, yet he
that hath not a better than that, hath none at all. I hope He
that ascended up on high, may give his gifts to whom he pleases,
and if those gifts be the seal of missions, are not you envious,
though Eldad and Medad prophesy ? You know who has bid us
covet earnestly the best gifts, but chiefly that we may prophesy ;
which the apostle explains to be, a speaking to instruction, edification, and comfort, which the instructed, edified, and comforted,
can best tell the energy and effect of.

"Now if this be evidence, take heed you envy not for your own
sakes, lest you be guilty of a greater fault than Moses reproved
in Joshua, when he envied for his sake. Indeed you err through
mistake of the Scriptures. Approbation is an act of convenience,
in respect of order, not of necessity, to give faculty to preach the
gospel. Your pretended fear, lest error should step in, is like the
man that would keep all the wine out of the country, lest men
should be drunk. It will be found an unjust and unwise jealousy,
to deny a man the liberty he hath by nature, upon a supposition

‡ Barclay's Apology, Prop. X. § XIII.

he may abuse it.   When he doth abuse it, then judge." And in
answer to the governor's complaint, that men of secular employments had usurped the office of ministry, to the scandal of the
reformed churches, he queries, "Are you troubled that Christ is
preached ? Doth it scandalize the reformed churches, and Scotland
in particular ? Is it against the covenant ? Away with the covenant if it be so. I thought the covenant and these men would
have been willing that any should speak good of the name of
Christ ; if not, it is no covenant of God's approving, nor the
kirk you mention, the spouse of Christ."*

It was in the time of the Commonwealth that the Society of
Friends arose in England, a time not only of great excitement in
the religious world, but also of great unsettlement in the State.
The Royalists had been subdued by the Parliamentarians, and Puritanism was in the ascendant. The Puritans, however, were far
from harmonious in their views on politics, and they differed still
more widely in matters of religion. The Presbyterians and
Independents formed the leading parties of the combination, and
whilst with common consent they abolished Episcopacy, there
was a rivalry between them as to the ecclesiastical government
which should be its substitute. The Presbyterians made great
efforts for the recognition of their form ; this, however, was
strenuously and successfully opposed by the Independents. The
intention of many of the leaders in parliament was to admit of
no established church, but leave every one to embrace whatever
sect was most congenial to them ; and to support such ministers
as met their approval. In 1653, the parliament actually took into
consideration the abolition of the clerical functions as savouring
of popery, and the taking away of tithes, which many of the members called a relic of Judaism. The Presbyterians were decidedly
opposed to these views ; but so strong was the feeling against the
application of tithes for the clergy, that in a house of one hundred
and eleven members, forty-three voted against such an appropria-
tion, although Cromwell, in this instance, had thrown the weight
of his influence on the Presbyterian side.† On the abolition of

* Cromwell's Letters and Speeches by Thomas Carlyle, vol. i. p. 61.
† Burton's Diary, vol. i. p. 3.

Episcopacy, the Liturgy was superseded in 1645, by another form of worship, called, the "Directory," and which continued in use until the restoration of the monarchy. The Directory was not an absolute form of devotion, but contained only some general directions to the ministers as to public prayer and preaching, and other parts of their functions, leaving them a discretionary power to fill up the vacant time. Whilst there was this general regulation as respected the form of worship, the pulpits were occupied variously by all kinds of professors. "Independent and Presbyterian priests, and some Baptist priests," observes George Fox in 1655, "had got into the steeple-houses,"* and who, now the Episcopalians were driven out, were said to hunt after a benefice as "crows do after a rotten sheep."†

Enlightened as were our early Friends on the subject of ministry and worship, they viewed with feelings of sorrow the routine of lifeless forms and ceremonies which prevailed among the various classes of the religious community;—a strong and a deep conviction rested on their minds, that the prevailing religious systems were essentially opposed to the pure and spiritual religion of Christ. They were not less fully persuaded of this, nor, it may be added, on less substantial grounds, than John Huss or Martin Luther was of the anti-christian character of the Romish church. They believed themselves called upon to testify, "in the name of the Lord," against a system which contained so woful an admixture of human invention.

Our early predecessors, when they first went forth to preach among their fellow-men, the spiritual and primitive doctrines of the gospel, frequently embraced the liberty granted in the days of the Commonwealth, of addressing the congregations in steeple-houses. As early as 1648, George Fox preached in these places. "I was moved," he observes at this date, "to go to several courts and steeple-houses at Mansfield, and other places, to warn them to leave off oppression and oaths, and to turn from deceit to the Lord, and do justly."‡ In the two succeeding years he also mentions preaching in steeple-houses. In 1651, he records several

* G. Fox's Journal, vol. i. p. 304.   † Ibid. p. 305.   ‡ Ibid. p. 105.

instances of this service. At Beverley, he writes, " I went up to the steeple-house where was a man preaching. When he had done, I was moved to speak to him, and to the people, in the mighty power of God, and turned them to their teacher, Christ Jesus. In the afternoon I went to another steeple-house, about two miles off. When the priest had done I was moved to speak to him, and to the people very largely. The people were very loving, and would have had me come again on a week-day, and preach among them."* At Malton the priest wished him to go into the pulpit, but having an objection to pulpits, he declined, and addressed the congregation from a less conspicuous place, and " having had a large opportunity among them, he departed in peace." At Pickering soon after, he had a similar opportunity.

George Fox, when he first visited Swarthmore, " went to Ulverstone steeple-house on a lecture or fast-day ; but he came not in," says Margaret Fell, " till the people were gathered : I, and my children, had been a long time there before. And when they were singing before the sermon, he came in ; and when they had done singing, he stood up upon a seat or form, and desired that he might have liberty to speak ; and he that was in the pulpit said, he might."† From Ulverstone he went to Aldenham and Ramside steeple-houses, where he also addressed the congregations. At the latter place, the priest " having acquainted " the people of G. Fox's visit, a large number attended. He also mentions preaching in several other steeple-houses during the same year.

In 1654, when Friends first visited London, they not unfrequently availed themselves of these opportunities. " Last Firstday but one," observes E. Burroughs in 1654, " I was at a steeple-house in the forenoon, and had free liberty to speak what I was free, and passed away to [our] meeting in the afternoon."‡ About the same date F. Howgill writes, " I went to E. B., who was gone to Lombard street to a public steeple-house, where most of the high notionists in the city come, and so I came to him

---

* G. Fox's Journal, vol. i. p. 154.
† Testimony of M. Fox concerning G. Fox in G. Fox's Journal.
‡ Letter to Margaret Fell, Caton MSS.

before the priest had done, and after he ceased, Edward stood up
upon a seat and spoke with a loud voice, and in much power, and
all was still and quiet ; and he spoke about one hour, and the
people were very calm ; and afterwards, I spoke, and we cleared
our consciences and passed away in peace."* In the following
year when Richard Hubberthorne visited the eastern counties, he
occasionally preached in steeple-houses. On one occasion he says,
that he " staid all day in the steeple-house with the people ;"
and on " the same day," he remarks, " James Parnell was at
another steeple-house, where the priest suffered him to speak."†
It is also notorious, that John Bunyan, who was a Baptist, held
disputations with Friends in Bedford steeple-house.

The circumstance of our early Friends entering the public
places of worship in the times of the Commonwealth, is one which
has been much misunderstood, and greatly misrepresented. For
these acts of dedication they have been calumniated as disturbers
of religious congregations, and as outraging the peace and order
of the churches. This estimate doubtless has been formed with
reference to usages of more modern date ; but to decide upon the
conduct of Friends in this particular, from a consideration of
present circumstances, would be exceedingly erroneous. In preaching in the national places of worship, they did but avail themselves of a common liberty, in a period of extraordinary excitement
on religious things. There were numerous other religious meetings held in those times, but into none of these did Friends ob-
trude themselves. Some, probably, will argue, that the fact of
their being so severely punished for persisting in this practice,
may be adduced in support of its irregularity ; but it may be answered, that the preaching of Friends almost everywhere at that
time, whether in steeple-houses or private houses, or in-doors or
out of doors, equally called down the rigour of ecclesiastical vengeance. It was not, in fact, because Friends preached in these
places so much as for what they preached, that they suffered.
When George Fox was committed to Derby prison in 1650, after
preaching in the steeple-house at " a great lecture," the mittimus
states, that his offence was for " uttering and broaching of

* Letter to Margaret Fell, Caton MSS.   † Ibid.

divers blasphemous opinions." In 1659, Gilbert Latey went to
Dunstan's steeple-house in the West, where the noted Dr. Manton
preached.   At the conclusion of the sermon Gilbert Latey
addressed the assembly relative to some errors in Manton's sermon, for which he was seized by a constable and taken before a
magistrate, who, however, gave G. Latey leave to speak for himself.
The statement he made satisfied the justice, and he replied, that
he had heard the people called Quakers were a sort of mad, whim-
sical folks ; " but," said he, " for this man, he talks very rationally, and I think for my part, you should not have brought him
before me."*   To which the constable replied, " Sir, I think so
too."   This occurred eleven years after G. Fox first visited a
steeple-house, and during that time Friends had suffered very
much for speaking in steeple-houses, yet now a magistrate
declares, that speaking rationally after the preacher had finished
in a steeple-house, is not an offence for which a man ought to be
brought before him. But the ministry of Friends struck at the very
foundation of all hierarchical systems, and the discovery of this circumstance prompted the priests to call in the aid of the civil
power to suppress the promulgation of views so opposed to
ecclesiastical domination.

The arrival of so many ministers in New England during the
summer of 1657, and more particularly the visits of Mary
Clark to Boston, and of Christopher Holder and John Copeland
to Sandwich and Plymouth, together with the marked success
which attended their labours in the propagation of their principles, caused no small degree of alarm and excitement among
those who were striving for the entire ascendancy of Puritan
orthodoxy in that country.   The safety and freedom which Rhode
Island afforded to the persecuted and banished of every country,
including the poor banished and hunted Friends, proved very
annoying to the rulers of church and state in Massachusetts.   In
their estimation it was an evil of such magnitude, and so fraught
with danger to the true interest of that religion for which they
and their forefathers had suffered, as to require counteracting

* Life of Gilbert Latey.

measures of a very decided character. The Commissioners of the United Colonies, lending a ready ear to the suggestions of intolerance, determined to exert their power and influence to effect the desired object, and, if possible, to compel the authorities of Rhode Island to unite with the other colonies of New England, in expelling Quakers from their territory. In the early part of the Seventh Month, 1657, a general meeting of this body took place at Boston, at which, in pursuance of their purpose, the following minute and letter were prepared for the governor of Rhode Island.

"*Sept.* 12*th,* 1657. The Commissioners, being informed that divers Quakers are arrived this summer at Rhode Island, and entertained there, which may prove dangerous to the colonies, thought meet to manifest their minds to the governor there, as followeth :—

" GENTLEMEN,—We suppose you have understood that the last year a company of Quakers arrived at Boston, upon no other account than to disperse their pernicious opinions, had they not been prevented by the prudent care of the government, who by that experience they had of them, being sensible of the danger that might befall the Christian religion here professed, by suffering such to be received or continued in the country, presented the same unto the Commissioners at their meeting at Plymouth ; who, upon that occasion, commended it to the general courts of the United Colonies, that all Quakers, Ranters, and such notorious heretics, might be prohibited coming among us ; and that if such should arise from amongst ourselves, speedy care might be taken to remove them ; (and as we are informed) the several jurisdictions have made provision accordingly ; but it is by experience found that means will fall short without further care by reason of your admission and receiving of such, from whence they may have opportunity to creep in amongst us, or means to infuse and spread their accursed tenets to the great trouble of the colonies, if not to the ———————— professed in them ; notwithstanding any care that hath been hitherto taken to prevent the same ; whereof we cannot but be very sensible and think no care too great to preserve us from such a pest, the contagion whereof (if received) within your colony, were dangerous to be diffused to the others by means of the intercourse, especially to the places of trade amongst us ; which we desire may be with safety continued between us ; we therefore make it our request, that you as the rest of the colonies, take such order herein that your neighbours may be freed from that danger. That you remove these Quakers that have been received, and for the future prohibit their coming amongst you ; whereunto the rule of charity to yourselves and us (we conceive), doth oblige you ; wherein if you should we hope you will not be wanting ; yet we could not but signify this our desire ; and further declare, that we apprehend that it will be our duty seriously to consider, what provision God may call us to make to prevent the aforesaid mischief ; and for our further guidance and direction herein, we desire you to impart your mind and resolution to the General Court of Massachusetts, which assembleth the 14th of October next. We have not further to trouble you at present, but to assure you we desire to continue your loving friends and neighbours, the Commissioners of the United Colonies.

"*Boston, September* 12*th*, 1657."

The letter of the Commissioners, being received by the governor of Rhode Island, was presented by him to the " Court of Trials," held at Providence, the 13th of the Eighth Month following. It was the desire of that body to maintain friendly relations with all the settlements of New England ; but, acting in unison with the law of their colony, " that none be accounted a delinquent for doctrine,"* they resolved that no settler or stranger within the limits of their jurisdiction, should be persecuted for whatever opinions in religion he might either hold or teach. The " Court of Trials," however, desiring to avoid any immediate collision with their neighbours, thought it best to return a cautious answer to the Commissioners, informing them that the subject would obtain further consideration at their own general assembly, which was to meet early in the following year. The reply, although it speaks of the doctrines of Friends as tend-

* Enactment of 1641.

ing to the " very absolute cutting down and overturning relations and civil government among men, if generally received," which had reference only to their testimony against war, evidently admitted that, although several had visited the colony, and some had received the doctrines they preached, yet the civil authorities had no complaint to prefer against them.* The general assembly of Rhode Island adverted to, met in the First Month, 1658. The communication of the Commissioners of the United Colonies, being then brought under their consideration, resulted in the preparation of the following answer :—

" *From the General Assembly to the Commissioners of the United Colonies.*

" HONOURED GENTLEMEN,—There hath been presented to our view, by our honoured president, a letter bearing date September 25th last, subscribed by the honoured gentlemen, commissioners of the united colonies, concerning a company of people, (lately arrived in these parts of the world,) commonly known by the name of Quakers ; who are generally conceived pernicious, either intentionally, or at least-wise in effect, even to the corrupting of good manners, and disturbing the common peace, and societies, of the places where they arise or resort unto, &c.

" Now, whereas freedom of different consciences, to be protected from enforcements, was the principal ground of our charter, both with respect to our humble suit for it, as also the true intent of the honourable and renowned Parliament of England, in granting the same unto us ; which freedom we still prize as the greatest happiness that men can possess in this world ; therefore, we shall, for the preservation of our civil peace and order, the more seriously take notice that those people, and any other that are here, or shall come among us, be impartially required, and to our utmost constrained, to perform all duties requisite towards the maintaining the dignity of his highness, and the government of that most renowned Commonwealth of England, in this colony ; which is most happily included under the same

---

* See answer in Appendix to vol. i. of Hutchinson's History of Massachusetts.

dominions, and we so graciously taken into protection thereof. And in case they the said people, called Quakers, which are here, or shall arise, or come among us, do refuse to submit to the doing all duties aforesaid, as training, watching, and such other engagements as are upon members of civil societies, for the preservation of the same in justice and peace ; then we determine, yea, and we resolve (however) to take and make use of the first opportunity to inform our agent residing in England, that he may humbly present the matter (as touching the considerations premised, concerning the aforesaid people called Quakers,) unto the supreme authority of England, humbly craving their advice and order, how to carry ourselves in any further respect towards those people—that therewithal there may be no damage, or infringement of that chief principle in our charter concerning freedom of conscience. And we also are so much the more encouraged to make our addresses unto the Lord Protector, for his highness and government aforesaid, for that we understand there are, or have been, many of the aforesaid people suffered to live in England ; yea, even in the heart of the nation. And thus with our truly thankful acknowledgments of the honourable care of the honoured gentlemen, Commissioners of the United Colonies, for the peace and welfare of the whole country, as is expressed in their most friendly letter, we shall at present take leave and rest. Yours, most affectionately, desirous of your honours and welfare

" John Sandford, *Clerk of the Assembly.*

"*From the General Assembly of the Colony of
Providence Plantation,*

" To the much honoured John Endicott, Governor of Massachusetts. To be also imparted to the honoured Commissioners of the United Colonies at their next meeting ; these."

The reply of the general assembly of Rhode Island was just such as might have been expected from men enlightened on the subject of religious freedom ; and the special reference which they make " to the freedom of different consciences," as being the principal ground of their charter, manifests their desire to impress on the minds of the rulers of Massachusetts, how greatly they prized that privilege. The absence of any thing like a response to the feelings which dictated the message from Massachusetts, and the probable effect of their answer in inducing a hostile feeling towards them, led them doubtless to refer in the manner they did to their being "graciously taken into protection" by England. It is evident that they wished to convey the idea, that in the event of compulsory measures being resorted to, the assistance of the Commonwealth would be sought; and the parallel which they draw between their own position and that of the mother country, by referring to the circumstance of Friends "being suffered to live in England—in the very heart of the nation," was significant of their hope, that in case of need, that assistance would not be sought in vain.

The general assembly of Rhode Island, feeling the peculiarity of their position in extending toleration to Quakers within their borders, thought it advisable to put their representative in England in possession of the facts of the case. The following extract from a letter addressed to him on the subject, still further shows the manner in which they regarded the communication of the Commissioners :—

"The last year we had laden you with much employment, which we were then put upon, by reason of some too refractory among ourselves; wherein we appealed unto you for your advice, for the more public manifestation of it with respect to our superiors. But our intelligence it seems fell short, in the great loss of the ship, which is conceived here to be cast away. We have now a new occasion, given by an old spirit, because of a sort of people, called by the name of Quakers, who are come amongst us, and have raised up divers, who seem at present to be of their spirit, whereat the colonies about us seem to be offended with us, because the said people have their liberty amongst us, as entertained into our houses, or into our assemblies. And for the present, *we have no just cause* to charge them with the breach of the civil peace; only they are constantly going forth among them about us, and vex and trouble them in point of their religion and spiritual state, though they return with many a foul scar on their bodies for the same. And the offence our neighbours take against us is, because we take not some course against the said people, either to expel them from among us, or take such courses against them as themselves do, who are in fear lest their religion should be corrupted by them. Concerning which displeasure that they seem to take ; it was expressed to us in a solemn letter, written by the Commissioners of the United Colonies at their sitting, as though they would bring us in to act according to their scantling, or else take some course to do us greater displeasure. A copy of which letter we have herewith sent unto you, wherein you may perceive how they express themselves. As also we have herewith sent our present answer unto them, to give you what light we may in this matter. There is one clause in their letter, which plainly implies a threat, though covertly expressed.

" Sir, this is our earnest and present request unto you in this matter, as you may perceive in our answer to the United Colonies, that we fly, as to our refuge in all civil respects, to his highness and honourable council, as not being subject to any others in matters of our civil state ; so may it please you to have an eye and ear open, in case our adversaries should seek to undermine us in our privileges granted unto us, and to plead our case in such sort as we may not be compelled to exercise any civil power over men's consciences, so long as human orders, in point of civility, are not corrupted and violated, which our neighbours about us do frequently practice, whereof many of us have large experience, and do judge it to be no less than a point of absolute cruelty."

Returning to Christopher Holder and John Copeland, whom we left in Rhode Island after their expulsion from Plymouth, we find them, about the middle of the Seventh Month, 1657, passing northwards to Salem, within the settlement of Massachusetts. In that vicinity they held meetings, and made converts to the doctrines they preached. Referring afterwards to this visit they thus speak : " Having obtained mercy from God, and being baptized into his covenant Christ Jesus, [we] preached freely unto them the things we had seen and heard, and our hands had handled, which as an engrafted word took place in them, such as never can be rooted out, so that our hearers in a short time became our fellow-sufferers."*

On First-day, the 21st of Seventh Month, they went to the Puritan place of worship at Salem ; and, after the priest had concluded, Christopher Holder felt a religious call to address the assembly. Here, however, as in Martha's Vineyard, he was not allowed to proceed, one of the Commissioners, " with much fury" seized him, and, " haling him back by the hair of his head,"† violently thrust a glove and handkerchief into his mouth. Samuel Shattock, who afterwards became convinced, on witnessing the furious conduct of the Commissioner, and fearful lest the Friend might be choked, interfered, and, taking the hand of the incensed ruler, drew it away. Shattock, though a man of " good reputation,"‡ had to suffer severely for thus evincing his kindness to the stranger ; being sent the next day, as a prisoner with the two Friends to Boston. The course taken by the authorities of Boston with the strangers, was to examine them separately, in order " to find them in contradictions ;" and for this purpose, Bellingham, and the secretary, accompanied by " the Elder and Deacon" of the place, visited the prisoners. " But," remark the Friends, " we abiding in the truth, which is but one, spake one thing, so that they had no advantage against us, neither could take hold of any thing we had spoken." The inquisitors, however, not being willing to acknowledge that their labour was altogether lost, declared that their answers " were delusive, and that the devil had taught them a deal of subtilty."§

A few hours after this interview, Christopher Holder and John Copeland were ushered into the presence of the Governor and Commissioners ; and, after undergoing a frivolous examination, were sentenced, under " the law against Quakers," to receive thirty lashes. The brutal manner in which the sentence was carried out, was in accordance with the spirit that prompted the rulers to pass the cruel law. A three-corded knotted whip was used on the occasion ; and the executioner, to make more sure of his

---

* Norton's Ensign, p. 60.   † New England Judged, p. 40.
‡ New England Judged, 41.   § Norton's Ensign, p. 61.

blows, "measured his ground," and then "fetched his strokes with all his might."* Thirty strokes thus inflicted, as will be readily imagined, left the sufferers miserably torn and lacerated ; and in this state they were conveyed to their prison cell. Here, without any bedding, or even straw to lie on, the inhuman gaoler kept them for three days without food or drink ; and in this dismal abode, often exposed to damp and cold, were these faithful men confined for the space of nine weeks. We may wonder that under such aggravated cruelties, their lives were spared, but He, for whose holy cause they thus suffered, was near to support and console them. His ancient promise was fulfilled in their experience, and they rejoiced in the comforting presence of his living power.

Samuel Shattock, who was committed to prison on the charge of being " a friend to the Quakers,"† was released on his giving a bond in the sum of twenty pounds, to answer the charge at the ensuing court, " and not to assemble with any of the people called Quakers at their meetings."‡ Lawrence and Cassandra Southwick, " an aged and grave couple"§ of Salem, who had entertained the two gospel messengers, were also arrested on a similar charge. Lawrence, being a member of the Puritan church, was released to receive his punishment in the shape of church censure. Cassandra, who had long dissented from the " Pilgrim Fathers," in both doctrine and worship, and who was not therefore amenable to their discipline, was obliged to expiate her offence by an imprisonment of seven weeks in Boston gaol.

Richard Doudney, who left the " Woodhouse " at New Amsterdam, was engaged for several weeks in that vicinity. He then directed his course towards Rhode Island, and, again proceeding northwards, entered Massachusetts. In the early part of the Ninth Month he reached Dedham, where, on being discovered by his speech to be a Friend, he was apprehended, and forthwith carried before the authorities at Boston. In less than three hours after he had entered this place, he was subjected to a cruel

* New England Judged, p. 40.　　† Ibid, p. 41.　　‡ Ibid, p. 41.
§ Ibid, p. 42.

whipping of thirty lashes, and was then sent to share the lot of his friends in Boston gaol.

It will be readily supposed that the course pursued by the priests and ruling powers of Massachusetts towards Friends, must have raised in the minds of many of the honest-hearted settlers no inconsiderable degree of prejudice against them. The distorted views of Quaker tenets, which were industriously circulated throughout New England, in justification of the cruelties practised, could scarcely fail to produce such a result. In the American colonies, as well as in England, calumny and misrepresentation were too generally favourite weapons of the enemies of the new Society. From a very early date it had been the practice of Friends, in order to correct the public mind in reference to their principles, to put forth declarations of their christian faith, and this course Christopher Holder and John Copeland felt it right to adopt whilst imprisoned at Boston. The document they issued, an imperfect copy of which has been preserved, is rendered the more interesting, as being, it is believed, the first written exposition of the doctrinal views of the Society,* and containing, as it does, clear evidence of the soundness of the views of our early Friends, is additionally valuable. Richard Doudney, on joining his imprisoned friends, also attached his signature to the declaration. There is but little doubt that this document is the " paper of exhortation " ‡ referred to by the historian Sewel ; it is as follows :

A Declaration of Faith, and an exhortation to obedience thereto, issued by Christopher Holder, John Copeland and Richard Doudney, while in Prison at Boston in New England, 1657.

" Whereas it is reported by them that have not a bridle to their tongues, that we, who are by the world called Quakers, are blasphemers, heretics, and deceivers ; and that we do deny the

---

* The first Declaration or Confession of Faith published in England, of which any record exists, appears to have been the one put forth by Richard Farnsworth, in 1658.—*Vide*, Evan's " Exposition of the Faith of the Religious Society of Friends," p. xiv.

† Sewel's History, p. 172.

scriptures, and the truth therein contained : therefore, we, who are here in prison, shall in few words, in truth and plainness, declare unto all people that may see this, the ground of our religion, and the faith that we contend for, and the cause wherefore we suffer.

" Therefore, when you read our words, let the meek spirit bear rule, and weigh them in the equal balance, and stand out of prejudice, in the light that judgeth all things, and measureth and manifesteth all things.

" As [for us] we do believe in the only true and living God, the Father of our Lord Jesus Christ, who hath made the heavens and the earth, the sea and all things in them contained, and doth uphold all things that he hath created by the word of his power.   Who, at sundry times, and in divers manners, spake in time past to our fathers by the prophets, but in these last days he hath spoken unto us by his Son, whom he hath made heir of all things, by whom he made the world.   The which Son is that Jesus Christ that was born of the Virgin ; who suffered for our offences, and is risen again for our justi- fication, and is ascended into the highest heavens, and sitteth at the right hand of God the Father.   Even in him do we be- lieve ; who is the only begotten Son of the Father, full of grace and truth.   And in him do we trust alone for salva- tion ; by whose blood we are washed from sin ; through whom we have access to the Father with boldness, being justified by faith in believing in his name.   Who hath sent forth the Holy Ghost, to wit, the Spirit of Truth, that proceedeth from the Father and the Son ; by which we are sealed and adopted sons and heirs of the kingdom of heaven.   From the which Spirit, the Scriptures of truth were given forth, as, saith the Apostle Peter, ' Holy men of God spake as they were moved by the Holy Ghost.'   The which were written for our admonition, on whom the ends of the world are come ; and are profitable for the man of God, to reprove, and to exhort, and to admonish, as the Spirit of God bringeth them unto him, and openeth them in him, and giveth him the understanding of them.

" So that before all [men] we do declare that we do believe in God the Father, Son and Holy Spirit, according as they are [declared of in the] Scriptures ; and the Scriptures we own to be a true declaration of the Father, Son and Spirit ; in [which] is declared what· was in the beginning, what was present, and was to come.

"Therefore, all [ye] people in whom honesty is ! stand still and consider. Believe not them that say, Report, and we will report it—that say, Come, let us smite them with the tongue ; but try all things, and hold fast that which is good. Again we say, take heed of believing and giving credit to reports ; for know that the truth in all ages was spoken against, and they that lived in it, were, in all ages of the world, hated, persecuted, and imprisoned, under the names of heretics, blasphemers, and

    [Here part of the paper is torn off; and it can only be known, by an unintelligible shred, that fourteen lines are lost. We read again as follows :]

" that showeth you the secrets of your hearts, and the deeds that are not good. Therefore, while you have light, believe in the light, that you may be the children of the light ; for, as you love it and obey it, it will lead you to repentance, bring you to know Him in whom is remission of sins, in whom God is well pleased ; who will give you an entrance into the kingdom of God, an inheritance amongst them that are sanctified. For this is the desire of our souls for all that have the least breathings after God, that they may come to know Him in deed and in truth, and find his power in and with them, to keep them from falling, and to present them faultless before the throne of his glory ; who is the strength and life of all them that put their trust in Him ; who upholdeth all things by the word of his power ; who is God over all, blessed for ever. Amen.

Thus we remain friends to all that fear the Lord ; who are sufferers, not for evil doing, but for bearing testimony to the truth, in obedience to the Lord God of life ; unto whom we commit our cause ; who is risen to plead the cause of the innocent, and to help him that hath no help on the earth ; who will be avenged on all his enemies, and will repay the proud doers.

" CHRISTOPHER HOLDER,
" JOHN COPELAND,
" RICHARD DOUDNEY,

" *From the House of Correction the* 1*st of the*
    " *Eighth Month*, 1657, *in Boston.*"

I certify that the foregoing is an accurate and true copy of the original document, issued by the above-named Friends, so far as the same can in its present mutilated state be read ; and that it exactly corresponds with the original, except that, for the sake of perspicuity, some additional points have been inserted, the orthography has been adapted to modern usage, some words, not legible, have been supplied within crotchets, and a few grammatical errors have been corrected.

GOOLD BROWN.*

New York, Ninth Month 23rd, 1829.

In addition to the foregoing, Christopher Holder and John Copeland prepared a document, shewing how contrary to the tenor of the New Testament was the persecuting spirit exhibited in New England ; with a warning to those who indulged therein. This paper gave great offence to the magistrates. The malevolent Endicott told the prisoners that they deserved to be hanged for writing it ; and if he had possessed power to execute his desires, the gibbet on Boston Common would, in all probability, soon have terminated the labours of these good men. The governor and deputy-governor, who, in their hatred to Quaker doctrines, were resolved to crush every appearance of them in Massachusetts, determined that those whom they had imprisoned in Boston gaol should feel the utmost weight of their hand, and, overstepping the bounds of their existing laws, cruel as they were, they ordered all the Friends then in prison to be " severely whipped twice a week," the punishment to commence with fifteen lashes, and to increase the number by three, at every successive application of the degrading sentence.

Severe as the Massachusetts law of 1656 had been against the Quakers, its promoters found, to their disappointment and dismay, that it failed to accomplish its purpose. The rulers of Boston, with Endicott at their head, urged blindly on by their

---

* The original was obtained by Goold Brown from a distant relative, whose ancestors were members of our religious Society of Pembroke, in Plymouth county, Massachusetts. He has forwarded to us a copy of the words remaining in the mutilated part of the document referred to ; they are, however, so few and isolated as not to have any intelligible meaning. They are therefore not inserted.

animosity to the new sect, concluded to try the effect of yet severer measures, and at their court in the Eighth Month, 1657, passed the following law:

" As an addition to the late order, in reference to the coming, or bringing in any of the cursed sect of the Quakers into this jurisdiction, It is ordered, that whosoever shall from henceforth bring, or cause to be brought, directly or indirectly, any known Quaker or Quakers, or other blasphemous heretics into this jurisdiction, every such person shall forfeit the sum of £100. to the country, and shall, by warrant from any magistrate, be committed to prison, there to remain, until the penalty be fully satisfied and paid ; and if any person or persons within this jurisdiction, shall henceforth entertain or conceal any Quaker or Quakers, or other blasphemous heretics (knowing them to be so) every such person shall forfeit to the country forty shillings for every hour's concealment and entertainment of any Quaker or Quakers, &c., and shall be committed to prison till the forfeitures be fully satisfied and paid : And it is further ordered, that if any Quaker or Quakers shall presume (after they have once suffered what the law requireth) to come into this jurisdiction, every such male Quaker shall, for the first offence, have one of his ears cut off, and he kept at work in the house of correction, till he can be sent away at his own charge ; and for the second offence, shall have his other ear cut off, and kept at the house of correction as aforesaid. And every woman Quaker that hath suffered the law here, that shall presume to come into this jurisdiction shall be severely whipped, and kept at the house of correction at work, till she be sent away at her own charge ; and so also for her coming again, she shall be used as aforesaid : And for every Quaker, he or she, that shall a third time offend, they shall have their tongues bored through with a hot iron, and kept at the house of correction close to work till they be sent away at their own charge. And it is further ordered, That all and every Quaker, arising from amongst ourselves, shall be dealt with and suffer the like punishment, as the law provides against foreign Quakers.

" EDWARD RAWSON, *Secretary.*"
" *Boston, 14th day of October, 1657.*"

The barbarous and illegal proceedings of Endicott and Bellingham, in ordering the imprisoned Friends to be whipped twice a week in the manner described, raised loud murmurs among many inhabitants of the town, who felt that such cruel indignities were alike repugnant to humanity and justice. The compassion thus excited towards the sufferers, effected their release, and on the 24th of the Ninth Month, they obtained their discharge. The law which had been enacted in the previous month was then read to them, when they were forthwith banished from the colony, except Cassandra Southwick, who was permitted to return to her home at Salem. In addition to Christopher Holder, John Copeland and Richard Doudney, we find that Mary Clark was banished on this occasion.

Humphrey Norton, who landed from Robert Fowler's vessel at Rhode Island, appears to have been engaged in that colony during the Sixth and Seventh Months, and in the following month, within the limits of Plymouth colony. On entering the latter he proceeded forthwith to Sandwich, where he laboured in the work of the ministry among those who had now become his fellow-professors. He was not, however, allowed to remain long undisturbed. A warrant was issued against him on the vague charge of being an extravagant person, and he was arrested and conveyed to Plymouth. Having been detained there a considerable time without examination, Humphrey began to fear that the court then sitting would adjourn without giving him a hearing; he therefore sent this brief message to the magistrates.

" Seeing you have apprehended me publicly as an evil doer, and have continued me [a prisoner] contrary to law, equity, and good conscience, I require of you a public examination, and if found guilty, to be publickly punished ; if not, cleared."*

The magistrates accordingly had the prisoner brought before them. Several of them evinced a feeling of moderation, but not so the governor, who commenced an attack on the doctrines of Friends, denying that the light which enlightened every man was sufficient for salvation. But Humphrey Norton showed him by

---

* Norton's Ensign, p. 25.

the declaration of Holy Writ, that "the grace of God, that bringeth salvation hath appeared unto all men ;" and that Christ had said "my grace is sufficient for thee." The governor then asked him "whether the Scriptures were not the rule of life and ground of faith." He replied, that it was only "through faith in Christ Jesus," the great Author and Finisher of our faith, and the true Rule and Guide of life, that the Scriptures were able to make wise unto salvation.* Unable to convict him of any breach of their laws, they nevertheless sentenced him to banishment. Having been taken by the officers fifty miles in the direction of Rhode Island, he proceeded to that settlement, within the limits of which he laboured for some months in the work of his Great Master. Towards the close of the year, he passed over to Long Island, and arriving in the Twelfth Month at Southhold, he was arrested and taken to New Haven in Connecticut, where he was heavily ironed, and imprisoned for twenty-one days, and, notwithstanding the severity of the season, was also denied the use both of fire and candle. To his further sufferings at New Haven, we shall have occasion again to refer.

William Brend, who we may here remark, was an aged person, after landing with his companions at Rhode Island, appears to have confined his gospel labours to that province until the Eleventh Month of 1657 ; when, being joined by his young friend John Copeland, who had been but a few weeks before banished from Boston, he set out on a visit to the colony of Plymouth. They first proceeded to Scituate, (now Pembroke) where they met with their fellow-voyager Sarah Gibbons, who had lately come from New Netherlands. At Scituate there were those who rejoiced in the spread of the doctrines declared by Friends, and at the house of James Cudworth, a magistrate, the three gospel labourers met with a cordial reception. Their presence in the colony again disturbed the rulers at Plymouth, and, anticipating that neither Cudworth, nor his fellow-magistrates of Scituate, would prosecute them, officers were dispatched for their arrest. Timothy Hatherly, another magistrate of Scituate, on

* Norton's Ensign, p. 33.

examining the warrant of the officers, significantly observed, " Mr. Envy had procured this ;" and, on his own responsibility refused to permit the arrest to take place.   Thus shielded from their enemies, William Brend and John Copeland pursued their religious engagements without interruption.   The heart of Timothy Hatherly had evidently been tendered by the Day-spring from on high, awakening his interest for the spread of vital religion, and for the preservation of its advocates from the hands of evil men.   With this feeling, the worthy magistrate, on the departure of William Brend and John Copeland, furnished them with the following pass :—

" These are, therefore, to any that may interrupt these two men in their passage, that ye let them pass quietly on their way, they offering no wrong to any.
                                        " TIMOTHY HATHERLY."*

With this pass, the two Friends left Scituate, intending to proceed without delay to the colonies of Rhode Island and Connecticut ; and in their journey they passed through Plymouth. On hearing this, the magistrates immediately issued a warrant for their arrest, which was soon accomplished.   Being brought before the authorities, they were required to enter into an engagement to leave that jurisdiction within forty-eight hours.   They replied that it was with the intention of proceeding elsewhere that they were pursuing the journey, but that they felt restrained from making a promise to do so.   This being construed by the bench into contemptuous perverseness, the travellers were sentenced to a severe scourging.   It was in vain that these persecuted men pleaded their rights as Englishmen, to travel in any part of the dominions of their country ; " the protector's instrument of government" was unheeded by the persecuting magistrates.

The rulers of the colony of Plymouth, like their fellow professors at Boston, found that their efforts for the suppression of

* Norton's Ensign, p. 28.

Quakerism were abortive. Ministers of the new Society continued to arrive within their limits, and the doctrines which they preached had been received by many, who rejoiced to welcome them to their homes. The noble conduct of Cudworth and Hatherly, in protecting the persecuted Friends, tended greatly to increase the gloomy apprehensions of the Puritans. These alarming indications of the spread of the " Quaker contagion," having obtained the grave consideration of the Court at Plymouth, induced it to enact the following law.

" Whereas there hath several persons come into this Government commonly called Quakers, whose doctrine and practices manifestly tend to the subversion of the fundamentals of Christian religion, church order, and civil peace of this Government, as appears by the testimonies given in sundry depositions and other. It is therefore enacted by the Court and authority thereof, that no Quaker or person commonly so called, be entertained by any person or persons within this Government, under the penalty of five pounds for every such default or be whipped. And in case any one shall entertain any such person ignorantly, if he shall testify on his oath that he knew not them to be such, he shall be free of the aforesaid penalty, provided he, upon his first discerning them to be such, do discover them to the constable or his deputy."

The passing of the foregoing order brings us to the close of the year 1657, a year memorable in the early history of Friends in America. In addition to those who landed from the " Woodhouse," New England was also visited towards the close of this year by John Rous, William Leddra, and Thomas Harris from Barbadoes. There were, therefore, at least ten Friends who were travelling at this period in the work of the ministry in that province. From what has already been related, it is evident that the work in which they were engaged was not of human appointment, and that, under the divine blessing, the precious truths they advocated, had taken root, and were spreading in the western world.

BOSTON, FROM DORCHESTER-NECK.

CHAPTER VI.

Humphrey Norton's sufferings at New Haven—He proceeds, accompanied by John Rous, to Plymouth ; their sufferings at that place—William Brend, Mary Dyer, Mary Wetherhead, John Copeland, and John Rous, visit New Haven—William Leddra passes into Connecticut ; is banished thence, and returns to Rhode Island — Sarah Gibbons and Dorothy Waugh proceed to Massachusetts ; their perilous journey thither—They arrive at Boston ; are imprisoned and scourged—They go to Providence and Connecticut ; are banished from Connecticut—Robert Hodgson visits New England—Richard Doudney, Mary Clark, and Mary Wetherhead are shipwrecked and drowned—Ten Friends in the ministry meet on Rhode Island—Thomas Harris goes to Boston, and William Brend and William Leddra to Salem — Their sufferings at those places — Humphrey Norton and John Rous visit Boston — They are imprisoned and scourged—The inhabitants of Boston subscribe money for the liberation of Friends from gaol.

HUMPHREY NORTON, whom we have noticed as a prisoner at New Haven, in Connecticut, in the latter part of 1657, was brought before the court there, in the beginning of the First Month following. On his examination he was not charged with any breach of the civil law, but his persecutors considered that they had more serious things to allege against him on doctrinal grounds, and a priest undertook to prove to the court, that he was guilty of heresy. Humphrey attempting to reply to his allegations, a large iron key was placed to his mouth, and so tied, as to prevent his speaking. He was told that when the priest had concluded he might answer the charges, but before he had an opportunity of doing so, the priest " had fled."* The trial occupied two days, and, after a long and frivolous examination, and many attempts on the part of the authorities, to entrap the prisoner in

* Norton's Ensign, p. 50.

his words, he was re-committed. After ten days he was again brought before the court, when he received a sentence from which humanity recoils. He was first to be whipped, then burnt in the hand with the letter H, to signify that he was a condemned heretic ; to be fined ten pounds for the costs and charges of the trial, and finally to be banished from the colony of New Haven, "upon the utmost penalty that the law could inflict."* The court determined that no time should be lost in subjecting this victim of their displeasure to the cruel decree ; and, in the afternoon of the same day, amidst a large concourse of people, gathered by beat of drum, the whipping and burning were carried into execution. The first act was to place him in the stocks "in view of all the people," and when he had been stripped to the waist, "with his back to the magistrates," the flogging commenced. Thirty-six "cruel stripes" were inflicted : and probably more would have been given, had not the inhuman exhibition disgusted the by-standers. "Do they mean to kill the man ?"† was the language of dissatisfaction which broke from the crowd. Humphrey, how-ever, who was remarkably freed from the feeling of pain observed that "his body was as if it had been covered with balm."‡ This part of the sentence being executed, the officers turned the face of the sufferer to the magistrates, and having fastened his right hand in the stocks, burnt the letter H upon it, "more deep," says John Rous, "then ever I saw an impression upon any living creature."§ The presence of Him, who supports his devoted children under every variety of trial, was, however, very near this faithful man, and on being loosed from the stocks, "the Lord opened his mouth in prayer, and he uttered his voice towards heaven, from whence came his help, to the astonishment of them all."‖ He was enabled to rejoice and give thanks, for the peace, and love, and joy, with which his heart abounded. He was now told that he might have his liberty, on paying the fine and prison fees. To this he replied, that if the sum of two-pence only would

* Norton's Ensign, p. 50.
† The Secret Works of a cruel people, p. 6.
‡ Norton's Ensign, p. 51.   § Ibid, p. 51.
‖ New England Judged, p. 155.

obtain his discharge, he could not pay it, or consent for others to do so for him. The authorities, being evidently ashamed of their cruel proceedings, then told him, that if he would only promise to pay the amount hereafter, he should be released ; but this also he declined. A Dutch settler, touched with compassion for the sufferer, now came forward, and, offering twenty nobles, obtained his discharge. " His spirit within him," the friendly settler remarked, " made him do it."* Humphrey Norton was then banished the colony of New Haven, from whence he proceeded to Rhode Island. These sufferings of Humphrey Norton, afford the first instance of the persecution of Friends in Connecticut.

After remaining for several weeks in the province of Rhode Island, Humphrey Norton believed it to be required of him to attend the next general court for the colony of Plymouth ; and John Rous, who had recently returned from a visit to some parts of Connecticut, felt it his duty to accompany him. The immediate object of Humphrey Norton's visit to Plymouth, was to plead with the authorities of that colony, on account of their intolerant and cruel proceedings towards Friends ; and in order that the governor might know the object of his coming, he forwarded previously, an epitome of the sufferings which his fellow-professors had endured in that settlement, with some remarks upon them. " These," he observes, " and what further may be presented to remembrance by the Lord, are the just grounds whereupon my intent and desire is, to appear before your court and country, and all who may be concerned therein, if God permit."†

On the 1st of the Fourth Month, 1658, the two Friends arrived at Plymouth, where they were immediately arrested and imprisoned, and two days after, they were brought before the court and questioned, as to their motives in coming. Humphrey referred them to the paper he had forwarded. The governor, however, unwilling to admit that he had received it, uttered several falsehoods and unfounded charges, which called forth a rebuke from Humphrey Norton. John Rous, feeling that, as a free-born Englishman, he had an undoubted right to visit any part of the

* Norton's Ensign, p. 51.   † Ibid, p. 39.

British dominions, denied the authority of the law, by which they sought to exclude Friends from the territory. The examination, however, ended in their being re-committed to prison. The Plymouth records charge them with having acted turbulently on the occasion. Humphrey Norton's reproof to the governor for his falsehoods, and the pleading of John Rous for his rights as a British subject, appear to have constituted the only ground for the charge.

Two days after the two Friends had been remanded, they were again brought before the court; for the object, it would appear, of being charged with heresy, by an individual who was anxious for the support of Puritan orthodoxy. The prisoners, confident of being able to disprove the obnoxious charge, desired a public opportunity of doing so; but the magistrates, fearing the result of a disputation, remanded them a second time; their accuser with some others being requested to visit them in prison, to hear what they had to say in answer to the charge. The interview having ended, it was reported to the court, that there was "very little difference betwixt what Winter affirmed, and the said Humphrey Norton owned;" from which it seems that their accuser failed to sustain his allegation. On being again brought into court, Humphrey Norton desired that he might be permitted to read the paper which he had written, in explanation of the object of his visit to the colony. The governor, however, who .still pretended to be ignorant of its contents, not only refused the request, but again used abusive language, calling the prisoners "inordinate fellows," "Papists," "Jesuits," and many other opprobrious epithets. Humphrey, indignant at these malicious expressions, replied, "Thy clamorous tongue I regard no more than the dust under my feet."*

The rulers at Plymouth, disappointed in not having sufficient evidence to convict the two Friends of heresy, and, determined that they should suffer for thus venturing within the limits of the colony, concluded to tender them the oath of allegiance, a snare in which they well knew that these conscientious men would be

---

* Colonial Records.

entrapped. On their refusal of the oath, the magistrates at once ordered them to be flogged ; Humphrey Norton being sentenced to receive twenty-three, and John Rous fifteen lashes. On their leaving the court, several of the inhabitants, desirous to express the sympathy which they felt for the strangers, shook hands with them as they passed ; but the envious rulers, disturbed at these tokens of Christian kindness, ordered three of them to be placed in the stocks for the act. The prisoners on arriving at the place of punishment, felt their minds influenced by the spirit of prayer, and in the midst of the assembled multitude, they supplicated the Most High. The flogging, although executed with great severity, was borne by the sufferers with marked patience and meekness. Being informed at its conclusion, that on the payment of the fees they might have their liberty, they answered, that if anything was due, they might go to the keeper of that purse, which had been filled by robberies on the innocent. A Puritan minister, who had been banished from Virginia for nonconformity to Episcopacy, was heard to remark, in reference to this exciting occasion ;—" On my conscience, you are men of noble spirits ; I could neither find it in my heart to stay in the court to hear and see the proceedings, nor come to the stocks to see your sufferings." " This persecution," remarks John Rous, " did prove much for the advantage of truth, and their [the magistrates] disadvantage ; for Friends did with much boldness own us openly in it, and it did work deeply with many." After a further imprisonment of a few days, they were released, and returned to Rhode Island.

The sufferings of Humphrey Norton at New Haven, and his banishment from thence, did not deter other gospel labourers from visiting that settlement. William Brend, Mary Dyer, and Mary Wetherhead, went thither from Rhode Island, to bear a public testimony against the cruelty and bigotry of the rulers, and arrived in the Second Month, 1658 ; but they were immediately arrested, and forcibly carried back to Rhode Island.

During the same month, John Rous and John Copeland, under a sense of religious duty, visited the colony of Connecticut. They first proceeded to Hartford, where resided John Winthrop, the

governor, who was an enlightened man, and averse to persecution.
At Hartford lived also a noted Puritan disputant, with whom
John Copeland and 'John Rous had a discussion in the presence of
the governor, and several of the magistrates. The priest proposed
several questions, with a view to confound the two Friends :
" What is God ?" he asked. " A spirit," replied the Friends.
The priest hoping by a syllogistic mode of reasoning to show the
contrary, denied their assertion. " A spirit is an angel," said he,
" an angel is a creature ; God is not a creature, and therefore God
is not a spirit." But the Friends, confident in the truth of their
assertion, replied that his conclusion was contrary to Scripture,
and that " it shewed he had learned more of logic than of God ;
for had he known God, he dared not thus to have spoken."* The
priest, supposing that he had to deal with two ignorant men, proceeded to other subjects ; but in these also, notwithstanding his
artful mode of reasoning, he signally failed ; " much," says John
Rous, " to the glory of truth, and his own shame." Much of
the day having been thus spent in polemical discussion, the magistrates informed the strangers that, by a law of the colony, their
presence could not be allowed within its limits. Their visit to
Connecticut was short, but it appears to have been instrumental
for good ; "the Lord," says John Rous, "gave us no small
dominion, and after some stay there we returned to Rhode Island."
After remarking that the four colonies of Massachusetts, Plymouth, New Haven, and Connecticut, had united in the unholy
purpose of banishing Friends, John Rous says of Connecticut,
" amongst all the colonies, found we not the like moderation as
in this ; most of the magistrates being more noble than those of
the others."†

About the Third Month of this year, William Leddra, who
had lately arrived at Rhode Island from Barbadoes, in company
with Thomas Harris, also felt drawn to visit the colony of Connecticut. After having had some religious service there, he was
arrested and banished, and subsequently returned to Rhode Island.
Sarah Gibbons, and Dorothy Waugh, who had been engaged in

---

* Norton's Ensign, p. 52.　　　　† Ibid, p. 53.

Rhode Island, left that colony in the Second Month of 1658, and proceeded on a gospel mission to Salem. The journey, which was performed on foot, occupied them several days. Their way was through a wilderness country of more than sixty miles, and being performed in the winter season, they were exposed to " great storms and tempests of frost and snow," while their only shelter at night was such as the forests afforded. " They lodged," says Humphrey Norton, " in the wilderness day and night— through which they cheerfully passed to accomplish the will and work of God, who, for their reward, brought them, beyond their expectation, to their appointed place, where their message was gladly received."* Having been occupied in gospel labours at and about Salem for two weeks, they believed it required of them again to go to the persecuting town of Boston. Arrived here, they felt it their duty to attend the weekly lecture given at the place of public worship, and, after waiting quietly until the lecturer had finished, Sarah Gibbons began to address the company. She had not, however, uttered many sentences, before she was taken into custody by the sergeant. Dorothy Waugh then rose, and having repeated the Scripture passage, " Fear God and give glory to his name,"† she also was stopped, and with her companion was hurried to prison, in the midst of a concourse of excited people. After being closely confined for three days, these faithful women were brought before the intolerant Endicott and Bellingham, who sentenced them to be whipped ; an order which was cruelly executed, " with a threefold cord, having knots at the ends for tearing the flesh." The whipping being over, " the people were astonished" to hear these innocent sufferers vocally offering praise and thanksgiving to their Heavenly Father, for the help of His sustaining presence in the time of their extremity. From this scene they were conveyed back to the prison-house, the gaoler refusing to let them go without the payment of his fees. Here they were detained for four days, when a kind-hearted inhabitant of Rhode Island obtained their release.

On leaving Boston, they proceeded southward to Providence

* Norton's Ensign, p. 69.   † Ibid p. 70.

and Rhode Island, where they remained for some weeks. They then felt drawn to pay a visit to Connecticut ; and, leaving the company of many of their dear and sympathizing friends, they travelled to Hartford. Of the nature of their religious services at this town we are uninformed. In consequence of the laws of the colony, however, they were soon placed under confinement,* and in a short time banished from its soil. Excepting that some extra apparel, which they took with them, was sold by the gaoler to pay his fees, no act of persecution befel them at Hartford.

Robert Hodgson, who, on reaching the shores of America, proceeded to visit New Netherlands and Long Island, arrived early in 1658, within the limits of Rhode Island, from whence he passed eastward as far as Marshfield, in the colony of Plymouth.

Excepting Mary Dyer, of Rhode Island, and John Rous, William Leddra, and Thomas Harris, from Barbadoes, up to the Third Month, 1658, the eleven who had crossed the Atlantic in the "Woodhouse," were the only Friends labouring in the work of the gospel in New England ; making in the whole fifteen, who were publicly pleading the cause of their Lord in this interesting part of the world. But it pleased the All-wise Disposer of events, whose purposes, however mysterious, we dare not question, to reduce the number of this devoted band. We have previously stated that Richard Doudney and Mary Clark were fellow-prisoners at Boston, and that they were liberated in the Ninth Month, 1657, after which, it appears, they were mostly engaged within the colony of Rhode Island. Mary Wetherhead had landed at New Amsterdam, but her presence not being allowed, either in the Dutch colony, or at New Haven, she also went to Rhode Island in the Second Month, 1658. Soon afterwards, these three Friends suffered shipwreck and were drowned.

About the middle of the Fourth Month following, ten of the remaining number met on Rhode Island, but they were not permitted long to enjoy this favoured retreat. On the 15th, William Brend, Thomas Harris, and William Leddra, proceeded

* Secret Works, p. 6.

northward for Massachusetts : in a day or two after, Christopher Holder and John Copeland passed eastward to Plymouth ; and two weeks later, Humphrey Norton and John Rous felt it to be their religious duty to go to Boston ; the three women Friends, Sarah Gibbons, Dorothy Waugh, and Mary Dyer, still remaining on Rhode Island. We next proceed to some particulars of the services of the respective parties.

William Brend and William Leddra passed onwards to Salem ; but Thomas Harris arrived at Boston on the 17th, the usual " lecture-day" of the week, and, under a feeling of religious duty, he attended the meeting. Having waited until the priest had finished his lecture, Thomas Harris began to address the company, but he was quickly interrupted and stopped. He again attempted to speak, declaring that, " the Lord God was risen, and the coverings of the persecutors were found too narrow, for their nakedness appeared to all them that feared God."* He was then seized and forthwith taken to prison, but in a short time was brought before the magistrates for examination, or more properly, to receive a cruel sentence. The formal and haughty Endicott, observing the prisoner enter the court with his hat on, thus sternly addressed him :—" Do you know before whom you are come ? *Thomas Harris.* Yea. *Endicott.* Why then do you not put off your hat ? *Thomas Harris.* I do not keep it on in contempt of authority, but in obedience to the Lord."† His hat being pulled off, and Bellingham having observed that his hair was longer than their rules admitted, ordered the marshal to bring a pair of shears and cut it off. After being questioned by Endicott from whence he came, and what was his object in coming, he was sent back to prison ; instructions being given that no one should be allowed to visit him. The gaoler, a cruel and heartless man, refusing to allow or sell his prisoner food, told him on the second day, that for every shilling which he earned at work, he might have the value of four-pence in diet. Thomas Harris, however, believed it right to bear a decided testimony against such unreasonable conduct, and declined working. The refusal

* Norton's Ensign, p. 73.   † Ibid, p 74.

was almost immediately followed by a whipping, after which the gaoler told him that, as he had suffered the penalty of the law for venturing within their limits, he might have his liberty provided he paid the marshal to convey him away. "If the doors be set open, I know no other but I shall pass," said Thomas, "but to hire a guard, that I cannot."* His imprisonment was consequently continued. The gaoler, who still refused to sell him food, brought some before him, with the taunting assurance that he should not taste it unless he promised to work. He again declined, and for five days, in the dismal prison of Boston, he was kept without nourishment of any kind. On the fifth night, a sympathizing friend, undiscovered in consequence of the darkness which prevailed, managed to convey him some food through the prison window. "In all probability, starved he had been," says Bishop, "had not the Lord kept him those five days, and ordered it so after that time, that food was conveyed to him by night at a window, by some tender people, who, though they came not into the profession of truth openly, by reason of the cruelty [of the rulers,] yet felt it secretly moving in them, and so were made serviceable to keep the servants of the Lord from perishing ; who shall not go without a reward."† On the sixth day of his imprisonment, Thomas Harris still refusing to work at the bidding of the merciless gaoler, was again subjected to the lash. Twenty-two strokes were given him on this occasion ; and, with the view of additional torture, a *pitched rope* was used instead of the whip. Leaving him in the gaol, lacerated and torn by this cruel infliction, we now turn to the proceedings of his late companions.

Reaching Salem, William Brend and William Leddra were warmly welcomed by the few faithful Friends of that place, with whom they were favoured to hold several meetings to their mutual refreshment and comfort. On First-day, the 20th of Fourth Month, they attended one held at the house of Nicholas Phelps, in the woods, about five miles from Salem. A magistrate of the town hearing of the intended meeting, came with a constable, for the purpose of breaking it up, and securing the two strangers ;

* Norton's Ensign, p. 75. † New England Judged, p. 49.

but failing in his purpose, he left the company, with a threat that he would prosecute the Friends who were present. From Salem the two gospel messengers travelled to Newburyport, where also they had some religious service. Their passing thus from place to place, in the very heart of the Puritan population of New England, and by their powerful ministry making converts to the doctrines they professed, aroused the fears of the local magistracy to this new state of things. After leaving Newburyport, they were soon overtaken by a zealous ruler of the place, who arrested them and carried them to Salem. The court, which was then sitting in the town, had the Friends brought up for examination. Here they were interrogated respecting the doctrines they were promulgating, but their answers were so clear and convincing, and they appealed so effectually to the consciences of the magistrates, that the latter confessed they discovered nothing heretical or dangerous in their opinions. The court, however, told the prisoners that they had a law against Quakers, and that that law must be obeyed. An order for their committal immediately followed, and in a few days they were removed to Boston prison. Six Friends of Salem were also committed for having attended the meeting at the house of Nicholas Phelps.

On their arrival at Boston, William Brend and William Leddra, who were deemed special offenders, were separated from their companions. They were placed in a miserable cell, the window of which was so stopped, as not only to deprive them of light, but also of ventilation, whilst all intercourse between them and the citizens was strictly forbidden. The gaoler, following the cruel course which he had pursued towards Thomas Harris, refused to allow them an opportunity of purchasing food, offering them occasionally a little pottage and bread, if they would work for it. The sufferers, however, declining to sanction such prison discipline, were kept for five days without food of any description. On the 5th of the Fifth Month, they were subjected to a whipping, after which they were told that they might obtain their liberation on payment of the prison fees, and the expenses of the marshal to convey them from the colony. The offer, as might be anticipated was rejected. William Brend, still refusing to work, underwent on the following day a new description of punishment. The inhuman gaoler, having fastened an iron fetter round his neck, and one on each leg, with great exertion drew them together, and left the aged man locked in that painful position for the space of sixteen hours. On the following morning, the gaoler, on releasing his victim from the iron fetters, ordered him to work, a requisition with which he still refused to comply. The baffled official, bent upon reducing his prisoner to submission, now changed his mode of treatment ; and, taking a pitched rope, an inch in thickness, commenced beating him " over his back and arms with all his strength."* Bruised and torn by this cruel infliction, the innocent old man was taken to his dark and dismal cell. On the same day the gaoler unavailingly repeated his command to him to work. " He haled me down," observes William Brend, " into the lower room again, and bid me work, which I could not do for all the world." The disappointed gaoler, overcome with passion, renewed his work of cruelty with increased violence, and, " foaming at the mouth,"† continued beating William Brend until exhaustion alone stopped his barbarity, but not until he had inflicted on the object of his rage, ninety-seven blows with his pitched rope. On leaving the prisoner, he uttered a threat that on his return in the morning, he would inflict as many more.

The lacerated condition to which William Brend was reduced by the successive floggings, together with the weakness produced by the closeness of his cell, and by the privation of food for five days, seemed likely to be the means of soon liberating him for ever from the hands of his persecutors. He now sank rapidly, and " his body turning cold,"‡ he appeared to be dying. His critical situation having become known, the magistrates and the gaoler were much alarmed. Endicott, fearing the consequences which might arise in the event of the death of the sufferer, sent his physician to attend him, and various means were resorted to for the resuscitation of the dying man. The physician, after examining his mangled body, to the dismay of his persecutors, pronounced his recovery impracticable ; intimating that the flesh

* Besse, vol. ii. p. 186.   † Ibid, vol. ii. p. 186.
‡ Ibid, vol. ii. p. 186.

was so torn and bruised, that it would rot from his bones. The idea of a murder committed under such aggravated circumstances, by a public officer of the colony, roused the feelings of the citizens of Boston. The magistrates, " to prevent a tumult,"* and fearful of being involved in serious responsibility, used efforts to fix the odium of the transaction on the gaoler ; whilst Endicott, to appease the public mind, issued a hand-bill, declaring that this official should be summoned to the next court to answer for his conduct. But the circumstance, although one of such atrocious barbarity, had its defenders, among whom John Norton, the popular minister of Boston, made himself conspicuous. If the gaoler was called in question for the act, this persecuting ecclesiastic declared that he would appear on his behalf. William Brend, he said, had " endeavoured to beat the gospel ordinances black and blue, and it was but just to beat him black and blue,"† and " if they dealt with him, he would leave them."‡ The uneasy forebodings of the rulers of Massachusetts, in the prospect of the death of their prisoner, were, however, soon dissipated ; for William Brend, contrary to all expectation, rapidly recovered.

Humphrey Norton, soon after the departure of William Brend and his companions for Massachusetts, was brought under a deep religious exercise to follow them in the same direction as far as Boston. " The sense of the strength of the enmity against the righteous seed" greatly distressed him, and took from him both rest and sleep. In this tried condition of mind, he informed John Rous of his prospect, who believed the same to be required of him ; he being sensible," remarks Humphrey Norton, " of the necessity of our repairing thither, to bear our parts with the prisoners of hope, which at that time stood bound for the testimony of Jesus."§ Anxious to reach Boston as early as possible, they travelled day and night, and arrived there the day after that on which William Brend had been so barbarously treated. One of the inhabitants of the town, being affected at the wicked course which the rulers were pursuing, and observing the arrival of the two Friends, informed them of the cruelties that had been exer-

---

* Besse, vol. ii. p. 186.   † Norton's Ensign, p. 78.
‡ Secret Works, p. 8.   § Norton's Ensign, p. 8.

cised towards William Brend, and begged them, "if they loved
their lives," not to remain in that place of persecution ; they
were dead men," he added, "if they did not depart." It was
evident that the honest "freeman" in his kind endeavours to
save the strangers from suffering, did not understand the nature
of their mission. " Such was our load," says Humphrey Norton,
" that beside Him who laid it upon us, no flesh nor place could
ease us."* The day on which the two devoted men entered
Boston, was that of John Norton's usual lecture, and both of
them believed it right to be present on the occasion. The public
mind of the city being at this juncture much excited by the
arrival of several Quaker ministers, the lecturer was not willing
to lose so favourable an opportunity, of endeavouring to impress
his audience with the danger of their principles. John Rous,
in describing the discourse of this intolerant minister, says, " he
began his sermon, wherein, amongst many lifeless expressions, he
spoke much of the danger of those called Quakers, and did much
labour to stain their innocency with many feigned words—sure I
am, little but gall and vinegar fell from him while I was there,
with which many of his hearers are abundantly filled." The
lecture being over, Humphrey Norton, who had listened quietly
to the slanderous language of the minister, feeling himself called
to bear a public testimony against it, stood up and began thus to
address the assembly. " Verily, this is the sacrifice which the Lord
God accepts not, for whilst with the same spirit that you sin, you
preach and pray, and sing ; that sacrifice is an abomination."† It
was evident to the minister and his company, that Humphrey
Norton was about to plead against the wicked conduct of the
Bostonians, in their misrepresentations and persecution of Friends.
From their first arrival at that place, the rulers had studiously endeavoured to suppress all such remonstrances ; and on this occasion Humphrey was soon haled down, and, with his companion
John Rous, taken off to the magistrates. Before these authorities,
a charge of blasphemy was preferred against Humphrey Norton, for
the words he had uttered in the assembly. A long examination

* Norton's Ensign, p. 79.   † Ibid, p. 79.

took place, and the charge of blasphemy being disproved was withdrawn ; they were however Quakers, and as such, were sentenced to be in prison and whipped. During the examination, John Rous was treated by the authorities with more respect and attention, than it had been customary for them to show to Friends. This arose from the circumstance of Lieutenant Colonel Rous, the father of John Rous, having resided in the colony, and being well known and respected. Vainly imagining that, by their acquaintance with his father, they might be able to prevail on John Rous to relinquish his fellowship with the despised and "heretical Quakers," the magistrates began to flatter and praise him. He was, however, too firmly established in the truth, to be shaken by their hypocritical flattery ; and not only boldly upheld his doctrines before them, but, as an English citizen, demanded his privilege of having his case tried in the courts of the mother country. An exposure of the judicial proceedings of Massachusetts in reference to Friends was, however, what Endicott and Bellingham shrank from : they well knew that such a course would inevitably bring disgrace upon the colony, and might be attended with serious results in respect to their charter. It is then no matter of surprise that the appeal of John Rous should have been vigorously resisted. " No appeal to England ! No appeal to England !"* was the language of these intolerant rulers on the occasion. Before his removal from the court, John Rous referred to the inhuman practice of preventing his imprisoned Friends from obtaining food, and demanded that he and his companion might be supplied with proper nourishment for their money. The exposure had its good effect, and neither of them was subjected to this species of New England cruelty.

After an imprisonment of three days, Humphrey Norton and John Rous, underwent the whipping to which they had been sentenced. Liberty was then offered to them, on payment of the prison fees, and of the cost of conveyance beyond the limits of the colony ; but declining to recognise these impositions they were again taken to gaol. The law which had been enacted for

* Besse's Sufferings, vol. ii. p. 188.

the punishment of "Quakers and such accursed heretics," not being, in the estimation of the magistracy of Boston, sufficiently severe for those now in prison, an order was issued to the gaoler that, if the Quakers refused to work, they were to be whipped regularly twice a week ; the first whipping to be with ten strokes, the second with fifteen, and every subsequent whipping with an addition of three "until further orders." The victims upon whom the efficacy of this fresh order was to be tried, were Humphrey Norton, John Rous, William Leddra, and Thomas Harris, and on First-day, the 18th of Fifth Month, each of them received ten strokes. The gaoler, eager in his work of cruelty, in a few days had the whip again applied with the stated number of fifteen lashes to each. On this second application of the lash, the blood flowed profusely from the unhealed wounds of the prisoners. The inhabitants of Boston, already much excited by the barbarities which had been committed on William Brend, and increasingly disgusted by these renewed cruelties, opened a public subscription, for the purpose of discharging the prison fees of the sufferers, and for defraying the cost of conveying them out of the colony. The necessary amount was quickly raised, and, soon after, William Brend, and his four companions, were conveyed to the safe and quiet retreat of the settlement at Providence.

CHAPTER VII.

Christopher Holder and John Copeland's travels and sufferings in Massachusetts—John Rous visits Boston a second time and is again imprisoned—His letter to Margaret Fell—The barbarous usage of Christopher Holder, John Copeland, and John Rous—Josiah Cole and Thomas Thurston proceed on a religious visit to America—Their gospel labours among the Indians—Josiah Cole's mission among those of Martha's Vineyard and Massachusetts—He is joined by John Copeland—They are imprisoned at Sandwich—Josiah Cole's further labours among the Indians of New England—Extract from his letter to George Bishop, containing a narrative of these engagements—Peter Cowsnooke, Edward Eades, and Philip Rose, embark for New England—Brief notices of the lives of Mary Clark, Richard Doudney, Mary Wetherhead, Sarah Gibbons, Dorothy Waugh, William Brend, Humphrey Norton, Christopher Holder, John Copeland, John Rous, Thomas Harris, and Robert Fowler.

CHRISTOPHER Holder and John Copeland, as we have already noticed, left Rhode Island about the middle of the Fourth Month, 1658, for the colony of Plymouth. On the 23rd, they attended a meeting of the little company of Friends at Sandwich. The marshal, on hearing of their arrival, immediately went to the meeting and arrested them. The orders which this functionary had received from the authorities, were, to banish all such without delay ; and, should any so banished return, that then " the select men appointed for that purpose, were to see them whipped."* Conformably to his instructions, he ordered the two Friends to leave the township : to which Christopher Holder and his companion replied, that, should they feel it to be the will of their divine Master, they would do so ; but on no other ground could

---

* Norton's Ensign, p. 39.

they promise to leave Sandwich. With a view to the infliction of the punishment referred to, the " select men" were informed of the continued presence of the Friends ; but this body, entertaining no desire to sanction measures so severe towards those who differed from them in religion, declined to act in the case. The marshal, disappointed at the refusal, determined to take them before a neighbouring magistrate at Barnstaple, about two miles distant, who, he anticipated, would lend a ready hand to assist in punishing Quakers,—an expectation which was fully realized. This functionary, after a frivolous examination of the prisoners, ordered them to be tied to the post of an out-house ; and then, turning executioner, he gave each of them thirty-three lashes. The Friends of Sandwich, aware of the hatred which the Barnstaple magistrate had to Quakerism, and well assured that no mercy was to be expected from him, with a view to cheer their brethren in bonds, accompanied them thither on the occasion, and were " eye and ear witnesses of the cruelty" inflicted on them. These were new proceedings at Barnstaple, and caused no little sensation among the quiet settlers of the district. They felt that however erroneous Quakerism might be, such conduct on the part of their rulers did not consist with the religion of Jesus. " Who would have thought," said one of them, " that I should have come to New England to witness such scenes ?" On the following day, the two Friends were taken back to Sandwich, from whence they were carried towards Rhode Island, and liberated.

After labouring for some weeks in the work of the ministry, in the vicinity of Providence and Newport, Christopher Holder and John Copeland, felt a religious call to proceed to Boston. At this place they had already experienced both imprisonment and the lash of the knotted scourge ; and they were not ignorant that, on the return of those who had been banished from Massachusetts, as they had been, the loss of one of their ears would probably be the penalty inflicted. But these faithful men, feeling assured that their call was from on high, humbly obeyed the requisition, believing that He who had hitherto been their help and their shield, would not forsake them in any extremity to which they might be exposed for the truth's sake. Leaving

Providence on the 3rd of Sixth Month, 1658, they arrived on the same evening, at the town of Dedham. Their presence within the limits of Massachusetts was soon made known to the magistracy; and early on the following morning, the travellers were arrested, to be conveyed as prisoners to Boston. On reaching this city, they were taken without delay to the residence of Endicott. "You shall have your ears cut off,"* were the first words, which, angry and agitated, the cruel governor uttered on seeing them. That men, who had been imprisoned, and whipped, and banished for their religious opinions, should still persist in the advocacy of them with the certainty of incurring increased severities, was what the darkened mind of Endicott could not comprehend; "What, you remain in the same opinion you were before?" he said. "We remain in the fear of the Lord;" the prisoners meekly replied; adding, "the Lord God hath commanded us, and we could not but come." "The Lord command you to come! it was Satan," vociferated the governor. The examination ended in the issue of the following order:—

"To the Keeper of the House of Correction.

"You are, by virtue hereof, required to take into your custody the bodies of Christopher Holder and John Copeland, and them safely to keep close to work, with prisoners' diet only, till their ears be cut off; and not to suffer them to converse with any while they are in your custody.

"Edward Rawson, *Secretary.*"†

In pursuance of this order, the two Friends were kept closely confined; and the unmerciful gaoler, pursuing his usual course towards such prisoners, prevented them for several days from having food, because they declined to work at his bidding.

John Rous, although he had been recently banished from Massachusetts, felt it required of him again to visit Boston. He reached it on the 25th of Sixth Month, and was arrested and taken before Endicott on the same day. After ordering him to

* New England Judged, p. 71.　　　† Besse Sufferings, vol. ii. p. 189.

be searched for letters and papers, the governor sent him to join
Christopher Holder and John Copeland, in the city gaol. About
a week after he had been thus imprisoned, he wrote a letter to
Margaret Fell, containing many interesting particulars of the
proceedings of the Society in New England, of which the following, taken from the original, is a copy :—

JOHN ROUS TO MARGARET FELL.

" DEARLY BELOVED SISTER, M. F.

"About the last of the Sixth Month, 1657, I came from
Barbadoes with another Friend, an inhabitant of the island ; and,
according to the appointment of the Father, landed on Rhode
Island in the beginning of the Eighth Month, on an out part of
the island ; and being come thither, I heard of the arrival of
Friends from England ; which was no small refreshment to me.
After I had been there a little while, I passed out of the island
into Plymouth Patent, to Sandwich, and several other towns
thereabouts ; where, in the winter time, more service was done
than was expected. Some time after, I was in Connecticut with
John Copeland, where the Lord gave us no small dominion, for
there we met with one of the greatest disputers of New England,
who is priest of Hartford, who was much confounded, to the
glory of truth, and to his shame. After some stay there, we
returned to Rhode Island, where Humphrey Norton was, and
after some time, he and I went into Plymouth Patent, and they
having a Court while we were there, we went to the place where
it was ; having sent before to the Governor, the grounds of our
coming ; but we were straightway put in prison, and after twice
being before them, where we were much railed at, they judged us
to be whipped. Humphrey Norton received twenty-three stripes,
and I fifteen with rods, which did prove much for the advantage
of truth, and their disadvantage ; for Friends did with much
boldness own us openly in it, and it did work deeply with many.
After we were let forth thence, we returned to Rhode Island, and
after some stay there, we went to Providence, and from thence to
Boston, to bear witness in a few words, in their meeting-house

against their worship, till they haled us forth and had us to their house of correction, and that evening we were examined and committed to prison. On the seventh day in the evening, they whipped us with ten stripes each, with a three-fold whip, to conclude a wicked week's work, which was this ; on the Second-day, they whipped six Friends ; on the Third-day, the gaoler laid William Brend, (a Friend that came from London), neck and heels, as they call it, in irons for sixteen hours ; on the Fourth-day, the gaoler gave William Brend one hundred and seventeen strokes with a pitched rope ; on the Fifth-day, they imprisoned us ; and on the Seventh-day we suffered. The beating of William Brend did work much in the town, and for a time, much liberty was granted ; for several people came to us in the prison ; but the enemies, seeing the forwardness and love in the people towards us, plotted, and a warrant was given forth that, if we would not work, we should be whipped once in every three days, and the first time have fifteen stripes, the second eighteen, and the third time twenty-one. So on the Second-day after our first whipping, four of us received fifteen stripes each ; the which did so work with the people, that on the Fourth-day after, we were released. We returned to Rhode Island, and continued there awhile, and after some time, Humphrey Norton went into Plymouth Patent to Friends there, and I was moved to come to Boston ; so that, that day five weeks [after] I was released, at night I was put in again. There were Christopher Holder and John Copeland, two of the Friends which came from England ; and we do lie here, according to their law, to have each of us, an ear cut off; but we are kept in the dominion of God, and our enemies are under our feet. It is reported that we shall be tried at a Court that is to be held next week, and if the ship do not go away from hence before then, thou shalt hear further how it is ordered for us, (if God permit). There was a great lamenting for me by many when I came again, but they were not minded by me ; I was much tempted to say, I came to the town to take shipping to go to Barbadoes, but I could not deny Him who moved me to come hither, nor his service, to avoid sufferings. This relation, in short, I have given thee, that thou might know how it hath fared with me since I came into this land.   About five weeks since, six Friends,* having done their service here, took shipping for Barbadoes ; two whereof were to go to Virginia and Maryland, two for London, and the other two were inhabitants of Barbadoes ; so that there are only four of us in the land.

" Dear Sister, truth is spread here above two hundred miles, and many are in fine conditions, and very sensible of the power of God, and walk honestly in their measures.   Some of the inhabitants of the land who are Friends have been forth in the service, and they do more grieve the enemy than we ; for they have hoped to be rid of us, but they have no hope to be rid of them.   We keep the burden of the service off from them at present, for no sooner is there need in a place, but straightway some or other of us step to it ; but when it is the will of the Father to clear us of this land, then will the burden fall on them.   The seed in Boston and Plymouth Patent is ripe, and the weight very much lies on this town, the which being brought into subjection unto the truth, the others will not stand out long.   The seed in Connecticut and Newhaven Patents, is not as yet ripe, but there is a hopeful appearance, the gathering of which in its time, will much redound to the glory of God.   We have two strong places in this land, the one at Newport in Rhode Island, and the other at Sandwich, which the enemy will never get dominion over ; and at Salem there are several pretty Friends in their measures ; but being very young, and the enemy exercising his cruelty much against them, they have been something scattered, but there are some of them grown pretty bold through their sufferings. Humphrey Norton, we hear, hath been with them this week, and had a fine large meeting among them, and they received much strength by it.   One of the inhabitants of Salem was whipped three times in five days, once to fulfil their law, and twice for refusing to work ; after eleven days' imprisonment he was let forth, and hath gotten much strength by his sufferings.   Great

* These doubtless were William Leddra, and Thomas Harris, of Barbadoes, and William Brend, Richard Hodgson, Dorothy Waugh, and Sarah Gibbons.   The four left in New England being Humphrey Norton, John Copeland, Christopher Holder, and John Rous.

have been the sufferings of Friends in this land, but generally they suffer with much boldness and courage, both the spoiling of their goods, and the abusing of their bodies. There are Friends, few or more, almost from one end of the land to the other, that is inhabited by the English. A firm foundation there is laid in this land, such an one as the devil will never get broken up. If thou art free to write to me, thou may direct thy letter to be sent to Barbadoes for me ; so in that which is eternal, do I remain,

> " Thy brother, in my measure, who suffers for the Seed's sake, earnestly thirsting for the prosperity and peace of Zion, the City of the living God,

From a Lion's Den called Boston Prison, this 3rd day of the Seventh Month, 1658.
         John Rous.

" My dear fellow-prisoners, John Copeland and Christopher Holder, do dearly salute thee. Salute me dearly in the Lord to thy children, and the rest of thy family who are in the truth."

According to the statement of John Rous in the foregoing letter, Christopher Holder, John Copeland, and himself were examined, on the 7th of the Seventh Month, by the " Court of Assistants" assembled in Boston. After a tedious questioning relative to their object in visiting those parts, they were remanded, and on the 10th were again brought before the court, but for the purpose only of receiving the cruel sentence, that each should have his right ear cut off.* The prisoners, feeling the injustice of the proceedings, and not doubting such cruelties would be condemned by the tribunals of the mother country, informed the court that they desired to appeal to Cromwell against its decision. So little regard, however, had the civil

---

* This degrading punishment for ecclesiastical offences had been practised in England towards Puritans. By order of the Star Chamber, William Prynne in 1634, and Henry Burton and Dr. Bastwick in 1637, had their ears cut off in public on a scaffold in Palace Yard, Westminster.

powers of Massachusetts for the laws of the empire, in pursuing their intolerant course towards Friends, that the only reply elicited by the appeal was a threat that, unless they were quiet, the gag would make them so.   In about one week after this wicked sentence had been pronounced, it was privately carried into execution by the hangman, within the walls of Boston gaol. " In the strength of God," say the prisoners, " we suffered joy-fully, having freely given up not only one member, but all, if the Lord so required, for the sealing of our testimony which the Lord hath given us." On the 7th of the Eighth Month, John Rous, Christopher Holder, and John Copeland, were released from prison ; the first having been confined for six, and the other two for nine weeks.

Excepting the visit of John Rous, William Leddra, and Thomas Harris, no fresh arrival of Friends in the ministry appears to have taken place in New England for more than a year after the landing of those from Robert Fowler's vessel.   About the Eighth Month, 1658, however, Josiah Cole and Thomas Thurston, who had been engaged in religious labours among the Indians in Virginia and New Netherlands, reached Rhode Island, having travelled through the interior of the country.   This inland journey extended through some hundreds of miles of forest country.   The Indians who inhabited these uncultivated wilds had been greatly exasperated by the European settlers, with whom they were fre-quently involved in most murderous conflicts, and in sudden onsets from the forest whole villages of the Dutch had been laid waste.   The circumstance, therefore, of two or three unarmed and defenceless Englishmen venturing among these irritated and re-vengeful natives, excited considerable surprise.   But they were the bearers of peace and goodwill to these benighted sons of the forest.   Their mission also was from on high, and they went forth divested of fear.   Trusting in the unfailing arm of the Shepherd of Israel, they passed through the wigwam towns of the interior in perfect safety.

The annexed sketch, taken from a Dutch map of that period, represents one of the towns of an Indian tribe visited by Josiah Cole and his companions on this occasion.

Maniere van Woonplaetsen ofte Dorpen der Mahicans ende andre Natien haer geburen

"*Plan of the dwellings or villages of the Mohegans, and other nations, their neighbours.*"

An original manuscript account of this extraordinary journey is yet preserved, from which we give the following extract :—

JOSIAH COLE TO GEORGE BISHOP.

" We went from Virginia [on the] 2nd of Sixth Month, 1658, and after about one hundred miles travel by land and water, we came amongst the Susquehanna Indians, who courteously received us and entertained us in their huts with much respect. After being there two or three days with [word indistinct,] several of them accompanied us about two hundred miles further, through the wilderness or woods ; for there was no inhabitant so far, neither knew we any part of the way through which the Lord had required us to travel. For outward sustenance we knew not how to supply ourselves, but without questioning or doubting, we gave up freely to the Lord, knowing assuredly that his presence was (and should be continued) with us; and according to our faith, so it was, for his presence and love we found with us daily, carrying us on in his strength, and also opening the hearts of those poor Indians, so that in all times of need they were made helpful both to carry us through rivers, and also to supply us with food sufficient. After this travel, we came to a place where more of them inhabited, and they also very kindly entertained us in their houses, where we remained about sixteen days, my fellow-traveller [Thomas Thurston] being weak of body through sickness and lameness; in which time these Indians shewed very much respect to us, for they gave us freely of the best they could get. Being something recovered after this stay, we passed on towards the Dutch plantation, to which one of them accompanied us, which was about one hundred miles further—

           " I am thy friend in the truth,

             Josiah Cole

After reaching Rhode Island, Josiah Cole very soon felt drawn to visit the Indians on the island of Martha's Vineyard. " I had a meeting amongst them," he observes, " and they were very loving, and told me they much desired to know God." From thence he crossed over to the colony of Plymouth, and laboured in the love of the gospel among the aboriginal tribes of that district. " Some of these," he writes, " had true breathings after the knowledge of God." Here he was joined by John Copeland, and they proceeded from tribe to tribe, among the natives of Massachusetts, " sounding the day of the Lord," being received with courtesy and kindness; but on reaching the town of Sandwich, and the dwellings of the civilized, an opposite treatment awaited them. The arrival of two English Quaker ministers becoming known to the authorities, they were soon subjected to the laws of the colony against such, and whilst at a Friend's house in Sandwich they " were haled out by violence,"* and committed to prison. On his liberation, Josiah Cole returned to the untutored Algonquins, preaching the unsearchable riches of Christ, and inviting them to Him as the Leader, the Comforter, and all-sufficient Saviour of his people. Though these untutored sons of the forest knew that the youthful preacher† had but just come from within the prison walls of his persecutors, they nevertheless listened attentively to his ministrations. The hatred which the rulers of Massachusetts entertained towards Friends, was a circumstance of which the Indians were not ignorant, but acting according to their own sense of right and wrong, they were not disposed to follow the malevolent example. " The Englishmen did not love Quakers," remarked the Indian king to Josiah Cole on this occasion, " but," he added, " the Quakers are honest men and do no harm, and this is no Englishman's sea or land, and Quakers shall come here and welcome." The love and favour that Josiah Cole found amongst these Indians deeply impressed his mind. " I do confess," he wrote, " this to be the Lord's hand of love towards me ; through the goodness of the Lord we found these Indians more sober and Christian-like towards us than the Christians so called."‡ This indefatigable labourer in the service of truth, having now been absent for a considerable time from his native country, felt at liberty to return home. Thomas Thurston made but a short stay in Rhode Island, and then passed southward again to Virginia.

About this time, Peter Cowsnooke, a Friend of the north of England, was directing his course towards North America, in company with Edward Eades and Philip Rose of Warwick. His desire was, if possible, to sail direct from some English port to New England ; but not being able to effect this, he proceeded first to Barbadoes, being accompanied by Henry Fell and some other Friends, including the two from Warwick. They reached Barbadoes in the Seventh Month, 1658, and in the following month, Peter Cowsnooke, Edward Eades, and Philip Rose,

* New England Judged, p. 180.
† His age was then about twenty-four.
‡ Letter to George Bishop, 1658.

made arrangements for proceeding to Rhode Island, by way of Virginia,* but whether they reached the shores of New England has not been ascertained.†

In the future pages of this history, we shall have occasion to refer but little to those who crossed the Atlantic in Robert Fowler's vessel, or to the other gospel messengers whose visits to New England have also been noticed, excepting William Robinson, William Leddra, Robert Hodgson, and Josiah Cole. A sketch, therefore, of the lives of those dedicated servants of the Lord, from whom we are now about to turn our attention, may not be inappropriately given in this chapter. They doubtless possessed gifts and qualifications in the service of their Lord, differing widely from each other, but, seeking to be led by His unerring voice, they were preserved in unity and love, and in a harmonious labour in His holy cause, and were made eminently instrumental in the spread of vital religion among men.

Mary Clark.

Mary Clark was the wife of John Clark, a tradesman of London, and united herself in religious fellowship with Friends, very early after their rise in that city. She came forth as a minister soon after, and in 1655 travelled into Worcestershire, to expostulate with the local magistracy respecting their cruel treatment of Friends;

---

* Letter to Henry Fell, 1658.

† A short time previous to the embarkation of Peter Cowsnooke on this religious visit, he addressed a letter to Margaret Fell, in which he notices a conversation he had with George Fox, in reference to his religious prospect, and respecting which, at times, he appears to have had feelings of discouragement. " I asked George concerning it," he says, " when I was first with him, and he left it to me. I was since with him at the General Meeting, at John Crook's, and as before, he said he would leave it to me. But I being somewhat troubled, he asked what I would have him to say, had I freedom in myself to pass back again? I answered, I did not at present see it; so he said again he would leave it to me." The care observed by George Fox, in not interfering in a matter where individual apprehension of duty was concerned, and his solicitude that the party might not lean on the judgment of others, affords a striking instance of his watchful care in regard to such important matters.

in the course of which visit she was placed in the stocks at Evesham for three hours on the market-day,* and exposed to other sufferings. Leaving her husband and children in 1657, she proceeded on the visit to New England. The first member of the Society who experienced the application of the lash in Great Britain was Mary Fisher ; but it fell to the lot of Mary Clark to be the first among Friends to suffer in this revolting manner in America. She was liberated from Boston gaol in the Ninth Month, 1657, and was occupied in religious service in New England until the early part of 1658, when, as we have already mentioned, with two of her companions in the ministry, Richard Doudney and Mary Wetherhead, she was shipwrecked and drowned. Thus, we may reverently believe, was she suddenly called from a tribulated path, to ineffable and unfading glory. The sufferings which she endured in New England, were borne with marked Christian patience ; " her innocency preaching condemnation to her adversaries," and, " for her faithfulness herein," said her companions, " the Lord God is her reward."†

RICHARD DOUDNEY.

Prior to Richard Doudney's visit to America, we find no incident respecting him. After his engagement in New England, in 1657, he joined Christopher Holder in a visit to some of the West India islands ; ‡ he however, returned to Rhode Island in the spring of 1658, soon after which the melancholy shipwreck took place, in which he was drowned. He is described as an " innocent man," and one who " served the Lord in the sincerity of his heart,"§ and he doubtless was prepared to meet the awful summons.

MARY WETHERHEAD.

Mary Wetherhead appears to have been an inhabitant of Bristol; no particulars, however, of her life previous to her crossing the Atlantic in 1656, have been met with. She is spoken of as being unmarried, and, it is believed, was young at the time of her death.

* Besse's Sufferings, vol. ii. p. 60.   † Norton's Ensign, p. 60.
‡ Letter of Peter Evans to George Fox, 1658.
§ Norton's Ensign, p. 62.

SARAH GIBBONS.

The narrative of the visit of the little company of gospel messengers to Boston, in 1656, first introduces the name of this Friend to our notice.   After her expulsion from Connecticut in the early part of 1658, she appears to have been engaged for some months within the limits of Rhode Island, from whence, in company with Dorothy Waugh, the aged Brend, and three other Friends, she proceeded on religious service to Barbadoes.*   In 1659, we find her again on Rhode Island ; her earthly pilgrimage, however, was now nearly accomplished, and its termination was an awfully sudden and affecting one.   Whilst attempting to land from a sloop at Providence, she was drowned.   The melancholy accident is thus referred to in a letter of William Robinson's, under date of Fifth Month, 1659.   "As they came near to the shore, near that town, there came a man in a canoe to fetch them from on board, wherein they went with some others, not minding that the canoe was a bad one, and soon after they were in it, the canoe filled with water and did sink. All that were in the canoe did escape and got to the shore, except Sarah Gibbons who was drowned. When it was low water they found her, and the next day buried her in Richard Scott's orchard."   After alluding to the trial of her being thus unexpectedly taken from her friends, William Robinson adds, "but herein were we comforted, that she was kept faithful to the end."

DOROTHY WAUGH.

Dorothy Waugh, who resided, it is believed, in London, united with Friends, very soon after their rise in that city, and is mentioned as being both young and unmarried.   Towards the close of 1654, she travelled in the work of the ministry into Lancashire, and from thence to Norwich, where, for exhorting the people in the market,† she was imprisoned for the space of three months.   On her release from Norwich gaol, she proceeded to London to meet George Fox.‡   During 1655, she travelled in gospel labours, to

---

* Letter of Henry Fell, 1658.   † Letter of R. Hubberthorne, 1655.
‡ Letter of T. Willan, 1655.

the western counties as far as Cornwall, and northward as far as Cumberland. In the course of this service she was imprisoned at Truro, and at Carlisle was subjected to barbarous treatment for preaching in the streets. In the early part of 1656, she visited some of the southern counties of England. The Berkshire sufferings for that year records her committal to the county gaol, for addressing the congregation in the public place of worship at Reading.* Her imprisonment, however, on this occasion, was but a short one, as she soon after embarked on her first visit to New England. The travels and sufferings of Dorothy Waugh, in New England, to the Fourth Month, 1658, have been already related, and after this period, the only remaining notice that we have respecting her, is of a visit to the West India Islands, towards the close of the same year. It is a remarkable circumstance that of the four women Friends, who formed a part of the little company of gospel ministers who crossed the Atlantic in the " Woodhouse" that within two years from the date of their landing in America, Dorothy Waugh was the only one surviving ; her female companions having all found a watery grave. The following is a fac-simile of her signature.

Dorthie waugh

WILLIAM BREND.

Among the ministers of the Society who were called thus early to labour in the work of the gospel in New England, the characters of few present features of greater interest than that of William Brend. The powerful preaching of Burrough and Howgill had not long been heard within the City of London, ere this ancient and venerable man appeared in the ranks of the ministers of the new Society. Having attained the age of manhood about the time of Queen Elizabeth's death, he witnessed the oppression and persecution inflicted on the Puritans in the time of James I.; but what was his own religious profession during this reign, and in the times of the civil wars of Charles I., or during the religious excitement which followed in the days of the Commonwealth, it

* MS. Account of Sufferings, vol. i.

does not appear.   His good natural abilities and general intelligence, warrant the supposition, that at least he could not have been an unconcerned spectator of what was passing around him in reference to these things ; his being alluded to as " a man fearing God in his generation," and who was " known to many of the inhabitants of the City of London,"* encourages this belief.   Although his call to the work of the ministry was not until the evening of his day, it nevertheless pleased his Divine Master to lead him in the exercise of his gift into distant countries, and thus in 1656, he embarked with seven others for North America, and again in the following year.   On both these occasions, William Brend occupied an interesting position, for, with the exception of one, or at most two, who were of middle age, all his fellow-labourers in the ministry were young and unmarried. The presence, therefore, of one, who as respects age was as a father among them, and who was also experienced in the truth, must have made his company peculiarly acceptable.   The foregoing chapters detail his travels and sufferings in New England.   It may however be remarked, that except in the martyrdom of four individuals, amidst all the cruelty which sectarian intolerance inflicted on the early Friends in New England, none was more severe, or more repugnant to the feelings of humanity, than that endured by this good and aged man.   In 1658, it appears that he left RhodeIsland on a visit to the West Indies :† in 1659, however, we again find him pleading the cause of true religion at Boston. This was subsequent to the passing of the Massachusetts law for banishment on pain of death, and under which, in the Third Month, he was expelled the jurisdiction.   For some months after this, his religious engagements were confined within the limits of Rhode Island.   He was a prisoner in Newgate, London, in the Ninth Month, 1662.   When his incarceration there commenced, it is difficult to ascertain.   In the Eleventh Month, 1664, some of his published pieces are dated " from Newgate :" and in the previous month, Besse records his being sentenced with several others to transportation to Jamaica.

* Howgill's Popish Inquisition, p. 64.
† Letter of Henry Fell, 1658.

The outbreak of the Fifth monarchy men in England at the close of the Protectorate, furnished a pretext to the Royalists for the adoption of severer measures towards nonconformists. Tendering the oath of allegiance was the most prominent of these measures, and objecting as the Society of Friends did to oaths of every description, it fell with peculiar force upon them ; but notwithstanding the numerous imprisonments which arose from this cause, towards the close of 1661, the legislature passed an act to prohibit the meetings of dissenters, in which " Quakers" were especially alluded to. The penalties under which the act was to be enforced, were such, to use the language of its promoters, " as might be profitable to work upon the humours of such fanatics,"* and " to cure the distempers of these people."† The Society of Friends had borne a large amount of cruel sufferings by the revival of laws originally directed against Papists ; it had, however, in 1662, to feel a more formidable oppression in this attempt of the legislature to crush them. The torrent of persecution which swept over it in consequence of the enactment in question, and the noble stand which Friends were strengthened to make against it, forms one of the most remarkable circumstances in the history of this people. In a very short time after the passing of the cruel law, there was not a county gaol in England which did not number among its prisoners, Friends who had been committed under its provisions, whilst some of the prisons, were literally crammed with them. In Newgate alone, William Brend could count hundreds of his fellow-professors. The wretched places into which they were thrust during these imprisonments are almost past belief.‡ The loathsomeness of Newgate was such, that during 1662, and the two subsequent years, no less than fifty-two of William Brend's fellow-prisoners died from disease contracted there. Edward Burrough, who was one of these martyrs, speaks of an hundred being " in one room"§ at a time.

During this storm of persecution, many christian exhortations

* Commons Journal in Kennett, p. 448.
† Journal of the Lords, May 28th, 1661.
‡ See " The Cry of Newgate, by R. C.," 1662.
§ Letter of E. Burrough to Friends, 1662.

to faithfulness and constancy, were addressed to the sufferers by
the more prominent Friends of that day, among which we find
one from the pen of William Brend, entitled " A loving salutation to all Friends every where, in this great day of trial, to stand
faithful unto God over all sufferings." The following extracts
from this piece, evidences the qualification of the writer for such
services, and the strong desire which he felt for the maintenance
of love and harmony among his persecuted and tried brethren
every where :—

" It hath been upon my heart when in the sweet repose of the
streams of my Father's love and life, by which my heart, soul
and spirit, hath been overcome, to visit you with a loving salutation from the place of my outward bonds and imprisonment, for
the gospel sake.

" O come, my dear lambs and dear babes, it is a time for us
to flock together into our Father's fold, and to get into his tent
of safety, and to lie down in the arms of his dear love, and to be
covered with the wing of his power, now the wild boar of the
forest is abroad to make his prey, and the wolvish devourers are
seeking to scatter the sheep of the Lord's pasture.   O let us feel
and know the safe harbour, in which alone is safety, whilst the
boisterous storms and tempests are all about us, and the foaming
rage of the troubled seas are casting up their waves, one after
another.—

"Oh, dear lambs and babes of God, our Rock is sure and stedfast, our Refuge and Harbour safe and unmoveable, and our Pilot
wise and exceeding skilful ; there is not a danger near that can
attend us in our voyage to our everlasting land of rest, but he
doth foresee, and knows right well how to avoid them all—he
never failed any that trusted in him, and in the Arm of his
salvation—may we all stand fast, and quit ourselves like men,
and be strong in the power of his might.

" Oh, dear lambs ! we have a great portion ; for I can say in the
secret of my soul, The Lord is my portion, and hath been and is
yours also, who have waited for him, and in whom is your delight.

" Oh ! in the love and life of the Lamb, look over all weakness in one another, as God doth look over all the weakness ·in every one of us, and doth love us for his own Son's sake—in so doing, peace will abound in our borders, it will flow forth amongst us like a river, and it will keep out jars, strifes and contentions from us, and so we shall be kept as a beautiful and amiable family, and in the order of God.

" These few lines do manifest something that was upon my heart towards you in the feelings of my Father's love, as I lay in my bed in the night season, this 11th of the Ninth Month, 1662."

" *Newgate Prison in London.*"   *William Brend*

Several other pieces were also written and published by William Brend during his imprisonment in Newgate.

Although William Brend had received sentence of transportation it was not carried into execution. This did not result from any change of feeling on the part of his persecutors, but simply from the difficulty they experienced to procure vessels for the purpose. With but one or two exceptions, the ship owners and captains declined to engage in the nefarious business, for, conscious of the uprightness and integrity of the sufferers, they felt no desire thus to countenance proceedings which evidently bore the stamp of cruelty and injustice. The number of Friends who received sentence of banishment gradually increased. In the summer of 1665, they amounted in Newgate to one hundred and twenty, and had not the great plague of London appeared, the number, doubtless, would have been considerably augmented. About the time when this devastating pestilence had reached its height, the prison doors of the metropolis were opened for the liberation of Friends, but not until the spirits of some scores* of the innocent victims of intolerance had been for ever freed, by the hand of death from all earthly oppression.

In 1672, the Yearly Meeting, as usual, was held in London. It was an important occasion in the history of Friends, and William Brend, aged and feeble as he was, attended, and his

---

* Besse, vol. i. pp. 388, 404, 407.

name, with that of eleven others, appears on the records of the meeting as having prepared one of the Epistles issued at that time.   The only remaining notice that we find respecting him, is that which records his death about four years later.   His age could not have been much, if at all, under ninety.   The burial record is as follows—" William Brend of the liberty of Katherines, near the Tower, a minister, died the 7th of the Seventh Month, 1676, and was buried at Bunhill Fields."

HUMPHREY NORTON.

The earliest notice which we find respecting Humphrey Norton, occurs in a manuscript letter addressed to Margaret Fell in the Seventh Month, 1655, by Thomas Willan of Kendal ; from this it appears that he was then residing in London, and acting as the accredited agent or officer of the Society there, for the assistance of Friends travelling in the ministry.   Whilst thus occupied, he maintained a frequent correspondence with Thomas Willan and George Taylor of Kendal, who were actively engaged in superintending the affairs of the body at large, more parti-cularly in reference to its provisions for defraying the travelling expenses of ministering Friends.*   The rise of the Society of Friends in London, took place about one year previous to the date of the letter referred to, but as it had existed as a distinct asso-ciation in the midland and northern counties, for nearly ten years before, the fact of Kendal being then the central place of the body, is explained.

The precise date when Humphrey Norton came forth as a minister, it is difficult to ascertain ; but as early as 1655, he appears to have travelled as such in the North of England, and it is known that, in the following year, he was extensively engaged in the ministry in Ireland.   During this period he had become acquainted with that nursing mother in the church, Margaret Fell, with whom he kept up a correspondence.†   In the course of his travels in Ireland, he visited the provinces of Leinster,

* Vide letters of Thomas Willan and George Taylor to Margaret Fell, 1655 and 1656, in the Swarthmore MSS.

† Letter of Richard Hubberthorne, Tenth Month, 1655.

Munster, and Connaught ; during which, in common with most of the early ministers of the Society, he experienced the persecuting hand of an envious and intolerant hierarchy. In Galway, he was " taken violently out of a meeting by a guard of soldiers, and driven from the city.* At Wexford, whilst at " a peaceable meeting," he was again seized by the soldiery, " taken to the steeple house, and thence committed to gaol till the next assizes.† His return from Ireland was in the early part of 1657.‡ In the Fourth Month, as has been already related, he went on board the "Woodhouse" for New England. The revolting cruelties which he endured in that land while prosecuting his gospel labours, need not be repeated. From New England, Humphrey Norton proceeded to visit some of the more southern English colonies. In 1660, he was again in Rhode Island, and, it is singular, that, after that date, no notice of him has been met with.

CHRISTOPHER HOLDER.

Previously to his visit to New England in 1656, Christopher Holder resided at Winterbourne, in Gloucestershire. He is referred to as a " well educated" man, and of " good estate," and was one of those who, in the south-west of England, very early professed with Friends. The following is the first notice found respecting him : " Christopher Holder, in ye year 1655, was sent to ye gayle at Ilchester, for speaking to ye priest at Keinsham steeple house ; and from thence after a while, upon bayle brought to ye next sessions, and so discharged."§ Having been called by the Great Head of the Church to plead his holy cause among men, in 1656, he believed it required of him to visit New England : which visit he repeated in 1657, with the little band of gospel messengers who sailed for that country. His religious engagements there continued until near the close of 1657, when he proceeded on a visit to some of the West India islands. His absence, however, from North America was but short, for in a letter received by George Fox from Barbadoes, ‖ he is men-

---

* Sufferings of Friends in Ireland.   † Ibid.
‡ Swarthmore Collection of MSS.   § MSS. Sufferings, vol. i.
‖ Letter of Peter Evans, 1658.

tioned as having sailed from that island in the Second Month, 1658, for Bermuda and Rhode Island ; the latter place, as we have already stated, he reached in the Fourth Month of that year. After his liberation from Boston gaol in the Eighth Month, 1658, he proceeded southward, and united with William Robinson and Robert Hodgson, " for some time," in gospel labours in Virginia, returning again to Rhode Island in the early part of 1659.* William Robinson, who was soon after imprisoned at Boston, mentions his having received in the Fifth Month, a letter from Christopher Holder, " who," he says, " was in service at a town called Salem, last week, and hath had fine service among Friends in these parts." In a short time after, Christopher Holder became a fellow-prisoner with William Robinson at Boston, having gone thither to seek a vessel bound for England. After an imprisonment of two months he was liberated, and taking passage in a vessel about to sail for Great Britain, he reached his home in safety. A few months after his return to England, he was united in marriage to Mary Scott, mentioned in the register as of " Boston, in New England," and the marriage was solemnized at Olveston, near Bristol, in Sixth Month, 1660. Mary Scott was the daughter of Richard and Katherine Scott of Providence.

Christoper Holder repeatedly visited America,† and it was the lot of this faithful minister, whilst travelling in distant countries, to endure a large amount of suffering and trial in the cause of his Great Master. On his return from America, he also suffered severely for his testimony to the truth. In the Third Month, 1682, he was again committed to Ilchester gaol for refusing to swear. After two months, he was premunired, and was continued a prisoner for more than four years and a half, till the Twelfth Month, 1685, when he was released with a large number of Friends in different parts of the country, under the general discharge granted by James II. He died about two years afterwards. In the burial

* William Robinson's letter, Fifth Month, 1659.
† Vide letter of Ellis Hookes to Margaret Fell, 1669, Swarthmore MSS., and Journal of George Fox, 1672.

register, his death is thus recorded, "Christopher Holder of Puddimore, in the county of Somerset, died at Ircott, in the parish of Almondsbury, on the 13th of Fourth Month, 1688, and was buried at Hazell." Having been described as "a young man," during his first visit to New England, his age probably did not exceed sixty. He was a minister about thirty-three years, and to him, we doubt not, the language of the Psalmist may be fitly applied, "mark the perfect man, and behold the upright, for the end of that man is peace."

JOHN COPELAND.

The relation of the visit of the eight Friends to New England, in the summer of 1656, contains the first reference that appears to John Copeland. Like his beloved companion, Christopher Holder, he was at that time young and unmarried : he is also spoken of as having been "well educated." His residence appears to have been in Holderness, in Yorkshire, and hence the probability of his early acquaintance with Robert Fowler of Bridlington Quay, in that county, a fellow-labourer in the gospel, and in whose little vessel he again visited America in 1657. How long John Copeland was absent from his native land during this visit it is difficult to ascertain ; but in the latter part of 1658, he was at Sandwich, in company with Josiah Cole, when they were violently taken from a Friend's house and carried to prison. In 1661, we meet with him in London,* and in 1667, he married. In the register of his marriage he is described as of "Lockington, North Cave, in the county of York." His wife dying about eight years after their union, he married a second time, in 1677. Ten years later, we find him again in America; in a letter addressed to George Fox from that land, he is mentioned as being in Virginia. After his return from this visit, he entered, in 1691, for the third time into the marriage covenant. It pleased Him, who holdeth the breath of every living thing, to grant to this dear Friend, length of days ; and having survived his first visit to North America, more than sixty years, he had reason to

* Sewel, p. 279.

rejoice, that the cause for which he both laboured and suffered, had spread itself widely among the settlers in that land. He died on the 9th of First Month, 1718, and was buried at North Cave.

JOHN ROUS.

John Rous was the son of Thomas Rous, a wealthy sugar planter of Barbadoes, and both father and son were among the early members of our religious Society in that island. At the time of John Rous's visit to New England, he was evidently but a young man. After his release from Boston gaol, in the Eighth Month, 1658, except a visit which he paid to the island of Nevis* towards the close of that year, we lose all trace of him until his marriage with Margaret, the eldest daughter of Judge Fell, which was solemnized at Swarthmore Hall, in the First Month, 1662. On his marriage John Rous settled in London, in which, and its vicinity, he appears to have resided during the remainder of his life. But few particulars of the life of John Rous have been preserved, and except a visit to the county of Kent in 1670, accompanied by Alexander Parker and George Whitehead; to Barbadoes in the following year with George Fox; and to the counties of York and Durham in 1689,† we know nothing of his gospel labours after he settled in England. In his will, which is dated from Kingston in the county of Surrey, " October, 1692," he describes himself as a merchant, and his property, which it appears was considerable, lay chiefly in Barbadoes. It is singular that no record of his death has been found, but as his will was proved in 1695, the probability is that it took place in that year.

THOMAS HARRIS.

The particulars given of the visit of Thomas Harris to New England is about all that we know of his history. As he is mentioned as " of Barbadoes," he must have been one of the earliest who embraced the views of our religious Society on that island.

* Besse's Sufferings, vol. ii. p. 352.
† Letter of John Rous to George Fox, 1689.

ROBERT FOWLER.

The biographical sketches of the early ministers of the Society, who were instrumental in the introduction and spread of its principles in New England, may be suitably followed by some allusion to Robert Fowler, the master and owner of the "Woodhouse." His home was at Bridlington Quay, in Yorkshire, his business being that of a mariner. A record in an ancient minute book of the Monthly Meeting of Holderness, entitled "A memorial of the first manifestation of the truth in the eastern parts of Yorkshire," written, as it professes, "for the view of posterity," states that Robert Fowler, "with many others gladly received the word of life in the year 1652." "Great fear and dread and the power of the Lord," continues the account, "wrought mightily in us, and made the strong man bow himself, and the keepers of the house to tremble, and those that were patient and staid in the light and power of God, increased in their faith, and loved one another fervently out of a pure heart, so that nothing was lacking unto any ; for self-denial, the true simplicity of the gospel, and charity which thinks no evil, flourished amongst us, and the wiles of Satan were manifest, and a way to escape his snares was seen in the light ; for the Lord anointed us with his Holy Spirit, and that led us into truth and righteousness ; and some were fitted to labour in his vineyard—unto the Lord be all the praise and glory, for it is his due, through all ages and generations."

In 1656, whilst building his little vessel, he became strongly impressed with the belief, that it would be required for some particular service in furtherance of the cause of truth ;—an impression, which, as we have seen, was remarkably realized. It was in the summer of 1657 that he landed his devoted friends on the shores of North America, and, as in the following year we find him for " some weeks a close prisoner" in Lincolnshire, for exhorting an assembly in one of the national places of worship, we may conclude that he returned without much delay from that country. The first notice of his exercising a gift in the ministry occurs in 1658; there is, nevertheless, good reason to believe, that he was for some years before, engaged in this important work. In the Eleventh Month of 1660, whilst assembled with his friends at Bridlington Quay, for the solemn purpose of worship, he was seized and carried to York Castle for refusing to take the "oath of allegiance," a snare which the enemies of the Society in that day, used to a great extent, and by which many thousands of its members were subjected to imprisonment ; at one time in 1660, no less than 4230 Friends were confined in the gaols and castles of the kingdom. His imprisonment on this occasion lasted about two months. The year following his committal to York Castle, we find that he was violently taken from a meeting at South Shields, and confined for four weeks in one of the dismal holes of Tynemouth Castle. Robert Fowler, it appears, had six children, the youngest of whom was born in 1665, and after this date we are unable to trace the incidents of his Christian course. The following indorsement made by George Fox on a letter which he received from Robert Fowler, but which is without date, contains the only remaining facts we have been able to gather respecting him :—" Robert Fowler, who often went to the steeple houses to declare the truth, and was a master of a ship, and died in the truth, and was often in prison for it." The fulness of George Fox's brief testimony needs no comment ; he " died in the truth." The date of his decease has not been ascertained.

CHAPTER VIII.

OUR attention in the preceding chapters, has been chiefly directed to the proceedings and treatment of those gospel ministers who had crossed the Atlantic, to promulgate the spiritual views of the Society of Friends, among the settlers in New England. We now enter upon the subject of the religious labours and sufferings of those in that land, who had embraced their views. The first of this class to be noticed, is Hored Gardner of Newport, on Rhode Island. In 1658, this faithful woman, under an apprehension of religious duty, left her family, consisting of " many children," to go on a visit to Weymouth, in the province of Massachusetts. This trial of her faith was rendered additionally severe, from her having at the time, a young infant to care for. Concluding to travel on foot, she took a girl with her to assist in carrying and caring for her child. Her journey was through a wilderness of above sixty miles, and "according to man," as a writer of the day remarks, " hardly accomplishable."* She was, however, favoured

* New England Judged, p. 47.

to reach Weymouth in safety ; her ministry was well received ; "the witness in the people answering to her words."* It was scarcely to be expected that, travelling thus in the same holy cause which had subjected her friends in the ministry, from England, to fines, whippings, imprisonments and banishments, she should herself escape persecution ; and accordingly, on the day after her arrival at Weymouth, she was placed under arrest, and conveyed to Boston. Endicott, who had recently evinced his hatred to Quakers, by causing Sarah Gibbons and Dorothy Waugh, to be imprisoned and whipped, on seeing a New England proselyte to Quakerism, brought before him for promulgating its doctrines, broke forth into abusive language to the prisoner, and ordered both her and her young attendant, to receive ten lashes "on their naked bodies." This species of punishment towards females, is at all times revolting, but in the present instance, it was rendered additionally so from the fact, that during its infliction, the inno- cent babe of Hored Gardner was on her breast, protected only by the arms of its agonized mother. The whipping being over, the scene was quickly changed, and instead of the sound of the knotted scourge, the voice of prayer arose from the unoffending sufferer, that her persecutors might be forgiven ; for she said that "they knew not what they did." The meek christian spirit thus strikingly displayed, struck the bystanders with astonish- ment. "Surely," said one of them, "if she has not the spirit of the Lord, she could not do this thing."† They were at once con- veyed to Boston gaol, in which they were confined for fourteen days, all communication with her Friends being strictly forbidden. One of the early sufferers in New England, in commenting on this heartless case, observes, that such instances distinctly mark the difference between the faith of those who professed with the maltreated Quakers, and that of their persecutors :—" the one, manifesting theirs through travails, trials, patience and sufferings ; the other, through wrath, malice, cruel mockings, reviling lan- guage, scourgings, and imprisonments." And he adds, "whether of these faiths stands in God, seeing there is but one Lord and

* Norton's Ensign, p. 72. † Ibid, p. 72.

one faith unto salvation, we leave it unto that of God in all people to judge.'*

The next sufferer whom we shall notice, is Katherine Scott of Providence, who in the Seventh Month, 1658, proceeded to Boston, to testify against the cruel proceedings of the magistracy towards Friends. Soon after her arrival, Christopher Holder, John Copeland, and John Rous, having been sentenced to the loss of their ears, Katherine Scott believed it to be her religious duty to remonstrate with the rulers on this barbarous act. For her christian boldness, however, she was imprisoned for three weeks, and also subjected to the ignominious torture of the lash. In the course of her examination, being told that they were likely to have a law to hang her if she came there again, she said, " If God call us, woe be to us if we come not ; and I question not but He whom we love, will make us not count our lives dear unto ourselves, for the sake of His name." Endicott maliciously replied, " And we shall be as ready to take away your lives, as ye shall be to lay them down."†

The case of Katherine Scott derives additional interest from the fact of her being a woman of considerable note and standing in New England. She was a sister of the celebrated Anne Hutchinson,‡ the leader of the Antinomians, and of John Wheelwright, both of whom were banished from Massachusetts in 1637, for their religious opinions. A narrator of Katherine Scott's sufferings, describes her as " a grave, sober, ancient woman, of blameless conversation," and of good education and circumstances.§ Hutchinson the historian says, she " was well bred, being a minister's daughter in England."‖ Her husband, Richard Scott, and eight or nine of her children, also became convinced of our principles. " The power of God," writes John Rous, " took place in all their children,"¶ One of her daughters spoke as a minister in the following year, although but eleven years of age.

Arthur Howland, an aged and venerable settler, residing at Marshfield in the colony of Plymouth, was also a sufferer for his

* Norton's Ensign, p. 72.   † Norton's Ensign, p. 97.
‡ Secret Works, p. 10.   § New England Judged, p. 75.
‖ Hutchinson's Massachusetts, vol. i. p. 200.
¶ Norton's Ensign, p. 95.

conscientious attachment to the principles of the new Society.
He was one of those who had long sought the Lord, and " Simeon
like," had waited for his salvation. Convinced that a ministry
for hire, and of mere human appointment, was a fearful usurpation
of the prerogative of the Great Head of the Church, he felt bound
to bear a christian testimony against it, by declining any longer
to contribute towards its support. His conscientious refusal, however, subjected him to considerable loss. The minister, incensed
by this innovation, and copying the example of those of his order
in the mother country, forcibly seized upon his property. In
1658, Robert Hodgson, in the course of his religious engagements
visited Marshfield, and was warmly received by Arthur Howland.
The good old man, believing the stranger to be a disciple of
Christ, entertained him gladly ; having faith in the declaration of
our Lord to his disciples, " He that receiveth you, receiveth me :
and he that receiveth me, receiveth him that sent me."* Whilst
Robert Hodgson was there, a constable came to the house to
arrest him. The aged Friend, feeling bound to do what he could
to protect his guest, demanded of the officer a warrant of his
authority. The constable replied that he had none, but that the
magistrate would justify him in taking a Quaker without one.
Arthur Howland, seeing that he had no legal authority for proceeding, told the officer that, in accordance with the constitution
of the colony, and the allegiance which he owed to the Protector,
he should resist his attempt ; and the constable, thus unexpectedly opposed, left the house. The local magistrates, vexed at
losing their prey, and at the course adopted by Arthur Howland,
fined him five pounds ; to satisfy which, a distraint was made
upon his cattle. " But such was their rage at the old man,"
observes Bishop, " that this would not satisfy them." A commitment to prison soon followed the fine. These arbitrary
measures, being considered by the sufferer as an invasion of the
rights of a British subject, and at variance with the colonial laws
of the empire, he demanded his liberty, in order that he might
" repair to England, to make his case known to the powers."†
His appeal, however, was unheeded, and had not a brother interfered, and obtained his release " by giving a bond," the aged

* Matthew x. 40.   † Secret Works, p. 5.

colonist would have had to endure the severity of a winter season within the precincts of a prison.

Among the early converts to the Society in New England, were some who resided at Sandwich, and who had been convinced in 1657. William Newland and Ralph Allen were two of these, and their attachment to the principles which they had embraced, was soon tested by suffering. Both of them were called to serve on a jury, and, acting on the injunction of their Lord, " Swear not at all," they declined to take the oath. William Newland was fined ten shillings for his refusal ; and on his request, during the sitting of the court, that his friends Christopher Holder and John Copeland, might be furnished with a copy of the warrant on which they had been arrested, he was fined another ten shillings for his interference : a distress was levied on his goods for the recovery of these sums. They were then arraigned before the court for keeping disorderly meetings at their houses. The charge, it appears, rested on the fact of a few Friends having met in silence to wait upon God. Their so assembling, however, being viewed by the magistrates as a grave offence, a fine of twenty shillings was imposed on each of the Friends, with an order, that they should find sureties in the sum of eighty pounds for their good behaviour during the ensuing six months. As an acquiescence in this demand would imply an acknowledgment of the offence, and a relinquishment of that spiritual worship of the Most High, which had become precious to them, they unhesitatingly refused to comply. They were then committed to the custody of the marshal, and were kept close prisoners for five months. When half the period had expired, they were offered their liberty on engaging not to receive or listen to a Quaker ; but the request was met by an immediate and a decided negative. Their settlement in the truth was too firm to be shaken by offers of this description.

Towards the close of 1657, the individuals who had been newly convinced at Sandwich, suffered considerably for continuing to meet for the purpose of religious worship. This little company included the six brothers and sisters of Ralph Allen just referred to. The father of the family, who had been an Anabaptist, and had also entertained a conscientious scruple against judicial swearing, had "laid down his head in peace" before Friends had visited those parts. His children had resided upwards of twenty years in Sandwich and its vicinity, and were much respected by their neighbours. But their reception of Quakerism was peculiarly annoying to the ministers and magistracy, whose persecuting hand was specially directed against them : the only individuals to whom the "oath of fidelity" was tendered, being those of this family.

In 1658, the sufferings of Friends of Sandwich were much aggravated by increased distraints on their goods, and by being prevented from holding their religious meetings. The levies were made for fines, on account of their conscientious refusal to take the "oath of fidelity," tendered purposely to ensnare them ; and also for absence from the public worship. In the Eighth Month, sixteen Friends of this place were summoned to the court held at Plymouth, and were fined five pounds each for refusing to take the oath. Some of them had been fined already on the same charge.* Some of

* Besse records the following distraints made about this period from Friends resident in and near Sandwich, to satisfy the fines imposed :—

	£	s.	d.
Robert Harper	44	0	0
Joseph Allen	5	12	0
Edward Perry	89	18	0
George Allen	25	15	0
William Gifford	57	19	0
William Newland	36	0	0
Ralph Allen, Jun.	18	0	0
John Jenkins	19	10	0
Henry Howland	1	10	0
Ralph Allen, Sen.	68	0	0
Thomas Greenfield	4	0	0
Richard Kirby	57	12	0
William Allen	86	17	0
Thomas Ewer	25	8	0
Daniel Wing	12	0	0
Peter Gaunt	43	14	6
Michael Turner	13	10	0
John Newland	2	6	0
Matthew Allen	48	16	0
	£660	7	6

these faithful sufferers, alluding to the persecution to which they were subjected for refusing the oath, remark, that it was "contrary to the law of Christ," "whose law," they add, "is so strongly written in our hearts, and the keeping of it so delightsome to us; and the gloriousness of its life daily appearing, makes us to endure the cross patiently, and suffer the spoiling of our goods with joy."*

While recording the sufferings of those who professed with Friends in the colony of Plymouth, we must not omit to notice the case of Cudworth and Hatherly, the two magistrates of Scituate. These worthy men appear never to have joined our religious Society, but being enlightened on the subject of religious toleration, and rejoicing in the extension of the kingdom of the Redeemer by whatever means He might use, they not only boldly opposed the authorities of New England in persecuting Friends, but also welcomed those who came to Scituate, and entertained them at their houses. This liberality was offensive to the rigid professors of Massachusetts, and several attempts being made to displace them from the magistracy, they both ultimately resigned their appointments. "He that will not whip and lash, persecute and punish men that differ in matters of religion," says one of them, "must not sit on the bench." Cudworth, who held a military captainship was discharged, "because," he says, "I entertained some of the Quakers at my house."

Turning from the Friends of Plymouth to their fellow-professors in the other part of Massachusetts, we find that suffering was also their lot for the cause of truth. The banishment of Nicholas Upshal from Boston in 1656, and the imprisonment of Samuel Shattock, and of Laurence and Cassandra Southwick of Salem, in the following year, have already been mentioned. Towards the close of 1657, the Salem Friends suffered severely for maintaining their meetings; and in order, as Bishop says, "to terrify the rest," the magistrates subjected Laurence and Cassandra Southwick, with their son Josiah, to a cruel whipping and an imprisonment for eleven days, for absenting themselves from public worship; and in the meanwhile, goods to the value of four pounds thirteen

* Norton's Ensign, p. 42.

shillings were taken from them for fines on account of such absence.*

Another who suffered at Salem, was Edward Harnet, a settler aged nearly seventy years. So many fines were levied upon him for not attending the authorised place of worship, as to make it probable that all the little property which he possessed, and which was his main dependence in declining life, would be sacrificed to the cruelty and rapacity of his enemies. To prevent this result, he felt free to emigrate to Rhode Island, after disposing of his house and land ;† and several others, who were similarly harassed, concluded to leave the scene of persecution. John Small, Josiah Southwick, and John Buffum were of this number, and whilst proceeding to Rhode Island, in order to fix upon some spot in this favoured province, on which to settle with their families, they were arrested and carried to Boston. This, however, was an outrage on the liberty of the colonist, which even the intolerant Endicott refused to sanction; and on appealing to him the Friends were liberated.

Reference has been made in a previous chapter to a meeting held by William Brend and William Leddra, at the house of Nicholas Phelps, in the woods, about five miles from Salem, and to a threat made by one of the authorities who attended, that he would prosecute the Friends who were present. The threatening magistrate, true to his intolerant purpose, applied to the court then sitting at Salem, for an order to arrest six of the Friends who were present at the meeting in question. The application was readily responded to, and in a short time Samuel Shattock, Laurence and Cassandra Southwick, their son Josiah, Samuel Gaskin, and Joshua Buffum, were seized by the officers. After an imprisonment of two days, they were brought before the court for examination. The charges preferred against them were, for absenting themselves from public worship—for assembling by themselves, and for meeting with the Quakers. They were committed, and sent to join William Brend and William Leddra, who were already in Salem prison.

* F. Howgill's Popish Inquisition, p. 35.
† Ibid, p. 34.

A few days after the committal of the six Friends, a warrant was issued to convey them all to Boston, and on the 2nd of the Fifth Month, preparations were made for the purpose. The Friends of Salem, finding that their companions were about to be separated from them, and conveyed to a place already notorious for scenes of persecution, came to take a sorrowing farewell of the sufferers ; and " before our departure," remarks one of them, " the Lord gathered us together, and we had a meeting of Friends some part of the way thither."* They were all on foot, and as the little company proceeded towards Boston, the solemnity of a religious meeting was maintained. When the time came for them to part, the prisoners engaged in prayer, and committed themselves in faith to the sustaining arm of the Shepherd of Israel. Having arrived at Boston, four of the Salem Friends were sentenced to undergo the cruelties of the lash, from which even Cassandra Southwick was not exempted. For Laurence Southwick and his son Josiah, the remaining two, a more severe punishment was reserved. In accordance with the last revolting law against Quakers, they both suffered the loss of their ears.

Being detained as prisoners after the liberation of the English Friends who were committed about the same period, the six Friends drew up a remonstrance to the court at Salem, under whose authority they had been sent to gaol. " Let it not be a small thing in your eyes," said they, " thus to expose, as much as in you lies, our families to ruin—as for our parts, we have true peace and rest in the Lord in all our sufferings, and are made willing in the power and strength of God, freely to offer up our lives in his cause, yea, and we find (through grace) the enlargement of God in our imprisoned state, to whom alone we commit ourselves and our families, for the disposing of us, according to his infinite wisdom and pleasure ; in whose love is our rest and life."† The Christian meekness and patience breathed in the language of these faithful individuals, and the inward peace and consolation which they enjoyed amid their sufferings, strikingly exemplifies the gracious promise of our Redeemer, " In

---

* Norton's Ensign, p. 76.　　† New England Judged, p. 60.

the world ye shall have tribulation, but in me peace." The court, on receiving the remonstrance, directed the liberation of the prisoners, excepting the Southwicks, who were continued under close confinement for twenty weeks.

Previously to the holding of the meeting at his house, Nicholas Phelps, being convinced of the spiritual character of divine worship, had absented himself from the public assemblies, and had been fined five shillings per week, for thus adhering to his religious convictions. Having rendered himself additionally obnoxious to the magistracy by allowing meetings to be held at his house, he was summoned before the court held at Salem, in the Fifth Month, 1658.* The presence of Quakers in New England being adverted to, one of the justices, with a view to prejudice the court against them, remarked, that they denied both magistrates and ministers. Nicholas Phelps, hearing the charge, and being sensible of its injustice, undertook to disprove it, and presented to the bench, a paper setting forth the sentiments of the Society on those questions. The document being read, and its contents found to be opposed to puritan opinions, the minds of the bigoted rulers were further incensed, and they determined that Nicholas Phelps should suffer for thus boldly advocating heresy. He was now asked, if he owned the document, and answering in the affirmative, was fined forty shillings for the paper, also forty shillings for having had a meeting at his house, and was finally committed to Ipswich gaol for being a Quaker.† The gaoler of Ipswich, following the example of his fellow-official at Boston, ordered Nicholas Phelps to work, and having received a refusal to his unjust demand, subjected him to three severe whippings in the short space of five days. The punishment inflicted upon this conscientious man was the more cruel in consequence of the very weak state of his health, and a physical deformity under which he laboured, but he endured it all with christian meekness and patience, and "being strong in faith,"‡ "all their cruelty

---

* F. Howgill's Popish Inquisition, p. 38.
† New England Judged, p. 61.
‡ F. Howgill's Popish Inquisition, p. 38.

could not bend his spirit, for the Lord upheld him."* The magistrates, finding that their prisoner was not to be shaken from his resolutions, either by fines, whippings, or imprisonments, seemed anxious to give up the fruitless task of attempting to reduce him to orthodoxy, and after fourteen days' confinement, he was set at liberty. This imprisonment, being in the time of harvest, occasioned him considerable loss.

In the Seventh Month, 1658, Joshua Buffum and Samuel Shattock, who had been but lately released from an imprisonment of twenty weeks, were committed to Ipswich gaol with Nicholas Phelps, for holding a meeting in the vicinity of Salem. They were detained on this occasion for three weeks, and were also severely scourged. In addition to these severities, Samuel Shattock had "half of his house and the ground belonging to it"† seized for the fines imposed—a very unusual and unwarranted stretch of arbitrary power. He was a man in good circumstances, and is spoken of as "the most considerable man at Salem." But, said he, in a letter to a friend, "In the Lord I rejoice, that I have something to suffer the loss of, for the Truth's sake."‡ A few days only had elapsed, after the liberation of these Friends, when with Laurence, Cassandra and Josiah Southwick, they were forcibly taken and carried to Boston, to hear from the lips of the authorities of that town, a law which they had just enacted, for banishing Friends on pain of death. Francis Howgill, alluding to the sufferings of Friends at Salem, says, "Now after all this there was a court held at Salem, the last day of November, 1658. This court sent for about fifteen of the inhabitants for not coming to their meeting, twelve of whom did appear ; of these, nine were fined for sixteen weeks' absence £4. a-piece ; one was fined £3. 15s., and one £1. The sum of what was fined by this court, was £40. 15s."§

We now pass on to Boston. This was much the most considerable town in the two colonies of Massachusetts,—the seat of government of one of them, and conspicuous, above all other places in New England, for bigotry and for excessive persecutions. The

* Norton's Ensign, p. 81.   † Ibid, p. 103.

‡ F. Howgill's Popish Inquisition, p. 60.   § Ibid, p. 43.

cruelty of Endicott and Bellingham towards the gospel messengers of the new Society, naturally led to much inquiry respecting the principles of Friends : but the watchful and unceasing efforts of the authorities, prevented those who came from publicly advocating the truth, as they had been enabled to do at Salem, Sandwich, and some other places in Massachusetts. To this cause may be attributed the few convincements which took place at Boston. From the time of Nicholas Upshal's banishment in 1656, to the close of 1658, but one of the inhabitants openly professed with Friends. This individual was William Shattock. Being convinced that the worship of the Divine Being must be performed in spirit and in truth, and that ability to preach or pray aright must be waited for, instead of frequenting the usual place of divine worship, he sought retirement for this purpose in his own dwelling. His non-attendance of public worship was soon noticed by the jealous eye of the rulers, and in the First Month of 1658, he was arrested for the offence, and brought before the court. Endicott, who presided, after questioning him on several points, sentenced him to be taken to the house of correction—to be severely whipped, and to be kept from all intercourse with his friends and neighbours. William Shattock was but poor as to the things of this world, and, having a wife and four children who were dependent upon his labour, the case of his family became truly distressing. Under these urgent circumstances, the wife of William Shattock interceded for his liberation, but the authorities, bent on clearing their capital at least, of " heretics," replied, that until he promised to leave the colony, the prison would be his habitation, and that his children would be taken and placed in servitude. In this painful situation, William Shattock " sought counsel of the Lord," and, he observes, " their arm of cruelty was so great, I found freedom to depart." The magistrates, impatient for his banishment, allowed him but three days to prepare for his departure. Thus exiled from Massachusetts, he proceeded to Rhode Island, where he found a peaceful home for himself and his family, and once more Boston appeared to be free from the "accursed heretics."

In these details, the case of William Marston of Hampton must not be forgotten. Notwithstanding the precautions taken by the authorities, to prevent the introduction and circulation of the writings of Friends, means had, it appears, been found for their distribution. William Marston was suspected of having some of these in his possession; his house was searched, and a copy of William Dewsbury's "Mighty day of the Lord," and of John Lilburne's "Resurrection," being found, he was subjected to the excessive fine of £10. Subsequently, he was "rated in the sum of £3. to the priest for his wages," and also fined £5. for absence from the authorised worship. To satisfy these claims, goods to the value of £20. were taken from him.*

In concluding the present chapter, which brings this narrative down to the close of 1658, being about two years and a-half from the time of the first landing of Friends in New England, it may be well to consider the extent of the footing which their principles had obtained in that country. Very early after the landing of the few gospel messengers from the "Woodhouse," meetings for worship were established and regularly kept up at Providence, and on Rhode Island. Of the number of members which constituted those meetings at this early period, it is difficult to speak with much precision : they could not, however, have been inconsiderable. Already several of their number had received a gift in the ministry, and four had travelled, in the exercise of that gift, to the neighbouring colonies of New England. The official documents of Rhode Island, as early as the First Month of 1658, alluding to the visits of English Friends, state that they had "raised up divers who seem to be of their spirit."† We must not forget, however, that Friends there, so far from experiencing persecution from the authorities, were received by them with favour. William Coddington and Nicholas Easton who had both filled the office of governor of the colony, inclined towards them from the first, and soon after, openly professed with them : meetings for worship, and also the Yearly Meetings, were held at the house of the former at Newport until the time of his decease in 1688.‡

---

* Besse, vol. ii. p. 195.

† Letter from the "General Assembly of the colony of Providence Plantations" to their agent in England.

‡ Morse and Parish's History of New England, p. 88.

The spread of Quakerism, however, in other parts of New England, was not dependent, as has been already seen, on the smiles of its rulers. An opposite policy in Massachusetts signally failed to suppress the rising ·society, and the persecutions in its two intolerant colonies, seemed fruitful in results. "Their patience under it," observes James Cudworth, in writing of the sufferers to his friend in London, "hath sometimes been the occasion of gaining more adherents to them, than if they had been suffered openly to preach a sermon."* At Sandwich, where the magistracy harassed them with great severity, the largest meeting in New England was held. It is stated that in 1658, no less than eighteen families of this place recorded their names in one of the documents of the Society.† Meetings were also held at Duxbury,‡ and some other places in this jurisdiction, whilst convincements had taken place at Marshfield and Barnstaple ; and at Scituate its ministers found a welcome reception from the local authorities. A magistrate of this latter town, addressing his friend, in 1658, thus remarks in reference to the progress of the Society, "They have many meetings, and many adherents, almost the whole town of Sandwich is adhering towards them." "I am informed," he adds "of three or four-score last court presented for not coming to public meetings."§ In the more persecuting colony of Boston, many had also received the spiritual views of the Society, and rejoiced that they were counted worthy to suffer for so holy a cause. It is true, that in the town of Boston, whilst many sympathized with the sufferers, under the revolting cruelties to which they were subjected, two individuals only openly professed with Friends, and these two had been banished from the colony. At Hampton the truth had found an entrance ; during 1658, a family at this place suffered largely in distraints for their testimony.‖ But it

* Secret Works, p. 21
† See Brief Account of Meetings in New England. Providence, Printed 1836, p. 20.
‡ Norton's Ensign, p. 49.
§ Letter of J. Cudworth,—See Secret Works, p. 20, and Neal's History of New England, vol. i. p. 321.
‖ F. Howgill's Popish Inquisition, p. 42.

was at and near Salem, about sixteen miles north of Boston, that the largest number of convincements in this colony took place. In 1657, it is stated that there were "divers Friends" in that locality. During the summer of 1658, the sufferings of eight families are distinctly recorded, and in the Ninth Month, fifteen individuals were summoned at one time to the court held at Salem, for not attending the Puritan meetings. Neal states, that about this time as many as twenty were taken at once from a meeting held at the house of Nicholas Phelps, about five miles from Salem.* Joscelyn, in his chronological observations on America at this period, remarks, that "the Quakers' opinions were vented up and down the country,"† and John Rous writing to Margaret Fell, from New England, observes, "the truth is spread here above two hundred miles, many are in a fine condition, and very sensible of the power of God, and some of the inhabitants who are Friends, have been forth in the ministry. We have," he continues, "two strong places in this land, the one at Newport in Rhode Island, and the other at Sandwich. At Salem, there are several pretty Friends in their measures—there are Friends, few or more, almost from one end of the land to the other, that is inhabited by the English."‡

In noticing the progress of the Society at this early period in New England, it should be borne in mind, that, being a newly settled country, its towns were few, and the number of its population was comparatively small. In 1643, there were but thirty-six churches, or places of authorized worship, in New England; in 1650, there were forty, containing 7750 communicants.§ Twenty-five years later, the whole population of Massachusetts and Rhode Island did not exceed 33,000.|| The settlements were chiefly agricultural communities, planted near the sea-side, or on the rivers, and cultivation had not extended far into the interior.

---

* Neal's History of New England, vol. i. p. 304.
† See Massachussett, Hist. Society's Pub. vol. iii. 3rd Series.
‡ Swarthmore Collection of MSS.
§ Morse and Parish's History of New England, p. 165.
|| Bancroft's History of the United States.

CHAPTER IX.

The priests and rulers of Boston petition the colonial legislature for a
law to banish Friends on pain of death—The proceedings of the
authorities respecting it—The law is passed by a majority of one
vote—A copy of the law—W. Brend and six Friends of Salem banished under its provisions—Daniel and Provided Southwick, for not
attending Puritan worship, are fined and ordered to be sold as slaves
—The authorities are unable to carry out the sentence—Samuel
Gaskin ordered to be sold as a slave—The constabulary empowered
to break open the doors of those suspected to be Quakers—William
Leddra and Peter Pearson are imprisoned at Plymouth—Letter
of Peter Pearson—William Robinson and Marmaduke Stevenson
arrive at Rhode Island—They proceed to Boston, and are imprisoned
—Nicholas Davis and Patience Scott also go to Boston, and are
imprisoned—Some account of Patience Scott, who came forth in the
ministry when eleven years of age—Observations on the ministry of
young persons— Extract of a Letter from William Robinson to
George Fox, written in Boston gaol.

For two years had the rulers of the church and of the state in
New England been strenuous in their endeavours to check the
introduction and spread of Quakerism, and lent themselves to
acts of great cruelty in pursuance of their purpose. The various
laws, however, which they had passed for this object, all signally
failed, for, notwithstanding the opposition which it had to
encounter, the little Society rapidly increased in numbers, and
neither imprisonments, whippings, nor banishments, deterred its
ministers from preaching their doctrines among the colonists.
" Such was the enthusiastic fire of the Quakers," observes an
early historian of the country, " that nothing could quench it :
the sect grew under these disadvantages."*

The bigoted religionists of Massachusetts, alarmed at the progress of these innovations, and disappointed in their exertions to
prevent them, now suffered themselves, in their deep-rooted aver-

---

* Neal's History of New England, vol. i. p. 306.

sion to dissent from the authorised religion, to be led on to the commission of extreme acts of persecution ; and the ministers, among whom the notorious Norton of Boston,* was foremost, petitioned the local legislature to banish Friends upon pain of death. The magistrates of the colony, who had evinced an eagerness in the work of persecution, listened to the unchristian suggestion ; and, at their general court held at Boston in the Eighth Month, 1658, the inhuman statute was enacted for exiling all Friends, both colonists and strangers, on pain of death. The laws of the British nation, based on the foundation of Magna Charta, made it imperative that the life of the subject should not be taken without trial by jury ; but the authorities of Massachusetts, to forward their wicked purpose of exterminating this harmless people, thus arbitrarily setting aside this safeguard of liberty, resolved that the awful sentence of death might be passed by a majority of a county court, consisting of even three magistrates only.

The legislature of the colony consisted of two houses, the one composed of the magistracy, and the other of representatives elected by the freemen of the respective towns ; each house being independent of the other. To enact a law, a majority of both houses was necessary ; the magisterial one, therefore, having passed the law in question, sent it to the representatives for confirmation. The deputies, however, were much divided in opinion on the proposed measure. Several of them had viewed with dissatisfaction the harsh and unchristian laws already passed in reference to Friends ; but the extreme severity of the bill in question was such, that, out of twenty-six members of their house, fifteen were decidedly opposed to it. This becoming known, the authorities, civil and ecclesiastical, being determined to carry their bold and wicked scheme, exerted all the power and influence they possessed, to induce the representatives to pass the extirpating enactment. Their efforts were unhappily successful ; two of the deputies were prevailed upon to alter their opinions,† and, in the absence, through illness of a third, (a deacon named Wozel,) who was opposed to the

* Oldmixon in his " British Empire in America," says " Norton was at the head of all the Quakers' sufferings" in New England.
† Neal's History of New England, vol. i. p. 307.

proposition, the assembly of twenty-five representatives passed the sanguinary law by a majority of one ; thirteen being for it, whilst the speaker and eleven others were opposed to it.* The absent member, it appears, felt such a conscientious repugnance to the proposed measure, that, although suffering from severe indisposition, he determined, nevertheless, to be present when the votes on the question should be taken ; and " he earnestly desired the speaker and some of the deputies, to send for him when the time came ;"† but to nullify his opposition, care had been taken by those favourable to the bill, to divide before he could arrive.‡ Wozel, being informed of the stratagem which had thus been practised, and of the law having been carried by a majority of one voice only, which his presence would have negatived, hastened to the assembly, and, expressing his sorrow that it should have passed by his absence, desired his vote to be taken ; and said that if he had not been able to go, he would have crept on his hands and knees to prevent it.§ But the exertions of the humane deputy were unavailing ; his vote was refused, and the blood-stained and unconstitutional measure was published as the deliberate act of the legislature of Massachusetts.

The twelve deputies who had voted in the minority, having entered their protest against the law, as being repugnant to those of the realm, the magistrates, fearful of proceeding under such circumstances, subsequently agreed to an amendment of the law, and admitted trial by special jury. The lives of some of the most conscientious inhabitants of New England were now placed in the hands of men who were known to be their most determined foes, and who were vindictively bent on their destruction. Such was the legislation of those who, to erect a church free from all the blemishes of popery, and to escape the persecuting hand of Laud, had fled to the wilds of America ; but, says a modern historian, " Laud was justified by the men whom he had wronged."|| The " foul enactment," contrary to the laws both of God and man, and from which the mind turns with feelings of abhorrence, will go down to posterity as a monument of lasting disgrace to Puritan New

* Neal's History of New England, vol. i. p. 307.
† New England Judged, p. 80. ‡ Ibid, p. 80. § Sewel, p. 198.
|| Bancroft, vol. ii. p. 190.

England. What a humiliating proof does this dark transaction furnish, of the extent to which man may err, through haughty self-righteousness, and a mistaken and fiery zeal for certain religious opinions. The law was as follows :—

AN ACT MADE AT A GENERAL COURT HELD AT BOSTON, THE 20TH OF OCTOBER, 1658.

" Whereas, there is a pernicious sect, commonly called Quakers, lately arisen, who by word and writing have published and maintained many dangerous and horrid tenets, and do take upon them to change and alter the received laudable customs of our nation, in giving civil respect to equals or reverence to superiors, whose actions tend to undermine the civil government, and also to destroy the order of the churches, by denying all established forms of worship, and by withdrawing from orderly church-fellowship, allowed and approved by all orthodox professors of truth, and instead thereof, and in opposition thereunto, frequently meeting by themselves, insinuating themselves into the minds of the simple, or such as are at least affected to the order and government of church and commonwealth, whereby divers of our inhabitants have been infected, notwithstanding all former laws made upon the experience of their arrogant and bold obtrusions, to disseminate their principles amongst us, prohibiting their coming into this jurisdiction, they have not been deterred from their impetuous attempts to undermine our peace and hazard our ruin.

" ·For prevention thereof, this court doth order and enact, that every person or persons of the *cursed sect of Quakers,* who is not an inhabitant of, but is found within this jurisdiction, shall be apprehended without warrant where no magistrate is at hand, by any constable, commissioner, or select man, and conveyed from constable to constable to the next magistrate, who shall commit the said person to close prison, there to remain (without bail) unto the next court of assistants, where they shall have a legal trial ; and being convicted to be of the sect of Quakers, shall be sentenced to be banished upon pain of death :

And that every inhabitant of this jurisdiction, being convicted to be of the aforesaid sect, either by taking up, publishing, or defending the horrid opinions of the Quakers, or the stirring up mutiny, sedition, or rebellion against the government, or by taking up their abusive and destructive practices, viz : denying civil respect to equals and superiors, and withdrawing from our church assemblies, and instead thereof frequenting meetings of their own in opposition to our church order, or by adhering to or approving of any known Quaker, and the tenets and practices of the Quakers that are opposite to the orthodox received opinions of the godly, and endeavouring to disaffect others to civil government and church order, or condemning the proceedings and practices of this court against the Quakers, manifesting thereby their compliance with those whose design is to overthrow the order established in church and state ; every such person, upon conviction before the said court of assistants *in manner aforesaid,* shall be committed to close prison for one month, and then, unless they choose voluntarily to depart this jurisdiction, shall give bond for their good behaviour, and appear at the next court, where continuing obstinate, and refusing to retract and reform the aforesaid opinions, they shall be sentenced to banishment upon pain of death ; and any one magistrate, upon information given him of any such person, shall cause him to be apprehended, and shall commit any such person to prison, according to his discretion, until he come to trial as aforesaid."

This wicked and sanguinary measure, although passed into law, from some cause or other, was not brought into operation for more than six months. Although congenial to the persecuting ecclesiastics and rulers of Boston, it was not so to the inhabitants generally. The dissatisfaction excited in the colony, by the barbarities recently inflicted upon the English Friends who had been banished, had not yet sufficiently subsided, to allow the authorities to exhibit with impunity, the revolting spectacle of the gallows in support of their religion.

The first individual upon whom the efficacy of the new law was tested, was William Brend, whilst on a visit to Boston in the

Third Month, 1659.   This aged minister of Christ, whose
scarred body testified abundantly to the severity of the persecutors of Massachusetts, was the first Friend who entered its
territory after the passing of the act.   Having received sentence
of banishment on pain of death, and being informed by the
authorities, that, if within two days he was found within the precincts of their jurisdiction, death would be his inevitable portion,*
he returned to Rhode Island.   His testimony to the truth had
been most unflinching among the high professors of this land, and
for his faithfulness he had already been brought near the gates of
death ; his withdrawal to Rhode Island therefore, must not be
understood to have been in order to avoid an ignominious death, in
violation of his duty, for his former course is opposed to such a conclusion : but rather let us believe that it was in compliance with the
apprehended will of his Great Master on that particular occasion.

The next victims to the application of the barbarous law, were
Nicholas Phelps, Joshua Buffum, Samuel Shattock, Laurence and
Cassandra Southwick, and their son Josiah.   These Friends all
resided in and near Salem, and had already smarted under intolerance and tyranny.   They had been twice imprisoned, some for
ten, and others for twenty weeks ; three had been once subjected
to the lash, two others twice, and the remaining one no less than
four times ; whilst property to a large amount had been taken
from them ;† and all for not conforming to the dominant ideas in
religion.   The date of their arraignment under this act, was the
11th of the Third Month, 1659, and no specific charge having
been made for their arrest, they desired the court to point out the
crime of which they had been guilty.   The governor replied, that
" it was for contemning authority, in not coming to the ordinances
of God, and for rebelling against the authority of the country in
not departing according to their order."‡   In answer to this exposition of the governor, they said, " that they had no other
place to go to, but had their wives, children, families, and
estates, to look after, nor had they done any thing worthy of
death, banishment, or bonds, or of any thing which they had

---

* Secret Works, p. 19.   New England a Degenerate Plant, p. 8.
† New England Judged, p. 82.   ‡ Besse, vol. ii. p. 197.

suffered."* Conscience smitten with the truth of the prisoners' reply, the governor remained silent, on which Denison, a Major-general, told them, that "they stood against the authority of the country in not submitting to their laws," adding, "you and we are not able well to live together, and at present the power is in our hand, and, therefore, the stronger must fend off."†

The six Friends were taken out of court, but in a short time were called back, and received the dreadful sentence of death, should their persons be found within the limits of the colony within two weeks from that day. The following, taken from the records of the General Court at Boston, is a copy of the minute on the occasion :—

AT A GENERAL COURT HELD AT BOSTON, THE 11TH OF MAY, 1659.

"It is ordered, that Laurence Southwick, and Cassandra his wife, Samuel Shattock, Nicholas Phelps, Joshua Buffum, and Josiah Southwick, are hereby sentenced, according to the order of the General Court in October last, to banishment, to depart out of this jurisdiction by the eighth day of June next, on pain of death ; and if any of them after the said eighth day of June next, shall be found within this jurisdiction, they shall be appre-hended by any constable or other officer of this jurisdiction, and be committed to close prison, there to lie till the next Court of Assistants, where they shall be tried, and being found guilty of the breach of this law, shall be put to death."

The prisoners urged the necessity of a longer period to allow them to settle their affairs, and to find an opportunity of pro-ceeding to England, but this reasonable request was denied, and they were ordered summarily to leave their country, their families and friends, to seek a home and subsistence in some land of strangers. Four days after, a vessel being about to sail for Barbadoes, Nicholas Phelps, Samuel Shattock and Josiah South-wick, embraced the opportunity it afforded for proceeding by that

* New England Judged, p. 84.   † Besse, vol. ii. p. 198.

route to England, to seek redress for these despotic proceedings. The aged Laurence and Cassandra Southwick took their course for Shelter Island, which lay at the eastern end of Long Island, and at that time belonged to Nathaniel Silvester, a Friend ;* whilst Joshua Buffum made his way to Rhode Island. The circumstance of being thus suddenly and rudely torn from their children, and banished from a home dear to them by many fond ties and recollections, was too great a shock for the aged Southwicks. Soon after reaching Shelter Island, and within three days of each other, the exiled couple were called from all the tribulations of time, in the good hope of a better and more peaceful inheritance.†

The family of the Southwicks, appear to have been the special objects of sectarian malignity ; which, not satisfied with driving the aged parents and their eldest son into banishment, now placed its unrelenting hand on the two remaining members of the family, a son Daniel, and a daughter named Provided. Daniel and Provided had wisely " Remembered their Creator in the days of their youth ;" the cause of truth had become precious to them, and for its sake they were now orphans in the world. Their absence from public worship continued to bear a clear though negative testimony against its lifeless forms and ceremonies ; and for this offence, although it was well known that they had no estate of their own, and it was notorious that their parents had been reduced to poverty by their rapacious persecutors, these innocent young persons were fined ten pounds each, and as an expedient for raising this unjust penalty, the General Court at Boston resolved to sell them as slaves, under the following order.

" Whereas, Daniel Southwick and Provided Southwick, son and daughter of Laurence Southwick, absenting themselves from the public ordinances, having been fined by the courts of Salem and Ipswich, pretending they have no estates, and resolving not to work : The court, upon perusal of a law which was made upon account of debts, in answer to what should be done for the satis-

---

* MS. letter of William Robinson, 1659.   † Besse, vol. ii. p. 198.

faction of the fines resolves, That the treasurers of the several counties, are and shall be fully empowered to sell the said persons to any of the English nation at Virginia or Barbadoes, to answer the said fines."

The heartless mandate having been issued, steps were now taken to put it in force, and the brother and sister, subjects of the British realm, were offered first to one Barbadoes captain, and then to another, as slaves for the southern markets. The atrocity of the attempt was, however, too glaring to meet with success, and the refusal of all the sea captains to lend themselves to the furtherance of such barbarity, offered a strong rebuke to the self-righteous ministers and rulers of Boston. One captain, less bold in his refusal than his companions, as an excuse for declining to purchase them, said, "they would spoil the ship's company." "No," said the officer, "you need not fear that, for they are poor harmless creatures that will not hurt any body." The captain, struck with this inconsistent avowal of the truth, at once replied, "Will you then offer to make slaves of such harmless creatures?"* Thus foiled in their wicked work, and at a loss how to dispose of their prey, as winter approached, the brother and sister were set at liberty to provide for themselves, until an opportunity could be found to accomplish the cruel purpose.

In framing the laws of New England, the Pilgrim Fathers, enlightened beyond most of their contemporaries on the subject of jurisprudence, had considerably reduced the number of offences, to be punished by the extreme penalty of the law.† The abhorrence also, with which they viewed the sinful and disgusting traffic in men, practised at that period by most, if not every christian nation, prompted them to constitute as one of their capital offences, a participation in this wicked and odious commerce. When, therefore, we compare these bright spots in their history, with the revolting conduct of their successors in the affair of the youthful Southwicks, how is the heinousness of the transaction heightened, and a palliation of such cruel inconsistencies

---

* New England Judged, p. 90, Sewel, p. 224.
† They had reduced the number of capital offences to eleven.

rendered impossible ! The authorised commission of a crime, for which their own laws had imposed the forfeiture of life, can only find its explanation in the excesses of a blind and barbarous bigotry, an explanation equally applicable to the darkest deeds of the Romish inquisition.

The failure of the rulers of Massachusetts to sell the two children of Laurence and Cassandra Southwick into bondage, did not deter them from making a similar attempt respecting others who were older. Edward Wharton and Samuel Gaskin, two Friends of Salem, who had already suffered severely for their religion, were soon after arrested for the non-attendance of public worship, and fined in the respective sums of £5. 10s. and £8. One of them, having no visible property to distrain upon for the fines, was sentenced to be sent to Barbadoes and sold as a slave. The cruel order, however, was never executed, arising it is supposed from the same cause which had frustrated the previous attempt. The authorities of Boston, it is evident, had not calculated upon the difficulties which presented in their attempt to make slaves of their conscientious neighbours. Their design undoubtedly was, to carry out to some considerable extent this plan for extinguishing heresy ; in pursuance of which the General Court made a law in the Third Month, " That all children and servants and others, that for conscience' sake cannot come to their meetings to worship, and have not estates in their hands to answer the fines, must be sold for slaves to Barbadoes or Virginia, or other remote parts ;"* and so unblushingly did the rulers of the province proceed in this disgusting business, that the slave making order was " proclaimed throughout the province."† The more effectually to hunt down the poor unresisting Quakers, the officers were instructed to use at their own discretion, all the powers of a search warrant. The following is a specimen of an order of this description given to the constable of Salem.

" You are required, by virtue hereof, to search in all suspicio houses for private meetings; and if they refuse to open the doors,

---

* New England a Degenerate Plant, p. 10.　　† Ibid, p. 10.

you are to break open the door upon them, and return the names
of all ye find to Ipswich court."*

" WILLIAM HATHORN."

While the authorities of the Boston division of Massachusetts,
were thus pursuing religious persecution, those of the Plymouth
patent, were not idle in the same wicked work. In the Fourth
Month, 1659, William Leddra, and Peter Pearson, whilst travelling in gospel labours in that colony, were arrested, and imprisoned for ten months at Plymouth. The following extract
from a letter written by Peter Pearson during his imprisonment, gives a few particulars of the movements of himself and
some of his friends prior to his arrest.

" Upon the Ninth-day of the Fourth Month, 1659, the Fourth-
day of the week, all of us English Friends that were abroad in this
country, had a meeting upon Rhode Island. The Sixth-day following, at a Ferry side, upon Rhode Island, one Friend, William
Leddra, and I, parted with Christopher Holder, Marmaduke
Stevenson, and William Robinson, we being about to pass over
the ferry, to travel into this part of the country called Plymouth
colony At the end of two days' journey we came to a town
therein, called Sandwich, and the day following had a pretty
peaceable meeting, and it was with us, if we did escape apprehension in this colony, to have travelled into Boston's jurisdiction ; but in the second meeting that we had at Sandwich, we
were apprehended, and had before the governor and magistrates,
and by them committed to this prison, where we have remained
five months and upward."†

*" Written in Plymouth prison, in New Eng-
land, the 6th of the Tenth Month,* 1659."　　*Peter Pearson*

Turning again to Boston, we find intolerant zeal fast approach-
its climax of atrocity. William Robinson who arrived in

* New England Judged, p. 91.
† Call from Death to Life, &c., printed 1660, p. 30.

New England in 1657, but whose gospel labours had been mostly in Virginia, came in the early part of 1659, to Rhode Island; where he met with Marmaduke Stevenson, who had recently arrived from Barbadoes, with Peter Pearson. Whilst there, William Robinson was much affected on hearing of the sufferings of his fellow-professors in Massachusetts, under the cruel law of banishment on pain of death, and, under a feeling of deep religious exercise, he believed it required of him to proceed to that arena of cruelty to bear a testimony against such unholy proceedings. In alluding to this prospect of religious duty a short time after, he thus writes, "On the Eighth-day of the Fourth Month, 1659, in the after part of the day, in travelling betwixt Newport and the house of Daniel Gould on Rhode Island, with my dear brother Christopher Holder, the word of the Lord came expressly unto me, and commanded me to pass to the town of Boston, my life to lay down in his will, for the accomplishing of his service; to which heavenly voice I presently yielded obedience, not questioning the Lord, who filled me with living strength and power from his heavenly presence, which at that time did mightily overshadow me: and my life said Amen, to what the Lord required of me."* A similar impression of religious duty was felt by his companion Marmaduke Stevenson; who had, even whilst in Barbadoes, a sense that such a service might be required of him, but which, he says, "I kept in my heart, and after I had been in Rhode Island a little time, visiting the seed, which the Lord had blessed, the word of the Lord came to me, saying, Go to Boston with thy brother William Robinson; and at His command I was obedient, and gave up to his will."†

Under such impressions, these dedicated men proceeded to Boston, and reached it about the middle of the Fourth Month, 1659. Their arrival was on one of the public fast days, and proceeding to one of the assemblies, they attempted to address the congregation, after the minister had concluded.

The presence of Quakers, thus boldly manifested, whilst it struck the company with surprise, excited the malevolent feelings

* New England Judged, p. 95.   † Ibid, p. 108.

of the minister and rulers, and, as will be readily supposed, they were quickly arrested by the constabulary, and summarily committed to prison.

It happened that about the same period, Nicholas Davis of Sandwich, and Patience Scott, a young Friend of Providence, were also in Boston, and being Quakers, were committed to prison with William Robinson and Marmaduke Stevenson, under the same warrant; of which the following is a copy:—

"TO THE KEEPER OF THE PRISON,

"You are by virtue hereof, required to take into your custody the persons of Nicholas Davis, William Robinson, Marmaduke Stevenson, and Patience Scott, Quakers; according to the law made in October, 1658: to be sure to keep them close prisoners till the next Court of Assistants, whereby they are to be tried according to law; not suffering any to come at them, or discourse with them, without special order from this court; and allow them only prisoner's fare, unless it be in times of sickness.

"EDWARD RAWSON, *Secretary.*"
"*Boston, June 19th,* 1659."*

The object which drew Nicholas Davis to Boston on this occasion, was one of business only; "to reckon," says Bishop,† "with those with whom he traded, and to pay some debts." But that of Patience Scott "was to bear witness against the persecuting spirit" of the rulers. The extreme youthfulness of Patience Scott renders her case a remarkable one, and deserving of further notice. She was one of the children of Richard and Katherine Scott of Providence, already mentioned. Though but a child of eleven years of age, it pleased the Most High to employ her in his holy cause, and to call her to go and plead with the cruel religionists of Massachusetts; and she seems to have been several weeks in the city before her imprisonment. In the course of her examination before the magistrates, she gave evidence of being endued with a wisdom above that of this world, " and spoke

* Secret Works, p. 19.   † New England Judged, p. 93.

so well to the purpose, that she confounded her enemies."*   A
narrative of the sufferings of Friends in New England, printed in
1659, thus mentions her.   "They have imprisoned three men
and a woman, whom they cast in prison with her clothes wet, and
a child between ten and eleven years of age, who was moved of
the Lord to go from her outward habitation 105 miles to Boston,
where she was cast into prison, and being examined, her answers
were so far beyond the ordinary capacity of a child of her years,
that the governor confessed there was a spirit in her beyond the
spirit of woman ; but being blind, and not seeing God perfecting
his praise out of the child's mouth, he said it was the devil."†
William Robinson, in writing to George Fox about a month after
their imprisonment, thus alludes to her.   "Here is a daughter of
Katherine Scott, who is a prisoner in the gaoler's house : she is
a fine child, and is finely kept : she is about eleven or twelve
years of age, and is of good understanding."‡   After an imprisonment of about three months, Patience Scott was brought up for
trial.   The court, however, was somewhat perplexed with her case.
Formally to banish a mere child for professing Quakerism, partook too much of the ridiculous to be enforced, and at last it was
concluded to discharge her.   The record made on this occasion
was singular.   "The court duly considering the malice of Satan
and his instruments, by all means and ways to propagate error
and disturb the truth, and bring in confusion among us,—that
Satan is put to his shifts to make use of such a child, not
being·of the years of discretion, nor understanding the principles
of religion, judge meet so far to slight her as a Quaker, as only
to admonish and instruct her according to her capacity, and so
discharge her ; Captain Hutchinson undertaking to send her
home."§   "Strange," observes an historian of the colony, "that
such a child should be imprisoned ! it would have been horrible
if there had been any other severity."‖

Before we turn from this notice of Patience Scott, it may be
observed that the fact of a person young as she was being called

---

* Sewel, p. 224.   † Secret Works, p. 19.
‡ MSS. Letters of Early Friends.
§ Hutchinson's Massachusetts, vol. i. p. 199.
‖ Ibid, vol. i. p. 200.

to the ministry, is not a solitary one in the history of Friends. George Newland, a youth of Ireland, entered upon this gospel service in his twelfth year; he died about the age of nineteen, and about six years before his death, laboured in the churches in his native land, to the comfort and edification of his friends. Ellis Lewis, of North Wales, felt constrained to engage in the ministry in his thirteenth year. His first communication was made in the English language, with which he was not familiar, and it is stated to have been "remarkable and tendering." Another instance of early dedication and submission to this divine call, was that of the noted William Hunt, of North Carolina. He entered upon gospel labours when about fourteen. At eleven years of age he had remarkable openings in divine things. Christiana Barclay, the daughter of Robert Barclay the Apologist, also entered on this important work when about fourteen years old. Many other young persons among Friends in the fourteenth, fifteenth, sixteenth, and seventeenth years of their age, it is well known, were also called by Him whose "Spirit bloweth where it listeth," to proclaim to others, the unsearchable riches of his heavenly kingdom. As an illustration of the power and efficacy which has attended the ministry of some of our youthful preachers, may be instanced the remarkable fact, that the Society of Friends in the counties of Norfolk, Suffolk, Essex, and Cambridge, was first raised, and became very numerous, chiefly through the instrumentality of James Parnel, William Caton, and George Whitehead, before either of them had attained the age of twenty years.

During his imprisonment, William Robinson, being desirous that his friends in Great Britain should be acquainted with the state of things in New England, addressed a letter to George Fox, the original of which is still preserved. The rarity of such documents relating to America, together with the interesting particulars it contains, makes it valuable and worthy of being included in these pages.

FROM WILLIAM ROBINSON TO GEORGE FOX.

G. F.

Oh! beloved of God, and highly honoured and esteemed among the children of the Lord, who hath made thee a father unto thousands; and hath given thee the spirit of wisdom and of understanding. I was refreshed when I was constrained to write, to give thee an account of our travels and labours in these countries. I who am one of the least among my brethren, have been for some time in Virginia with Robert Hodgson and Christopher Holder, where there are many people convinced; and some that are brought into the sense and feeling of Truth in several places. We left Thomas Thurston a prisoner in a place called Maryland; his sentence was, to be kept a year and a day. We came lately to Rhode Island, where we did meet with two of our brethren, named Peter Pearson and Marmaduke Stevenson, in whom we were refreshed, and Friends on the island were glad to see us, and the honest-hearted were refreshed.

Peter Pearson and one William Leddra, are prisoners in this country, at a town called Plymouth, as I did understand by a letter I received from my brother Christopher Holder, who was in service at a town called Salem, last week, some fifteen miles from Boston, where I am now a prisoner, (with my brother Marmaduke Stevenson) for the testimony of Jesus. Soon after I came to Rhode Island, the Lord commanded me to pass to Boston, to bear my testimony against their persecution and to try their bloody law which they have made, with laying down of my life, if they have power to take it from me; for truly I am given up in my spirit into the hand of the Lord to do with me as He sees meet; for verily, my life is laid down, and my spirit is freely given up for the service of God, whereunto he hath called me.

The rulers, priests, and people, do boast much in their hearts, that they have caused some to fly, for they have banished six Friends upon death, from their outward beings which was at Salem, and they have stooped to them in flying the cross in departing. Three of them are gone towards Barbadoes, and intend for England, it may be for London, whose names are Samuel Shattock, Nicholas Phelps, and Josiah Southwick; Josiah's father and mother are passed to a place called Shelter Island, which belongs to a Friend, one Nathaniel Silvester, who is a fine, noble man; and the other of the six are gone to Rhode Island. Oh! God knows how near this went to me, when I did hear that they were departed, and soon did the Lord lay it upon me to try their law ; yea, on the same day that I heard of their departure was I constrained, and soon made willing to give up my life, Boston's bloody laws to try ; and was given up frequently in my spirit into the Lord's will, even to finish my testimony for the Lord, against the town of Boston ; not knowing of any Friend to pass with me at that time, but the Lord had compassion on me, seeing how willingly I was given up to do his will, not counting my life dear to me, so that I might finish my course with joy ; and on the day following, the Lord constrained my brother, M. S. [Marmaduke Stevenson] to pass along with me to Boston, who is freely given up to suffer with me for the seed's sake, who doth dearly salute thee.   Oh ! my dearly beloved, thou who art endued with power from on High ; who art of a quick discerning in the fear of our God ; Oh ! remember us—let thy prayers be put up unto the Lord God for us, that his power and strength may rest with us and upon us ; that, faithful, we may be preserved to the end.   Amen.

WILLIAM ROBINSON.

From the Common Gaol in Boston,
the 12th of the Fifth Mo. '59.

CHAPTER X.

Mary Dyer leaves her home on Rhode Island, and proceeds to Boston—is imprisoned—M. Stevenson, W. Robinson, N. Davis, and M. Dyer are sentenced to banishment on pain of death—M. Dyer returns home—W. Robinson and M. Stevenson go to Salem, &c.—M. Dyer returns to Boston, and is again arrested—Mary Scott, Robert Harper, Daniel and Provided Southwick, and Nicholas Upshal are imprisoned at Boston—W. Robinson and M. Stevenson return to Boston, and are again imprisoned—Daniel Gould and several Friends of Salem also imprisoned at Boston—W. Robinson, M. Stevenson, and Mary Dyer are sentenced to be executed—The procession to the place of execution described—W. Robinson and M. Stevenson are executed—M. Dyer is reprieved, and returns home—Brief notices of the lives of W. Robinson and M. Stevenson—John Chamberlain, Edward Wharton, Daniel Gould, and several others are scourged—Christopher Holder banished on pain of death — Persecutions in Plymouth Colony — John Taylor visits New England.

MARY DYER has already been noticed, both as an Antinomian exile from Massachusetts, and as having been expelled from Boston in 1657, and from New Haven in 1658, when visiting those places as a minister of the Gospel. This dedicated woman, hearing of the new species of persecution, and of the imprisonment of four of her fellow-professors at Boston, believed herself called to visit them, in order to comfort and encourage them under their trials. On reaching the city, she was very soon brought before the magistrates for examination as a Quaker, which resulted in her committal until the next Court of Assistants.

The Court of Assistants referred to, was a court consisting of the governor, deputy governor, and magistrates of Boston. It met in the early part of the Seventh Month, then called September. Before this tribunal the imprisoned Friends, were exar..ined, and, excepting‧ Patience Scott, all received sentence of banishment, on pain of death, if found within the limits of that jurisdiction within two days after their release from prison. William Robinson, being desirous that the magistrates should fully understand that they came to those parts under a feeling of religious duty, and not in their own wills only, pleaded with them on the iniquitous course they were pursuing. " If they did put them to death," he said, " for transgressing their law, they would become guilty of shedding innocent blood ;"* " with many more expressions,"† observes Peter Pearson, " that cut them to the quick." But the persecuting court were not inclined to listen to the remonstrances of their victim, and he was silenced by having a handkerchief rudely thrust into his mouth. Again he attempted to address them respecting their cruel law, when the magistrates " in a great rage," and " looking upon him as a teacher,"‡ sentenced him to receive twenty lashes. He was forthwith taken into the streets of the city, stripped to the waist, and subjected to the degrading punishment.

The wicked sentence having been passed, Rawson, pursuant to the direction of the court, issued the following warrant to the gaoler :—

" You are required by these, presently to set at liberty, William Robinson, Marmaduke Stevenson, Mary Dyer, and Nicholas Davis ; who, by an order of the court of council, had been imprisoned, because it appeared by their own confession, words, and actions, that they are Quakers ; wherefore a sentence was pronounced against them, to depart this jurisdiction on pain of death ; and that they must answer it at their peril, if they, or any of them, after the 14th of this present month, September, are found within this jurisdiction, or any part thereof.

" EDWARD RAWSON, *Secretary.*"
" *Boston, September 12th,* 1659.§"

* Call from Death, &c. p. 31.
† Peter Pearson's letter in Call from Death, &c. p. 31.
‡ New England Judged, p. 96.
§ Sewel, p. 226.

Having thus received their discharge, Nicholas Davis proceeded to his home at Sandwich, and Mary Dyer felt liberty to return to Rhode Island. But William Robinson and Marmaduke Stevenson, under a deep sense of religious duty, believed it required of them to remain in the colony, and on the day following their liberation they proceeded to Salem, where they endeavoured to strengthen and encourage their friends to stand fast in this day of trial. Daniel Gould of Rhode Island, who had become acquainted with these two servants of the Lord, thought it right to be with them under their perilous circumstances, and joined them at Salem.* Here, he remarks, "the people were much exercised in their minds concerning them ; and some were willing to hear ; but by reason of their cruel law, were afraid to have meetings at their houses. They had a meeting in the woods, not far from Salem, and great flocking there was to hear. The Lord was mightily with them, and they spake of the things of God boldly, to the affecting and tendering the hearts of many."† William Robinson, writing to Christopher Holder from this place, says, " we were, and are gladly received here, and the seed hath been reached in many—we have had two fine meetings."‡ Leaving Salem, they proceeded northward as far as Piscattaway, and as they went, "found the people very tender and loving."§ Their continued presence in the colony was regarded by many of the inhabitants, as a proof of great devotedness to their Lord ; and gave rise to much inquiry concerning the doctrines they were promulgating. "Divers," says Peter Pearson, "were convinced, the power of the Lord accompanying them ; and with astonishment confounded their enemies before them : great was their service abroad in that jurisdiction for four weeks and upwards."‖

Whilst William Robinson and Marmaduke Stevenson were thus travelling in the service of their Great Master, Mary Dyer, under a feeling of religious constraint, returned to Boston, accompanied by Hope Clifton, a Friend of Rhode Island. They entered the city on the 8th of Eighth Month, and on the following morn-

---

* A Narrative, &c., by D. Gould, p. 5.   † Ibid, p. 5.
‡ Call from Death, &c., p. 20.   § D. Gould's Narrative, p. 5.
‖ P. Pearson's Letter in Call, &c. p. 31.

ing proceeded to the gaol to visit Christopher Holder, who, after labouring in the gospel, in the north of Massachusetts, came to Boston, with an intention to take shipping for England, where he was arrested and imprisoned. Mary Dyer was soon recognised and placed under arrest, together with her companion Hope Clifton. On the same day was also committed Mary Scott, who came to visit Christopher Holder, with whom she was under an engagement of marriage. Robert Harper, of Sandwich, who had come to Boston on business, was also arrested as a Quaker, and imprisoned with them. In addition to these, the gaoler had in his custody Daniel and Provided Southwick, and the good old Nicholas Upshal, who, after a banishment of three years, had returned to see his wife and family. But although this conscientious man had been an exile for so long a period, it was not considered a sufficient expiation of his crime in favouring Quaker opinions, and he was thus given to understand, that he was still regarded as a criminal in their estimation.

But a very few days had elapsed after the committal of Mary Dyer, before William Robinson and Marmaduke Stevenson again made their appearance in Boston. Having finished their religious engagements in the north of the province, they returned by way of Salem, accompanied by several Friends of that place ;* having been absent rather more than four weeks. The Friends who came with them on this perilous occasion were Daniel Gould, Hannah the wife of the exiled Nicholas Phelps, William King, Mary Trask, Margaret Smith, and Alice Cowland, the latter of whom " brought linen to wrap the dead bodies of those who were to suffer."† " These," says Bishop, " all came together, in the moving and power of the Lord, as one man, to look their bloody laws in the face, and to try them."‡

This return of William Robinson and Marmaduke Stevenson, forms one of the most striking and remarkable incidents in the history of Friends. Banished the colony of Massachusetts on pain of death, instead of obeying, they disregard the unrighteous mandate, and proceed at once to preach within its limits, and to make converts

---

* New England Judged, p. 97.   † Ibid, p. 97.
‡ Ibid, p. 97.

to the doctrines, for the profession of which, the dreadful sentence had been passed upon them. Engaged thus for the space of a month, they next go, under the apprehended constrainings of a divine call, to lay down their lives a willing sacrifice, and to evince to highly professing New England, the impotence of their persecuting edicts to stay the work of the Lord. The conclusion, thus to offer their lives for the cause of truth, excites in the minds of their newly convinced brethren the tenderest emotions, and, regardless of the consequences of the step, seven of them, under a sense of duty, accompany the exiled strangers to Boston. The mournful little company, as they left Salem, bearing with them the habiliments for the dead, partook much of the character of a funeral procession; and as they drew towards the persecuting city, they felt that they were approaching the spot, where they were to witness the martyrdom of two beloved servants of Christ.

The constabulary, having been apprised of the approach of the banished Friends and their companions, went forth " with a rude company,"* and arrested them. After a mocking and scoffing examination by the magistrates, the whole of them were committed to prison, the gaoler being specially instructed to place William Robinson and Marmaduke Stevenson in chains, and to keep them in a separate cell. They were also searched, and all their papers, including William Robinson's journal, were taken from them.† There were now no less than seventeen persons in the gaols of Boston for professing Quakerism. " Their prisons," observes Bishop, "begin to fill." Thus, notwithstanding the extreme nature of the persecuting law, at no previous date had the city witnessed the presence of so many of the sect which the rulers were vainly endeavouring to crush. This extraordinary circumstance has attracted the notice of historians. " The Quakers," remarks a modern writer, " swarmed where they were feared."‡

The rulers had now in custody three individuals whose continued presence in the colony subjected them, under the late sanguinary law, to the forfeiture of their lives. These three, William Robinson, Marmaduke Stevenson and Mary Dyer, were brought before the General Court on the 19th of the Seventh

* Gould, p. 6.   † Gould, p. 6.   ‡ Bancroft's United States.

Month, 1659. Endicott, who presided, "demanded why they came again into that jurisdiction after being banished upon pain of death."* To this the prisoners severally replied, that they came only in obedience to a Divine call.† The situation of the court was peculiar. The law that had been passed for proceeding to the extreme penalty of death, was clearly applicable to the parties arraigned. But vindictive and cruel, as Endicott and Bellingham and their fellow-magistrates had shown themselves, they evidently shrank from the horrible deed of imbruing their hands in blood. After telling the prisoners "that he desired not their death, and that they had liberty to speak for themselves,"‡ and querying with them why sentence of death should not be passed upon them, Endicott directed the gaoler to take them away. Baffled as these bigoted and intolerant rulers were, they yet paused, ere they put forth their hands to slay their fellow-professors of the christian name, for merely dissenting from certain religious opinions.

On the following day, being one of the public meeting days, the officiating minister, in addressing his auditory, alluded to the presence of so many of the "cursed sect" among them. Instead of endeavouring to inculcate feelings of tenderness and love, he prostituted his eloquence to the wicked purpose of exciting his hearers to hatred and revenge, and urged them on to one of the darkest deeds of ecclesiastical power. The rulers, says Bishop, thus "heated by their priest, and prepared to shed the blood of the innocent, sent for the prisoners again."§ On their being brought into court, Endicott, after directing the gaoler to pull off their hats, and without any preparatory proceedings, began to pass sentence of death upon them in these words, " We have made many laws, and endeavoured by several ways to keep you from us ; and neither whipping, nor imprisonment, nor cutting off ears, nor banishment on pain of death, will keep you from among us. I desired not your deaths : give ear and hearken to your sentence."‖ Here Endicott, whose proceedings had been

---

* New England Judged, p. 97.   † Ibid, p. 98.   ‡ Ibid, p. 98.
§ Ibid, p. 98.   ‖ W. Robinson's Letter in Call, &c. p. 24.

marked " with much fear,"* made a stop, for, observes Bishop,
" he spoke faintly as a man whose life was departing from him,
for the hand of the Lord was upon him."†   At this juncture
William Robinson requested permission to read a document
which he had prepared, setting forth the reason why he had
not departed the colony.   But Endicott, excited by the interruption, replied, " you shall not read it, nor will the court hear
it read."‡   William Robinson then calmly laid it on the table,
and it was handed up to Endicott, who, after having quietly read
the document to himself, proceeded thus to finish the horrible
sentence, " You shall be had back to the place from whence you
came, and from thence to the place of execution, to be hanged on
the gallows till you are dead."§

William Robinson having been removed, Marmaduke Stevenson
was called to receive a similar sentence.   Endicott, before proceeding, said to him,‖ " If you have any thing to say, you may
speak ;" but the prisoner seeing the manner in which his companion had been treated, made no reply.   The governor then
pronounced the awful sentence of death against him in the
usual form, after which, Marmaduke, under a feeling of Diviné
authority,¶ thus addressed the court, " Give ear, ye magistrates,
and all who are guilty, for this the Lord hath said concerning
you, and will perform his word upon you.   That the same day ye
put his servants to death, shall the day of your visitation pass
over your heads, and you shall be cursed for evermore; the mouth
of the Lord of Hosts hath spoken it.   Therefore, in love to you
all, I exhort you to take warning before it be too late, that so the
curse may be removed.   For assuredly, if you put us to death,
you will bring innocent blood upon your own heads, and swift
destruction will come upon you."**   Mary Dyer was next called,
and the same dreadful sentence having been pronounced on her,
she meekly replied, " The will of the Lord be done."††   Endicott,
irritated at the calm and dignified manner in which the sentence

---

* Nicholson's Standard of the Lord lifted up, p. 22.
† New England Judged, p. 98. Call, &c., p. 24.   ‡ Ibid, p. 98.
§ Ibid, p. 99.   ‖ Nicholson, p. 22.
¶ Nicholson, p. 23.   ** Besse, vol. ii. p. 199.   †† Call, &c., p. 26.

was received, impatiently said, "take her away marshal;" but she, undisturbed by the unfeeling order, replied, "yea, joyfully shall I go;"* and so favoured was she with heavenly joy and consolation, that on her way to the prison, she frequently uttered praises to the Most High, for the evidences of His love, and that she was counted worthy to suffer for His name. Whilst under sentence of death, she wrote a close remonstrance to the General Court relative to their wicked law.

"Were ever such laws," she says, "heard of among a people that profess Christ come in the flesh? Have you no other weapons but such laws, to fight against spiritual wickedness withal, as you call it? Woe is me for you. You are disobedient and deceived. Let my request be as Esther's to Ahasuerus. You will not then repent that you were kept from shedding of blood, though it was by a woman."†

The day appointed for the execution, was the 27th of the Seventh Month, being one week after the condemnation, and the usual meeting day of the Church in Boston. The week which thus intervened, was a memorable one in the history of that city. The fact of the gallows being about to be called into requisition for the support of religion, produced an excitement of no ordinary character. It was a fresh shock to the feelings of most of the inhabitants. "They stood amazed, and wondered at such cruelty."‡ "The thing struck among them," says a narrator of the circumstance, "and struck a fear in the magistrates, where no fear had been." Throughout the persecution of Friends in New England, it had been an especial object with the rulers, to prevent their having any intercourse with the colonists, during their imprisonment. On the present occasion, however, the sympathy of the people was stronger than the words of their rulers, and they flocked to the prison windows to hear the ministrations of the conscientious victims."§ On the morning of the day on which the execution was to take place, "there came," says Daniel Gould, "a multitude of people about

* Call, &c., p. 26.　　　　　　　　　† Besse, vol. ii. p. 202.
‡ William Robinson's letter, in Besse vol. ii. p. 244.
§ New England Judged, p. 99.

the prison, and we being in an upper room, William Robinson, put forth his head at a window, and spake to the people concerning the things of God ; at which the people flocked about, earnest to hear, and gave serious attention.　But," he continues, " quickly it was noised in the town that much people was about the prison to see the Quakers, and that the Quakers were speaking to them, upon which came Oliver, (a captain, a very fit man for their purpose) and a company with him, to disperse the people ; but they being so many, and willing to hear, he could not drive them away."* The captain, anxious to stop the preaching of the Friends, and finding himself unable to disperse the assemblage, proceeded to take other means to accomplish his purpose.　" He came," says Daniel Gould, "in a fret and heat to us within, and furiously hurling some of us down stairs, left us not, till he had shut us up in a little low dark cub, where we could not see the people."† But though thus persecuted for the cause of their dear Lord, they felt Him near to sustain them, and realized his ancient promise, " Lo ! I am with you alway, even unto the end of the world."　" As we sat together waiting upon the Lord," observes one of them, " it was a time of love ; for as the world hated us, and despitefully used us, so the Lord was pleased in a wonderful manner, to manifest his supporting love and kindness to us in our innocent sufferings ; especially to the worthies who had now near finished their course—for God had given them a sure word, that their souls should rest in eternal peace.　God was with them, and many sweet and heavenly sayings they gave unto us, being themselves filled with comfort."‡

Whilst these things were passing at the prison, the magistrates and others were assembled at their meeting.　Here, as on the week previous, the minister spoke abundantly of " the diabolical doctrines" and horrid tenets of, as he was wont to term them, "the cursed sect of Quakers."　" Their lecture being ended ; the priest having sharpened and hardened them for the service,"§ the officers, in pursuance of the bloody work, proceeded to the

---

* Gould's Narrative, p. 8.　　† Ibid, p. 8.
‡ Ibid, p. 9.　　§ Ibid, p. 9.

prison with an escort of two hundred "armed men, with drums and colours, and halberds, guns, swords and pikes, besides many horse-men."* "While we were yet embracing each other, and taking leave, with full and tender hearts," observes one of the prisoners, "the officers came in and took the two from us, as sheep for the slaughter."† These two were William Robinson, and Marmaduke Stevenson ; the house of correction having been selected as the place of Mary Dyer's imprisonment. Every thing being prepared, the procession began its march towards Boston Common, the destined place of execution, being about one mile distant. The authorities, as though conscious of the wickedness of the deed, and fearing the excitement of the citizens, directed the course to be taken by a back-way, and not through the direct thoroughfare of the city.

The motley concourse, as it proceeded with its Boston priest, and Boston soldiery, the city officials, and the condemned ; with colours flying, and drums beating, together with the unmarshalled multitude which the impending demonstration had attracted, presented a scene strongly analogous to the procession of an *auto-da-fè* of Roman Catholic Spain. Except, indeed, that in the one case, the victims were to be led to the gibbet, and in the other to the stake, there seems such an identity of proceeding, that it is difficult to realize the idea that the abettors of this revolting spectacle, professed to be the uncompromising opposers of papacy.

It might have been expected that at least some little regard would be paid to the feelings of those who were now so soon to be launched into eternity, but the want of decorum exhibited towards the condemned at this awful period, was revolting in the highest degree. The rulers, dreading the voice of public remonstrance from the victims of their malignity, in order to frustrate any such attempt, directed the drummers to walk immediately before them, with special instructions for a louder beat, should either of them begin to speak : when therefore, William Robinson began to

* E. Burrough's declaration of the sad and great persecution, p. 24.
† Gould's Narrative, p. 9,

address the people, his voice was quickly drowned amid the increased din, and all that could be heard was, "this is your hour and
[the] power of darkness." The drums having ceased a little,
Marmaduke Stevenson said, " This is the day of your visitation,
wherein the Lord hath visited you."* He said more, but the
drums being again beaten, it could not be heard.

The pious sufferers, although deprived of outward quiet and
solemnity at this awful time, were nevertheless wonderfully supported, and favoured with great serenity of mind, and, under
the feeling of the Divine presence which was largely vouchsafed
to them, they rose superior to all the clamour and indignities
to which they were exposed ; and, as they proceeded, walking
hand in hand, to the place of execution, " glorious signs of
heavenly joy and gladness were beheld in their countenances,"†
and they rejoiced that the Lord had counted them worthy to
suffer for his name's sake.

It can excite no surprise that many of those engaged in this
wicked work were strangers to sensibility of mind, and the
marshal appears to have been one of these. This active official,
observing that Mary Dyer walked between her condemned companions, coarsely and tauntingly said to her, " Are you not
ashamed to walk thus between two young men ?" " No,"
answered Mary Dyer, to the repulsive observation, " this is to
me an hour of the greatest joy I ever had in this world. No ear
can hear, no tongue can utter, and no heart can understand, the
sweet incomes and the refreshings of the Spirit of the Lord,
which I now feel."‡ Wilson, the " minister of Boston,"
appears to have been another of this class. Having made himself
conspicuous in urging the rulers to the use of the gallows against
Friends, he countenanced the present proceedings in a manner
which stigmatizes him as a ruthless and hardened persecutor.
Whilst the dismal group was on its way, this high professor
joined in the train, and wickedly glorying in the transaction,
began " taunting William Robinson ;" and " shaking his

* Sewel, p. 224.   † Ibid, p. 224.
‡ Sewel, p. 231.

hand in a light scoffing manner," in low and vulgar language thus addressed him. " Shall such Jacks as you come in before authority with their hats on ?" The observation occasioned William Robinson to say to the spectators, " Mind you, mind you, it is for not putting off the hat we are put to death."*

Having reached the Common, the faithful sufferers now took a final farewell of each other. William Robinson was selected as the first to undergo the sentence, and having ascended the ladder, he thus addressed the multitude : " we suffer, not as evil doers, but as those who have testified and manifested the truth. This is the day of your visitation, and therefore I desire you to mind the Light of Christ, which is in you, to which I have borne testimony, and am now going to seal my testimony with my blood." Short as the address was, it was too long for Wilson. This implacable professor, vexed at beholding the martyrs display so little fear of death, and the fortitude and joyful resignation with which they were favoured, interrupted William Robinson, and vented his impetuous virulence by saying, " hold thy tongue—be silent— thou art going to die with a lie in thy mouth."† The executioner having fastened the rope around his neck, bound his hands and feet, and drawn his neckcloth over his face, he said " Now are ye made manifest ;" his last words being, " I suffer for Christ, in whom I live, and for whom I die." Marmaduke Stevenson was the next to suffer, and having mounted the ladder, he thus addressed the spectators—" Be it known unto you all this day, that we suffer not as evil-doers, but for conscience' sake ;" adding a few moments before he was turned off, " this day shall we be at rest with the Lord."‡

Mary Dyer, who saw the lifeless bodies of her companions suspended before her, was now called to undergo the like ignominious death. She calmly ascended the ladder—her clothes were bound around her feet—her face was covered and the halter adjusted, and in a few seconds her resigned and purified spirit would have been for ever free from all the trials of time ; but at

---

* New England Judged, p. 101.   † Ibid, p. 101.
‡ Sewel, p. 224.

this awful moment the silence which prevailed over the gazing assembly was suddenly broken by the distant cry, " Stop ! she is reprieved."* Her life had been granted at the intercession of her son. The announcement though heard with gladness by many who witnessed the horrid spectacle, bore no tidings of joy to Mary Dyer. So entirely resigned was she to the prospect of death, and so favoured with divine consolation, that she seemed to be already participating in the joys of eternity. " Her mind," says a historian, " was already in heaven, and when they loosened her feet and bade her come down, she stood still, and said she was there willing to suffer as her brethren had, unless they would annul their wicked law."† The officers, however, disregarding her expressions, pulled her down, and under the care of the marshal she was re-conducted to prison, where her son was waiting to receive her.

Having thus sacrificed two victims to their intolerance, these persecutors had done enough to satisfy even an extreme malignity, but not enough it appears, to glut their desires for blood. To add to the atrocities of the spectacle, even the remains of the sufferers were subjected to the revenge which characterised these proceedings. The bodies after hanging the usual time were cut down, and no pains being taken to prevent it, they fell violently to the ground, the skull of William Robinson being fractured by the fall. They were then stripped, thrown into a pit, and there left uncovered. Those who had been denied the request to provide coffins, and to give the remains a decent interment, fearing that the bodies thus exposed would be devoured by the wild animals which then infested the country, requested permission to erect a fence around the pit, but even this reasonable application was disregarded ; and had not the hole been soon filled with water, the bodies would in all probability have been food for the beasts of the forest. To complete this wicked and disgusting business, the notorious Wilson, as a yet further exhibition of his malice, actually made a song on the two martyrs. For the cause of humanity and for the cause of religion, it is well that the pages

* Sewel, p. 232. † Ibid. p. 232.

of Anglo-Saxon history are not sullied by many such exhibitions of human malevolence. Protestantism at least has not an equal to so atrocious a transaction. May it never be stained by a similar exhibition !

Before passing from the martyrdom of William Robinson and Marmaduke Stevenson, it may be well to notice a few particulars of them that have been preserved.

WILLIAM ROBINSON.

The earliest notice that we find respecting William Robinson, is that of his voyage to New England in the "Woodhouse," in the

The accompanying plan of Boston, is taken from an ancient one in the British Museum. About the year 1663, Boston was described in Johnson's *Wonder Working Providence*, in the following manner :—

" Invironed it is with brinish flood, saving one small istmos, which

year 1657. He was a man of good education, and in very respectable circumstances, his occupation being that of a merchant in the City of London.* His father was living at the time of his execution, and instituted some inquiry respecting it. On the day when he received sentence of death, he addressed the following epistle to his fellow-prisoners :—

"DEAR BRETHREN AND SISTERS,

" To whom my love abounds ; I am filled with pure love unto you all ; dear lambs, feel it in your own lives, and receive it into your own hearts as new oil ; for truly the fear of the Lord is our strength, and the blessing of the Lord is our portion, which the Lord doth daily give unto us ; blessed be his name for ever. Oh ! let us all keep in lowliness, and holiness, and meekness, and tender love one towards another, which is the seal and witness that the Lord is with us ; where the Lord for ever keeps us stayed on him, to receive our daily bread, which satisfieth the hungry soul.

" Dear friends, brethren and sisters, this I am constrained to let you know, how mightily the love of the Lord our God abounds in my heart, towards you all ; it runs forth as a living stream,

gives free access to the neighbouring towns by land, on the south side, on the north-west and north-east. Two constant fairs are kept for daily trafique thereunto. The form of this town is like a heart, naturally situated for fortifications, having two hills on the frontier part thereof next the sea, the one well fortified on the superficies thereof, with store of great artillery well mounted : the other hath a very strong battery built of whole timber, and filled with earth. At the descent of the hill, in the extreme point thereof, betwixt these two strong arms, lies a cove or bay, on which the chief part of this town is built, overtopped with a third hill ; all these, like overtopping towers, keep a constant watch to see the approach of foreign danger, being furnished with a beacon, and loud babbling guns, to give notice by their redoubled echo to all the sister towns. The chief edifice of this city-like town is *crowded* on the sea-banks, and wharfed out with great labour and cost ; the buildings beautiful and large, some fairly set forth with brick, tile, stone, and slate, and orderly placed with seemly streets, whose continual enlargement presageth some sumptuous city."

* Bishop, p. 93.

refreshing the spirit and life—I was the first that our heavenly
Father did lay this thing upon, for which I now suffer bonds
near unto death ; from the first day until now, the weight of the
thing lay upon me from the Lord God, and in obedience to his
holy will and command I gave up ; in which obedience the arm
and power of the Lord hath been, and is with me this day ; and
the thing which the Lord had said unto me, still remains with
me, that my life must accomplish the thing, and by it must the
powers of darkness fall, and yet will they seek and labour to take
it from me, and through much difficulty will they be suffered, to
the glory of our God, and to the rejoicing of the elect.

" So, my dear brethren and sisters, my love and my life feel in
your hearts, for I am full unto you all in heavenly joy. The
Lord for ever keep us all as we are now, to the glory of his name,
Amen.　　This was I moved to write unto you all, my dear brethren
and sisters, my fellow-prisoners, that have any part, or do partake
with me herein.

" Your dear brother, in holy and heavenly joy, and true love
and peace.

" WILLIAM ROBINSON."*

" *Written in the Hole of the Condemned, in*
Boston *gaol in* New England, *the First-*
day of the week, being the 16*th day of*
the Eighth Month, 1659."

Four days before his death he wrote an epistle " To the Lord's
people." The heavenly state of his mind, and the complete resignation with which he was favoured at this awful season, is
very fully developed in this address, and we cannot better close
the notice of him than by inserting the following extract
from it :—

" The streams of my Father's love run daily through me, from
the Holy Fountain of Life, to the seed throughout the whole
creation. I am overcome with love, for it is my life and length
of my days ; it is my glory and my daily strength.—

" I am full of the quickening power of the Lord Jesus Christ,
and my lamp is filled with pure oil, so that it gives a clear light

* Besse, vol. ii. p. 247.

and pleasant smell ; and I shall enter with my beloved into eternal rest and peace, and I shall depart with everlasting joy in my heart, and praises in my mouth, singing hallelujah unto the Lord, who hath redeemed me by his living power from amongst kindreds, tongues, and nations. And now the day of my departure draweth near. I have fought a good fight ; I have kept the holy faith ; I have near finished my course ; my travailing is near at an end ; my testimony is near to be finished, and an eternal crown is laid up for me, and for all whose feet are shod with righteousness, and the preparation of peace, even such whose names are written in the book of life, wherein I live and rejoice with all the faithful for evermore.

" Written by a servant of Jesus Christ,

" WILLIAM ROBINSON."

The 23rd of the Eighth Month, 1659.*

MARMADUKE STEVENSON.

Marmaduke Stevenson was an agriculturist of Shipton, near Market Weighton, in Yorkshire. The earliest account of him is contained in a paper which he put forth at Boston shortly before his execution, designated his " Call to the work and service of the Lord." It begins thus :—" In the beginning of the year 1655, I was at plough in the east part of Yorkshire, in Old England, and as I walked after the plough, I was filled with the love and presence of the living God, which did ravish my heart when I felt it, for it did increase and abound in me like a living stream, which made me to stand still. And as I stood a little still, with my heart and mind stayed upon the Lord, the word of the Lord came to me in a still small voice, which I heard perfectly, saying to me in the secret of my heart : ' I have ordained thee a prophet unto the nations ;' and at the hearing of the word of the Lord I was put to a stand, seeing that I was but a child, for such a weighty matter. So at the time appointed, Barbadoes was set before me, unto which I was required of the Lord to go, and leave my dear and loving wife and tender children ; for the Lord said unto me, immediately by his

* Besse, vol. ii. p. 248.

Spirit, that he would be as an husband to my wife, and as a father to my children, and they should not want in my absence, for he would provide for them." Notwithstanding the prospect which he thus had in 1655, he did not leave his native land until the Fourth Month, 1658, when he embarked for Barbadoes with several other gospel messengers.

During his imprisonment at Boston, he wrote his " Call to the work and service of the Lord," already referred to, and also a long address to his " neighbours and the people of the town of Shipton, Weighton, and elsewhere," entitled " A Call from Death to Life, out of the dark Ways and Worships of the world, where the Seed is held in bondage, under the Merchants of Babylon." In this piece he affectionately warns those who were living in forgetfulness of God, " to lend an ear to His call, while he knocked at the door of their hearts." " Oh," he writes, " my love runs out to you all in compassion and pity to your souls, which lie in death, as mine hath done ; but the Lord in his eternal love and pity to my soul, hath redeemed me from my fallen estate, and raised my soul from death to life, out of the pit, wherein it lay dead in trespasses and sins. And seeing the Lord hath done this for me, I cannot but declare it to the sons of men, and praise his Name in the land of the living, who hath done great things for me. When I consider, and ponder it in my heart, my soul is ravished with his love, and broken into tears at his kindness towards me, who was by nature a child of wrath as well as others. Oh ! the consideration of his love hath constrained me to follow him, and to give up all for his sake, if it be the laying down of my life ; for none are the disciples of Christ, but they that follow him in his cross, and through sufferings, *and they that love any thing more than him, ' are not worthy of him.'* The Lord knows I do not forget you, though I be thousands of miles from you, because of the simplicity that was in some of you, who were my neighbours and acquaintance ; for I am one who has obtained mercy from the Lord, through judgment and great tribulation, which all must pass through before they come into the land of Canaan : they must be regenerate and born again, and know a dying to sin, and that which they have delighted in, before they witness a living to righteousness : the old man must be put off with his deeds, before the new man Christ Jesus, be put on, the Son of the living God." " The desire of my soul is," he continues, " that you may not perish in your gainsayings, and for this end was this written unto you, as I was moved of the Lord, knowing that you are where I once was, in the perishing state, like the prodigal from the Father's house, in the far country, feeding upon the husks, with the swine. This was my state and condition for many years ; but in the time appointed the Lord looked upon me with an eye of pity, and called me home to himself, out of the far country, where I was feeding on the husks with the swine, into the banqueting house, where my soul is refreshed, nourished, and fed with the hidden manna and bread of life."*

He also wrote a few days before his martyrdom, a letter " To the Lord's People," which strikingly evidences the prepared state of his mind in the near prospect of death, as will appear from the following extract :—

" Oh ! my dear and well-beloved ones, who are sealed with me in the holy covenant of our Father's love, my love and life runs out to you all who are chosen of God and faithful ; for you are dear unto me, the Lord knows it, and are as seals upon my breast. You lambs of my Father's fold, and sheep of his pasture, the remembrance of you is precious to me, my dearly beloved ones, who are of the holy seed, and bear the right image, which springs from the true vine and offspring of David, the stock of Abraham, the father of the faithful, and the redeemed ones, who are reconciled to God and one to another, in that which sea and land cannot separate ; here you may feel me knit and joined to you, in the spirit of truth, and linked to you as members of his body ; who is our head, and rock of sure defence to fly unto ; here we are kept safe in the hour of temptation ; and in the day of trial shall we be preserved in the hollow of his hand ; here his banner of love will be over us, to compass us about ; here we shall have recourse to the living springs, which come from the pure fountain and well-spring of life, which issues forth abundantly to refresh the hungry, and strengthen the feeble-minded ; here you may

* Besse, vol. ii. p. 256.

feel me, my beloved ones, in the green pastures, among the lilies of the pleasant springs, where our souls are bathed and refreshed together, with the overcomings of God's love, and the virtue of his presence, which is as precious ointment poured forth, giving a pleasant smell.

" So my dear friends ! let us always wait at the altar of the Lord, to see the table spread ; that so we may sit down and eat together, and be refreshed with the hidden manna, and living food of life, that comes from Him who is our life, our peace, our strength, and our Preserver night and day.   O ! my beloved ones ! let us all go on in his strength, who is our Prince and Saviour, that his image we may bear, who is meek and lowly in heart, and mind the true and sure foundation of many generations, the chief Corner Stone, elect and precious ; the Rock of Ages on which the saints were built ; and if we all abide thereon, we shall never be moved, but stand for ever as trees of righteousness, rooted and grounded in Him, who will be with us in all our trials and temptations ; and here will the Lord our God be honoured by us all that are faithful unto death : and we shall assuredly have a crown of life which will never be taken from us.

" Oh ! my beloved ones, what shall I say unto you, who drink with me at the living fountain, where we are nourished and brought up : where I do embrace you in the bond of peace which never will be broken.   O ! feel me and read me in your hearts ; for I am filled with love when I think upon you, and broken into tears ; for the remembrance of you doth refresh my soul, which makes me often to think upon you, you jewels of my Father, and first fruits of his increase.   If I forget you, then let the Lord forget me.   Nay, verily, you cannot be forgotten by me : so long as I abide in the vine, I am a branch of the same nature with you, which the Lord hath blessed, where we grow together in his life and image, as members of his body ; where we shall live together to all eternity, and sit down in the kingdom of rest and peace, with Abraham, Isaac and Jacob, to sing the songs of deliverance to the Most High that sits on the throne, who alone is worthy of all honour and living praise, to whom it is due now and for ever.   AMEN."*

* Besse, vol. ii. p. 249.

On the day following the execution of her two Friends, Mary Dyer addressed their persecuting judges, in a strain of sublimity, displaying a boldness and fortitude of mind, with such a deep sense of their iniquitous proceedings, as was calculated strongly to impress them. " Once more to the General Court assembled in Boston, speaks Mary Dyer, even as before. My life is not accepted, neither availeth me, in comparison of the lives and liberty of the truth, and the servants of the living God, for which, in the bowels of meekness and love, I sought you." After reproving them for resisting the power of divine grace, she thus concludes, " when I heard your last order read, it was a disturbance to me, who was freely offering up my life to Him that gave it me, and sent me hither so to do ; which obedience being his own work, he gloriously accompanied with his presence, and peace, and love, in which I rested from my labour."

Mary Dyer's reprieve directed that she should remain a prisoner for forty-eight hours, after which the magistracy thought it most prudent to commute her sentence into banishment, on penalty of death in the event of her return. In accordance with this decision, she was sent with a guard of four men, fifteen miles in the direction of Rhode Island, where she was left with a man and horse to convey her forward ; but declining the offices of her guard, she proceeded to her home without his assistance. The disgust with which the executions had been witnessed by the people, and their growing discontent at such cruel and unconstitutional proceedings, induced the rulers to adopt the plan of sending Mary Dyer to her home, in order to allay the excitement which prevailed.

A feeling of indignation was not the only effect produced on the minds of the colonists on this occasion. The Christian constancy and holy resignation of the victims, excited a desire in some of the serious people to become more intimately acquainted with the principles of those, who were strengthened and upheld joyfully to suffer even the loss of their lives for the cause of religion. The consequence of this inquiry was a further accession of numbers to the little persecuted band. John Chamberlain was one of these. On attending the execution, he was so much affected that he became convinced of the truth of the principles for which the sufferers died. His sympathies being awakened, he was led to visit the prisons at Boston, to comfort and encourage those, whom he now claimed as brethren of the same religious faith. This did not escape the notice of the magistracy, and in a short time he was not only an inmate of the gaol, but had more than once severely to feel the effect of religious bigotry, in the application of the knotted scourge.* Edward Wharton of Salem, was also deeply affected by the circumstance of the executions; and spoke boldly among his fellow-townsmen of the wickedness of the act. But his testimony against these unrighteous proceedings drew down the anger of the rulers, and Edward, " as a peremptory fellow," was visited not only with a whipping of twenty lashes, but also with a fine of twenty pounds.†

Returning to the other Friends who were imprisoned at Boston, we find that after about two months' confinement, they were brought before the General Court for examination. At this tribunal, Daniel Gould was sentenced to receive thirty strokes; Robert Harper, and William King, each fifteen; and Margaret Smith, Mary Trask, and Provided Southwick, ten strokes each; whilst Alice Cowland, Hannah Phelps, Mary Scott, and Hope Clifton were " delivered over to the governor to be admonished."‡ To Christopher Holder, the only English Friend of the company, was reserved the sentence of banishment on pain of death.§ The lash, at best a barbarous and degrading punishment, was in this instance rendered additionally repulsive by its application in " the open streets of the city;"|| the female as well as the male prisoners being stripped for the purpose, before the gazing multitude. These cruelties caused much excitement and commotion in the city, and the gaol was at last so crowded by sympathizing citizens, that a guard was sent to prevent their approach. " The compassion of the people," observes an early writer, " was moved; many resorted to the prison by day and by night, and upon a representation of the keeper, a constant watch was kept round the prison, to keep people off."¶ The punishment being inflicted, the court

* New England Judged, p. 110. † Ibid. p. 111. ‡ Ibid. p. 112.
§ Besse, vol. ii. p. 205. || New England Judged, p. 112.
¶ Hutchinson's Massachusetts, vol. i. p. 201.

ordered the liberation of the prisoners, on their paying the gaoler's fees, but the sufferers objecting in any manner to recognize their unjust imprisonment, refused the payment of this demand. The inhabitants, however, grieved at the scenes of persecution which had disgraced their country, undertook to pay the amount, and procured their discharge.

The magistrates of Boston, finding that the sympathies of the colonists were now much awakened in favour of the victims of their intolerance, and that murmurs of dissatisfaction with their illegal conduct, were increasing, endeavoured to remove this feeling, by publishing a justification of their proceedings. Throughout, the defence is but a lame one, and " the miserable apology,"* as it has been justly called, concludes in an incoherent manner, worthy of men who could perpetrate such deeds of darkness. " The consideration of our gradual proceedings," say they, " will vindicate us from the clamorous accusations of severity ; our own just and necessary defence calling upon us, other means failing, to offer the point which these persons have violently and wilfully rushed upon, and thereby become *felones de se*, which, might it have been prevented, and the sovereign law, *salus populi*, been preserved, our former proceedings, as well as the sparing of Mary Dyer, upon an inconsiderable intercession, will evidently evince we desire their lives absent, rather than their deaths present." " It is said," remarks Bancroft, in allusion to this manifesto, " the Quakers themselves rushed on the sword, and so were suicides." " If it were so," he continues, " the men who held the sword were accessaries to the crime." The same fallacious plea might be urged by the most unrelenting persecutors for religion.

The rulers of the colony of Plymouth, though not so severe in their measures for oppressing Friends, as their neighbours of Boston, continued, nevertheless, to harass them by heavy fines, for the non-attendance of meetings. Thomas Ewer of Sandwich, in addition to severe distraints, was " laid neck and heels together,"† for reproving his persecutors, for these unjust proceedings. Peter Pearson and William Leddra, who were committed to Plymouth

* Bancroft's United States.   † New England Judged, p. 148.

gaol, in the Fourth Month of 1659, did not obtain their liberty until the early part of the following year ; the period of their imprisonment, being more prolonged than that of any Friend who suffered in New England.

During the year 1659, three Friends only appear to have arrived from Great Britain, for religious service in New England ; these were Marmaduke Stevenson, and Peter Pearson, already referred to ; and John Taylor, of York. Respecting the religious labours of the last, but a very brief account has been met with. It appears that in the previous year, he felt a call to proceed to America, but being a young man, and of a diffident disposition, he was reluctant to venture on so important an engagement, without first consulting some of his friends. Acting on this conclusion, he laid the subject before George Fox, Francis Howgill and Edward Burrough, who all encouraged him to proceed, under the persuasion that he was called to the work. He accordingly embarked for the new country, from London, being then only in the twenty-second year of his age, and, after a voyage of ten weeks, he landed " at his desired haven in New England." How long he was occupied within the limits of this province it is not stated, but his religious services were not confined to the English settlers. Trusting to the never-failing arm of divine guidance and protection, he travelled alone among the Indian tribes, and " had meetings in the woods and wilderness, to declare the truth to them," as he remarks, " and to turn them from darkness to the light of Christ Jesus, in their own hearts." By these untutored sons of the forest, the stripling preacher was " received with kindness," and in their wigwams he became a welcome guest. " They heard me soberly," he says, " and did confess to the truth I spake, by an interpreter ; and they were loving and kind afterwards to Friends." In the course of this history we shall have again to refer to John Taylor, but it may be observed here, that he is described by a contemporary, " as an able minister of the New Testament ; in the publishing of which, the Spirit of God and of glory rested upon him, to the comforting and true refreshment of the churches, where the Lord ordered him, or his lot was cast."

CHAPTER XI.

THE last notice of Mary Dyer, mentioned her expulsion from Massachusetts on the reprieve of her life, and her subsequent return to Rhode Island. Shortly afterwards she believed herself called again to leave the comforts and happiness of home, to travel in the service of her Divine Master. Her course on this occasion was directed to Long Island, where she spent most of the winter ;* thence proceeding to Shelter Island, to the mainland about Narragansett, and on to Providence. Here she was introduced into a deep religious exercise of soul, under the apprehension that it was required of her once more to visit Massachusetts, to finish, as she expresses it, "her sad and heavy experience in the bloody town of Boston." Leaving, therefore, the quiet retreat of Providence, she journeyed towards the persecuting city, and arrived there on the 21st of the Third Month, 1660.

* Besse, vol. ii. p. 206.

Having been so nearly a victim to the gallows for venturing within its confines before, her presence now took the rulers by surprise. They had cherished the hope, that the dreadful example of their cruelty in the execution of her late companions, would have been sufficient to deter her from again coming amongst them. But they were blind to the character and motives of Mary Dyer, and ignorant of the efficacy of that Divine Power by which she was led and supported.

So vigilant had the magistracy been to prevent the propagation of the views of Friends in the province, that on all previous instances, no time had been lost in immediately arresting those who came to Boston for the purpose ; but, whether from the perplexity the rulers felt on the return of Mary Dyer, as shewing the futility of their barbarous enactment for excluding Friends ; or, from a fear of increasing the excitement of the public mind, or, from whatever other cause it might be, for ten days after the arrival of this devoted Friend, no attempt was made to interrupt the course of her gospel labours.

On this occasion, the general court was sitting. There were at the time several Friends in the gaols of the city, some of whom came to "sojourn" in the province, and, like Mary Dyer, much to the perplexity of Endicott and his fellow-magistrates, had returned after being banished on pain of death. Since her reprieve, several of the colonists also, had, according to the law against Quakers, forfeited their lives ; yet this extreme penalty the rulers hesitated to enforce. But Mary Dyer was a stranger, and one whose avowed object in coming, was to preach those doctrines against which the whole weight of authority was vehemently directed. To exempt her, therefore, from the operation of the law, after she had been once reprieved, would have been a virtual abandonment of the enactment ; a course for which they were not yet prepared, and on the 31st of the Third Month, she was once more arraigned before the general court. Endicott, who undertook the examination, asked her if she was the same Mary Dyer that was there before ? To which she unhesitatingly replied, " I am the same Mary Dyer that was here at the last general court.'' Endicott said, '' Then you own yourself a Quaker, do you not ?'' '' I own myself to be reproachfully called so," answered Mary Dyer. Endicott, after saying, "I must then repeat the sentence once before pronounced upon you," thus proceeded, "You must return to the prison, and there remain till to-morrow at nine o'clock; then from thence you must go to the gallows, and there be hanged till you are dead." "This," said Mary Dyer calmly, "is no more than thou saidst before." To this observation, Endicott replied, "But now it is to be executed; therefore, prepare yourself for nine o'clock to-morrow." This dignified woman, unmoved by the dreadful sentence, and unshaken in her belief that her call to come amongst them was from on high, thus addressed the court: "I came in obedience to the will of God, to the last general court, praying you to repeal your unrighteous sentence of banishment on pain of death; and that same is my work now, and earnest request, although I told you, that if you refused to repeal them, the Lord would send others of his servants to witness against them." Endicott, disturbed by her address, tauntingly said to her, "Are you a prophetess?" "I spoke the words," she replied, "which the Lord spoke to me, and now the thing is come to pass." She then proceeded to speak further of her religious call, but the governor impatiently cried, "Away with her," and she was speedily reconducted to prison.

The departure of Mary Dyer to Boston on this occasion, plunged her family into the greatest distress; for the consequence, they were well assured, would be the sacrifice of her life. Her husband, whose religious views did not harmonize with those of Friends, nevertheless loved her tenderly, and, anxious for her preservation, addressed the following touching appeal to Governor Endicott:—

"HONOURED SIR,

"It is with no little grief of mind and sadness of heart, that I am necessitated to be so bold as to supplicate your honoured self, with the honourable assembly of your general court, to extend your mercy and favour once again to me and my children. Little did I dream that I should have occasion to petition in a matter of this nature; but so it is, that through the Divine Providence, and your benignity, my son obtained so much pity and mercy at your hands, to enjoy the life of his mother.   Now, my supplication to your honours is, to beg affectionately the life of my dear wife.   'Tis true, I have not seen her above this half year, and cannot tell how, in the frame of her spirit, she was moved thus again to run so great a hazard to herself, and perplexity to me and mine, and all her friends and well-wishers.

"So it is, from Shelter Island, about by Peynod, Narragansett, &c., to the town of Providence, she secretly and speedily journeyed, and as secretly from thence came to your jurisdiction.   Unhappy journey, may I say, and woe to that generation, say I, that gives occasion thus of grief (to those that desire to be quiet), by helping one another to hazard their lives to, I know not what end, nor for what purpose.

"If her zeal be so great as thus to adventure, Oh ! let your pity and favour surmount it, and save her life.   Let not your love and wonted compassion be conquered by her inconsiderate madness ; and how greatly will your renown spread, if by so conquering, you become victorious !   What shall I say more ?   I know you are all sensible of my condition ; you see what my petition is, and what will give me and mine peace.

"Oh ! let Mercy's wings soar over Justice's balance, and then whilst I live, I shall exalt your goodness ; but otherways, 'twill be a languishing sorrow—yea, so great, that I should gladly suffer the blow at once, much rather.   I shall forbear to trouble you with words, neither am I in a capacity to expatiate myself at present.   I only say this, yourselves have been, and are, or may be, husbands to wives ; so am I, yea, to one most dearly beloved. Oh ! do not deprive me of her, but I pray give her me once again. I shall be so much obliged for ever, that I shall endeavour continually to utter my thanks, and render you love and honour most renowned.   Pity me !   I beg it with tears, and rest your humble suppliant,

W. DYER.*

* The Friend, a Philadelphia journal, vol. iv. p. 165, Third Month 5th, 1831.   This, it is believed, was the first publication of the letter.

What answer was returned to this appeal is not ascertained, if indeed, Endicott condescended to answer it at all ; it was, however, unavailing.   On the morning following her condemnation, being the 1st of the Fourth Month, Mary Dyer was led forth to execution.   The officer, on coming to her cell, exhibited an unbecoming degree of impatience ; but, still preserved in great calmness, she desired him to "wait a little, and she would be ready presently."   The coarse and unfeeling official, more at home in such cruel business than most others, replied, " He could not wait upon her, but she should now wait upon him."*

The demonstrations of sympathy by the townspeople towards the victims of these wicked proceedings, gave Endicott much uneasiness ; and fearing that the populace might show it in a very inconvenient manner, he deemed it prudent that a "strong guard" of soldiers should be in attendance.   Mary Dyer being brought forth, and the drummers placed both "before and behind her," the procession commenced its march towards the Common.

Thus guarded, and amid the incessant beat of the drums, the procession arrived at the place of execution.   Having ascended the ladder, she was told, that "if she would return home, she might come down and save her life ;" but to this she replied with much Christian firmness, " Nay, I cannot ; for in obedience to the will of the Lord I came, and in his will I abide faithful unto death."†   She was then charged with being guilty of her own blood ; to which she answered, " Nay, I came to keep blood-guiltiness from you, desiring you to repeal the unrighteous and unjust law of banishment upon pain of death, made against the innocent servants of the Lord ; therefore my blood will be required at your hands, who wilfully do it ; but for those that do it in the simplicity of their hearts, I desire the Lord to forgive them.   I came to do the will of my Father, and in obedience to his will, I stand even to death."‡

Whilst on the scaffold, with the eyes of the mixed multitude fixed intently upon her, she was asked whether she would have

* Sewel's History, p. 234.   † Ibid. p. 234.
‡ Ibid, p. 234.

the elders to pray for her? " I know never an elder here," was
her reply.   Will you then have any of the people to pray for
you? continued the attendant.   " I would have all the people of
God to pray for me," she said.   As on the former occasion, so
now, the approbation of the ministers of Boston was evinced by
their presence.   " Mary Dyer! Oh repent! Oh repent!" cried
out Wilson, "and be not so deluded, and carried away by the
deceit of the devil."   " Nay, man," she answered, " I am not
now to repent."   After some further conversation between her
and her persecutors, she was reproached with having said, she
had already been in Paradise.   To this she unhesitatingly answered, " Yea, I have been in Paradise several days."   Her
mind was in the same peaceful and favoured condition as when
she had been previously brought to the place of execution.   Other
expressions dropped from the lips of this devoted woman, descriptive of the happy and unclouded state of her mind, in the prospect
of that eternity into which she was about to enter.   The executioner now did his awful office ; and her purified spirit passed, it
may be humbly believed, into the glorious presence of Him for
whose cause she died.

But few particulars of her previous history are recorded in the
writings of Friends.   It appears, however, that long before she
embraced our principles, she was a prominent character in New
England.   As early as 1637, or about twenty years before she
professed with Friends, she was a distinguished leader in the
Antinomian secession in that country.   Oldmixon, in his history
of the English colonies in America, speaks of her as " the companion" of Anne Hutchinson in that controversy ;* and, in a
work of more modern date, she is mentioned as her " devoted
follower."†   In common with others who dissented from the
Puritan church in Massachusetts, Mary Dyer and her husband
were banished from Boston, and, with most of the Antinomians,
they settled on Rhode Island.   Her husband was one of eighteen
who formed the " body politic" on the settlement of Rhode

* Oldmixon's British Empire in America, vol. i. p. 76.
† Life of Anne Hutchinson in Sparke's American Biography. Boston
printed.

Island,* and afterwards held the office of secretary to the colony.†
It is clear that Mary Dyer was endowed with mental qualities of
no ordinary kind. Her addresses to the court, and her conduct
when led to execution, evince that she possessed considerable
ability and great fortitude of mind. John Taylor, who was united
with her in some gospel labours on Shelter Island, a short time
previous to her execution, said, " she was a very comely woman
and grave matron, and even shined in the image of God."‡
Sewel, who bears a similar testimony, says, she had "extraordinary qualities," and " was of good family and estate, and the
mother of several children."§ Croese, a Dutch writer, states, that
she was reputed as a " person of no mean extract and parentage,
of an estate pretty plentiful, of a comely stature and countenance,
of a piercing knowledge in many things, of a wonderful sweet and
pleasant discourse, so fit for great affairs, that she wanted nothing
that was manly, except only the name and the sex."‖

At the time of Mary Dyer's execution several Friends were
lying in the prisons of Boston, and among them Joseph and Jane
Nicholson of Cumberland. By a letter addressed in the Second
Month, 1660, to Margaret Fell, it appears that it was their
intention to make Boston their home, at least for a time. This
letter recites several interesting incidents, as follows :—

FROM JOSEPH NICHOLSON TO MARGARET FELL.

From the Prison at Boston, this Third-day of the Second Month, 1660.

M. F.,

—— Upon the 7th of the First Month, I was called forth
before the court at Boston, and when I came, John Endicott bade
me take off my hat, and after some words about that, he asked me

---

* Callender's Historical Discourse of Rhode Island, edited by Romeo
Elton, p. 84.

† Hutchinson's Massachusetts, p. 199.

‡ Journal of John Taylor, p. 8.

§ Sewel's History, p. 233.

‖ The General History of the Quakers, &c., by Gerard Croese. Second
Book, p. 148.

what I came into the country for ; I told him he had my answer already. Then he asked, who sent me. I told him I was moved of the Lord to come hither with my wife, to sojourn in this land. He then asked, where I came from. I told him from Cumberland, where I formerly lived. Then he said, what would I follow when I had my liberty. I told him, labour with my hands the thing that was honest, as formerly I had done, if the Lord called me thereto.—He said, would I not go a preaching. I told him if I had a word from the Lord to speak, wherever I came I might speak it.—He asked if my wife was able to come to the court : I told him she was ; then he bid the gaoler fetch her, and the two other Old England Quakers. When they came, after some tempting questions, we were returned to prison. The next day we were called forth again, and were sentenced by the court to depart their jurisdiction before the sixteenth-day of the month, not to return upon pain of death. We could not have liberty to speak in our own defence, but, several times they stopped my mouth, and threatened to gag me, and to whip me when I could not forbear to speak. Bellingham boasted in open court, and said their law was too strong for us : he threatens much with their gallows.—My wife was not able to leave prison till the last day of their limited time, and then we passed to Salem, a place where are some Friends, and there stayed until the 20th, and then came two constables and took us both and carried us to prison. As we passed along the street we met the gaoler, who said I was come again to see if the gallows would hold me. The other two Friends that were banished with us, were one that did belong to the ship, and a maid that came with us in the ship, who was in prison about a week before the court began. They are at present gone out of the jurisdiction, but will hardly be clear, but come again.—I have had peace more than ever since this thing was made known to me, before I told thee of it : so the will of the Lord be done in it, what ever it be.

Joseph Nicholson

According to Boston law, Joseph Nicholson and his wife, by

continuing in Massachusetts, had forfeited their lives, and the gaoler, presuming that he had another victim for the gallows, laid Joseph in irons. On the day of Mary Dyer's execution, they were brought before the general court, " to see," observes Bishop, " if the terror thereof could have frighted them." " But," he continues, " the power of the Lord in them was above all, and they feared them not, nor their threats of putting them to death.*   It was whilst lying in Boston prison, that Joseph Nicholson wrote a remonstrance to the rulers of the province, which he called *"The Standard of the Lord lifted up in New England,"* &c.

The bold and unflinching manner in which Friends were strengthened to resist the banishing enactment, impressed the rulers of Boston with fear ; and, hesitating to pursue their sanguinary course, they again liberated Joseph and Jane Nicholson from prison.   Having obtained their liberty, these Friends proceeded to the contiguous colony of Plymouth.   The rulers, however, of this district, sympathised with those of Boston, and the two Friends were not allowed a resting-place amongst them ; " if they had turned them away at Boston," said the magistrates at Plymouth, " they would have nothing to do with them."†   From Plymouth the exiled couple proceeded to Rhode Island, from whence Joseph Nicholson addressed a letter to his friend Margaret Fell, from which the following is an extract :—

FROM JOSEPH NICHOLSON TO MARGARET FELL.

From Rhode Island, the 10th of Fifth Month, 1660.

M. F.,

We have found the Lord a God at hand, and although our lives were not dear unto us, yet He hath delivered us out of the hands of blood-thirsty men.   We put our lives in our hands for the honour of the truth, and through the power of God we have them as yet.   Although we pressed much to have our liberty to go as we came, yet could not, but are banished again.   How it will be ordered afterward, if they let not their law fall, as it is

---

* New England Judged. Second Edition, p. 221.   † Ibid, p. 223.

broken, we know not ; for if the Lord call us again to go, there we must go, and, whether we die or live, it will be well. His powerful presence was much with us in Boston. We found much favour in [the] sight of most people in that town. The power of God sounded aloud many times into their streets, which made some of them leave their meetings, and come about the prison, which was a sore torment to some of them.

I think I shall pass towards Shelter Island ere long, and some places that way where I have not yet been ; and, for ought we know at present, Jane may remain here awhile. Boston people were glad at our departure, for there were not many, I believe, would have had us to have been put to death. We are well in the Lord.

Thy friend in the Truth,

JOSEPH NICHOLSON.

I was prisoner in Boston [about] six months, and my wife a prisoner eighteen weeks.

Joseph and Jane Nicholson soon returned to England ; but scarcely had they regained the shores of their native land, ere they were immured within the walls of Dover Castle.* Writing from hence in the Second Month, 1661, Joseph Nicholson says, " If the Lord make way for my liberty from these bonds shortly, I shall pass to Virginia in the Friends' ship, and so to New England again, but which way Jane will go, or how it is with her, I cannot say."† We shall have hereafter to refer to these Friends.

When writing from Boston, Joseph Nicholson spoke of several Friends who were fellow-prisoners with him. These were Mary Trask, John Smith, Margaret Smith, Edward Wharton, and some others of Salem. About the same time, Robert Harper and his wife were also committed to the same wretched abode, and after them William Leddra, who it appears had returned to Boston, after having been banished upon pain of death. " These," observes Bishop, " were in Boston gaol in the Tenth Month, 1660,"

---

* Besse says they were imprisoned there for refusing to swear just after they had landed at Deal from New England. See vol. i. p. 291.

† Swarthmore MSS.

where, he adds, " they had been continued long."* William King, of Salem, who is noticed in the preceding chapter as having been imprisoned and whipped, had, we find, together with Wenlock Christison of Salem, Mary Wright of Oyster Bay, in Long Island, and Martha Standley, a young Friend of England, had sentence of banishment on pain of death passed upon them. Martha Standley is without a doubt " the maid" referred to in Joseph Nicholson's letter from Boston, who " came with him in the ship." Wenlock Christison after his banishment, went on a visit to his brethren at Sandwich. Here, however, like the Nicholsons, he was not permitted to remain. On arriving at the town, he was arrested and conveyed to Plymouth, where he was not only imprisoned for fourteen weeks, but subjected to a severe flogging, once " tied neck and heels together,"† and robbed of his Bible and clothes, to the value of four pounds, for the payment of the prison fees. " All this," adds Bishop, "was but for coming into their jurisdiction, when he was banished from the other."‡

The date of the transactions just alluded to, brings the narrative for New England, down to the close of 1660. In the closing chapter for 1658, a notice of the meetings established up to that period, is given. During the two subsequent years, the progress of the Society was rapid, and Monthly Meetings were established there, as in some parts of Great Britain. In a recent pamphlet relative to the meetings in New England, it is stated, that " Sandwich Monthly Meeting was the first established in America,"§ and that Scituate, now known as Pembroke Monthly Meeting, was established prior to 1660.‖ No authentic records of the Society appear to be in existence, by which the precise date of these can be ascertained, but the fact that meetings of this description were established by Friends of New England at this time, is corroborated by the ancient provincial manuscripts of

* New England Judged, Second Edition, p. 220.
† Ibid. p. 222.　　　　　　　　‡ Ibid. p. 223.
§ Brief account of the Yearly Meetings in New England. Providence, printed, p. 20,
‖ Ibid, p. 21.

Massachusetts. In the minutes of the Court of Plymouth for the year 1660, the following order is recorded :—

"Whereas there is a constant Monthly Meeting of Quakers from divers places in great numbers, which is very offensive, and may prove greatly prejudicial to the government, and as the most constant place for such meetings is at Duxburrow, the court have desired and appointed Constant Southworth and William Paybody to repair to such meetings, together with the marshal or constable of the town, and to use their best endeavours by argument and discourse, to convince or hinder them."*

The circumstance of Monthly Meetings having been thus set up in America, before they had been generally established in England, is an interesting feature in the progress of the Society in the new country, and deserving of particular notice. There does not appear to have been any systematic organization attempted at this early period. The new association consisted of pious individuals, who, forsaking the lifeless forms and ceremonies of the day, and a dependence upon man in spiritual things, found in the principles of the gospel enunciated by George Fox, and his associates, that rest and peace which their souls desired. As a gathered church, they acknowledged Christ only as its living and ever present Head. He was felt to be " their all in all ;" " their Teacher to instruct them, their Counsellor to direct them, their Shepherd to feed them, their Bishop to oversee them, and their Prophet to open divine mysteries unto them ;"† and remarkably indeed did the Chief Shepherd condescend to visit and " appear in the midst of them," refreshing and comforting their spirits, and cementing them in a precious feeling of unity and love.

Separated as the Early Friends were from other religious professors ; with their numbers gradually increasing, and the zeal of new converts warm and active, it was found that in the right exercise of the " diversities of gifts," there arose a necessity for those important duties and for that mutual Christian care, which

* See notes on Duxbury in the Massachusett's Historical Society. Second Series, vol. x.

† Journal of George Fox.

we understand by the term *Discipline ;* to be regulated and upheld under the authority of frequent periodical meetings.   The
first meeting for discipline established in the Society, appears to
have been held in the county of Durham, in the year 1653. This
was a Monthly Meeting.   George Fox mentions in his journal,
that some meetings of this description were settled in the north
of England at this date.*   Among the Swarthmore manuscripts
is a document which has been recently discovered, relative to the
establishment of the Monthly Meeting in Durham.   It is signed
by sixteen Friends, and endorsed by George Fox.†   This paper,
setting forth the object which our early Friends had, in thus
establishing a meeting for discipline, is valuable, and will, doubtless, be read with interest.   It is as follows :—

" Dear Friends, in the measure of the light of Christ, we being
brought to feel and see the estate and condition of the Church in
these parts, and the danger that many lie in, because of the
oppressors, and [that] thereby the enemy of the soul may come
to have advantage over us, therefore in the fear of the Lord, being
moved thereunto by the Lord, and being subject henceforth every
one to bear his burden, the strong with the weak, that the weak
be not oppressed above his strength, but all drawing on hand in
hand, that the weak and the tired may be refreshed, and so all
become a joint witness to the everlasting truth, in word and conversation ; our lives and minds being set free from that, that daily
may tempt or trouble in the particular.   Therefore, dear friends,

---

* See vol. ii. p. 229.   Leed's Edition.
† The endorsement by George Fox runs thus :—" The setting up the
men's meeting in Bishoprick, 1653."   And the following are the Friends
who signed it :—

Christ : Eyon.	Anth : Pearson.
John Higgington.	Robt : Selbye.
Christr : Richmound.	Richard Wilson.
Peter Young.	Will : Trewhitt.
William Cotsworth.	Jo : Langstaff.
Martin Richmound.	Rich : Ewbanke.
James Whyte.	Andrew Rawe.
John Hopper.	Thomas Shaw.

we, who are met together, do think it convenient that some of
every several meeting, do meet together, the first Seventh-day of
every month, beginning with the Third Month, and to declare
what necessities or wants are seen in their several meetings, there
to be considered on by Friends, and as necessity is seen, so to
minister.   And, seeing at present there is a great need for a
collection, by reason of some great sums of money that have been
laid out, and more is to be laid out, we recommend it to your
several meetings, to do herein every one according to your freedom
in the present necessity, and to give notice the next First-day,
that it may be collected for the poor, the First-day following, and
to be paid over to John Langstaffe ; and a note of the same subscribed by some Friends from every meeting."

Quarterly Meetings constituted of representatives from the
several meetings in a county, were established in some parts, a
few years subsequently ; their office in the body being then similar
to that which Monthly Meetings now exercise.   But the setting
up of Monthly Meetings did not generally take place throughout
Great Britain, until about thirteen years after the date of that
above referred to.   In an early epistle which George Fox wrote
in reference to these meetings, he thus counsels his friends, " Admonish all them that be careless and slothful, to diligence in the
truth and service for God, and to bring forth heavenly fruits, and
that they may mind the good works of God, and do them in believing on his Son, and showing it forth in their conversation, and
to deny the devil, and his bad works, and not to do them ; and to
seek them that be driven away from the truth into the devil's
wilderness, by his dark power.   Seek them again by the truth,
and by the truth and power of God, bring them to God again."

CHAPTER XII.

William Leddra's imprisonment and sufferings at Boston—His examination before the Court—Is sentenced to be executed—His conduct
at the place of execution—Letter of a spectator respecting it—The
character of William Leddra—His epistle to Friends, written the day
previous to his martyrdom—The examination and banishment of
Edward Wharton—The return of Wenlock Christison after banishment—His Christian boldness before the rulers; examination and sentence—His address to the Court—The restoration of the monarchy in
England—The rulers at Boston are agitated on hearing it, and release W. Christison and twenty-seven Friends from prison—The law
for banishing on pain of death superseded by a law for banishing on
penalty of being whipped from town to town out of the colony—The
sufferings of Friends under this new law—Nicholas Phelps and
Josiah Southwick return from banishment—The cruel scourging of
the latter—George Rofe, of Essex, visits New England—His letter
relative to the service—The first General Meeting of Friends in
America held on Rhode Island.

In the previous chapters, much has been recorded that sullies
the historic pages of Puritan New England. We have seen that
its religious zealots, under cover of high spirituality, had con-
summated their persecutions in the murder of three individuals
of unspotted lives and conversation, and of whom it may be
justly said, "The world was not worthy." Injustice and cruelty
in any form afford a humiliating exhibition of the depravity of
man; but when presented to us under the mask of superior sanctity, the mind is wont to turn with feelings of deepened abhorrence
from such a desecration of the name of religion. In every religious profession, conscientious feelings should be respected, but
the persecutions in Massachusetts violated even the plainest laws
of humanity. The rulers of this province, in justification of their
wicked acts, represented Friends as moving under extreme delusion; but what greater or more shocking delusion can there be,
than to slay our fellow-creatures and to believe that we are thereby

promoting the sacred cause of religion.   Of all the acts to which
the grand adversary influences man, this we conceive to be the
most flagrant violation of the Divine law.

We have used the term murder, and used it advisedly ; for
the martyrdom of the three Friends on Boston Common had been
perpetrated contrary to the laws of the realm.   The charter of
Massachusetts in no degree empowered the local authorities to
enact laws contrary to the fundamental principles of English
jurisprudence and English liberty.   In pursuing their despotic
course, they did so likewise with the consciousness that it was
repulsive to the feelings of the community.   Towards the close
of 1660, this was so intelligibly manifested, that for a time they
deemed it prudent to suspend the operation of the law for execut-
ing Friends, and thus the life of Joseph Nicholson was saved.

It has been stated in the preceding chapter, that among those
imprisoned at Boston in the Tenth Month, 1660, was William
Leddra, who had returned to the city, after having been exiled
on pain of death.   This faithful man appears to have been in
no ordinary degree the object of Puritan displeasure.   During
his former imprisonment at Boston, the sufferings to which he
was subjected had been so extreme that his life was endangered.
On the present occasion, he was fettered to a log of wood, being
chained night and day in an open prison ; and that, also, during
the severities of a New England winter.   His persecutors would
probably have been glad, had these inhumanities put an end to
his existence ; but it pleased Divine Providence to support him
through them.

On the 9th of the First Month, 1661, he was again brought
before the Court of Assistants.   Thus arraigned, with the chains
about him, and still bound to the log, he was told that having
returned after sentence of banishment, he had incurred the penalty
of death.   On hearing this, the sufferer asked what evil he had
done ?   The Court replied, he had owned those that were put to
death ; had refused to put off his hat in court, and said thee and
thou.   He then asked them if they would put him to death for
speaking English, and for not putting off his clothes ?   To this,
one of the magistrates made the absurd reply, " A man may

speak treason in English." William Leddra then inquired if "it was treason to say thee and thou to a single person."* Broad-street, a violent persecuting magistrate, now undertook to question the prisoner, and asked him "If he would go to England." He replied that he had no business in England. Then, said Broadstreet, significantly pointing to Boston Common, "You shall go that way." "What," replied William Leddra, "will you put me to death for breathing in the air of your jurisdiction? What have you against me? I appeal to the laws of England for my trial. If by them I am found guilty, I refuse not to die."† The arbitrary Court, however, overruled his appeal; and then, like some other persecutors of old, endeavoured to persuade him to recant, and conform to their own religion. The wretched attempt was at once rejected, and rejected, too, with magnanimity and disdain. "What! join with such murderers as you are," said William Leddra; "then let every man that meets me say, Lo, this is the man that hath forsaken the God of his salvation."‡

The Court, finding their victim unshaken in his religious convictions, passed the sentence of death upon him, and appointed the 14th of the month for its execution. On this day it was also arranged that a morning lecture should be given; and now, as on the former occasions, the officiating minister exerted his eloquence, to urge the magistracy onward in their dreadful work. "Priests and Papists," writes a contemporary, "served to whet them on."§ The lecture, or, as a modern writer terms it, "this shocking preamble to the execution,"|| being concluded, the governor, with a guard of soldiers, proceeded to the prison. Here the irons that had long hung on William Leddra were knocked off, and, taking a solemn farewell of his imprisoned companions, he "went forth to the slaughter in the meekness of the spirit of Jesus."¶ On leaving the prison walls, he was immediately surrounded by the soldiery, with a view to prevent

---

* New England Judged, p. 316.   † Ibid, p. 317.
‡ Ibid, 318.   § Ibid, 326.
|| Tuke's Biographical Notices, p. 55.
¶ New England Judged, p. 327.

him from speaking to his friends. Edward Wharton, observing
the manœuvre, exclaimed that it was worse than the·conduct of
Bonner's men. "What," said he, "will you not let me come
near my suffering friend before you kill him." One of the company replied that "it would be his turn next;" and an officer
threatened to stop his mouth, if he spoke another word.

The procession was similar in character to those before-mentioned; and having reached the place of execution, William
Leddra exhorted his friend, Edward Wharton, to faithfulness,
and bade him a final farewell, saying, "All that will be Christ's
disciples must take up his cross." While standing on the ladder,
some one having called out, "William, have you anything
to say to the people?" he replied, "For bearing my testimony
for the Lord against the deceivers and deceived, am I brought
here to suffer." These expressions, together with the heavenly
mindedness which he manifested at this awful period, awakened
the tender feelings of many of the spectators, in a manner that
conveyed keen reproof to the instigators of the revolting scene.
The ministers observed the manifestation of this feeling with
uneasiness; and Allen, who was one of them, with a view to
check the current of sympathy, said, loudly, "People, I would
not have you think it strange to see a man so willing to die, for
it is no new thing; you may read how the apostle saith, that
some shall be given up to many delusions, and even dare to die
for it." Truly, the apostle said that many should be given
up to delusions; but the persecuting priest committed a great
error, when he quoted the apostle as saying that such should
dare to die for them.

The executioner now proceeded to complete his work. Whilst
the halter was being adjusted, the martyr meekly and resignedly
said, "I commend my righteous cause unto thee, O God." His
last expressions being, as the ladder was turning, "Lord, Jesus!
receive my spirit."* The body, on being cut down, was allowed
to be removed by his friends for interment; this, however, would
not have been granted, but for the outcry of the people against

* New England Judged, p. 329.

the barbarous indecencies exhibited to the remains of the former victims.

Before the execution, it was currently reported that William Leddra had liberty to leave the prison, and to save his life. This was a gross falsehood, propagated, doubtless, with a view to lessen the odiousness of the wicked proceedings. There was present a stranger, who was much affected on witnessing the scene. A letter addressed by him to a friend at Barbadoes, alluding to this report, and describing the execution, has been preserved, and will be read with interest.

Boston, *March* 26, 1661.

" On the 14th of this instant, one William Leddra was put to death here. The people of the town told me, he might go away if he would ; but when I made further inquiry, I heard the marshal say that he was chained in prison, from the time he was condemned, to the day of his execution. I am not of his opinion : but yet, truly, methought the Lord did mightily appear in the man. I went to one of the magistrates of Cambridge, who had been of the jury that condemned him, as he told me himself; and I asked him by what rule he did it ? He answered me, that he was a rogue, a very rogue. But what is this to the question, said I ; where is your rule ? He said, he had abused authority. Then I went after the man, and asked him, whether he did not look on it as a breach of rule to slight and undervalue authority ? And I said that Paul gave Festus the title of honour, though he was a heathen. (I do not mean to say these magistrates are heathens.) When the man was on the ladder, he looked on me and called me friend, and said, ' know that this day I am willing to offer up my life for the witness of Jesus.' Then I desired leave of the officers to speak, and said, ' gentlemen, I am a stranger both to your persons and country, yet a friend of both :' and I cried aloud, for the Lord's sake, take not away the man's life ; but remember Gamaliel's counsel to the Jews—' If it be of man, it will come to nought ; but if it be of God, ye cannot overthrow it : but be careful ye be not found fighters against God.' And

the captain said, why had you not come to the prison ? The
reason was, because I heard the man might go if he would ; and
therefore I called him down from the tree, and said, come down,
William, you may go away if you will. Then Captain Oliver
said it was no such matter ; and asked me what I had to do
with it ; and bade me begone : and I told them I was willing,
for I could not endure to see this. And when I was in the
town, some did seem to sympathize with me in my grief. I
told them, they had no warrant from the word of God, nor
precedent from our country, nor power from his Majesty, to
hang the man.

" I rest your friend,

" THOMAS WILKIE."

" To Mr. George Lad, master of the *America*,
    of Dartmouth, now at Barbadoes."*

Of the history of William Leddra previous to his joining in
religious fellowship with Friends, but very little is known. His
home was in Barbadoes, but he is said to have been by birth a
Cornishman ;† and his occupation, it appears, was that of a
clothier.‡ We find him engaged very early in visiting the West
Indies as a minister, and in 1657 he proceeded in that character
to New England. The particulars of the sufferings he underwent
in pursuing this labour of love have already been set forth.
Christian constancy, and patient endurance under extreme sufferings for the cause of his Lord, remarkably distinguished William
Leddra. Addressing his friends of New England, from Boston
prison, a few weeks before his death, he says—" I testify in the
fear of the Lord God, and witness with a pen of trembling, that
the noise of the whip on my back, all the imprisonments, and
banishing upon pain of death, and after returning, the loud
threatening of a halter from their mouths, did no more affright
me, through the strength of the power of God, than if they had
threatened to have bound a spider's web to my finger ; which
makes me to say with unfeigned lips—" Wait upon the Lord, O

* Sewel's History, p. 269.   † Whiting's Catalogue, p. 61.
‡ New England Persecutors Mauled, by Thomas Philathes, p. 45.

my soul, for ever. I do not seek to withdraw my cheek from the smiter, nor to turn aside my feet from the footsteps of the flock, as witness this chain and this log at my leg; but I desire, as far as the Lord draws me, to follow my forefathers and brethren, in suffering and in joy; wherefore my spirit waits and worships at the feet of Immanuel, unto whom I commit my cause."*

The state of William Leddra's mind, in anticipation of his death, may be truly called a triumphant one. The heavenly enjoyments which he was permitted to experience, and the fore-taste he had of a glorious immortality, were such as are rarely vouchsafed to humanity. On the day preceding his execution, he wrote the following :—

" To the Society of the little Flock of Christ.

" Grace and Peace be multiplied.

" Most dear and inwardly beloved !

" The sweet influences of the morning star, like a flood, dis-tilling into my habitation, have so filled me with the joy of the Lord in the beauty of holiness, that my spirit is as if it did not inhabit a tabernacle of clay, but is wholly swallowed up in the bosom of eternity, from whence it had its being.

" Alas! Alas! what can the wrath and spirit of man that lusteth to envy, aggravated by the heat and strength of the king of the locusts which came out of the pit, do unto one that is hid in the secrets of the Almighty, or unto them that are gathered under the healing wings of the Prince of Peace? under whose armour of light they shall be able to stand in the day of trial; having on the breastplate of righteousness and the sword of the Spirit, which is their weapon of war against spiritual wickedness, principalities and powers, and the rulers of the darkness of this world, both within and without.

" Oh, my beloved! I have waited like a dove at the windows of the ark; and have stood still in that watch, which the Master, without whom I could do nothing, did at his coming reward with

* New England Judged, p. 297.

the fulness of his love ; wherein my heart did rejoice, that I might, in the love and life of God, speak a few words to you, sealed with the spirit of promise ; that the taste thereof might be a savour of life to your life, and a testimony in you of my innocent death.   And if I had been altogether silent, and the Lord had not opened my mouth unto you, yet he would have opened your hearts, and there have sealed my innocence with the streams of life, by which we are all baptized into that body which is of God, with whom and in whose presence there is life ; in which as you abide, you stand upon the pillar and ground of truth.   For the life being the truth and the way, go not one step without it, lest you should compass a mountain in the wilderness ; for to everything there is a season.

" As the flowing of the ocean doth fill every creek and branch thereof, and [as it] then retires again towards its own being and fulness, and leaves a savour behind it ; so doth the life and virtue of God flow into every one of your hearts, whom He hath made partakers of his Divine nature ; and when it withdraws but a little, it leaves a sweet savour behind it, that many can say they are made clean through the word that He hath spoken to them ; in which innocent condition you may see what you are in the presence of God, and what you are without Him.

" Your brother,

" WILLIAM LEDDRA."

Boston Gaol, the 13*th of the*
First Month, 1661.

Thus died this devoted Christian, in the full assurance of a blessed resurrection unto eternal life, and doubtless he now forms one of that innumerable company, who " have come out of great tribulation, and have washed their robes, and made them white in the blood of the Lamb."

During the sitting of the General Court at which William Leddra was condemned, Edward Wharton, who had been a prisoner in Boston for nearly a year, was brought up for judgment.   Being a man of great Christian courage, he spoke boldly against these persecutions, and, consequently, he was very obnoxious to the ecclesiastics and rulers. When brought forward, he asked the governor what he had to lay to his charge? Endicott answered by referring to his not having taken off his hat, and hypocritically observed that he was sorry to see him so deluded.

Edward Wharton. " Wearing my hat is no just cause for persecuting me,—the truth deluded no man, and by the grace of God I am made willing to suffer for His name's sake, which grace I witness in my measure."

Endicott, scoffingly. " In my measure? This is right the Quakers' words. Hast thou grace?"

E. Wharton. " Yes."

Endicott. " How dost thou know thou hast grace?"

E. Wharton. " He that believeth on the Son of God, needs not go to others, for he hath the witness in himself, as said John, and this witness is the Spirit."

Endicott having ordered the gaoler to be sent for, Edward Wharton, desirous of knowing the ground of his committal, thus addressed him. " Since thou hast warrant, and caused the constable to take me out of my house, and to lead me through the country, from town to town, like an evil-doer, I would know what thou hast to lay to my charge?" To this Endicott replied, " Nay, you shall know that afterwards." The gaoler was then directed to reconduct him to prison, where he was kept day and night closely confined with William Leddra, " in a very little room, little larger than a saw-pit."*

On his being soon brought back to the Court, Edward Wharton repeated his former question—" Wherefore have I been fetched from my habitation, where I was following my honest calling, and here laid up as an evil-doer?"

The Court. " Your hair is too long, and you have disobeyed that commandment which saith, ' Honour thy father and mother.' "

E. Wharton. " Wherein?"

---

* Besse, vol. ii. p. 220.

The Court. " In that you will not put off your hat to magistrates."

E. Wharton. " I love and own all magistrates and rulers, who are for the punishment of evil-doers, and for the praise of them that do well."

Rawson. " Edward Wharton, come to the bar."

E. Wharton. " Yea, and to the bench too, for thou hast no evil justly to lay to our charge."

Rawson. " Hold up your hand."

E. Wharton. " I will not. Thou hast no evil to charge me with."

Rawson. " Hear your sentence of banishment."

E. Wharton. " Have a care what you do, for if you murder me, my blood will lie heavy upon you."

Rawson. " Edward Wharton, attend to your sentence of banishment. You are, upon pain of death, to depart this jurisdiction, it being the eleventh of this instant, March, by the one-and-twentieth of the same, on the pain of death."

E. Wharton. " Friends, I am a single man, and I have dealings with some people ; it were good I had time to make clear with all, and then if you have power to murder me, you may."

Endicott, after consulting with Rawson. " If we should give him an hundred days, it is all one."

E. Wharton. " Nay, I shall not go away ; therefore be careful what you do."*

The prisoner then addressed the numerous assembly, on the injustice of the proceedings ; " They have nothing to charge me withal," said he, " but my hat and my hair." Rawson now calling the attention of the Court, read the record he had made— " that, contrary to law, the prisoner had travelled up and down, with William Robinson and Marmaduke Stevenson." Edward Wharton replied, " What readest thou that for ?" and alluding to the whipping he underwent in 1659, said, " Have ye not ploughed furrows on my back for that already, although ye had no law for it ?" The reply having silenced Rawson, Bellingham,

* Besse, vol. ii. p. 221.

the deputy governor, interfered, with a threat to send him back to prison, and to have him whipped. He was, however, released, and commanded immediately to depart the colony ; but, undaunted by their threats or their law, he attended the execution of his friend William Leddra, at which he bore an unflinching testimony against such atrocities, and then returned to his home at Salem.*

The case of Edward Wharton was an unpalatable one to Endicott and his fellow-magistrates ; but they were still more perplexed by that of Wenlock Christison, than whom none distinguished himself more by Christian constancy and firmness, in the time of these cruelties. In the previous chapter, he is stated to have been banished under penalty of death ; and on proceeding to the adjacent colony of Plymouth, to have been driven also from that territory. Wenlock Christison, not counting his life dear unto him for the truth's sake, believed it required of him to return to Boston, although in the expectation that ere long he should be added to the list of martyrs. He came back boldly, and entered the general court to face his persecutors, at the very moment they were passing sentence of death on William Leddra. The magistrates, on seeing him enter, were struck with consternation. The unexpected event so petrified them, that for some time it produced an entire silence. Their extreme surprise, however, soon gave place to other feelings, and one of the Court cried out, " Here is another, fetch him to the bar."†

Rawson. " Is not your name Wenlock Christison ?"

Wenlock. " Yes."

Endicott. " Wast thou not banished upon pain of death ?"

Wenlock. " Yea, I was."

Endicott. " What dost thou here, then ?"

Wenlock. " I am come to warn you, that you shed no more innocent blood ; for the blood that you have shed already cries to the Lord for vengeance."

Being handed over to the custody of the gaoler, he was then taken to prison. On the same day on which William Leddra

* New England Judged, p. 342.   † Sewell, p. 226.

was put to death, he was again placed at the bar, the magistrates presuming that the circumstance of his companion's execution would terrify him into submission ; but, as will be seen, they greatly mistook the character of their prisoner. On this occasion, both Endicott and Bellingham endeavoured to shake his Christian firmness. Except he would renounce his religion, they said he should surely die. But undismayed by their menaces, he replied, " Nay, I shall not change my religion, nor seek to save my life ; neither do I intend to deny my Master ; but if I lose my life for Christ's sake, and the preaching of the gospel, I shall save it."* The prisoner's reply touched the hearts of some of the magistrates, and being divided in sentiment about putting him to death, they ordered him to be remanded until the next General Court. Endicott, it appears, was so disconcerted with the conduct of those on the bench who took the more humane view, that for two days he refused to preside again.†

The time having arrived, Wenlock Christison was brought from his prison-house, and being placed at the bar, the Governor asked him what he had to say for himself, why he should not die ?

Wenlock. " I have done nothing worthy of death : if I had, I refuse not to die."

Endicott. " Thou art come in amongst us in rebellion, which is as the sin of witchcraft, and ought to be punished."

Wenlock. " I came not in among you in rebellion, but in obedience to the God of heaven ; not in contempt to any one of you, but in love to your souls and bodies ; and *that* you shall know one day, when you and all men must give an account of the deeds done in the body. Take heed, for you cannot escape the righteous judgments of God."

Major-General Adderton. " You pronounce woes and judgments, and those that are gone before you pronounced woes and judgments ; but the judgments of the Lord are not come upon us yet."

Wenlock. " Be not proud, neither let your spirits be lifted

* New England Judged, p. 335.   † Ibid, p. 335.

up ; God doth but wait till the measure of your iniquity be filled up, and you have run your ungodly race ; then will the wrath of God come upon you to the uttermost.   And as for thy part, it hangs over thy head, and is near to be poured down upon thee, and shall come as a thief in the night suddenly, when thou thinkest not of it.*   By what law will you put me to death ?"

Court. " We have a law, and by our law, you are to die."

Wenlock. " So said the Jews of Christ, we have a law, and by our law he ought to die.   Who empowered you to make that law ?"

Court. " We have a patent and are patentees ; judge whether we have not power to make laws ?"

Wenlock. " How ! have you power to make laws repugnant to the laws of England ?"

Endicott. " Nay."

Wenlock. " Then you are gone beyond your bounds, and have forfeited your patent, and this is more than you can answer.   Are you subjects to the king, yea or nay ?"

Rawson. " What will you infer from that, what good will that do you ?"

Wenlock. " If you are, say so : for in your petition to the king, you desire that he will protect you, and that you may be worthy to kneel among his loyal subjects ?"

Court. " Yes."

Wenlock. " So am I, and for any thing I know, am as good as you, if not better ; for if the king did but know your hearts, as God knows them, he would see that your hearts are as rotten towards him as they are towards God.   Therefore seeing that you

* Events seemed to indicate that Wenlock Christison, in speaking thus prophetically to Adderton, did so under the influence of that wisdom which is from above. Some time after, this daring and hardened persecutor was suddenly cut off in a very remarkable manner. Returning home one day, after he had been exercising the soldiery, his horse took fright, and threw him with such violence as to cause instant death. His lifeless corpse presented a shocking spectacle, his eyes being forced out of his head, and his brains out of his nose, whilst the blood flowed in profusion from his ears.— Vide *Besse's Sufferings*, vol. ii. p. 270.

and I are subjects to the king, I demand to be tried by the laws of my own nation."

Court. " You shall be tried by a bench and jury."

Wenlock. " That is not the law, but the manner of it : for if you will be as good as your word, you must set me at liberty, for I never heard or read of any law that was in England to hang Quakers."

Endicott. " There is a law to hang Jesuits."

Wenlock. " If you put me to death, it is not because I go under the name of a Jesuit, but a Quaker ; therefore I appeal to the laws of my own nation."

Court. " You are in our hands, and have broken our laws, and we will try you."

Wenlock. " Your will is your law, and what you have power to do, *that* you will do ; and seeing that the jury must go forth on my life, this I have to say to you in the fear of the living God : ' Jury, take heed what you do, for you swear by the living God, that you will true trial make, and just verdict give, according to the evidence ; What have I done to deserve death ? Keep your hands out of innocent blood.' "

A Juryman. " It is good counsel."

The jury retired, but not before " they had received their lesson." They soon returned, and either from a fear of offending the Court, or from a prejudice against Quakers, brought the prisoner in guilty.

Wenlock. " I deny all guilt, for my conscience is clear in the sight of God."

Endicott. " The jury hath condemned thee."

Wenlock. " The Lord doth justify me, who art thou that condemnest ?"

The Court then proceeded to vote on the sentence of death ; there were, however, several who were opposed to this extreme measure ; for the innocency and Christian magnanimity of the prisoner, had produced a counter feeling in their minds. Endicott, vexed, and disappointed at this want of unanimity, passionately throwing something down on the table, told the Court that he " could find it in his heart to go home."

Wenlock replied, " It were better for thee to be at home than here, for thou art about a bloody piece of work."

Endicott. " You that will not consent record it. I thank God, I am not afraid to give judgment. Wenlock Christison, hearken to your sentence : You must return to the place from whence you came, and from thence to the place of execution, and there you must be hanged until you be dead, dead, dead, upon the thirteenth day of June, being the fifth day of the week."

Wenlock. " The will of the Lord be done : In whose will I came amongst you, and in whose counsel I stand, feeling his eternal power, that will uphold me to the last gasp, I do not question it. Known be it unto you all, that if you have power to take my life from me, my soul shall enter into everlasting rest and peace with God, where you yourselves shall never come : and if you have power to take my life from me, the which I question, I believe, you shall never more take Quakers lives from them. Note my words : Do not think to weary out the living God by taking away the lives of his servants. What do you gain by it ? For the last man you put to death here are five come in his room.* And if you have power " to take my life from me, God can raise up the same principle of life in ten of his servants, and send them among you in my room, that you may have torment upon torment, which is your portion : for there is no peace to the wicked, saith my God."

Endicott. " Take him away."†

Wenlock Christison was reconducted to his cell, where in " sweet peace" and pious resignation of soul he waited the arrival of the day, when he should be called upon to offer up his life for the sake of his dear Redeemer. The circumstances, however, which followed, evince that in his concluding address to the Court, he spoke under that holy influence which is profitable to direct, and which verifies the Scripture declaration, that " there is a spirit in man, and the inspiration of the Almighty giveth them understanding."

* The five were, Elizabeth Hooton, Joane Brocksoppe, Mary Mallins, Katharine Chattam, and John Burstow.

† New England Judged, p. 336.

The day drew near on which it was determined to enact on the person of Wenlock Christison, another of the dreadful scenes on Boston Common. But whilst the infatuated rulers of the colony were thus pursuing their barbarous career, not only had the news of their cruelties reached the shores of Old England, but an echo of the indignation excited there was now heard in Massachusetts. The fall of the Puritan government in the mother country, and the accession of Charles II. were circumstances which the bigoted governors of the province heard about this time with much anxiety. They were conscious that, independently of their Quaker persecutions, they had violated the laws of the realm, and had assumed powers which the charter did not confer upon them. The sympathy existing between the Puritans of New England and the government at home had, during the times of the Protectorate, quieted any feelings of uneasiness and calmed all apprehension. But the case was now changed. The royalists were again in power, and instead of having in the British government, powerful partisans of their cause, they had to deal with authorities who watched them with a jealous eye, and from whom they could expect at least no favour. They, therefore, naturally felt that their situation was a critical one, and that no time should be lost in endeavouring to redeem their character, as good colonial subjects. The life of Wenlock Christison was saved, and not only so, but, on the day preceding that fixed for his exe- cution, an order was issued for his liberation, and for that of twenty-seven other Friends then in Boston prison.*

The fear which actuated the zealots of New England to aban- don their murderous course towards the unresisting sufferers, had the effect, not of inducing them to relinquish religious persecution altogether, but to render it less manifestly illegal. As a sub- stitute for the law of banishment on pain of death, they passed

---

* The names of most of those who were liberated on this occasion were John Chamberlain, John and Margaret Smith, Mary Trask, Judith Brown, Peter Pearson, George Wilson, John Burstow, Elizabeth Hooton, Mary Mallins, Joane Brocksoppe, Katherine Chattam, Mary Wright, Hannah Wright, Sarah Burden, Sarah Coleman and three or four of her children, Ralph Allen, William Allen and Richard Kirby.

a new one for banishment on pain of a whipping from town to town out of the province. When the officers came to open the prison doors to Wenlock Christison and his companions, they informed them that their liberation was in consequence of the passing of the new law. On hearing this Wenlock said, " What means this ?—You have deceived the people,—they thought the gallows had been your last weapon ; your magistrates said your law was a good and wholesome law, made for your peace and the safe-guard of your country. What ! are your hands now become weak ? The power of God is over you all."*

Peter Pearson and Judith Brown, two of those who were released, were, however, first whipped through Boston streets, both having been stripped to the waist, and fastened to the tail of a cart in preparation for the inhuman punishment. These Friends were strangers in the colony, and the cause of their being thus singled out for the application of the whip, we presume, was that they had been previously banished.

That the new enactment might appear to have the authority of English law, those that suffered under it were wrongly stigmatized as vagabonds. Great were the severities to which its provisions still subjected Friends, as will appear in the ensuing pages. Indeed it was not until those who had been foremost in instigating these persecutions, had been summoned by the angel of death to stand before a higher tribunal, that such inhumanities ceased in that highly professing country.

The faithful messengers of the Lord, who were thus unex-pectedly released from bondage, were concerned almost immediately on leaving the gaol, to preach to the inhabitants those truths for which they had suffered. The magistrates, already at their wits end, in fruitlessly endeavouring to arrest the spread of Quaker principles, being impatient at this fresh manifestation of devoted-ness, ordered a guard of soldiers to drive all the Friends out of their territory into the wilderness ; an order which was speedily executed. John Chamberlain an inhabitant of Boston, and George Wilson, were among those who were thus forcibly

* New England Judged, p. 341.

expelled; but, undismayed by the new law for the application of the whip, they returned at once to their homes. There they were quickly apprehended, and were sentenced to undergo a flogging through three towns and to be put out of the limits of the colony. The executioner, desirous of lending his ingenuity to increase the severity of the sentence, provided himself with a singularly constructed whip, or as it is called a " cruel instrument," with which he " miserably tore" the bodies of the two sufferers. Such was the new and barbarous character of the weapon used on this occasion, that Friends endeavoured, though unsuccessfully, to obtain it, in order to send it to England, as another proof of the malignant cruelty which actuated the rulers of Massachusetts towards the new Society.

At the conclusion of the whipping at Boston, George Wilson, in the midst of his persecutors, knelt in solemn supplication to the Most High. John Chamberlain became convinced of the principles of Friends, by witnessing the triumphant end of William Robinson and Marmaduke Stevenson. In common, however, with others in Boston, who embraced these views, it was his lot to suffer severely for his conscientious convictions. Within two years from the time of his convincement, he was not only imprisoned and banished, but subjected to cruel whippings through three towns, of Massachusetts: yet, observes a contemporary, "so far from beating him *from* the truth, it rather drove him nearer to it."* Through all his sufferings he appears to have been supported in much christian cheerfulness.

Josiah Southwick and Nicholas Phelps, who, on their banishment, in 1659, proceeded to England, together with Samuel Shattock, to obtain redress for their grievances, having been unsuccessful in their endeavours, by reason of the favouritism still shewn to the province of New England, returned to their homes about the time that the new law for whipping was passed. Nicholas Phelps, whose constitution was much weakened, died soon after. Josiah Southwick, desirous that the rulers might know that he had returned, proceeded to Boston, and appeared

* New England Judged, p. 353.

boldly before them.   He was soon placed under arrest, and after an imprisonment of nine weeks, was brought before the court of assistants in the Seventh Month, 1661.   The governor told him that he would have been tried for his life, had not their new law been passed, and then pronounced on him the sentence of whipping.   Josiah, with arms outstretched, and in a spirit which rose superior to their cruelty, said " Here is my body ; if you want a further testimony to the truth I profess, take it and tear it in pieces ; it is freely given up ; and for your sentence I matter it not.   It is no more terrifying to me, than if ye had taken a feather and blown it up in the air."   " Tongue cannot express," said he, " nor declare the goodness and love of God to his suffering people."*

The sentence was executed, as usual, with great severity, but the faithful sufferer was so divinely supported, that during its infliction he broke forth in praises to the Lord.   " They that know God to be their strength," he said, " cannot fear what man can do."   On the First-day he was whipped through Boston and Rocksbury, and the next morning at Dedham, from whence he was carried fifteen miles into the wilderness.   Disregarding, however, the threats, and unmoved by the cruel conduct of the magistrates, he immediately returned to his home at Salem, which he reached on the following morning.

While these scenes were passing in Massachusetts, the truth was steadily gaining ground in the more charitable territory of Rhode Island.   George Rofe of Halstead, in Essex, one of the earliest ministers in the Society, having travelled much in his own land, and on the continent of Europe, visited the latter colony and some parts adjacent in 1661.   Afterwards being in Barbadoes, he wrote to Richard Hubberthorne ; and as his letter contains some interesting particulars of his religious engagements in America, it is subjoined.

* New England Judged, p. 356.

From George Rofe to Richard Hubberthorne.

Barbadoes [date not discoverable.]

" Dear Brother R. H.

" The last winter, I wintered in Maryland and Virginia, in great service for the establishing of many, and bringing others into the truth ; many Friends are in those parts in whom the precious life is. From thence I sailed in a small boat, with only two Friends, to New Netherlands and so to New England, having good service among both Dutch and English ; for I was in the chief city of the Dutch and gave a good sound, but they forced me away ; so we got meetings through the islands in good service, and came in at Rhode Island, and we appointed a general meeting for all Friends in those parts, which was a very great meeting and very precious, and continued four days together, and the Lord was with his people and blessed them, and all departed in peace : there is a good seed in that people, but the enemy keeps some under through their cruel persecution, yet their honesty preserves them, and the seed will arise, as way is made for the visitation of the power of good to have free liberty amongst them. From thence I came about four months ago to this island, where the truth hath good dominion, and Friends are very precious, and grow in the feeling and sensibleness of the power of God : Fare-well, I am in great haste at present,

" Thy truly loving brother,

G Rofe

A circumstance mentioned in this letter deserves our particular notice. George Rofe refers to a General Meeting held on Rhode Island, " for all Friends in those parts." Several meetings of this character had already been convened in England. The first of which we have any account took place at Swanington in Leicestershire in 1654.* One was held at Edge Hill in the

* Sewel, p. 93.

same county in 1656 ;* another in that year at Balby in Yorkshire ;† and in 1658 a very memorable one was convened at the
house of John Crook in Bedfordshire.‡　That referred to, however, by George Rofe appears to have been the first of the kind
held on the continent of America.　Bishop alludes to this meeting and says, under date of 1661, "about this time the General
Meeting at Rhode Island was set up."§　The numbers who
attended it were so considerable that at Boston, the enemies of
the Society raised "an alarm that the Quakers were gathering
together to kill the people.‖　It is to be regretted that no further
account of this "very great meeting" has been preserved, for
doubtless, though it was probably for the most part a meeting for
worship, the transactions during the four days which it occupied,
would have presented to our notice many points of interest.

* G. Fox's Journal, vol. i. p. 383, and Life of W. Caton.
† Rules of Discipline, 3rd Edition, Introduction.
‡ Sewel, p. 172.　　　　　　　§ New England Judged, p. 351.
‖ Ibid, p. 351.

CHAPTER XIII.

THE rulers of Massachusetts, soon after the restoration of the monarchy under Charles II., sent an address to the king, expressive of their loyalty to his person and government. In this address they alluded to the fact of their having put to death some Friends at Boston, which, they were aware, excited much notice in Britain. And with a view to justify their conduct in this respect, they represented Friends of New England as a people of the most odious and audacious description. " Open blasphemers, open seducers from the glorious Trinity, the Lord's Christ, the blessed gospel, and from the holy Scriptures as the rule of life ; open enemies to the Government itself, as established in the hand of any but men of their own principles ; malignant promoters of doctrines directly tending to subvert both our Church and State."* With this strain and these

* Burrough's Works, p. 758.

epithets they sought to villify before the king the objects of their malice.

The presentation of the address was watched with considerable interest by Friends in England. Edward Burrough entered deeply into the case of his suffering brethren in America, and in order to undeceive the king, sent him " some considerations" on the address in question. " Oh King," he commences, " this my occasion to present thee with these considerations is very urgent, and of great necessity, even in the behalf of innocent blood, because of a paper presented to thee, called ' The humble petition and address of the General Court at Boston, in New England ;' in which are contained divers calumnies, unjust reproaches, palpable untruths, and malicious slanders against an innocent people. It is hard to relate the cruelties that have been committed against this people by these petitioners : they have spoiled their goods, imprisoned many of their persons, whipped them, cut off their ears, burned them, yea, banished and murdered them : and all this I aver and affirm before thee, O King, wholly unjustly and unrighteously, and without the breach of any just law of God or man ; but only for and because of *difference in judgment and practice concerning spiritual things.*"* After refuting the charges of blasphemy, &c., Edward Burrough refers to another, in which they are represented as persons of " impetuous and desperate turbulency to the State, civil and ecclesiastical." " Let it be considered," he says, " what their dangerous and desperate turbulency was to States, civil and ecclesiastical. Did ever these poor people, whom they condemned and put to shameful death, lift up a hand against them, or appear in any turbulent gesture towards them ? Were they ever found with any carnal weapon about them ? or, what was their crime, saving *that they warned sinners to repent, and the ungodly to turn from his way ?* We appeal to the God of heaven on their behalf, whom they have martyred for the name of Christ, that they had no other offence to charge upon them, saving *their conversations, doctrines, and* [religious] *practices.*

* Burrough's Works, p. 758.

It is fully believed by us, that these sufferers did not go into New England in their own cause, but in God's cause, and in the movings of his Holy Spirit, and in good conscience towards him. They did rather suffer the loss of their own lives for their obedience towards God, than to disobey him to keep the commandments of men. The blood of our brethren lieth upon the heads of the magistrates of New England. They are guilty of their cruel death ; for they put them to death, not for any evil doing between man and man, but for their obedience to God, and for good conscience sake towards him."*

Edward Burrough continues thus :—" Again, these petitioners fawn and flatter in these words—' Let not the king hear men's words ; your servants are true men, fearers of God and the king, and not given to change ; zealous of government and order. We are not seditious to the interest of Cæsar, &c.' In answer to this, many things are to be considered ; why should the petitioners seem to exhort the king not to hear men's words ? Shall the innocent be accused before him, and not heard in their lawful defence ? Must not the king hear the accused as well as the accusers, and in as much justice ? I hope God hath given him more nobility of understanding, than to receive or put in practice such admonition ; and I desire it may be far from the king ever to condemn any person or people upon the accusation of others, without full hearing of the accused, as well as their enemies, for it is justice and equity so to do, and thereby shall his judgment be the more just."† " Thus," he concludes, " these considerations are presented to the king, in vindication of that innocent people called Quakers, whom these petitioners have accused as guilty of heinous crimes, that themselves might appear innocent of the cruelty, and injustice, and shedding of the blood of just men, without cause. But let the king rightly consider of the case between us and them, and let him not hide his face from hearing the cry of innocent blood. For a further testimony of the wickedness and enormity of these petitioners, and to demonstrate how far they had proceeded contrary to the good laws and authority of England,

---

* Burrough's Works, p. 760. † Ibid, p. 762.

and contrary to their own patent, hereunto is annexed, and presented to the king, a brief of their unjust dealings towards the Quakers."*

Edw: Burrough

What effect this appeal of Edward Burrough had on the mind of Charles II. has not been stated, but there is good reason to believe that it was the means of opening the eyes of that monarch to the intolerant disposition of his subjects in Massachusetts. In the early part of 1661, George Bishop of Bristol, published his "New England Judged," a work to which we have made frequent allusion, and wherein is set forth a very circumstantial account of the sufferings of Friends in that Province. A copy of the work soon found its way to the palace. The king, evidently interested with the book, was much struck with that part of it, wherein Denison, an active persecutor, is stated to have said, in contempt of the authorities at home, to a Friend who appealed to the laws of England, against his cruel and illegal course. "This year ye will go and complain to the Parliament; and the next year they will send to see how it is; and the third year the government is changed."† The language of Denison forcibly impressed the king with the idea, that the loyalty of his subjects in that colony, was not that which they had professed towards him in their recent address. He paused in his reading, and calling his courtiers about him, directed their attention to the passage, and very significantly remarked, "Lo, these are my good subjects of New England, but I will put a stop to them."‡

Friends in England had not been unmindful of their persecuted brethren in America, throughout their sufferings, but in the apprehension that the law for banishing them on pain of death had been suspended, the anxiety before felt was considerably relieved. This was the state of feeling on the subject, until the summer of 1661, when news arrived, that another

* Burrough's Works, p. 763.   † p. 66.   ‡ Sewell, p. 272.

Friend, viz. William Leddra, had been brought to the gallows at
Boston.

On hearing the affecting intelligence, and also that others were
sentenced to suffer in like manner, Friends in England saw the
necessity of making immediate and strenuous efforts to stay the
martyring hand in Massachusetts.   Edward Burrough, who was
a courageous and powerful advocate on behalf of the persecuted
Society, determined at once to seek an interview, and to plead in
person with the king on the subject.   It was also now pretty well
known, that Charles II. looked with a suspicious eye on the professed loyalty of his New England subjects.   Puritan ascendancy
had brought his father to the scaffold, and Puritan power and
influence had long deprived him of his legitimate accession to the
throne.   The remembrance of these things, and his knowledge of
the recent unconstitutional proceedings of the colonists, in not
permitting appeals to England, according to the express condition
of their charter, were likely to produce a jealous feeling in the
mind of the king.   The application of Burrough met with a
hearty response, and the monarch readily listened to the charges
against the authorities at Boston.

On being admitted to the presence of the king, Edward Burrough informed him, " that there was a vein of innocent blood
opened in his dominions, which, if it were not stopped, would
overrun all."   His anxiety for the jeopardied lives of his
brethren was soon relieved.   The king replied decisively, " but
I will stop that vein."   " Then do it speedily," rejoined Edward
Burrough, " for we know not how many may soon be put to
death."   " As speedily as ye will," answered the king ; and
turning to his attendants he said, " call the Secretary and I will
do it presently."   The Secretary having arrived, the following
mandamus was immediately granted :—

" CHARLES R.

" Trusty and well-beloved, we greet you well, Having been
informed, that several of our subjects among you, called Quakers,
have been and are imprisoned by you, whereof some have been
executed, and others (as hath been represented unto us) are in

danger to undergo the like; we have thought fit to signify our pleasure in that behalf for the future; and do hereby require, that if there be any of those people called Quakers, amongst you, now already condemned to suffer death, or other corporal punishment; or that are imprisoned, and obnoxious to the like condemnation, you are to forbear to proceed any further therein; but that you forthwith send the said persons (whether condemned or imprisoned) over into their own kingdom of England, together with their respective crimes or offences laid to their charge; to the end such course may be taken with them here, as shall be agreeable to our laws and their demerits. And for so doing, these our letters shall be your sufficient warrant and discharge.

" Given at our Court, at Whitehall, the 9th day of September, 1661, in the 13th year of our reign.

" To our trusty and well-beloved John Endicott, Esq., and to all and every other the governor or governors of our plantations of New England, and of all the colonies thereunto belonging, that now are, or hereafter shall be; and to all and every the ministers and officers of our plantations and colonies whatsoever, within the continent of New England.

" By his Majesty's command,
" WILLIAM MORRIS."*

That much more passed between the king and Edward Burrough, on this interesting occasion cannot be doubted. The brief relation we have given, is however, all that history has handed down respecting the interview.

The mandamus having been granted, Friends were anxious for its speedy transmission to Boston. The indefatigable Burrough, fully alive to the importance of preventing any unnecessary delay in a matter wherein the lives of his friends were concerned, a day or two after sought another audience of the king. As in the former instance, the interview was readily granted. Edward Burrough having expressed his desire for dispatch in the business, the king replied that " he had no occasion at present to send a ship to New England; but if they (meaning Friends) would send

* Sewel, p. 272.

one, they might do it as soon as they could."*   The king, with a
view to facilitate the object, having thus proposed to depart from
the usual mode of conveying official despatches, Edward Burrough
was encouraged to ask him, " If he would grant his deputation,
to carry the mandamus to New England, to a Quaker."   The
king replied, " Yes, to whom you will."†   This favourable
answer led Edward Burrough to propose to the king the name of
the banished Samuel Shattock.   The proposal undoubtedly was a
bold one.   Samuel Shattock was the only remaining exile from
Massachusetts, then in England, and the penetrating mind of
Edward Burrough quickly perceived that to entrust the mandamus to an individual so circumstanced, would be a most effective
and significant mode to adopt, in the Sovereign manifesting his
indignation at the cruel and illegal transactions of his New
England subjects.   The king approved of the suggestion, and the
persecuted Shattock was forthwith authorized to proceed to New
England, as the king's messenger with the mandamus.

The attention of Friends was next directed to the most speedy
mode of conveying Samuel Shattock to Boston.   The subject
was of so urgent a character, that expense was felt to be a
secondary consideration.   An agreement was soon made with
Ralph Goldsmith, a Friend, the master of a " good ship,"
to sail " goods or no goods," in ten days for Boston, for
the sum of three hundred pounds.   The master immediately
prepared for sailing.   The voyage was a prosperous one, and
in about six weeks, the vessel anchored in Boston harbour ; the
day of their arrival being on First-day.   A ship with English
colours having entered the harbour, some of the citizens anxious
to have the letters, and also to learn the news which she might
bring from the old country, soon went on board.   It had been
previously arranged by Samuel Shattock and the master, that the
object of their coming should be kept strictly private until after
their interview with Endicott the governor.   The citizens who
came on board, were told that no letters would be delivered on
the First day.   They returned and reported that a ship-load of

Quakers had arrived, and among them the banished Shattock. The report, whilst it was calculated to produce consternation among the authorities, must also have singularly impressed the inhabitants at large.

In pursuance of the plan agreed on, none of the ship's company were permitted to land on the day of their arrival. On the following morning Samuel Shattock, bearing with him the official document, and accompanied by the Captain, went on shore. The boatmen having been ordered to return to the ship, the two Friends immediately proceeded to the residence of the governor. Here the porter desired to know their business. " Our business," they replied, "is from the king of England." And having desired him to inform his master " that they would deliver their message to none but the governor himself,"* they were forthwith ushered into his presence. Endicott observing Samuel Shattock enter with his hat on, ordered it to be taken off. Shattock now produced the mandamus and his credentials as the king's messenger. Endicott was amazed and confounded. The despised Quaker colonist, whom he had driven from his country and his home, stood before him as the representative of his Sovereign, bearing with him a crushing token of the royal anger. Endicott however did not forget the requisitions of court etiquette. The hat of the banished Quaker was ordered to be handed to him, and as a recognition of the presence of the king's deputy, he immediately took off his own. Having read the papers, and withdrawn for a short time, the governor returned and requested the two Friends to accompany him to the house of Bellingham, the deputy governor. At this place the two authorities conferred together on the new position in which the colony was placed, by virtue of the mandamus, and then briefly said to Shattock and his companion, " We shall obey his Majesty's commands."†

After these interviews, Captain Goldsmith returned to his ship, and landed the passengers, who speedily held a religious meeting with their friends of the town, to return thanksgiving to the Father of all their sure mercies, for so signal a manifestation of

* Sewel, p. 274.   † Ibid. p. 274.

his providence, in delivering them from the oppression of bigoted and cruel men.

The purport of the royal mandamus, together with the fact of a banished Quaker being sent as its official bearer, as might be imagined, greatly disconcerted the rulers of Massachusetts. The royal instructions took all power of adjudicating the case of any Friend then in prison, out of the hands of the colonial authorities. They were " to forbear to proceed any further therein," but immediately to send all under condemnation or imprisonment to England. Endicott and his fellow rulers saw that the effect of sending their Quaker prisoners to England, in the manner authorised by the mandamus, would be to furnish the king with potent witnesses against themselves. To avoid so dangerous a dilemma was therefore important. To effect this, however, but one safe course was open to them, and that was, to have no such prisoners to send ; and, acting upon this conclusion, all the Friends then in the gaol were quickly liberated by the following order.

" To WILLIAM SALTER, keeper of the prison at Boston.

" You are required, by authority and order of the General Court, to release and discharge the Quakers, who at present are in your custody. See that you do not neglect this.

" By order of the Court, ,

" EDWARD RAWSON, *Sec.*"*

" *Boston, 9th December*, 1661."

A day of reckoning for the despotic and illegal course which the zealots of New England had pursued, appeared now to be hastening upon them, and conscious of their guilt, they exerted themselves to avert the dreaded result of their misrule. Immediately on the liberation of Friends from Boston prison, they deemed it advisable to dispatch a special messenger to the king, to inform him of their ready compliance with his royal will ; and soon after to send a deputation to England to palliate their unlicensed severities, and to watch proceedings in connexion with the business. The parties chosen for this unenviable

* Sewel, p. 274.

task were, Norton, a minister of Boston, who had been conspicuous in promoting these cruelties, and Simon Broadstreet, a persecuting magistrate. The deputies having arrived in England, proceeded to London, where, remarks Sewel, " they endeavoured to clear themselves as much as possible, but especially priest Norton, who bowed no less reverently before the archbishop, than before the king."*

During the stay of Norton and Broadstreet in London, Friends had several interviews with them, on the object of their mission. It was notorious that they had themselves been deeply concerned in the New England barbarities ; Norton, however, fearing the consequence of admitting the fact, denied all participation in the extreme proceedings at Boston. This departure from truthfulness failed to protect him, for John Copeland, who had had an ear cut off, happening to be in London at the time, came forward and confronted his statement. Broadstreet, less equivocating, did not deny that he was one of the magistrates who had given his voice for the execution of Friends, and openly attempted to justify his conduct.

George Fox being present at one of these interviews, remonstrated strongly with them on their horrible proceedings, and asked them whether they would acknowledge themselves to be subject to the laws of England. Broadstreet replied, " They were subjects to the laws of England, and they had put his friends to death by the same law as the Jesuits were put to death in England."

George Fox. " Do ye believe that those Friends whom ye have put to death were Jesuits, or jesuitically inclined ?"

Deputies. " No."

George Fox. " Then you have murdered them, for since ye put them to death by the law that Jesuits are put to death here, and yet confess they were no Jesuits ; it plainly appears ye have put them to death in your own wills, without any law."

Broadstreet finding himself and his companion ensnared by their own words, asked, if he came " to catch them ?"

George Fox. " Ye have caught yourselves, and may be justly

* Sewel, p. 279.

questioned for your lives ;" and added that if the father of
William Robinson were in town, it was probable he would question
them, and bring their lives into jeopardy.*

The deputies alarmed at their perilous situation, began,
says George Fox, " to excuse themselves, saying ' there was no
persecution now amongst them ;' but, the next morning we
had letters from New England, giving us account that our
friends were persecuted afresh.   Thereupon we went to them
again, and showed them our letters, which put them both to
silence and to shame."†

Norton and Broadstreet thus confronted, were perplexed and
in great fear lest they should be indicted for murder.   Broadstreet
became particularly uneasy, because he had openly confessed himself a party to the executions, though subsequently he attempted
to dispute it.   Some of the old Royalists, who had no sympathy
with Puritan dissent, earnestly endeavoured to prevail upon
Friends to commence a prosecution ; but George Fox and his
friends declined, saying, that " They left them to the Lord, to
whom vengeance belongeth, and he would repay."‡

The father of William Robinson who was not a Friend, being
unwilling to let the murder of his son pass so quietly by, proceeded to London§ with a view to institute an inquiry and to
interrogate the deputies respecting his death.   Norton and
Broadstreet, dreading the consequences of his investigation, and
feeling there was no safety for their lives whilst in England,
prudently determined to return home, and thus a meeting between
them and Robinson was avoided.‖

This mission to England was a complete failure.   The colonists,
indeed, were so sensible of this, that the two deputies on their
return to Massachusetts, met with a cool reception.   " Whether,"

* Journal of George Fox, Leeds Ed. vol. i. 549 ; and Sewel's History,
p. 280.

† Ibid, vol. i. p. 549.   ‡ Sewel, p. 280.

§ By an observation in a letter written by Alexander Parker about
this time, there is reason to believe that William Robinson's father lived
in Cumberland.

‖ See Coddington's Demonstration, p. 8.

remarks the historian Neal," they flattered the Court too much, or promised more for their country than they ought, is uncertain; but when Norton came home, his friends were shy of him, and some of the people told him to his face that he had laid the foundation of the ruin of their liberties; which struck him to the heart, and brought him into such a melancholy habit of body, as hastened his death."

Before we pass on to other subjects, it may be well to notice the attempts which have been made, to explain and justify the cruelties exercised by the Pilgrim Fathers to the Society of Friends in New England. The attempted vindications, from that time down to the present day, have greatly misrepresented the motives and the conduct of the early Friends in that country, and charges have been preferred against them wholly unfounded. It was natural to expect that the Puritan writers would endeavour, to the utmost, to defend the character of their brethren from the stigma which their persecuting policy had so justly fixed upon them, and thus we find Cotton Mather, the favourite historian of New England, reiterating the charges of " heresy," " blasphemy," " undermining civil government," &c., which the colonial authorities made to Charles II. " I appeal," says this partial writer, " to all the reasonable part of mankind, whether the infant colony of New England, had not cause to guard themselves against these dangerous villains."[*] The strictures which Edward Burrough presented to the king, on the charges in question, and to which allusion has already been made, render it unnecessary for us to expose their injustice. Mather, however, notwithstanding his extreme partiality on the subject, was conscious that his co-religionists had violated the laws of humanity and justice, a feeling which the following language plainly exhibits. " A great clamour," he observes, " hath been raised against New England, for their persecution of the Quakers; and if any man will appear in the vindication of it, let him do as he please; for my part I will not."[†]

* Cotton Mather's Magnalia Christi.   Book 7. Chap. 4.
† Ibid.   Book 7. Chap. 4.

But it is not so much to the early apologists of the New England persecutors, as to the mis-statements of their modern defenders, that we wish more particularly to direct our remarks. It was asserted a few years since in the *North American Review*, that Mary Fisher and Anne Austin were banished from Boston, for interrupting ministers in their places of worship. The same assertion was made in a discourse lately delivered in Philadelphia, on the anniversary of the landing of the Pilgrim Fathers, with the additional statement that they went naked into the place of worship. The truth, however, is, that Mary Fisher and Anne Austin, before they had set foot on American ground, were arrested in the vessel in which they came, and taken directly to Boston gaol, where they remained until banished by the colonial authorities. So far, therefore, from going at all into the public religious assemblies of the town, as has been represented, the only building which they entered in New England was the place of their incarceration. The parties who made these unfounded statements did not probably know them to be false ; but charges of this grave description, asserted without proper authority against innocent persons, for the purpose of vindicating the conduct of their persecutors, betray not only a culpable ignorance of the real facts, but also too eager a disposition to excuse wrong or justify oppression at the expense of truth.

Other recent publications characterise our early sufferers in that land, as " turbulent spirits, who disturbed the worship, and outraged the decent customs of the pious pilgrims ;"* as a sect " not rising up on the soil of New England and claiming simply the right of separate worship ;" but as " invaders, who came from Old England, for the sole and declared purpose of disturbance and revolution ;" whose principles " struck at all order and of society itself." They are represented as " outraging peace and order; openly cursing and reviling," the magistrates and ministers, and the worship of the " Fathers," and interrupting the sermon " with outcries of contradiction and cursing ;" " outraging natural

* Vide *The Knickerbocker,* an American periodical of Sixth Month, 1843.

decency itself," by "one of their women preachers," going unclothed through the streets of Salem, and "in other instances
coming in the same plight into the public religious assemblies."*

The authors of this language, in their admiration of the
general character of the Pilgrims of Massachusetts, and their
descendants, and in the desire to extenuate, if not to justify, their
cruel conduct towards Friends, have not only accepted as undeni-
ably true, the refuted aspersions of the persecutors themselves,
but have so blended these with erroneous statements of their own,
and with transactions of a later period, as to give their readers
the impression, that the Friends who were executed at Boston,
were wild ungovernable fanatics. We may well exclaim with an
early writer on this subject, "What will not envy misrepresent?"†

The assertion that the Early Friends in New England were a
sect "not rising up on its soil," but "coming as invaders from
Old England, for the *sole* and *declared* purpose of disturbance
and revolution," is as wide a departure from truth, as it is calum-
nious in its character. Of the four who were executed at Boston,
two it is true were from Old England, another came from Barbadoes; but the fourth, Mary Dyer, was one of the early settlers
in the province. Almost the first indeed, who suffered under the
law of banishment on pain of death, were inhabitants of Salem,
and that too for "claiming simply the right of separate worship."
No one conversant with the early history of New England, can be
ignorant that a large amount of the sufferings of Friends in that
province, was for merely absenting themselves from the authorized worship. Neal, partial as he was, admits that "several
persons and families" were entirely ruined by the excessive fines
and imprisonments imposed on this account.‡ The magistrate, in
his eager pursuit after the victims of his bigotry, no longer recognised the ancient principle of English law, that every man's house
is his asylum and castle. The sanctuary of home was violently

---

* Vide *Thirteen Historical Discourses on the completion of the two
hundred years, from the beginning of the first church in New Haven*, by
Leonard Bacon. New Haven, printed, 1839.

† Whiting's answer to Mather, p. 78.

‡ Neale's History of New England, vol. i. p. 304.

invaded by the authorities, to drag to church the lukewarm and disaffected.* Had some of the modern writers on these excesses, sufficiently borne in mind what were the views of the Pilgrims of Massachusetts on the subject of religious toleration, they would probably have felt less anxious to darken the characters of the early Friends, in order to shew that they merited their severities. " It is said," remarked a clergyman of Ipswich in Massachusetts, in 1645, " that men ought to have liberty of conscience, and that it is persecution to debar them of it. I can rather stand amazed than reply to this. It is an astonishment, that the brains of a man should be parboiled in such impious ignorance."† President Oakes said in 1673, that he looked " upon toleration as the first born of all abominations."‡ To the prevalence of sentiments such as these, among the rulers and ecclesiastics of New England, and the practical application of them by the State, and not from any misconduct of our Friends, may be traced the cause of all their sufferings in that land ; a view which we find thus ably expressed in one of the recent publications of the Historical Society of Pennsylvania. " We contemplate with horror the fires of Smith-field; the dungeons and auto da fes of the Inquisition; the massacre of St. Bartholomew, and the penalties of the Star Chamber. But the unpitying and remorseless sentence of Endicott the governor, who, on one occasion, told his prisoner, ' renounce your religion or die,' and the sanguinary denunciations of the General Court, fill us with equal dismay. That they who had preached such purity of life and conduct to mankind ; that they who had been exposed to the terrors of persecution and fled from it ; that they, forgetful of their own precepts, and the lessons of their own sad experience, should pursue to banishment and death, almost every species of nonconformity ; displays to us recesses in the human mind, which point to a dark and unexplored labyrinth in its devious and impenetrable depths."§

* Felt's Annals, p. 257.
† Ward in Belknap.
‡ Belknap's History of New Hampshire, vol. i. p. 71.
§ Vide Discourse on the Colonial History of the Eastern and some of the Southern States, vol. iv. part 2.

Much that is untrue has been written of Friends for venturing into the public places of worship in Massachusetts. They are said on these occasions, to have " thrust themselves into worshipping assemblies, and interrupted the worship or the sermon, with outcries of contradiction and cursing."*   In New England, as in Old England, some of our early ministers believed it required of them to enter the public places of worship, but in no one instance do we find, as has been alleged, that they interrupted the minister in his sermon.   The few occasions on which they presented themselves before the congregations in New England, they did not attempt to address the assembly until the minister had concluded ; and then they were stopped, violently assailed and dragged to prison.   Excepting Marmaduke Stevenson, however, the four Friends who were put to death at Boston, do not appear to have apprehended that this service was required of them ; the plea, therefore, of disturbing religious assemblies does not apply in the most extreme cases of Puritan cruelty.   These suffered martyrdom for the mere profession and promulgation of their religious views.

It has been adduced as evidence of the grave misconduct of the early Friends in New England, and as palliating circumstances for the severities to which they were subjected, that natural decency was outraged by two women Friends going unclothed, one into the public place of worship in a small town, and the other through the streets of Salem. On investigation, however, it will be found that these extraordinary circumstances will not avail the apologists of the Fathers.   When Deborah Wilson and Lydia Wardell went partially unclothed, in the manner described, a particular explanation of which will appear in the following chapter, it was not until nine years after the commencement of the New England cruelties of Friends, and four years after the last case of martyrdom, and when the persecution had very much subsided.   This is a fact which the modern defenders of the Pilgrims have omitted to state, and by the absence of which, their readers are led to believe, that it was in consequence of these and other acts of misconduct, that the

* L. Bacon's Thirteen Discourses.

rulers of Massachusetts adopted their extreme measures towards Friends.

In justification of the policy of the Pilgrim Fathers, it has been alleged that the motive which led them to emigrate to Massachusetts, was in order that they might enjoy their religion to the exclusion of all others, and that to guard it from danger, defensive laws became needful. If this was their original design, they practised a deception on the parent state. Not only had they no warrant in their charters for such conduct, but their professions before obtaining them were opposed to such intentions. The miserable plea of necessity was but a plea for the adoption of ecclesiastical tyranny.; a principle which, if admitted, at once justifies the Popish atrocities of Queen Mary's reign, and the Star Chamber and High Commission Court of her Protestant successors. The Jews and Roman Pagans, because their religion was in danger, persecuted the early Christians. On the same principle, the Roman Catholic Church persecuted the Protestants, and the Protestants the Puritans. If we excuse the heartless legislation of New England on this ground, we admit the plea in defence of cruelty and despotism from time immemorial.

Again, it has been said, that the political policy of the age was one of religious intolerance. This apology, however, is not a strictly true one. The Puritans in England, and the Huguenots in France, we know, tasted the bitter fruits of a dominant hierarchy ; but in Holland, religious liberty was fully recognized by the State, and, indeed, the Puritans themselves lived there in perfect freedom. The same may be said of the dominions of the enlightened Gustavus of Sweden. Lord Baltimore, in the settlement of Maryland, pursued no restrictive legislation ; and Roger Williams, in the settlement of Providence, and William Coddington and his Antinomian brethren, in founding the colony of Rhode Island, also adopted an universal toleration as the basis of their system. A few years later, the same liberal policy was recognized in the colonies of New York, Carolina, the Jerseys, and Pennsylvania. The colonial policy of New England, in the unrelenting treatment of dissidents to the religion of the Fathers, and the persecuting power of the church in its connection with the State, fearfully invaded the rights of the subject, and which, in fact, were better secured in Britain during the times of Laud, than in New England in the days of Endicott.   The severities endured by the Puritans in England were " lenient and indulgent, in comparison of the sufferings which they inflicted on those they termed heretics."*   " In your heart," says Isaac Pennington, " ye have mistaken and dealt more injuriously with others, than ye yourselves were ever dealt with."†

* Vide European Settlements in America, vol. ii. p. 144.
† Works, Ed. 1681, p. 223.

CHAPTER XIV.

THE fear which had prompted the rulers at Boston to release Friends from prison on receiving the mandamus of their sovereign, and which also induced them to send Norton and Broadstreet to England, soon began to subside, when they saw that no further act followed, expressive of the king's displeasure towards them. The danger to which the colonial charter had been exposed by these zealots, and the critical situation of the lives of some of them, for abetting the executions on Boston Common, did not teach them a lasting lesson of wise forbearance, or convince them of the error of their cruel legislation. The narrow bigotry, that had already urged them to expatriate every sect that dared to dissent from their own religious opinions, was not corrected by these circumstances. It is true, that after the restoration of the monarchy, they no longer banished settlers on account of their faith, or executed persons for professing the doctrines of Friends. Prudential motives alone dictated the policy of discontinuing these excesses. But the authorities of Massachusetts adhered with extraordinary tenacity to their exclusive system, in their zealous support of which, as our narrative will shew, they acted with great cruelty.

The first who suffered under the revival of persecution in New England in 1662, were Mary Tomkins, Alice Ambrose and Ann Coleman, three Friends from England who had come on a gospel mission to that country. We first meet with Mary Tomkins and Alice Ambrose on their way to Dover, a town on the river Piscattaway in the northern part of Massachusetts, in company with Edward Wharton and George Preston of Salem. At Dover none had yet been convinced of our principles, and the four ministers took up their quarters at an inn. Soon after their arrival they were visited by many persons, who desired to know on what foundation Friends rested their faith and hope of salvation. With these inquirers they " had a good opportunity," and " some of them confessed to the truth."* The priest of Dover, being much disturbed by the preaching of the strangers among his people, accused them of " denying magistrates, ministers, the churches of Christ, and the three persons in the Trinity." These allegations were first replied to by Mary Tomkins, who after some dispute with the priest, said, " Take notice, people, this man falsely accuseth us ; for godly magistrates, and the ministers of Christ, we own, and the churches of Christ we own, and that there are three that bear record in heaven, which three are the Father, Word, and Spirit, that we own." The priest then entered on a dispute with George Preston ; but failing to maintain his argument, he became much excited, and " in a rage" left the company. The doctrines of the gospel were then unfolded to the people " in demonstration of the Spirit and of power ;" a great and good meeting was held, and many were convinced of the truth.†

* New England Judged, p. 361.   † Ibid, p. 363.

From Dover the four Friends travelled into the province of Maine, where Major Shapley, a magistrate, who is described as " an inquiring man after truth," invited them to his house. Being desirous of promoting the cause of religion, he had for some time employed a priest to officiate at meetings which were held under his own roof, and with the same desire, he suggested that the priest and Friends should have some discussion. The priest, however, who was not so inclined, precluded an opportunity for it by going to a distant part. A meeting was soon held with the inhabitants, to whom the truth was declared. Major Shapley and his wife were convinced, and not only ceased to employ the priest, but permitted the meetings of Friends to be held in their house. The four gospel messengers after labouring in the province of Maine, where it is said, " they had very good service for the truth," proceeded to the western parts of New England.*

In the Tenth Month, 1662, Alice Ambrose and Mary Tomkins, visited in the love of the gospel, the individuals newly convinced on the Piscattaway, in which service they were joined by Ann Coleman. The success that attended the gospel labours of Friends on the former visit, had greatly disconcerted the priest of Dover ; and on the occasion of the visit of these three ministers, he instigated the authorities to persecute them. They were accordingly apprehended and taken before a magistrate. This functionary, as a prelude to the sentence he was about to impose, told them of the law that had been passed for whipping Friends out of the Colony. Mary Tomkins replied, " So there was a law that Daniel should not pray to his God." " Yes," rejoined the magistrate, " and Daniel suffered, and so shall you." The following warrant, drawn up by the priest, who acted as the magistrate's clerk on the occasion, was then issued.

" To the Constables of Dover, Hampton, Salisbury, Newbury, Rowley, Ipswich, Wenham, Lynn, Boston, Roxbury, Dedham, and until these vagabond Quakers are carried out of this jurisdiction.

" You and every of you are required, in the king's majesty's

* New England Judged, p. 364.

name, to take these vagabond Quakers, Ann Coleman, Mary Tomkins, and Alice Ambrose, and make them fast to the cart's tail, and driving the cart through your several towns, to whip them on their backs, not exceeding ten stripes a-piece on each of them, in each town, and so convey them from constable to constable, till they come out of this jurisdiction, as you will answer it at your peril : and this shall be your warrant.

" Per me,

" RICHARD WALDEN."

" *At Dover, dated Dec. 22nd,* 1662."

An order thus to expose and torture three innocent women through eleven towns, extending over a distance of nearly eighty miles, under the inclemencies of a wintry season, was little, if any thing short of an order to persecute them to death. The cruel sentence was inflicted upon them at Dover, and the priest, to whom the revolting scene seems to have been attractive, " laughed," as he watched the lacerating effects of the knotted scourge on the naked bodies of his victims. The unfeeling conduct of this ecclesiastic called forth a reproof from two of the spectators ; but the magistrates, urged on by him, ordered them both to be placed in the stocks for this manifestation of sympathy. From Dover the sufferers were conveyed to Hampton, and from thence to Salisbury, at which places the lash was severely applied. In this season of extremity, the persecuted Friends were remarkably sustained by the Divine Arm, and the comforting presence of their Lord was so abundantly vouchsafed, " that they sang in the midst of their sufferings, to the astonishment of their enemies."*

The condition of the prisoners as they passed through Salisbury, fastened with ropes to the cart's tail with their " torn bodies and weary steps," excited the commiseration of the spectators ; and one of the inhabitants, after persuading the constable to pass the prisoners and the warrant into his hands as deputy, immediately gave them their liberty. The three Friends, being still impressed with the belief that it was required of them to return to Dover and its

* New England Judged, p. 367.

vicinity, on leaving Salisbury proceeded to the hospitable residence of their friend Major Shapley. Near his house they had
a meeting, to which the minister of the place came. At the
conclusion, hoping to confound the Friends before the people, he
stood up and said, " Good women, ye have spoken well, and
prayed well ; pray what is your rule." " The Spirit of God,"
they replied, " is our rule, and it ought to be thine, and all men's
to walk by."* Except that he denied the Spirit to be his guide,
the priest, it appears, was not inclined to proceed further in the
discussion.

Leaving Maine, the three gospel labourers returned to Dover.
On the First-day of the week they assembled with their friends
of this place for the solemn duty of worship, during which two
constables entered ; and whilst Alice Ambrose was engaged in
prayer, they violently seized her, and in the most inhuman
manner, dragged her through deep snow and over "stumps and
trees for the distance of one mile."† Mary Tomkins was also
taken and subjected to the same barbarous treatment. On the
following morning, the constables, at the instigation of a "ruling
Elder," informed the two Friends and Ann Coleman, that they
should take them to the mouth of the harbour, where they should
" put them in and so do with them that they should no more
be troubled with them."‡ Their lives being thus atrociously
threatened, the Friends objected to go to the harbour ; the constables, however, impetuous in their wicked work, immediately
seized Mary Tomkins, and dragged her on her back with such
violence over the snow and stumps of trees, that she frequently
fainted. Alice Ambrose shared no better ; having been brought
to the river, she was forcibly immersed to the imminent peril of
her life. Ann Coleman was also unmercifully treated, so as
greatly to endanger her life. The constables, whilst thus pursuing their abominable work, and encouraged it would appear by
the approving presence of the Puritan " Elder," were providentially stopped from persisting in their wicked career, by the
sudden rising of a " great tempest," which drove them to seek

* Sewel, p. 325.   † New England Judged, p. 371.
‡ Ibid, p. 371.

refuge in the house where their victims had been placed on the previous night. The three Friends were also taken back to the house, and at midnight, thrust forth to find such shelter as the woods might afford during the rigours of a wintry season. The preservation indeed, of the lives of these devoted women under such accumulated sufferings, must be attributed to a higher power than that of man.

Continuing their gospel labours in the northern parts of Massachusetts, Mary Tomkins and Alice Ambrose felt called, on a First-day, to go to the public place of worship at Hampton ; at the instance of the minister, however, they were not allowed to remain ; but they, nevertheless, found an opportunity to " declare the truth among the people." The enunciation of views differing from those of the ruling church " much tormented," some of the strict and formal professors of this town, more particularly a persecuting magistrate, who caused Mary Tomkins to be beaten, and Alice Ambrose to be placed in the stocks. Feeling that they had accomplished the service required of them in New England, the two Friends left it, and proceeded on a visit to other parts of America.

It has been already noticed that in the summer of 1661, Elizabeth Hooton and Joane Brocksoppe, two ministers from England, were prisoners at Boston, and that on their liberation they were forthwith driven from the colony into the wilderness ; through which, " amidst many dangers," they travelled until they arrived at Rhode Island. From this colony they went on a visit to the West Indies ; but believing that it was required of them to revisit New England, and testify against the spirit of persecution, they soon after returned to Boston. The authorities, however, being bent on their expulsion, caused them to be arrested and conveyed back to the ship in which they came. In this they returned to Virginia, and soon after to their native land.*

---

* The following letter, written by Joane Brocksoppe to Margaret Fell, after her first banishment from Boston, is still preserved among the Swarthmore MSS. Joane Brocksoppe was from Derbyshire in England.

" *Barbadoes, this 9th of the Sixth Month,* 1661.

" M. F.,

" Dear in the unchangeable love and life of my heavenly Father, do I

Elizabeth Hooton had not been long at home, before the duty of returning to New England, more particularly to Massachusetts, revived with increased weight and clearness. In making a third attempt to visit this persecuting colony, she deemed it advisable, in order to prevent banishment, to obtain if possible, a license from the king to settle in any of the colonies of Britain, and " to buy a house for herself to live in, Friends to meet in, and ground to bury their dead in."* She was in very sufficient circumstances, and the king, on being informed of her repeated expulsions from Massachusetts, readily granted the license. Thus authorized, she set sail in a ship bound for Boston, accompanied by her daughter Elizabeth. The captain of the vessel was not ignorant that those who should land Friends in that colony were liable to a heavy fine ; but as his passenger was fortified with a royal permission, he felt secure against such an imposition. On their arrival at Boston, the authorities attempted to enforce a fine

dearly salute thee, who, in his everlasting love, hath called me to bear his testimony for his Name's sake, in which love and life I embrace thee, and have oft been refreshed in the remembrance of thee. Dear heart pray for me, that I may be kept in it for evermore ; and as thou hast freedom and opportunity, remember my love to George Fox and R. W. ; and my dear love is to all thy children, who am one of the least.

" Dear heart, I shall not make mention much of passages, because I expect other Friends have given large information; only this, by order of the Court at Boston, I and twenty-seven more Friends were set out of prison and driven out from constable to constable, till we were out of their jurisdiction. I am not yet clear of that country, but do expect to return thither again in some short time. I came at land here on this island, about a week since, where I found dear A. C. [Ann Cleaton] with Josiah Cole, whose dear love is remembered to thee. Several other Friends I found here also, by whom I was much refreshed, so fare thee well.

" Thy dear,

Joane Brooksopp

" Elizabeth Hooton my companion dearly salutes thee."

* New England Judged, p. 411.

of one hundred pounds upon the captain, and they were only deterred from seizing his goods for the amount by the license in question.

Desirous of speedily accomplishing the object for which she came, Elizabeth Hooton made efforts to obtain a dwelling for herself and for the entertainment of her friends. The rulers, who had hitherto expelled every English Quaker preacher that had ventured within their limits, resolved that Elizabeth Hooton should not settle amongst them ; and, in contempt of the royal order, peremptorily refused to recognise her right to purchase land in the territory. After repeated but ineffectual solicitations to the authorities at Boston on this subject, she proceeded on her gospel mission to the northern parts of Massachusetts, in the course of which she was subjected to much cruel suffering. At Hampton she was imprisoned for testifying against the rapacity of a priest in seizing the goods of a Friend. At Dover, during very cold weather, she was placed in the stocks, and imprisoned for four days. Passing through Cambridge on her return, she felt called to exhort the inhabitants to repentance, an act of dedication for which she suffered still greater severities. At the instance of the magistracy, she was arrested, and for two days and two nights confined in a " noisome dungeon," without food, and without any thing to lie down or even to sit upon. It may be difficult to estimate the actual amount of physical hardship endured by one under such painful circumstances, but it will be readily imagined, that with the damp floor of a pestilential dungeon as the only resting-place of an aged female for forty-eight hours, in cold weather and without sustenance, her sufferings must have been exceedingly great. Whilst in this distressed condition, a Friend, touched with sympathy for her, brought her a little milk ; but for this act of Christian kindness, the authorities of Cambridge arbitrarily fined him five pounds, and committed him to prison. On the third day of her imprisonment, Elizabeth Hooton being brought before the Court, was sentenced to be whipped through three towns and expelled the colony. The sentence was executed with great rigour ; at Cambridge she was tied to the whipping-post, and received ten lashes ; at Watertown she was beaten with ten strokes from willow rods ; and at Dedham ten lashes more " laid on with exceeding cruelty at a cart's tail." Miserably torn and bruised by these severities, the aged sufferer was now placed on horseback and carried into the wilderness, where she was left towards night in a defenceless condition to the inclemencies of winter.   According to all human probability, her life would be sacrificed under such aggravated circumstances, and this, it seems, her inhuman persecutors had in view ; they hoped as they said, on leaving her in the forest wild, never to see her more.   Their wicked design was, however, frustrated.   She was remarkably cared for by her divine Master, and through " dismal deserts," and " deep waters," she was favoured at length to reach the town of Rehoboth, from whence she proceeded to her friends on Rhode Island, praising and magnifying Him who had so signally supported her under these grievous cruelties, and who had counted her worthy to suffer for his great Name.

Elizabeth Hooton, on her banishment from Cambridge, had not been permitted to take away her clothes and some other articles; after staying, therefore, on Rhode Island, until she was '' refreshed," she returned, in company with her daughter, to claim her property.   Having obtained her object, and being on the way back to Rhode Island, with her daughter, and with Sarah Coleman an aged Friend of Scituate who happened to meet them in the woods, she was arrested and taken again to Cambridge, where they were all three immediately imprisoned.   The autho-rities, in unison with their previous conduct, ordered the pri-soners to be whipped in three towns, and to be sent out of their jurisdiction ; on the following morning, therefore, they received the usual number of ten stripes at Cambridge, and the same number in each of two other towns lying in the direction of Rhode Island.

Notwithstanding the cruelties to which Elizabeth Hooton had thus been repeatedly exposed, for entering Massachusetts, when she believed it was required of her by her Divine Master, she did not hesitate again to visit that colony.   Before the close of the year in which she had been twice so cruelly expelled from its limits, she proceeded a third time to Boston, to preach, as it is

expressed, " repentance to the people ;" but her message was
received with scorn, and her warnings were unheeded. Here, as
at Cambridge, she was committed to prison, and received the usual
sentence of " vagabond Quakers." Pursuant to the cruel order,
she suffered at the whipping-post in Boston, and at the cart's tail
in the towns of Roxbury and Dedham, and was afterwards during
the night, in her lacerated state, carried into the wilderness ;
she was however, enabled, though with great difficulty, to reach
Rhode Island on the following day. Soon again she was impressed with the belief that it was required of her to return to
Boston, and without " conferring with flesh and blood" this persecuted minister of Christ was faithful to the divine call. This
act of dedication, however, was again followed with severe suffering. She was whipped from the prison in Boston, " to the end
of the town," and afterwards in other towns and out of the jurisdiction ; the threat being added, that " if ever she came thither
again, they would either put her to death, or brand her on the
shoulder."*

It does not appear how long Elizabeth Hooton remained in
New England on the occasion of this visit; the grievous sufferings, however, to which she had been subjected, did not cause her
to shrink from again visiting that land, when religious duty called
her. At the time of Endicott's death, in the First Month, 1665,
we find her again at Boston ; and as she was imprisoned for
attending the funeral of this notorious bigot, the probability is
that she attempted to exhort the company against persecution,
and to call their attention to the judgment of the Most High
upon the deceased, as evinced in the miserable condition in which
he died.† Twice afterwards she was imprisoned at Boston, once

* Besse, vol. ii. p. 231.

† " He was visited," says Besse, " with a filthy and loathsome disease,
so that he stunk alive, and died with rottenness." It is a remarkable
fact that many of those who were foremost in the persecution of Friends
in New England, were either suddenly cut off, or ended their days
miserably. Bellingham died distracted—Adderton, it has already been
stated was thrown from his horse and died instantly—Norton, minister
of Boston died suddenly, his last words being " the hand" or " judg-

at Braintree, and once at Salem ; at the latter place her horse
was also taken away, which obliged her, in order to get to Rhode
Island, to travel seventy miles on foot. Through all her trials
and afflictions in this country, she was greatly comforted with the
presence of her Saviour, in the precious enjoyment of which, she
felt willing to endure much more for his sake, and for that of her
fellow-creatures. " Yea," she observed, " the love that I bear
to the souls of men, makes me willing to undergo whatsoever can
be inflicted on me."*

ELIZABETH HOOTON.

As we shall not have occasion, in this division of the work, to
refer again to Elizabeth Hooton, and as some brief sketch of her
life will be expected, it may be suitably given in this place. She
was born, it appears, at Nottingham, about the year 1600. Respecting her early life, but very few particulars can be collected.
She was married to Samuel Hooton, of Skegby, in Nottinghamshire, who occupied a respectable position in society.

In 1647, she formed one of a company of serious persons, who
occasionally met together ; and at this date George Fox mentions
her as being " a very tender woman."† For three years subsequently, little is known of her life ; " the meetings and discourses," however, that she had with George Fox, appear to have

ment of the Lord is upon me."—Danfort, Captain of the Castle, was
struck dead by lightning.—Webb, who led Mary Dyer to execution,
was drowned.—Captain Johnson who led William Leddra to execution,
became insane.—Dalton, a persecutor of Hampton, was killed by the
falling of a tree—Marshall Brown of Ipswich, another persecutor, died
" in great horror of mind."—Norris, minister of Salem, whilst vindicating in his pulpit the cruelties towards Friends, was struck dumb,
and died soon after. " Many other particular persons," says Besse, " who
had been noted instruments in carrying on the work of persecution,
were afterwards observed to fall under several calamitous disasters and
casualties, which were esteemed by those who knew them as tokens of
the Divine displeasure manifested against them, by reason of the particular share of guilt which their personal concern in shedding innocent
blood had brought upon them."—*Besse's Sufferings*, vol. ii. p. 270.

* New England Judged, p. 420.   † G. Fox's Journal, vol. i. p. 90.

been the means of convincing her of the spiritual views of Friends. Sewel says that in 1650, " from a true experience of the Lord's work in man, she felt herself moved publicly to preach the way of salvation to others."* George Fox had hitherto been the only one who publicly preached our doctrines ; she was, therefore, not only the first of her sex, but the second individual who appeared in this character in our religious Society. The preaching of women at this period was not considered singular. Several were known to be thus engaged among the various religious sects then in England. Elizabeth Hooton had not long followed her Lord in this high vocation, before her sincerity and faithfulness were tested by persecution. In 1651, she was imprisoned at Derby for reproving a priest ; in the following year, while travelling in Yorkshire, she was apprehended at Rotherham for addressing the congregation at the close of public worship, and taken to York Castle, where, with her friend Mary Fisher, she was confined for sixteen months. In 1654, whilst on a gospel mission in Lincolnshire, she was imprisoned for five months at Beckingham, " for declaring the truth in the place of public worship." In the following year, she suffered three months imprisonment in the same county, " for exhorting the people to repentance." In the course of her early travels in the work of the ministry, she was also subjected to other kinds of suffering.

The extreme cruelties to which Friends in New England had been exposed, excited deep sympathy among their fellow-members at home : in this feeling, Elizabeth Hooton largely participated ; and, though conscious that suffering was almost sure to await her, she left her home in 1661, under an apprehension of a religious call to this persecuting province. This transatlantic visit, and another which quickly followed it, occupied her for several years.

As a gospel minister, she appears to have stood high in the estimation of her friends ; and although far advanced in age, when George Fox visited the West India islands and America in 1671, she was among those who accompanied him in this

* Sewel's History, p. 35.

capacity. They proceeded first to Barbadoes ; and after labouring there in word and doctrine, they sailed for Jamaica, where they arrived in the Eleventh Month. About a week after they landed on this island, Elizabeth Hooton was suddenly taken ill, and on the following day she died, being then about seventy years of age, having been a minister twenty-one years. In allusion to her death, George Fox makes this brief remark :— " She departed in peace, like a lamb, bearing testimony to truth at her departure."* Her call from time to eternity was sudden ; but, like the wise virgins in the parable, she was prepared, when the midnight cry was heard, to meet the Bridegroom at his coming, with her lamp trimmed and her light burning ; and is now, without doubt, participating in the full fruition of everlasting joy.

Annexed is a fac-simile of her signature :

Elizabeth: Hooton

Another of those who, in 1661, were driven from Boston into the wilds of New England, was Katherine Chattam, of London. Soon after her arrival at Boston, she submitted, under a deep sense of religious duty, to the humiliating exposure of going among the people clothed in sackcloth, as a sign of the indignation of the Lord against the highly professing and cruel oppressors of that place. An imprisonment in the city gaol followed this act of dedication ; and at the time of her banishment, referred to in a previous chapter, she was also cruelly whipped at Dedham. These sufferings, however, did not deter her from again visiting Massachusetts ; and in the following year she proceeded a second time to Boston, to plead with its intolerant rulers. On this occasion, she was again arrested and imprisoned " for a long time ; her life being greatly endangered by the hardships to which she was subjected during the winter season. She was afterwards married to John Chamberlain, a Friend of Boston, who has already been mentioned as a sufferer for the truth, and thus she became a settled inhabitant of that persecuting city.

* G. Fox's Journal, vol. ii. p. 154.

Some of the travels and sufferings of Ann Coleman in New England, during the year 1662, have already been noticed. Early in the following year, she was engaged in the work of her divine Master, on Rhode Island, together with Joseph Nicholson, John Liddal, and Jane Millard, all of whom had recently come from England. In the summer of 1663, they believed it required of them to go on a gospel mission to the northern and eastern parts of New England. Passing northward, they visited Salem, where, at the instance of Hathorn, a persecuting magistrate, they were arrested ; and, together with Thomas Newhouse, another gospel messenger to those parts, sentenced to be whipped as vagabonds in three towns, and expelled from the jurisdiction. The sentence was executed with such severity, and the thongs of the whip so lacerated the body of Ann Coleman, that for some time it was feared she would not survive the barbarous treatment.*

* A short time previous to her leaving Rhode Island on this visit, Ann Coleman addressed the following letter to George Fox :—

ANN COLEMAN TO GEORGE FOX.

" DEAR GEORGE FOX,

" Dear friend, the love of the Lord constraineth me to write to thee ; Oh, the love of the Lord, who hath kept his handmaid that put her trust in Him. Dear George, if I should write all the cruelty that hath been acted to me, it would be much ; five times I have been a prisoner ; in their towns I have been whipped, beside stonings, and kickings, and stockings ; but oh the power of the Lord which hath supported me. Dear George, good is the Lord, whose presence is with me ; for this I can truly say, my life is over the enemies who rise up against the lambs of my Father's fold, who taketh them in His arms : Oh what shall I say unto thee of the love of my Father. And now I have seen the travail of my soul, and dwell in peace, and none can make me afraid : glory, glory unto the Lord saith my soul. Much service for the Lord in this land, and it hath not been in vain, and so my dear friend, let thy prayers be unto the Lord for me. Dear Jane Millard is in New England ; Friends are much refreshed in her, and we both are bound in spirit to the East of New England, where there is a people newly raised ; much service for the Lord I have had amongst them ; it is in my heart to visit them. Jane Millard's dear love is to thee. Joseph Nicholson and John Liddal are at Rhode Island, where we have had some meetings

Subsequently these Friends proceeded to Dover. Here Joseph Nicholson was exposed to some cruel abuse, whilst his four companions were imprisoned for two weeks. They next journeyed to Hampton, where they were violently assaulted. Whilst at a meeting with their friends, "the constables with a rude company," actually destroyed a part of the building in which they were met, and then took them to prison.

Thomas Newhouse, on leaving this part of Massachusetts, went southward. At Boston, he attended the public place of worship, and on attempting to address the assembly, he was immediately taken before the magistrates, who sentenced him to be whipped there, at Roxbury and at Dedham, and then to be carried into the wilderness. Not feeling at liberty to leave this colony, after the infliction of this severity, he proceeded to Medfield, which at that time was one of the most inland towns of the province. He entered this place on a First-day, and finding it difficult to obtain a meeting with the inhabitants, he endeavoured to address them on their coming out of their meeting-house. In this attempt he received from some of the company "several sore blows;" he was also placed in the stocks at Medfield, and on the following day was whipped both there and at Dedham, and again driven into the wilds of the interior. While confined in the stocks, the interest excited caused the people to visit him, and he had, he observes, "good service for the Lord."*

The four other Friends, soon after their visit to Massachusetts, left New England for Barbadoes, from which place Joseph Nicholson addressed the following letter to George Fox, "The young man," who he says, "came with him from England," was doubtless

which have much refreshed us. Elizabeth Hooton is here, and their dear love is to thee. It is pretty well with Friends here. Dear friend, in that life and love that is unchangeable art thou near me. I cannot but say again, pray for me. I should be much refreshed to hear from thee, and so I rest thy dear friend and sister in the truth.

"ANN COLEMAN."

"*Rhode Island, this 6th day of the*
    Fifth Month, 1663."

* New England Judged, p. 471.

John Liddal, and the "little maid that came out of Kent," was Ann Coleman :—

JOSEPH NICHOLSON TO GEORGE FOX.

"Barbadoes, the 10th day of the last Month, 1663.

"G. F.,

" Dearly and well-beloved in the Lord, my love is to thee. I should be glad to hear from thee if it might be. I received a letter from thee in New England, written to Christopher Holder and me, wherein I was refreshed. I wrote to thee from Virginia about the last First Month, and since then I have been in New England about eight months. I passed through most parts of the English inhabitants, and also the Dutch. I sounded the mighty day of the Lord which is coming upon them, through most towns, and also was at many of their public worship houses. I was prisoner one night amongst the Dutch, at New Amsterdam ; I have been prisoner several times at Boston, but it was not long, but [I was] whipt away. I have received eighty stripes at Boston, and some other of the towns ; their cruelty was very great towards me, and others ; but over all we were carried with courage and boldness ; thanks be to God ! We gave our backs to the smiter, and walked after the cart with boldness, and were glad in our hearts in their greatest rage. Here is a young man that came with me from England ; he hath been with me for the most part ; since which we have had several meetings where never any were before, and many people were made to confess to the truth ; but the wicked rulers still keep the people much under by their cruelty. We had good service up and down amongst them while we stayed. I came to this island about twenty days ago from Rhode Island, and the young man with me ; and Jane Millard, and a little maid that came out of Kent, came with us ; they also suffered in New England, and did very good service indeed. The little maid hath thoughts to go to Nevis ; their dear love is to thee, and the young man's also. The power of God hath accompanied us all along ; to His name be the praise for evermore, who hath kept us faithful in all our trials. We hope thou will not forget us, and so I rest thy friend."

Joseph Nicholson

It has been stated that Mary Tomkins and Alice Ambrose on leaving New England in 1662, proceeded on a visit to Maryland and Virginia. Early in 1664, they both returned to Boston, when Mary Tomkins was taken so dangerously ill, that it was doubtful whether she would survive the attack. Her illness having become known to Friends of Salem, Edward Wharton and Wenlock Christison went to see her. While the sick stranger was lying in this critical state, two constables, who had watched the Salem Friends to her lodgings, entered the house, and in a most brutal manner took her and her companions before Endicott. The shock was so great to the invalid, that on her way to the house of the governor, she fell down in an apparently lifeless condition ; but so hardened had the constables become in pursuing the reckless work of persecution, that instead of conveying Mary Tomkins to her lodgings, they waited until she had a little revived, and then hurried her before the Court. Endicott evinced, on this occasion, that his malice towards Friends had in no degree abated ; and he actually sentenced the almost dying Friend and her companions, to be whipped in three towns and banished. The sentence, however, was regarded as such an outrage on humanity, and so great a fear was entertained that the sick woman would not survive its infliction, that at the intercession of Colonel Temple, it was not enforced, except on Edward Wharton.

Another gospel labourer who visited New England about this period was Ann Richardson, formerly Ann Burden, who had been banished from Boston with Mary Dyer in 1657. In the Tenth Month, 1663, we find her addressing George Fox from "Kittery Eastward in New England."* Subsequently she appears to have laboured in Maine and the northern parts of Massachusetts for several months, and for a time, to have been joined in her religious service by Elizabeth Hooton and Jane Nicholson. Early in 1665, she was engaged on Rhode Island.

John Tysoe, a tradesman of London, prepared soon after to leave his home on a gospel errand to Massachusetts. He arrived in Boston harbour early in 1667. Bellingham, who had succeeded Endicott as governor, hearing that a Quaker preacher had

* Swarthmore, MSS., vol. iii.

arrived from England, forthwith dispatched a constable to arrest him, and before John Tysoe had an opportunity of landing, he was seized and brought before the authorities. The governor, after venting his displeasure, questioned him as to his object in coming, and the intended duration of his visit. John Tysoe replied, that he "did not know how long he should stay, or whither he should go;" but that he "stood in the will of the Lord." After some conversation, introduced by Bellingham, on the subject of freedom from sin, which was disputed by Mather, a priest of Boston, but sustained by John Tysoe, they committed him to prison, and also fined the captain of the ship in which he came £100, unless he removed his passenger from their jurisdiction on "the first opportunity." In the Fourth Month, 1667, whilst in Boston prison, he wrote a remonstrance to the governor on their persecuting conduct. The address was couched in language of much Christian boldness. "Oh ye wretched men," he says, "God will plead with you! Was ever the flock of Christ Jesus found in your practices? Did ever the lambs kill wolves?" Alluding to their restrictive laws, he says, "and it seems in prison I must lie, till by your law I am forced to another land; but unto your cruel laws herein I dare not bow; for I may come again to this town, and honest men, who fear the Lord, may live here when your laws are vanished as smoke. In vain do ye strive, ye mortal men, the fruit of your doings will fall on your own heads, a weight too heavy for you to bear."* How long John Tysoe's imprisonment lasted does not appear. At this period he was in the 42nd year of his age. He died in 1700, aged 74, having been a minister for more than forty years. He suffered many imprisonments for his religion, one of these lasted nearly three years, and he was one of the Friends who, under sentence of banishment, were placed on board the vessel at Gravesend, in 1665, for transportation to Jamaica.

Respecting the lives of several of the gospel ministers mentioned in this chapter, but little information has been obtained. MARY TOMKINS and ALICE AMBROSE, before they crossed the Atlantic, appear to have been companions in the work of the ministry. It is recorded that in 1660 they were both imprisoned

---

* A Glass for the People of New England, by S. G., p. 35, 39.

at Lancaster for reproving a priest. JOHN LIDDAL, it is believed,
was of Cumberland. Whilst travelling in Lancashire, in 1665,
he was much abused on account of his religious profession.
JOANE BROCKSOPPE, was the wife of Thomas Brocksoppe, of
Little Normanton, in Derbyshire ; she died in 1680. ANN
COLEMAN, soon after her visit to New England, went on a visit to
Bermuda, where, writes George Fox, "she died in the truth."
Of JANE MILLARD, KATHERINE CHATTAM, and JOHN BURSTOW,
we have no particulars further than what have been related in the
previous pages. PETER PEARSON was of Greysouthen, in Cumberland ; his death is recorded to have taken place in 1713.
MARY MALLINS was of Bandon Bridge, in Ireland, and in 1656,
she was imprisoned for preaching in the steeple house at that
place. GEORGE PRESTON appears to have been a resident of
York, where in 1659 he was much abused by the soldiery whilst
attempting to enter a meeting of Friends, and in the following
year he was committed to Ousebridge prison in that city for
refusing to swear. His decease took place in 1666, and he was
interred in Friends' burial-ground at York. JOSEPH NICHOLSON
was of Cumberland. He professed with Friends as early as 1653,
in which year George Fox, whilst on a visit to that county, was
entertained at his house. From this period, to the time of his
first visit to New England in 1659, no incidents of his religious
course have been met with. In 1660 he returned to England,
but in 1663 he proceeded on a second gospel mission to America,
which occupied him for several years. After his return from
this visit, he removed to Settle, in Yorkshire, and as late as
1704 we find him a member of that meeting. No record of
his death has been found ; he must, however, at this period have
been considerably advanced in years. JANE NICHOLSON, his wife,
died at Settle, in 1712.

Having thus far noticed the travels and sufferings of Friends
from Great Britain, we now proceed to relate some further hardships, which were endured by those who were residents in New
England. Edward Wharton, after receiving the sentence of
banishment at Boston, in 1661, returned quietly to his home at
Salem, from whence he addressed the rulers at Boston, informing
them of his continuance in the colony, and remonstrating with

them for their wickedness in attempting his exile.* In the following year he travelled on a gospel mission with George Preston, Mary Tomkins, and Alice Ambrose, to Dover and the province of Maine, some particulars of which have been given in the early part of this chapter. From this locality Edward Wharton proceeded to Rhode Island. How long he remained within the limits of this colony does not appear, but on leaving it he went to the adjacent town of Taunton. No Friends resided in this place, and he took up his quarters at an inn. The puritan minister having heard of his arrival, and fearing lest his hearers should imbibe the " Quaker heresy," evinced no little anxiety for the departure of Edward Wharton, and a deacon was immediately sent to him to request it. " Friend," said Edward Wharton, " what hast thou to lay to my charge ? Whose ox have I stolen? or whose ass have I taken away ? or whom have I wronged ? And as for my being in town, I purpose to stay here until I have accomplished my business wherefore I came." The message being unheeded, a constable was next sent, with the threat that unless it was attended to he should be whipped out of the colony, in conformity with their law. " As for thy law," replied Edward Wharton, " thou mayst execute it if thou wilt, but thou hadst best take heed what thou dost ; for the king hath lately sent over to the rulers in New England a charge that they inflict no more sufferings upon such as I am."† When the constable came to Edward Wharton he was " engaged" with the people, but his answer having quieted the official, he was left to proceed without interruption.

Leaving Taunton, Edward Wharton felt a religious call to visit the settlers in the most northern parts of New England, whom some self-righteous professors regarded as " outcasts " from church and state. Having passed through several towns and " escaped the danger of being apprehended," he reached Saco in the district of Maine. The people received him kindly, and he proceeded on the coast as far north as Casco Bay. The " outcasts" of this region were not insensible to the touches of Divine love, and they heard the ministry of the exiled Friend " with gladness." There

* New England Judged, p. 342.   † Ibid, 395.

were "tender people" among them, who wept at parting when they understood that, at the risk of his life, Edward Wharton intended to return to Boston. Turning southward, he visited the settlers at Black Point, and on Cape Porpoise, and at Wells ; from thence proceeding by way of the river Piscattaway, Greenland, and Hampton, to his home at Salem.

In 1663 or soon after, he was engaged in gospel service with some English Friends in the vicinity of Newbury. In the Fifth Month he again visited Piscattaway, and on hearing of the cruel treatment which some of his friends had received from the magistrates at Dover, he was " pressed in spirit " to go and remonstrate with them. His language to these authorities was that of warning ; it was however not only unheeded but even resented. They immediately had him placed in the stocks, and issued a warrant to scourge him in the three towns of Dover, Hampton, and Newbury.

As usual, the sentence was executed with much severity ; but under it, Edward Wharton was preserved in patience and resignation, and rejoiced " that he was counted worthy to suffer for righteousness sake." Soon after being thus forcibly brought to Salem, he was again subjected to the cruelties of the lash, for " testifying " against the barbarous usage which some Friends of that town had received. Early in 1664 he went to Rhode Island on secular business, and, whilst there, met with George Preston, and with Wenlock Christison his fellow-townsman, who had just returned from a gospel visit to Virginia. These Friends believed it required of them to proceed to Boston, a service in which Edward Wharton felt it right to join. On reaching this place, they held a meeting with their brethren, " wherein," says G. Bishop, " their hearts were made glad by the living power and presence of God,—and their souls rejoiced in His salvation." The intolerant Rawson, on hearing of their arrival and of the meeting referred to, proceeded thither. At the time he entered, Edward Wharton was preaching, and many of the citizens, anxious to hear him, had collected about the house. Rawson was much disturbed on witnessing the assemblage, and was not sparing in his threats and epithets of anger to those who composed it. With a view to suppress these meetings, he immediately issued the following order :—

"To the Constable of Boston.

"You are hereby required, in his Majesty's name, forthwith to repair to Edward Wanton's house, where a stranger, and a Quaker, with several others there, the said stranger publicly amongst many, endeavouring to seduce his Majesty's good subjects and people to his cursed opinions, by his preaching amongst them : you are to carry the said strangers before the honoured Governor, to be proceeded with as the law directs, and return the names of such as are their hearers.

"Edward Rawson, *Commissioner.*"
Dated at Boston, the 4th of May, 1664.

The " stranger" referred to in the warrant was Edward Wharton, who was soon apprehended and sentenced to the degrading severity of the lash, as a vagabond, through Boston and Lynn, and then to be taken to his home at Salem. The authorities of Boston were evidently very anxious to prevent Edward Wharton from visiting their city, and hoping to effect their object by a show of lenity, they told him that, " if he would promise the governor to come no more to the Quaker's meeting at Boston," they would forego the execution of the sentence and liberate him. But these persecuting zealots had mistaken the character of their prisoner ; " Not for all the world," was his unflinching reply ; " I have a back to lend to the smiter, and I have felt your cruel whippings, and the Lord hath made me able to bear them, and as I abide in his fear, I need not fear what you shall be suffered to do unto me." " But surely," he continued, " The Lord will visit you for the blood of the innocent, and your day is coming, as it is coming upon many, who but as yesterday were higher in power than ever you were, or are likely to be, but now are made the lowest of many, and truly my soul laments for you."* In pur-

* New England Judged, p. 438.

suance of the cruel order, on the day following he was whipped
through Boston for nearly a mile, and passed on to Lynn.   At
this place, the constable, who knew that the prisoner was an
inhabitant of Salem, and that the order was, therefore, an illegal
one, refused to recognise it, and set him at liberty.   At the conclusion of his punishment at Boston, his persecutors told him,
that every time he entered their city, he should be subjected to a
similar treatment.   The threat, however, was unavailing; Edward
Wharton with his wonted courage replied, "I think I shall be
here again to-morrow;" an intimation which was realised.   He
knew that the rulers, in treating him as a vagabond, had acted
illegally; and with Christian boldness he determined to assert
his rights.   His undaunted conduct proved more than a match
for the intention of his persecutors; and when, on this occasion,
he appeared openly before them, they hesitated to commit him.
Observing this, Edward Wharton asked them, "How it could be
that he should be a vagrant yesterday and not to-day."   His
Christian firmness had been blessed with success, and in peace he
returned to his home at Salem.   In the course of the following
year he again visited Boston, where he met with several English
Friends.   An order for their arrest was quickly issued, and
Edward Wharton, for the alleged offence of standing in the Court
with his hat on, whilst Bellingham was at prayer, was sentenced
to receive fifteen lashes, and to be imprisoned for one month.*

Among the sufferings of Friends of New England, the case
of Eliakim and Lydia Wardel, of Hampton, deserves particular
notice.   On one occasion, Eliakim Wardel had a horse worth
fourteen pounds taken from him, for merely receiving the
banished Wenlock Christison into his house.   He was also
frequently fined for absenting himself from the Puritan worship;
and to satisfy these unjust demands, nearly the whole of his
property was carried off.   The case of Lydia, his wife, was a
very peculiar one.   Having become convinced of the principles
of Friends, and consequently ceasing to attend the Puritan
worship, she was several times requested to attend the congre-

* New England Judged, p. 461.

gation, and give a reason for the change of her opinion and practice. She at last went, but under circumstances which were extraordinary and humiliating. She had been deeply impressed with the want of true religion among many of the high professors and rulers of New England, and with their unblushing violation of the plainest doctrines of Christ in the persecution of Friends ; but more especially with the immodest and revolting manner in which females had been publicly stripped and scourged. Although stated to have been a " chaste and tender woman," and of " exemplary modesty," she believed it required of her to appear similarly unclothed* in the congregation at Newbury, as a token of the miserable state of their spiritual condition, and as a testimony against the frequent practice of publicly whipping females in the manner referred to. It was to be expected that the appearance of Lydia Wardel under such circumstances, would be resented by those for whom the sign was intended. She was immediately arrested, and hurried before the authorities of the neighbouring town of Ipswich, where she was barbarously scourged ; her husband was also severely whipped for countenancing this apprehended act of duty on the part of his wife. The transaction appears to have taken place in the year 1665.†

About the same time, Deborah Wilson, who is described as " a young woman of a very modest and retired life, and sober conversation,"‡ under an impression of religious duty, went in a similar state through the streets of Salem, as a sign against the " cruelty and immodesty" of the authorities, " in stripping and whipping" females. The punishment to which Lydia Wardel had been exposed was soon inflicted on Deborah Wilson.

The sufferings of Friends of Hampton and Salem, for absenting themselves from the Puritan worship, were very severe about this time. John Hussey and his wife, of Hampton, were grievously plundered of their property for fines on this account.

* Vide " A New-England Fire-brand Quenched," by G. Fox and J. Burnyeat, p. 224.

† Besse's Sufferings, vol. ii. p. 235.

‡ New England Judged, p. 583.

John Small, of Salem, had his best yoke of oxen taken from him during the ploughing season, when he most required them Samuel Shattock was fined five pounds. John Kitching had his horse taken from him under circumstances which were peculiarly aggravating. Philip Verrin, for expressing his abhorrence of the martyrdom of his friends at Boston, underwent a cruel scourging. Several other Friends in the colony of Massachusetts, also received great severity from the hands of its persecuting zealots.

Wenlock Christison, of Salem, before spoken of, was still a sufferer for the cause of truth about this period. On visiting Boston in the early part of 1664, he was apprehended, with some other Friends, and brought before the Court. Bellingham, who then presided, told him that he should be whipped under their law against vagabonds. After proving to the Court that he was not a vagabond, he said to them—" At this bar, time was, that sentence of death was passed upon me ; yet, by the help of God, I continue unto this day, standing over the heads of you all, bearing a faithful witness for the truth of the living God. Some of your associates are gone, and the Lord hath laid their glory in the dust, and yours is a fading flower."* He was soon committed to prison, and on the following day was sentenced to be whipped with ten stripes in each of the towns of Boston, Roxbury, and Dedham, and then to be expelled from the colony. Conscious that they were violating the laws of the realm, he appealed against their decision ; but his request was unheeded. " If thou hadst been hanged," said one of the magistrates, " it had been well." " You had not power," he rejoined, " to take away my life, but my blood is upon you, for you murdered me in your hearts." Pursuant to the order, he was whipped in the towns named, and with some others, driven into the wilderness of the interior ; " but," writes a contemporary, " the Lord was with them, and the Angel of his presence saved them, who had none in Heaven beside God, nor in the earth in comparison of Him."†

It was now about ten years since Friends first landed in

* New England Judged, p. 458.   † Ibid, p. 459.

Massachusetts, and during nearly the whole of that period they had been exposed to a cruel and relentless persecution. The authors and abettors were urged on in their ungodly career by feelings of extreme sectarian bigotry, by the powerful influence of which sect after sect had been suppressed. Not only the Episcopalians, but Roger Williams and his party, as well as the Antinomians and the Baptists, had severally suffered themselves to be driven as exiles from the country. The anti-christian legislation of the ruling sect had triumphed over all opposition, and it was not until it joined issue with Quakerism, that it had to contend with principles more potent than its own. On the Society of Friends devolved the noble work of contending successfully against the exclusive principle of sectarian legislation in New England, and of ecclesiastical tyranny in North America. The struggle truly was a severe one—more severe doubtless than we in this day can rightly estimate. We may point to the memorial which is furnished by the scenes exhibited on Boston Common, and talk of the sufferings of William Brend and his companions; —of the revolting barbarities practised towards unoffending females;—of whippings, of banishments, and of ruinous distraints; but the aggregate sufferings of Friends in New England, in their faithful and unflinching support of the truth, is known only to Him who seeth and knoweth all things. With ancient Israel, they could feelingly say, "If it had not been the Lord, who was on our side, when men rose up against us, then had they swallowed us up quick, when their wrath was kindled against us: then the waters had overwhelmed us, the stream had gone over our soul.—Blessed be the Lord, who hath not given us a prey to their teeth."

For this faithful stand no praise is due to man; it belongs alone to Him, whose work we reverently believe it was; and who, in the wise economy of his divine purposes, qualifies and strengthens his devoted servants for every emergency and every trial. Those of our early Friends who were foremost in this fearful conflict were, under the divine anointing, given clearly to see, that on the passing of the law for exiling on pain of death, nothing short of the sacrifice of some of their lives would be called for, to break down the barrier which the self-righteous professors of New England, in their determination to enforce their own sectarian views on the community, had raised against the progress of true religion.   William Robinson, before ever he entered Massachusetts, was impressed with this belief.   " The word of the Lord," he says, " came expressly unto me and commanded me to pass to the town of Boston *my life to lay down.*"   " To which heavenly voice," he continues, " I presently yielded obedience, not questioning the Lord, who filled me with living strength and power from his heavenly presence, which at that time did mightily overshadow me : and my life said Amen to what the Lord required of me."*   The feeling under which William Robinson went to Boston, also pervaded the minds of his fellow-martyrs.   When the reprieve came for Mary Dyer, just in time to save her life, she told the authorities, that " unless they would annul their wicked law, she was there willing to suffer as her brethren had."   They were strengthened with might in the inner man, thus willingly to surrender their lives, and He who called them to the sacrifice also upheld their brethren under other suffering.   Thus, Wenlock Christison and Edward Wharton, were enabled to display a degree of christian courage and firmness that was altogether extraordinary.   Conscious of the truthfulness and righteousness of their cause, and upheld by the Spirit of their God, they wearied out injustice and cruelty.   The religious constancy of Friends confounded and subdued the priests and rulers of Massachusetts, and not only led to the spread of those spiritual views which distinguished them from others of the christian name, but also materially assisted in the emancipation of North America from the miseries of priestly tyranny and oppression.

The relation of acts of intolerance and oppression exercised by one section of the christian name towards another, must ever be felt a humiliating task to the right-minded historian and could he consistently do so, he would gladly consign to merited oblivion, transactions so much at variance with true religion.   But, when, in pursuance of his work, he has to detail instances of cruelty and

* New England Judged, p. 95.

injustice by a people so enlightened, and in many respects too, a people so much in advance of most of their day, as were the Puritans of New England, the task is rendered additionally painful. In recording the persecution of Friends in New England, we wish to impress on the mind of the reader, a circumstance which, in perusing the foregoing pages, has probably attracted his notice ; that to the rulers and ecclesiastics, and not to the people at large, belongs the disgrace of these antichristian proceedings. In support of this view it may be further remarked, that throughout the sufferings of Friends in New England, there is scarcely a single instance on record, in which the public evinced a spirit of persecution. Had this disposition been manifested by the people, and had the truths which Friends proclaimed been rejected by them with indignation and contempt, the ministers of Massachusetts would have nothing to fear from the presence of Quakers. But it was because in New England, as in Old England, many who were piously disposed, were willing to hearken to their gospel declarations, and because they laboured to turn the attention of the people from outward teachers, and a dependence upon man in the things of God, to Christ their inward teacher, and to the efficacy of his free grace, that the ecclesiastics of that day resorted to persecution to maintain their unholy dominion amongst men.

The ultimate prevalence of religious toleration in the western world, through the constancy and faithfulness of Friends, is a subject calculated to furnish much profitable reflection. Had they given way to fear, and shrunk from suffering, it is impossible to say to what extent religious freedom might have been checked in its emancipation from the trammels of ecclesiastical rule. The doctrines and practice of our early Friends were, however, such only as the New Testament recognizes ; and these, it may be fearlessly asserted, when made the rule of our conduct, will ever lead us to condemn all interference with the inalienable rights of conscience.

CHAPTER XV.

In commencing another chapter, it is with feelings of satisfaction that we are enabled to turn the attention of the reader, from scenes of persecution, to events connected with religion, under a civil and political condition of society more consistent with the laws of truth and righteousness.

The rigid professors of Massachusetts having, in the progress of their restrictive legislation, excluded Episcopalians, as well as Friends, from their territory, received from the throne four years after the restoration of Charles II., an emphatic injunction, " To permit such as desire it to use the Book of Common Prayer, without incurring any penalty, reproach, or disadvantage; it being very scandalous," continues the admonition, " that any person should be debarred the exercise of their religion, according to the laws and customs of England, by those who were indulged with the liberty of being of what profession or religion they pleased."*
About a year after, a similar monition was addressed to the

* Hutchinson's Hist. of Massachusetts, vol. i. p. 219.

government of Connecticut that, " All persons of civil lives might freely enjoy the liberty of their consciences, and the worship of God in that way which they think best."*

By these and other concurrent circumstances, religious persecution in New England received at length an effectual check, and henceforward there will be but few instances to record, wherein the liberties of the subject were outraged, or the rights of conscience invaded. Not but that heart-burnings existed for a time, but by degrees, the clouds that had long obscured the religious horizon of this province were gradually dispelled, and its thrifty and energetic population began to enjoy in mutual confidence and goodwill, the sunshine of religious freedom. An eloquent writer, referring to the causes by which the fury of sectarian bigotry was thus stayed, remarks, " Charles was restored—Endicott died, and when the sun seemed to be turning into darkness and the moon into blood, the wheels of the car of destiny appeared suddenly to roll backward, and a glimmer of humanity began to dawn."†

The first individual who appears to have visited Massachusetts under the new and more favourable state of things was John Taylor, who had travelled in New England about seven years previously. He arrived at Boston, on this occasion, in the Third Month, 1666. The vessel in which he came was bound for Barbadoes, but being short of provisions the captain put in at this port for fresh supplies. He stayed three weeks at Boston, and during that period, Ann Coleman and others also arrived there. From thence, John Taylor sailed to Rhode Island, where he remarks, " Friends received me very kindly." Here he remained for about six months, " having good service for the Lord, and in the country thereabouts."‡

The next gospel minister who is recorded to have visited New England, was John Burnyeat of Cumberland. He reached Rhode Island early in 1666 ; and, after " a comfortable service" among Friends of that island, he travelled to Sandwich in the adjacent colony of Plymouth. From thence he proceeded by way of

* Massachusetts Hist. Coll., 2nd Series, vol. viii. p. 76.
† Vide " The Churchman, vol. v. p. 857. May 2nd, 1835."
‡ Journal of J. Taylor, p. 29.

Duxbury, Marshfield, and Scituate, to Boston," visiting Friends and having meetings" as he went. After going to Salem, and northward as far as Piscattaway, he returned to Plymouth and Sandwich, travelling through the woods, until he arrived at Ponigansit, from whence he crossed over to Rhode Island. Having spent "some time" in declaring the gospel message to the inhabitants of this favoured locality, he passed to Long Island. In the winter, however, he returned again to Rhode Island, where he was engaged until the First Month, 1667.

In the year 1669, we find that Joseph and Jane Nicholson were again labouring in New England in the cause of their Redeemer, and during that summer they appear to have visited Boston.*

The care of the churches in America, rested with much weight on the mind of John Burnyeat; and in 1670, he again visited that country. Proceeding by way of Barbadoes, he landed at New York, in the Second Month, 1671, and after some gospel service, he reached Rhode Island in the Fourth Month following, in time to attend the Yearly Meeting. There is good reason to believe, that the Yearly Meetings of Rhode Island had been regularly held from 1661, the year in which Bishop says, "it was set up."† No minutes of its proceedings prior to 1683, have, however, been preserved; the records for several years after its origin having been, it is supposed, destroyed by fire, by the burning of the dwelling-house where they were deposited.‡ "It begins," says John Burnyeat, "in the ninth of the Fourth Month every year; and continues for much of a week, and is a general meeting once a year for all Friends in New England.§ The first Yearly Meeting in Great Britain was in Yorkshire in the year 1658, where it was held successively for three years. "In 1661," says George Fox, "it was removed to London, where it hath been kept ever since."‖ Excepting, therefore, that of London, New

* Letter of Jos. Nicholson, 1669, in Swarthmore MSS.

† New England Judged, p. 351.

‡ Vide "Brief Account of the Meetings of Friends in New England," p. 7.

§ Journal of John Burnyeat.

‖ Letters of Early Friends, p. 313.

England Yearly Meeting is clearly the most ancient in the Society. The circumstance, that at this early period, it " continued for much of a week," shews that it was of considerable importance. It was not, indeed, a Yearly Meeting for New England only, but for " the other colonies adjacent,"* including doubtless Friends of the Half-year's Meeting of Long Island, those resident in the Jerseys, and probably as far south as Virginia and Maryland.

From Rhode Island John Burnyeat passed to Massachusetts, and held meetings at Sandwich, Duxbury, Marshfield, Scituate, and Boston, thence to Salem, Hampton, and as far north again as Piscattaway, returning by the same route to Rhode Island. Speaking of this journey, he says, "I had many precious meetings, and the Lord was with us, and his power was over all." After visiting Friends at Providence, he sailed in the Seventh Month, 1671, to the colonies in the south, accompanied by Daniel Gould.

The year 1671 was another memorable period in the history of our religious Society in the western world. We have seen that, on several occasions, many of the gospel ministers who visited that land proceeded to it in companies; it was, however, during this year, that the largest number embarked from England at one time on religious service, in that direction,—a circumstance which is rendered additionally interesting from the fact that George Fox formed one of the party, consisting altogether of thirteen Friends. It was now about twenty-eight years since George Fox had entered upon the important work, to which he had been called by the Great Head of the Church. He had within that period travelled in almost every part of England and Wales, had also visited Scotland and Ireland ; and notwithstanding the torrent of persecution which had assailed the new Society from the rulers and ecclesiastics of the land, he had seen it gradually enlarging until it had extended itself throughout the three kingdoms, in some parts of the European Continent, in the West India Islands, and in North America. The welfare of the religious community which he was the chief instrument in gathering, was peculiarly

* Journal of George Fox, vol. ii. p. 160.

dear to him everywhere ; but in no part was it more so than in the western world. Almost as soon as companies of his fellow professors were collected in this hemisphere, he endeavoured by frequent epistolary communications to encourage them in the path they had chosen, and in the faith they had embraced.

Those who accompanied George Fox on this occasion were William Edmundson, John Stubbs, Thomas Briggs, John Rous, Solomon Eccles, James Lancaster, John Cartwright, Robert Widders, George Pattison, John Hull, Elizabeth Hooton, and Elizabeth Miers, who were all well known to him, and whose faithful labours in the gospel had clearly indicated their love for the truth, and their desires for the salvation of their fellow-men. They embarked at London in the Sixth Month, 1671, for Barbadoes. From this island George Fox and several of the company passed to Jamaica, and from thence to Maryland, where they met with John Burnyeat. From this part James Lancaster and John Cartwright went by sea to New England, whilst George Fox, John Burnyeat, Robert Widders, and George Pattison proceeded thither by land, and arrived at Rhode Island in the Third Month, 1672. They were gladly received by Friends, and all of them became the welcome guests of Nicholas Easton, the governor of the colony. On the First day, following their arrival they had a large meeting, and the deputy governor and several justices who attended " were mightily affected with the truth."*

The usual time for holding the Yearly Meeting on Rhode Island was in the following week, and before that time James Lancaster and John Cartwright had arrived, and also John Stubbs, from Barbadoes. There were, therefore, at this Yearly Meeting, at least seven ministers from England, and it appears to have been a memorable occasion. Friends came to it " from most places in New England," and also from " the other colonies adjacent." The transactions were important, and are thus described by George Fox :—" This meeting lasted six days, the first four days were general public meetings for worship, to which abundance of other people came ; for they had no priest in the island, and so

* Journal of George Fox, vol. ii. p. 166.

no restriction to any particular way of worship ; and both the governor and deputy governor, with several justices of the peace, daily frequented the meetings. This so encouraged the people that they flocked in from all parts of the island. Very good service we had amongst them, and truth had a good reception. I have rarely observed people, in the state wherein they stood, hear with more attention, diligence, and affection, than generally they did, during the four days together. After these public meetings were over, the men's meeting began, which was large, precious, and weighty ; and the day following was the women's meeting, which also was large and very solemn. These two meetings being for ordering the affairs of the church, many weighty things were opened and communicated to them, by way of advice, information, and instruction in the services relating thereunto ; that all might be kept clean, sweet, and savoury amongst them. In these two meetings several men's and women's meetings for other parts were agreed and settled, to take care of the poor, and other affairs of the church ; and to see that all who profess truth walk according to the glorious gospel of God. When this great general meeting in Rhode Island was ended, it was somewhat hard for Friends to part ; for the glorious power of the Lord, which was over all, and his blessed truth and life flowing amongst them, had so knit and united them together, that they spent two days in taking leave one of another, and of the Friends of the island ; and then, being mightily filled with the presence and power of the Lord, they went away with joyful hearts to their habitations, in the several colonies where they lived."*

At the conclusion of the Yearly Meeting, George Fox and Robert Widders, remained " for some time" on Rhode Island, where, " through the great openness of the people," they had " many large and serviceable meetings."† Passing from this locality, accompanied by Nicholas Easton, the governor, they directed their course to Providence. Here they had a large and memorable meeting, which, in order to accommodate the people,

---

* Journal of George Fox, vol. ii. p. 161.　　　† Ibid.

was held in a " great barn."   " The glorious power of the Lord,"
observes George Fox, " shined over all."*   They next proceeded
to the Narragansett country, where a meeting was held at the
house of a Justice ; and notice having been previously circulated,
the settlers from the surrounding country, and even from the
adjacent colony of Connecticut, flocked together, and it " was
very large."   " Most of these," writes George Fox, " were such
as had never heard Friends before, and they were mightily
affected with the meeting."†   From hence the Friends returned
to Rhode Island,

The other European Friends were travelling, at the same time
in gospel service, in Massachusetts.   John Burnyeat, John
Cartwright, and George Pattison, on leaving Rhode Island,
took their course eastward to Sandwich, where, observes John
Burnyeat, " we had a blessed meeting, and were comforted and
richly refreshed.   The blessed presence of the Lord's holy power
was with us, and opened and enlarged our hearts."‡   They
then proceeded northward, passing through Plymouth, Duxbury,
Marshfield, and Scituate, to Boston.   The meeting at this place
is mentioned as a " blessed season," where " the truth was
cleared of those scandals which the priests and others had cast
upon it, and the people greatly satisfied."§   This meeting
appears to have made a deep impression on the minds of many
of the citizens of Boston ; and the visit of the Friends, to the
great annoyance of the priests, became the subject of general
conversation.   One of the ministers, displeased to hear his flock
speak favourably of Friends and their preaching, on the following
First-day, prostituted the sanctity of his office, and his pulpit,
in exciting the magistracy against the strangers.   His unholy
efforts were successful ; the authorities, urged on by the malicious
declarations of their minister, causing several Friends to be
arrested on the same day, while assembled for divine worship.
A few days after, John Stubbs and James Lancaster arrived
at Boston ; they were, however, immediately seized, imprisoned,

---

* Journal of George Fox, vol. ii. p. 162.   † Ibid.
‡ Journal of John Burnyeat.   § Ibid.

and summarily banished the colony. John Raunce, Thomas Eaton, and Robert Hornden, who are spoken of as "strangers," were imprisoned on this occasion ;* and about the same period Solomon Eccles, of London, and Nicholas Alexander, a justice of Jamaica, who came on a religious visit to New England, were also imprisoned and banished.† "Thus their old fruits," as John Burnyeat remarks, in reference to the priests and rulers, "were brought forth again."

From Boston, John Burnyeat and his two companions passed on to Salem and Hampton. The meeting held at the latter town was attended by many of the inhabitants, including some elders of the Puritan Church, who were very favourably impressed with what they heard on the occasion, and "gave a good report of the truth." The minister of Hampton, disturbed and "offended" at the favour which the people evinced towards Friends, assembled the heads of his church, with a view to induce them to pass a resolution "that no member, nor members' children, go to a Quakers' meeting." The illiberal feelings of the minister, however, were not responded to by his flock, and they declined to sanction his proposal. The travellers next visited Piscattaway, and had a meeting with the most influential Friends respecting the settlement of meetings for discipline for both men and women. "Friends," remarks John Burnyeat, "were very open, and all things were settled in sweet unity."

At Salem, some Friends had imbibed the notion of John Perrot, of not putting off the hat in time of prayer, under the delusive idea that it was a form to be testified against. This was cause of anxiety to John Burnyeat and his two fellow-travellers; and with a view to show the Friends of Salem the evil tendency of such opinions and practices, a meeting on the subject took place on their return. The occasion was blessed to the church of that place ; some of them saw their error, and condemned the unseemly practice. "Blessed be the Lord,"

* New England Judged, p. 489.
† Journal of John Burnyeat.

writes John Burnyeat, " who shows mercy, and restores out of
the snares of Satan."*

Having completed their religious engagements in Massachusetts, the three Friends returned to Rhode Island, where
they met with George Fox and Robert Widders, who had just
come from the Narragansett country. This was in the Sixth
Month 1672, and after they had been engaged about two months
in New England. From Rhode Island, George Fox, Robert
Widders, James Lancastar, and George Pattison, passed to
Shelter Island ; whilst John Burnyeat and John Stubbs proceeded to Providence and Warwick, returning again to Rhode
Island. On their return, they met John Cartwright, who had
parted from them at Piscattaway, to extend his journey northward into Maine.

It was at this period, that Roger Williams, of Providence,
made his proposal for a public disputation with Friends.
Williams, though one who had nobly advocated religious
liberty, was yet strongly opposed to some of the doctrinal views
of Friends ; and being very confident of the rectitude of his
own opinions, he sent a challenge to maintain fourteen propositions against Friends ; seven of which were to be argued at
Newport, and seven at Providence. At this juncture, William
Edmundson, who had been travelling in the south, arrived at
Rhode Island, and joined with his brethren in accepting the
challenge in question. The circumstance was one that excited
considerable interest among the settlers, and " a great concourse
of people of all sorts" assembled to hear the disputation. The
discussion of the seven propositions at Newport, says William
Edmundson, occupied no less than three days. " They were all
but slanders and accusations against Friends, and were turned
back upon himself." The remaining seven propositions were discussed at Providence ; and on the part of Friends, were opposed by
William Edmundson and John Stubbs alone ; John Burnyeat and
John Cartwright having left for Narragansett and Connecticut.
The disputation at Providence occupied a day ; and, as at New-

* Journal of John Burnyeat.

port, there " was a very great gathering of the people." The remaining propositions were similar in character to the former ones ; " but," observes William Edmundson, " we answered all his charges, and disproved them."* At the conclusion, he continues, " we had a seasonable opportunity to open many things to the people, appertaining to the kingdom of God, and way of eternal life and salvation. Prayer was made to Almighty God, and the people went away satisfied and loving."†

But a short time previous to this disputation, the government of Rhode Island had been placed, by the suffrages of the people, in the hands of Friends ; the governor, deputy governor, and magistrates, having been all chosen from among them.‡ This was a circumstance not at all congenial to the mind of Roger Williams. He was the founder of the plantation of Providence, and after it had been incorporated under one charter with Rhode Island, for several years he had filled the office of governor, though opposed by William Coddington and those who were now the rulers of the colony. Twenty years before, there had, indeed, been a strong rivalry between Williams and Coddington for the post of governor: the latter, in 1651, obtained from the government at home, a commission, constituting him governor of Rhode Island for life. This appointment gave great discontent to Roger Williams and to the settlers in and about Providence, and he and another were sent to England for the purpose of obtaining a repeal of Coddington's commission. After much difficulty this was effected in 1652, and in 1654, after Williams had returned, he was elected governor.§ Roger Williams was also in religious profession a very decided Baptist ; a body from among whom the Society of Friends in Rhode Island obtained many converts. This, doubtless, was another circumstance that disturbed his equanimity, and under the excitement it produced, together with the transfer of the civil power to Friends, he was led to make charges against them, which he was unable to sustain.

On leaving Providence, William Edmundson and John Stubbs,

---

* Journal of William Edmundson, 3d edit., p. 95.   † Ibid.
‡ Bancroft's United States.
§ The Early History of Rhode Island, by Romeo Elton, p. 268.

proceeded to Warwick, a few miles distant.   The meeting held there was a very large one, being attended by most of those who had been present at the disputation at Providence.   "The Lord's power and presence," observes William Edmundson, "were largely manifested, and the people were very loving—like Friends."* From this place John Stubbs went to Narragansett to join John Burnyeat, whilst William Edmundson took boat for Rhode Island.   After some meetings with Friends on this Island, he travelled eastward to Sandwich and Scituate, and from thence to Boston ; where, feeling that the service required of him in America was accomplished, he embarked in a ship bound for Ireland.

In the year 1675, William Edmundson, under the constraining influence of heavenly love, again left home on a gospel visit to his transatlantic brethren.   He sailed from Cork in a vessel bound for Barbadoes, from whence, after labouring among his friends for about five months, he was taken to Rhode Island in a yacht belonging to a Friend.   At this period New England was engaged in a disastrous war with the Indians, who, headed by their bold and ingenious king Philip, evinced their savage revenge for conceived wrongs in murderous onsets upon the settlers.   The sudden inroads of these exasperated Algonquins made it exceedingly dangerous to travel ; but William Edmundson, trusting in the unfailing succour of the Most High, pursued his gospel errand in faith.   " I travelled," he writes, " as with my life in my hand, leaving all to the Lord, who rules in heaven and earth."   After having some meetings on Rhode Island, he proceeded to Sandwich, " one Friend," he remarks, " having ventured to go with me, to guide me through the woods."†   At Sandwich, " Friends were glad of his coming."   " There was an honest tender people there, that loved the Lord and His truth."   He had two meetings with them, and, he writes, " we were well refreshed in the Lord, and one in another."‡   From this town he travelled by way of Scituate, Boston, and Salem, as far north as Piscattaway ; holding meetings at these towns and in " several other places."   His

* Journal of W. Edmundson, p. 96.   † Ibid. p. 104.
‡ Ibid, p. 105.

mode of travelling through this new country was on horseback ; on reaching Piscattaway, however, he left his horse and took boat for Dover. At this place, Nicholas Shapley, who had been convinced about fifteen years before, still resided. He continued to fill the office of a magistrate, and "was a man of note in that country."* At and near Dover there were many who had embraced the principles of Friends, and the meeting held there having been attended by settlers who "came from far to it," was not only " a precious one," but " a very large one " also. Before leaving this part, they had " a men's meeting about church affairs."

William Edmundson, on his return from Dover, hearing that some "tender people" resided at Reading, felt attracted in the love of the gospel towards them, and with some other Friends proceeded on a visit to the place. The settlers, to protect themselves against the incursions of the Indians, were living in a garrisoned house, and at the time when Friends arrived they were assembled for religious worship. William Edmundson, under an apprehension of duty, mentioned his desire to address the company. The request was readily acceded to, " And," he writes, " my heart being full of the word of life, I spoke of the mysteries of God's kingdom, in the demonstration of the spirit and power of the Lord ; so that their consciences were awakened, and the witness of God in them answered to the truth of the testimony : they were broken into tears, and when I was clear in declaration, I concluded the meeting with fervent prayer."† The settler at whose house the company were assembled, and who is described as " an ancient man," was deeply affected on the occasion. " We had heard," said he, " that Quakers denied the Scriptures, and denied Christ, who died for us : which was the cause of that great difference between their ministers and us : but he understood this day that we owned both Christ and the Scriptures ; therefore he would know the reason of the difference between their ministers and us ?" " Their ministers," replied William Edmundson, " were satisfied with the talk of Christ, and the Scriptures ; but we could not be satisfied without the sure, inward,

---

* Journal of W. Edmundson, p. 105.　　　† Ibid, p. 107.

divine knowledge of God and Christ, and the enjoyment of those comforts the Scriptures declared of, which true believers enjoyed in the primitive times."* The old man, affected to tears, replied, "that those were the things he wanted."

At Boston, and in the parts adjacent, William Edmundson had several meetings, and laboured to reclaim some, who, though professing with Friends, were lax in their practice, and brought dishonour on the truth.

From Massachusetts, he returned to Rhode Island, in a little vessel belonging to Edward Wharton. His presence there just at this period, was a source of much comfort to Friends; who, in consequence of the Indian war, were placed in circumstances of some difficulty. The government was in the hands of Friends, who had a testimony to bear against all wars and fightings, as opposed to the clear and unequivocal doctrines of Christ; consequently, they refused to join in the colonial compact of New England for a campaign against the natives. The forbearing conduct of the government was much opposed by the people at large, many of whom "were outrageous to fight."† Under these circumstances of trial, William Edmundson was enabled to strengthen his brethren; and was favoured to have "many blessed and heavenly meetings."

Leaving Rhode Island, this faithful minister proceeded westward, to the towns of New London and Hartford, in Connecticut. The rulers and ecclesiastics of this colony regarded Friends with great aversion, in consequence of which, when John Burnyeat visited it four years previously, he found it very difficult to hold meetings among the inhabitants. On the present occasion, however, the authorities were strongly disposed to evince their hatred to Quakerism in a more decided manner, and at a meeting which William Edmundson held at New London, " the constable and other officers came with armed men and forcibly broke it up." In this persecuting spirit the inhabitants generally did not participate, and when the "armed men" were "haling and abusing" Friends, " the sober people were much offended."‡ At Hartford,

* Journal of William Edmundson, p. 107.　　† Ibid, p. 108.
‡ Ibid, p. 112.

he felt it required of him to attend the places of public worship. In the first that he entered, the congregation listened quietly to his ministry, and offered no molestation. In the afternoon of the same day he attended another, where for a considerable time he was enabled "to declare the way of salvation." The doctrine preached offended the priest of this congregation, and, at his persuasion, the officers "haled him out," and took him off to the guard-house. His detention, however, was but short, and he soon proceeded to Long Island. The religious labours of William Edmundson, at Hartford, excited much enquiry among the people respecting divine things, and he was afterwards told that he "had set all the town a talking of religion."

The spirit of oppression, which in former years had been so notoriously displayed at Boston, although in great measure kept down by the Government at home, occasionally gave very decided manifestations that it was not wholly extinguished. The regular holding of a Friends' meeting there, and the visits of ministers from Britain, caused much uneasiness to the bigoted rulers of Boston, who, again outstepping the bounds of their authority, in 1675, passed a law that every person found at a Quakers' meeting should be apprehended, *ex-officio*, by the constable, by a warrant from a magistrate be committed to prison, " have the discipline of the house applied, and be kept to work on bread and water for three days ;" or otherwise should pay a fine of five pounds. It also included a provision that their old law " against the importation of Quakers," should be more rigidly enforced ; and that the penalty, which originally was £100, should in no case be mitigated to a sum less than £20.*

The first individuals, at least from Britain, against whom this law was enforced, were William and Alice Curwen, of Lancashire. Alice Curwen had for some years been under the apprehension that it would be required of her to go on a gospel mission to America, and that it would be laid upon her husband to accompany her, when he should be released from an imprisonment for tithes. They accordingly left England for Rhode Island in

---

* " Cain against Abel," by George Fox, p. 41.

1676, from whence they travelled to Boston, and northward as far as Dover. " The power of the Lord," they remark, " was with us, and was our support, for which we cannot but bless his name."* The law against Friends' meetings, although passed in the previous year, had not yet been proclaimed. Probably its bigoted promoters were half ashamed that this proof of their persecuting disposition should be publicly announced to their fellow-citizens. But the visit of the Curwens seems to have given a fresh impulse to the intolerant feelings of the rulers ; and whilst they were absent on their journey to Dover, the restrictive law was proclaimed. In returning from the north, they again visited Boston, and while assembled with their brethren for divine worship, were seized by the constabulary and taken to prison. This outbreak of violence gave rise to no little commotion in the city ; and in the excitement which prevailed, numbers flocked to the prison. " Many people," remarks Alice Curwen, " both rich and poor, came to look upon us." The circumstance was overruled to the promotion of the truth, and afforded the prisoners a favourable opportunity for declaring the things of God to the people. " The Lord was with us," she says, " our service was great, and some were convinced."† The authorities, vexed at witnessing results so opposite to their wishes, determined to revive the old practice of whipping ; and on the third day the two Friends were publicly subjected to this degrading punishment ; " but," remark the sufferers, " the presence of the Lord was manifested there also, which gave us dominion over all their cruelty, and we could not but magnify the name of the Lord, and declare his wonderful works." On the following day they were released, but, undismayed by the cruelty that had been inflicted upon them, these faithful Friends again assembled with their brethren, and after a good meeting, left them and proceeded to visit other meetings on their way to Rhode Island, from whence they sailed to the colonies in the south.

In 1677, a circumstance which caused considerable excitement took place at Boston. Margaret Brewster, a Friend of Barbadoes,

---

* A Relation of the Labours, &c., of Alice Curwen, p. 5.   † Ibid.

whilst on a gospel mission in New England, having a foresight given her of the afflictive visitation called the " black pox," believed it was required of her to enter one of the public places of worship in Boston, clothed in sackcloth and ashes, with her face blackened, as a prophetic warning of the event ; the realization of which quickly followed. This unusual manifestation greatly offended the authorities, and she was immediately apprehended, together with four others who accompanied her. On her examination she told the court, that for three years this service had been required of her by her divine Master, and that it was not until she had been visited with sickness which brought her near the gates of death, that she " could give up to bear a living testimony for the God of her life, and to go as a sign among them ;" and that " if they were suffered to take away her life, she was contented."* Whatever might be the opinion of the Puritans of Massachusetts respecting prophetic manifestations, the rulers of Boston were not prepared to recognize the service of Margaret Brewster as of divine origin. For this act of dedication, she was sentenced " to be stripped to the waist," and to receive twenty lashes.

The case of Margaret Brewster appears to have served as a pretext to the rulers of Boston for a revival of acts of cruelty ; and in forgetfulness of the claims of either justice or humanity, within a few days after she had been scourged, no less than twenty-two of her fellow-professors were subjected to the same punishment, simply for attending their own meetings for the worship of the most High.† This sudden fit of persecution, so far from promoting the object of its authors, tended greatly to augment the excitement that prevailed ; and when Friends on the following day assembled at their meeting, so many of the citizens attended, as to cause no inconsiderable degree of alarm to the bigoted ecclesiastics and rulers of the city. The news of this fresh outbreak of violence having reached London, William Penn, William Mead, and some other Friends, had interviews with the authorities

* Besse, vol. ii. p. 262.
† Letter of W. Coddington in Besse, vol. ii. p. 261.

respecting it.*   The voice of public disapprobation in the colony, was also raised against these proceedings, and from that period, the rulers of New England never resorted to the lash in their endeavours to stem the progress of Quakerism.

For the first ten or fifteen years of the Society's existence in New England, its meetings had been mostly held in the dwellings of its members, but as their numbers increased, meeting houses were built for their better accommodation, and we find that Friends of Scituate erected one as early as 1672.   The mere profession of a religious belief differing from that held by the pre-vailing sect of Massachusetts, had been sufficient in former years to draw down the resentment of the civil power, and the holding of religious meetings of the same character met with their uncom-promising opposition ; it was not, therefore, to be expected that the rulers, when they began to see other edifices than their own provided for the purposes of divine worship, should remain quiet spectators of the innovation.   Notwithstanding the progress of dissent, they had fondly hoped, that at least the only buildings in Massachusetts set apart for the worship of the most High, would be those indicated by their favourite spires ; and they were not willing to see this hope extinguished without a decided struggle.   In 1679, therefore, the general Court at Boston, with a view to meet the apprehended evil, passed a law to prevent the erection of meeting-houses without leave of the " freemen of the town" and of the county court ; and in the event of any trans-gression of the law, such houses were to be forfeited " to the use of the country."   The evil thus proscribed, is set forth in the preamble as "attempts made by some persons, to erect meeting-houses on pretence of the public worship of God on the Lord's day, thereby laying a foundation (if not for schisms and sedition, for error and heresy) for perpetuating divisions, and weakening such places where they dwell, in the comfortable support of the ministry orderly settled amongst them."   The restrictive enact-ment, however, was never enforced, but this must be ascribed to the intimations of displeasure from Whitehall, rather than to any change of sentiment on the part of the colonial authorities.

* Minutes of the Meeting for Sufferings, vol. i.

During 1678, and a few years subsequently, several Friends from Europe visited New England. Of these are mentioned John Boweter, John Haydock, Benjamin Brown, John Hayton and Joan Vokins from England, and Jacob Tilnor from Ireland. We have no particulars of the services of these Friends, excepting John Boweter and Joan Vokins. The former was of Worcestershire, and his visit took place in 1678 ; his travels extending from Rhode Island eastward to Scituate, and northward as far as Salem. Joan Vokins was of Reading in Berkshire. She arrived at Rhode Island in 1680 in time to attend the Yearly Meeting, which, she remarks, lasted four days. She had "good service" amongst her friends, and during their important deliberations, she writes that "God's eternal, heart-tendering power, was over all."[*] Accompanied by Mary Wright of Oyster Bay, she next proceeded on a visit to Boston, where she held several meetings without any interference from the magistracy. On these occasions the baptising power of the Lord appears to have been strikingly manifested, and the hearts of the people were much tendered under her ministry. She says, "There were hardly any that I saw but shed tears."[†] This dedicated servant of Christ was one who had a very low estimate of her qualifications as a gospel minister, describing herself to be " the poorest and most helpless that ever I did see concerned in such a service : but it was the more to the honour of the power of my God, that so wonderfully wrought in my poor, weak, and helpless vessel. Honoured and renowned be it for ever, saith my soul ; for its manifestation made the hearts of the people glad."[‡]

---

[*] Vokins' God's Mighty Power Magnified, p. 35.   [†] Ibid, p. 36.
[‡] Ibid, p. 36.

CHAPTER XVI.

The progress of Friends in New England—Their increase on Rhode Island, and influence with the local authorities—Friends are elected as the rulers of the colony of Rhode Island—Their adoption of the principles of peace in its government—The sentiments of the Society of Friends on war—Peace a distinguishing feature of the religion of Christ—This principle recognized during the first three centuries of the Christian era—The circumstances under which it was abandoned by professing Christendom—The principle maintained by the Cathari of Germany, Wickliffe, Erasmus, and by the Society of Friends.

FROM the time when Mary Fisher and Ann Austin first landed in New England to the concluding date of the foregoing chapter, rather more than a quarter of a century had passed away ; and during the whole of that period the principles of the Society of Friends had been gradually gaining ground in the country. Of their numbers it is difficult to speak with any degree of exactness ; five Monthly Meetings, however, appear to have been established, and there were regularly settled meetings for worship, extending over the country from Rhode Island to Maine. The population of the colonies of Plymouth, Massachusetts and Maine about 1682 did not number 40,000, and that of Rhode Island was under 6,000. The progress of the Society was steady in the eastern and northern parts of New England, but in Rhode Island it more especially flourished. Very soon after Friends visited that district, the most influential of its inhabitants embraced their doctrines, among whom may be mentioned William Coddington, Nicholas Easton, and Henry Bull, each of whom filled the office of Governor. The increase of Friends in this colony by convincements was rapid ; as early as 1666 they were sufficiently numerous and influential to cause the General Assembly to refuse the proposition of the royal commissioners for enforcing the oath of allegiance, and in the following year an engagement of even milder form was repealed to satisfy the conscientious scruples of members of the Society.

The government of Rhode Island about 1667, though considerably influenced by Friends, was not under their absolute control. In 1672, however, the governor, deputy governor, and magistrates were all chosen from among them, and the affairs of the colony came under their entire management. This circumstance was an extraordinary one, and formed not only a new era in the history of the enlightened inhabitants of that territory, but a new era also in the history of this religious Society, and indeed, it may be said, in the history of the Christian world. The principles of the Society of Friends not only struck at the foundation of all hierarchical systems, and the intervention of a human priesthood between man and his Maker in the things of eternal life, but tended also to exemplify the excellency of the primitive doctrines of Christianity in their application to the civil affairs of mankind. Since the commencement of the Christian era, nearly seventeen centuries had elapsed, but that peculiar characteristic of the Gospel which is opposed to war, had not been reduced to practice in the government of any state; the non-resisting principles of Friends, however, led to its adoption in the colony of Rhode Island through their being chosen as its rulers.

It is not intended in this history to enlarge on those religious views which distinguish Friends from others of the Christian name, but so incalculably does the subject of war affect the present and eternal well-being of man, and to such an extent has this evil been sanctioned by the professors of Christianity, producing an amount of misery and ruin which it is frightful to contemplate, that we are inclined to offer some observations on a matter which thus so largely involves the happiness of our species.

From its rise, the Society of Friends has always borne a decided testimony against war, as being altogether incompatible with the glorious dispensation of the Gospel, displayed in the conduct and precepts of Christ, and of his Apostles and immediate followers. They believe that the religion of Jesus was to be distinguished pre-eminently by the law of love and peace, and that as mankind come under His government, they will, in unison with the language of prophecy, "beat their swords into ploughshares, and their spears into pruning-hooks ; nation shall not lift up sword against nation, neither shall they learn war any more."*

Wars and fightings are emphatically the bitterest fruits of our fallen nature. They have their origin in the degenerate and unrenewed nature of man. "Come they not hence," says an Apostle, "even of your lusts which war in your members."† But Christ came to destroy the works of the devil, and to bring in everlasting righteousness ; He was to be the remedy for the spiritual disease which, through the disobedience of our first parents, had found entrance into the world ; and by and through Him, mankind were to be brought into that renewed condition, in which those corrupt passions from whence wars have their rise should be subdued.

In the inscrutable wisdom of the Most High, wars, under the Mosaic dispensation were, in some special cases commanded, but this gives no sanction to wars under the Gospel. Christianity also forbids many things which, in condescension to the weakness of man, were in that age of the world allowed to the Israelites. It was so regarding oaths and the law of marriage. The Law, however, for "the weakness and unprofitableness thereof," gave place to the more spiritual dispensation of Christ, and the law of retaliation and revenge was annulled. "Ye have heard," said our Lord, in reference to the law of Moses, "that it hath been said, Thou shalt love thy neighbour and hate thine enemy. But I say unto you, Love your enemies, bless them that curse you, do good to them that hate you, and pray for them which despite-fully use you and persecute you, that ye may be the children of your Father which is in heaven."‡ The Apostle Paul, in ad-dressing the converts at Rome, surrounded as they were with trophies of military glory, was anxious that they should be guarded against these pernicious influences, and be fully im-pressed with the non-resisting religion of Jesus. "Avenge not yourselves ; if thine enemy hunger, feed him ; if he thirst, give him drink. , Recompense no man evil for evil—overcome evil

---

* Isaiah ii. 4, 5.   † James iv. 1, 2.   ‡ Matthew v. 38—45.

with good."* This was the language of the great Apostle of the Gentile world. "They who defend war," says Erasmus, "must defend the dispositions which lead to war." But here we see that such are entirely forbidden.

The character of Him who was our great pattern was entirely opposed to war. He was pre-eminently distinguished by a meek, non-resisting, and forgiving spirit. "Whosoever shall smite thee on thy right cheek, turn to him the other also," was his own language ; and that of the Apostle Paul to the primitive believers was, "Let this mind be in you which was also in Christ Jesus."†
His holy religion was designed for the renovation of man ; and as its benign influence prevails. warfare and bloodshed must certainly cease. There is scarcely a divine truth that is more clearly set forth in the Holy Scriptures than this. The prophet Isaiah, in describing the glorious results of the gospel of Christ, thus speaks, in reference to its peaceable character—"The wolf also shall dwell with the lamb, and the leopard shall lie down with the kid : and the calf and the young lion, and the fatling together : and a little child shall lead them, &c."‡ When we turn from this delightful picture of the reign of Messiah in the hearts of the children of men, to the wars which have afflicted mankind ; the awful destruction of human life, and the devastation and ruin which have followed in their train ; when we compare the harmony and love which should ever characterise the followers of Christ, with the scenes which contending armies present in their mutual fiend-like struggles, how are we led with the Apostle to exclaim, "What communion hath light with darkness ? and what concord hath Christ with Belial ?"§

That the views which the Society of Friends take concerning war harmonize with divine truth, is abundantly confirmed by the practice of the early Christians. Both in the time of the Apostles, and for about two centuries after the Christian era, the primitive believers bore a decided testimony to the peaceable nature of the kingdom of their Redeemer. Those of them who lived in the time of our Lord and his immediate followers—a time, it should

* Romans xii. 19, 20.			† Phil. ii. 5.
‡ Isaiah xi. 6.			§ 2 Cor. vi. 14, 15.

be remembered, when the rulers of the world were Pagans, whose religion fostered that spirit which seeks distinction and honour in military conquests—could not well fail to understand this doctrine aright ; and with the unquestionable evidence before us that they condemned war, it is surprising that there should be found among Christians of the present day, those who plead for its consistency with the principles of their holy religion. But however unfaithful its professors may be, Christianity is unchangeable, for its Founder is " the same yesterday, to-day, and for ever." Ages of error can give no prescriptive sanction for a departure from so distinguishing a feature of the religion of Jesus ; and the widespread defection in Christendom on this subject, affords no plea to the awakened soul, for the guilt of upholding this violation of the divine law.

It is not within the scope of this history to give a treatise on the melancholy declension of professing Christians in regard to war ; but as the conduct of the Society of Friends, in their faithful adherence to the principles of peace, bears a striking analogy to that of the primitive believers ; and as it is important to understand under what circumstances this genuine doctrine of the gospel was abandoned by Christians, we may not inappropriately follow the subject a little further.

Notwithstanding the opposition which Christianity had to encounter from both Jew and Pagan, its progress among mankind was rapid ; and at the time when, about forty years after the crucifixion, the Roman legions encamped before the walls of Jerusalem for the purposes of siege, there were thousands in that city who had embraced its faith. The calamities of that memorable siege, it is well known, exceed anything before recorded in history ; but these followers of the Prince of Peace, having no part or lot in these carnal struggles, under a divine intimation, left the land of Judea and resorted to a village lying beyond Jordan. Here, under the unfailing protection of the Almighty arm, they dwelt in perfect safety ; and amidst all the carnage which attended the destruction of Jerusalem, it does not appear that a single Christian perished.*

* Eusebius Ecc. Hist., Bk. iii. c. 5.

In the second century the maintenance of the peace principles among christians, is spoken of by several of the fathers of that period. Justin Martyr, about A.D. 140, in alluding to the prophecy of Isaiah, which declared that the swords should be turned into ploughshares, and the spears into pruning-hooks, remarks that it was fulfilled in his time, for "we who were once slayers of one another do not now fight against our enemies."* Ireneus, thirty years later, in speaking of the same prophecy, makes a similar observation. "The Christians," he says, "have changed their swords and their lances into instruments of peace, and they know not how to fight."† Tatian who was a disciple of Justin Martyr, in his oration to the Greeks, declares war as unlawful, and Clemens of Alexandria, his contemporary, uses expressions which affirm the same doctrine; he calls Christians "followers of peace," and says that they "used none of the implements of war."‡

There cannot be more conclusive evidence adduced of the practice of Christians in the second century in this respect, than from the attacks of Celsus, their bitter opponent. One of his charges against them was, "that they refused in his times to bear arms for the Emperor, even in case of necessity." "If," he added, "the rest of the Empire were of their opinion, it would soon be overrun by the barbarians."§ The testimony of Origen, a talented and learned writer, is also important on this subject. He was born A.D. 183, and became a pupil of Clemens of Alexandria. Nearly the whole of a long life was spent by him in writing, teaching, and expounding the scriptures; and Jerome calls him "the greatest teacher since the apostles." He wrote largely for the promotion of true religion, and replied to the attacks of Celsus. On the subject of war, however, we find Origen freely admitting the facts advanced by Celsus, but vindicating the conduct of his brethren, on the principle that wars were forbidden.

Tertullian, whose father was a centurion at Carthage, was a contemporary with Origen, and became a convert to Christianity. Before he renounced heathenism he was a distinguished rhetorician or advocate. He also wrote much in support of his religion,

* Clarkson's Essay on the Practice, &c., of the Early Christians on War, p. 7.   † Ibid, p. 6.   ‡ Ibid, p. 6.   § Ibid, p. 7.

repeatedly making the avowal that any participation in war was unlawful for a Christian, because Christ " had forbidden the use of the sword and the revenge of injuries." He also informs us that " many soldiers, who had been converted to Christianity, quitted military pursuits in consequence of their conversion."*

Towards the close of the third century, under the reign of Dioclesian, a large number of Christians refused to serve in the army, and many of them suffered martyrdom for their faithful adherence to this doctrine of Christ. Maximilian was one of these. Having been brought before the tribunal to be enrolled as a soldier, he boldly declared his opinions. " I cannot fight," said he, " for any earthly consideration. I am now a Christian."†
Lactantius, one of the most learned and eloquent of the Latin Fathers, and who wrote about this period, makes the explicit declaration that " to engage in war cannot be lawful for the righteous man, whose warfare is that of righteousness itself."‡

In the purest age of the Church, and for at least two centuries from the dawn of Christianity, so universally was war held to be unlawful by its professors, that there does not appear to have been a single writer among them during this period, who notices the subject, except with this view. " It is as easy," remarks a learned writer, " to obscure the sun at mid-day, as to deny that the primitive Christians renounced all revenge and war."§ In the third century some declensions were apparent, and among them that of some entering the army. In the fourth century, under the Emperor Constantine, this defection from primitive principle and practice made woeful progress. Constantine was a convert from paganism; but not so entirely a convert as to adopt the peace principle and disband his legions. The countenance thus given to war by the first Christian Emperor, had the effect of inducing a large number of Christians to enter the army ; and on the other hand many of the heathen, finding that the profession of Christianity did not subject them to a renunciation of arms, out of compliment to the Emperor imitated his example, and embraced the new religion.||

* Gurney on War. † Clarkson's Essay, p. 12.
‡ Gurney on War. § Barclay's Apology, prop. xv.
|| Vide Moshiem's Ecc. Hist., vol i. p. 304 ; also Clarkson's Essay, p. 20.

The Most High, as though to fix a mark of reprobation for the violation of his gospel, appears to have hid his face in anger ; for his erring children, being left to their own unaided capacities in the things of God, departed widely from his law. It is a remarkable fact that during the century in which Christians relaxed their principles respecting peace, most of the evils in the Church were introduced, and by a strange infusion of heathen practices, christianity became gradually metamorphosed into what is now understood by Romanism. Ceremonies were greatly multiplied ; Pagan rites were imitated ; and a desire for pompous display in religion, manifested itself to an enormous extent. Transubstantiation, or something analogous to it, was maintained ; the ceremony of the elevation used in the celebration of the eucharist was introduced ; pilgrimages were performed ; their places of worship were held to be sacred ; saints were invoked ; relics were adored ; images used and the cross worshipped ; monasteries were founded ; magnificent public processions in imitation of those which the Pagans used to appease their gods, frequently took place ; and the clerical orders were augmented by archbishops, archdeacons, and other ecclesiastical dignitaries.

The religion of the Greeks and Romans differed, indeed, very little in externals, from that now adopted by Christians. Both were distinguished by a most imposing and splendid ritual. In the churches of both were to be seen pictures, images, gold and silver vases, wax tapers, gorgeous robes, mitres, tiaras, crosiers, &c. In imitation of the temples of the heathen deities, magnificent buildings were erected, which bore also a resemblance to them, in their outward form as well as their inward decorations. As among the Pagans, so also among the Christians, priestly power and influence had gained a dominion over the minds of the people ; fraud and artifice were resorted to in the most unblushing manner to impose on their credulity.

These declensions sprang up under the auspices of the half-converted and warlike Constantine and his immediate successors ; and were among the means employed in their day, to allure the Pagan nations to embrace Christianity ; and these truly, as an eminent ecclesiastical historian has observed, " All contributed to establish the reign of superstition upon the ruins of Christianity."*

That amidst all these corruptions, among a people who had been conspicuous for their love of arms ; and obscured as genuine Christianity was by so much of Paganism, the distinguishing feature of the religion of Him who was emphatically called " the Prince of Peace," which proclaims against all wars and fightings, should be no longer recognised, can excite no surprise ; neither are we unprepared, amidst these desecrations, to hear that armies were employed to promote ecclesiastical rule, and that uncivilized nations were forced into the profession of Christianity under the terror of the sword.   The most important doctrines of Christ being discarded, we now see the Church torn with strife and divisions; and the secular arm for a long period was resorted to in support of the views of the contending parties, in a manner which not only disgraces religion but outrages humanity itself.†

Although professing Christendom from the time when it first sanctioned the use of the sword, down to the present hour, has more or less given sad proof of its defection, yet God has not been without his witnesses for this precious principle of the gospel.   Towards the close of the fourth century, there were those who suffered for faithfully objecting to all war.   The church itself, indeed, even in its declension, did not at once forget the practice of its brighter day, and there was yet a lingering reverence for the doctrine of peace.   At the Council of Nice, A.D. 325, under Constantine, a penalty of excommunication for a lengthened period was imposed on those who, after having renounced a military life, should again return to the army.   Two hundred years later, Pope Leo declared it to be " contrary to the rules of the church, that persons after the action of penance should revert to the warfare of the world."‡   It may also be noticed, as a remarkable fact, that the Goths who, in the third century, had been converted to Christianity, in the next, whilst having the

* Moshiem's Ecclesiastical History, vol. i. p. 327.   Ed. 1826.

† In the Arian controversy, eighty ecclesiastics, who were opposed to its views, were placed in a ship, which was set on fire when it had cleared the coast.—Vide Moshiem's Ecc. Hist.   ‡ Gurney on War.

bible translated into their language, proposed the rejection of the books of Kings and Chronicles, lest the recital of the wars between the kingdoms of Israel and Judah, should awaken those feelings of military ardour which had been subdued under the benign influence of the gospel.* In the tenth century the Paterines, a numerous sect, scattered throughout Italy and France, maintained the non-resisting principle,† in which, during the eleventh, twelfth, and thirteenth centuries, they were joined by the Cathari, or Puritans, of Germany, who held that it was not lawful to bear arms or to kill mankind. In the fourteenth century, Wickliffe, the first English reformer, proclaimed the same views. In the fifteenth century, the United Brethren of Bohemia,‡ and during the Reformation the great Erasmus, also bore an uncompromising testimony against all war; in the century following, this doctrine was more conspicuously revived by the Society of Friends.

Recognizing the principle of peace as the genuine fruit of the everlasting gospel, it will be interesting to mark the conduct of the Society under their new circumstances in the government of Rhode Island. From the foundation of the colony to the time when it came under the government of Friends, was comprehended a period of about thirty-four years, during which the settlers had been involved in conflicts with the Indians; "garrisoned houses were appointed;" "armed boats were fitted out;"§ troops were raised; and lives were lost, in their war with the aborigines. In 1652, during the hostilities between the English and Dutch, the "colony and island were put to considerable expense to put and keep themselves in a posture of defence." We see, then, that in Rhode Island, in common with other governments of the time, warlike preparations had been resorted to, and the aid of the sword was sought in deciding disputes.

Within a few years after Friends became the rulers of Rhode Island, no circumstance arose to test the practical application of their non-resisting principle, and no active measures appear to

---

* Hoyland's Epitome of the History of the World, p. 367, and compare Moshiem's Ecclesiastical History, vol. i. p. 304.

† Jones's Hist. of the Waldenses, vol. i. p. 427.

‡ Crantz's Hist., vol. i. p. 200.   § Callender's Hist. Discourse, p. 125.

have been taken by them in which this doctrine was involved,
except in the passing of an act which provided for the entire right
of those colonists who had a conscientious scruple against war, to
refuse a participation in military operations without being liable
to any penalty for such refusal ; this exemption was, nevertheless,
clearly defined not to extend to services of a purely civil character.
Respecting the latter, the law in question was as follows : " Provided, nevertheless, that such said persons who cannot fight nor
destroy men, it being against their conscience, and not against
their conscience to do and perform civil services to the colony,
though not martial services, and to preserve, so far as in them
lies, lives, goods, and cattle, &c., that when any enemy shall
approach or assault the colony, or any place thereof, that then it
shall be lawful for the civil officer for the time being, as civil
officer, and not as martial or military, to require such said persons
as are of sufficient able body and of strength, though exempt from
training and fighting, to conduct, or to convey out of the danger
of the enemy weak, aged, and impotent persons, women and children, goods and cattle, by which the common weal may be better
maintained, and works of mercy manifested to distressed, weak
persons ; and shall be required to watch to inform of danger (but
without arms in martial manner or matter), and to perform any
other civil service by order of the civil officers, for the good of the
colony and inhabitants thereof."*

In 1675, the peace principles of the government of Rhode
Island were severely tested, in consequence of a formidable confederacy among the Indian tribes, to exterminate the settlers in
New England by falling upon them " everywhere at once." With
a view to provide against this fearful combination, it was proposed
for the several colonies of New England to unite in military preparations. To this proposal, however, the government of Rhode
Island could not conscientiously accede, and in dependence on the
protecting care of Him who hath the hearts of all men at his
disposal, they refrained from engaging in the war. This was a
course which involved Friends in considerable trial, for although
the governors, and most of the inhabitants of the island were dis-

* Colonial Records, 1673. At an extra session held in consequence of
an apprehended attack from the Dutch whilst at war with the English.

posed to peace, yet in that part of the colony which lay on " the main," the majority of the settlers held different views, being " outrageous to fight," and loud in their declamations against the rulers for refusing to give, as was said by a Friend, " commissions to kill and destroy men."* The government at home were apprized, in the language of complaint, of this novel policy. It was said that " the colony would never yield any joint assistance against the common enemy, no, not so much as in their own towns ;" and that they refused " to garrison " the towns of Providence and Warwick, which lay much exposed to incursions from the revengeful natives. The war was carried on by the Indians with great determination, and though it resulted in their defeat, its cost was terrible to the colonists. Twelve towns were destroyed, six hundred men fell in the conflict, and no less than six hundred houses were burnt. Of the able-bodied men in the province of New England, one in twenty had perished, and one family in every twenty had been burnt out ; altogether, the cost of this Indian war amounted to half a million sterling. Amidst the dreadful scenes which characterised this conflict, and whilst so many towns on the main were either wholly or partially destroyed, it is remarkable that the habitations of the peace-loving settlers on Rhode Island itself remained safe, and not a settler thereon received personal injury.

It has been remarked by some that Friends did not wholly abstain from taking means to protect their territory from the ravages of the Indians, and that boats were employed to ply around the island and keep them off. No account, however, appears, of any attempt on the part of the natives to land, or at least to do so in any forcible or aggressive manner. It is very easy to imagine that precautions might be taken for the protection of life and property under such circumstances, without violating in the slightest degree the doctrine which holds in abhorrence the slaying of our fellow-creatures ; precautions, indeed, which, if omitted, would imply culpable neglect. The settlers on the island entertained the opinion that the Indians had in many respects been wronged by the whites, and of this opinion the

* Journal of W. Edmundson, p. 108.

Indians doubtless were not ignorant.* Friends, also, had evinced considerable interest in the welfare of the natives. In the year following the election of some of their body to the government of the colony, a Committee of the Assembly was appointed to "treat with the Indian Sachems, to prevent drunkenness among them."† Important civil rights were also granted to them under the administration of Friends ; natives were allowed to serve on juries in cases affecting themselves, and their testimony was received in the courts as evidence.‡ The Indians, also, were unquestionably aware that the governors of Rhode Island were guided by principles of peace, and were not parties in the combination against them. They had, therefore, no incitement to kill and ravage the country of those who befriended them, and we find that they acted accordingly.

The rise and progress of the Society in New England down to about the year 1682 has now been related, and every year of its history to this period evinces that its planting was of the Lord. The early Friends of this province were deeply sensible of this, and their hearts were often lifted up in praise for this manifestation of divine goodness. "Blessed," they said, "were the feet of them that were sent to visit us, and brought the glad tidings of peace and the message of salvation." The Lord did indeed largely bless this portion of his visible church with the energy of his life-giving presence and power, and caused it to increase and flourish, and to rejoice in Him as the Rock of their salvation. "God is good to his spiritual Israel," they wrote ; "many are grown and growing to that state to tell others what he hath done for their souls, and are instruments to draw and persuade many to taste and see how good He is." "We enjoy our meetings peaceably," was their language on another occasion, "and the Lord's presence and powerful word of life doth often fill our assemblies. Glory to His name for ever, who feeds his faithful ones with the finest of the wheat, and gives them honey out of the rock."

* Collection of Rhode Island Hist. Society, vol. iii. p. 93
† Ibid, p. 80. ‡ Ibid, p. 80.

NIEUW AMSTERDAM.
Op't Eylant Manhattans.

NEW AMSTERDAM, now NEW YORK.
Taken from a Dutch Map of 1656.

CHAPTER XVII.

COEVAL with the rise of the Society of Friends within the province of New England, was its origin in that of New York, then termed New Amsterdam. The first individual of this part who professed our religious views was Richard Smith, of Long Island. He had come to Great Britain on some particular object, which is not explained ; and whilst in this country became convinced of the principles of Friends, which he steadily maintained in after life. In the summer of 1656, he arrived at Boston with eight Friends from London, and together with them was in a summary manner banished from the shores of Massachusetts. The English Friends were obliged to return in the vessel in which they came, but Richard Smith was taken to Long Island.

Though under the jurisdiction of the Dutch authorities of New
Netherlands, at least as far eastward as Oyster Bay,* Long
Island was colonized chiefly by English, who had " fled" from
Puritan New England to enjoy, under Dutch legislation, that
religious liberty and civil protection which had been denied them
by their own countrymen. Richard Smith was one of this class.
In 1641, he " purchased of the Sachems a tract of land in the
Narragansett country, remote from English settlements, where
he erected a house of trade, and gave free entertainment to all
travellers."† Callender, in his " Historical Discourse," states
that about 1643 there were two trading houses set up in the
Narragansett country, one of which belonged to Roger Williams
and another party, the other to Richard Smith.‡ His land lay
in the vicinity of the present town of Warwick ; and the probability is, that on the breaking out of the war between the
Narragansett Indians and the United Colonies of New England, Richard Smith left it for the more peaceful territory of
Long Island. Subsequently, however, he returned to Narragansett ; and John Burnyeat, who visited that part in 1672,
mentions having a meeting at his house.§ Roger Williams,
who was intimately acquainted with him, says he was of a very
respectable family. In a testimony which he gave, relative to
Richard Smith's title to some land, he thus speaks : " Mr.
Richard Smith, for his conscience to God, left faire possessions
in Gloucestershire, and adventured with his relations and estate
to New England ; he was a most acceptable inhabitant, and
prime leading man in Taunton, in Plymouth colony. For his
conscience sake (many differences arising) he left Taunton and
came to yᵉ Narragansett country, where, by God's mercy and yᵉ
favour of yᵉ Sachems, he broke the ice (at his great charge and

---

* By a treaty made in 1654 with the colonies of New England, it was
agreed that the Dutch territory should extend on Long Island as far
east as Oyster Bay.

† See Holmes' Annals, and Massachusetts Historical Society Transactions, vol. v.

‡ Callender's Historical Discourse, published by Romeo Elton, p. 92.

§ Journal of John Burnyeat, Barclay's Series, p. 212.

hazards), and put up in y⁰ thickest of y⁰ barbarians, y⁰ first English house amongst them." "There," he continues, " in his owne house, with much serenity of soule, and comfort, he yielded up his spirit to God, y⁰ Father of spirits, in peace."*

The gospel messengers who crossed the Atlantic in Robert Fowler's vessel in 1657, were the first, of whom we have any account, that visited New Netherlands. Of the eleven who reached the shores of the new world on that occasion, five, viz., Robert Hodgson, Richard Doudney, Mary Weatherhead, Dorothy Waugh, and Sarah Gibbons, landed at New Amsterdam on the first of the Sixth Month, 1657. On the day following, being First-day, Robert Fowler and Robert Hodgson paid a religious visit to Stuyvesant, the governor. " He was moderate," remarks Robert Fowler, " both in words and actions." The friendly disposition which he evinced towards Friends on their landing, was, however, but of short duration. The change is attributed to the influence of some Puritans, more particularly of Captain Willet, a persecuting magistrate of Plymouth, who was then at New Amsterdam, and who laboured successfully to embitter the mind of the governor against the strangers, inducing him to adopt the exiling policy pursued in Massachusetts. The persecuting course adopted by the governor, and which directly contravened the express directions of the Colonial Proprietaries for the toleration of all religious classes, seems unaccountable ; but it is partly explained by the fact, that a short time previous to the arrival of the Friends, a dispute had arisen between Stuyvesant and the authorities of New England, on the question of boundary ; when the former, feeling himself the weaker of the two, was anxious to conciliate the New Englanders, to avoid an appeal to arms.

On the day following the visit of Robert Fowler and Robert Hodgson to the governor, Mary Weatherhead and Dorothy Waugh, under a feeling of religious duty, went into the streets of New Amsterdam and publicly exhorted the people. The scene was new to the Dutch citizens ; and the magistrates, angry at such public ministrations, caused the two Friends to be arrested,

---

* Collections of the Rhode Island Hist. Society, vol. iii.

and committed them to noisome and filthy dungeons apart from each other. So unhealthful, indeed, were these places, that it was thought by some that the prisoners would not survive their incarceration.* After a confinement of eight days in these wretched abodes, they were brought out, and, having their hands bound behind them, were led to a boat about to sail for Rhode Island, and taken thither. The unsectarian soil of this colony, which the Puritans designated the " Island of error," was, in the apprehension of Stuyvesant, the most fitting abode for " Quaker heretics."

In the meantime, their fellow-labourers in the ministry, Robert Hodgson, Richard Doudney, and Sarah Gibbons, proceeded to visit the settlers on Long Island, who were mostly English. Among them were many sincere seekers after heavenly riches, who were prepared to appreciate those spiritual views of religion which these gospel messengers had to declare. They proceeded first to Gravesend, where their " testimony was received ;" and from thence passed to Jamaica, " where they were received with gladness ;"† and next to Hampstead, where also they met with settlers who welcomed them to their homes, and rejoiced in the spread of those living truths which were preached among them. Richard Doudney and Sarah Gibbons left their companions at Hampstead, and travelled, it is believed, to the eastern division of Long Island, then part of the colony of New Haven, from whence they crossed to Rhode Island.

On the First-day after Robert Hodgson arrived at Hampstead, he appointed a meeting to be held in an orchard, to which the inhabitants were invited. There lived in the town an Englishman, who was a magistrate under the Dutch government, and who having heard of the intended meeting, sent a constable to arrest Robert Hodgson. The officer arrived at the place of meeting before the appointed time, where he found his victim alone, pacing the orchard in quiet meditation. Robert Hodgson was immediately seized and carried before the magistrate, " who," he observes, " kept me a prisoner in his house," but

* Secret Works, p. 12.   † Howgill's Popish Inquisition, p. 6.

while he went to his worship in the fore-part of the day, many staid and heard the truth declared." The magistrate on his return finding that his house had answered the purpose of a chapel, and that his prisoner had had so favourable an opportunity for gospel labour, wrote a mittimus for his removal to another house. The change, however, did not prevent the people from visiting him. " In the latter part of the day," he remarks, " many came to me, and those that had been mine enemies, after they had heard truth, confessed to it."*

There resided at Hampstead another magistrate, who disapproved of the course adopted by his colleague towards the stranger, a feeling in which most of the respectable inhabitants of the town also participated. But the persecuting magistrate, " taking counsel of the baser sort,"† committed R. Hodgson to prison, and then set off for New Amsterdam to inform the governor of what had taken place. The proceedings met with the approval of Stuyvesant, who, determining to proceed with vigour in the suppression of the " Quaker heresy," forthwith despatched the sheriff and gaoler, with a guard of twelve musketeers, to bring the prisoner and those who had entertained hm to new Amsterdam. On the arrival of these at Hampstead, Robert Hodgson was searched, and his bible, papers, and some other articles, being taken from him, he was pinioned in a barbarous manner and so kept until the following day. During this interval, the officers were busy in searching " for those who had entertained" the stranger, and on this ground two hospitable women were arrested. On the following day preparations were made for conveying the arrested parties to New Amsterdam. The two females were placed in a cart, to the hinder part of which they fastened Robert Hodgson in his pinioned condition. The distance they had to travel was nearly thirty miles, over bad roads, and through the woods. The journey, which was performed mostly during the night, was a very painful one to the prisoners, especially to R. Hodgson, who was much bruised and torn.

Having reached their destination, the two women were im-

* Howgill's Popish Inquisition, p. 7.　　　† Norton's Ensign, p. 15.

prisoned, but the period of their detention was short.   The
punishment of R. Hodgson, however, was one of great severity.
Being loosed from the cart, he was led by the gaolor to one of the
dungeons of the city, a place "full of vermin," says the prisoner,
and "so odious, for wet and dirt, as I never saw."* On the
following day, he was brought before the Court for examination,
an English captain officiating as interpreter, but of the nature of
the examination, or what passed on the occasion, we are uninformed.   He was brought up the next day, when the sentence of
the Court was read to him in their own language, and afterwards
thus interpreted to him,—"It is the General's pleasure, seeing
you have behaved yourself thus, that you are to work two years
at a wheelbarrow with a negro, or pay or cause to be paid 600
guilders."†   Robert Hodgson, conscious of his innocency, and
that he had committed no breach of the laws of Holland, attempted
to make his defence against the cruel decision.   Stuyvesant,
however, would not suffer him to speak, but remanded him to the
wretched dungeon, with orders that none of his countrymen should
be allowed to visit him.   In a few days, he was again brought
out, when a paper in the Dutch language was read to him. Of the
nature of its contents he was ignorant, but the Dutch people who
heard it "shook their heads" in token of disapprobation, and
sympathized with the sufferer.
   After a further incarceration of several days, he was brought
out, and having been chained to a wheelbarrow, was commanded
to work on some repairs of the city walls, which were then going
forward.   He felt restrained from recognising the dictation of
his persecutors, and declined to obey.   Excited at the unexpected
refusal, the authorities, in order to reduce him to submission,
directed "a lusty crabbed negro slave,"‡ to beat him with a
tarred rope.   The negro, obedient to the order of his masters,
commenced the cruel task, and continued it until Robert Hodgson,
faint from suffering, fell to the ground.   The beating, severe as
it had been, was not severe enough to satisfy the sheriff who
superintended the affair.   At his bidding the sufferer was raised,

* Howgill's Popish Inquisition, p. 7.   † Norton's Ensign, p. 16.
   ‡ Gerard Croese's History of Friends, part ii., p. 156.

and the negro commanded to renew his work. After an infliction
of about one hundred blows, the prisoner fainted a second time.
Having failed in their attempts to force him to work, the officers
conducted him to the governor to complain of his obstinacy. The
governor resided at the fort, and here Robert Hodgson was left the
whole of the day. Towards noon the heat of the sun became
oppressive, when, being unsheltered from its rays, and having for
some time had but little food, oppressed also with his lacerated
condition, he again fainted. On the following day he was again
commanded to work, but steadfast to his convictions, he still
refused. During these sufferings, his mind, he observes, " was
staid upon the Lord," and he was sweetly refreshed and strengthened by His living power.

Having been closely confined in the dungeon for about a week,
Robert Hodgson had to endure sufferings of a still more barbarous description. The hard-hearted Stuyvesant, by some of the
settlers in milder tone called " hard headed," unrelenting towards
the victim of his displeasure, now ordered him to be stripped to
the waist, to be hung up by the hands with weights attached to
his feet, and, thus suspended, to be beaten severely with rods.
The sentence was executed with great cruelty, after which he was
again led to his miserable abode, and for two days and nights kept
without food.   " Afterwards," remarks the sufferer, "they took
me forth again, and asked me if I would pay the fine ; but I
told them I could not." The command to work was then repeated, and continuing to refuse, he was a second time suspended
by the hands, and cruelly beaten.

Being greatly exhausted by his sufferings, Robert Hodgson
solicited that some of the English inhabitants of the city might
be allowed to visit him. His request having been granted, he
was soon visited by a feeling woman, who gave the needful attention to his wounds, and administered to his wants ; but his body
was so torn, and his strength so reduced, that she expected
death in another day, would terminate all his sufferings. The
tender-hearted woman on her return home, informed her husband
of Robert Hodgson's critical state. It excited his commiseration,
and in his anxiety for the recovery of the sufferer, he immediately

offered the authorities "a fat ox" to be allowed to remove him from the dungeon to his own dwelling, where he might receive proper attention, and have those comforts of which his miserable abode was destitute. The offer of the humane settler being communicated to Stuyvesant, this mercenary governor refused to allow the removal of the prisoner, unless the fine were paid of six hundred guilders. The sufferings of Robert Hodgson had excited the sympathy of many others in New Amsterdam, "both Dutch and English," and on the refusal of the governor to accept the ransom, a number of them came forward and offered to raise the amount requisite to obtain his release. He, however, did not feel easy to accept his liberation on this principle, and in a belief that the Lord would heal him, and that strength would be given him to labour for his sustenance during his imprisonment, he declined the kind offer of the citizens. He now rapidly recovered, and in a few days was sufficiently strong to work, "not being free," he observed "to partake of the coarse prison diet, without labouring for it."

The cruelties to which Robert Hodgson had been subjected, caused no small degree of excitement among the settlers in New Netherlands. The colony had been famed for its religious toleration, and emigrants from different regions had sought it as a land where freedom of conscience was especially recognised. It soon became known that the persecution of Friends was mainly attributable to the malevolent whispers of Captain Willett, of Massachusetts, who received very intelligible intimations from the colonists of their dissatisfaction with his conduct. Willett, anxious to regain the esteem which he had so justly forfeited, now petitioned the governor for Robert Hodgson's release. A sister of Stuyvesant, whose sympathies were enlisted on behalf of the sufferer, also exerted her influence for his liberation. The aversion of the colonists to religious persecution, together with the entreaties of Willett and the governor's sister, obtained the object, and thus, without paying any portion of the fine, Robert Hodgson was again at liberty to pursue his gospel labours. His discharge took place about the middle of the Seventh Month, 1657, soon after which he proceeded to Rhode Island.

Persecution within the limits of New Netherlands, was not confined to the gospel labourers who visited it from England. Several of the inhabitants of Long Island, who had embraced the principles of Friends, were also subjected to suffering for their religion, among the earliest of whom were John Tilton, Joane Chatterton, Henry Townsend, Tobias Feak or Fecco, and Edward Hart. In the Seventh Month, 1657, Henry Townsend, who resided at Jamaica, was fined eight pounds for having assisted Robert Hodgson in holding a meeting. Stuyvesant, imitating the intolerant legislation of Massachusetts, enacted a law which provided that if any of the settlers should receive a Friend into their houses, but for a night, they should be fined fifty pounds; one-third of which was to be paid to the informer, whose name, in order to promote the operation of the law, was to be kept secret. Another provision was, that if any Friends should be brought into that jurisdiction, the vessel in which they came should be forfeited, with all its goods.*

The law which Stuyvesant had passed for the suppression of Quakerism, being a new feature in the government of the colony, produced considerable dissatisfaction among the settlers on Long Island, particularly among those residing at Flushing. Tobias Fecco, the sheriff, and Edward Hart, the town clerk of that place, were prominent in the expression of this feeling; and the latter, having drawn up a remonstrance to the governor on the subject, convened a meeting of the inhabitants of Flushing and its vicinity, in order that the document might receive their sanction. The document was approved by the meeting, signed, and committed to the care of the sheriff, to be forwarded to the governor.

The protest was presented to the governor and council on the twenty-ninth of the Tenth Month. Stuyvesant was highly indignant at its presentation. The spirit of independence which it breathed, was construed to be "mutinous;" and orders were immediately issued for the arrest of the sheriff as the bearer of it. The fact that two of the magistrates of Flushing, and Edward Hart, the town clerk, had attached their names to the document,

---

* New England Judged, p. 218.

attracted the special attention of the governor and council, and warrants were forthwith dispatched to Long Island, requiring their personal appearance. In three days, Edward Farrington and William Noble, the two magistrates, were arraigned before the council, and in a summary manner committed to prison. These arbitrary proceedings were, in the opinion of the two enlightened magistrates, altogether unconstitutional, and at variance with that liberty of conscience which the proprietors designed should be recognised in the province, and after a week's imprisonment they concluded to represent their views to the authorities, and addressed a letter to them on the subject. "Our patent," they said, "we call our charter; we have heard it read, and do conceive it grants liberty of conscience without modification, either of brevet or benefice." Their construction of the liberal meaning of the patent was clearly the correct one, but they wished to avoid the appearance of self-confidence. "If we are in the dark therein," they continued, "we desire your honours to direct us." Stuyvesant, however, was inflexible. Anxious to escape from their miserable abode, the prisoners on the following day, addressed a short petition to the court, praying for pardon; this met with a more favourable reception, and Farrington and Noble were released from gaol, but with the restriction to "remain on the Manhattan, under promise to appear at the first summons." Edward Hart appeared before the court on the 3rd of the Eleventh Month, and having been charged with the authorship of the protest, was sent to gaol to wait their further orders.

The council of New Amsterdam, following up their intolerant proceedings, issued a summons in a few days, for the appearance of Henry Townsend. The complaint preferred against him was for having entertained and corresponded with Friends. In about a week he obeyed the summons, when, "as an example for other transgressors and contumelious offenders," he was condemned "in an amende of three hundred guilders, to be applied as it ought to be, and that he shall remain arrested till the said amende shall be paid, besides the costs and mises of justice."

John Tilton of Gravesend was another victim of Stuyvesant's hatred to Friends. A warrant having been issued for his apprehension, for receiving and entertaining a banished woman Friend, he forwarded to the Court a defence of his case, in which he stated, that the Friend came to his house during his absence ; his statement, however, was unavailing, and on the 10th of the Eleventh Month he was sentenced to pay "an amende of £12. Flanders, with costs and mises of justice." His offence is thus set forth in the records of the council : "Whereas, John Tilton, residing at South Gravesend, now under arrest, has dared to provide a Quaker woman with lodging, who was banished out of the province of New Netherlands ; so, too, some other persons of the adherents, belonging to the abominable sect of the Quakers, which is directly contrary to the orders and placards of the director-general and council of New Netherlands, and therefore, as an example to others, ought to be severely punished."

The day on which John Tilton received his sentence, John Townsend was brought before the Court. He was one of those who had signed the protest at Flushing, and there were circumstances which led the authorities to suspect that he was otherwise favourably disposed towards Friends. He was therefore committed to prison, while the attorney-general made enquiry if he had in any manner contravened the orders of the governor.

Whether any others of those who signed the protest adopted at the meeting at Flushing, were proceeded against, it does not appear. The Flushing remonstrance, however, was a subject of grave deliberation with the governor and council, and with a view to discourage such expressions of opinion in future, in the First Month, 1658, a minute in council was drawn up, from which the following is extracted :—

"We, director-general and council in New Netherlands, having maturely considered the mutinous orders and resolutions adopted by the sheriff, clerk, magistrates, and the majority of the inhabitants of the village Vlessingen, signed on the 27th of December, 1657, and delivered a few days after to the director-general by the sheriff, Tobias Fecco, by which resolution they not only contemn, infringe, and oppose the aforesaid order of the director-general and council against the Quakers, and other sectarians, daring to express themselves in so many words, that they cannot stretch out their arms against them, to punish, banish, or persecute them by imprisonment; that they, so as God shall move their consciences, will admit each sectarian in their houses and villages, and permit them to leave these again, which, as said before, is contrary to the orders and placards of the director-general and council, and directly in opposition of these ; a case, indeed, of the worst and most dangerous tendency, as treading, absolutely, the authority of the director-general and council under their feet, and, therefore, well deserved to be corrected and punished, for an example to others, with the total annihilation of the privileges and exemptions which were granted from time to time to the aforesaid village ; and besides this, with a corporal punishment and banishment of each one who signed the aforesaid mutinous resolution. But the director-general and council, in the hope of greater prudence in future, are actuated towards their subjects more by mercy than by the extremes of rigorous justice ; more so, as they were inclined by several circumstances to believe that many, yea, the majority, were encouraged by the previous signatures of the sheriff, clerk, and some of the magistrates. Wherefore, the director-general and council pardon, remit, and forgive this transgression against the authority of the director-general and council." The minute then refers to the appointment of a magistrate for Flushing more versed in the Dutch language, and provides " that in future no similar meetings shall be convocated or holden, except for highly interesting or pregnant reasons, which shall previously be communicated to the director-general and council by the sheriff, &c. ;" and it concludes by commanding the inhabitants of Flushing " to look out for a good, pious, and orthodox minister," and that such an one should be " encouraged," by their providing for him " a decent maintenance."

About one year after the landing at New Netherlands of the Friends who came in the " Woodhouse," Josiah Cole and Thomas Thurston arrived in the province. They had travelled inland from Virginia, and had religious service among the Indians, who received them kindly and heard them with attention, but soon after they had entered the territory of the Dutch, they were arrested, imprisoned for a few hours, and then carried under an escort of soldiery, to an adjacent island, supposed to be Staten Island. A few Dutch families had settled at this place ; special orders, however, were given that none of them should entertain the strangers, or assist them to leave the island. The sufferers, after remaining there for two days, met with some kindly disposed Indians, who conveyed them to Long Island, "where," observes Josiah Cole, "we found some Friends in the Truth, by whom we were much refreshed."* Soon after their arrival in Long Island, Josiah Cole left his companion, "he not being of ability," he remarks, "to travel on so fast as it lay upon me." Having travelled about one hundred and fifty miles on Long Island, he crossed over to New England.

The inhabitants of Long Island were settled chiefly on that part of it which lay contiguous to the continent. At its eastern extremity, however, and in the small Islands adjacent, there were those who had embraced the principles of Friends, among whom the name of Nathaniel Silvester deserves notice. He was the sole proprietor of Shelter Island,† which lies in an inlet of the sea near the eastern point of Long Island, measuring in extent about five miles from east to west, and about seven miles from north to south. Of the period when he became possessed of this interesting little domain, or when he joined in religious profession with Friends, we are uninformed, but as early as the Third Month, 1659, he is referred to as one who had adopted our principles. It was in that year, that Laurence and Cassandra Southwick, on being driven from their home in Massachusetts, sought and found an asylum in the territory of this island ; there is, indeed, good reason to believe, that its name is derived from the refuge which it afforded to the victims of intolerance. William Robinson, writing to George Fox about this time, speaks of its owner as " a fine noble man." The liberality and kindness of Nathaniel Silvester became known to Friends in

* Letter of Josiah Cole to G. Bishop, 1658.
† Journal of John Taylor, p. 5 ; and Letter of W. Robinson to George Fox, 1659.

England, and John Taylor of York, when he visited America in 1659, first landed on the shores of Shelter Island,* and was, he says, "very kindly received." Except this island, and the colony of Rhode Island, there was not at this time a nook in the colonies of North America, on which a Friend could land, without exposing himself to severe suffering, and the ship-master to a heavy penalty. The possession, therefore, of the island in question, by one who loved the truth, was a providential circumstance, peculiarly favourable to Friends at this juncture, and not to be viewed as one of mere chance.

John Taylor next passed to Long Island, "to seek," as he remarks "the lost." In its villages and towns, he found "many sober people that feared God, and were convinced of the blessed Truth;" and who, he continues, "received me and my testimony readily with gladness, and many meetings of the people were settled under the teachings of the Lord Jesus Christ, our Free Teacher, at Gravesend, Seatancott, Oyster Bay, Hemstead and other places." In the "woods and wilderness" on Long Island, he adds, "we also had meetings." While thus pursuing his gospel labours, he was joined in the winter of 1659, by Mary Dyer; "several brave meetings," he writes, "we had together, and the Lord's power and presence was with us gloriously."†

The next gospel minister who appears to have visited New Netherlands, was George Rofe. After labouring in Virginia and Maryland, he reached the Dutch province in 1661, "having sailed in a small boat with only two Friends." I had good service, "he writes," among both Dutch and English. I was in the chief city of the Dutch, and gave a good sound, but they forced me away; and so we had meetings through the islands in good service."‡

Among the convinced who resided at Gravesend on Long Island, Croese the Dutch historian mentions the "Countess of Mordee" who had previously professed with the Puritans, and whom he terms "a noble lady." The meetings of Friends at

* Journal of J. Taylor, p. 5.   † Ibid, 8.
‡ Letter of G. Rofe, to R. Hubberthorne, 1661.

Gravesend were held in her house: "but," says Croese, "she managed it with that prudence and observance of time and place, as gave no offence to any stranger, or person of another religion, and so she and her people remained free from all molestation and disturbance."* At Flushing, however, things were different; and, unprotected by the influence of the rich, Friends were driven to hold their meetings in the adjacent woods. These were occasionally attended by other professors, among whom was Hannah Bowne, who soon united with the persecuted community. Her husband John Bowne, desirous to ascertain more particulars of the sect to which his wife had now become united, went on one occasion to see Friends during the time of their meeting in the woods. The beauty and simplicity of their worship, made a deep and lasting impression on his mind, and having his heart expanded in love towards the hunted little company, he generously invited them for the future to hold their meetings at his house, an offer which, it appears, was readily accepted. Dwelling near the fountain of all true knowledge and wisdom, John Bowne was soon given to see that the principles which his wife had embraced, harmonized with the doctrines of Christ his Saviour, and under this conviction, he also openly professed with the united, small, persecuted flock.

The conscientious course pursued by John Bowne drew down the displeasure of the authorities of New Amsterdam, and in the Sixth Month, 1662, a complaint was preferred against him for permitting the meetings of Friends to be held at his house.† He was accordingly arrested, sentenced to pay a fine of £25. Flemish, together with the court charges, and expressly admonished to discontinue the meetings under the penalty of banishment. Having refused to pay the unjust imposition, he was committed to a noisome dungeon at New Amsterdam, where, says Bishop, "he was kept very long, and well nigh famished to death."‡ The governor, finding that this punishment was ineffectual to reduce the prisoner to submission, determined to enforce the threat of banishment. Having been taken to the

* Albany Records.   † Croese Hist. of Friends, part II. p. 157.
‡ New England Judged, p. 422.

Stadthouse, where his wife and friends were permitted to see him, J. Bowne was informed that it was resolved he should pay the fine within three months, or be exiled from the country. The cruel edict, however, did not induce him to deny his Lord, and continuing steadfast, he was in the Tenth Month, placed on board a Dutch vessel, and conveyed to Holland. The banishment of a settler on account of religion, from the dominions of the Dutch, was a circumstance so extraordinary, that the colonial authorities at New Amsterdam deemed it prudent to forward a despatch to the directors of the West India Company, by the ship which bore John Bowne into exile, in which the nature of his offence was explained. The following is a copy of the despatch.

" Honourable, right respectable Gentlemen,—We omitted in our general letter the troubles and difficulties which we, and many of our good inhabitants, have since some time met with ; and which are daily renewed, by the sect called Quakers, chiefly in the country, and principally in the English villages, establishing forbidden conventicles, and frequenting those against our published placards ; and disturbing, in a manner, the public peace ; in so far, that several of our magistrates and well-affectioned subjects remonstrated and complained to us, from time to time, of their insufferable obstinacy, unwilling to obey our orders or judgment.

" Among others, one of their principal leaders, John Bowne, who, for his transgression, was, in conformity to the placards, condemned in an amende of 150 guilders ; who has been now under arrest more than three months, for his unwillingness to pay, obstinately persisting in his refusal, in which he still continues, we at last resolved, or were rather compelled to transport him in this ship from this province, in the hope that others might by it be discouraged. If, nevertheless, by these means, no more salutary impression is made upon others, we shall, though against our inclinations, be compelled to prosecute such persons in a more severe manner. On which we previously solicit to be favoured with your honours' wise and foreseeing judgment, &c.

" *Fort Amsterdam, New Netherlands, Jan. 9th,* 1663."

John Bowne arrived in Holland in the Second Month, 1663, and feeling that the cause for which he suffered was a just and righteous one, and that his political rights had been outraged, he naturally sought redress for his wrongs. Benjamin Furly and William Caton, who were at that time in Holland, assisted him; and in company with them he obtained several interviews with the Directors of the West India Company. These were men of enlightened consciences, who prized religious freedom as one of the greatest blessings of their land. They could not, therefore, sanction the illiberal and persecuting policy of the colonial legislature, and in a few weeks after John Bowne had landed in Holland, the directors reversed his sentence, and returned the following enlightened reply to the rulers at New Amsterdam:—

" Amsterdam, 16th April, 1663.

" We finally did see, from your last letter, that you had exiled and transported hither a certain Quaker, named John Bowne, and although it is our cordial desire that similar and other sectarians might not be found there, yet as the contrary seems to be the fact, we doubt very much if vigorous proceedings against them ought not to be discontinued, except you intend to check and destroy your population; which, however, in the youth of your existence, ought rather to be encouraged by all possible means: Wherefore, it is our opinion, that some connivance would be useful; that the consciences of men, at least, ought ever to remain free and unshackled. Let every one be unmolested, as long as he is modest; as long as his conduct in a political sense is irreproachable; as long as he does not disturb others, or oppose the government. This maxim of moderation has always been the guide of the magistrates of this city, and the consequence has been that, from every land, people have flocked to this asylum. Tread thus in their steps, and, we doubt not, you will be blessed.

" ABRAHAM WILMENDONK.
" DAVID VAN BAERLE."

Having received full permission from the directors of the West

India Company to return to his home, with a guarantee of protection and of entire religious liberty, John Bowne, after visiting some of his relatives and friends in England, and also the island of Barbadoes, reached Flushing again in the early part of 1664. From this period full toleration was enjoyed by the Society of Friends in the Dutch possessions of North America. It is said that Stuyvesant on meeting John Bowne, soon after his return from banishment, expressed his regret for the course he had pursued, and assured him that neither- he nor his friends would be molested for the future. The letter of the directors, doubtless, under the divine blessing, produced this change in the conduct of the governor. His opportunity, however, of exhibiting a different policy was but short ; preparations were then making by the English for the war by which, before the conclusion of the same year, New Netherlands was wrested from the Dutch, and became a British colony under the name of New York.

CHAPTER XVIII.

Mary Tomkins, Alice Ambrose, and others visit the colony of New York
—The religious services and sufferings of John Liddal—John Burnyeat's gospel labours in New York and on Long Island—George Fox
and other ministers visit the province : their religious labours on
Long Island—William Edmundson visits the colony in 1672 and
again in 1676—The gospel services of William and Alice Curwen,
John Boweter and Joan Vokins—Epistle of Joan Vokins—Brief
notice of the lives of Robert Hodgson and John Taylor—Remarks
on the increase of Friends in the colony of New York, Meetings for
Worship, and the general state of the Society in 1682.

During the time of John Bowne's banishment, in 1663, the
colony of New Netherlands was visited by several gospel labourers.
Mary Tomkins, and Alice Ambrose, on leaving New England
proceeded to Oyster Bay, accompanied by Edward Wharton and
William Reap.   From Oyster Bay they journeyed to Flushing,
where " they were much refreshed,"* on witnessing " the faithfulness and fellowship" of Friends. They then passed on to Gravesend,
where they met with their fellow-labourers in the ministry, Joseph
Nicholson, John Liddal, and Jane Millard, who had just returned
from a visit to Virginia and Maryland.   The unexpected meeting of these gospel messengers in a foreign land, was a source of
much joy to them, and they were comforted "in the love and
fellowship of the Lord, and one another !"†

Whilst the Friends above referred to were at Gravesend, they
felt it to be their religious duty to proceed to New Amsterdam ;
a service in which they were joined by John and Mary Tilton
of the former place.   On their way they visited Flatbush, a town
about ten miles from the capital.   In passing through this place,

* New England Judged, p. 422.   † Ibid, p. 424.

John Liddal felt constrained publicly to exhort the inhabitants to repentance. With a view to deter Friends from visiting the colony, the governor had issued instructions to the officers, immediately to seize and place in irons all "Quakers who should preach amongst them."* John Liddal was, therefore, immediately arrested, ironed, and conveyed under an escort of Dutch soldiery to New Amsterdam. The rest of the company followed, and the entrance of the motley group into the city of New Netherlands, gave rise to much excitement. As they passed through the streets, John Liddal again felt called to address the people; "the trumpet of the Lord," observes Bishop, "sounded with great dread, and was very terrible, and much people came together." On approaching the Fort, where the governor resided, the company were met by the Fiscal, who, displeased on seeing so many of the inhabitants assembled and listening to Quaker ministrations, committed all the Friends to prison. To have nine Friends in the prisons of New Amsterdam at one time, was a new circumstance in the history of that city, and the Fiscal appeared somewhat ashamed of his proceeding; but, wishing to make it appear a mild policy, in comparison of the persecutions at Boston, he remarked "that they did not hang them, as their countrymen in New England did." After a few days' imprisonment, at the request of a humane Dutch Captain, who offered to convey them from the colony, they were all released, except John and Mary Tilton. About this time, Thomas Newhouse visited New Netherlands. He also was imprisoned, and soon after, banished to New England.† After their expulsion from New Amsterdam, Alice Ambrose, and Mary Tomkins, in company with George Preston, again visited Long Island.

In the year 1666, that unwearied labourer in the work of the gospel, John Burnyeat, landed at New York. No particulars, however, of his services in this province have come down to us; and the only reference which he himself makes to them is, that he "spent some time there amongst Friends in going through their

---

* New England Judged, p. 424.　　† Ibid, p. 425.

meetings.* In 1671, during John Burnyeat's second visit to the western continent, he again laboured in this province. He landed on this occasion at New York, in the Second Month, and proceeded without much delay to visit his brethren of Long Island, and attended the half-yearly meeting held at Oyster Bay. The first notice of the existence of a meeting for discipline, among Friends of Long Island, is that of the one in question ; but there is good reason to believe, that this meeting had been established for some years prior to this date. After a journey of some months in New England, John Burnyeat returned to Long Island, and was present at the half-yearly meeting in the Eighth Month, 1671, and which, he remarks, was " a blessed time."

On Long Island, as in some other parts of America, there were those who had imbibed the notions of John Perrot, and who were opposed to the establishment of meetings for discipline. The most prominent of these attended the half-yearly meeting for the purpose of promoting their schismatical opinions. Their object, however, was not accomplished, for John Burnyeat was enabled, under the influence of that wisdom which is profitable to direct, to point out this snare to his brethren, and to confirm them in " the blessed order of the truth into which they were gathered and sweetly settled." " The Lord's power," he writes, " broke in upon the meeting, and Friends' hearts were broken, and great meltings in the power there were amongst us ; and in the same we blessed the Lord, and praised him."† Leaving Oyster Bay, he proceeded to Flushing, Gravesend, and New York ; at each of which places, he was enabled publicly to preach the way of salvation with convincing energy and power.

It was the intention of John Burnyeat to quit the shores of America soon after leaving New York ; but having unexpectedly met with George Fox, Robert Widders, and George Pattison, in the south, he returned with them to Oyster Bay in time to attend the half-yearly meeting held there in the Third Month, 1672. The presence of George Fox and his companions on this occasion,

---

* Journal of J. Burnyeat.　　　† Ibid.

is mentioned as having been of " great service to the truth, and of great comfort to Friends." The meeting lasted four days ; the first and second of which were occupied in holding meetings for the inhabitants at large, the third to meetings for discipline, and the fourth to a meeting with the " dissatisfied ones." Respecting the proceedings of the fourth day, George Fox remarks, " the Lord's power broke forth gloriously, to the confounding of the gainsayers,—and the glorious truth of God was exalted and set over all, and they were all brought down and bowed under."* After visiting some other parts of Long Island, the English Friends took boat for New England.

The next gospel labourer who visited the province of New York, was William Edmundson, who arrived soon after the departure of George Fox for New England. Although there were many Friends on Long Island, yet up to this period none, it appears, had united with the Society in the city of New York, and William Edmundson on landing took up his abode at an inn. It is somewhat singular, that New York and Boston, the capitals of their respective provinces, and at that time the only two places of much importance in North America, were alike unfavourable to the progress of Quakerism. With respect to New York, we do not find that Friends had been much drawn to preach their enlightened views in this rising emporium of the new world ; William Edmundson, however, felt it right to convene a meeting ; and in the dining-room of his hostess, he met many of its citizens. Here, he remarks, " we had a brave large meeting ; some of the chief officers, magistrates, and leading men of the town were at it ; very attentive they were, the Lord's power being over them all."†

On leaving New York, William Edmundson proceeded to Long Island, where, he observes, " were many honest tender Friends." He held several meetings with his brethren on this island, in which, he says, " we were well refreshed, and comforted together in the Lord." From thence he passed to Shelter Island, where he met with George Fox. Here, in the enjoy-

* Journal of George Fox, vol. ii., p. 159.
† Journal of William Edmundson p. 93.

ment of the generous hospitality of Nathaniel Silvester, these two eminent servants of the Most High related their travels and their services on the western continent; and, under a sense of the Divine presence and blessing that had attended their labours, their hearts were lifted up in praise to their Great Master for these tokens of his goodness.

From Shelter Island George Fox and his companions, who now included James Lancaster, and, it appears, also Christopher Holder, took shipping for Oyster Bay, where they arrived in the Sixth Month. At this place, and also at Flushing, they had very large meetings, some of those who attended them having come from a distance of thirty miles. Whilst George Fox was engaged in the work of his Redeemer at thesè places, Christopher Holder and some others were similarly occupied in the town of Jamaica. At Gravesend, George Fox held three meetings, "to which," he says, "many would have come from New York but that the weather hindered them." About two months after, John Burnyeat, on his return from New England, again visited Long Island, and New York, being accompanied on this occasion, by John Cartwright; from whence he proceeded to Maryland, and in a few weeks after embarked for Ireland.

In the year 1676, William Edmundson went on a second visit to the churches in America. He landed on this occasion at Rhode Island, and, after much religious service in New England, he came to Long Island, where "Friends received him gladly." "We stayed in that part," he observes, "for some time, and had large and precious meetings." His labours were also blessed to some of those who had been led astray under the delusive notions of Perrot, and who had, at times, been troublesome. "Some of them," he remarks, "were reached and brought back to the truth."*

During the year 1676, this portion of America was also visited by William and Alice Curwen. Their services were extended to Shelter Island, Long Island and New York. The interest of these devoted ministers was much awakened on behalf

---

* Journal of William Edmundson, p. 117.

of Friends in these localities, and, after leaving them, they endeavoured by epistolary communications to strengthen them in their christian course. In the following year, John Boweter arrived in the province ; he, however, gives us no particulars of his religious engagements, further than that he held meetings at New York, Gravesend, Flushing, and Oyster Bay. The next gospel labourer whom we have to notice is Joan Vokins, who landed at New York in 1680. At this place there had been, she says, " hurt done by some," and which had led to the discontinuance of their week-day meeting. " I laboured to settle it again," she continues, " and God's eternal power wrought wonderfully in me, in several meetings with his people, and we were well refreshed." From this city she crossed over to Long Island, and laboured in the love of the gospel among her brethren in the towns of that locality. " The Lord," she remarks, " had a tender people there, and his power was amongst them, and we were sweetly refreshed together." Like her friends William and Alice Curwen, Joan Vokins was also engaged, when separated from this part of the Society, to cheer and encourage them on their heavenly way, by written exhortations. The following, selected from one of these, shows the ardency of her soul for the welfare of her brethren :—

For Friends at Gravesend, in Long Island, and elsewhere.

Dear Friends,—My love and life salutes you, and in that which unites unto our God, and endears us in the heavenly relation, you are often in my remembrance ; and my soul's desire is, that we may feel each other in a living growth in that life and love of God which reaches over sea and land, and satisfieth our souls.

The breathing of my soul to the God of my life is, that we may all keep low in the valley of our Father's love, where the well-spring of life doth overflow, that our souls through its sweet refreshings may live unto him ; that through its arising, we may magnify his name, and celebrate his praise.

Oh ! dear hearts, feel his love, for it requires love, my

soul can truly say.　Oh! what manner of love, is this, that he hath loved us with, that, when we were afar off and strangers to him, he made known his precious truth unto us, and revealed a measure thereof in us, to help our infirmities and to teach us, when we could find no comfort of all the teachings of the idol shepherds, nor any help for our infirmities.　Oh, how precious was his voice, and comely was his countenance, and how tenderly were our hearts affected therewith, in the day of our convincement!　Oh, it was a day of love never to be forgotten!　And how hath he surrounded us by his power ever since.　Surely his fatherly love hath been, and is, sufficient to oblige us to obedience.

Therefore, let our hearts magnify his name, and our souls, and all that is within us, return praises and thanksgiving unto him ; for he is worthy, who is God blessed for ever, and evermore. Amen, saith my soul, who am a traveller in spirit for the tender seed, and a rejoicer in its prosperity.

JOAN VOKINS.

*Written, it is supposed, soon after her
　return home from America.*

A notice of the lives of several of the gospel ministers who laboured in the colony of New York has already been given.　We here insert a similar brief sketch respecting Robert Hodgson and John Taylor.

ROBERT HODGSON.

The first notice that we find respecting Robert Hodgson occurs in 1655, while on a gospel mission in Berkshire ; in the course of which he was imprisoned at Reading, for refusing to take the oath of allegiance when tendered to him by the mayor, before whom he was brought for ministering to the people.*　In the following year he again visited Reading, and, as on the former occasion, he was again taken before a magistrate, who sent him to gaol for not taking off his hat when in his presence, and for not having, as it is stated, " a certificate of his travel."　Of the place of his

* MS. Sufferings.

residence it is difficult to speak with certainty, but the probabilities are, that it was near Skipton· in Yorkshire. After his release from the dungeon at New Amsterdam, he proceeded to New England, and towards the close of 1658, he appears to have joined his aged friend William Brend and a few others in a visit to the West India islands ; from whence he sailed to Virginia. For about ten years from this date, he appears to have been occupied in the service of his Lord in the colonies of North America, his return to England having taken place in 1669.* After remaining in England about two years and a half, he embarked a second time for the shores of America, and five years later we find him engaged on Rhode Island, being the latest account which we have been able to find respecting him. It appears somewhat probable that he settled and died in America.

JOHN TAYLOR.

John Taylor was born about the year 1638. His parents at a later date were residing in Huntingdonshire, and there is reason to believe his birth took place in that county. At an early age he had living desires after a knowledge of the truth, and in his youthful years, when the meetings of Friends were first established in Huntingdonshire, he occasionally attended them ; but the persecution and derision, to which Friends were then exposed, caused him to hesitate in openly professing with them. In 1656, George Fox first visited this county, and, under his baptizing ministry, John Taylor was fully convinced of the spiritual views of Friends, and " by whom," he remarks, " I was thoroughly resolved of all doubts, and settled in the blessed truth." He was then about eighteen years of age. George Fox became deeply interested in the best welfare of his convert, and a free conversation took place between them. John Taylor observed, that Friends " were a people despised, hated, and persecuted by all ;" that he " saw nothing to be had among them but a righteous life ; and that," he continued, " one might have among others that were not so hated and persecuted." George Fox saw the conflict of his

* Letter of Ellis Hookes to Margaret Fell, 1669.

mind, and that he was struggling to reconcile an easier path as the pathway to peace "He then," says John Taylor, "took me by the hand, and said, 'Young man, here are three scriptures thou must witness fulfilled. Thou must be turned from darkness to light, and from the power of Satan unto God, and so thou mayst come to the knowledge of the glory of God ; and thou shalt be changed from glory to glory ; and this is the word of the Lord unto thee.' "*

Following on to know the Lord, John Taylor "grew in the truth," and "in a little time," he writes, "I was moved of the Lord to travel into the West of England, to preach the everlasting gospel, and to tell to others what the Lord had done for my soul." On his return from this journey he proceeded to London, and soon after embarked on his religious visit to America. He sailed in the Second Month 1659, being then only about twenty-one years of age. After a long and tedious voyage, he arrived at Shelter Island, where he was kindly received by Nathaniel Silvester. He then proceeded to Long Island, New England, and thence to the West Indies, and returned after an absence of about three years.

Soon after John Taylor's return from his transatlantic visit, he went on gospel service to London. His arrival there was during the severe persecution of Friends which followed the outbreak of the Fifth monarchy men, and in common with a large number of his friends, he was taken from a meeting and committed to gaol, from which, however, he was released in the Second Month, 1661. "After awhile," he observes, "it was upon me from the Lord to go into America again." Obedient to the heavenly call, he left London, in 1662, for the West Indies, and visited the Islands of Nevis, Barbadoes, and Jamaica. At Jamaica he believed it was required of him to settle. Having lived about one year on this island, he returned to London to accomplish an intended marriage, after which he resided for about two years longer at Jamaica as a merchant. Early in 1666, he left Jamaica with his wife and family, in a ship "bound for Barbadoes, through the gulf of Florida." But

* Journal of John Taylor, p. 2.

the vessel having been carried out of its course, the voyage was so prolonged that at last it was deemed needful to sail to New England for supplies. They reached Boston in the Third Month, where John Taylor and his family landed. At this place he stayed three weeks and then removed to Rhode Island, from whence, after remaining about six months, he proceeded to Barbadoes and resided there until the year 1676, when he returned to England and settled at York, as a sugar refiner. During his residence in Barbadoes he was frequently from home in the service of his Divine Master, not only in the islands of the West Indies, but also in England, Ireland and Holland. After he settled at York he was also largely engaged in the work of the ministry in different parts of the nation, to the comfort and edification of his friends. He died in the Twelfth Month, 1708, aged about seventy years, having been a minister about fifty years.*

As in New England, so also in the province of New York, the Society of Friends from its rise made a gradual and onward progress, and many of those who had embraced its doctrines, shone brightly in the cause of truth, and were as lights to the inhabitants of the land. They were concerned in their daily walk, to adorn the doctrine of God their Saviour ; and by their faithfulness, they were instrumental to the gathering of others to the enjoyment of the substantial realities of religion. The blessing of the Lord was upon this portion of his people, and the heavenly dew evidently rested upon them. Under the constraining influences of divine love and life, the mouths of several were opened to declare of the riches of the heavenly kingdom, and of the peace and joy which was to be found within the safe enclosure of the fold of Christ.

The churches in the province of New York had been abundantly watered by servants and hand-maidens from other lands, and in the divine economy, it pleased the Great Head of the Church, to call some of his devoted ones of this part to travel in

* Journal of John Taylor. Preface.

other countries in his holy cause. About the year 1664, Mary Wright of Oyster Bay, proceeded on a gospel mission to New England, and again in 1677. She also visited most of the other colonies of North America. Her sister, Hannah Wright, when only fourteen years of age, visited Boston to warn the persecutors of that place, " in the name of the Lord," to cease from their wicked work. She entered one of the courts, and, it is said, the authorities were dumb with astonishment at the " dread and power of the Lord," that attended her on the occasion.*　In 1680, Lydia Wright, another Friend of Oyster Bay, also travelled to the neighbouring colonies, in the work of the gospel. John Bowne of Flushing, and Elizabeth Bowne, his wife, who were both called to the work of the ministry not only visited the colonies of America, but, about the year 1675, extended their labours to Great Britain.

About the year 1682, meetings for worship appear to have been settled on the mainland at New York, and Westchester, and on Long Island, at Oyster Bay, Flushing, Gravesend, Jamaica, and also on Shelter Island. How many Monthly Meetings had been established, it does not appear. In an epistle addressed by the Half-Yearly Meeting to the Yearly Meeting of London about this period, meetings for worship and discipline are thus alluded to : " First, as touching our worship ; we keep our meetings according to the wholesome order and institution of Friends, to wit, Weekly, Monthly, Quarterly, and Half-Yearly Meetings, both men and women's ; the same meetings we enjoy in great peace, and [they are,] many times attended with an extraordinary heavenly sense of the holy power and presence of God, to our great joy and comfort ; and are, thereby, many times occasioned to render living praises and thanksgiving unto the Lord."

It has already been mentioned, that Friends of Long Island, had been tried by some who had fallen from their first love, and who, in a spirit of opposition, had, at times, disturbed the meetings of Friends. These troubles, however, gradually disappeared: " through patience and quietness," continues the epistle

---

* New England Judged, p. 461.

referred to, " we have overcome in and through the Lamb ; and we of a truth have found, that the Lord takes care of his people, and makes them ashamed who grieve his heritage.   So that our testimonies go forth without any hinderance, and return not unto us wholly empty again, but have their fruitful workings upon both Dutch and English nations ; in the sense of which, our hearts rejoice in the Lord, for that his holy light of life breaketh through darkness as the dawning of the day, to the redemption and salvation of the poor creature, and to the praise, honour, and glory of his holy name."*

* MS. Epistle.

CHAPTER XIX.

THE colony of Virginia, was another district in the new world, to which the attention of the Society of Friends, soon after its rise, was directed. At a very early date, several of its ministers were attracted in gospel love to this plantation, among whom was Elizabeth Harris of London, who appears to have been the first who visited that country. No account of the precise date of her embarkation for Virginia has been preserved, but it is evident that it took place as early as the year 1656. Her religious labours were blessed to many in that province, who were sincere seekers after heavenly riches, and she was instrumental in convincing many, of the primitive and spiritual views of the christian religion professed by Friends.

Elizabeth Harris returned from Virginia in the Fifth Month, 1657, but, solicitous for the welfare of her converts in that land,

she endeavoured to strengthen and encourage them by epistolary exhortations, and by supplying them with books illustrative
of our religious principles.   One item in the national stock
accounts for 1657, is, " For books to Virginia £2. 5s."*

Among those in Virginia who were convinced by the ministry
of Elizabeth Harris, was Robert Clarkson, an influential settler,
who resided at Severne, and who is spoken of by Thomas Hart
of London, in a letter to George Taylor, of Kendal, as being, he
supposed, the " governor of that part." Robert Clarkson took
much interest in the prosperity of the little community of
Friends in that colony, and a letter addressed by him to Elizabeth Harris, in 1657, contains some particulars of its state, from
which we give the following :—

"From Robert Clarkson to Elizabeth Harris.

" Elizabeth Harris, dear heart,—I salute thee in the
tender love of the Father, which moved thee towards us, and do
own thee to have been a minister, by the good will of God, to bear
outward testimony, to the inward word of truth in me and others ;
even as many as the Lord in tender love and mercy, did give an ear
to hear.   Praises be to his name for ever.   Of which word of life,
God hath made my wife partaker with me, and hath established
our hearts in his fear, and likewise Ann Dorsey in a more large

* The following letter, addressed by Gerard Roberts of London, to
George Fox, refers to the return of Elizabeth Harris from Virginia,
and of her services there :—

"Dear G. F.—These enclosed papers I received from John Stubbs,
who is now in Kent : my dear love is to thee. I could not but write
these few lines to thee to acquaint thee that the Friend who went to
Virginia is returned in a pretty condition ; and there she was gladly
received by many who met together. The governor is convinced. Our
meetings here are pretty quiet. Dear E. Burrough is not very well :
his service is and hath been very great of late. Glad should I be to see
thee this way.   John Perrot is gone to Turkey.   Friends to New
England went two months since, who may be there by this time.

                              " Thy dear friend,

                                        Ger. Roberts."

"London, 9th of Fifth Month, 1657."

measure ; her husband I hope abideth faithful ; likewise John Baldwin and Henry Caplin ;—Charles Balye, the young man who was with us at our parting, abides convinced, and several others in those parts where he dwells. Elizabeth Beaseley abides as she was when thou wast here. Thomas Cole and William Cole have both made open confession of the truth ; likewise Henry Wool-church ; and many others suffer with us the reproachful name. William Fuller abides unmoved : I know not but that William Durand doth the like ; he frequents our meetings but seldom ; indeed we have but a small company. Nicholas Wayte abides convinced. Thus I have been moved to write thee word, briefly concerning the work of the Lord amongst us, both in myself and others, since thy departure from hence, as the Lord hath given me to discern it. Though absent in body, yet being kept present in that love which did first move in thee towards us ; I say, being kept abiding in that, we may rejoice together ; there being joy in heaven at the conversion of one sinner ; and truly in the remem-brance of it, I have been filled with refreshment and joy unspeak-able. Glory be to his name, who is the living fountain which fills all that abide in Him.

" The two messengers thou spoke of in thy letters, are not yet come to this place ; we heard of two come to Virginia in the fore part of the winter, but we heard that they were soon put in prison, and not suffered to pass ; we heard further that they desired liberty to pass to this place, but it was denied them, whereupon one of them answered, that though they might not be suffered, yet he must come another time. We have heard that they are to be kept in prison till the ship that brought them be ready to depart the country again, and then to be sent out of the country. We have disposed of the most part of the books which were sent, so that all parts are furnished, and every one that desire it, may have benefit by them ; at Herring Creek, Roade River, South River, all about Severen, the Brand Neck, and thereabout, the seven mountains, and Kent ; all these parts are so furnished that every one may have also of them. Some we have yet to dispose of ; as the Lord gives opportunity we shall give them forth to those that desire them.

" With my dear love I salute thy husband and the rest of Friends [at London], and rest with thee, and the rest of the gathered ones in the Eternal Word, which abideth for ever. Farewell.

" ROBERT CLARKSON."

" From Severn, the 14th of the Eleventh Month, 1657.
" This is in Virginia."

About the time that Elizabeth Harris embarked for the shores of Virginia, Josiah Cole and Thomas Thurston, who both resided in Gloucestershire, also had an impression of religious duty to visit that land. They appear to have sailed from Bristol, and reached Virginia towards the close of 1657, and they are, without doubt, the " two messengers" referred to in Robert Clarkson's letter. Their religious labours were continued in this province until the Sixth Month, 1658, when they proceeded on their memorable visit to the Indians, and travelled through the forests of the interior, to New England.*

---

* The following letter, in reference to this religious prospect, was addressed by Josiah Cole to Margaret Fell some months previous to his embarkation. It is without date, but endorsed by George Fox, " From Josiah Cole to M. F., 1656."

" FROM JOSIAH COLE TO MARGARET FELL.

"Dear heart, when I was with thee I saw little of my going to Virginia with Thomas Thurston ; but since, I have been made sensible of the groanings of the oppressed seed in that place ; unto which my soul's love dearly reacheth, and I am much pressed in spirit to go there, and to pass through the Indian's country amongst them, and to go into New England : and it is also upon my dear brother Thomas Thurston to go through with me. Dear, let thy prayers be, that in unity and love we may be preserved and kept together faithful to the Lord, in his power and wisdom to stand continually ; that wheresoever the Lord calls us, we may have a good savour unto God in all his servants which shall come after us, which is the desire and breathings of my soul ; that the Lord alone may be honoured and glorified, who is worthy.

Josiah Cole

Although Josiah Cole makes no mention of his being imprisoned in Virginia, yet it is evident by the reference which Robert Clarkson makes to the imprisonment of the two strangers, that the rulers of this province, like those of New England and New York, were disposed to exert their power to prevent the principles of Friends from spreading in their territory, and in 1658 they passed a law for the banishment of Friends, and making it an act of felony, should they venture to return.*

Thomas Thurston, soon after he had reached Rhode Island, returned to Virginia, where he was again imprisoned. In a letter which Josiah Cole sent to Margaret Fell, about this period, the circumstance is thus alluded to :—" As concerning my dear brother Thomas Thurston, when I parted from him at Rhode Island he was very well ; and since, I hear, he is returned to Virginia, where he has been imprisoned, but is now at liberty again, and the governor of that place hath promised that he shall have his liberty in the country ; where there is like to be a great gathering, and the living power of the Lord goes along with him."†

The colony of Virginia having been founded by rigid Episcopalians, they insisted that their doctrines should be the only ones recognised in its jurisdiction, and in 1643, when a considerable number of Puritans in New England, were making preparations to settle on the inviting lands of the province, they passed a law that no minister should preach or teach but in conformity to the English church.‡ Under the commonwealth, however, the cords of religious bigotry were loosened, and but for the law passed in 1658, for the banishment of Friends, religious freedom would, at that period, have been universal in Virginia. On the restoration of the monarchy, a political revolution followed, opposed to the principles of popular liberty, and the former exclusive policy was revived. One of the first acts of the royalist assembly of Virginia, in 1661, was the disfranchisement of " Major John Bond," a magistrate, for " factious and

---

* Bancroft's United States.   † Manuscript Letters of Early Friends.
‡ Act 64, Hening, i. p. 277.

schismatical demeanours ;"* and though there was not a minister in more than one parish in five, every settler was, nevertheless, required to contribute to the maintenance of the English church, and, following the example of the rulers at home, the laws made against Papists in the reign of Elizabeth, were directed with great severity against Friends ; a monthly fine of twenty-pounds was imposed upon them for absence from church, and their own meetings were forbidden under heavy penalties.

These exhibitions of Episcopalian intolerance in Virginia, were identical with the outburst of persecution towards Friends in England, and under the new enactments, large numbers of Friends were arraigned as nonconformists. On one of these occasions, one of the sufferers, after pleading for "tender consciences," informed the authorities that he and his friends felt bound to "obey the law of God, however they might suffer." But the hearts of his judges were untouched by his appeal, and the answer he received was, that with them there was "no toleration for wicked consciences."†

It was during this period of persecution that George Wilson of Cumberland went on a gospel mission to Virginia, and, as a victim to the reigning intolerance, he was soon incarcerated in the dungeon at James's Town. The circumstances of his case evinced great barbarity on the part of his persecutors. The place of his imprisonment was an extremely loathsome one, without light and without ventilation. Here, after being cruelly scourged and heavily ironed, for a long period, George Wilson had to feel the heartlessness of a persecuting and dominant hierarchy ; until at last his flesh actually rotted from his bones,‡ and within the cold damp walls of the miserable dungeon of James's Town, he laid down his life a faithful martyr for the testimony of Jesus.§

Four Friends had been publicly executed in New England, for nonconformity to Puritan opinions, and the cruelty exhibited towards George Wilson, for simply dissenting from Episcopacy,

* Hening, ii. p. 39.   † Richmond Records, No. 2, in Bancroft.
‡ New England Judged, p. 351.
§ Testimony concerning W. Coale, printed 1682.

was of nearly equal atrocity. The American wilderness had been sought as a refuge by men of almost every shade of religious opinion, but, excepting the colony of Rhode Island, and Nathaniel Silvester's little domain of Shelter Island, the new world at this period, presented nothing inviting to the persecuted Quaker. The Puritans in New England, the Episcopalians in Virginia, the Papists of Maryland, and the Calvinistic authorities of New Amsterdam, whilst differing with and persecuting each other joined in a common effort to crush this rising and harmless people.

Respecting the life of George Wilson, but few particulars have been met with. His home, it appears, was in Cumberland, and as early as 1657 he suffered imprisonment in that county "for reproving a priest."* When he left his native land for the shores of the new world it is not mentioned, but in 1661 we find him a sufferer in New England for the truth. In this year he was imprisoned at Boston, and, preparatory to banishment, he was subjected to the torture of the lash in three towns of Massachusetts; soon after which he proceeded on a gospel mission to Virginia. The patience and resignation with which he bore his aggravated sufferings in this province, and his faithfulness unto death, form another striking instance of the inflexible adherence to conscientious conviction, which so remarkably characterised our early Friends. Living near Him who is the fountain and fulness of love, his enemies also became the objects of his solicitude; and whilst lingering in the wretched dungeon of James's Town, his heart was lifted up in prayer for his persecutors. " For all their cruelty," he writes, " I can truly say, Father forgive them, for they know not what they do."† During his imprisonment in Virginia, he gave forth, it is said, " many precious writings," which were, after his death, forwarded to Friends in England.

William Coale of Maryland, was another who experienced the cruelty of Episcopalian bigotry in Virginia. He was a fellow-

---

* Besse, vol. i. p. 128.   † Ibid, ii. p. 384.

prisoner with George Wilson in James's Town, and he never entirely recovered the cruelties he endured during this imprisonment. His visit to Friends in this part was blessed; "some were turned to the Lord through his ministry, and many were established in the truth."*

The rulers of Virginia pursuing their restrictive policy, imposed, in 1662, heavy fines on those, who, to use their own language, were "so filled with the new-fangled conceits of their own heretical inventions, as to refuse to have their children baptised."† Ship-masters were also forbidden, on pain of banishment, to receive nonconformists as passengers, and John Porter, one of the colonial representatives, who became a Friend, was expelled the assembly in 1663, "because he was well-affected to the Quakers."‡

Towards the close of 1658, the feet of other gospel messengers were directed towards Virginia; these were, William Robinson, Christopher Holder, and Robert Hodgson, three of those who crossed the Atlantic in the "Woodhouse." Of their gospel labours in this province we have but little information, but by some remarks in a letter from William Robinson, it appears that their ministry was blessed to not a few. "There are many people convinced," he says, "and some that are brought into the sense and feeling of truth in several places."§ In the course of the following year it seems probable that Humphrey Norton also visited this province.

The religious welfare of Friends in Virginia, was a subject in which few felt a deeper solicitude than Josiah Cole, and during his second visit to the western world in 1660, he was again drawn to visit them. Writing to George Fox from Barbadoes in the following year, he says, "I left Friends in Virginia generally very well, and fresh in the truth; of my departure from hence I know not at present, but I believe it will be to Virginia again."||

During the year 1661, George Rofe, in the course of his travels

* Piety Promoted, Part i.   † Hening, ii. p. 166.   ‡ Ibid, ii. p. 198
          § W. Robinson's Letter, 1659. || Swarthmore MSS.

in America, also visited Virginia. He has left us no very circumstantial account of his services in this land; but a letter addressed by him to his intimate friend Stephen Crisp, briefly adverting to them, is worthy of insertion.

FROM GEORGE ROFE TO STEPHEN CRISP.

Barbadoes, 15th of Ninth Month, 1661.

" DEAR S. C.—My life salutes thee in that which is pure and eternal; wherein the Lord hath prospered my soul according to my desire, and blessed me and his work in my hands, and hath made me an instrument of good to many through these countries; to the gathering many into the knowledge of the truth, and the settling of many in a good sense of the life and power of the Lord; whereby they bless the Lord for his visitation, knowing it is life unto them, and virtue to their souls, who believe and obey it; though it brings anguish upon the souls of all who do not believe unto obedience; so that the gospel is a savour of life unto life, and a savour of death unto death.

" But to mention passages at large I cannot now; but this thou mayst understand, that the truth prevaileth through the most of all these parts, and many settled meetings there are in Maryland, and Virginia, and New England, and the islands thereabouts; and in the island of Bermuda; through all which places I have travelled in the power of the Spirit, and in the great dominion of the truth, having a great and weighty service for the Lord; in which I praise Him, he hath prospered me in all things to this day.

" I remain, thy dear brother,"

G Rofe

In the year 1661, Elizabeth Hooton and Joan Brocksoppe also visited this colony. They came to it direct from England, and at a subsequent date, on their expulsion from Massachusetts, returned to it; but no particulars of their services in this colony have been met with. The next gospel labourers who appear to have visited Virginia, were Joseph Nicholson, John Liddal, and Jane Millard ; this was about the latter end of 1662. In reference to the visit of these Friends, it is said that " they had many hard travels and sufferings in the service of the Lord."* In the following year Mary Tomkins and Alice Ambrose also visited this colony. How long they were occupied in gospel labours there it does not appear ; their visit, however, was very opportune in checking the progress of the schism occasioned by John Perrot, who had recently arrived in that part. The following letter, addressed by these dedicated women to George Fox, contains some particulars of their services in Virginia.

The Cliffs in Maryland,
the 18*th of the Eleventh Month,* 1663.

" DEAR G. F.—The remembrance of thee, and the precious words which thou spoke unto us when we were with thee, remaineth with us a seal on our spirits. Dear George, we are well, and God is with us. We have been in Virginia, where we have had good service for the Lord. Our sufferings have been large amongst them. John Perrot is now amongst them ; many there are leavened with his unclean spirit. He has done much hurt, which has made our travels hard, and our labours sore ; for which we know he will have his reward, if he repent not. What we have borne and suffered concerning him, have been more and harder than all we have received from our enemies ; but the Lord was good, and was with us, and in his power kept us over him. We have not time to acquaint thee of much more. We are now about to set sail for Virginia again. We are not clear of New England ; if the Lord will, we may pass there in a little time, if he maketh way for us. Dear George, it is our desire, if it were the will of God, to go to England again as soon as we can see our way there, for we greatly desire to see thee and Friends again. Let thy prayers be to the Lord for us, that we may live unto him for ever.

" MARY TOMKINS.
" ALICE AMBROSE."

* New England Judged, p. 423.

Agreeably to the intimation contained in the foregoing letter, Mary Tomkins and Alice Ambrose returned to Virginia. In the course of their first visit to that colony, they appear to have suffered much from its Episcopalian rulers, but on this occasion the conduct of their persecutors was extremely barbarous. The lash was resorted to with great cruelty, each of the sufferers having been subjected to " thirty-two stripes" from a knotted and " nine-corded whip." Their goods were then seized, and in the Fourth Month, 1664, they were expelled the colony.*

In every age of the world, the church has been more or less subject to troubles arising from the unfaithful within its own borders, who, through unwatchfulness, have fallen from their first love, and become a prey to the snares of Satan. The early Christian church had painful experience of these things. Judas, though one of the chosen twelve, fell from his apostleship and sold his Lord. Hymenæus and Philetus departed from the truth, and became dangerous corrupters of the brethren. " Their word eat as a canker," and, it is recorded, " overthrew the faith of some."† Alexander the coppersmith was another painful instance. " He did me much evil," writes Paul, and " greatly withstood our words."‡ The Nicolaitan heresy was also another fruitful source of evil to the primitive church, and although its doctrines were so utterly at variance with the purity of the religion of Christ, there were, nevertheless, not a few of the early Christian converts, who embraced its sin-pleasing principles.§ If, then, in the purest age of the church, such afflictions were permitted to befal it, it ought, surely, to excite no surprise, that the followers of Him who was betrayed by Judas, should, in after times, have to experience similar dispensations from the wickedness of unregenerate man, and the malice of the unwearied adversary of the church.

The Society of Friends, arising as it did, in a time of peculiar excitement in reference to religious things, was remarkably preserved in harmony and love, and from the withering influence of

* New England Judged, p. 440. † 2 Timothy i. 17, 18.
‡ 2 Timothy iv. 14, 15. § Revelations ii. 1-5.

jars and contentions. It was not, however, entirely free from troubles of the kind to which we have adverted. The schism produced by John Perrot, was a melancholy proof of this ; and which also extended itself to Friends in America.

The division occasioned by John Perrot commenced in 1661, and arose by his endeavouring to introduce among Friends what George Fox calls " the evil and uncomely practice of keeping on the hat in time of public prayer."* Perrot, whom Sewel describes as " a man of great natural parts,† united at a very early period with Friends ; and in 1660, travelled in the ministry to Rome, with a view, it is said, to convert the Pope.‡ Whilst at Rome, he bore a public testimony against the idolatrous usages of the Papists, but for which he was soon subjected to the terrors of the Inquisition. Notwithstanding the appearance of great sanctity which marked the character of John Perrot, it was the sense of some discerning Friends of that day, that he proceeded to Rome, more in his own will, than from a divine call. During his imprisonment in that city, he evinced no inconsiderable degree of spiritual pride ; and his addresses were written in a style so affected and fantastic, as induced the belief that he was of unsound mind, and the inquisitors accordingly selected Bedlam as the place of his incarceration.§

The imprisonment of Perrot at Rome was a very prolonged one ; and his sufferings there, together with the great outward sanctity which he manifested, brought him into much notoriety among Friends. His true character, however, soon began to show itself ; and, declaring that he was more enlightened than George Fox and his brethren, he maintained that the practice of uncovering the head in time of prayer, was a mere form, and one which ought to be testified against. To such a woeful extent had forms and ceremonies, altogether unauthorised by Scripture, crept into the professing churches of Christendom, that Friends, in bearing a testimony against these inventions, at once became a peculiarly distinguished people. Drawn off as our early Friends

* Journal of G. Fox, vol. i. p. 555.   † Sewel, p. 249.
‡ Life of Thomas Ellwood, p. 241.   § Ibid, p. 242.

were, from the routine of lifeless observances, and participating so
abundantly as they did in the true refreshment and consolations
of the gospel without such outward means, it is not at all surprising that a readiness to listen to suggestions against forms of
every kind should be a besetment ; and, unhappily, the notions
of Perrot found an entrance.

There is no doubt but that Perrot was a man of much plausibility of manner, and of some eloquence.   The number of Friends
who were led away with his new notion was considerable, and
caused no little anxiety to those faithful watchmen, who saw in it
a snare of the enemy.   Another extravagancy adopted by Perrot,
was to let his beard grow ; a practice in which many of his followers joined.   With a view to propagate his opinions, he proceeded to America and the West India islands, where, by his
" show of greater spirituality,"* he was successful in gaining
many adherents from among the newly-convinced ; and particularly in Virginia.   Subsequently, Perrot also discouraged the
attendance of meetings for worship, under the notion that this
also was a mere form ; and so greatly were Friends of Virginia
led astray by him, that most of them followed his pernicious
example, and forsook their religious assemblies.

John Perrot resided for some time in Barbadoes, where a considerable number professed with us.   On his arrival there, Friends,
several of whom were in affluent circumstances, in the hope of
reclaiming him, showed him much kindness, and contributed
largely to his wants.   " He was even loaded with the love and
kindness of Friends," writes John Taylor, " in the hope that he
would become a reformed man ; but," he continues, " he, like an
unhappy and unworthy man, abused all the kindness of Friends,
and the very mercies of God unto him."†   He afterwards removed
to Jamaica, and became clerk of the court on that island.   Here,
he manifested a degree of depravity which clearly evinced that
he was out of the truth ; for he not only exhibited much haugh-

* Life of Ellwood, p. 243.
† John Taylor's " Loving and Friendly Invitation to all Sinners to
Repent, with a Brief Account of John Perrot," printed 1683, p. 7.

tiness of manner, and pride in dress, but he fell also into gross
sensuality.　He afterwards practised as a lawyer in Jamaica, but
died soon after, and so much in debt, that all his property was
seized by his creditors.*

Though most of the influential Friends in England continued to
bear a very decided testimony against the unsound notions of
John Perrot, yet it was some years before "this strange fire," as
Sewel calls it, was entirely extinguished.　The manifest departure of the author of this schism, not only from a religious life,
but from the paths of morality also, tended to open the eyes of
his followers to their error, and prepared them for a restoration to
their brethren.　In the year 1666, at the express desire of
George Fox, a meeting on this painful subject was held in
London.　It lasted several days, and was a memorable and
solemn occasion.†　"Those that had run out from the truth
and clashed against Friends," observes George Fox, "were reached
unto by the power of the Lord, which came wonderfully over
them—and the Lord's everlasting power was over all."‡　"In
the motion of life," writes Thomas Ellwood, "were the healing
waters stirred, and many through the virtuous power thereof
restored to soundness ; and, indeed, not many lost."§

The effects of the unsound notions were sorrowfully apparent
in Virginia.　The Friends of this part, in their conscientious
endeavours to follow their Lord, had borne much suffering, and
under it had been bright examples of faithfulness.　They were a
tender-hearted people, who had received the truth in the love of
it, and who were ready to embrace whatever might appear to
make for the glory of God, or to advance that holy cause which
had become dear to them.　When, therefore, John Perrot came
amongst them, and preached a seemingly higher degree of spirituality, many listened to his specious declarations, and, under the
idea that his views were founded in truth, they adopted them.
The enemy of their soul's peace appeared to them in the character

---

* J. Taylor's "Loving and Friendly Invitation, &c., p. 9.
† Life of Ellwood, p. 244.　　‡ Journal of G. Fox, vol. ii., p. 86.
§ Life of Ellwood, p. 244.

of an angel of light ; they were dazzled by the luminous manifestation, and betrayed into his snares. One wrong step having been taken, others followed ; and, deviating little by little from the true path, they at last went so far astray as to become even careless in regard to religion, and " much one with the world in many things."*   But it pleased Him who watcheth over his church, to look with an eye of tender regard on these his erring children, and by his servants to point out their delusions and their dangers.   About the time that the meeting referred to was held in London, John Burnyeat, whom George Fox mentions as " a pillar in the house of God," arrived on a gospel mission in Virginia, and laboured in the love of Christ among his brethren ; especially among those who had been led aside by the unsound notions of Perrot.   He had some difficulty in obtaining a meeting with them, but at last one was held, in which the gathering arm of the Great Shepherd was manifested.   " The Lord's power," remarks John Burnyeat, " was with us, and amongst us ; several were revived and refreshed, and through the Lord's goodness, and his renewed visitations, raised up into a service of life, and in time came to see over the wiles of the enemy."†

During a second visit which, in 1671, John Burnyeat made to America, he again visited Virginia, accompanied by Daniel Gould of Rhode Island.   Their services on this occasion are thus described by John Burnyeat : " I went down to Virginia to visit Friends there, and found a freshness amongst them ; and they were many of them restored, and grown up to a degree of their former zeal and tenderness ; and a great openness I found in the country, and I had several blessed meetings.   I advised them to have a men's meeting, and so to meet together to settle things in good order amongst them, that they might be instrumental to the gathering of such as were cold and careless ; and so to the keeping of things in order, sweet, and well amongst them."‡

A few months after the visit of John Burnyeat and his companion, William Edmundson arrived in Virginia.   His attention was also directed to the settlement of meetings for discipline in

* Journal of J. Burnyeat.   † Ibid.   ‡ Ibid.

these parts. After having had " several powerful meetings, I
appointed," he says, " a men's meeting for the settling of them
in the way of truth's discipline."* He then proceeded to Carolina ; but on his return to Virginia, renewed his labours in
establishing meetings for discipline. At a meeting specially convened for this object, he remarks that the Lord's power was with
them, and that " Friends received truth's discipline in the love
of it, as formerly they had received the doctrine of truth."†
William Edmundson laboured in the cause of his Redeemer in
several parts of Virginia, to the convincement of some, and the
confirmation of others. At Green Springs, he was instrumental
to the gathering of some who had been scattered, through the
unfaithfulness of one who had been a minister among them.
" These," he writes, " were much comforted, as sheep that had
been astray, and returned again to the shepherd, Christ Jesus ;
so I left them tender and loving." His meetings were frequently
attended by " persons of note" in that country ; General Bennett,
and Major-General Colonel Dewes were of this number. Colonel
Dewes was one who sought after the substantial enjoyments of
religion, and who rejoiced in the revival of those truths which
Friends had to declare, and which he afterwards openly professed.
" He was a brave, solid, wise man," observes William Edmundson,
" and who received the truth and died in the same."‡

The next gospel labourers from Britain who visited Virginia
were George Fox, Robert Widders, James Lancaster, and George
Pattison. This was in the Ninth Month, 1672, and after George
Fox had travelled through most of the colonies in the north. At
Nancemum they had " a great meeting of Friends and others,"
at which Colonel Dewes, and several others of the civil and military
authorities were present, and who, observes George Fox, " were
much taken with the truth declared."§   Another meeting was
held about four miles distant, and a third at William Parrett's,
at Pagan Creek.   The latter was so largely attended, that it was
found needful to hold it in the open air.   The powerful preach-

* Journal of W. Edmundson, p. 88.   † Ibid, p. 90.
‡ Ibid, p. 93.   § Journal of G. Fox, vol. ii. p. 171.

ing of George Fox and his companions, among the planters of Virginia, roused many of them to a serious consideration of their spiritual condition. The truths they had heard sank deep into their hearts, and to many " were as nails fastened in a sure place." " A great openness," remarks George Fox, " there was ; the sound of truth spread abroad, and had a good savour in the hearts of the people."

After visiting Carolina, these indefatigable labourers in the work of the gospel returned to Virginia, where they were engaged for about three weeks," having many large and precious meetings." At one held at Crickatrough, George Fox says, " many considerable people" were present. On leaving Virginia, George Fox proceeded to the adjacent colony of Maryland, from whence he embarked for England, after having, as he remarks, " travelled through most parts of North America, and visited most of the plantations ; having alarmed people of all sorts where we came, and proclaimed the day of God's salvation amongst them."*

The gospel labours of Burnyeat and Edmundson in America, and their exertions in settling meetings for discipline, largely benefited the rising Society in that land ; but the labours of George Fox were, in no ordinary degree, blessed to the settlers in the western world. In almost every place where he came, numbers were convinced of the doctrines he preached ; and in no part was this more strikingly apparent than in Virginia. It is stated that the number of Friends in this province was nearly doubled by his powerful ministrations ; and among the newly-convinced were individuals both of influence and station.

At a very early period of the Society's history, George Fox was impressed with the advantages to be derived by mutual epistolary intercourse between Friends in England and their distant brethren ; but up to this date, no correspondence had, it appears, taken place between London Yearly Meeting and the churches in other countries. On his return from America, he landed at Bristol, where a numerous body of Friends resided ; and, as there were frequent opportunities at that place of sending

* Journal of G. Fox, vol. ii. p. 181.,

to Virginia and Maryland, he suggested an epistolary intercourse with Friends of those provinces. The recommendation was approved, and in a few months, Bristol Monthly Meeting forwarded an epistle to Friends of Virginia. The communication was cordially received ; and in a feeling of true Christian love and fellowship, they responded to the interest thus manifested towards them, and returned the following answer :—

FROM FRIENDS OF VIRGINIA, TO BRISTOL MONTHLY MEETING.

" Dear friends, in the endless love of the Almighty, do we reach unto and kindly salute and embrace you. These are to let you understand, that we received your loving letters, and have had them read in our meetings, to the refreshment of ourselves and other Friends, in hearing and considering your declared love unto us, chiefly and above all things desiring of the Lord, that, by the operation of his power, we may grow up together with you, in the life and power of God ; to the praise of his great and glorious name, and to the establishment of our everlasting unity and fellowship, in the same life and power. The four books you sent by Lot Ricketts, by the ship *Comfort,* we have received, and have also disposed of them according to your order ; and we are also greatly refreshed, and glad to hear that truth prospers so well amongst you in England, than which nothing can be more welcome tidings unto us ; and we, also, in some measure, can give you the like intelligence. Everlasting praises be given to God. Since our dear friend George Fox's departure hence, (whose coming amongst us, hath been very prosperous,) our meetings, which at that time were not large, are at this time, (as we suppose,) more than doubled ; and several of them, (we do believe,) are very true and savoury Friends ; and not only so, but (as we judge,) a large convincement is upon many who as yet stand off ; and some there are amongst us, as well as amongst you, that through their miscarriages and disobedience, do give advantage to the enemies to speak reproachfully of truth ; which at some times doth cause some dissettlement amongst us, and doth so at this present also, we being not many in number ; but as the power of God hath in a large measure expelled all former slights of the enemy, and cleared up the understandings of Friends to a new gathering into his truth, so we trust, that by the same power, all things that are contrary to truth, and the prosperity thereof, shall be brought to nought ; and we do hope, that he that hath begun the work amongst us will carry it on in power, to the eternal praise of his name, and to the everlasting welfare of such as abide in it.

" We kindly bid you farewell, and remain your friends and brethren."

> " WILLIAM DENSON,
> " WILLIAM PARRATT,
> " THOMAS JORDAN."

" *Nansemum, 25th of Fourth Month,* 1674."

A few months previous to the return of George Fox from America, the works of Edward Burrough, in one thick folio volume, had issued from the press. It was ten years since the death of this remarkable man had taken place, but his memory was still fresh in the remembrance of his friends, and many of his powerful addresses to them under suffering, and to the rulers of the nation who persecuted them, were revived in the volume in question. Like many others of our early Friends, Edward Burrough had a clear apprehension of the rights of conscience, and his views of civil and religious liberty on the one hand, and of the duty which, as christian citizens, we owe to the government under which we live, on the other, were set forth by him, on several occasions, in clear and powerful language. George Fox, ever alive to what might promote the cause of righteousness, was desirous that some of the rulers and influential persons he had met with in the course of his transatlantic journeyings, should peruse the works of his deceased friend. He was persuaded that the truth would be promoted by such a step, and, acting upon this conclusion, he sent a copy of the work to sixteen individuals of the class referred to. The care of forwarding them was entrusted to Friends of Bristol, who thus write to the parties in America to whom they were consigned. " Our beloved George Fox, when at Bristol, was refreshed in the remembrance of the free-passage of the gospel in America, and of the many kindnesses shown to him there by some in authority, and with the remembrance of his love to them, doth send to each of them a large book, being the memorable works of a servant of the Lord, Edward Burrough; which, when come to your hands, we desire your care to convey unto each man one, whose names we here underwrite, being the persons he nominated to us."*

A few years after William Edmundson returned from America, he proceeded on a second gospel mission to that land, and in 1676, again arrived in Virginia. His visit to the province at this period was peculiarly acceptable to Friends, who were placed in circumstances of considerable difficulty in consequence of a civil commotion which then raged in the colony. " Friends," he

* MSS. of Bristol Monthly Meeting. The following is a list of the several parties to whom the book was to be presented, prepared evidently by George Fox himself.

Colonel Thomas Dews, at Nansemum.

Major-General Bennett.

Lieutenant-Colonel Waters, in Accomack.

Judge Stephens, at Anemessy.

Thomas Taylor, one of the Council, and Speaker of the Assembly.

The Judge at Wye River, to be left with Robert Harwoods.

The Judge of the Court and his wife, at Sassifrax River.

Justice Frisby.

Major-General Maleverate.

Deputy-Governor Gransuck, in Rhode Island.

Governor Winthrop, in New England.

The Governor of Delaware.

The Governor of New York.

Nicholas Easton, Governor of Rhode Island.

Dr. Winsor, and the Judge that liveth near him, in Chopthank, in Maryland.

One of the Council and his wife, that liveth near Margaret Holland, in Maryland.

The Judge that liveth near Henry Wilcox, in Maryland.

 Let Thomas Turner deliver the books to the Judge and Justices on that side; he liveth at Seaverne.

Justice Jordan, near Accomack, in Potomac.

One Floyd, about Wye, in Maryland.

Justice Jonson and Coleman, at Anemessy.

The Governor of Carolina.

remarks, " stood neuter, and my being there was not vain on that account." The quarrel was one of a very exciting character. The revolutionary party, as they were considered, were urged on by real or supposed grievances, and a cry for popular liberty, with which the authorities, who were strongly attached to the aristocratic views of the old royalists, did not sympathize. The former, though including most of the colonists, were nevertheless held by the government at home, as rebels, and a force was despatched to suppress them. The affair ended in the restoration of the governor, who evinced his revenge on the subdued party; twenty-two of whom he had executed, and he would have proceeded further in his sanguinary course, had he not been stopped by a resolution of the assembly. Amidst these distractions, William Edmundson was favoured to pursue his gospel errand without obstruction, and held " many precious meetings" with his Friends.

About the year 1678, John Boweter visited Virginia. He appears to have travelled through most of the settled parts of the province; but no particulars of his religious engagements, have been preserved, further than the names of the places he visited.*

We shall conclude the present chapter by inserting a brief memorial of the lives of George Rofe and Josiah Cole.

* In a list of " The names of places and Friends in America, where John Boweter was received and had meetings and service for the Lord in the gospel of peace," the following in Virginia are mentioned :—

James River in Virginia.

James River at Chuckatuck	Eliz. Outland.
Pagan Creek - - -	Wm. Parretts, Wm. Bodilie.
Southward - - -	Edward Perkins.
Nansemun - - - -	Matthew Atkinson.

Accomack.

Pongaleg by Accomack shore.

Pocomock Bay.

Annamesiah - - -	Ambrose Dickson.
Moody Creek in Accomack -	George Johnson.
Savidge Neck - - -	Robert Harris.
Nesswatakes - - - -	George Brickhouse.
Ocahanack - - -	Jonas Jackson.
Moody Creek - - -	John Parsons.
Annamesiah - - -	George Johnson and George Wilson.

GEORGE ROFE.

On the rise of the Society of Friends in the eastern parts of England, George Rofe was residing at Halstead in Essex, and was by trade a glazier. No particulars of his convincement have been handed down to us ; it must, however, have been at a very early date, as in 1655 we find him on a gospel mission in Kent.* During the same year, whilst travelling in Suffolk, he was imprisoned at Bury for being, as the mittimus expresses it, " a Quaker," and at the ensuing sessions, together with George Whitehead and John Harwood, he was indicted as a " common disturber of magistrates and ministers." George Fox the younger was present at the trial, and observing that the accusing parties were themselves the judges, he remonstrated with them on such injustice. But his Christian boldness offended the authorities, and he also was committed to prison. The place in which they were confined was a very miserable one, and for about seven months their only resting-place was on the damp earthen floor, and subsequently the gaoler, a cruel and heartless man, placed three of the sufferers in a small dungeon about twelve feet under ground. Considerable exertion was made for their release, and at last their case was laid before Cromwell and his council, " wherein," says Besse, " Mary Saunders, a waiting gentlewoman in the Protector's family, was very serviceable."† After an im-

---

* Besse, vol. i. p. 289.

† Mary Saunders at this time was a Friend, having been convinced by the ministry of Francis Howgill, on his visit to the Court in 1654, and it is interesting to notice that her acceptance of our religious views did not subject her to expulsion from the Protector's family. During George Fox's visit to London in 1656, he met with Cromwell at Hyde Park, when he remonstrated with him on the persecuting conduct of the authorities towards Friends. Cromwell, on his return to the palace, said to Mary Saunders with much meaning that he would tell her " some good news." Mary, whose attention was much excited by the remark, asked him what it was. Cromwell answered, " George Fox is come to town." " That," replied Mary, " was good news," and on the following day she hastened to his lodgings.

prisonment of more than a year, an order for their liberation was issued from Whitehall in the Eighth Month, 1656.*

In the year 1657, George Rofe was again subjected to imprisonment for his religion, and passed five months in one of the gaols of his own county, and in the Ninth Month of the same year, whilst travelling in Suffolk, he was placed in the stocks. Towards the close of 1657, his religious engagements were more extended, and he proceeded, in company with William Ames, to the Continent of Europe. At Creishiem, a village in the Palatinate of the Rhine, they were instrumental in the convincement of a little company, who, in after years, emigrated in a body to Pennsylvania, and settled at a place which they named Germantown. How long George Rofe was occupied in gospel labours on the continent is not ascertained, neither have we any further account of his religious engagements until near the close of 1659, when he proceeded on a visit to the West India islands and America. He was accompanied in the early part of this transatlantic visit by Richard Pinder of Westmoreland, who, in writing to George Fox, from Barbadoes, in the Sixth Month, 1660, remarks thus, " I have lately been at an island called Bermuda, where I left George Rofe. Great service," he adds, " is done in that place."† The success, indeed, that attended his ministry on this island greatly disturbed the priests, and at their instigation he was committed to prison.‡

Towards the latter end of 1660, he proceeded to North America, and for about one year laboured in the service of his Lord in most of the English colonies of that region, after which he returned to the West Indies. In the early part of 1663, he paid a second visit to North America, during which he was much engaged in New England, and on Long Island.

In addition to his labours in the ministry, George Rofe also endeavoured to promote the cause of his divine Master through the aid of the press, and from 1656, to 1663, several small pieces issued from his pen. The work of this dedicated Friend was now nearly accomplished. Soon after leaving Long Island, in

* Besse, vol. i. p. 663.   † Swarthmore MSS.
‡ Besse, vol. ii. p. 366.

1663, he was drowned during a storm in Chesapeake Bay. In a letter addressed to Stephen Crisp by William Caton, dated from Amsterdam, in the Fifth Month, 1664, the circumstance is thus referred to:—" I had lately a letter out of Maryland, with a book of dear George Rofe's, from a Friend there, who did absolutely confirm the truth of the report of dear George's being cast away in a little boat upon Maryland's river, in a storm."* The following remark respecting him occurs in an ancient American manuscript:—" And so having visited Friends in these parts, of whom he was well beloved and accepted, he lastly went to Maryland, and there finished his course and ended his life."

JOSIAH COLE.

Josiah Cole was convinced of the principles of our religious Society through the instrumentality of John Camm and John Audland, during their memorable visit to the city of Bristol in the year 1654. He was then about twenty-one years of age, of a highly respectable family, and resided at Winterbourne, near Bristol. Before his convincement, his mind had been much turned to the consideration of divine things, and he became deeply impressed with the emptiness and lifelessness of forms and ceremonies in religion. " I saw nothing of God in them," he observes, " for they were but as a shadow, vanity, and nothing—and in my heart I could not join with them. But how to come into the way of life I was still a stranger, until the Lord in his eternal power sent the ministers of the word of life, who were anointed of Him, and endued with power from on High, to preach the glad tidings of the Gospel, whose voice I rejoiced to hear, and whose testimony I gladly received ; for they declared the way of life, that it was in the midst of the paths of judgment."† He subsequently passed through deep conflict of mind. " I saw," he says, " that my heart was polluted, and that there was no habitation for God, which caused me to mourn in desolation and to wander in solitary

---

* Swarthmore MSS.
† A Song of Judgment and Mercy, in his collected works, p. 132.

places, until I was ready to faint; and I said in my heart, never man's sorrow was like my sorrow." In this time of trial he cried earnestly unto the Lord, and covenanted with Him. "If thou wilt indeed bring me through thy judgments, and grant me thy everlasting peace; if thou wilt destroy the enemy of my soul, and give me rest from those that oppress me; then will I teach sinners thy way, and transgressors shall be converted unto thee; yea, I made many promises unto Him that I would give up my life unto his service, and that I would follow him whithersoever he would lead me."* Having in no ordinary degree experienced the baptizing and purifying power of Christ, he became an able and powerful minister of the Gospel; "his declarations to the ungodly world," says William Penn, who knew him well, "were like an axe, a hammer, or a sword, sharp and piercing, being mostly attended with an eminent appearance of the dreadful power of the Lord; but to the faithful and diligent, O the soft and pleasant streams of life immortal that have run through him to the refreshing of those of the Lord's heritage."† "In prayer and supplication," writes Croese, "he did it with so much effect, and with such a grace and mode of speech, though without affectation, that he infinitely surpassed many of his brethren."‡

Devotedness to the cause of truth and righteousness was a remarkable characteristic of our early Friends, but in no instance was it more strikingly exemplified than in the life and character of Josiah Cole. Almost from the time of his convincement to the time of his death, he laboured incessantly in the heavenly warfare. It has already been stated that he twice visited North America and the West India islands; subsequently he also went on a Gospel mission to Holland and the Low Countries, whilst in England his religious labours were extended to nearly every county. On several occasions he was interrupted in his Gospel travels by imprisonments. As early as 1654 he was imprisoned in Bristol, and two years later at Weymouth. In 1660 he was

---

* A Song of Judgment and Mercy, p. 133.
† W. Penn's Testimony concerning Josiah Cole; Works, p. 16.
‡ Croese Hist. of Friends, p. 52.

confined in the goals of Leicester and Cambridge. Under the provisions of the Conventicle Act, he was committed in 1664 to Newgate, and towards the close of the same year he was also imprisoned at Launceston, in Cornwall, and in the following year at Kendal, in Westmoreland. "For the sake of his blessed testimony," writes William Penn, "he baulked no danger, and counted nothing too dear for the name and service of the Lord."[*] Sewel, our historian, who knew him well, has left us this testimony respecting him:—"It was his life and joy to declare the Gospel, and to proclaim the word of God, for which he had an excellent ability ; and when he spoke to the ungodly world, an awful gravity appeared in his countenance, and his words were like a hammer and a sharp sword. But though he was a son of thunder, yet his agreeable speech flowed from his mouth like a pleasant stream, to the consolation and comfort of pious souls. Oh ! how pathetically have I heard him pray, when he, as transported and ravished, humbly beseeched God, that it might please him to reach to the hard-hearted, to support the godly, and to preserve them stedfast ; nay, with what a charming and melodious voice did he sound forth the praises of the Most High in his public prayers ! Though he went through many persecutions imprisonments, and other adversities, yet he was not afraid of danger, but was always valiant ; and he continued in an unmarried state that so he might the more freely labour in the heavenly harvest ; and many were converted by his ministry."[†]

The decease of this dedicated Friend took place in London, and his end was emphatically a triumphant one. " I have peace with the Lord ; his majesty is with me, and his crown of life is upon me." These were nearly his last words. Among the few who were present at his close were George Fox and Stephen Crisp ; and from their arms his spirit passed into the presence of Him, the promotion of whose cause among men had been his paramount delight. He had been a minister twelve years, during which he also published many religious treatises. He wrote zealously against Popery ; and one of his longest pieces was

* W. Penn's Testimony.   † Sewel's History, p. 463.

entitled " The Mystery of the Deceit of the Church of Rome
Revealed." The following is a copy of his burial register :—
" Josiah Cole, aged about thirty-five years, departed this life
the 15th day of the Eleventh Month, 1668, at Mary Forster's,
in John Street, having weakened and worn out his outward man
in the work and service of the Lord in the ministry of the everlasting gospel, and was interred in the burying-ground in Chequer
Alley." His death was a circumstance that was deeply felt by
his brethren ; and it is recorded that more than a thousand of
them attended his funeral.*

* Sewel's History, p. 465.

CHAPTER XX.

THE next in the order of date among the colonies of the New
world, where the Society of Friends arose, was that of Maryland.
Josiah Cole and Thomas Thurston, whilst visiting the Indians
of the interior in 1658, appear to have been the first who travelled
in this part of America. Towards the close of this year,
Thomas Thurston returned to the colony ; his object being now
to labour in the gospel among the settlers. In Maryland, as in
the other colonies of North America, there were piously-disposed
individuals whose hearts were much prepared to appreciate those
views of primitive Christianity which, in the convincing and
tendering power of Christ, the gospel ministers of the Society of
Friends preached to their fellow-men. When, therefore, Thomas
Thurston came amongst the colonists of Maryland, many of them

were given to feel that " the living power of the Lord" attended his ministrations ; and from them he met with a cordial welcome, and in several places little communities were soon gathered, who professed the doctrines he preached.

The prejudice which calumny and misrepresentation had raised against Friends in the mother country, had also found entrance into the unsectarian colony of Maryland ; and when, on the arrival of Thomas Thurston, it became known that he was a minister of the new sect, the courts of the colony for the first time lent their aid to religious persecution, and he was arrested and sentenced to an imprisonment of " a year and a day."* The excitement which prevailed in Maryland on the first appearance of Friends in that province, was considerable ; and the authorities, in their anxiety to prevent the introduction of views which they regarded as an evil of a grave character, imitating the example of the rulers of Massachusetts, imposed fines on any of the settlers who should " entertain Quakers," and four individuals were fined in the sum of £3. 15s. for evincing their hospitality to Thomas Thurston ; whilst another was cruelly whipped " for not assisting the sheriff to apprehend him."†

In the early part of the year 1659, Maryland was visited by other gospel labourers of the new society, but no attempts appear to have been made for their arrest ; these were William Robinson, Christopher Holder, and Robert Hodgson, and through the religious labours of these Friends, a considerable convincement took place.

For some years prior to the rise of Friends in Maryland, there had been great political strife and commotion among the colonists, arising from conflicting claims for the proprietary between Lord Baltimore, and a resolute man of the name of Clayborne. The pretensions of Clayborne resulted in a recourse to arms, in which his party was successful and obtained the power. In 1658, a compromise was effected, and the agent of Baltimore was allowed to rule under certain restrictions. In 1660, however, the colonists, influenced probably by the adoption at that period of an indepen-

* MS. Letter of W. Robinson, 1659.
† Besse's Sufferings, vol. ii. p. 380.

dent legislation in Virginia, followed the example, and also declared themselves independent. But this state of things was but of short duration, for, soon after the restoration of Charles II., the power of Baltimore was again established in Maryland. During the years 1658, and 1659, the period in which the Claybornites admitted the agent of Baltimore to rule, it was with the express stipulation that they should be allowed to retain their arms. Baltimore's representative, in order to strengthen the cause of his master, on the other hand organized a militia, a course which prominently developed the principles of the Society of Friends against all wars and fightings. The authorities of Maryland, finding that their orders for enrolling in this service were disobeyed by the settlers who had embraced our views, endeavoured to subdue their conscientious scruples by excessive fines and distraints. A list of thirty Friends who suffered on this account has been preserved, from whom property amounting in the aggregate to £172. 4s. 9d. was taken. Many Friends also suffered about the same time for conscientiously refusing to swear.*

* The following are recorded in *Besse's Sufferings* as having suffered about the year 1658.

FOR REFUSING TO BEAR ARMS.

	£.	s.	d.
William Fuller ⎱	8	15	6
Thomas Homewood ⎰			
Richard Keene . . .	6	15	0
William Muffit . . .	6	15	0
John Knap	7	10	0
Michael Brooks . .	4	10	0
Edmund Hinchman .	4	10	0
Henry Osborne . .	4	10	0
John Day	4	10	0
John Baldwin . . .	5	5	0
Thomas Mears . . .	5	0	0
Robert Clarkson . .	2	0	0
Henry Woolchurch .	5	5	0
John Homewood . .	7	10	0
Jonathan Neale . .	2	5	0
Carried forward .	75	0	6

	£.	s.	d.
Brought forward . .	75	0	6
Hugh Drew . . · .	4	10	0
William Davis . . .	4	10	0
William Cole . . .	16	0	0
Robert Dunn . . .	18	15	0
Francis Barnes . . .	6	5	0
John Ellis	6	5	0
William Eliott . . .	4	17	6
Edward Coppedge . .	5	7	0
Henry Carline . . .	5	13	6
John Walcott . . .	5	5	0
William Read . . .	7	10	0
Ismael Wright . . ⎱			
William Stockden . ⎰ 7	0	0
Guy White . . . ⎰			
John Holyday . . .	5	6	3
£172	4	9

Soon after the restoration of Charles II. the persecution of Friends in Maryland, as in some other parts of the new world, was, for a time, suspended. It was during this time of religious freedom that Josiah Cole arrived on a second visit to this colony. His presence among the newly convinced was peculiarly helpful at that time, for, owing to some who had "run into words without life," and others who "judged rashly," the harmony of the new society had been interrupted. After labouring about two months among his brethren, he had the heartfelt consolation to witness a change for the better. "These things," he writes, "are well over, and life ariseth over it all."* Whilst Josiah Cole was pursuing his gospel mission in Maryland, he addressed the following to George Fox :—

From Josiah Cole to George Fox.

The Province of Maryland,
this 21st of Eleventh Month, 1660.

Dear George,—Whom my spirit loveth, and whom I honour in the Lord, and who, in the life of truth, art dear and precious to me, in which, according to my measure which I have received, do I dearly salute and embrace thee. Dear George, as concerning passages here, all is quiet as yet in relation to the truth, and meetings are precious ; and the Lord manifests his precious presence and love amongst us in our assemblies ; and persecution doth not yet appear in this province of Maryland, but the spirit

FOR REFUSING TO SWEAR.

	£.	s.	d.
John Knap	3	10	0
Michael Brooks . .	7	10	0
William Stockley . .	3	15	0
Thomas Coale . . .	2	0	0
Thomas Mears . . .	8	5	0
Robert Clarkson . .	5	0	0
Edmund Burton . .	8	0	0
Carried forward . .	38	0	0

	£.	s.	d.
Brought forward . .	38	0	0
John Larkin . . .	15	0	0
Robert Harwood . .	11	0	0
Thomas Underwood .	7	10	0
Ralph Hawkins . .	10	5	0
Ismael Wright . . .	2	5	0
	£84	0	0

Francis Billingsley, 590 lbs. of Tobacco.

* MS. Letter of Josiah Cole, 1660.

thereof is chained down for a season, that the babes may renew their strength.—I have been amongst them about ten weeks, and have at present well nigh cleared myself in this province, and am upon passing down into Virginia to visit the remnant that is there, and to sound forth God's mighty day amongst the heathen; and as way is made, I shall pass to Barbadoes, and from thence to New England.   I remain thine in the truth,

Josiah Cole

Soon after the foregoing was written, religious intolerance was again manifested in Maryland, and Josiah Cole was banished from its jurisdiction. During the year 1661 George Rofe appears also to have visited this province; but no particulars of his services there have been met with, excepting the brief but full expression that he " travelled in the power of the spirit, and in the great dominion of the truth."*   Towards the close of 1662, Joseph Nicholson, John Liddal and Jane Millard proceeded on religious service to Maryland; and in the following year Mary Tomkins and Alice Ambrose, but of their religious engagements no account has been preserved.

During the year 1661, and the following year, several Friends in this colony had their principles against swearing and against bearing arms strongly tested.   Three were imprisoned for several months, and others were heavily fined for adhering to their conscientious convictions respecting these things.   Towards the close of 1662, no fewer than twenty-three Friends, who, in previous years had enrolled in the militia, but who now, in accordance with their altered views on the subject of war, declined to sanction such anti-christian proceedings, were each of them fined 500lbs. of tobacco for, as the warrant expresses it, "delinquency and breach of an Act, intituled ' An Act for military discipline.' "†   Reli-

* G. Rofe to Stephen Crisp, 1661.
† Besse's Sufferings, vol. ii. p. 381.

gious persecution, however, was but of short duration in this province, and for sixteen years from this date, no act of intolerance appears to have disgraced the colonial records of Maryland.

The European population of Maryland at this period was but small, not exceeding, it is estimated, 10,000. Unlike the Puritan colonies of the north, it possessed no towns, nor indeed any village of much importance ; the settlers being scattered up and down in log houses of one story high on the banks of the rivers or among the forests. The absence of towns was considered an evil, and attempts were made to form them under the provisions of law, but this proved an entire failure.

The schism in the Society arising from the notions of John Perrot extended itself also to Maryland. Thomas Thurston, who had " run well for a season," and who had been instrumental in gathering many to the truth, unhappily imbibed the opinions of Perrot, and for a while " drew a party after him." In the Second Month, 1665, John Burnyeat arrived in the colony, where he spent the whole of the summer in religious labours among the settlers. " Large meetings we had," he observes, " and the Lord's power was with us, and Friends were greatly comforted, and several were convinced."* The Perrot division was a subject to which the attention of John Burnyeat was much directed, and it was with much sorrow that he saw Thomas Thurston upholding the erroneous sentiments which led to it. " Great was the exercise and travail," he says, " which was upon my spirit day and night, both upon the truth's account, which suffered by him, and also for the people who were betrayed by him to their hurt ; but," he continues, " through much labour and travail in the Lord's wisdom and power, I and other faithful Friends of that province had to search things out, and to clear things to their understanding,—it pleased the Lord so to assist us, and bless our endeavours, that most of the people came to see through him, and in the love of God to be restored into the unity of truth again, to our great comfort, truth's honour, and their everlasting happiness."† Although John Burnyeat was favoured to be thus instrumental for the good of his brethren, he was not so as it regarded Thomas

* Journal of J. Burnyeat.   † Ibid.

Thurston.   Like John Perrot this deluded individual proceeded
from one wrong thing to another, until at last he had wandered
far from the true sheepfold.   " He was lost as to truth," writes
John Burnyeat, " and became a vagabond and fugitive as to his
spiritual condition, and little otherwise as to the outward."*
What a teaching lesson do instances of this kind furnish of the
frailty of man, and of the necessity there is for continued watchfulness and self-abasement.   A departure from true lowliness of
mind, and a self-confident spirit, are indubitable marks that our
foundation is not laid in Him who is the Rock of ages.

For more than five years after this visit of John Burnyeat, no
minister from England appears to have arrived in the province ;
in the Eighth Month, 1671, however, he again visited Maryland.
He had previously been in New England, and was accompanied
on this occasion by Daniel Gould, of Rhode Island.   In the
Second Month, 1672, after returning from the south, John
Burnyeat appointed a meeting to be held at West River, in
Maryland, for all the Friends in the province.   His object in
calling this meeting was, " that he might see them together
before he departed," for the purpose, it appears, of establishing
meetings for discipline among them.

At the date of the foregoing, George Fox, who had completed
his religious service in the West Indies, was making his way to
Maryland, together with James Lancaster, John Cartwright,
William Edmundson, Robert Widders, and George Pattison.
They had no knowledge of the meeting that John Burnyeat had
appointed, but, observes George Fox, " it was so ordered by the
good providence of God, that we landed just in time to reach
it."†   The gathering was a very large one.   Friends from all
parts of the province attended it, and it continued for four days.
But the attendance was not confined to Friends ; " many other
people," says George Fox, " came, divers of whom were of considerable quality in the world's account ; for there were amongst
them five or six justices of the peace, a speaker of their assembly,
one of the council, and divers others of note ; who seemed well

* Journal of J. Burnyeat.
† Journal of George Fox, vol. ii. p. 156.

satisfied with the meeting."*   "After the public meetings were ended," he continues, "the men's and women's meetings began." This General Meeting was an important occasion in the history of the Society in Maryland.   A few years previous, George Fox, in order to settle meetings for discipline, had travelled through most parts of Great Britain and Ireland ; and in addition to his public ministrations, an engagement for the same object attended him in the western world.   There had been meetings of the Society in Maryland for about fourteen years, but no attempt to establish those for discipline had been made.   The subject was, therefore, a new one to Friends of this province.   The benefits to be derived from such meetings, were largely explained to them by George Fox, who, observes John Burnyeat, "did wonderfully open the service thereof unto them, and they with gladness of heart received advice in such necessary things as were opened unto them ; and all were comforted and edified."*

After this memorable meeting at West River, George Fox and his companions proceeded to a place called the Cliffs, where another general meeting was held, to which, besides Friends, large numbers of the colonists came, including both Puritans and Papists.   Here also, as at West River, meetings for discipline were proposed and established.   From the Cliffs some of the European Friends proceeded to other colonies, but George Fox, John Burnyeat, Robert Widders and George Pattison crossed the Chesapeake to the Eastern shore of Maryland.   On the first day following they had a meeting in this district ; "a very large and heavenly one it was," remarks George Fox ; "several persons of quality in that country were at it, two of whom were justices of the peace,—many received the truth with gladness, and Friends were greatly refreshed."*

George Fox in the course of his transatlantic journeyings did not forget the aborigines.   They also were the objects of his gospel love, and he held two meetings with those of the eastern shore. "God," said he to them, "was raising up his tabernacle of

* Journal of George Fox, vol. ii. p. 156.
† Journal of J. Burnyeat.
† Journal of George Fox, vol. ii. p 157.

witness in their wilderness country, and was setting up his standard and glorious ensign of righteousness." The untutored North American Indian listened to his powerful ministrations with deep attention, and "confessed" to the truths he declared, and "carried themselves very courteously and lovingly." So deeply, indeed, had they been impressed with what had been said, that they evinced a desire to hear more, and enquiring where the next meeting would be held, expressed their desire to attend it.

On leaving Maryland, George Fox proceeded inland through Delaware and the Jerseys to Long Island. Excepting a few places on the coast, this portion of North America was untenanted by Europeans, and but an inhospitable wild, the difficulties of traversing which, were very great. They left the eastern shore at the head of Tredhaven Creek, and it occupied them ten days to reach Middletown in East Jersey. "It was," remarks George Fox, "a tedious journey through the woods and wilderness, over bogs and great rivers." At nights, by a watch fire, they sometimes lodged in the woods ; and at others in the wigwams of the friendly Indians. The country was so much of a wilderness that for a whole day together they travelled "without seeing man or woman, house or dwelling-place."

After George Fox had completed his religious engagements in New England and Long Island, he proceeded on a second visit to Maryland accompanied by Robert Widders, James Lancaster and George Pattison. His return was through the forest wilds of the Jerseys and Delaware. The journey occupied them nine days, and, as on the former occasion, they experienced many difficulties and dangers. In the course of this journey they passed through many Indian towns, and to the inhabitants of these humble dwellings, George Fox and his fellow-travellers were led to speak of the things of eternal life, and as he expresses it, to declare "the day of the Lord to them."

In the Seventh Month, 1672, these gospel labourers reached Miles river, on the Eastern shore, in the vicinity of which they had several meetings, and then proceeded to the Kentish shore, where two others were also held. Travelling about twenty miles further, they had another and a very memorable one, which was attended by several hundreds of the colonists, among whom were four justices and the high sheriff of Delaware. "A blessed meeting," says George Fox, "this was, and of great service, both for convincing and establishing in the truth those that were convinced of it. Blessed be the Lord who causeth his blessed truth to spread." George Fox now returned to Tredhaven Creek, and from thence, on the third of the Eighth Month, to a general meeting on the Eastern shore, appointed specially for all the Friends of Maryland.

The gospel mission of George Fox in the New World was a very remarkable one. The settlers everywhere evinced an eagerness to listen to his declarations, and by the effect of his preaching large numbers were added to the Society. His presence among his fellow-professors in this land was hailed as a blessing of no ordinary kind, and the churches were greatly strengthened by his labours. That double honour should be paid to such an one can excite no surprise. But it was not from those of his own Society only that George Fox received a welcome in America. Everywhere, governors, magistrates, and the authorities, both civil and military, received him with cordiality, and paid him marked attention. When we reflect upon the position which George Fox occupied, we need not wonder that this should have been so. The Society of Friends, of which it was understood that he was the founder, though of less than thirty years' standing, and notwithstanding the violent persecution it encountered, had now become, both at home and abroad, a numerous and increasing body, and included in its ranks men both of wealth and station. Another circumstance which caused the settlers in America to frequent the meetings of George Fox, was the rarity of ministers of any sort among them ; for, excepting in New England, there were at that period but few ecclesiastics in the land. None had yet settled in Carolina, and in Virginia they were so few that a bounty was offered to allure them ; and scattered as the settlers were along the banks of the rivers and creeks, it was a rare thing for them to hear a sermon of any kind. When, therefore, it was known that George Fox, "the head of the Quakers in England," had come amongst them, and was going to have a general meeting at Tredhaven Creek, the lonely settlers of both the Eastern and Western shore of Maryland, flocked from far and near to hear him. The following, penned by George Fox himself, gives us a graphic account of the meeting in question :—

" This meeting held five days ; the first three we had meetings for public worship, to which people of all sorts came ; the other two were spent in the men's and women's meetings. To those public meetings came many Protestants of divers sorts, and some Papists ; amongst these were several magistrates and their wives, and other persons of chief account in the country. There were so many, besides Friends, that it was thought there were sometimes a thousand people at one of those meetings. So that though they had not long before enlarged their meeting-place, and made it as large again as it was before, it could not contain the people. I went by boat every day four or five miles to the meeting, and there were so many boats at that time passing upon the river, that it was almost like the Thames. The people said ' there were never so many boats seen there together before.'* And one of the justices said ' he never saw so many people together in that country before.' It was a very heavenly meeting, wherein the presence of the Lord was gloriously manifested, and Friends were sweetly refreshed, the people generally satisfied, and many convinced ; for the blessed power of the Lord was over all ; everlasting praises to his holy name for ever ! After the public meetings were over, the men's and women's meetings began, and were held the other two days ; for I had something to impart to them which concerned the glory of God, the order of the gospel, and the government of Christ Jesus. When these meetings were over, we took our leave of Friends in those parts, whom we left well established in the truth."†

Leaving Tredhaven Creek, George Fox and his companions proceeded by way of Crane's Island, Swan Island, and Kent

---

* The mode of travelling in these parts at that period was mostly in boats on the creeks and rivers, or on horseback through the forests.

† Journal of George Fox, vol. ii. p. 168.

Island, to the other side of the " Great Bay." From thence they travelled about six miles to the house of a Friend who was a magistrate, where a meeting was held. On the following day, they had another meeting near the head of Hatton's Island ; and on the succeeding one, at a place about three miles distant. The next was held at Severn, to which " divers chief magistrates and many other considerable people" came ; " and a powerful, thundering testimony for the truth was borne." From this place he passed to the Western shore, and had a large meeting at William Coale's, " where," says George Fox, " the speaker of the Assembly" and several others " of quality" were present. The next meeting took place about seven miles off, and, two days later, another at the Cliffs, which was attended by " many of the magistrates and upper rank of people," and is mentioned as " a heavenly meeting." They next travelled to James Preston's, on the river Patuxent, where, remarks George Fox, " we had a meeting to take our leave of Friends, and a powerful meeting it was."

As stated in the preceding chapter, George Fox, on his return to England, encouraged his friends of Bristol to maintain a correspondence with their brethren in America ; and, acting on the suggestion, in 1673, an epistle, from which the following is extracted, was addressed by Bristol Monthly Meeting to Friends of Maryland : —

EPISTLE FROM BRISTOL MONTHLY MEETING TO FRIENDS IN MARYLAND.

" DEARLY BELOVED FRIENDS AND BRETHREN,—Although our abiding be at so great a distance, and we never had opportunity to see one another, yet are you very near and dear unto us in the Spirit ; in which we can and do embrace you as members of our body ; and are comforted in you ; and having heard of your obedience and faithfulness to the truth, by our beloved George Fox, and other Friends that came from you, we could not well forbear to write unto you, not only to manifest our unity with you, and the inward joy and consolation we have in you, but also to exhort you all to continue in the faith, and to walk worthy of that honour which the Lord God hath given you, in all lowliness of mind, and meekness of spirit ; every one waiting to feel a very hearty and willing subjection in themselves, to all the manifestations and revelations of the Truth ; and that none professing the truth, do walk, or move, or act in their own wills, or after the imaginations and thoughts of their own hearts ; but that every one wait to feel that will subjected, by the operation of the heavenly power mightily working in them ; yea, that the cross of Christ be known more and more, and abode in and daily taken up, until the creaturely will, or will of the flesh, be crucified, mortified, and slain ; not obeyed, not fed or nourished ; and so all giving up in the holy will that sanctifieth, may be able truly to say, I came to do thy will, O God. And so self in all its desires and lusts, being destroyed and baptized into death, the Lord God of life and power will be more and more manifested, and, in the overflowings of his own life and power, exalted and magnified ; and before the glory of his appearance, all crowns will be cast down before Him who liveth, and will reign for evermore.

" And now, dearly beloved friends, we give you to know that in this nation, the blessed truth which is pure, prospereth and spreadeth abundantly, and is of a good savour among men.—The meetings of Friends are very large and peaceful. Multitudes flock to hear the declaration of truth, and some come to abide in it.

" Our beloved George Fox, after his arrival from you in this place, stayed in and about the city about two months or more, and afterwards went for London, in and about which place he still remains, enjoying a good measure of bodily health and strength, which we esteem a very great mercy. The good report he gives of Friends in your country enlargeth the hearts of Friends here to love and embrace you ; and therefore let not the tender mercies and visitations of the Lord easily be forgotten or shut out of your remembrance, and glad shall we be as your freedom is, to receive some lines from you, whereby we may understand of your welfare and the prosperity of the precious truth in your hearts, and through your country, in the love of which truth we remain

" Your endeared friends and brethren,

" Tho. Gouldney.

" Thomas Callowhill.

" Charles Harford.

" William Ford.

" John Love."

" *From the Men's Meeting in Bristol,*
for ordering the affairs of truth, the
24th day of Ninth Month, 1673."

The epistle from Bristol was refreshing to the Friends of Maryland ; and, feeling that they were indeed brethren, baptized by the one Spirit into one body, and of the same household of faith, they responded to the address in the following affectionate language :—

Epistle from Maryland to Bristol Monthly Meeting.

" Dearly beloved Friends and Brethren,—In the blessed truth and covenant of the light, life, and peace, do we dearly salute you, whose lines of dear and tender love are come safe to our hands. Though absent in body, yet present in spirit, we dearly and truly embrace you, and truly receive your good exhortations ; and in the footsteps of you our beloved companions and elder brethren in the blessed truth, who are followers of the Lord in the way of holiness, we truly desire to tread and walk, truly blessing the Lord in the secret of our hearts through his Spirit, for his great loving-kindness and tender mercy to us-ward, who hath highly favoured us, and made us partakers of his heavenly gift, which is eternal life, and given us a part amongst them that are sanctified.—We do not write these things in commendation of ourselves, but of the living God, whose blessed work is begun in our hearts and carried on by his blessed power, that God over all may have the praise of his own work in us all, to whom be the glory of all, from us all for ever, amen. And that you, whom we dearly love, may more and more be comforted in us, and we in you, in the blessed truth, in which we truly and dearly salute you all, ye dear and faithful ones. And now, dearly beloved friends and brethren, we give you to understand that the enclosed paper of condemnation hath been of service amongst us ; and whereas you do very earnestly desire our watchfulness over any professing the truth that may come from your parts hither ; likewise, do we earnestly desire you to be very careful and watchful over any professing truth that may come from hence into your parts, that so as much as in us lieth, the worthy name of the Lord may not be dishonoured, nor his blessed truth and way of holiness reproached, to the grieving of any of his dear children. And now, dearly beloved, to acquaint you that the blessed truth of the Lord is more and more precious unto us, and the heavenly virtue of the same doth do us much good, blessed for ever be the Lord our God, whose mercy endures for ever, to all them that truly fear him. Much people there be in our country that comes to hear the truth declared, which in its eternal authority is over all, and many by it are convinced. But too many there be that doth not readily stoop to it, for that they come not to partake of the heavenly virtue of it. But blessed be the Lord God Almighty, for with the faithful and obedient it is not so. And now, dearly beloved brethren, we may not forget to make mention of our dearly beloved George Fox, with the rest of the servants of the Lord who accompanied him in the service of the blessed God in our country, whose labours, travels, and service, the Lord did exceedingly bless, to our great comfort, and consolation, and benefit, for which we then did and still do bless the Lord. Since their departure from us, we plainly understand their dear and tender love is toward us, which we feel the benefit of in our own hearts, and do return the salutation of our dear love in the blessed truth unto them all. And dearly beloved friends and brethren, glad shall we be, as you have opportunity and freedom, to receive some lines from you, whereby we may further understand of your welfare and the prosperity of the truth in England, in which blessed truth we once more dearly salute you, and remain your endeared friends and brethren.

"Signed by the order and appointment of the meeting, by

> "WILLIAM COALE.
> "WILLIAM RICHARDS.
> "JOHN GARY."

"*From the Men's General Meeting, at
West River, in Maryland, the 6th day
of the Fourth Month,* 1674."
"*To the Men's Meeting of Friends in Bristol.*"

"DEAR FRIEND,—The eight books sent by our friend Thomas Hucker, we had opportunity at our meeting to send away by safe hands to be delivered as directed, and with each book a note to signify to each person from whom and per what account they were sent. The other eight came by our friend George Hawes, which we have taken care to convey as speedily as opportunity presents, and so we remain.

"W. C."

On the 12th of the Eighth Month, 1674, Bristol Monthly Meeting again addressed an epistle of encouragement "To the General Meeting of men Friends at West River, in Maryland."

About the year 1676, William Edmundson was again drawn to visit the colonies of America. His labours in Maryland, though not extended, were blessed to his brethren. He held meetings both on the Eastern and Western shores of the Chesapeake. In the following year, John Boweter also visited this province. Of his religious services, however, we have no account further than a list of the places where "he was received and had meetings."*

* The following are those mentioned for Maryland :—

Chopthanck -   -   -   - {William Berry.
                                        {Walter Dickson.

About the year 1677, the faithfulness of Friends in Maryland, against judicial swearing, was severely tested by the imposition of excessive fines. In 1678, one Friend was fined 500 lbs. of tobacco for not taking the oath of a constable, and another was mulct in the same amount for refusing the oath of a juryman. The sufferings to which the Society in this plantation were exposed in this respect, obtained the notice of Friends in England, and, at the instance of the Meeting for Sufferings, William Penn had conferences with Lord Baltimore, the Proprietary, on the subject, in which he promised to adopt means to relieve his Quaker population from the grievance ; a promise, however, which he failed to fulfil until nearly ten years after. Considerable exertions were also made by friends of Maryland to obtain a legal absolution from swearing, by the recognition of a simple affirmation. In 1681 they presented a statement of their case to Lord Baltimore and his council. " It hath been sufficiently known" they state, " that we have been a suffering people, both ın our persons and estates, ever since the Lord was pleased first to raise us up to be a people, and particularly in the discharge of our consciences to God in refusing all oaths whatsoever, which command of Christ we dare not disobey ; for which cause we are

Tuchahow	-	-	-	-	{ Meeting-house and Betty Cove's.
					John Pitts.
					Ralph Fishborns.
Kent Island -	-	-	-		Sarah Thomas.
West Shore -	-	-	-		} Richard Snoden.
Rode River -	-	-	-		
West River -	-	-	-		Meetings.
Herring Creek	-	-	-		Meeting.
East Shore	-	-	-		Meeting.
Kent Island -	-	-	-		Hoil Powels.
Little Chopthanck		-	-		William Stevens.
Miles River -	-	-	-		Bryan Amaliell.
West River -	-	-	-		Thomas Taylor.
South River -	-	-	-		Thomas Linscomb's.
Herring Creek	-	-	-		Meetings.
The Cliffs	-	-	-	-	John Garie.
Patuxent	-	-	-	-	Benjamin Lawrence.

many ways laid open to our enemies, as a spoil both in our persons and estates. Nor are our sufferings like to terminate in our own persons, but also extend to the ruining of our wives and children."* After setting forth the impolicy of declining the civil services of Friends because they refused to swear, they add " We are made in many cases unserviceable to the Proprietary ; for although we are a considerable member of this province, and in many respects might be serviceable by bearing divers offices, yet because we cannot take the formal oaths, we are therefore made almost as useless."

The address was well received by the Upper House of Assembly, which, desirous of promoting the objects of Friends, made the following record on the occasion :—

" Upon reading the paper delivered yesterday by William Berry and Richard Johns, this House do say, That if the rights and privileges of a freeborn Englishman, settled on him by Magna Charta, so often confirmed by subsequent Parliaments, can be preserved by yea and nay, in wills and testaments, and other occurrents, the Lower House may do well to prepare such a law, and then the Upper House will consider of it."

The Lower House was also decidedly favourable to Friends in this matter ; many indeed of this representative assembly were members of the Society.† On receiving the minute, therefore, from the Upper House, they requested the two Friends who had presented the address, to prepare an answer to the question raised in reference to Magna Charta. This was readily undertaken, and a document on the subject prepared, entitled " Some reasons given to show, that this law desired in favour of tender consciences as to oaths, is not against Magna Charta, nor destructive to the ancient rights and privileges of Englishmen."‡ The " reasons" were satisfactory, and an Act was accordingly prepared and passed by the two Houses for the relief of Friends on this subject. An unexpected difficulty however now arose. For, it is said, " some particular reasons of state," Baltimore de-

---

* Besse, vol. ii. p. 383.

† MS. Letter of W. Richardson to Geo. Fox, Second Month, 1681.

‡ Besse, vol. ii. p. 384.

clined to sanction the measure, and it was not until the year 1688, that Friends of Maryland were relieved from the sufferings to which the anti-christian imposition of oaths subjected them.

The Society of Friends in Maryland, though less numerous than those professing with them in New England, and probably also than those in the province of New York, was, nevertheless, an increasing body. By their religious life and conversation, they had gained the esteem of the inhabitants at large, and on public occasions their meetings were numerously attended by them. William Richardson, of West River, a zealous and influential Friend, in a letter to George Fox in 1682, in speaking of their half-yearly meeting held in the spring of that year, says:—" We have had a very great meeting ; for number of people, never more in Maryland, and very peaceable to hear the truth declared." Of the Society itself he thus speaks:—" Friends are in general well, and in love and unity one with another, and I may truly say I never knew them more, or so much concerned for the truth, in the good order of our men's and women's meetings for keeping all things sweet and clean amongst Friends than they now are. Blessed be the Lord for it."

Almost from the commencement of the discipline, a strong jealousy was entertained by some, that its institution involved an undue interference with individual freedom of thought and action. Those who objected to meetings for discipline were for the most part persons whose conduct was more or less inconsistent with the self-denying professions of Friends, and who, consequently, were averse to the adoption of measures which would subject them to censure or control. There were some of this class in Maryland, and these, at times, proved troublesome to the Society. It was in order to expose the fallacious reasoning of those who objected to church discipline that William Penn wrote his " Brief Examination of Liberty Spiritual " and Robert Barclay his " Anarchy of the Ranters," in which the order of the discipline established among Friends is vindicated with great clearness and ability.

But notwithstanding these things, the Society in Maryland was favoured to enjoy much harmony and love, and in their epistle from the Half-yearly Meeting held in the early part of 1683, they could speak encouragingly of their state and condition. We close this chapter by the following, taken from the epistle referred to :—

An Epistle from the Half-year's Meeting in Maryland.

The 18th of Fourth Month, 1683.

" Dear George Fox,—Whom we dearly love and esteem in the blessed Truth and love of God, which is universal. Our Half-yearly Meeting in the Third Month last, having a sense of the care that is laid upon thee for the churches' welfare, did appoint us to give thee and Friends at London an account of the affairs of Truth in this province ; but we, finding the ships gone out of this province, so that sending is very difficult at this time, shall not enlarge as otherwise we might have done. So care may for the future be taken yearly from our Half-yearly Meeting in the Eighth Month, to give thee full account of Truth's concerns amongst us.

" At present Truth prospers in this province, and Friends that abide in the Truth are strong and valiant for God and the honour of his Truth.

" A heavenly time and great service we had at our Half-yearly men's Meeting in the Third Month last, which continued three days. The Lord crowned our meeting with his heavenly presence, which bound and chained down the enemy's power, which was felt to be great at that time, so that although he had made what strength he could, by his wicked, unruly instruments, to spoil, destroy, and devour, even in our assembly, the power of God they perceived to be amongst us in a mighty measure, so that shame and confusion covered their faces, and many young and tender Friends were thereby greatly strengthened, the Lord having evidently owned our proceedings ; for which we return glory and praise to God for ever. Amen. Here are many Friends of this province who find a concern laid upon them to visit the seed of God in Carolina, for we understand that the spoiler makes havoc of the flock there ; so here are many weighty Friends, intending [to go] down there on that service, and may visit Virginia and Accomack, and then we may inform thee how things are on Truth's account in those places. Our very dear love to thy wife, to A. Parker, W. Gibson, and G. Whitehead, and all the faithful. We remain thy friends in our measure of that glorious unerring Truth which the Lord hath manifested to us.

"Wm. Richardson,
"Wm. Berry,
"Richard Johns,
"Thomas Taylor."

NEW YORK

Newark

Elizabeth Town
Woodbridge
Raritan R.
Perth Amboy
Middleton
Shrewsbury
Freehold

New York
LONG I.

Staten I.

Sandy Hook

Trenton

Burlington

Woodbury

New Castle

Salem

Little Egg R.

Little Egg H.

Great Egg H.

Delaware R.

DELAWARE
BAY

Cape May

C. Henlopen

A MAP OF
NEW JERSEY.
IN 1682.

James Bowden, del.

Thomas Wells litho. 35 Basinghall St. Lond.

CHAPTER XXI.

THE territory of New Jersey previous to the year 1664 was included in the Dutch possessions of North America. At this date New Netherlands fell by conquest into the hands of the English, and the country between the Delaware and the Hudson was granted to Lord Berkley and Sir George Carteret, and in honour of the latter, who was then governor of the island of Jersey, it was called New Jersey. The number of settlers at the period when it first became an English plantation was but few, as but little attempt to colonize this district had as yet been made. In 1663, some Puritans from New England had settled on the banks of the Raritan, and in the following year a few families of the Society of Friends are said to have sought refuge near the same spot.* In 1665, several settlements took place in East New Jersey, and the towns of Middleton and Shrewsbury were beginning to rise, and Elizabethtown, with four houses only, was the capital of the province. Puritans from New England continued to arrive, and, under their influence, in 1668 a colonial legislature was convened at Elizabethtown. The proprietaries in England

* Bancroft's United States.

had appointed Philip Carteret governor of New Jersey, and things went smoothly on until the awkward question of quit-rents was mooted. The payment of this demand was resisted by the settlers ; angry disputes with the governor followed, and at last the colonists, claiming the right to legislate independently of the proprietaries, displaced the governor.

While the province was thus distracted, the English were at war with the Dutch, and a force having been sent by the latter to recover New Netherlands, and being successful, New Jersey in 1673 came a second time under Dutch control. But the change was of short duration ; in a treaty between the two powers, New Netherlands, in 1674, was finally transferred to British dominion.

The successful colonization of New Jersey, like that of New England, was a result of the Reformation, but not arising from efforts of the Church of Rome to regain her lost power and influence in Christendom, so much as from the antichristian and unwise policy of Protestant England in enforcing conformity to the national church. It is a remarkable circumstance, that when Western Europe became convulsed with religious persecution, the North American continent was the asylum to which its victims almost instinctively fled for refuge ; and it was thus that Puritans and Papists from England, exiled Covenanters from Scotland, and Huguenots from France, became inhabitants of the New World.

The Society of Friends soon after its rise suffered severely for the maintenance of views opposed to those of the ruling sects in England, but on the return of the Royalists to power the persecution towards them became most intense. During the hottest time of persecution, however, it was never contemplated by Friends to remove in a body to America in order to escape the cruelties of the mother country, but on the outbreak of persecution which ensued on the restoration of the monarchy, the idea of possessing a territory in the western world to which those of its members who desired it might flee for shelter, was seriously entertained by some of the most influential Friends of that day, and particularly by George Fox. To obtain land in North America for the foundation of a colony was, however, no easy matter, for the whole coast from Maine to Florida was either colonized or claimed by parties for that purpose. The Society of Friends, therefore, in pursuance of this interesting object, had to turn its attention to a territory inland. Josiah Cole, who had travelled extensively as a gospel minister in America, and particularly among the Indians of the interior, on his second visit to that country in 1660, appears to have been commissioned by his brethren at home to treat with the Susquehanna Indians, whom he had visited about two years before, for the purchase of land. For this purpose he had interviews with them, but their being at that time involved in a deadly war with some neighbouring tribes, together with the absence of William Fuller, a Friend of considerable influence in Maryland, and who had, it appears, taken some steps on this subject, presented an insurmountable obstacle to any progress in the matter at that time.*

On the restoration of New Netherlands to the English, Berkley and Carteret were again acknowledged as the proprietaries of New Jersey. Berkley, who was now a very old man, and whose expectations of colonial wealth, in the prospect of disputes with the independent settlers for quit-rents, was not likely to be realised, came to the conclusion to sell his moiety of the territory. The opportunity was a favourable one for Friends, and in the Third

---

* The following extract from a letter written from Maryland by Josiah Cole to George Fox in the Eleventh Month, 1660, which is preserved among the Swarthmore MSS., refers to this interesting subject :—

" DEAR GEORGE,—As concerning Friends buying a piece of land of the Susquehanna Indians, I have spoken of it to them, and told them what thou said concerning it, but their answer was, that there is no land that is habitable or fit for situation beyond Baltimore's liberty till they come to or near the Susquehanna's fort, and besides William Fuller, who was the chief man amongst Friends with the Indians, by reason he was late governor amongst the English, he is withdrawn at present, for there are of them who are in present authority that seek his life with much greediness for some old matter that they had against him, and their enemy is stirred up afresh, by reason he had a hand in changing of the government the last year, when they took away the

Month, 1674, a few months after George Fox had returned from his gospel mission in America, Berkley conveyed the whole of his right and interest in New Jersey to John Fenwick and Edward Billinge for the sum of £1000. Fenwick and Billinge were both members of the Society ; the former appears to have resided in Buckinghamshire, and the latter was a merchant of London ; and there is good reason to believe that the property was acquired by them for the advantage of the Society at large.

In the transfer of New Jersey from Berkley, the conveyance was made to John Fenwick in trust for Edward Billinge and his assigns. Subsequently, a disagreement arose between the two Friends as to their respective interests in the purchase ; but acting on the recognised views of the Society against " brother going to law with brother," they mutually agreed to submit their dispute to arbitration. The subject was an important one, and requiring, in its right disposition, the exercise of a sound judgment. William Penn then lived at Rickmansworth, in Hertfordshire, not far from the residence of John Fenwick ; and his talents and integrity pointed him out as a fit arbitrator of the question. He accepted the office, and, after considerable difficulty, finally awarded that one-tenth of the territory, with a con-

authority from Baltimore, which hath much stirred up their rage against him, so that without him there can little be done at present with the Indians ; and besides, these Indians are at war with another nation of Indians, who are very numerous, and it is doubted by some that in a little space they will be so destroyed that they will not be a people.

" Thine in the Truth,

Josiah Cole

William Fuller, before he united with Friends, took an active part in the quarrel between Clayborne and Baltimore for the proprietary of Maryland, and in 1656 acted as governor under an appointment by Clayborne. He therefore became obnoxious to Baltimore and his party, who, on regaining power, would doubtless have taken his life, had he fallen into their hands.

siderable sum of money, should be given to Fenwick, and that the remainder of the province should be the property of Edward Billinge.*

---

* The nature or cause of the dispute between John Fenwick and Edward Billinge is unknown. The former, however, appears to have been litigious and troublesome in the business. Among the Harleian MSS. in the British Museum, No. 7001, are three letters of William Penn to John Fenwick, upon this subject : these throw some light on the transaction, which we subjoin :—

London, 20th of Eleventh Month, 1674.

" John Fenwick,—The present difference betwixt thee and E. B. fills the hearts of Friends with grief, and a resolution to take it in two days into their consideration to make a public denial of the persons and accusation that offers violence to the award made, or that will not end it without bringing it upon the public stage. God the righteous judge will visit him that stands off. E. B. will refer it to me again. If thou wilt do the like, send me word ; and as oppressed as I am with business, I will give an afternoon to-morrow or next day to determine, and so prevent the mischief that will certainly follow divulging it in Westminster Hall ; let me know by the bearer thy mind. O, John, let truth and the honour of it in this day prevail : woe be to him that causeth offences ! I am an impartial man.

" W. Penn."

The foregoing letter has the following endorsement by Fenwick :—

" The Heads of my Answer to W. P.

" I desire to perform the award, and not to infringe it, but to receive my money securely, and to reserve my two parts entirely. To have up all my writs, and my reputation repaired and vindicated. All which W. Penn promised he would see performed.

" If any other thing be proposed contrary to the award, it must not be yielded unto, for several reasons, especially it will immediately open a door for a suit in Chancery."

Rickmansworth, 30th of Eleventh Month, 1674.

" J. F.,—I am sorry for thy arrest. E. B. I stopt from any proceed ; but for the Lord Berkley, it was not in my power. As to thy counsel, mine has told me that he was with him, and has stated it quite upon another footing, giving, as I perceive, a relation with all advantages for thee. Now, I must need complain of that proceeding. I took care to hide the offences on both hands, as to the original of the thing, because

It was not long ere a new difficulty arose. Edward Billinge became embarrassed in his circumstances, and was obliged to make a conveyance of his property in New Jersey for the benefit of his creditors ; and, desirous that the contemplated benefit to

it reflects on you both, and, which is worse, on the truth. Therefore, I undertook-it that I might hide your shame, and serve the truth ; and let me tell thee, that it was an unworthy, secret piece of undermining of my conduct in the matter, to give any such accompt, which concerned the present award. I cannot enough express my resentment of this thing. I intend to be to-morrow night at London, and design to make one essay more ; if that will not do, I intend no further concern therein. And for the award, I say that it is broke in nothing, but that of the way of raising money ; and if thou wilt not acquiesce in that particular, rather than come before the world, I am heartily sorry. I wish thee true felicity which stands in the blessed truth ; and thy conformity to it.

" Thy well-wishing friend,

" W. PENN."

London, 13th of Twelfth Month, 1674.

" J. F.,—I have, upon serious consideration of the present difference (to end it with benefit to you both, and as much quiet as may be), thought my counsel's proposals very reasonable ; indeed, thy own desire : the eight parts added was not so pleasant to the other party that it should be now shrunk from by thee as injurious ; and when thou hast once a proposal reasonable, and given power to another to fix it. 'Tis not in thy power, nor a discreet, indeed, a civil thing, to alter or warp from it, and call it a being forced. John, I am sorry that a toy, a trifle, should thus rob men of time, quiet, and a more profitable employ. I have a good conscience in what I have done in this affair ; and if thou reposest confidence in me, and believest me to be a good and just man, as thou hast said, thou shouldst not be upon such nicety and uncertainty. Away with vain fancies, I entreat thee, and fall closely to thy business. Thy days spend on, and make the best of what thou hast : thy great grand-children may be in the other world, before what land thou hast allotted will be employed. My counsel, I will answer for it, shall do thee all right and service in the affair that becomes him, whom, I told thee at first, should draw it up as for myself. If this cannot scatter thy fears, thou art unhappy, and I am sorry.

" Thy sincere friend,

" WILL. PENN."

the Society might not be lost through his embarrassments, he assigned his nine-tenths of the new territory to three of his fellow-members, viz., William Penn, Gawen Lawrie of London, and Nicholas Lucas of Hertford. The remaining tenth part being still held by John Fenwick.

Soon after Friends had become possessed of a territory in the New World, Fenwick, who was active in his endeavours to promote emigration, sold lands to those who had concluded to seek a home in the Quaker colony, an adventure in which he himself intended to embark. Fenwick, however, before he left England, obtained a sum of money from two individuals, John Eldridge and Edmund Warner, to whom he gave as security for its repayment, a lease on his portion of the province for 1000 years, with power for them to sell as much land as would repay the advances made. Notwithstanding the power which the lessees had thus acquired, Fenwick considered himself entitled to enter at once upon the territory, and to use it for his own particular benefit ; and, acting upon this conclusion, he set sail with a number of others, in the *Griffith*, from London, and in the Fourth Month, 1675, they landed on a pleasant fertile spot, on a creek of the Delaware, where a permanent settlement was made, to which they gave the name of Salem.* This was the first English ship which touched the shores of West Jersey. Fenwick, who claimed the authority of chief proprietor in the province, began to divide the land and to make grants to the several settlers, and also entered into treaty with the natives for the purchase of an extensive tract of country.

Whilst things were thus going forward, measures had been taken for a more general settlement of the province. William Penn and his co-assignees, in the exercise of their trust for the creditors of Edward Billinge, had disposed of considerable portions of the province ; several of the creditors, indeed, who were Friends,

---

* Among those who emigrated with Fenwick were Edmund Champ-ness, his son-in-law ; Edward Wade, Samuel Wade, John Smith, Samuel Nicholson, Richard Guy, Richard Noble, Richard Hancock, John Pledger, Hipolite Lefever, and John Matlock, who are all said to be " masters of families."

accepted lands in liquidation of their claims ; and thus, in common with the assignees, became proprietors.*

In the right settlement of West New Jersey as a colony, it was necessary that a form of government should be adopted. Previous, however, to any decided steps being taken for this purpose, it was considered needful that the boundary line between East and West New Jersey, should be clearly defined, and an agreement was accordingly entered into between Sir George Carteret, the proprietor of East New Jersey of the one part, and William Penn, Gawen Lawrie, Nicholas Lucas, and Edward Billinge, of the other part ; by which the line of division was settled to extend from Little Egg Harbour to a point on the Delaware in 41° of north latitude. After the boundary had been thus settled, Edward Billinge and his trustees re-conveyed the share that had belonged to Fenwick to Eldridge and Warner in fee, by which they were constituted proprietors.

The proceedings of Fenwick, in entering West Jersey and disposing of land as his own, after his conveyance to Eldridge and Warner, were regarded by the proprietaries with much dissatisfaction ; and with a view to assert their right to govern, and for conducting the affairs of the province until the form of government should be definitively settled, a provisional commission, dated Sixth Month, 1676, was given to Richard Hartshorne and Richard Guy, two Friends who resided in East Jersey, together with James Wasse, who was sent specially from England for the purpose.† The proprietaries, in a letter addressed to Richard Hartshorne at this period, refer to the principles which they intended to recognize in the future government of the colony.

---

* Thomas Hutchinson, Thomas Peirson, Joseph Helmsley, George Hutchinson, and Mahlon Stacey, Friends of Yorkshire, who were all principal creditors of Edward Billinge, and to whom several other creditors made assignments of their debts, accepted as an equivalent for their aggregate debts of £3,500., ten of the ninetieth parts of West Jersey.

† Richard Hartshorne was a Friend of London, who emigrated to East Jersey in the year 1669, and settled at Middleton. He is described as a " considerable settler," and " of good reputation and public character." Richard Guy emigrated to West Jersey in company with John Fenwick.

"We have made concessions by ourselves," they say, "being such as Friends here and there (we question not) will approve of, having sent a copy of them by James Wasse. There we lay a foundation for after ages to understand their liberty as men and Christians, that they may not be brought in bondage, but by their own consent; for we put the power in the people, that is to say, they to meet and choose one honest man for each proprietary, who hath subscribed to the concessions; all these men to meet as an assembly there, to make and repeal laws, to choose a governor, or a commissioner, and twelve assistants to execute the laws during their pleasure; so every man is capable to choose or be chosen. No man to be arrested, condemned, imprisoned, or molested in his estate or liberty, but by twelve men of the neighbourhood. No man to lie in prison for debt, but that his estate satisfy as far as it will go, and be set at liberty to work. No person to be called in question or molested for his conscience, or for worshipping according to his conscience; with many more things mentioned in the said concessions,"* "We hope," continues the letter, "West Jersey will soon be planted, it being in the minds of many Friends to prepare for their going against the spring." The place Fenwick had chosen for a town, was not, in the judgment of William Penn and co-proprietaries, the best for a "first settlement," and Richard Hartshorne was requested "to go over to Delaware side," and on "some creek or river, find out a fit place to take up for a town, and agree with the natives for a tract of land."†

The charter or fundamental laws of West New Jersey were settled and passed in the Third Month, 1676, under the designation of "Concessions and Agreements of the Proprietors, Freeholders, and inhabitants of the province of West New Jersey, in America," and was signed by one hundred and sixty-two persons. It consisted of forty-four chapters, and was framed with much method, and throughout the principle of democratic equality is fully and unconditionally recognized, and a full toleration of individual sentiment in religion prominently upheld. "No men,

* The History of Nova-Cæsaria, or New Jersey, by Samuel Smith, p. 80. † Ibid. p. 82.

or number of men upon earth, hath power or authority to rule over men's consciences in religious matters," says chapter xvi. ; " therefore it is consented, agreed, and ordained, that no person or persons whatsoever, within the said province, at any time or times, hereafter, shall be any ways, upon any pretence whatsoever, called in question, or in the least punished or hurt, either in person, estate, or privilege, for the sake of his opinion, judgment, faith or worship towards God, in matters of religion ; but that all and every such person and persons, may from time to time, and at all times, freely and fully have and enjoy his and their judgments, and the exercise of their consciences, in matters of religious worship throughout all the said province." In its civil arrangements, the members of the general assembly were to be chosen by the balloting box, and every man was eligible for election. The electors were empowered to give their representatives instructions, which, under hand and seal, they might be called upon to obey. The executive was to be vested in ten commissioners, to be appointed by the people ; and justices and constables were chosen directly by them. No man was to be imprisoned for debt ; courts were to be conducted without attorneys or counsellors. The aborigines were protected against encroachments ; the helpless orphan was to be educated by the state ; and " all and every person inhabiting the province, by the help of the Lord, and by these concessions and fundamentals, were to be free from oppression and slavery."*

For the information of Friends, a description of the province of West New Jersey was soon published, and many, invited by the prospects which were held out, made preparations for emigrating. William Penn, Gawen Laurie, and Nicholas Lucas, anxious that none of their brethren should take a step of so much moment without very deliberate consideration, published the following cautionary address to their friends on the subject :—

" DEAR FRIENDS AND BRETHREN,—In the pure love and precious fellowship of our Lord Jesus Christ, we very dearly salute you. Forasmuch as there was a paper printed several months

* Smith's History of New Jersey—Appendix, p. 521—539.

since, entitled *The Description of West New Jersey*, in the which our names were mentioned as trustees for one undivided moiety of the said province ; and because it is alleged that some, partly on this account, and others apprehending that the paper by the manner of its expression came from the body of Friends, as a religious society of people, and not from particulars, have through these mistakes weakly concluded that the said description in matter and form might be written, printed, and recommended on purpose to prompt and allure people to dis-settle and transplant themselves and families to the said province ; and lest any of them (as is feared by some) should go, out of a curious and unsettled mind, and others to shun the testimony of the blessed cross of Jesus, of which several weighty Friends have a godly jealousy upon their spirits ; lest an unwarrantable forwardness should act or hurry any beside or beyond the wisdom and counsel of the Lord, or the freedom of his light and spirit in their own hearts, and not upon good and weighty grounds ; it truly laid hard upon us to let Friends know how the matter stands, which we shall endeavour to do with all clearness and fidelity. [After setting forth the manner by which the province came into their hands, they thus proceed :]

" The ninety parts remaining are exposed to sale, on behalf of the creditors of Edward Billinge. And forasmuch as several Friends are concerned as creditors, as well as others, and the disposal of so great a part of this country being in our hands ; we did in real tenderness and regard to Friends, and especially to the poor and necessitous, make Friends the first offer, that if any of them, though particularly those that, being low in the world, and under trials about a comfortable livelihood for themselves and families, should be desirous of dealing for any part or parcel thereof, that they might have the refusal.

" This was the real and honest intent of our hearts, and not to prompt or allure any out.of their places, either by the credit our names might have with our people throughout the nation, or by representing the thing otherwise than it is in itself.

" As relating to liberty of conscience, we would not have any to think that it is promised or intended to maintain the liberty of the exercise of religion by force and arms ; though we shall never consent to any·the least violence on conscience ; yet it was never designed to encourage any to expect by force of arms to have liberty of conscience fenced against invaders thereof.

" And be it known unto you all, in the name and fear of Almighty God, his glory and honour, power and wisdom, truth and kingdom, is dearer to us than all visible things ; and as our eye has been single, and our heart sincere to the living God, in this as in other things ; so we desire all whom it may concern, that all groundless jealousies may be judged down and watched against, and that all extremes may be avoided on all hands by the power of the Lord ; that nothing which hurts or grieves the holy life of truth in any that go or stay, may be adhered to ; nor any provocations given to break precious unity.

" This am I, William Penn, moved of the Lord, to write unto you, lest any bring a temptation upon themselves or others ; and in offending the Lord, slay their own peace. Blessed are they that can see and behold Him their Leader, their Orderer, their Conductor and Preserver, in staying or going : whose is the earth and the fulness thereof, and the cattle upon a thousand hills. And as we formerly wrote, we cannot but repeat our request unto you, that in whomsoever a desire is to be concerned in this intended plantation, such would weigh the thing before the Lord, and not heavily or rashly conclude on any such remove ; and that they do not offer violence to the tender love of their near kindred and relations ; but soberly and conscientiously endeavour to obtain their good wills, the unity of Friends where they live ; that whether they go or stay, it may be of good savour before the Lord (and good people), from whom only can all heavenly and earthly blessings come.

" This we thought good to write for the preventing of all misunderstandings, and to declare the real truth of the matter ; and so we commend you all to the Lord, who is the watchman of his Israel. We are your friends and brethren,

" WILLIAM PENN.
" GAWEN LAWRIE.
" NICHOLAS LUCAS."

In the early part of the year 1677, many of those who had become proprietors in West New Jersey, left the shores of England to settle on their newly-acquired possessions. The ship sailed from London, and the emigrants, two hundred and thirty in number, consisted of two companies of Friends, one from Yorkshire, and the other from London. The circumstance of so large a number of Friends emigrating in a body to America, was a subject which attracted public attention. The King participated in this feeling, and, meeting the ship, whilst yachting on the Thames, and being informed that the passengers were Quakers who were bound for the new country, "he gave them his blessing."*

After a tedious passage, the ship anchored safely in the waters of the Delaware, and in the Sixth Month the passengers were all landed near Racoon Creek. Almost immediately after they had landed, the Commissioners, acting on the instructions received from William Penn and his colleagues, proceeded further up the Delaware, to the place where Burlington now stands, "to treat with the Indians about the land, and to regulate the settlements." Several purchases of land were made from the natives, but as Friends at the time had not goods sufficient to pay for all they had bought, it was further agreed not to occupy any part until it was all paid for.

A few months after the settlement at Burlington, another ship arrived from London, having on board about seventy passengers. Some of these settled at Salem, and others at Burlington. A vessel also arrived from Hull during the same year with one hundred and fourteen emigrants. In the following year another ship, called the *Shield*, left Hull with above one hundred passengers. In the course of 1678, another ship with emigrants also left London. The number of Friends who emigrated to the new colony during the years 1677 and 1678, is stated to be in all about eight hundred, a large number of whom were persons of property. Up to the year 1681, it is calculated that at least fourteen hundred persons had found their way to the new province.

* Smith's History, p. 93.—Ibid, p. 93.

In common with most of the early emigrants to the western world, the first settlers of West New Jersey were exposed to many hardships and privations. The country was, for the most part, a wilderness, and yielded nothing for the support of man but such as the chace afforded ; and the only dwellings of the settlers during the first winter, were hastily constructed wigwams. But the Christian conduct of Friends towards the Indians had gained their good-will, and enlisted their sympathies, and they were considerably relieved in their difficulties by supplies of corn and venison from these untutored aborigines. The providential manner in which the early settlers of this new colony were cared for, made a deep impression on the minds of many of them, and, sensible that they were regarded by Him who fed Israel in the wilderness, their hearts were lifted up in thanksgiving for the manifestation of his fatherly regard. The following, extracted from a paper written by one of the settlers who embarked from Hull in the *Shield,* in 1678, indicates this feeling, and will be read with interest.

" The first settlers were mostly of the people called Quakers, who were well-beloved where they came from, and had valuable estates : and though, while they lived in their native country, they had plenty of all necessaries, yet their desire to remove to America was so strong, that they could not be content without going thither ; and chose to venture themselves, their wives, children, and all they had, in the undertaking.

" But, notwithstanding the masters of families were men of good estates, yet, before they could get their land in order, and corn and stock about them, they endured great hardships, and went through many difficulties and straits ; nevertheless, 1 never perceived any of them to repine, or repent of their coming. As it is said in holy writ, the preparation of the heart in man is of the Lord, so it may well be believed that the hearts of these people were prepared for this service ; even to labour for the replenishing of the land ; it being a wilderness indeed, and they unacquainted with the nature of the soil, and also with the inhabitants ; altogether pilgrims and strangers at their first coming among them.

" A providential hand was very visible and remarkable, in many instances that might be mentioned ; and the Indians were even rendered our benefactors and protectors. Without any carnal weapon we entered the land and inhabited therein, as safe as if there had been thousands of garrisons ; for the Most High preserved us from harm, both of man and beast.

" The aforesaid people were zealous in performing their religious service ; for, having at first no meeting-house to keep public meetings in, they made a tent or covert of sail-cloth to meet under ; and after they got some little houses to dwell in, then they kept their meetings in one of them, till they could build a meeting-house. Thomas Olive and William Peachy were two of the first settlers who had a public ministry."*

The emigrant Friends to West New Jersey were individuals who had been awakened to the importance of religion, and who were zealous for the honour of the truth. From the time of their landing they were diligent in assembling for the public worship of the Most High, and having seen in their native land the benefits to be derived from meetings for discipline, in about seven months after Friends landed at Racoon Creek, a Monthly Meeting was regularly established at Burlington, the records of which commence with the following minute :—

" Since, by the good providence of God, many Friends with their families have transported themselves into this province of West Jersey, the said Friends in these upper parts have found it needful, according to the practice in the place we came from, to settle Monthly Meetings, for the well ordering of the affairs of the church ; it was agreed that accordingly it should be done, the 15th of the Fifth Month, 1678."

A care to discourage the sale of strong liquors to the Indians, and arrangements for the relief of their poor members, by instituting monthly collections, were some of the earliest acts of their discipline. Instituting the usual inquiries relative to proposals of marriage also formed no inconsiderable portion of their business. Within three years from the establishment of Burlington

* Proud's History of Pennsylvania, &c., vol. i. p. 157.

Monthly Meeting, thirteen couples, it appears, passed the Monthly Meeting with this object. Another subject which very early claimed their attention, was the propriety of having certificates of removal on behalf of Friends who had emigrated or might emigrate from England ; and with a view to forward this object, the Monthly Meeting, in the year 1680, addressed an Epistle to the Yearly Meeting of London.*

* This Epistle is the earliest, of which we have any record, that was received by the Yearly Meeting of London from any of the meetings in America : we subjoin a copy of it :—

" To our dear Friends and Brethren at the Yearly Meeting at London.

" Dear Friends and Brethren,—Whom God hath honoured with his heavenly presence and dominion, as some of us have been eye-witnesses (and in our measures partakers with you) in those solemn annual assemblies ; in the remembrance of which, our souls are consolated, and do bow before the Lord with reverent acknowledgment to him, to whom it belongs for ever. And, dear Friends, being fully satisfied of your love, and care, and zeal for the Lord and his truth, and your travail and desire for the promotion of it, hath given us encouragement to address ourselves to you, to request your assistance in these following particulars, being sensible of the need of it, and believing it will conduce to the honour of God and benefit of his people ; for the Lord having, by an over-ruling providence, cast our lots in these remote parts of the world, our care and desire is, that he may be honoured in us and through us, and his dear truth which we profess may be had in good repute and esteem by those that are yet strangers to it.

" Dear Friends, our first request unto you is, that in your several counties and meetings out of which any may transport themselves into this place, that you will be pleased to take care that we may have certificates concerning them ; for here are several honest and innocent people that brought no certificate with them from their respective Monthly Meetings, not foreseeing the service of them, and so never desired any, which for the future, in cases of which defect we do entreat you who are sensible of the need of certificates, to put them in mind of them ; for in some cases where certificates are required (and they have none) it occasions a great and tedious delay before they can be had from England, besides the hazard of letters miscarrying, which is very uneasy to the parties immediately concerned, and no ways grateful nor desirable to us ; yet in some cases necessity urgeth it, or we must act very unsafely, and particularly in cases of marriage in which we are often con-

In the year 1681, a considerable number of Irish Friends from Dublin and its vicinity settled in the province. The vessel in which they came belonged to Thomas Lurting, whose name is

cerned. So if the parties that come are single and marriageable at their coming away, we desire to be satisfied of their clearness or unclearness from other parties ; and what else you think meet for our knowledge. And if they have parents, whether they will commit them to the care of Friends in general in that matter, or appoint any particular person whom they can trust. And if any do incline to come that do profess truth, and yet walk disorderly, and so become dishonourable to truth, and the profession they have made of it, we desire to be certified of them and it by some other hand (as there are frequent opportunities from London of doing it), for we are sensible that here are several that left no good savour in their native land from whence they came, and it may be probable that more of that kind may come, thinking to be absconded in this obscure place ; but, blessed be the Lord, he hath a people here whom he hath provoked to a zealous affection for the glory of his name, and are desirous that the hidden things of Esau may be brought to light, and in it be condemned ; for which cause we thus request your assistance, as an advantage and furtherance to that work ; for though some have not thought it necessary either to bring certificates themselves, or require any concerning others, we are not of that mind, and do leave it to the wise in heart to judge whence it doth proceed ; for though we desire this as an additional help to us, yet not as some have surmised, that we wholly build upon it without exercising our own mediate sense as God shall guide us. Some, we know, that have been otherwise deserving, have been unadvisedly denied this their impartial right of a certificate, and very hardly could obtain it, merely through the dislike of some to their undertaking in their coming hither, which we believe to be an injury : and though we would not have any should reject any sound advice or counsel in that matter ; yet we do believe that all the faithful ought to be left to God's direction in that matter ; most certainly knowing by the surest evidence that God hath had a hand in the removal of some into this place, which we desire that all that are inclined to come hither, who know God, may be careful to know before they attempt it, lest their trials become insupportable to them : but if this they know, they need not fear, for the Lord is known by sea and land the shield and strength of them that fear him.

" And, dear friends, one thing more we think needful to intimate to you, to warn and advise all that come, professing of truth, that they be careful and circumspect in their passage.

" So, dear friends, this, with what further you may apprehend to tend

conspicuous in the history of Friends. Some of these emigrants settled at Salem, and others at Burlington, but most of them at a new settlement on Newtown Creek. A meeting was settled at this place, and in two years after a meeting-house was built. Previous to this date, a Monthly Meeting, including Friends on Cooper's and Woodbury creeks, had been set up ; and, some time after, Friends of Salem and Newtown Monthly Meetings constituted a Quarterly Meeting. Burlington Monthly Meeting consisted of Friends settled about the Falls, and of the particular meetings of Rancocas, Shackamaxon, and Chester, in Pennsylvania. There were also settlements of Friends at the Hoarkills and Newcastle. Burlington Quarterly Meeting appears to have been established in 1680 ; and in 1682, Shrewsbury Monthly Meeting, which had previously belonged to Long Island, was annexed to it. At Burlington Monthly Meeting, in the Third Month, 1681, it was concluded to establish a Yearly

to truth's promotion in this place, we desire your assistance in, which will be very kindly and gladly received by us, who are desirous of an amicable correspondence with you, and do claim a part with you in the holy body and eternal union, which the bond of life is the strength of ; in which God preserve you and us who are your friends and brothers.

Thomas Budd.	Rob. Powell.	Scath Smith.
Wm. Peachy.	John Bourton.	Walter Pumphrey.
Wm. Brightown.	Jo. Woolston.	Tho. Ellis.
Tho. Gardiner.	Daniel Leeds.	Samuel Jenings.
Rob. Stacey.	Jo. Butcher.	James Satterthwaite.
Tho. Barton.	Henry Grubb.	John Coips.
John Hollinshed.	William Butler.	

" Several Friends not being present at the said meeting, have since, as a testimony of their unity with the thing, subscribed their names.

Mahlon Stacey.	William Billes.	Abra. Hewlings.
Thomas Lambert.	Tho. Harding.	Peter Fretwell.
John Kinsey.	Wm. Hewlings.	Tho. Eaves.
Samuel Pleft.	Rich. Arnold.	Wm. Clark.
Wm. Cooper.	John Woolman.	John Paine.
John Shin.	John Stacey.	

" From our Men's Monthly Meeting, in Burlington, in West New Jersey, the 7th of the Twelfth Month, 1680."

Meeting, the first to be held in the Sixth Month following. A notice of this conclusion was circulated among Friends of the provinces of East and West New Jersey; and on the 28th of the Sixth Month, 1681, the meeting assembled at the house of Thomas Gardner, of Burlington. But very little information of the proceedings of this Yearly Meeting, which occupied four days, has been preserved; the times and places of holding meetings for worship and discipline, however, including a Yearly Meeting for worship to be held in the Second Month at Salem, formed an important part of its deliberations. It was also agreed that the next Yearly Meeting should be held in the Seventh Month of the following year.*

---

* In "An account of the first settlement of Friends' meetings, &c., in New Jersey," the following particulars appear:—

"About 1670, a meeting was settled at Shrewsbury, Monmouth county, being the first settled meeting of Friends in these provinces. Their first house was built in 1672. About 1670, a Monthly and General Meeting was also held there. The first settlers there were nearly, or quite all, Friends. The first child born there was Elizabeth, daughter of Eliakim Wardell, in 1667. Meetings were probably held there occasionally for a few years previous to the regular settlement of the meeting in 1670.

"At a very early day, a settlement of Friends at Middletown, in the same county, held meetings at each other's houses, but built no house. The Baptists built a meeting-house there, upon ground purchased from Richard Hartshorne, in which he reserved a privilege of holding Friends' meetings when strangers visited them.

"A meeting for worship was held at Amboy, from about 1680, for some time; then by turns at that place and at Woodbridge. At a very early day, a meeting was held once in three months, on Staten Island, for the sake of the families of John and Daniel Shotwell, who lived there.

"Meetings for worship were first settled at Burlington in 1677, and first held under tents. Afterwards they were held at Friends' houses, till the building of their great meeting-house in 1696.

"Friends at Chesterfield held meetings for some time at private houses.

"In 1687, the meeting-house at Newtown was built; previous to which meetings were there held at Friends' houses. In 1682, a Monthly Meeting was settled to be held there.

"Salem was the first part of West Jersey settled by the English. The Friends who came with John Fenwick, in 1675, first held their meetings

Among the settlers who had left Great Britain were several who had received a gift in the ministry, and who were felt to be as watchmen among their brethren, under their new circumstances; among these were John Butcher from London; Samuel Jennings from Aylesbury; John Skein from Scotland, Thomas Olive and William Peachey. Samuel Jennings and John Skein both filled the office of Governor.

The progress of Friends in West Jersey had proved in the highest degree satisfactory. "Let every man write according to his judgment," said one of the early settlers, "this is mine concerning this country; I do really believe it to be as good a country as any man need to dwell in.—I cannot but admire the Lord for his mercies, and often in secret bless his name, that ever he turned my face thitherward."* "This is a most brave place," writes another, "whatever envy, or evil spies may speak of it, I could but wish you all here."‡ "I would not have anything to remain as a discouragement to planters," writes the cautious Samuel Jennings, the governor, in 1680, "here are several good and convenient settlements already, and here is land enough, and good enough for many more."† The encouraging language of the settlers, proved inviting to their brethren in England, and in the year 1682, a ship of considerable size arrived in the Delaware, having on board three hundred and sixty emigrants, who were landed in West Jersey, on the country between Burlington and Philadelphia.

Whilst the English population of West Jersey was thus rapidly increasing, East Jersey made but very slow progress. Sir George Carteret, the proprietor of the latter, died in 1679, and by will directed that East Jersey should be sold in order to pay his debts.

for worship at each other's houses, and sometimes joined with Friends at what was called Robert Wood's landing (now Chester), on the west side of the Delaware. The Monthly Meeting was first set up in 1676. They built a large meeting-house in early times."

* Letter of D. Willis, in Smith's Hist. p. 115.
† Proud's Pennsylvania, vol. i. p. 152.   ‡ Smith's Hist.

The success that had attended the colony of West Jersey, under the auspices of Friends, led them very naturally to direct their attention to the intended sale of the adjoining province, and at the instance of William Penn and some other influential members of the Society, it was concluded to purchase East Jersey, and in the Second Month, 1681, it was conveyed by Carteret to the following twelve Friends, viz.: William Penn, Robert West, Thomas Rudyard, Samuel Groome, Thomas Hart, Richard Mew, Thomas Wilcox, Ambrose Rigge, John Haywood, Hugh Hartshorne, Clement Plumstead, and Thomas Cooper.

The date of this purchase was the era of those civil wars in Great Britain, during which the followers of Cameron in Scotland were hunted with great cruelty by the Royalists. The Quaker Colonies of East and West New Jersey had become popular, and by the persecuted Scots were hailed as a blessing, and considerable numbers of them left their mountainous region to bestow their industry on the forest lands of the Jerseys. The attention of the Scotch was immediately directed to East Jersey in consequence of the original twelve proprietors extending the proprietary to twelve others, several of whom were natives of Scotland and of rank and influence, among whom may be named the Earl of Perth, Lord Drummond, Robert Barclay, Robert Gordon, Aarent Sonnemans, and Gawen Lawrie. "Among the proprietaries," remarks Oldmixon the historian, in alluding to the purchase of East Jersey, "are several extraordinary persons besides Lord Perth, as Robert West, Esq., the lawyer; William Penn the head of the Quakers in England; and Robert Barclay the head of the Quakers in Scotland and Ireland." In the year following that of the purchase, "Robert Barclay of Urie" was elected by the proprietaries as governor for life of East Jersey, who appointed Thomas Rudyard as his deputy, and after him Gawen Lawrie.

Previous to the purchase of the Jerseys by Friends, but few of their gospel ministers who proceeded to America visited this part; the paucity of English settlers in that territory is sufficient to account for this. George Fox passed through it in 1672, and

William Edmundson visited it soon after the landing of John Fenwick. In 1681, Joan Vokins also visited the province.

The attention of George Fox was very early directed to his brethren in the Jerseys, and anxious that, under their new circumstances, the truth might be exalted by a right use of the political power which they had acquired, he was led to exhort them by epistolary communications. "Let your lives, and words, and conversations," he writes in 1676, "be as becomes the gospel, that you may adorn the truth, and honour the Lord in all your undertakings. Let that be your desire, and then you will have the Lord's blessing, and increase both in basket, and field, and storehouse; and at your lyings down you will feel him, and at your goings forth and coming in. And let temperance and patience, and kindness, and brotherly love, be exercised among you, so that you may abound in virtue and the true humility; living in peace, showing forth the nature of Christianity; that you may all live as a family and the church of God."* On another occasion he thus addresses them : "My Friends, that are gone and are going over to plant, and make outward plantations in America, keep your own plantations in your hearts with the spirit and power of God, that your own vines and lilies be not hurt."† "You that are governors and judges, you should be eyes to the blind, feet to the lame, and fathers to the poor, that you may gain the blessing of those who are ready to perish, and cause the widow's heart to sing for gladness. If you rejoice because your hand hath gotten much ; if you say to fine gold, 'Thou art my confidence,' you will have denied the God that is above.—The Lord is ruler among nations, he will crown his people with dominion."‡

* Epistles of George Fox, p. 401.   † Ibid. p. 477.
‡ Hazard's Register, p. 200.

CHAPTER XXII.

THE earliest Friends in the Carolinas of whom we have any account, are those of the family of Henry Phillips, who settled on the banks of the Albemarle about the year 1665. He previously resided in New England, where both himself and wife were convinced of the principles of Friends. The settlement of Henry Phillips in Carolina was prior to the scheme of English colonization under the " Constitutions " of Locke, and when some enterprizing adventurers had their attention turned to this portion of the new world. One of these, a Barbadoes planter, and the son of an English baronet, was anxious to encourage the influx of New England men. " Make things easy to the people of New England," were his instructions in 1663, " from thence the greatest supplies are expected."

The first gospel minister who appears to have visited Carolina was William Edmundson. He landed in Maryland in the early part of 1672, in company with George Fox and others, and whilst the latter passed northwards to New England, William Edmundson proceeded to visit the plantations in Carolina, accompanied by two Friends whose names are not given. The journey, which occupied them several days, was a very dangerous and tedious one, the country through which they passed "being all wilderness, and no pathways ;" and at times they " were sorely foiled in the swamps and rivers," and at nights, by a watch fire, their only shelter was such as the forests afforded. Having at last reached the river Albemarle, they were warmly received and hospitably entertained at the house of Henry Phillips, and, observes William Edmundson, " not having seen a Friend for seven years before, he and his wife wept with joy to see us."*

At the house of Henry Phillips, a meeting was proposed to be held, and many of the inhabitants attended. The important concerns of religion do not appear to have had much place in the minds of the settlers of Carolina. " They had little or no religion," remarks William Edmundson, " for they came and sat down in the meeting smoking their pipes ; but," he continues, " in a little time, the Lord's testimony arose in the authority of his power, and their hearts being reached with it, several of them were tendered and received the testimony." Among those who were present at the meeting was a magistrate, who resided about three miles off, on the south side of the Albemarle, and by whom the gospel truths declared on the occasion were much appreciated. He " received the truth with gladness," and at his desire a meeting was held at his house on the following day, " and," writes William Edmundson, " a blessed meeting it was, for several were tendered with a sense of the power of God, received the truth, and abode in it."† The visit of this gospel labourer to Carolina on this occasion was but short, for, having appointed a meeting for discipline with his brethren of Virginia, but little time was affoided him for religious service in the south.

The European population of Carolina at this period was but small, not exceeding, it is believed, three thousand. Neither city nor township had yet been founded, and scarcely a hamlet was to be seen in the province, or, indeed, one house within sight of another ; there were no roads, and the paths from house to house, which were mostly along the banks of the rivers and the inlets, were marked by notches in the trees ; and so far from religious

* Journal of W. Edmundson, p. 88.   † Ibid, p. 90.

edifices having been erected, there appears not to have been a religious sect in the colony. "From the commencement of the settlement," says an historian, "there seems not to have been a minister in the land; there was no public worship, but such as burst from the hearts of the people themselves, and when at last William Edmundson came to visit his Quaker brethren among the groves of Albemarle, he met 'with a tender people,' delivered his doctrine 'in the authority of truth,' and made converts to the Society of Friends. A Quarterly Meeting for discipline was established, and this sect was the first to organize a religious government in Carolina."*

Towards the close of 1672, George Fox, Robert Widders, James Lancaster and George Pattison, visited Carolina. "Having," writes George Fox "travelled hard through the woods, and over many bogs and swamps, we reached Bonner's Creek, and there we lay that night by the fire-side, the woman lending us a mat to lie on. This was the first house we came to in Carolina; here we left our horses over-wearied with travel."† From Bonner's Creek they passed down the river Maratuc or Roanoke to Connie Oak Bay and the river Albermarle. With the scattered planters of North Carolina, George Fox and his companions held several meetings, and he observes, "the people were very tender, and very good service we had amongst them." By the authorities they were received with much respect and attention, and they all became the guests of the governor, who, with his wife, "received them lovingly." From the hospitable residence of the governor they travelled about thirty miles to the house of Joseph Scott, "one of the representatives of the country," where they had "a sound and precious meeting." At another meeting "the chief secretary of the province," who "had been formerly convinced," was present, and by whom they were also kindly entertained.

The religious well-being of the Indians of North America was a subject that deeply interested the feelings of George Fox.

* Bancroft's United States, and Martin in Bancroft, vol. i. p. 155, 156.
† Journal of George Fox, vol. ii. p. 172.

He longed that the tribes of the western wilderness should be
brought to a knowledge of the truth, and in Carolina, as in other
parts, he was engaged to hold up to their view the blessings of
the everlasting gospel.   " I spoke to them," he writes, " concerning Christ, showing them that he died for all men, for their
sins, as well as for others, and had enlightened them as well as
others ; and that if they did that which was evil, he would burn
them, but if they did well, they should not be burned."*   Anxious
that the untutored red men might be instructed in the things of
eternal life, George Fox was also led to press their case upon the
attention of his American brethren."   In all places where you
do outwardly live and settle, " he wrote," invite all the Indians,
and their kings, and have meetings with them, or they with you ;
so that you may make inward plantations with the light and
power of God."   His exhortations were not unheeded.   In 1673,
we find him thus addressing his friends of Virginia.   " I received letters giving me an account of the service some of you
had with and amongst the Indian king and his council ; and if
you go over again to Carolina, you may inquire of Captain Batts,
the governor, with whom I left a paper to be read to the Emperor, and his thirty kings under him of the Tuscaroras."   At a
later date, in addressing Friends of Carolina, he says, " you
should sometimes have meetings with the Indian kings and
their people, to preach the gospel of peace, of life, and of salvation to them ; for the gospel is to be preached to every creature,
so that you may come to see the light of Christ's glorious gospel
set up in those parts."†

The visit of George Fox to Carolina occupied him about
eighteen days.   During his subsequent travels his mind, however,
was frequently introduced into a feeling of deep solicitude for
the religious welfare of his scattered converts in this part, and
before he quitted the shores of the western world he was led to
address them in the language of encouragement.   He exhorted
them in their lonely situation, to seek Him who is the fountain

* Journal of George Fox, vol. ii. p 173.
† Epistles of George Fox, p. 463.

and fulness of the Christian's strength ; " to keep their meetings and meet together in the name of Jesus, whose name is above every name, and gathering above every gathering ;" and he endeavoured to impress them with the important truth that " there is no salvation in any other name, but by the name of Jesus." " Gather in his name" he continues, " He is your Prophet, your Shepherd, your Bishop, your Priest in the midst of you, to open to you, and to sanctify you, and to feed you with life, and to quicken you with life ; wait in his power and light, that ye may be the children of the light, and built upon Him the true Foundation."*

During William Edmundson's second visit to America in 1677, the religious welfare of the little society in Carolina was not forgotten by him, and he again travelled south as far as the banks of the Albemarle. " I had," he writes, " several precious meetings in that colony, and several were turned to the Lord ; people were tender and loving ; there was no room for the priests (viz., hirelings), for Friends were finely settled, and I left things well among them."†

Although no gospel labourers had yet visited South Carolina, there were, nevertheless, settlers in that colony who professed with Friends ; and at an early date a Monthly Meeting appears to have been established among them. At Perquimons, in North Carolina, a Monthly Meeting had also been set up, and in 1681, we find George Fox proposing the establishment of a Yearly or Half-yearly Meeting. " If you of Ashley River and that way, and you of Albemarle River and that way," he writes, " had once a year, or once in a half-year, a meeting together, somewhere in the middle of the country, it might be well."

In South Carolina, and also in North Carolina, Friends enjoyed unlimited toleration in religion, and though their number was comparatively small, yet they occupied an influential position in the country. Almost, indeed, from the commencement of the colonial legislature, some of them had been active members of the Assembly. " North Carolina," says the historian Bancroft, who

---

* Epistles of George Fox; 1672. † Journal of W. Edmundson.

evidently considered Friends to be the ruling people of the province, "was settled by the freest of the free; by men to whom the restraints of other colonies were too severe. But the settlers were gentle in their tempers, of serene minds, enemies to violence and bloodshed; and the spirit of humanity maintained its influence in the paradise of Quakers."

The responsible position of Friends in Carolina did not escape the vigilant eye of George Fox. He was desirous that in their outward ease and prosperity, they might be preserved in the truth, and in his addresses to them he did not fail to exhort them to much circumspection in their daily walk, and to increased diligence in their heavenly calling. The following is a specimen of one of these communications :—

FROM GEORGE FOX TO FRIENDS IN CHARLESTOWN, CAROLINA.

"DEAR FRIENDS, of the Monthly Meeting of Charlestown, in Ashley Cooper river, in Carolina, I received your letter, dated the sixth day of the Eighth Month, 1682; wherein you give an account of your meeting, and of the country, and of your liberty in that province; which I am glad to hear of, though your Meeting is but small. But however, stand all faithful in truth and righteousness, that your fruits may be unto holiness; and your end will be everlasting life.—

" My desire is, that you may prize your liberty, both natural and spiritual, and the favour that the Lord hath given you, that your yea is taken instead of an oath; and that you do serve both in assemblies, juries and other offices, without swearing, according to the doctrine of Christ : which is a great thing, worth prizing. And take heed of abusing that liberty, or losing the savour of the heavenly salt, which seasons your lives and conversations in truth, holiness, and righteousness : for you know, when the salt hath lost its savour, it is good for nothing but to be trodden under the foot of men.—

" My love to you all in Christ Jesus.—The Lord God Almighty preserve and keep you all holy, pure and clean to his glory.

" *London, the 23rd of the Twelfth Month*, 1683."

It was about this time that John Archdale, an opulent Friend from England, and one of the eight proprietaries of North Carolina, was residing in the colony. Of the precise date of his arrival we have no account. During his stay he appears to have acted as governor, at least in the absence of Seth Sothel, a co-proprietor, who was elected governor by his partners in 1680. The administration of Sothel gave great dissatisfaction to the colonists. He endeavoured to enforce the obnoxious "Constitutions," but without success. He was accused of acting arbitrarily, and of employing his power to gratify a sordid desire for accumulation. After a few years the settlers deposed him, and the assembly, to whom he appealed, sentenced him to twelve months' banishment, and a perpetual incapacity for the government. It was after his banishment, that John Archdale appears to have been invested with the government.

Whilst engaged in the civil affairs of the province, John Archdale, aware of the strong interest felt by George Fox in the welfare of Friends in the New World, occasionally addressed him. The following is a copy of one of his letters :—

JOHN ARCHDALE TO GEORGE FOX.

"*North Carolina,* 25th *of First Month,* 1686.

" DEAR AND HIGHLY-ESTEEMED FRIEND,—I have written unto thee formerly but as yet have received no answer, which makes me doubt the miscarriage of mine : and, indeed, for the present, we have not immediate opportunities to send to England, by reason there is no settled trade thither ; which, notwithstanding, may conveniently be effected in its proper season ; there being commodities, as tobacco, oil, hides and tallow, to transport thither ; and Hollands Busses may come in safety of about 150 tons, drawing about nine feet of water. The country produces plentifully, all things necessary for the life of man, with as little labour as any I have known ; it wants only industrious people, fearing God. We at present have peace with all the nations of the Indians ; and the great fat King of the Tuscaroras was not long since

with me, having had an Indian slain in these parts: he was
informed it was by the English, but upon inquiry I found out the
murderer, who was a Chowan Indian, one of their great men's
sons, whom I immediately ordered to be apprehended; but the
Chowan Indians bought his life of the Tuscarora king for a great
quantity of wamp and bage. This Tuscarora king was very
desirous to cut off a nation of Indians called the Matchepungoes;
which I have at present prevented, and hope I shall have the
country at peace with all the Indians, and one with another. The
people are very fearful of falling into some troubles again if I should
leave them before my brother Sothell returns, which makes my
stay the longer. This Tuscarora king seems to be a very wise
man as to natural parts; some of the Indians near me are so
civilized as to come into English habits, and have cattle of their
own, and I look upon their outward civilizing as a good preparation for the gospel, which God in his season without doubt, will
cause to dawn among them: I wish all that had it had been
faithful, then had the day broken forth in its splendour as it
began. I am sure God forsakes none but the unfaithful; who by
disobedience are cut off, whereas the obedient come to be grafted
into the true stock, through the growth of the holy seed in their
minds and hearts. O! that my spirit were thoroughly purged and
established by that power which is the Rock of ages, the foundation of all generations; but blessed be God, I possess more than
I ever deserved, and desire patiently to wait for the accomplishment of his inward work of regeneration; which is a word easily
writ or expressed, but hardly attained. What I writ unto thee
in my former, I cannot but again repeat; which is a desire to be
had in remembrance by thee, having a faith in the power that was
by thee, in this last age of the world, first preached, and convinced
me in the beginning, and separated me from my father's house;
the sense of which love I desire may for ever dwell upon my spirit,
and in the end bring forth the true fruit of regeneration. I wish
these parts had been more visited by Friends, if it had been the
will of God: however, the immediate sense and growth of the
Divine Seed, is encouragement to all that witness the same. Thus

with my true and real love to thee in my measure of the truth, I rest thy loving friend.

A few biographical notices are again introduced. The following relate to some of those whose religious labours have been alluded to in the latter chapters of this volume.

WILLIAM EDMUNDSON.

By his own account, William Edmundson was born in Westmoreland in the year 1627, of parents who, he says, "were well accounted among men," and who apprenticed him to the trade of a carpenter and joiner, at York. In his youthful days he was much exercised in mind on religious things, and was often brought low under the consideration of his spiritual condition. "The priest and congregation," he remarks, "took notice of me; but none did direct me aright to the physician that could heal my wounded spirit."* On the expiration of his apprenticeship he entered the Parliament army, and in 1650, he served under Cromwell in his Scotch campaign, and in the following year was engaged in the great battle at Worcester. Having married in 1652, he left the army and united with a brother at Antrim, in Ireland, as a shopkeeper, or merchant, "promising," he says, "great matters to ourselves and religion besides."† In the Puritan army, religious subjects were the all engrossing topics of conversation, and William Edmundson heard frequent allusion made to the Quakers; "the priests every where," he found, "were angry against them, and the baser sort of people spared not to tell strange stories of them." But the more he heard of Friends the more he was attracted towards them, and "loved

* Journal, p. 42.   † Ibid. p. 44.

them." Having occasion, in 1653, to go on business to the North of England, he first met with Friends, and, by the ministry of George Fox and James Nayler, he was convinced of those spiritual views in religion which in after life he so powerfully advocated.

Subsequent to his uniting with Friends, William Edmundson experienced great spiritual conflicts : his change of view attracted the attention of his neighbours, "some of whom," he says, "would come to gaze on me, jangle and contend against the truth ; some would say I was bewitched ; and others that I was going mad." It was the design of the most High to prepare him as a chosen vessel of his mercy to others, and, patiently enduring all the turnings of his holy hand, he became an able minister of the gospel. He was profound in the mysteries of the heavenly kingdom, which were largely communicated to him, and, as a faithful steward, he brought out of his treasury things new and old. It is evident, by the many testimonies given of him, that he was a powerful instrument in turning many to righteousness. In the course of his gospel labours he visited the continent of North America and the West India Islands three times ; he also frequently went on gospel missions to England, and laboured abundantly in different parts of Ireland. During his early travels in the ministry he was several times imprisoned for the truth's sake. His contemporaries describe him as a minister of the gospel, "sound in doctrine and in judgment ; plain in preaching, and free from affectation : in apparel and gesture, grave ; in his deportment, manly ; of few words, and very exemplary in life and conversation ; a man of a thousand for promoting virtue in the many branches thereof, as well as a sharp instrument for threshing and cutting down that which was evil and hurtful in the churches." Although he was a man of but a limited education, he appears to have possessed considerable ability, and, observe some of his friends, " the truth invigorating his understanding, made him bold as a lion." So powerful was his ministry, that he was frequently called "the great hammer of Ireland." He died in the Sixth Month 1712, at the age of eighty-five years, having been a minister fifty-seven years.

JOHN BURNYEAT.

John Burnyeat was born in the parish of Lowswater, in Cumberland, about the year 1631. His parents, who are spoken of as being " of good repute," gave him an education, " suited," says Gough, " to his circumstances and line of life." From early life he was seriously inclined, and took much delight in perusing the Holy Scriptures. In his pursuit after a knowledge of divine things, he sought instruction from those who were regarded as persons of religious experience, but from whom he failed to obtain that true peace and consolation which he sought after. About the twenty-second year of his age George Fox visited Cumberland, by whom he was directed to the inward manifestations of Christ his Saviour, and whose ministry was blessed to his tossed and tried soul. He was now brought to see the emptiness of his former high professions in religion, and that a regenerated heart, and a holy life, were necessary to salvation· " Then," he writes, " began the warfare of true striving to enter the kingdom, and when this war was truly begun, all my high conceit in my invented notional faith, and my pretence and hopes of justification thereby, were overthrown." He subsequently passed through much deep conflict of mind, and after assembling for four years with a little company of Friends who waited mostly in silence, he came forth in the ministry.

The first gospel mission of John Burnyeat was to Scotland in 1658, and in the following year his religious labours were extended to Ireland. Both before and after his visits to America, he also travelled extensively in England. In 1685, he removed to Ireland. During his early travels in the ministry, he was twice imprisoned, once at Carlisle for about five months, and at Ripon in Yorkshire, for three months. In a testimony given forth by the Morning Meeting of London, he is described as an able and powerful minister of the gospel ; " a strengthener of the weak, and an encourager of the upright and sincere hearted— a skilful marksman, yea one of the Lord's worthies of Israel ; a valiant man in the camp of the Lord, and an undaunted warrior in his holy host ; and his bow abode in strength, and wisdom was given him to direct his arrows to the very mark ; so that the sturdy were wounded, the meek were comforted, the tender in spirit refreshed. He was a choice and seasoned vessel of Christ, the special workmanship of his power and wisdom, by which he was effectually qualified for the ministry of his everlasting gospel, thoroughly furnished, may we say, to every good word and work, which God called him unto:—deep and large in his gift, reaching what was seasonable to every state; in judgment sound, free in utterance, zealous for holiness; severe against unsound and dividing spirits; most tender to penitents and returning prodigals; affectionate to the brethren, and careful over the flock of God: of a grave and steady temper, yet sweet; hardy in constitution, and undaunted and unwearied in mind. He was the father of many children in Christ, who through his ministry were begotten again to a living hope; and the builder up of more, through the same, in the precious faith of God's elect. He laid down his head in peace with God, and love to his people, and good will to all men; and is entered into eternal habitations, to praise the God of his mercies in the living family of the spirits of the just for ever."

He died in the Seventh Month, 1690, in the fifty-ninth year of his age, having been a minister thirty-three years.

JAMES LANCASTER.

James Lancaster resided on the Island of Walney, in Lancashire, and was convinced by George Fox during his first visit to that county in 1652. In the following year he came forth as a minister, and in 1654, went on a gospel mission to Scotland, with Miles Halhead. In 1665, he visited many of the midland counties of England. There was not, perhaps, any one who was so much associated in gospel labours with George Fox as James Lancaster. He not only accompanied him throughout his visit to the western hemisphere, but he was also with him during his visit to Scotland in 1657, and to Ireland in 1669, and on these occasions it appears that he frequently acted as his amanuensis.

ROBERT WIDDERS.

Robert Widders was of Upper Kellet, in Lancashire, where,

Whiting tells us, he was born " of honest substantiantial parents, about the year 1618." In early manhood he appears to have had living desires after heavenly things, and in 1652, when George Fox visited Lancashire, he was fully convinced of the truths declared by him. He first travelled in the work of the ministry in 1653, to the adjoining county of Cumberland, where he suffered considerable abuse and was imprisoned at Carlisle for about one month. He also was much associated with George Fox in gospel travels. In 1657 he went with him into Scotland, and a few years later throughout most of the western counties of England. He was one who suffered much for his religious testimony, for, in addition to several imprisonments at Lancaster, he was subjected to excessive distraints for tithes. " Many sufferings, trials, and exercises," remarks Whiting, "he went through outwardly and inwardly, being a valiant man for God and his truth ; a grave solid man, and had a great discerning of spirits."* He was " a thundering man," says George Fox, " against hypocrisy, deceit, and the rottenness of the priests."† He died in the First Month, 1687, about the sixty-eighth year of his age.

George Fox.

George Fox was born at Drayton-in-the-Clay, in Leicestershire, in the year 1624. His parents, who were in respectable circumstances, and esteemed for their piety and integrity, gave him an education suited to the sphere in which they moved, and brought him up in the worship of the national church. His mother, who was a woman of superior qualifications, and accomplished beyond those of her class, took notice of the religious gravity and observing mind which he evinced even from his childhood. In the eleventh year of his age, he was, by his own account, favoured with clear views of righteousness and purity, and was taught of the Lord to be "faithful in all things—inwardly to God and outwardly to man." The questions he would put, and the answers he would give respecting Divine things, even in early boyhood, were such as to cause astonishment to those who heard him. His employment during his apprenticeship was mostly in keeping sheep, an

---

* Whiting's Memoirs.　　　† Journal of G. Fox, vol. i., p. 442.

engagement in which he was skilful, and took much delight. At
the termination of his apprenticeship, being then in his nineteenth
year, he returned to his parents ; religious things, however, had
the predominance in his mind, and he was led to be very circumspect
in all his words and actions. For about three years subsequently,
he spent his time in moving from place to place in some of the
midland counties of England, and during this period he underwent a variety of probations, and advanced in religious experience
and the work of sanctification.

At times in his solitary wanderings his mind was brought under
deep anguish, and he was tempted almost to despair. In reference
to this season he thus remarks : " I fasted much, and walked
abroad in solitary places many days, and often took my Bible and
went and sat in hollow trees and lonesome places till night came
on, and frequently in the night walked mournfully about by myself : for I was a man of sorrows, in the times of the first working
of the Lord in me." As his troubles were great, so also at times
his consolations abounded, and he adds, " Though my exercises
and troubles were very great, yet were they not so continual but
that I had some intermission, and was sometimes brought into
such a heavenly joy, that I thought I had been in Abraham's
bosom. As I cannot declare the misery I was in, it was so great
and heavy upon me ; so neither can I set forth the mercies of
God unto me in all my misery. Oh, the everlasting love of God
to my soul, when I was in great distress ! when my troubles and
torments were great, then was his love exceeding great."

About the twenty-third year of his age he came forth in the
work of the ministry, in which he laboured most devotedly
throughout the remainder of his eventful life. His interesting
journal contains a full account of his travels and services in the
gospel ; it is, therefore, needless for us to make any allusion to
them here. He was the first who preached the gospel principles
of our religious Society, and as such has been aptly called " the
founder of the Quakers." " He was a man," says Ellwood, raised up
by God in an extraordinary manner, for an extraordinary work, even
to awaken the sleeping world, by proclaiming the mighty day of
the Lord to the nations.—He was valiant for the truth, bold in
asserting it, patient in suffering for it, unwearied in labouring in

it, steady in his testimony to it; unmoveable as a rock.   Deep he was in divine knowledge, clear in opening heavenly mysteries, plain and powerful in preaching, fervent in prayer."*   There were few, if any, who had better opportunities of forming an estimate of the character of George Fox than William Penn, and to whom posterity is indebted for the following testimony respecting him :—

" He was a man that God endued with a clear and wonderful depth : a discerner of others' spirits, and very much a master of his own.   And though that side of his understanding which lay next to the world, and especially the expression of it, might sound uncouth and unfashionable to nice ears, his matter was nevertheless very profound; and would not only bear to be often considered, but the more it was so, the more weighty and instructing it appeared.   And as abruptly and brokenly as sometimes his sentences would seem to fall from him, about divine things, it is well-known they were often as texts to many fairer declarations.   And indeed it showed, beyond all contradiction, that God sent him, in that no arts or parts had any share in the matter or manner of his ministry ; and that so many great, excellent, and necessary truths, as he came forth to preach to mankind, had therefore nothing of man's wit or wisdom to recommend them.

" In his testimony or ministry, he much laboured to open truth to the people's understandings, and to bottom them upon Christ Jesus, the light of the world ; that by bringing them to something that was from God in themselves, they might the better know and judge of him and themselves.

" He had an extraordinary gift in opening the Scriptures.   He would go to the marrow of things and show the mind, harmony, and fulfilling of them, with much plainness and to great comfort and edification.

" The mystery of the first and second Adam, of the fall and restoration, of the law and the gospel, of shadows and substance, of the servant's and the son's state, and the fulfilling of the Scriptures in Christ, and by Christ the true light, in all that are his, through the obedience of faith, were much of the substance and

T. Ellwood's Testimony.

drift of his testimonies : in all which, he was witnessed to be of
God ; being sensibly felt to speak that which he had received of
Christ and was his own experience in that which never errs nor fails.

   " But above all, he excelled in prayer.   The inwardness and
weight of his spirit, the reverence and solemnity of his address
and behaviour, and the fewness and fulness of his words, have
often struck even strangers with admiration, as they used to
reach others with consolation.   The most awful, living, reverent
frame I ever felt or beheld, I must say, was his, in prayer.   And
truly it was a testimony, he knew and lived nearer to the Lord
than other men ; for they that know Him most, will see most
reason to approach Him with reverence and fear.

   " He was of an innocent life ; no busy-body, nor self-seeker ;
neither touchy nor critical : what fell from him was very
inoffensive, if not very edifying.   So meek, contented, modest,
easy, steady, tender, it was a pleasure to be in his company.   He
exercised no authority but over evil, and that every where, and in
all ; but with love, compassion, and long-suffering.   A most
merciful man, as ready to forgive as unapt to take or give
offence.   Thousands can truly say he was of an excellent spirit
and savour amongst them ; and because thereof, the most excellent spirits loved him with an unfeigned and unfading love.

   " He was an incessant labourer ; and as he was unwearied,
so he was undaunted, in his services for God and his people ;
he was no more to be moved to fear than to wrath : his behaviour
at Derby, Litchfield, Appleby, before Oliver Cromwell, at
Launceston, Scarborough, Worcester, and Westminster Hall,
with many other places and exercises, did abundantly evidence
it, to his enemies as well as his friends.

   " And truly I must say, that though God had visibly clothed
him with a divine preference and authority, yet he never abused
it ; but held his place in the Church of God with great meekness
and a most engaging humility and moderation ; for, upon all
occasions, like his blessed Master, he was a servant to all ;
holding and exercising his eldership in the invisible power that
had gathered them, with reverence to the Head, and care over
the body : and was received, only in that Spirit and power of

Christ, as the first and chief elder in this age ; who, as he was therefore worthy of double honour, so, for the same reason, it was given by the faithful of this day ; because his authority was inward, not outward, and that he got it and kept it by the love of God, and the power of an endless life. I write my knowledge, and not report ; and my witness is true, having been with him for weeks and months together on divers occasions, and those of the nearest and most exercising nature ; and that by day and by night, by sea and by land, in this and in foreign countries ; and I can say I never saw him out of his place, or not a match for every service or occasion."

The earnest solicitude of George Fox for the prosperity of the truth was the predominating feeling of his mind to his last moments, and shortly before his close he addressed an epistle " to the Churches of Christ throughout the whole world." But the welfare of his brethren in the western world claimed his particular attention at this solemn period, and " mind poor Friends in America" was nearly his last request. His decease took place at London in the Eleventh Month, 1690, in the sixty-seventh year of his age. "I have done," says William Penn, in concluding his testimony, "when I have left this short epitaph to his name :—Many sons have done virtuously in this day, but, dear George, thou excelled them all."

A history of the Society of Friends in America for about twenty-five years from its rise on that continent, has been now related. In that land, as in almost every other Protestant country where its principles had been enunciated, many, as we have seen, soon openly professed them, and at the period to which this history has been brought down, the Society had extended itself throughout all the English colonies of the New World. The Yearly Meetings of New England and Burlington had been established, and Half-Yearly Meetings were held respectively on Long Island, and in Virginia, Maryland, and Carolina. In Newfoundland also there were at this early period some who professed our principles,* whilst John

* Vide Appendix to Leonard Bacon's Thirteen Historical Discourses, &c., p. 378.

Bowron,* and, it appears, Henry Fell† also had declared them as far south as Surinam, now Dutch Guiana. But even in the short space of a quarter of a century the Society had not only become a numerous body in America, but highly influential also. The governments of Rhode Island, East New Jersey and West New Jersey were entirely in the hands of Friends; in North Carolina they were regarded as the ruling people of the province, and in Maryland they took a prominent in the local legislature; and all this was before the great colony of Pennsylvania had been founded.

The relation given in the foregoing pages, furnishes abundant evidence that it was in the ordering of Him who ruleth in the kingdoms of men, that this people occupied so conspicuous a place in the early history of the colonies of the New World. The testimony which they bore to the spirituality of the religion of Christ in the disuse of forms and ceremonies in worship, and to the unauthorised assumption of the priesthood in the things of God; to the perceptible guidance of the Holy Spirit, so little recognised by professing Christendom in that age, and to the peaceable character of the gospel dispensation, could not fail to exert a powerful influence for good on the rising population of that land, and to promote the kingdom of our Lord and Saviour Jesus Christ in the hearts of the children of men.

* Memoir of John Bowron, in Piety Promoted, part i.
† Swarthmore MSS.

LONDON:
PRINTED BY RICHARD BARRET, 13, MARK LANE.

THE HISTORY

OF THE

SOCIETY OF FRIENDS

IN

AMERICA.

By JAMES BOWDEN.

VOL. II

PENNSYLVANIA AND NEW JERSEY.

LONDON:

W & F. G. CASH, 5, BISHOPSGATE STREET WITHOUT.

1854.

THE HISTORY

OF THE

SOCIETY OF FRIENDS IN AMERICA.

CHAPTER I.

SETTLEMENT OF PENNSYLVANIA.

Pennsylvania granted to William Penn—His design in obtaining it—
His views on the nature and object of government—Laws for Pennsylvania—Many Friends prepare to emigrate to the new country—
William Penn's first visit—His reception and progress—Session of the
first General Assembly—Philadelphia founded—The rapid progress and
promising state of the colony—William Penn returns to England—His
farewell address to Friends of his province.

THERE are, perhaps, few circumstances connected with the
settlement of Europeans on the continent of North America, or
in the colonial history of the British empire, which are fraught
with greater interest, or the results of which have been more important, than the settlement of Pennsylvania. Until the year 1682,
this territory, lying immediately north of Maryland, and west of
the Jerseys, was little other than a wilderness, where the native
red man still held undisputed dominion. It measured about
three hundred miles long and about one hundred and sixty in
width, comprehending forty-one thousand square miles, or an area
very little short of that of England. The tribes of the Huron
Iroquois hunted over its northern portion, whilst the southern,
with the exception of some Swedish settlements, was occupied
chiefly by the Lenni Lenape, one of the tribes of the Algonquin
race of North American Indians.

Admiral Penn, the father of William Penn, who was a distinguished naval officer in the days of Cromwell and Charles II.,

had owing to him, at his decease, a considerable sum of money for the arrears of his pay, and for loans to the Government for naval purposes. As time passed on, the amount was augmented by interest, until in 1681, the debt had reached sixteen thousand pounds, the value of money at that period being at least threefold that of our present currency. In liquidation of this debt, William Penn petitioned for the grant of the territory in question.* The petition was strongly opposed by some of the most influential of the privy council, who, on the subject of government, and on civil and religious liberty, were hostile to his views. But he had powerful friends at Court. The Duke of York, the Earls Sunderland and Halifax, and Chief Justice North, favoured his cause, and his exertions to obtain the grant were ultimately crowned with success, and a charter, recognizing him as the sole proprietor of Pennsylvania, was issued in the Third Month 1681. "After many waitings, watchings, solicitings, and disputes in council," he writes, "my country was confirmed to me under the great seal of England." William Penn had now become the owner of a territory which, for extent and natural resources, could scarcely be equalled by any of the colonies of North America. "God," said he, "hath given it to me in the face of the world. . . . He will bless it, and make it the seed of a nation."†

In addition to the grant of Pennsylvania, William Penn obtained from the Duke of York a free gift of a portion of the territory belonging to the province of New York, now known as Delaware, and at that time inhabited by Swedish and Dutch settlers. This district was then called "the territories of Pennsylvania," or "the three lower counties upon Delaware."‡ In 1704 it was constituted a separate and independent province.

The name which he originally fixed for his province was New Wales. The Secretary, however, who was himself a Welshman, decidedly objected to this appellation. The proprietor thereupon,

* Pennsylvania Papers, June 14th, 1680, State Paper Office.
† Letter to Turner, Third Month 5th.
‡ Proud's History of Pennsylvania, vol. i. p. 202.

in reference to the wooded character of the country, proposed that it should be called Sylvania, to which the King, in honour of Admiral Penn, prefixed his name.

The design of William Penn, in obtaining the grant of this extensive territory in the new world, was one worthy of his liberal and enlightened mind. As a Christian citizen, alive to the interests of the community, he had watched the operation of the respective governments of his day, and, as a scholar, he was well acquainted with the forms and working of those of ancient times. But in none of these could he discover that the true end of government had been realized. " The nations," he observes, " want a precedent—and because I have been somewhat exercised about the nature and end of government among men, it is reasonable to expect that I should endeavour to establish a just and righteous one in this province, *that others may take example by it*—truly this my heart desires."* " I eyed the Lord in obtaining it," he writes on another occasion, "I have so obtained it, and desire to keep it, that I may not be unworthy of his love ; but do that which may answer his kind providence, and serve his truth and people, *that an example may be set up to the nations.* There may be room there, though not here, for such an *holy experiment.*"† His aim was truly a bold and noble one, such as no other founder of a colony, either in ancient or modern times, has attempted.

Actuated by these feelings, William Penn commenced his work of legislation for the new colony by publishing a frame of government, which, however, he concluded to refer for confirmation to the first provincial council to be held in Pennsylvania. In the preamble to these laws, the enlightened sentiments of the proprietor on the origin, nature, and object of government, are set forth. " Government," he says, " seems to me a part of religion itself ; a thing sacred in its institution and end.—They weakly err who think there is no other use of government than correction : daily experience tells us that the care and regulation of many other affairs make up much the greatest part.—I know

* Proud's History, vol. i. p. 169.   † Ibid.

what is said by the several admirers of monarchy, aristocracy, and democracy ; and [these] are the three common ideas of government when men discourse on the subject. But I choose to solve the controversy, with this small distinction, and it belongs to all three. *Any government is free to the people under it* (whatever be the frame) *where the laws rule, and the people are a party to those laws,* and more than this is tyranny, oligarchy, or confusion.—Governments, like clocks, go from the motion men give them, so by them they are ruined too. Wherefore governments rather depend upon men, than men upon governments. Let men be good, and the government cannot be bad; if it be ill, they will cure it. But, if men be bad, let the government be never so good, they will endeavour to warp and spoil it to their turn. It is the great end of all government to support power in reverence with the people, and to secure the people from the abuse of power ; for liberty without obedience is confusion, and obedience without liberty is slavery."

His frame of government did not exceed twenty-four articles, and his original code of laws consisted of but forty, to which, however, twenty-one were added before the whole received the sanction of the colonial assembly. As though to give prominence to the subject, the first in the new code had special reference to liberty of conscience. This important principle was recognized in the following words :—" That all persons living in this province, who confess and acknowledge the one Almighty and Eternal God to be the Creator, Upholder, and Ruler of the world, and that hold themselves obliged in conscience to live peaceably and justly in civil society, shall in no wise be molested or prejudiced for their religious persuasion or practice in matters of faith and worship ; nor shall they be compelled at any time to frequent or maintain any religious worship, place, or ministry whatsoever."

The penal laws of England did not harmonize with the feelings of William Penn, who had suffered severely under them ; and, excepting for wilful murder and treason, no crimes in Pennsylvania were punishable by death. In these cases his charter gave him no power to annul this awful penalty by positive enactment.* It should, however, be known that, during his life-time, Pennsylvania was not disgraced by the disgusting exhibition of the gallows, or by an execution in any other mode.

On the subject of prison discipline, he introduced a complete reform ; and every prison, instead of being a nursery of vice and idleness, was constituted a place of industry and education. Oaths were entirely abolished, and profane swearing, cursing, lying, and drunkenness, were punishable as crimes. The brutalizing scenes of bull-baiting, cock-fighting, &c., were also forbidden, as well as theatrical exhibitions, masques, and card-playing, as tending to "looseness and irreligion." On the first day of the week, "according to the good example of the primitive Christians, and the ease of the creation, people were to abstain from their daily labour, that they might the better dispose themselves to worship God according to their understandings." Vexatious law-suits were prevented by the appointment of arbitrators in every county court, whilst distinct courts were instituted for protecting and assisting orphans and widows. The rights of the native inhabitants of the country early claimed the attention of the governor, and one of his first acts was to protect their interests.†

Such was the early legislation of Pennsylvania, and such the endeavours of its rulers to promote religion and morality by the aid of civil checks and restraints upon the people. Well indeed might one of the freemen exclaim on the passing of these laws :— " It is the best day we have ever seen !" " Here," said another, " we may worship God according to the dictates of the divine principle, free from the mouldy errors of tradition ; here we may thrive, in peace and retirement, in the lap of unadulterated

* Vide Sec. v. and vii. of the Charter. Among Lord Chief Justice North's official notes on the draft of the Charter for Pennsylvania are these :—" W. Penn to pardon all offences committed within the limitts of his province, treason and murder excepted."

" Felonies and treasons to be the same as by the common laws, and tryalls to be in the same manner."—*State Paper Office, Penn. Papers, B. T. vol. I.*

† Vide his Conditions or Concessions, agreed upon in 1681, in Proud's History, Appendix I.

nature ; here we may improve an innocent course of life on a virgin Elysian shore."* The constitution of Pennsylvania, far in advance of the age, stood unequalled in excellence, and it is not too much to say that it contained the germ at least, if not the development, of every valuable improvement in government or legislation, which has been interwoven into the political systems of more modern times. When, more than a century later, Frederic, king of Prussia, read the account of its government, he involuntarily exclaimed, " Beautiful !"—" It is perfect if it can endure."† " And how happy," said Peter the Great of Russia, in alluding to Friends, " must be a community instituted on their principles."

On becoming the proprietor of Pennsylvania, William Penn, for the information of his friends, published a description of the province, so far as it was then known in England, and offered lands at forty shillings per hundred acres, to those who inclined to emigrate. Many of his brethren in religious profession were still exposed to grievous outrage and spoil from a rapacious and dominant hierarchy, and aware of the strong bias which the sufferers had to remove to a country where spiritual courts could no longer harass them, he was induced to accompany his liberal offer with a word of caution, " that none might move rashly, but to have an eye to the Providence of God ;" and their movements, thus guided, he believed, would " turn to the glory of His great name, and to the true happiness of them and their posterity."

The fame of William Penn as a champion for religious freedom, and as a man of universal benevolence, but above all as a devoted Christian, had spread itself widely, not only in the three kingdoms, but also on the continent of Europe : the announcement, therefore, that he now possessed an extensive territory in the new world, quickly drew people to him with proposals for emigration, and his generous terms brought many purchasers. The most considerable of these formed a company, called the " Free Society of Traders," consisting chiefly of Friends of London and Bristol ; a German company was also formed, headed

---

* " The Planter's Speech to his neighbours."
† Herder, xiii., p. 116, in Bancroft.

by Franz Pastorious. The former bargained for 20,000 and the latter for 15,000 acres.

The first emigrant ships that left the shores of Britain for Pennsylvania, sailed in the autumn of 1681, having on board a considerable number of persons from Wales, London, Bristol, and Liverpool. The ships were three in number, two from London, and one from Bristol. The "John and Sarah," from London, was the first that arrived; the other from that port was driven out of its course, and did not reach its destination till the following spring. The one from Bristol did not arrive until winter, and having ascended the Delaware as far up as Chester, was there frozen in the same night. In this dilemma, the emigrants were obliged to land and winter on the spot, and several of them had to take up their abode in huts hastily constructed, and in caves dug in the banks of the river.*

It appears that from the very first William Penn entertained the idea of settling in Pennsylvania, in order to promote, by a personal superintendence, the great object he had in view. For some time therefore, he had been making preparations for the voyage; and, in the Sixth Month, 1682, in company with about one hundred persons, who were mostly Friends from Sussex, the county in which he resided, he sailed for his transatlantic possessions. After a tedious and sickly voyage of nine weeks, during which no fewer than thirty of the passengers had been carried off by the small-pox, the "Welcome" anchored in the Delaware, and he landed at Newcastle, on the 27th of the Eighth Month.† The settlers of this district were mostly Dutch and Swedes, and on hearing of his arrival they hastened to meet their new governor, and greeted him with hearty demonstrations of joy.‡

* Watson's Annals of Philadelphia, p. 14.

† On this occasion the following entry was made in the public records of Newcastle:—" On the 27th day of October, 1682, arrived before ye Towne of New Castle, from England, William Penn, Esqe., whoo produced twoo deeds of feofment for this Towne and twelve myles about itt, and also for the twoo Lower Counties, ye Whoorekill, and St. James's— wherefore the said William Penn received possession of ye Towne the 28th of October, 1682."

‡ Watson's Annals of Philadelphia, p. 16.

At Newcastle, the agents of the Duke of York formally sur-- rendered to William Penn the territory on the Delaware.* Con- vening the settlers at the Court-house, he addressed them on the nature and object of government, stating his desire to exercise the powers he had obtained, for the general good of the com- munity, and concluded by renewing, under his own authority, the commissions of the existing magistrates. Leaving Newcastle, he ascended the Delaware to Upland, now Chester. Agreeably to his instructions, the Commissioners had already caused repre- sentatives to be elected for the first General Assembly ; and as Friends' Meeting-house was the most commodious building in Chester, it was fixed upon as the place of their deliberations. These primitive legislators of Pennsylvania were an unsophisti- cated people, and more practical than theoretical. In the course of their discussion they adopted the salutary restriction, " that none speak but once before the question is put, nor after, but once ; and that none fall from the matter to the person ; and that superfluous and tedious speeches may be stopped by the speaker." Their session lasted only four days, and notwith- standing their inexperience in the work of legislation, such was the good feeling and harmony prevalent among them, and such their confidence in the sincere desires of William Penn to pro- mote their welfare, that during this short space of time they passed the laws already referred to. At the conclusion, being addressed by the proprietor in the language of christian ex- hortation,† they retired to their new homes, under the pleasing reflection that those blessings of civil and religious freedom, which had been denied to them in the land of their nativity, were now, in the overrulings of a kind Providence, secured to them and to their posterity.

William Penn now proceeded on a visit to the authorities of New York, and next to meet Lord Baltimore in Maryland, to confer with him on the subject of boundary. Amidst the numerous important avocations which devolved upon him in this infant

---

* Hazard's Register, vol. v. p. 79.

† Votes and Proceedings of the House of Representatives, by B. Franklin, p. 7.

state of the colony, he was not, it appears, forgetful of his duties as a gospel minister. " I have been," he writes in the Tenth Month, 1682, " at New York, Long Island, East Jersey, and Maryland; in which I have had good and eminent service for the Lord.—I am now casting the country into townships for large lots of land. I have held an assembly, in which many good laws are passed; we could not safely stay till the spring for a government. I have annexed the lower counties (lately obtained) to the province, and passed a general naturalization for strangers, which hath much pleased the people.—As to outward things, we are satisfied ; the land good, the air clear and sweet, the springs plentiful, and provision good and easy to come at; an innumerable quantity of wild fowl and fish ; in fine, here is what an Abraham, Isaac, and Jacob, would be well contented with ; and service enough for God ; for the fields are here white for harvest : O, how sweet is the quiet of these parts, freed from the anxious and troublesome solicitations, hurries and perplexities, of woeful Europe !"*

Among the many objects which claimed his attention, few were more important than the selection of a site for a chief city. According to his express instructions, the Commissioners had been industrious in collecting information to assist in determining the point. Some thought Chester favourably situated for the capital, but William Penn fixed upon the narrow neck of land lying between the Delaware and the Schuylkill,† a situation " not surpassed by one among all the many places he had seen in the world." The establishment of a great city in Pennsylvania was very early his favourite object ;‡ while his choice of the situation, and the grand scale which he laid down for building it, would have made it inferior to few, whether of ancient or modern date. As originally designed, with its squares, gardens, and noble streets lined with trees, it would have covered no less than twelve square miles. The erection of detached dwellings surrounded by garden-ground, was quite a favourite idea of the governor ; for he wished the Quaker capital to resemble " a

---

* Proud, vol. i. p. 209.   † Day's Hist. Collections, p. 544-6.
‡ Vide his Concessions, Fifth Month, 1681.

greene country town, which might never be burnt, and might always be wholesome." Its name he decided should be Philadelphia, a Greek word, signifying brotherly love, and which he gave as indicating the spirit which he desired might pervade the minds of the colonists and rule in all their actions.

The colony of Pennsylvania was now fast peopling; so rapid indeed was the influx of settlers, that within three months after the landing of the governor, no less than twenty-three ships, filled with emigrants from Great Britain and Ireland, had entered the waters of the Delaware.* Within a few months from the foundation of Philadelphia, William Penn could announce that eighty houses and cottages were ready; that the merchants and craftsmen were busily engaged in their respective callings; that more than three hundred farms had been laid out and partly cleared; that ships were continually arriving with goods and passengers, and that plentiful crops had already been obtained from the soil.† At the time of his return from Pennsylvania, in the summer of 1684, the city could number three hundred and fifty-seven houses, "divers of them," he says, "large and well-built, with cellars;" and at least fifty townships had been settled :‡ one year later the houses had increased to no less than six hundred.§ In little more than two years from its settlement, ninety ships, bringing, according to the estimate of William Penn, an average of eighty passengers in each, or in all seven thousand two hundred, had arrived in the colony :‖ these, together with the previous colonists and those from the adjacent settlements, gave a population of about nine thousand to the province. Oldmixon says, that in 1684 the number was about seven thousand, of which two thousand five hundred were inhabitants of the new city; and that twenty-two townships had been established.¶ In

---

* Proud, vol. i. p. 209.

† W. Penn to the Free Society of Traders, Sixth Month 16th, 1683 ; Lord Baltimore, Seventh Month, 1683.

‡ Further Account of Pennsylvania and its improvements, by W. Penn.

§ Robert Turner to W. Penn, Sixth Month, 1685.

‖ Further Account, &c., by W. Penn.

¶ Oldmixon's British Empire in America.

three years from its foundation Philadelphia had gained more than New York had done in half a century, and the progress of the province was more rapid than even that of New England. Already schools had been established, and the printing press was at work, sowing broadcast the seeds of morality and religion. In the Tenth Month, 1683, Enoch Flower, in a dwelling formed of pine and cedar planks, commenced the work of education ; his terms being " to learn to read, four shillings a-quarter ; to write, six shillings ; boarding scholars, to wit—diet, lodging, washing and schooling, ten pounds the whole year."

One of the earliest production of the printing press was an epistle by John Burnyeat, in 1686. In New England the press was not in operation until eighteen years after its settlement. In New York seventy-three years elapsed before any book or paper was printed, and in North Carolina a still longer period ; whilst in Episcopal Virginia and Popish Maryland the printing press was discouraged as dangerous to religion.* " I must without vanity say," observes William Penn, in writing to Lord Halifax, " I have led the greatest colony into America that any man did on private credit ;" and to Lord Sunderland he says, " with the help of God, and such noble friends, I will show a province in seven years equal to her neighbours of forty years' planting."†

The boundary line between Pennsylvania and Maryland had for some time been a subject of dispute between William Penn and Lord Baltimore, and their conferences on the subject had issued without any satisfactory result. In the early part of 1684, Lord Baltimore proceeded to England, with a view to exercise his personal interest with the government on the disputed question. The subject was considered by William Penn to be of so much importance to the interest of his colony, that he deemed it needful to take some course to counteract the court influence of Baltimore. About this time also he received accounts of the renewed persecution of nonconformists, more especially those of his own Society. These things, together with the spread of malicious and unfounded reports affecting his reputation, and

* Memorials of the Penn. Hist. Soc. i. p. 103.
† Letter, Fifth Month 28th, 1683.

some matters of a private nature, led him to the conclusion that it was right for him to return to England ; and having appointed a Commission for conducting the affairs of the government during his absence, he went on board in the Sixth Month, 1684.

The prospect of leaving Pennsylvania at this interesting stage of its progress was deeply felt by William Penn. The temporal interests of the settlers was an object which he ardently sought to promote, but the spiritual advancement of his friends was that for which above all he was the most deeply solicitous, and, just before he sailed, he addressed them in the following beautiful exhortation :—

" To THOMAS LLOYD, J. CLAYPOLE, J. SIMCOCK, C. TAYLOR, and J. HARRISON, to be communicated in Meetings in Pennsylvania, and the Territories thereunto belonging, among Friends.

" My love and my life is to you, and with you, and no water can quench it, nor distance wear it out, or bring it to an end. I have been with you, cared over you, and served you with unfeigned love ; and you are beloved of me, and near to me beyond utterance. I bless you in the name and power of the Lord, and may God bless you with his righteousness, peace, and plenty, all the land over ! O that you would eye Him in all, through all, and above all the works of your hands, and let it be your first care how you may glorify Him in your undertakings ! for to a blessed end are you brought hither ; and if you see and keep in the sense of that Providence, your coming, staying, and improving, will be sanctified : but if any forget Him, and call not upon his name in truth, He will pour out his plagues upon them, and they shall know who it is that judgeth the children of men.

" O, you are now come to a quiet land ; provoke not the Lord to trouble it ! And now that liberty and authority are with you and in your hands, let the government be upon his shoulders in all your spirits, that you may rule for Him, under whom the princes of this world will one day esteem it their honour to govern and serve in their places. I cannot but say, when these things come mightily upon my mind, as the apostles said of old, ' What manner of persons ought we to be in all godly conversation ?'

Truly the name and honour of the Lord are deeply concerned in the discharge of yourselves in your present station, many eyes being upon you; and remember that, as we have been belied about disowning the true religion, so, of all government, to behold us exemplary and Christian in the use of it will not only stop our enemies, but minister conviction to many, on that account prejudiced. O that you may see and know that service, and do it for the Lord in this your day!

" And thou, Philadelphia, the virgin settlement of this province, named before thou wert born, what love, what care, what service, and what travail has there been to bring thee forth and preserve thee from such as would abuse and defile thee!

" O that thou mayst be kept from the evil that would overwhelm thee; that, faithful to the God of thy mercies, in the life of righteousness thou mayst be preserved to the end! My soul prays to God for thee, that thou mayst stand in the day of trial, that thy children may be blessed of the Lord, and thy people saved by his power. My love to thee has been great, and the remembrance of thee affects my heart and mine eye.—The God of eternal strength keep and preserve thee to his glory and peace!

" So, dear Friends, my love again salutes you all, wishing that grace, mercy, and peace, with all temporal blessings, may abound richly among you!—So says, so prays, your friend and lover in the truth."

14

CHAPTER II.

IN common with all those who were pioneers in settling the
colonies of North America, the early emigrants to Pennsylvania
underwent many privations, and no inconsiderable degree of personal suffering. Many of the settlers, it is true, were persons of
considerable means, and took with them houses in frame, together
with furniture, tools, and implements suited to their new circumstances. These, realized the full benefit and comfort of such
precaution ; but others, who were not so provided, were obliged

to content themselves with such shelter as the forest afforded, while the first homes of not a few were in caves dug in the high banks of the Delaware.

But amidst all the trials and difficulties which attended the emigrant Friends to these hitherto uncultivated wilds, and notwithstanding the excitement which naturally prevailed among them in entering upon their duties in the new world, they were not unmindful of the Heavenly kingdom, or of the duty which they owed to the Most High. " Our business in this new land," wrote one of the early settlers, " is not so much to build houses and establish factories, and promote trade and manufactures that may enrich ourselves, (though all these things, in their due place, are not to be neglected,) as to erect temples of holiness and righteousness, which God may delight in ;—to lay such lasting frames and foundations of temperance and virtue, as may support the superstructures of our future happiness, both in this and the other world."*

* " The Planter's Speech to his neighbours," &c. printed by A. Sowle, *Shoreditch,* 1684.

The following certificate from Settle Monthly Meeting, in Yorkshire, also shews that many of the early settlers in Pennsylvania did not emigrate merely on considerations of a worldly nature, but from a sense of religious duty :—

From SETTLE MONTHLY MEETING, *the 7th of the Fourth Month,* 1682.

These are to certify, all whom it may concern, that it is manifested to us that a necessity is laid upon several Friends belonging [to] this Monthly Meeting to remove into Pennsylvania, and particularly our dear friend Cuthbert Hayhurst, (his wife and family,) who has been, and is a labourer in the truth, for whose welfare and prosperity we are unanimously concerned, and also for our friends, Thomas Wrightsworth, and also his wife ; Thomas Walmsley, Elizabeth his wife, and six children ; Thomas Croasdale, Agnes his wife, and six children ; Thomas Stackhouse, and Margery his wife ; Nicholas Waln, his wife and three children ; Ellen Cowgill and her family ; who, we believe, are faithful Friends in their measures and single in their intentions to remove into the aforesaid Pennsylvania, in America, there to inhabit, if the Lord permit, and we do certify unity with their said intentions and desire their prosperity in the Lord, and hope what is done by them will lead

As early as 1684, it is stated that "there were about eight hundred persons in regular attendance on First and Week-days, at Friends' meeting in Philadelphia. This," observes the writer, "was remarkable for a people who were contending with the various difficulties incident to opening the wilderness.—No wonder they prospered."*

In respect to food the settlers were singularly provided for, considering that, with the exception of a strip of land about two miles in breadth, extending along the banks of the Delaware,

to the advancement of the truth in which we are unanimously concerned with them.

[Signed by eleven Friends.]

These came to America, in the ship "Welcome," with W. Penn, some of whom settled at Byberry.—*Memoirs of the Hist. Soc. of Pennsylvania,* vol. ii. part i. p. 182.

A memorandum in an ancient Register Book of Newton Meeting, settled by Friends from Ireland, who came over in Thomas Lurtin's vessel from London in 1681, presents a similar testimony. They at first settled at Burlington, but in the spring of 1682 removed to Newton. This was before William Penn arrived in Pennsylvania.

" Zeal and fervency of spirit was what in some good degree at that time abounded among Friends, in commemoration of our prosperous success and eminent preservation, both in our coming over the great deep, as also that, whereas we were but few at that time, and the Indians many, whereby it put a dread upon our spirits, considering they were a savage people ; but the Lord that hath the hearts of all in his hands, turned them so as to be serviceable to us, and very loving and kind; which cannot be otherwise accounted but to be the Lord's doing in our favour, which we had cause to praise his name for.

"And that the rising generation may consider that the settlement of this country was directed by an impulse upon the spirits of God's people, not so much for their ease and tranquillity, but rather for the posterity that should be after, and that the wilderness being planted with a good seed, might grow and increase to the satisfaction of the good husbandman. But, instead thereof, if, for wheat it should bring forth tares, the end of the good husbandman will be frustrate, and they themselves will suffer loss. This narration I have thought good and requisite to leave behind, as having had knowledge of things from the beginning.

" THOS. SHARP."

* Hazard's Register, vol. x. p. 92.

the country produced nothing for the support of human life but wild fruits, birds, and animals of the forest.   The early Friends of Pennsylvania were deeply sensible that their outward wants were supplied by the good providence of Him who fed Israel in the wilderness, and many of them were, in after years, often led to recount his mercies and the manifestation of his all-protecting and preserving care in this time of trial.   The following extract from " the testimony " of one of them on this subject is worthy of preservation :—

" THE TESTIMONY OF RICHARD TOWNSEND, SHOWING THE PRO-
    VIDENTIAL HAND OF GOD TO HIM AND OTHERS, FROM THE
    FIRST SETTLEMENT OF PENNSYLVANIA TO THIS DAY [about
    the year 1727].

" Whereas, King Charles the Second, in the year 1681, was pleased to grant this province to William Penn and his heirs for ever ; which act seemed to be an act of Providence to many religious, good people ; and the proprietor, William Penn, being one of the people called Quakers, and in good esteem among them and others, many were inclined to embark along with him for the settlement of this place.

" To that end, in the year 1682, several ships being provided, I found a concern on my mind to embark with them, with my wife and child ; and about the latter end of the Sixth Month, having settled my affairs in London, where I dwelt, I went on board the ship 'Welcome,' Robert Greenaway, commander, in company with my worthy friend William Penn, whose good con-versation was very advantageous to all the company.

" At our arrival we found it a wilderness ; the chief inhabitants were Indians and some Swedes, who received us in a friendly manner ; and though there was a great number of us, the good hand of Providence was seen in a particular manner, in that provisions were found for us by the Swedes and Indians, at very reasonable rates, as well as brought from divers other parts, that were inhabited before.

" Our first concern was to keep up and maintain our religious worship ; and, in order thereunto, we had several meetings in the houses of the inhabitants, and one boarded meeting-house was set up where the city was to be, near Delaware ; and, as we had nothing but love and goodwill in our hearts one to another, we had very comfortable meetings from time to time ; and after our meeting was over, we assisted each other in building little houses for our shelter.

" After some time I set up a mill on Chester Creek, which I brought, ready framed, from London, which served for grinding of corn and sawing of boards, and was of great use to us.   Besides, I, with Joshua Tittery, made a net, and caught great quantities of fish, which supplied ourselves and many others ; so that, not-withstanding it was thought near three thousand persons came in the first year, we were so providentially provided for, that we could buy a deer for about two shillings, and a large turkey for about one shilling, and Indian corn for about two shillings and sixpence per bushel.

" And as our worthy proprietor treated the Indians with extra-ordinary humanity, they became very civil and loving to us, and brought in abundance of venison.   As, in other countries, the Indians were exasperated by hard treatment, which hath been the foundation of much bloodshed, so the contrary treatment here, hath produced their love and affection.

" As people began to spread, and improve their lands, the country became more fruitful, so that those who came after us were plentifully supplied, and with what we abounded [in] we began a small trade abroad.   As Philadelphia increased, vessels were built and many employed.   Both country and trade have been increasing wonderfully to this day ; so that, from a wilderness, the Lord, by his good hand of Providence, hath made it a fruitful field ; on which to observe all the steps, would exceed my present purpose ; yet, being now in the eighty-fourth year of my age, and having been in this country near forty-six years, and my memory pretty clear concerning the rise and progress of the province, I can do no less than return praises to the Almighty, when I look back and consider his bountiful hand, not only in temporals, but in the great increase of our meetings, wherein he hath many times manifested his great loving-kindness, in reaching to and convincing many persons of the principles of truth : and those that were already convinced and continued faithful, were blessed not only with plenty of the fruits of the earth, but also with the dew of heaven.   I am engaged in my spirit to supplicate the continuance thereof to the present rising generation ; that as God hath blessed their parents, the same blessing may remain on their offspring to the end of time ; that it may be so is the hearty desire and prayer of their ancient and loving friend,

RICHARD TOWNSEND'S ORIGINAL DWELLING-HOUSE.

The establishment of meetings for both worship and discipline, was a subject that very early claimed the attention of Friends in Pennsylvania.   For a short time they held those for worship at the dwellings of some of the settlers, but these were soon exchanged for a more commodious though temporary meeting-house, built of boards, on a spot now occupied by the city of Philadelphia.   Towards the close of 1682, or in little more than two months after William Penn had landed on his new territory, it was concluded to establish a Monthly and also a Quarterly Meeting. The following, taken from the minutes of Philadelphia Quarterly Meeting, was the record made on this interesting occasion :—

c 2

" Friends belonging to the meeting in Philadelphia, in the province of Pennsylvania, being met in the fear and power of the Lord, at the present meeting place in the said city, the 9th day of the Eleventh Month, being the third day of the week, in the year 1682, they did take into consideration the settlement of meetings therein, for the affairs and service of Truth, according to that godly and comely practice and example, which they had received and enjoyed with true satisfaction amongst their friends and brethren in the land of their nativity, and did then and there agree, that the first third day of the week in every month shall hereafter be the Monthly Meeting day for the men's and women's meeting, for the affairs and service of Truth in this city and county ; and every third meeting shall be the Quarterly Meeting of the same."

With the influx of settlers meetings were multiplied, and in about three months from the date of the foregoing, no less than nine meetings for worship, and three Monthly Meetings, had been set up in the province. William Penn and some of his companions thus wrote to their brethren in England, in the First Month, 1683 : " The truth is in authority amongst us—our God hath engaged us, yea he hath overcome us with his ancient glory ; the desert sounds, the wilderness rejoices, a visitation inwardly and outwardly is come to America ; God is Lord of all the earth."*

---

* An early copy of this communication is still preserved by Cotherstone Meeting, in Yorkshire. It is doubtless the earliest document issued by Friends of Pennsylvania, and written to inform Friends in England of the state and condition of the Society in the new colony. Some interest, therefore, attaches to this paper, and claims a place for it in these pages :—

Philadelphia in Pennsylvania,
the 17th day of the First Month, 1683.

DEARLY BELOVED FRIENDS AND BRETHREN,—

In the everlasting kindred of the heavenly truth of our God, we who are therein as flesh of your flesh, and bone of your bone, send you the salutation of our endeared love. Friends, brethren, and sisters, parents and children, masters, mistresses, and servants, your whole families, whether you be little children, young men, or fathers in the honourable truth, the God of eternal love and power, that visited and gathered us in our own land, and kept us while we lived in it, who hath brought

As noticed in the former volume, a Yearly Meeting had been set up at Burlington, in West Jersey, as early as the Sixth Month,

us safely into this part of his earth, and that so unutterably appears to us and amongst us in all our assemblies, to refresh, bless, and establish us, hath laid it upon us in the name of many Friends present, at a select meeting of elders and faithful brethren of Pennsylvania and Jersey, at the city of Philadelphia (where the glory of the Lord did wonderfully overshadow us) to greet you all in the Lord Jesus Christ, and to let you know how it is with us both inwardly and outwardly. Blessed be the God of Abraham, and of Isaac, and of Jacob, that called us not hither in vain : this was the testimony of life in our living assembly through many faithful brethren, that God was with us and is with us, yea, he hath made our way for us, and proved and confirmed to us his word and faithfulness. For he hath adorned this wilderness with his presence, and contented our hearts in his providence ; yea, established our hearts with his goodness ; and while this humility, this brokenness, this self-abasement dwells with us, shall it not go well with us ? yea, and with all that so dwell. Our God hath engaged us, yea, he hath overcome us with his ancient glory, the desert sounds, the wilderness rejoices, a visitation inwardly and outwardly is come to America ; God is Lord of all the earth, and at our setting of the sun will his name be famous. Friends, we rejoice in his salvation, we see his work, we are in our places, and God with us, and much here is to do for him. It is in our heart to deliver up our days and lives and strength to him, and we pray God to be kept, and you to pray for us. O ! remember us, we cannot forget you ; many waters cannot quench our love, nor distance wear out the deep remembrance of you in the heavenly truth : we pray God preserve you in faithfulness, that, discharging your places and stewardships, ye may be honoured and crowned, with the reward of them that endure to the end. And though the Lord hath been pleased to remove us far away from you, as to the other end of the earth, yet are we present with you ; your exercises are ours, our hearts are dissolved in the remembrance of you, dear brethren and sisters, in this heavenly love ; and the Lord of heaven and earth, who is the father of our family, keep us in his love and power, and unite, comfort, and build us all more and more to his eternal praise, and our rejoicing.

And now, dear friends, know that God's truth is in its authority amongst us, yea, a terror to the wicked, and a praise to them that do well, and God daily gives the faithful dominion over the spirits of the people, and they that are not subject to the truth in themselves, are subject to its heavenly authority in those that fear God. The dominion under this part of the whole heaven is given to the saints of the

1681.   The second was held at the same place in the Seventh
Month of the following year, and by it an epistle of advice was
issued to its members.   This meeting concluded that single
young persons should bring with them from England certificates
of their clearness, or otherwise, in regard to marriage, and that
none should marry without the consent of parents or guardians.
In 1683, Burlington Yearly Meeting, in consequence of the
attendance of the newly-settled Friends of Pennsylvania, formed

Most High, and our part of the kingdoms of this end of the world
growing to be the kingdoms of the Lord and his Christ, whose authority
is setting up within and without, that we may be a society complete in
Him throughout, as well in body as in soul and spirit, which are his ;
so will the creation be delivered, and the earth obtain her sabbaths
again.

For our meetings, more especially of worship, there are in West
Jersey, one at the falls of the river Delaware, another at Burlington,
one at Assisconck, one at Rancocas, one at Newtown, and one at Salem,
and two Half-year Meetings, one at Burlington and one at Salem,
to which the Half-Yearly Meeting of Friends in East Jersey is joined,
who also have a Yearly Meeting of themselves, a men and women's
meeting, and a Yearly Meeting at Shrewsbury.

In Pennsylvania there is one at the Falls, one at the Governor's house,
one at Colchester River, all in the county of Bucks ; one at Tawsany
[Trelawny], one at Philadelphia, both in that county ; and at Darby at
John Blunsom's, one at Chester, one at Ridley at John Simcock's, and
one at William Ruse's, in Chichester in Cheshire.   There be three
Monthly Meetings of men and women for Truth's service : in the county
of Chester one ; in the county of Philadelphia another ; and in the
county of Bucks another ; and intend a Yearly Meeting in the Third
Month next.

And here our care is as it was in our native land, that we may serve
the Lord's truth and people, and keep, what in us lies, our holy profession
from the reflection of the enemies thereof.   And our desires are, that as we
are joined of the Lord, and so one people, by his own power we may live in
this dear and near relation, and have a mutual regard to the honour of the
Lord's truth, both here and there.   And in order to the same, that there
may be free communication, and holy advices and correspondences,
which on our parts we intend (the Lord willing) to observe, and tenderly
desire the same from you, that we may be comforted and edified in each
other, to the praise of the name of the great Lord of our heavenly family.
Particularly, we on the Lord's behalf do agree, that if any shall leave

a much larger assembly. The records of this meeting are still preserved, and by them we are informed, that one of the subjects under deliberation, was a very comprehensive proposal for the establishment of a Yearly Meeting for Friends of all the North American colonies. The minute made on the occasion runs thus :—

" Whereas this meeting judged it requisite, for the benefit and

these parts and incline homewards, they shall have a certificate of their clearness in respect of conversation, credit, marriage and unity amongst us, or else that you shall have cause of shyness towards them. So we intreat of you, that all desiring to come into these parts, may be cautioned to observe that good and comely care, as they hope to be received and helped of us. And such as are certified of by the faithful of the meetings where they have lived to be clear in life, credit, marriage engagements, and unity among God's people where they inhabited, we shall embrace and assist them as brethren in the service of love.

And for outward condition as men, blessed be God, we are satisfied ; the countries are good, the land, the water, and the air ; room enough for many thousands to live plentifully, and the back lands much the best ; good increase of labour, all sorts of grain, provision sufficient, and by reason of many giving themselves to husbandry, there is like to be great fulness in some time ; but they that come upon a mere outward account must work, or be able to maintain such as can. Fowl fish and venison, are plentiful, and of pork and beef no want, considering that about 2,000 people came into this river last year. Dear friends and brethren, we have no cause to murmur ; our lot is fallen every way in a good place, and the Son of God is among us. We are a family at peace within ourselves, and truly great is our joy therefore. So in the unchangeable love and life of Truth, into which we have been with you baptized, and so made to drink into one pure and eternal fellowship, where our souls dwell and feed together before the Lord, we once more salute you and embrace you, remaining, and praying that we may remain therein, your true, tender, and faithful brethren,

WILLIAM PENN,	JOHN SOUTHWORTH,	THOMAS BRASSEY,
SAMUEL JENNINGS,	WILLIAM YARDLEY,	JOHN SONGHURST,
CHRISTOPHER TAYLOR,	JOHN SYMCOCK,	GRIFFITH JONES,
JAMES HARRISON,	THOMAS FITZWATER,	WILLIAM CLAYTON,
JOHN KENNELL,	LEWIS DAVID,	ROBERT WADE,
ROBERT STACY,	HENRY LEWIS,	THOMAS DUCKET,
ISAAC MARRIOT,	WILLIAM HOWELL,	NICHOLAS WALNE,
ARTHUR COOK,	THOMAS WINN,	JOHN BLUNSOM.
WILLIAM FRAMPTON,	BENJAMIN CHAMBERS	

advantage of Truth, and mutual comfort of Friends, that a General Yearly Meeting might be established for the provinces in these parts, northward as far as New England, and southward as far as Carolina, that, by the coming of Friends together from the several parts where Truth is professed, the affairs thereof may be the better known and understood ; and to the end the same may be assented to by Friends in those parts and places, as above mentioned, it is agreed that William Penn, Christopher Taylor, Samuel Jennings, James Harrison, Thomas Olive, and Mahlon Stacey, do take sure methods, by writing to Friends, or speaking, as may best fall out for their conveniency, in order to have the same established."*

A few weeks after the holding of this Yearly Meeting at Burlington, one for the first time was held in Philadelphia. It met in the Seventh Month, 1683 ; no records of its proceedings have, however, come down to us, excepting a small notice preserved on the minutes of Bucks Quarterly Meeting, and having reference to the establishment of that meeting. Early in the Seventh Month, 1684, a Yearly Meeting was again held at Burlington, and in the latter part of the same month another at Philadelphia.† Except a general epistle to Friends on the American continent, and one to Friends of London, issued by the latter, the records of both these meetings have been lost. In the epistle to London, the holy influence which prevailed among Friends on these occasions is thus referred to : — " At the two aforementioned General Meetings we had such a blessed harmony together, that we may say that we know not that there was a jarring string amongst us—Glorious was God in his power amongst us. A great multitude came of many hundreds, and the gospel-bell made a most blessed sound. There was the men's and women's meeting, at both places, in their precious services, to

---

* Evidence of Thomas Evans, vol. ii. p. 174 of Foster's Reports.

† In Smith's History of Friends of Pennsylvania, it is stated that the first Yearly Meeting held at Philadelphia was in 1685. This, however, is clearly an error. The Epistle from London makes a distinct allusion to the one held in Philadelphia on the 24th of Seventh Month, 1684.

inspect into truth's matters, in what related to them ; and God gave them wisdom to do it, and all was unanimous. We are to send an epistle to Carolina, Virginia, Maryland, and all thereaway ; also the other way to New England, and Rhode Island, that it may be presented to them, if possible that from these remote provinces they may send two or three from each province to our Yearly Meeting here, being as a centre or middle place. That so communion and blessed union may be preserved amongst all. Some are stirred up in their spirits to travel in the work and service of the gospel."*

It is an interesting circumstance, that on this occasion women Friends also held a Yearly Meeting, and addressed an epistle to those of their sex in England, which was answered by a meeting of women Friends then held in London.†

" Things went on sweetly with Friends in Pennsylvania," writes W. Penn, in 1684 ; " many are increased finely in their outward things, and grow also in wisdom ; their meetings are also blessed, and there are no less than eighteen in the province." " We are now laying," writes Robert Turner, from Philadelphia, in the summer of 1685, " the foundation of a large plain brick house for a meeting-house, in the centre, sixty feet long and about forty broad ; a large meeting-house, fifty feet long and thirty-eight feet broad, also going up on the front of the river, for an evening meeting."

In the year 1685, the Yearly Meeting for the Jerseys again met at Burlington, and another was held in Philadelphia for the province of Pennsylvania. At the latter of these there were present by appointment some Friends from Rhode Island, and also from the Quarterly Meetings of Chopthank and Herring Creek in Maryland. From the last named Quarterly Meeting an epistle was also received. On this occasion it was concluded there should be but one Yearly Meeting for the Jerseys and Pennsylvania, to be held alternately at Philadelphia and Burlington ; the one for 1686, to be held at Burlington, under the title of " The General Yearly Meeting for Friends of Pennsylvania, East and West

Jersey, and of the adjacent provinces." At the Philadelphia Yearly Meeting of 1685, it was also concluded to establish a Yearly Meeting of ministers.*

From the year 1682, a Yearly Meeting was also held at Salem, in West Jersey. For some years this meeting seems to have been considered as one of a disciplinary character, and it exercised some control over the meetings in its vicinity until about the close of that century.

Agreeably to the conclusion of the previous year, the Yearly Meeting of 1686 commenced on the 8th of the Seventh Month, (O.S.) at Burlington. As on the former occasion, there were Friends under appointment from the two Quarterly Meetings of Maryland; none, however, being in attendance from Virginia or Carolina, " it was agreed that they be writ to again, to request their consent to have this as a General Yearly Meeting, as formerly proposed." There were no representatives from New England, but the presence of Friends from New York and Long Island is noticed. It was also agreed, " that two Friends or more be appointed out of every Quarterly Meeting, that are capable, to give an account of the affairs of truth, to attend this General Yearly Meeting to be held from time to time until the said meeting shall be ended."† The following is an extract from their epistle to the Yearly Meeting of London :—

" We had a good and great opportunity for the Lord at our yearly assembly; many were the testimonies, weighty was the power, and living was the Holy Presence that was with us, as we gathered and sat together in his dread.—We had many Friends with us from Long Island, New York, and Maryland.—A glorious day of the Lord is dawning more and more in these regions ; his light goes forth as the morning, and the brightness his appearance as the rising of the sun. He is dispelling the darkness, removing weights and burdens, and bringing several to a near station to himself; so that being fitted and prepared by his divine power, they may be able ministers and instruments in his hand to bring many to the lowly path of righteousness."

---

* Evidence of T. Evans, in Forster's Reports, vol. ii. p. 473.   † Ibid.

Agreeably to the conclusion of the Yearly Meeting of 1686, representatives were regularly appointed to attend it in the following year. The meetings noticed as sending them in 1688, were the Quarterly Meetings of Philadelphia, Bucks, Chester, Burlington, Salem and Gloucester, and Shrewsbury; and in the following year the same with the addition of some from Delaware.*

The Yearly Meeting of 1687 was "as to numbers very considerable, and several useful and wholesome admonitions were recommended to the notice and observation of the respective meetings."† In the following year also it was "large and full, many Friends," they record, "having come from all these three provinces, and some from New York, Long Island, and Maryland —many living precious testimonies were borne and held forth in our meeting, which continued four days, in all which we were livingly refreshed, comforted and strengthened."‡ In 1690 they write that "the appearance of Friends at this [annual] assembly was very numerous. Several of our ministering brethren visit yearly the neighbouring colonies, and some of us had a door opened to a nation or two of our bordering Indians."§ A Yearly Meeting collection was first made in 1691.

For several years subsequent to the date of the foregoing, the Yearly Meetings were considerably agitated by the apostacy of George Keith, and by the schism which he endeavoured to effect in the Society, of which a full and circumstantial account will be given in another chapter. The Yearly Meeting of London pronounced its decision on the appeal of George Keith against the Yearly Meeting of Pennsylvania, confirming the judgment of the said meeting, and condemning the conduct of Keith. This had a favourable effect upon the Society in America, and in 1695, their epistle to English Friends was cheering and encouraging. "The Lord," they write, "hath in a very eminent manner appeared amongst us, the rays of his glory have covered us,

* Records of Philadelphia Yearly Meeting.
† Epistle to London Yearly Meeting, 1687.
‡ Ibid. 1688.   § Ibid. 1690.

and his heart-melting and tendering power he hath distilled upon us as the gentle rain, to our mutual refreshment and solace in Him, which rests and dwells livingly upon our souls; so that we can truly say it hath been a season of love, and a time of harmonious concord." "This assembly," they add, "has been larger than any heretofore, being not less by a modest computation than twelve hundred."*

During the controversy with Keith and his party, Friends were much misrepresented by them, more especially in reference to their faith in the divinity of our Lord and Saviour Jesus Christ, in his propitiatory sacrifice for the sins of mankind, and with respect to their acceptance of the Holy Scriptures as an inspired record. Soon after Keith's disownment from membership in our religious body, Friends of Pennsylvania and the Jerseys, with a view to disabuse the public mind of the mis-statements which had been extensively circulated, published their belief on these important points of Christian doctrine. As a declaration of the faith of the Society, a considerable degree of interest attaches to this document, and being somewhat brief, it cannot with propriety be omitted from these pages. It is as follows:—

" OUR ANCIENT TESTIMONY RENEWED CONCERNING OUR LORD AND SAVIOUR JESUS CHRIST, THE HOLY SCRIPTURES, AND THE RESURRECTION." "GIVEN FORTH BY A MEETING OF PUBLIC FRIENDS, AND OTHERS, AT PHILADELPHIA IN PENN-SYLVANIA." 1695.

" TO THE READER.—That we faithfully and sincerely own and confess Christ Jesus our Lord and Saviour, according to he divine testimonies of the Holy Writ, and according to his spiritual manifestation upon our souls; and it is for our Christian vindication herein, and not for controversy (for a contest with contentious persons is endless), this following confession is writ, and submitted to thy perusal.

---

* Epistle to London Yearly Meeting, 1695.

" OUR SCRIPTURE CONFESSION CONCERNING OUR LORD JESUS CHRIST.

"I. *Concerning his Divinity, and his being from the beginning.*

" We believe that in the beginning was the Word, and that the Word was with God, and the Word was God, the same was in the beginning with God ; all things were made by him, and without him was not anything made that was made.* Whose goings forth have been from of old, from everlasting.† For God created all things by Jesus Christ, who is the image of the invisible God, the first-born of every creature, the brightness of the Father's glory, and the express image of his substance.‡

"II. *Concerning his appearance in the flesh.*

" We believe that the Word was made flesh ; for he took not on him the nature of angels, but took on him the seed of Abraham, being in all things made like unto his brethren.§ [He was] touched with a feeling of our infirmities, and in all things tempted as we are, yet without sin. He died for our sins, according to the Scriptures, and he was buried, and he rose again the third day, according to the Scripture.||

"III. *Concerning the end and use of that appearance.*

" We believe that God, sending his own Son in the likeness of sinful flesh, and for sin, condemned sin in the flesh.¶ For this purpose the Son of God was manifested, that he might destroy the works of the devil.** Being manifested to take away our sins, for he gave himself for us, an offering and a sacrifice to God for a sweet smelling savour ; having obtained eternal redemption for us.†† And through the Eternal Spirit offered up himself without spot to God, to purge our consciences from dead works to serve the living God.‡‡ He was the Lamb that was slain from the foundation of the world ; of whom the Fathers did all drink ; for they drank of that Spiritual Rock that followed them, and

* John i. 1, 2, 3.
† Micah v. 2.
‡ Eph. iii. 9 ; Col. i. 15 ; Heb. i. 3.
§ John ii. 14 ; Heb. ii. 16.
|| Heb. iv. 15 ; 1 Cor. xv. 3.
¶ Rom. viii. 3.
†† Eph. v. 2 ; Heb. ix. 12.
** 1 John iii. 8.
‡‡ Heb. ix. 14.

that Rock was Christ, the same yesterday, to-day, and for ever.*
Who suffered for us, leaving us an example, that we should follow
his steps, that the life also of Jesus may be made manifest in our
mortal flesh; that we may know him, and the power of his
resurrection, and the fellowship of his sufferings, being made conformable to his death.†

" IV. *Concerning the inward manifestation of Christ.*

" We believe that God dwelleth with the contrite and humble
in spirit ; for he said, I will dwell in them, and walk in them ;
and that Christ standeth at the door and knocketh ; if any man
hear his voice, and open the door, he will come in to him, and
sup with him.‡   And therefore ought we to examine ourselves,
and prove our own selves, knowing how that Christ is in us, unless
we be reprobates ; for this is the riches of the glory of the mystery which God would make known among (or rather in) the
Gentiles, Christ within the hope of glory.§

" V. *Concerning his being our Mediator and Advocate.*

" We believe there is one God, and one Mediator between
God and men, even the man Christ Jesus, who gave himself a
ransom for all, to be testified in due time.‖   My little children,
these things write I unto you, that ye sin not ; and if any man
sin, we have an advocate with the Father, Christ Jesus the
righteous.   And he is the propitiation for our sins, and not for
ours only, but for the sins of the whole world.¶   He sits on the
right hand of God the Father, and ever lives to make intercession
for us.**

" VI. *Concerning his unity with the saints.*

" We believe that he that sanctifieth, and they who are sanctified, are all of one ; for by the exceeding great and precious
promises that are given them, they are made partakers of the
Divine nature ; because for this end prayed Christ, saying, " That
they all may be one ; as thou, Father, art in me, and I in thee,

* 1 Cor. x. 4 ; Heb. xiii. 8 ; Rev. xiii. 8.
† 1 Pet. ii. 21 ; 2 Cor. iv. 11 ; Phil. iii. 10.
‡ Isa. lvii. 17 ; 2 Cor. vi. 16 ; Rev. iii. 20.
§ 2 Cor. xiii. 5 ; Col. i. 27.   ‖ 1 Tim. ii. 5.
¶ 1 John ii. 1.   ** Heb. vii. 25.

that they also may be one in us:" "and the glory which thou gavest me I have given them ; that they may be one, even as we are one : I in them, and thou in me, that they may be made perfect in one."*

" VII. *Concerning his coming to Judgment.*

" We believe that we must all appear before the judgment-seat of Christ, that every one may receive the things done in his body, according to that he hath done, whether it be good or bad. Knowing therefore the terror of the Lord, we persuade men.†

"VIII. *Concerning the Resurrection.*

" We believe there shall be a resurrection of the dead, both of the just and unjust ; they that have done good to the resurrection of life, and they that have done evil to the resurrection of damnation.   Flesh and blood cannot inherit the kingdom of God, neither doth corruption inherit incorruption.   Nor is that body sown that shall be, but God giveth it a body as it hath pleased him, and to every seed his own body : It is sown in dishonour, it is raised in glory ; it is sown in corruption, it is raised in incorruption ; it is sown in weakness, it is raised in power ; it is sown a natural body, it is raised a spiritual body.‡

" IX. *Concerning the Scriptures.*

" We believe that whatsoever things were written aforetime, were written for our learning ; that we through patience and comfort of the Scriptures might have hope—which are able to make wise unto salvation through faith, which is in Christ Jesus.§ All Scripture given forth by inspiration of God (as we believe the Holy Scriptures of the Old and New Testament are), is profitable for doctrine, for reproof, for correction, for instruction in righteousness, that the man of God may be perfect, throughly furnished unto all good works.   And knowing also that no prophecy of the Scriptures is of any private interpretation ; for prophecy came not in old time by the will of man, but holy men of God spake as they were moved by the Holy Ghost.‖

---

* John xvii. 21 ; Heb. ii. 11 ; 2 Pet. i. 4.
† 2 Cor. v. 10.
‡ 1 Cor. xv. 37.
§ Rom. xv. 4 ; 2 Tim. iii. 15.
‖ 2 Pet. i. 20.

"OUR SOLEMN CONFESSION, IN THE HOLY FEAR OF GOD, CONCERNING OUR LORD AND SAVIOUR JESUS CHRIST, ACCORDING TO THE SEVERAL TESTIMONIES GIVEN FORTH BY OUR FAITHFUL BRETHREN.

"We sincerely believe, own and confess no other Lord and Saviour than our Lord Jesus Christ, the Son of the Living God, to whom the Prophets and Apostles give witness, and who in the fulness of time took flesh of the seed of Abraham, and of the stock of David. We confess to his miraculous conception by the power of the Holy Spirit overshadowing of the Virgin Mary; and to his being born of her (according to the flesh), and that he took upon him a real body, and that he was a real man; and that in the days of his flesh he preached righteousness, wrought miracles, was crucified, being put to death by wicked hands; and that he was buried, and rose again the third day, according to the Holy Scriptures; and after he rose he really appeared to many brethren, and afterwards he ascended into glory according to the wisdom and power of the Heavenly Father, and is glorified with the same glory, which he had with the Father before the world began, being ascended far above all heavens, that he might fill all things, whose glory is incomprehensible. And we also believe that he is that one Mediator between God and man, viz. that entire, perfect, heavenly, and most glorious man, Christ Jesus, who ever lives, and endures in his soul (or spirit) and glorious body. We further believe, that according to his promise to his disciples before he left them, viz. that he would come unto them again, and that he that was with them should be in them, and they in Christ, and Christ in them.* And that accordingly he came; and that he who appeared in that body, which was prepared for him, was full of grace and truth, and received the spirit not by measure, appeared by a measure of his grace and spirit in his apostles and disciples, and doth since in all his faithful followers; and that he is their King, Prophet, and High-Priest, and intercedes and mediates in their behalf, bringing in everlasting righteousness, peace, and assurance for ever into their hearts and consciences; to whom be everlasting honour and dominion. Amen.

* John xiv. 20.

"CONCERNING THE SOUL'S IMMORTALITY AND THE RESUR-
RECTION.

" We believe our souls are immortal, and shall be preserved in
their distinct and proper beings, and shall have spiritual, glorious
bodies, such as shall be proper for them, as it shall please God to
give them in the resurrection ; that we may be capable of our
particular rewards, and different degrees of glory after this life in
the world to come."

As time passed on, the tide of emigration from Europe to
Pennsylvania does not appear to have slackened.   During 1686,
many Friends from Germany and Holland arrived in the province.*   Most of the Germans settled at Germantown, about six
miles from Philadelphia, where some of their countrymen had
already located.   They came from Gersheim, a town near Worms,
and had been convinced of our religious doctrines through the
ministry of William Ames.   Within four years from the settlement of Pennsylvania, about twenty meetings for worship were
established in that province, and seven more in the Jerseys.
No statistical account has been preserved of the number of
Friends who arrived in the subsequent years ; but it is evident
that, from the continued increase in the number of meetings
in the respective provinces, they could not have been few.†
In 1700, the Yearly Meeting numbered at least forty particular
meetings.   This increase of the Society did not arise from immigration only—the bright example of godliness which was evinced
in the daily life and conversation of most of the early Friends in
these parts—their lowly, humble walk, together with the gospel
truths which were livingly and powerfully declared among the
people, were circumstances which drew not a few to unite with
them on the ground of religious conviction.   Of this latter class

* Proud, vol. i. p. 304.
† In a letter written in 1698 by Thomas Camm, of Westmoreland, he
thus briefly notices the inclination which still prevailed among Friends
for settling in America : "A great deal of the younger sort of Friends
hereaway are intending for Pennsylvania."—*Bristol Monthly Meeting
MSS.*

were a number of Welsh people who had settled at Gwynned, and who, in 1698, set up the meeting at that place. Ellis Pugh, himself a Welshman, frequently visited them, and was instrumental to the convincement and establishment of many. He afterwards became a member of that meeting, and ended his days among his countrymen there, most of whom were unable to speak any other than the Welsh language.*

Education was a subject that early claimed the attention of Friends in Pennsylvania. The opening of Enoch Flower's school in 1683, has already been noticed. In 1689, an important step in furtherance of this object was taken, by the establishment of a public school in Philadelphia, in which the poor were to be taught gratis.† George Keith was engaged as the head master, and, on the petition of several influential Friends, this school was incorporated by charter in 1697. Four years later, William Penn confirmed it by another charter, the powers of which were extended in 1708, and 1711. This institution was intended not only for teaching the usual branches of an English education, but also to furnish a means for the acquisition of classical learning. In the preamble to the charter the design is thus set forth : " Whereas the prosperity and welfare of any people depend, in great measure, upon the good education of youth, and their early introduction in the principles of true religion and virtue, and qualifying them to serve their country and themselves, by educating them in reading, writing, and learning of languages, and useful arts and sciences, suitable to their sex, age, and degree, which cannot be effected in any manner so well as by erecting public schools, for the purposes aforesaid," &c.‡

Four years after the establishment of the school in question, or eleven years from the foundation of the colony, the Assembly passed an Act making it imperative for every child to be taught reading and writing.§ In 1645, or twenty-five years after their landing in Massachusetts, the Puritans had formed similar insti-

* Smith's Hist., chap. xiv.
† Proud, vol. i. p. 343 ; and Smith's Hist., chap. vii.
‡ Proud's Hist. vol. i. p. 344.   § Acts of Pennsylvania, 1693.

tutions, in which, observes Bancroft, " lies the secret of the success and character of New England.":* Education, both among the Puritans and the early Friends, was regarded as a most important element in their social and religious condition. Great, indeed, would have been the inconsistency, if they, who held religious considerations to be paramount to every other, had been indifferent to the education and moral training of their offspring. As early as the year 1667, George Fox recommended the establishment of a boarding-school for each sex in the neighbourhood of London, for the purpose, as he states, of instructing them " in all things, civil, and useful in the creation." In that for boys, the languages were taught under the superintendence of Christopher Taylor, a Friend of learning and classical literature. In 1691, it was reported to the Yearly Meeting in London, that no less than fifteen establishments of this description were kept by Friends in different parts of England.† Our early Friends have been charged with undervaluing learning ; but no real ground existed for the imputation. The error has probably arisen from their boldly avowing that human learning was not needful to qualify any for the work of a gospel minister. But whilst both they and their successors have been most emphatic on this point, their history, so far from furnishing evidence of indifference to literary instruction, proves, that in this respect, as in many others, they were in advance of most of their day. We may at least point to Pennsylvania as corroborative of this fact.

The difficulties which the early settlers experienced in obtaining a subsistence from the soil, soon gave place to plenty and abundance. They were sensible that the divine blessing had rested on their labours, and in their prosperity they were not slack in deeds of charity. In 1692, they co-operated with Friends in England, in raising a considerable sum of money for the redemption of those of their brethren who were held in captivity in the Barbary States ;‡ and in 1697, Friends of Philadelphia for-

* Bancroft's History of the United States.
† Minutes of London Yearly Meeting, vol. i. p. 269.
‡ Proud's Hist. vol. i. p. 370.

warded about two hundred pounds for the relief of their fellow-members in the eastern parts of New England, who had suffered by a severe prevailing sickness.*

Very early after the settlement of Pennsylvania, many ministers of the Society of Friends from England visited it in the love of the gospel. The first of these of whom we have any account, is James Martin of London, who arrived there in 1684, " and stayed," says Smith, " several years, and whose diligent labours of love were well received."† He had already visited America in 1682, but his services did not at that time extend to Pennsylvania. James Martin joined Friends in 1672, and on several occasions, in after years, suffered imprisonment for the principles he had embraced.‡ Although a man of a weakly constitution, he was much devoted to the work and service of the gospel. He died in 1691, whilst on a religious visit in Essex, at the age of forty-five, his last moments being so richly and abundantly attended with divine consolation, as to cause him to sing forth, in a remarkable manner, the praises of the Most High.§

In the year 1687, Roger Longworth, of Lancashire, paid a religious visit to Pennsylvania.‖ It appears that he also had visited it once before, but in what year we are not informed.¶ His second visit was but of short duration : after a few months religious labour, he was seized with fever, and died in the Sixth Month of the same year, at the age of fifty-seven. Roger Longworth was a most devoted minister, and travelled largely in the cause of truth. In addition to extensive labours in his own land, he visited Scotland once, the West India islands and North America twice, Ireland five times, and the continent of Europe no less than six times. For the last twelve years of his life he was wholly given up to the work and service of the ministry. "The Lord," say Friends of Pennsylvania, "made him a successful instrument in his hand ; he settled and established meetings in many parts where he came, to the great comfort and refreshment of the upright in heart, by which he got a name

* Smith's Hist., chap. xiv.   † Ibid., chap. vi.
‡ Besse, vol. i. pp. 452, 463.   § Piety Promoted, part ii.
‖ Whiting's Memoirs, p. 368.   ¶ Penn. Memorials, p. 5.

amongst the ancients, and is recorded among the worthies of the Lord."*

Thomas Wilson, and James Dickinson, were the next gospel messengers from Europe whose labours are recorded. They arrived in 1691, a period of much agitation among Friends, arising from the apostacy of George Keith, and they were eminently serviceable to their brethren under the trials of this peculiar case. They attended the Yearly Meeting, which was held at Salem, in West Jersey, in the Second Month of the following year, and lasted several days.† "Here we met," says James Dickinson, "with Friends from most parts of the country; had many glorious meetings; and were livingly opened to proclaim the everlasting gospel and day of God's love to the mourners in Sion, encouragement to the weak and feeble, and judgment to the fat and full. The meeting ended in love and unity, and our hearts were filled with praises to the Lord."‡

After some further service in this part, these vigilant watchmen passed on to New England. They were, however, much affected at the troubles introduced by George Keith, and, whilst on their journey eastward, their minds often turned with deep solicitude to their brethren in Pennsylvania and the Jerseys, to whom they addressed an epistle of exhortation, dated from Rhode Island, in the Fifth Month, 1692. "Dear Friends," they write, "Truth is the same that ever it was, and the power of it as prevailing as ever; and where it is kept to, and dwelt in, hath the same effect as ever; as many of you are witnesses, who keep your nabitations therein; with whom our souls are bound up in God's everlasting covenant of light; in which, as we walk, we have true fellowship one with another, and the blood of Jesus Christ his Son, cleanseth us from all unrighteousness."§ These Friends, a few years subsequently, paid a second visit to Pennsylvania; a reference will, therefore, be again made to them.

In 1694, Thomas Musgrave of Yorkshire arrived. Some years previously he had visited the more northern parts of the American continent, but this appears to have been the first time

---

* Penn. Memorials, p. 5.   † Wilson's Journal.
‡ Dickinson's Journal.   § Ibid.

he travelled in the provinces on the Delaware : his visit, says Smith, was " to the satisfaction of his brethren."* On returning to England, he attended the Yearly Meeting of London, and gave an account of his gospel services ; alluding to Pennsylvania, he said there were " about eighteen meetings of Friends, who are in great love and unity."† In 1699, Thomas Musgrave left his native land with the intention of settling in America, but died on the passage.‡

In the course of 1694, Robert Barrow of Westmoreland, and Ralph Wardell of Sunderland, visited their transatlantic brethren in these parts. They are described as "ancient Friends ;" the former, as being eminently gifted in the ministry—the latter, as having an "extraordinary talent as to discipline." In the year following, Jonathan Tyler of Wiltshire, a young man about twenty-six years of age, referred to as a "noble instrument in the hand of God,"§ also arrived in the province. He travelled about three years in America, and many, it is recorded, "were turned from darkness to light by his living and powerful ministry." He died in 1717, at the age of forty-eight, in the full assurance of a glorious and unspeakably blessed change : "Lord Jesus, come quickly," were nearly his last words. Jonathan Tyler attended the Yearly Meeting held at Burlington in 1696, where he was joined by Jacob Fallowfield from Hertford, and also by James Dickinson before referred to. Jacob Fallowfield died a few years after, whilst on a voyage from Barbadoes to Pennsylvania.‖ During the same year Henry Payton, and his sister Sarah Clark, of London, also crossed the Atlantic, and visited Friends in these provinces, and, together with Jonathan Tyler, were present at the Yearly Meeting held at Philadelphia, in 1697, much to the satisfaction of their brethren.

The year 1698 was marked by the arrival in Pennsylvania of an increased number of gospel labourers from other parts. These were William Ellis and Aaron Atkinson ; Thomas Chalkley and

* Smith's Hist., chap. x.
† Minutes of London Yearly Meeting, 1697.
‡ Letter of N. Waln, in Ellis's Life, p. 148.
§ Piety Promoted, part vi.   ‖ W. Ellis's Life, p. 148.

Thomas Turner ; Elizabeth Webb and Mary Rogers ; Thomas Story and Roger Gill, all from England ; and Mary Gamble, from Barbadoes. The services of these will be noticed in the order in which they are named.

William Ellis and Aaron Atkinson were companions in their travels ; the former came from Airton, a village in Yorkshire, and was at that time about forty years of age. He came forth in the ministry soon after reaching manhood, and in the certificate furnished to him by his Monthly Meeting on this occasion, he is stated to have been " a faithful labourer in the work of our Lord Jesus Christ, not only in word and doctrine, but in propagating of every good work."* Aaron Atkinson, from Cumberland, was then about thirty-three years of age. He had been brought up among the Presbyterians, but at the age of twenty-nine was convinced of the principles of Friends, by the ministry of Thomas Story. Soon afterward he came forth as a minister, and was instrumental, according to the testimony of his friends, in " bringing many, not only to the acknowledgment of the truth, but to sit under the teaching of Christ our Lord, the only Shepherd and Bishop of souls."†

These two gospel labourers landed in Maryland, in the First Month, 1698, and, after visiting the meetings in those parts, they reached Pennsylvania in the Sixth Month following, and passed on to the Yearly Meeting of ministers then held at the house of Samuel Jennings, at Burlington, in the same month. The proceedings of this meeting were deeply interesting in many respects. William Ellis took notes of them, which are still preserved among his papers, and, as showing the character of the meeting in question, they may be appropriately inserted in these pages. It will be observed that among other matters which came before them, was the revision of manuscripts intended for publication—a regulation which had existed in England from the establishment of the Morning Meeting of ministers in 1672. The notes are as follows :—

---

* Life of W. Ellis, p. 38.   † Ibid. p. 40.

AT A MEETING OF MINISTERING FRIENDS, HELD IN BUR-
LINGTON, AT THE HOUSE OF SAMUEL JENNINGS, THE 17TH,
18TH, 19TH, 20TH, 21ST, 22ND, AND 23RD DAYS OF THE
SEVENTH MONTH, 1698.

The meeting was large and full, and divers travelling Friends
that were strangers were present, as William Ellis, Aaron
Atkinson, Mary Rogers, Elizabeth Webb, from England, and
Elizabeth Gamble, from Barbadoes, with divers others from
neighbouring provinces ; and the Lord's eternal power was with
us, in which divers living, sound testimonies were borne ; our
hearts were united by the bond of Truth, and we proceeded to
inspect the necessary affairs of the meeting.

A Testimony concerning our dear friend, Thomas Janney,
given forth by Griffith Owen, was read and approved.

The meeting adjourned until the morrow morning.

18th day.—Friends being met together, and the Lord's power
and presence eminently attending the meeting, divers testimonies
and cautions were delivered in the power and life of Truth, which
then overshadowed the meeting.

First,—Though some that had a public testimony, might think
within themselves, that the weight of the service of the Yearly
Meeting might not be upon them, believing it would rather
become the concern of those who had come from far to visit
Friends here ; yet that they should beware of an unconcernedness
in that respect, but be weightily and carefully concerned to
travail, spiritually, with them who might be in the exercise, that
thereby they might be helped and strengthened through their
spiritual travail with them.

As also, that whereas it was the way of the world to forget
God, yet the Lord had gathered us, his people, to himself, that
we could not forget him ; for though we came poor and empty
together, yet the Lord in his wisdom, and goodness, and love,
met us with a full hand, to comfort and strengthen us, that we
might not faint in our minds, but be renewed in our strength ;
and as Friends kept in that, the Lord would be praised, and his

Truth advanced. As also, that Friends might keep to the power of Truth, and not to be over forward, but to mind it ; and when things were well, not to offer any thing that might do hurt, or hinder the Lord in his spiritual work amongst his people. And though this caution might seem then to be well received, as it had been formerly, yet it was seldom but some things in these great meetings were offered that did hurt, wound, and grieve the honest-hearted ; and several cautions were given, that it should not be so at this meeting, or for the future.

As also, that Friends in the ministry should not run before their Guide, but be weightily concerned, and not strive to utter words out of the power of Truth : but as the power fell in them, though there might be an openness and a desire to speak in that power, yet rather to leave off, that the Lord might have his way. For many things which might open at such times, if the power withdrew, might be better spoken to by another, who might afterward be put forth to speak to it, if the Lord saw good to order it.

Adjourned until the morrow morning.

19th day.—Friends being again met this morning, some testimonies and cautions were given, viz :—

As to the difference between the wisdom of God and of man, and that though the wisdom of man was in the power of many, yet the wisdom of God was to be waited for ; therefore Friends were cautioned to wait for it in silence, and know a renewing of their strength therein, and not to stir without it carried them along ; but rather to rest when it withdrew or did not put them forth.

As also, that as the Lord had formerly appointed priests and Levites to serve him, so the Lord had now appointed the chosen vessels to bear public testimonies to his name and truth : with caution, that none should go before or stay behind the power of that which had called them, lest their offerings should be those of strange fire.

And not only so, but to be good patterns and examples in their lives and conversation, and to see that it should be so with their wives and children and servants, that in all things the Lord through them might be praised.

William Ellis and Aaron Atkinson, for good order and example's sake, were willing, and of their own accord, offered their certificates, that Friends in England had given them, of their unity with them, and of Friends' satisfaction in their coming to visit us here, which were read and well accepted and approved.

A letter from Thomas Turner, and his certificate, read from Friends in England, were well received; and it was agreed that a certificate be drawn on his account, to go from this meeting.

The answer written by Caleb Pusey and John Wood, to Daniel Leed's book, called "News of a Trumpet," agreed to be read next Fifth-day morning.

Adjourned until the morrow, at eight in the morning.

20th day.—Adjourned again until four in the afternoon.

Ann Dilworth proposed her intentions of going for England, to visit Friends there, and she was advised of the weight of so great a concern; but if it rested still with her, the meeting left her to her liberty.

Walter Fawcitt laid before this meeting his intention of going to England to visit Friends, and he was left to his liberty.

An epistle from the Yearly Meeting at London was read, and referred to be considered by the Yearly Meeting here.

A paper of condemnation was brought into this meeting, signed by Griffith Jones, about his joining with George Keith in his separation; but [Friends] being informed it had not yet orderly passed the Monthly Meeting at Philadelphia, to which he belonged, he was therefore referred to give the said meeting satisfaction in the first place.

Adjourned until eight in the morning.

21st day.—Adjourned until evening.

Adjourned until eight in the morning.

22nd day.—Mary Rogers, in much brokenness, laid before Friends, how that it had not been her own choice to choose exercises, trials and difficulties, but it had been the Lord's pleasure to draw her beyond her expectation, as now he had laid it upon her to visit Barbadoes; and though she had tried several ways to have evaded it, if the Lord had seen good, yet every way, except that, seemed as darkness to her. But she was willing to lay it before the meeting, that she might have the concurrence of Friends in so weighty an undertaking; which caused much tenderness in the meeting, and divers testimonies were borne of the satisfaction of Friends concerning her and her exercises; and with several prayers for her preservation, in much love and brokenness, the meeting gave her up to the will of the Lord.

Agreed that a certificate be drawn on her behalf, and that the Monthly Meeting at Philadelphia be desired to take care that it be done.

It was proposed to this meeting, that Richard Hoskins had it on his mind to visit the meetings in Maryland and thereaway, and in Virginia, and he was left to his liberty.

Thomas Turner's certificate signed.

23rd day.—Caleb Pusey's answer to Daniel Leed's " News of a Trumpet sounding in the Wilderness," &c. was read, and [the meeting] agreed that it be published with amendments, and the additions noted to be made.

The meeting ended.

After attending the Yearly Meeting at Burlington in 1698, William Ellis and his companion passed onwards to New England, and then returned southward, and to England in the following year. Referring to his services among the settlers in Pennsylvania, William Ellis says, " The Lord blessed my travels greatly amongst them; disciples increase. It is thus also in most parts of West Jersey : there is little [or but few] in East Jersey."*

Thomas Chalkley crossed the Atlantic in company with Thomas Turner and the two Friends just referred to. Speaking of his labours in Pennsylvania, he says, " I had many large and precious meetings, the power of the eternal Son of God being wonderful— there are many Friends in that province, and many sober young people, which greatly rejoiced my spirit. The Lord is with his people there, and prospereth them spiritually and temporally."†

* Letter to W. Edmundson.   † Chalkley's Journal.

Passing from this province he proceeded to the Jerseys, and visited the meetings in those colonies. At Crosswicks he mentions having a large meeting under the trees. It appears to have been a memorable occasion, at which he adds, "some were convinced of the truth." It was at this meeting that Edward Andrews, who afterwards became a valuable minister, was, as he expresses, "mightily reached."* He also held meetings with the Indians. Thomas Chalkley returned to England in 1699, but within a few years after settled in Pennsylvania: to his services in promotion of the cause of truth, reference will be made hereafter.

Thomas Turner was from Coggeshall Monthly Meeting in Essex. He travelled for a while in company with Thomas Chalkley, and his religious labours were edifying to his brethren in America; his stay, however, on this occasion, was but short, as he appears to have returned to England in the latter end of the same year.†

Elizabeth Webb and Mary Rogers landed in Virginia in the Twelfth Month, 1697. But little is recorded of their religious services, either within the province of Pennsylvania or in the other colonies of America. Mary Rogers, who is mentioned in the minutes of the Yearly Meeting of Ministers in 1698, as having been liberated to visit Barbadoes, died in the following year whilst passing from Nevis or Antigua to Jamaica.‡ Elizabeth Webb came from Gloucester. She was brought up as an Episcopalian, but at an early age was convinced of the principles of Friends. We are not informed at what time she came forth in the ministry, but respecting the visit in question, she has left the following remarkable record:—" In the year 1697, in the Sixth Month, as I was sitting in the meeting in Gloucester, which was then the place of my abode, my mind was gathered into perfect stillness for some time, and my spirit was as if it had been carried away into America; and, after it returned, my heart was as if it had been dissolved with the love of God, which flowed over the great ocean, and I was constrained to kneel down and pray for the seed of God in America. The concern never went

* Phil. Friend, vol. xix. p. 47.   † Life of W. Ellis, pp. 90 and 118
‡ Carpenter's Letter, in Life of W. Ellis, p. 168.

out of my mind day nor night, until I went to travel there in the love of God, which is so universal, that it reaches over sea and land."* She and her husband, John Webb, about 1708, settled in Pennsylvania, and in 1712, she went on a religious visit to Friends in Great Britain.

The Epistle from the Yearly Meeting held at Burlington, in 1698, to the Yearly Meeting in London, notices the attendance of most of the foregoing Friends:—"We may in truth say," they add, "through the large mercy and wonderful goodness of our God, we have had a very blessed and heavenly meeting.—The presence of the great God overshadowing us, many living and powerful testimonies were delivered."†

Thomas Story, and Roger Gill, reached the shores of the new world in the Twelfth Month, 1698. Of the life of the former eminent minister some particulars will be given. Roger Gill was from London. In his youth he had professed with the Baptists, and joined Friends at the early age of nineteen.‡ He also was an able minister of Christ, faithful and diligent in his calling. In 1699, they attended Philadelphia Yearly Meeting. This was a time of great affliction in that city, arising from the fatal ravages of the yellow fever. It broke out in the early part of the Sixth Month, and, by the latter end of the Eighth Month following, no less than two hundred and thirty persons had fallen victims to this terrible disease ; but few if any houses, being free from its attacks.§ In reference to this visitation Thomas Story thus writes : " Great was the majesty and hand of the Lord ! Great was the fear that fell upon all flesh ! I saw no lofty or airy countenance; nor heard any vain jesting to move men to laughter ; nor witty repartee to raise mirth ; nor extravagant feasting to excite the lusts and desires of the flesh above measure. But every face gathered paleness, and many hearts were humbled, and coun-tenances fallen and sunk, as such that waited every moment to be summoned to the bar, and numbered to the grave. But the just appeared with open face, and walked upright in the streets, and

---

* E. Webb's Letter to A. W. Bœhm.   † MS. Epistle.
‡ Piety Pro., part iii.   § T. Story's Life, p. 224.

rejoiced in secret, in that perfect love that casteth out all fear; and sang praises to Him who liveth and reigneth, and is worthy for ever, being resigned unto his holy will in all things, saying, Let it be as thou wilt, in time and in eternity, now and for evermore ; nor love of the world, nor fear of death, could hinder their resignation, abridge their confidence, or cloud their enjoyments in the Lord."*

In the Morning Meeting of Ministers and Elders which preceded the Yearly Meeting, the question of postponing the time of holding the latter, in consequence of the prevailing sickness, was considered. " But," observes Thomas Story, " the testimony of truth went generally against the adjournment or suspension, and the Lord's presence was greatly with us to the end."—" Friends," he continues, " were generally much comforted in the divine truth ; the fear of the contagion was much taken away, and the testimony of truth was exceeding glorious in several instruments, and over the meeting in general, and so continued to the end, which was the first, second and third days for worship, and the fourth for business, which was managed in wisdom and unanimity, and ended in sweetness and concord."†

During the early stage of the awful visitation referred to, Roger Gill was in New England. He was deeply affected at the circumstance, and impressed with the belief that it was required of him to go at once to the scene of his brethren's affliction. " When one hundred miles off," he said in one of his public meetings, " his love in the Lord was such to them, that had he had wings he would fly to Philadelphia."‡   The strong feeling of Christian sympathy and love which drew him thus to visit the sick and the dying, and to expose himself to the contagion, did not lessen as he saw his friends one after another suddenly snatched from time. On one occasion, during the Yearly Meeting, he was drawn fervently to supplicate the Most High to stay his hand, and he added, " if He would be pleased to accept of his life for a sacrifice, he freely offered it up for the people." Under a belief that his prayer had been heard, and that his life had been indeed accepted

* T. Story's Life, p. 224.   † Ibid.   ‡ Piety Pro. part iii.

as a free-will offering to the Lord, Roger Gill intimated to his friends that his work was nearly finished.   He went on a visit to Burlington Meeting, and soon after his return to Philadelphia was seized with the prevailing disease.   During the illness some of his friends expressed a hope for his recovery ; but he replied, " Truly I have neither thoughts nor hopes about being raised in this life ; but I know I shall rise sooner than many imagine, and receive a reward according to my works."*   He died after a few days' illness, the closing scene being one of great sweetness and solemnity. It is remarkable, that almost immediately after the death of this dedicated man, the ravages of the yellow fever ceased.†   " I was fully satisfied," writes Thomas Story on hearing of his death, that " he had obtained a crown of everlasting peace with the Lord ; many hearts in America had been tendered by him, many souls comforted, and several convinced : all [being] through that divine power by which he is now raised to glory, to sing praises to Him who sitteth on the throne, and ruleth and reigneth, and is alone worthy, for ever and ever." ‡

Towards the close of 1699, Thomas Story, who had been travelling in some of the southern states, returned to Pennsylvania, and held public meetings in various parts of that province, where no meetings of Friends had hitherto been settled.   He also attended many of the meetings in this province and in the Jerseys.   At Salem, he preached " against the world and apostates." At Cohanzie, " several were melted and comforted."   At Chester Creek he had the heartfelt pleasure of meeting William Penn on his again landing from England.   From thence he passed on to Concord, where he remarks the meeting "was large and well." The next was held at John Bowater's, about three miles distant, and was "a good and tender meeting, for the Lord was with them."   " Several also were tendered by the virtue of truth " at a large meeting held at Thomas Minshall's near by.   Another was then held about four miles off : this also appears to have been a tendering opportunity, after which he writes, " I was very easy,

---

* Piety Promoted, part iii.   † Ibid.
‡ T. Story's Life, p. 227.

and much comforted in the divine truth." He then passed on to Philadelphia.*

After spending about a week in the city, Thomas Story proceeded with William Penn to witness the proceedings of the Quarter Sessions at Chester, where he had a "large and open" meeting. He then visited his Welsh friends at Haverford West and Radnor. At Merion also he had a "very large meeting—many important truths," he remarks, "were opened, and we were comforted in the blessed truth, and mutually one in another therein." After this he again visited Philadelphia, whence he proceeded to the meetings of Germantown, Neshaminy, The Falls, Frankfort, Darby, and Burlington, and after another visit to Philadelphia he attended most of the meetings in East and West Jersey.†

In the early part of 1700, Thomas Story felt that he had completed the religious service required of him in America, and was, as he expresses it, "ready to return to England." There were, however, many Friends in his native land, who were conscious that he possessed abilities and qualifications which would render him a most useful member of the new and rising Commonwealth of Pennsylvania, and who were desirous to see them applied in that direction. William Penn, with whom he was on terms of the most intimate friendship, was also alive to the subject. He saw in his younger friend, those qualities of mind which could not fail to exert a beneficial influence on the people and government of his province, and he earnestly solicited him to remain. Thomas Story yielded to the wishes of his friends, and William Penn at once nominated him a member of the "Council of State," and soon afterwards "Keeper of the Great Seal," "Master of the Rolls," and one of his "Commissioners of Property." In the patent appointing him to these offices a proviso was inserted, which enabled him "to have deputies therein respectively, when and so often as his calling in the truth, and service thereof, might require it." Two years later, Thomas Story was appointed first Recorder of the city of Philadelphia. He was, however, always averse to this office, and resigned it as soon as the Corporation

T. Story's Life, p. 237–240.   † Ibid. p. 240–3.

was regularly settled.   He resided in Pennsylvania until the year 1714, when, after an absence of about sixteen years, he returned and settled in his native land.   During his residence in America, he was largely engaged in religious labours to promote the kingdom of his Redeemer, and visited most of the meetings from New England to Carolina, and the islands of the West Indies.

Intimately connected as Thomas Story was with Pennsylvania, a brief sketch of his life will not be inappropriate in these pages. He was born in Cumberland, of parents who were opulent, and who brought him up in the established church.   From very early life he was piously inclined: "the Lord," he remarks, "in his great mercy and kindness, had an eye upon me for good, even in my infancy, inclining my heart to seek after him in my tender years."   He delighted much in the study of the Holy Scriptures, and in religious contemplation.   His education, however, conflicted with this inclination of mind; the fashionable accomplishments of the day, such as music, dancing, and fencing, ill accorded with his aspirations after heavenly good, and, as he advanced towards manhood, his mind "suffered many flowings and ebbings." His father having designed to bring him up in the profession of the law, he was placed with a barrister in the country previously to his entering one of the Inns of Court.

Having been mercifully preserved in a tender and seeking state of mind, he was, through divine illumination, given to see that some of the ceremonies of the Church in which he had been educated, were inconsistent with the simplicity and character of the gospel of Christ.   Bowing at the sound of the name of Jesus, turning the face towards the east on the reading of the Apostles' Creed, kneeling towards the altar table, and infant baptism, were some of those observances against which he first had a religious scruple.   Continuing to follow on to know the Lord, he grew in Christian experience, and was favoured with deeper and clearer views of divine truth.   He saw that there were many evils in his nature, which were to be consumed by the spirit of judgment and of burning, and, resigning himself to the operations of the divine hand, he witnessed the carnal mind to be mortified and slain.   "I became," he observes, "simple as a little child;

the day of the Lord dawned, and the Son of Righteousness arose in me, with divine healing and restoring virtue in his countenance, and he became the centre of my mind. I was filled with perfect consolation, which none but the Word of Life can declare or give. It was then, and not till then, I knew that God is love, and that perfect love which casteth out all fear. It was then I knew that God is eternal light, and that in Him is no darkness at all."*

These, were the secret and silent operations of the power of God upon his mind, but the fruits of the Spirit were soon apparent to those around him. His manners were no longer jovial; his sword, which he had worn as a "manly ornament," was laid aside; his instruments of music were committed to the flames; and superfluous apparel no longer adorned his person or ministered to his pride. He also felt it to be his duty to discontinue his attendance of the national place of worship, but not with the view of uniting with any other sect; and a secret impression arose in his mind, that one day he should be called upon "to oppose the world in matters of religion; but when, or how, that should be brought to pass, he did not foresee."†

Being led into much retirement, he was at seasons remarkably favoured with Divine openings, as well as with spiritual enjoyments. "The Lord," he writes, "gave me joy which no tongue can express, and peace which passeth understanding. My heart was melted with the height of comfort; my soul was immersed in the depths of love; my eyes overflowed with tears of greatest pleasure." On one occasion, during a time of retirement, "Friends," he says, "were suddenly, and with some surprise," brought to his mind; and this circumstance induced a strong inclination to enquire respecting them. He soon after attended one of their meetings. The occasion appears to have been a favoured one, which tended to draw him in a feeling of sweet unity towards them. Alluding to this meeting, he says, "I sat still among them in an inward condition and mental retirement." A Friend spoke in the ministry, but his own attention was more directed to what was passing in his mind than to the doctrines which were

* T. Story's Life, p. 14.   † Ibid. p. 16.

declared—his object being, "to know whether they were a people gathered under a sense of the enjoyment of the presence of God in their meetings." His desire was abundantly answered. He had not sat long before "a heavenly and watery cloud," as he expresses it, "overshadowed his mind, and brake into a sweet abounding shower of celestial rain," and under the divine influence which prevailed, most present were contrited and comforted. "Our joy," he says, "was mutual and full—and mine as the joy of salvation from God, in view of the work of the Lord, so far carried on in the earth, when I had thought, not long before, there had scarce been any true and living faith, or knowledge of God in the world.*

This was in the year 1691 ; and from henceforth he openly professed with Friends, and in a few years after spoke in the character of a minister. At first his communications were confined to a few sentences only ; but, dwelling in the root of divine life, his gift was enlarged, and he became a mighty instrument in the hand of the Lord, for the awakening and conversion of others. Friends of his Monthly Meeting spoke of him as "a man of great parts, and these, sanctified and made instrumental in Divine wisdom, rendered his ministry very convincing and edifying ; so that he was acknowledged not only by our Society, but even by other people, to be a truly great and evangelical minister."† He travelled very extensively in the exercise of his gift as a minister of the Gospel in the United Kingdom, as well as in America, and he also once visited Holland and Germany. The greater portion, indeed, of his long life was given up to the service of his Lord. He died in Cumberland in the Fourth Month, 1742, and was buried at Carlisle, having been a minister nearly fifty years. He married the daughter of Edward Shippen of Philadelphia, but it does not appear that he left any family.

Thomas Story

---

* In 1716, Thomas Story delivered a memorable testimony in the Yearly M eting of London, in which he adverted to this meeting, and the impression then made on his mind "that Friends were the Lord's people."—*MS. Account.*

† MS. Testimonies of deceased Ministers, vol i.

Whilst the great Head of the Church sent his messengers from Europe to edify and to strengthen this portion of his visible church, he was also pleased to call some of his ministers in Pennsylvania and New Jersey to visit other parts of America, as well as to labour in word and doctrine among their brethren on the other side of the Atlantic. These things gladdened the hearts of their friends in England, and in an epistle dated from London in the Fourth Month, 1685, we find expressions of joy, " that some were stirred up in the spirit and power of the Lord to visit the churches of Christ in New England, Virginia, Maryland, and Carolina." In the year 1685, Thomas Olive, of New Jersey, and Edward Luffe, visited the meetings in Maryland,* and in the summer of 1688, several Friends of that province went on a gospel mission to their brethren in New England.† Soon after this date, James Dilworth, of Neshaminy, in Pennsylvania, visited his friends in Maryland.‡ In 1692, John Delavall accompanied Jacob Tilner to New England, and in the next year Richard Hoskins, who had recently settled in the province, visited Friends in Maryland, Virginia, and North Carolina.§ In 1694, Thomas Ducket and William Walker of Pennsylvania proceeded on a visit to Great Britain and Ireland. The latter died whilst on the service. Griffith Owen, of Philadelphia, also crossed the Atlantic soon after in the love of the gospel. It was during 1694 that Robert Ewer, in company with Thomas Musgrave, travelled in the work of the ministry to the colonies in the south ;‖ and in the following year Griffith Owen and William Gabitt attended the Yearly Meeting in Maryland.¶

The gospel labours of ministering Friends of Pennsylvania and the Jerseys, who travelled within the limits of other Yearly Meetings, were more generally about this time directed to New England. In 1695 Hugh Roberts and Joseph Kirkbride visited the churches in those parts ; in the year following, Richard

* Smith's Hist., ch. vi.   † Epist. to London Yearly Meeting, 1688.
‡ Smith's Hist., ch. vii.
§ MS. Letter to George Whitehead—Papers of London Yearly Meeting.
‖ Smith's Hist., chap. x.
¶ Epistle to London, 1695 ; Smith's Hist., chap. x. ; Ellis's Life, p. 90.

Hoskins and George Gray, and soon after them Hannah Delavall. It appears that Ann Dilworth and Jane Biles, of Pennsylvania, and Ann Jennings, of New Jersey, had on a previous occasion so visited the Friends of New England, but the date is not given. Hannah Delavall went thither a second time in 1697, and in the following year no less than six Friends of Pennsylvania travelled in that country; these were Thomas Janney, John Simcock, James Dilworth, William Biles, John Willsford, and Nicholas Waln; and in 1699 Thomas Ducket and Samuel Jennings. In 1698, Richard Hoskins, Richard Gove and Thomas Chalkley, visited their brethren in Maryland and Virginia, and in the year following they all three extended their gospel labours to Friends in England.*   About this time also, Walter Fawcett, and Ann Dilworth, were left at liberty to cross the Atlantic on a similar service.†

* Smith's Hist., chap. xiv.   † Ellis's Life, p. 89.

FRIENDS' MEETING-HOUSE AT MERION PENNSYLVANIA.

CHAPTER III.

IN taking a review of the history of the colonies on the American continent, it is humiliating to observe how little regard has been paid by nations even civilized, and professing the name of Christ, to the just rights and claims of the aborigines. From the time of Cortereal's kidnapping expeditions to Labrador, and the cruel enormities of Cortez and Pizarro in Mexico and Peru, the European adventurers to the western world, with some honourable exceptions, not only entered on the territory of the red man without either purchase or treaty, but, in too many instances they were regarded as the property of the invaders, to be bought and sold as the cattle of the field.

According to the views and practices of civilized nations, the mere discovery of lands occupied by uncivilized tribes, gives right of sovereignty over such lands to the nation making the discovery, and, in many instances, it has been held to confer also an actual claim of ownership to the soil. A title resting on such a basis, and entirely setting at naught the immemorial claim and possession of the natives, is, however, an unrighteous usurpation by the strong of the rights of the weak, and opposed alike to justice and to reason.

The right of the North American Indians to their lakes and their hunting grounds, could only cease by a voluntary surrender. But, if forcible possession be taken by invaders, the title is as unsound as the violence or fraud by which it was acquired was unjust and wicked. Europeans could not by possibility claim a legitimate right, even on the ground of conquest; for no injury had been received from the Indians to justify a war. It was not, indeed, until the guns of the white man were heard on their coasts, that the unsuspecting natives of America were aware of the existence of such people. The indisputable rights of the aborigines of America yielded, however, before the cupidity of its discoverers, and, with little exception, its vast region was unrighteously parcelled out among a few of the Christian states of Europe.

With regard to the actual ownership of the soil, a considerable difference of opinion appears to have existed, followed by a diversity of practice. The Dutch and Swedes obtained their freeholds by purchase from the various tribes,* whilst the French and Spanish nations, less scrupulous than their Protestant neighbours, took possession of the land without such preliminaries. The course pursued by the English in this particular was unfixed and varied. In Virginia, Maryland, and North Carolina, there is but little evidence of treaties for land, and the same also may be said of Massachusetts. New Hampshire appears to have been

---

* An original deed, conveying lands from the Indians to the Swedes, is still preserved in the national archives at Stockholm. The instructions given by Christina, the daughter and successor of Gustavus Adolphus, to Governor Printz in 1642, thus refer to purchases from the Indians :—" When the governor shall, God willing, arrive in New Sweden, he must carefully observe the limits of the country which our subjects possess, by virtue of the contract made with the savage inhabitants, *as legitimate owners of it,* according to the deeds."—Vide *Penn. Hist. Soc.*, vol. i. part i. p. 63.

purchased, "acquiring thereby," says Belknap, "a more valuable right, in a moral view, than any European prince could give."* Roger Williams, in founding the colony of Providence, before "he broke ground," made a full and complete purchase of the Indians; and the settlers on Rhode Island did the same. A considerable portion of Connecticut was also thus honourably obtained, whilst other parts of it were claimed on the more than doubtful grounds of conquest.

In the previous volume it has been stated, that the Society of Friends, in emigrating to the Jerseys, were careful not to occupy lands without first effecting a full and complete purchase from the natives, and this principle is well known to have been rigidly observed by William Penn in the settlement of Pennsylvania. In his opinion the sovereignty of Charles II. did not extinguish the right of the Indians to the territory; and although the charter recognised him as the absolute proprietor of the soil, yet he himself never claimed a single acre, until it had been acquired by purchase from its original occupiers.

It was not only in the acquisition of territory that William Penn followed the best examples of the early settlers in the western world—he aimed at something more. He was aware that the aborigines had been deeply injured by Europeans, and that the white man was justly regarded by them as their foe and their oppressor. Excepting the Jerseys and Rhode Island, there was not one among all the colonies in America which had not, more or less, been involved in almost exterminating wars with the natives. The cruelties of Narvaez in Florida, and of Cortereal in Labrador, are of historical notoriety. Raleigh's failure in Carolina may be traced to his unhappy conflicts with the Indians; and the terrible slaughter of the Virginian settlers in 1618, and again in 1644, was the result of a deep-rooted feeling of wrongs received from those whom they regarded as invaders of their country. By the Puritans of New England the aborigines were called "Dragons of the Desert," and "Amalekites,"—beings to be "rooted out of the world;"† and, thus regarded, they were hunted as the wild beasts of the field. In New Netherlands the

* Belknap's New Hampshire, vol. i. p. 12.   † Mather's Magnalia Christi.

Dutch were continually at war with the Algonquins. "When you first arrived on our shores," said a chief of Long Island to them in 1643, "you were destitute of food ; we gave you our beans and our corn ; we fed you with oysters and fish ; and now for our recompense you murder our people. The traders, whom your first ships left on our shores to traffic till their return, were cherished by us as the apple of our eye : we gave them our daughters for their wives ; among those whom you have murdered were children of your own blood."*

From Florida to Labrador, the prevailing feeling of the Indian towards the European was, as a necessary consequence, one of distrust and hatred, and the murderous tomahawk was not unfrequently wielded to satiate his revenge for the wrongs he had received. On the other hand the generality of the settlers unhappily regarded the natives as but wild and irreclaimable savages —as a race wholly unfitted to live in the presence of civilized beings. And the superior intelligence and acquirements of Christians, instead of being employed to ameliorate the condition of the untutored red man, and in exhibiting to him examples of justice and mercy, have been miserably prostrated at the shrine of avarice and cruelty. It was reserved for William Penn more fully to manifest, not only that such a course was foolish and wicked, and absurdly impolitic, but that the tribes of North America were naturally a confiding people, who could be won by justice and kindness, and that they were recipients of that divine grace which can contrite and soften even the hearts of the uncivilized.

In one of the ships that first sailed with emigrants to Pennsylvania, William Penn sent Markham, his deputy-governor, who, together with several commissioners that accompanied him, was specially charged to confer with the Indians in reference to the sale of lands, and to make arrangements with them for entering into a firm and lasting league of peace. With a view to facilitate this object, they were also directed to treat the natives with all possible kindness, and in all their transactions with them, to act with such justice and candour as should erase all suspicion

* Bancroft's History of the United States.

of the sincerity of their motives. In order, also, to impress them with a just sense of the love which he entertained for them, he sent them the following friendly letter, remarkably adapted to their understandings and feelings, and calculated to inspire them with confidence towards himself and the settlers:—

London, *the* 18*th of the Sixth Month,* 1681.

My Friends,—

There is a great God and power that hath made the world, and all things therein, to whom you and I, and all people, owe their being and well-being, and to whom you and I must one day give an account for all that we do in the world. This great God hath written his law in our hearts, by which we are taught and commanded to love, and help, and do good one to another. Now this great God hath been pleased to make me concerned in your part of the world; and the king of the country, where I live, hath given me a great province therein; but I desire to enjoy it with your love and consent, that we may always live together as neighbours and friends; else what would the great God do to us, who hath made us, not to devour and destroy one another, but to live soberly and kindly together in the world. Now, I would have you well observe, that I am very sensible of the unkindness and injustice that have been too much exercised towards you by the people of these parts of the world, who have sought themselves, and to make great advantages by you, rather than to be examples of goodness and patience unto you, which I hear hath been a matter of trouble to you, and caused great grudgings and animosities, sometimes to the shedding of blood, which hath made the great God angry. But I am not such a man, as is well known in my own country. I have great love and regard towards you, and desire to win and gain your love and friendship by a kind, just, and peaceable life; and the people I send are of the same mind, and shall, in all things, behave themselves accordingly; and, if in anything any shall offend you or your people, you shall have a full and speedy satisfaction for the same, by an equal number of just men on both sides; that by no means you may have just occasion of being offended against them.

I shall shortly come to you myself, at which time we may more largely and freely confer and discourse of these matters; in the mean time I have sent my commissioners to treat with you about land, and a firm league of peace. Let me desire you to be kind to them and the people, and receive these presents and tokens which I have sent you, as a testimony of my good will to you, and my resolution to live justly, peaceably, and friendly with you.

I am, your loving friend,

Unlike most of the previous adventurers to the western world, the emigrants to Pennsylvania proceeded thither entirely unprovided with weapons of war. They confidently relied on the protecting power of the Almighty, and, on the efficacy of Christian principle, believing that courtesy and kindness would win the North American Indian to their friendship, and, that neither the sword, nor the soldier, would be required in the colony of the friends of peace. The sequel shows that they had not miscalculated.*

* The King, who had no sympathy with the pacific views of William Penn, in granting him the Charter of Pennsylvania introduced a clause empowering him to make war upon the aborigines, or "savages," as he was wont to call them. The clause contrasts singularly with the principles of the Governor. It runs thus:—

"And because, in so remote a country, and situate near so many barbarous nations, the incursions as well of the savages themselves, as of other enemies, pirates and robbers, may probably be feared; therefore, we have given, and, for us, our heirs, and successors, do give power, by these presents, unto the said William Penn, his heirs and assigns, by themselves, or their captains, or other their officers, to levy muster and train all sorts of men, of what condition soever, or wheresoever born, in the said province of Pennsylvania, for the time being, and to make war, and pursue the enemys and robbers aforesaid, as well by sea as by land, yea even without the limits of the said province,

Before William Penn had landed on the shores of the New World, Markham had completed extensive purchases of land

and (by God's assistance), to vanquish and take them ; and, being taken, to put them to death, by the law of war, or to save them at their pleasure ; and to do all and every other thing, which unto the charge and office of a Captain Generall of an army belongeth, or hath accustomed to belong, as fully and freely as any Captain Generall of an army hath ever had the same."—*State Paper Office. Penn's Charter,* 1681. *B. T.* vol. i.

Weem, in his life of William Penn, gives the following conversation, which is said to have taken place between him and Charles II., previous to his embarkation for America. The dialogue displays William Penn's policy in contrast with the legislators of that day, and the confidence he had in a sincere appeal to the moral feelings of the Indians.

King.—"What ! venture yourself among the savages of North America ! Why, man, what security have you that you will not be in their war-kettle in two hours after setting your foot on their shores ? I have no idea of any security against these cannibals, but in a regiment of soldiers, with their muskets and their bayonets ; but, mind you, I will not send a single soldier with you."

W. Penn.—"I want none of thy soldiers. I depend on something better than soldiers—I depend on the Indians themselves—on their moral sense—even on the grace of God which bringeth salvation, and hath appeared to all men."

King.—"If it had appeared to them, they would hardly have treated my subjects so barbarously as they have done."

W. Penn.—"That is no proof to the contrary ; thy subjects were the aggressors. When they first went to North America, they found these poor people the kindest and fondest creatures in the world. Every day they would watch for them to come on shore, and hasten to meet them and feast them on their best fish, their venison, and their corn, which was all they had. In return for this hospitality of the savages, as we term them, thy christian subjects, as we term them, seized on their country and their rich hunting grounds for farms for themselves. Now is it to be much wondered at, that these much injured people, driven to desperation by such injustice, should have committed some excesses ?"

King.—"But how will you get their lands without soldiers ?"

W. Penn.—"I mean to buy their lands of them."

King.—"Why, man ! you have bought them of me already."

W. Penn.—"Yes ; I know I have, and at a dear rate too : I did this to gain thy good will, not that I thought thou hadst any right to their lands—I will buy the right of the proper owners, even of the Indians from the natives.* He had first explained to them the bene-volent intentions of the proprietor towards them, and that, although the King of England had granted to him the whole country of Pennsylvania, yet he would not occupy a single rood of their hunting grounds, without previously buying it from them, with their full consent and goodwill. Markham also informed them, that laws had been enacted to prevent the settlers from cheating them in the market-place—that a fair price would be paid to them for their furs and their wild game, and that any articles they might purchase should be fairly charged—that if a dispute arose between a white man and a red one, twelve men, six of the former, and six of the latter, should decide the controversy—that "no man shall, by any ways or means, in word or deed, affront or wrong an Indian, but he shall incur the same penalty of the law as if he had committed it against his fellow planter;" and, "that the Indians shall have liberty to do all things relating to improvement of their ground, and providing sustenance for their families, that any of the planters shall enjoy."† When the Deputy-Governor had told the Indians of these things, and laid before them the presents which he had brought for them as a token of friendship and goodwill, they were touched with a sense of such christian conduct, and declared that they would "live in peace with Onas and his children as long as the sun and moon shall endure."‡

It was in the summer of 1682, that the lawgiver of Penn-sylvania first beheld the native forests of his new domain. For several weeks after his landing he was, as we have already stated, busily engaged on many important subjects connected with the settlement of the colony, after which he went on a visit to New York, the Jerseys, and Long Island. It is generally agreed, that his great and memorable treaty with the Indians, took place

themselves : by doing this, I shall imitate God in his justice and mercy, and hope, thereby, to insure his blessing on my colony, if I should ever live to plant one in North America."

* Smith's Laws of Pennsylvania, p. 109.

† W. Penn's Concessions, in Proud, vol. ii. Append. ix., p. 3.

‡ Smith's Laws of Pennsylvania, p. 109.

immediately on his return from this journey. The records made
on that celebrated occasion are, it is to be regretted, now lost ;
but of the time and place of the transaction we are not left in
doubt. An envelope, accidentally discovered in the office of the
secretary at Harrisburgh, among some papers relating to the
Shawnese Indians, has the following brief endorsement, which
sets this matter at rest : " Minutes of the Indian Conference, in
relation to the great treaty made with William Penn, at the Big
Tree, Shackamaxon, on the 14th of the Tenth Month, 1682."*
Shackamaxon was situate on the banks of the Delaware, in the
suburbs of Philadelphia, within the present limits of Kensington.
It is described as a fine natural amphitheatre, and had been used
as a place of meeting by the Indian tribes from time immemorial,
and Sakimaxing, corrupted to Shackamaxon, signified that it was
the locality of kings.† Here, under the wide-spread branches
of a great elm tree, a century and a half old, which adorned the
already venerated spot, William Penn met the assembled tribes with
their chiefs and warriors, and proclaimed to them those sublime
sentiments of peace and love, which he sought to promote amongst
mankind, ratifying at the same time a deed of concord with the
aborigines, that has won the admiration and praise of the world.

Excepting some Mingoes and Susquehanna tribes, the Indians
who met William Penn on this highly interesting occasion, were
chiefly the Lenni Lenape, or Delaware Indians, and their number,
altogether, was considerable. " On William Penn's arrival,' says
Clarkson, " he found the sachems and their tribes assembling.
They were seen in the woods as far as the eye could carry, and
looked frightful both on account of their number and their
arms."‡ This negotiation is unequalled in history. A mere
handful of defenceless men go forth in the midst of the wilderness, to confer with the assembled warriors of the forest, depending alone on the righteousness of their cause, and the all-
protecting arm of Him who hath the hearts of all men at his

* See Gordon's Hist. of Pennsylvania, p. 603.
† This etymology is given in the Penn. Hist. Soc. Mem. vol. iii. part
ii. p. 183.
‡ Clarkson's Life óf Penn, vol. i. p. 341.

disposal. William Penn, at that time in the thirty-eighth year of his age, met the swarthy foresters in simple costume, undistinguished either by crown or sceptre, and, excepting a silken sash which he wore, by any other emblem of power, attended only by his friends, and holding in his hand the roll containing his terms of peace and friendship. The reception being over, the sachems retired to consult, after which, Taminent their king returned, and placed on his head a chaplet, into which was twisted a small horn. This was his symbol of kingly power, and, whenever placed on his brow, it proclaimed the place sacred, and the persons of all present inviolable. The scene was now immediately changed. The Indians threw down their weapons of war, and, having ranged themselves in the form of a crescent or half-moon, Taminent intimated to the governor, through an interpreter, that "the nations" were prepared to hear and consider his words.* William Penn then proceeded to address them to the following import:— "The Great Spirit," he said, "who made you and me, who rules in heaven and the earth, and who knows the innermost thoughts of man, knows that I and my friends have a hearty desire to live in peace and friendship with the Indians, and to serve them to the utmost of our power. It is not the custom of me and my friends to use weapons of war against our fellow creatures, and for this reason we have come to you without arms. Our desire is not to do injury and thus provoke the Great Spirit, but rather to do good. We are now met on the broad pathway of good faith and good will, and no advantage will be taken on either side, but all is to be openness, brotherhood, and love."† After some further expressions, in which he assured them that he and his friends believed that their brethren of the red race were just, and that they were prepared to confide in their friendship,‡ he unrolled the parchment containing the treaty, and explained in detail the words of the compact made for their future union. After having spread before them some presents of mer-

---

* W. Penn's Letter to Sunderland, Fifth Month 28th, 1683.
† Clarkson's Life of William Penn, vol. i. p. 338.
‡ Penn. Hist. Soc. vol. iii., part ii. p. 189.

chandise, he laid the roll on the ground, observing that the spot
should be free and common to both, and that he should consider
them as brethren of the same flesh and blood, and children of the
same heavenly Father. William Penn then presented the roll to
Taminent, and desired that it might be carefully preserved, that
future generations might know what had passed between them, just
as if he himself had remained to repeat it. We have no account of
the speeches made by the Indians on the occasion. Their hearts,
however, were touched with the pure and heavenly doctrines which
were declared to them, and, renouncing all feelings of revenge,
they solemnly, in the usages of their people, pledged themselves
to live in love with William Penn and his children for ever.*

* The roll containing the great treaty was shown by the Mingoes,
Shawnese and other Indians, at a conference with Governor Keith in
1722 ; no copy of it is now known to exist, and no full report of the
proceedings has been handed down. The only authentic account of the
covenants entered into on the occasion, is contained in a speech made
by Governor Gordon to the Susquehanna Indians, at a treaty held at
Conestego in 1728, and which is as follows :—

"My brethren !—You have been faithful to your leagues with us !
. . . . Your leagues with William Penn and his governors are in
writing on record, that our children and our children's children may
have them in everlasting remembrance. And we know that you preserve
the memory of those things amongst you, by telling them to your children, and they again to the next generation ; so that they remain
stamped on your minds, never to be forgotten. The chief heads or
strongest links of this chain I find are these nine, to wit :—

1st. "That all William Penn's people, or Christians, and all the
Indians should be brethren, as the children of one father, joined together
as with one heart, one head, and one body.

2nd. "That all paths should be open and free to both Christians and
Indians.

3rd. "That the doors of the Christians' houses should be open to the
Indians, and the houses of the Indians open to the Christians, and that
they should make each other welcome as their friends.

4th. "That the Christians should not believe any false rumours or
reports of the Indians, nor the Indians believe any such rumours or
reports of the Christians, but should first come as brethren to inquire
of each other ; and that both Christians and Indians, when they have
any such false reports of their brethren, should bury them as in a
bottomless pit.

William Penn's Treaty with the Indians.

This treaty of peace made an abiding impression on the hearts of the simple sons of the wilderness. In their wigwams they kept the history of this great deed by strings of wampum, and long after, with delight, would they recall to their memory, and repeat to their children and the stranger, their covenant of peace with the Quaker.* The memory of William Penn became venerated among them, and to be a follower of Onas, was at all times, a passport to their protection and their hospitality.†

But the praise of this memorable transaction has not been confined to the aborigines of North America. It has been alike the theme of the philosopher, the song of the poet, and the scene of the painter. It was not confirmed by oaths, or ratified by seals, but accepted on both sides by simple assent. "It is the only treaty," says the learned and philosophic, though infidel Voltaire, that was never confirmed by an oath and never broken. The Abbé Raynal has paid to it a high tribute of praise, and Noble in his

5th. "That if the Christians hear any ill news that may be to the hurt of the Indians, or the Indians hear any such ill news, that may be to the injury of the Christians, they should acquaint each other with it speedily, as true friends and brethren.

6th. "That the Indians should do no manner of harm to the Christians, nor to their creatures, nor the Christians do any hurt to the Indians ; but each treat the other as brethren.

7th. "But as there are wicked people in all nations, if either Indians or Christians should do any harm to each other, complaint should be made of it by the persons suffering, that right might be done ; and when satisfaction is made, the injury or wrong should be forgot, and be buried as in a bottomless pit.

8th. "That the Indians should in all things assist the Christians, and the Christians assist the Indians, against all wicked people that would disturb them.

9th. "And lastly, that both Christians and Indians should acquaint their children with this league and firm chain of friendship made between them, and that it should always be made stronger and stronger, and be kept bright and clear without rust or spot, between our children and our children's children, while the creeks and rivers run, and while the sun, moon, and stars endure."

* Heckwelder, Hist. Trans. American Phil. Soc., p. 176.

† Watson's Annals of Philadelphia, and Oldmixon's British Empire in America, vol. i., p. 171.

continuation of Granger, notices, with warm approbation, that here "the Christian and the barbarian met as brothers."

The scene at Shackamaxon furnishes to mankind an instructive lesson. In other colonies the settlers maintained their possessions with the sword, and almost every adventurer was a soldier. The planters of Pennsylvania, however, though surrounded by the angry and incensed Algonquin, believing that war was opposed to the will of their God, built no forts and maintained no soldiers. The Indians saw that they came unarmed, and had they been disposed, might have made them the very sport of their rage. But whilst they ravaged the neighbouring states with desolation and slaughter, the horrors of the scalping-knife and the toma-hawk were unknown in the territory of William Penn. His people went forth to their daily occupations in conscious security, whilst those around them trembled for their existence. "This little state," says Oldmixon, "subsisted in the midst of six Indian nations without so much as a militia for its defence." "New England," remarks Bancroft, "had just terminated a disastrous war of extermination; the Dutch were scarcely ever at peace with the Algonquins; the laws of Maryland refer to Indian hostilities and massacres. Penn came without arms; he declared his purpose to abstain from violence; he had no message but peace; and not a drop of Quaker blood was ever shed by an Indian."* That Pennsylvania should have been prosperous can excite no surprise. Relying on the Most High for protection, they realised that his promises were unfailing, and, though surrounded by a nation of uncivilised warriors, they were preserved in peace and blessed with plenty. "Without any carnal weapon," said one of the early immigrants, "we entered the land and inhabited therein as safe as if there had been thousands of garrisons; for the Most High preserved us from harm, both of man and beast." "We have done better," said another in 1684, "than if, with the proud Spaniards, we had gained the mines of Potosi. We may make the ambitious heroes, whom the world admires, blush for their shameful victories. To the poor dark souls around us we teach their rights as men."†

* Bancroft's Hist. of the United States.   † Planter's Speech, 1684.

The reputation of William Penn and his contemporaries in the government of Pennsylvania, is no glittering bubble destined to pass into oblivion ; but as mankind become more and more enlightened with the rays of heavenly truth, the more will they be led to appreciate the motives which produced this Christian conduct. Men have too generally gazed with admiration on military fame, and the triumphs and glories of war have obtained almost unqualified praise. If, however, we believe in the declarations of Holy Writ, we may confidently look forward to the period, when the heroes of Cressy and Agincourt, of Austerlitz and Waterloo, will be remembered in connexion only with the follies and wickedness of mankind, and when the character of William Penn, as a legislator whose acts were based on the laws of immutable righteousness, will be increasingly admired, and society will award to his name, the enduring renown, of having been a pioneer to that happier and better day.

The Christian motives and enlightened policy, which actuated William Penn in these memorable proceedings, did not stop short with forming a friendly alliance with the tribes of North America. Though it was wise and right, in his estimation, to obtain the confidence and good will of the natives, and to live on terms of friendly relations with them, yet he felt also that they had still higher claims on his attention ; and his expansive benevolence embraced other objects for their good. The blessings of civilization were among these ; but, above all, the blessings of Christianity. From deep and heartfelt experience he could testify that the religion of Jesus was "no cunningly devised fable," but a substantial reality ; and having largely participated in its consolations, he had, in the constraining influence of gospel love, earnestly invited his fellow-men to the same heavenly enjoyment. In his intercourse with the Indians, he was sensible that they were not forgotten by Him " whose tender mercies are over all his works." He found that they believed " in a God and immortality," and that they had a strong idea of " the great Spirit ;" but he felt that, ignorant of the great truths of Christianity, they were " under a dark night in things relating to religion," and strong was his desire for their appreciation of these divine principles.

In this work William Penn had long been much interested, and years before he crossed the Atlantic it had become a settled object of his attention. In his petition to Charles II. in 1680, for the grant of Pennsylvania, he distinctly declares that in making the application, " he had in view the glory of God by the civilization of the poor Indians, and the conversion of the Gentiles, by just and lenient measures, to Christ's kingdom." The crown evidently regarded this as a favourite object of the petitioner, and in the preamble to his charter, among other things, his desire in obtaining the province is stated to be, " to reduce the savage natives, by just and gentle manners, to the love of civil society, and the Christian religion." During William Penn's first visit to Pennsylvania, in order to promote the carrying out of these views, he took pains to make himself thoroughly acquainted with the character, genius, customs, and language of the natives, and for this purpose he often made journeys into the interior. " I have made it my business," he says, " to understand their language, that I might not want an interpreter on any occasion."* In his frequent conferences with them, he sought to imbue their minds with the transcendent excellency of the religion of Christ their Saviour, and to direct them to the inshinings of his Light and good Spirit in their hearts. " Nothing," remarks Clarkson, " could exceed his love for these poor people, or his desire of instructing them, so as to bring them by degrees to the knowledge of the Christian religion ; and in this great work he spared no expense."† Oldmixon states " that he laid out several thousand pounds to instruct, support, and oblige them."‡ William Penn returned to England, as before related, in the summer of 1684, after a residence of little more than twenty months in his province, and notwithstanding the onerous engagements which pressed upon him in settling his infant state, so assiduous had he been in his efforts among the Indians, that, during this period, he had had interviews, and had made treaties of friendship, with no less than nineteen distinct

* Letter to the " Free Society of Traders."
† Clarkson's Life of Penn, vol. i. p. 415.
‡ Oldmixon's British Empire in America.

tribes.* Before his departure he had a meeting with the chiefs of all the Indians in the vicinity of Pennsbury, to reiterate to them his desire for their welfare, and to obtain from them a solemn promise, that they would live in love and peace with each other, and with the settlers, telling them that he was going beyond the seas for a little while, but would return to them again, if the Great Spirit permitted him to live.†

In the exertions made for ameliorating the condition of the Indians, and for instructing them in the blessed principles of the Gospel, other Friends of station and influence in. Pennsylvania and the Jerseys also took a deep interest. Samuel Jennings, and Thomas Olive, who had both been elected to the high office of Governor of West Jersey, participated warmly in it; while several ministers of the Society in these provinces, and, as Proud tells us, " divers preachers from abroad, often had meetings and serious discourse with them."‡ So general was the desire among Friends to forward this good work, that it formed a subject of deliberation in the Yearly Meeting held at Burlington in 1685. The practice of selling strong liquors to the Indians had always been discouraged by Friends ; but, at the meeting in question, additional measures were taken ·to prevent its members from engaging in this evil practice. Prior to this date religious meetings had been frequently held with the natives ; a particular appointment, however, about this time, was made by Burlington Quarterly Meeting, for the special purpose of "instructing them in the principles of Christianity, and a practice of a true Christian life."§

The exertions of Friends for the religious improvement of the Indians, met with the cordial sympathy and encouragement of their brethren in England. In an epistle addressed by the Yearly Meeting of London in 1685, to that of Philadelphia, the subject is distinctly referred to, with a request that information respecting the meetings held with these people, both in their own and in

---

* Clarkson's Life of W. Penn, vol. i. p. 415.
† Dixon's Life of W. Penn, p. 280.
‡ Proud's Hist. of Pennsylvania, vol. i. p. 301.
§ Ibid. vol. i. p. 300.

the adjacent provinces, might, from time to time, be forwarded. George Fox, whose ministrations among the tribes of the new world have been already noticed, felt particularly interested in the work, and, in his epistolary communications to the churches in that land, he alludes to it with approbation. "Let them know the principles of truth," he writes to Friends in Pennsylvania and West Jersey in 1687, "so that they may know the way of salvation, and the nature of true Christianity, and how Christ hath died for them." Writing to Friends in the ministry in America, a short time previous to his decease, he exhorts them to "have meetings with the Indian kings, and their councils and subjects everywhere. Bring them all," he continues, "to the baptising and circumcising Spirit, by which they may know God, and serve and worship Him."* His exhortation was not un-heeded: in a letter addressed to London Yearly Meeting in 1690, they were enabled to state that "ministering Friends had visited the neighbouring countries, and some had visited some of the nearest plantations of Indians."†

Among those whose public ministrations were directed to the Indian tribes about the close of this century, may be mentioned Thomas Turner from Essex, Thomas Story, and, a few years later, Thomas Chalkley. William Penn also, during his second visit to his province, was still unremitting in his endeavours to promote the well-being of this interesting people. At the time of his memorable treaty with them in 1682, it was his intention, twice every year, to call a council of the chiefs for the purposes of renewing the covenants, adjusting matters of trade, and hearing and rectifying any grievances that they might have suffered, an intention which it appears was carried out during his first residence in Pennsylvania.‡ In the First Month of the year 1700, he introduced the subject of maintaining a more frequent intercourse with the Indians to the Monthly Meeting of Philadelphia, and expressed an earnest desire that Friends might be found fully discharging their duty to these untutored tribes,

* Epistles of George Fox.
† Yearly Meeting Minutes, vol. i., 1692.
‡ Fishbourne's MSS. in Watson's Annals, p. 455.

more especially in that which concerned their spiritual interests. The meeting sympathized with the views and feelings of the humane Governor, and agreed to adopt a plan for more frequently visiting them ; to facilitate which, he offered to provide the meeting with interpreters.

The Indians were often great sufferers from unprincipled traders taking advantage of their ignorance in commercial matters. William Penn, however, determined, if possible, to correct the evil in the territory over which he ruled. For this purpose he proposed to the local legislature, that the Indian trade should be carried on by a company of individuals selected for their integrity. They were to have a joint stock, and to trade only under specified regulations and restrictions, more particularly with regard to the sale of spirituous liquors. It was also provided, that the company should use all reasonable means to inspire the natives with a sense of the inestimable value of Christianity. "This," says Clarkson, "was probably the first time that trade was expressly made subservient to morals, and to the promotion of the Christian religion."*

The Indian tribes on the Susquehanna and the Delaware, had now for nearly twenty years past, been in the enjoyment of that peace and friendship with the settlers, which was ratified under the great treaty held at Shackamaxon. The blessings resulting from this amicable league had been rehearsed to other and more distant tribes, and had kindled in the hearts of those dwelling on the banks of the Potomac, an anxious desire to form a similar covenant of peace with the "Great Onas."† Their wishes were promptly met, and, early in 1701, William Penn met in a public conference Connoodaghtah, King of the Mingoes—Wopatha, King of the Shawnese—Weewhinjough, King of the Gamasese, inhabiting the head waters of the Potomac—and Ahookassong, brother of the great Emperor of the Five Nations, together with about forty of their chiefs. On this occasion, these representatives of warrior and hostile tribes

* Clarkson's Life of Penn, vol. ii. p. 246.

† Proprietary Papers, April 23, State Paper Office. "*Onas*," in the language of the Indians is the word for pen or feather.

agreed by their " hands and seals," with each other, with William
Penn and his successors, and with other Christian inhabitants of
the province, " to be as one head and one heart, and to live in
true friendship and amity, as one people."*

A few months later, the Governor, attended by all the officers
of the provincial legislature, held a great Indian council at his
residence at Pennsbury. This was for the purpose of taking
leave of them prior to his returning to England, and for renewing
the existing covenants of peace and friendship.† This farewell
meeting was a highly interesting one, and afforded William Penn
an opportunity for reiterating to the aborigines of his province,
the love and christian interest which he entertained towards
them.

In his negociations for the purchase of land, William Penn
appears to have given in all about twenty thousand pounds to the
Indians. Some have insisted that he gave no equivalent for the
land—that in fact his purchase was merely the semblance of one.
A close investigation of the subject will, however, show that the
allegation is unfounded. We must bear in remembrance that
during his lifetime but a comparatively small portion of his
province had been occupied by settlers—that the Indians possessed
large territories, which were used by them only as hunting
grounds, and that in the infancy of the colonies it was difficult to
estimate the value of the land. He sold vast tracts at the almost
nominal price of forty shillings per hundred acres; and that it
was generally set at low prices, may be further inferred from the
fact, that he gave away large sections in some of the most advantageous localities.

Before passing from William Penn and the Indians, there are
two important features in his conduct towards them which his
biographers have omitted to notice. One is, that notwithstanding
his purchase of the land from them, he on no occasion desired
their removal from it. Expatriation formed no part of his policy,
and the Algonquin had equal liberty with the European in the
choice of settlements. The other is, that he not only admitted

* Proud, vol. i. p. 429.   † Watson's Annals, p. 442.

them to the full participation of the rights of citizens in the benefits and protection of the laws, but, as already stated, passed other enactments for their special welfare, lest, from inferiority in knowledge, they should become the victims of the designing. He also provided that, in cases of dispute between the whites and the Indians, they should sit in equal numbers on juries.*

The conduct of William Penn and his government in their treatment of these Indians, is one which the philanthropic mind delights to contemplate, and forms a bright spot in English history. Would that in the colonizing enterprises of modern times his example had been followed ! Then had the hearts of the humane been no longer saddened with details of cruel and exterminating wars waged against the uncivilized—wars which, in our own and other countries, may be justly regarded as some of the darkest in the catalogue of national sins, causing that holy name by which we are called, to be "blasphemed among the Gentiles."

It would occupy more space than can be suitably given in this history, to particularize the various acts of the legislature of Pennsylvania, and of Friends in that province and the Jerseys, for protecting and promoting the interests of the aborigines. "The province of Pennsylvania," says Proud, "was constantly at a considerable expense for the preservation of the friendship of the Indians." So impressed in fact were the settlers with the importance of this subject, that treaties were constantly held with them. The attention of the Yearly Meeting was also at different times directed to the same object, and its continued solicitude for the full recognition of the just and inalienable rights of the natives was expressed in sundry advices issued to its members. The following is selected from them :—

"In these provinces we may say, the Lord hath, as a gracious and tender parent, dealt bountifully with us, even from the days of our fathers : it was He who strengthened them to labour through the difficulties attending the improvement of a wilderness,

---

* These points were ably alluded to by Thomas Hodgkin, M.D., in evidence given before a Committee of the House of Commons in 1837, on the subject of the aborigines in British settlements.

and made way for them in the hearts of the Indian natives ; so that by them they were comforted in times of want and distress. It was by the gracious influence of his Holy Spirit that they were disposed to work righteousness, and walk uprightly one towards another and towards the natives, and in life and conversation to manifest the excellency of the principles and doctrines of the Christian religion ; whereby they retained their esteem and friendship, which ought ever to be remembered with grateful thankfulness by us." Another minute at a later date expresses its " solid sense and judgment that Friends should not purchase, or remove to settle on such lands as have not been fairly and openly first purchased of the Indians, by those who are or may be authorised by the government to make such purchases."*

For more than seventy years, or during the period Pennsylvania was under the government of Friends, there was no interruption of cordial friendship between the settlers and the natives. The advantages which, in a temporal point of view, resulted to the colonists by the adoption of a kind and Christian conduct towards the Indians were unquestionably great, and they form a striking contrast to the melancholy conflicts and troubles in which other colonies were involved, by resorting to a course adverse to the principles of peace, to a sound and prudent policy, and, in many instances also, to the most obvious requisitions of justice and humanity. Motives of mere worldly policy did not actuate the members of the Society of Friends in their treatment of the aborigines. They were incited by others of a far higher and purer nature.

* Minutes of 1759 and 1763, in Rules of Discipline of Philadelphia Yearly Meeting.

CHAPTER IV.

FOR the space of fifteen years from the first landing of Friends
in the Jerseys, the Society, both in that colony and in the more
recently founded one of Pennsylvania, had experienced an onward
and harmonious course. Towards the close of 1691, however,
the unity which had thus so strikingly characterised it was
unhappily broken by the apostacy of George Keith. The schism
to which the defection of this individual gave rise, was an event
of unusual and painful interest, and forms an important epoch in
the history of Friends in America.

George Keith was a native of Scotland, a man of considerable
ability and literary attainments, and formerly a rigid Presbyterian.
He received a learned education at the University of Aberdeen,
where he obtained the degree of Master of Arts.* Of the circumstances attending his convincement of our principles, history
is silent. The first notice which we find of him as a Friend, is
under date of 1664, when he came from his home in the south of
Scotland on a gospel mission to his brethren at Aberdeen, on

* Barclay's Jaffray, p. 548.

which occasion he suffered an imprisonment of ten months.* Possessed of superior talents for composition, during the time of his incarceration he wrote and published two pieces, one entitled ". A salutation of dear and tender love to the Seed of God arising in Aberdeen," and the other, "Help in time of need, from the God of Help, to the people of the Church of Scotland (so called)."† In the following year, he was subjected to much personal abuse in Aberdeen for preaching in "the great steeple-house," and for many years after we find him suffering long imprisonments and pecuniary confiscations for the cause of Truth, all of which he bore with a spirit of meekness and resignation, that much endeared him to his friends.

Quick in perception, and acute in argument, few of our early Friends possessed stronger powers for public disputations than George Keith, and he not unfrequently employed them in defending the Society from the unjust aspersions of envious professors. In 1674, he was united with William Penn, George Whitehead, and Stephen Crisp, in a dispute with the Baptists in London, and in the following year, with Robert Barclay, in defending his Theses against the students of Aberdeen.‡ He also wrote several powerful treatises in defence of the doctrines of the Society. In 1677, he travelled with William Penn and Robert Barclay on an interesting gospel mission to the Netherlands.

About the year 1682, he left Scotland to succeed Christopher Taylor, in conducting a Friends' school at Edmonton, in the county of Middlesex. So little had England, at that period, advanced in religious toleration, and so much was it under ecclesiastical dominion, that even the languages were forbidden to be taught, except by persons licensed by a bishop ; and on many occasions were our early friends called to suffer, for imparting classical knowledge without the sanction of the church dignitaries.§ George Keith was one of these. He was cited to appear at the Quarter Sessions for the offence, and, on

---

* Besse, vol. ii. p. 497.   † Whiting's Cat. p. 82
‡ Sewel's History.   § Besse, vol. i. p. 204.

refusing to take the oath then tendered to him, was committed to Hertford gaol.* From Edmonton he removed to London, where he hoped to follow his profession without ecclesiastical interference and persecution. But protection from priestly domination was no more to be found in the capital than in the country ; and in 1684, he was imprisoned for five months in Newgate.†

The declension of this talented man has been dated from about this period. He became impatient under suffering, and also manifested a spirit of self-importance among his brethren, incompatible with that lowliness of mind, and abnegation of self, which ever characterises the true disciples of Christ. His change, to some extent, has been attributed to his indulging in some vain and speculative notions which Van Helmont, a German enthusiast, sought to promote ; among which may be mentioned, the transmigration of souls.‡ George Keith also held some strange ideas respecting our first parents, and alleged, that much of the Mosaical account was to be regarded as allegorical. A work which he published in 1694, entitled "Wisdom advanced in the correction of many gross and hurtful errors," contains ample evidence of the absurd doctrines, and wild mysticisms, in which he indulged. Although he was careful not to express his new opinions in public, yet he took pains to advocate them privately and anonymously. These, however, found no place with Friends, some of whom faithfully warned him of the dangerous consequences of entertaining such speculative notions.§

Under the conviction that his opinions had lessened him in the esteem of his brethren, George Keith became increasingly uneasy ; and to this cause, together with his desire to fly from persecution, may be traced his resolve to proceed to America. Soon after his release from Newgate he emigrated to New Jersey, where he was employed in determining the boundary line between East and West Jersey ; and in 1689, he removed to Philadelphia, to undertake the head mastership of the grammar school,

* Min. of Meeting for Sufferings, vol. iii. p. 49.   † Besse, vol. i. p. 473.
‡ Sewel's History, p. 616.   § Ibid, p. 616.

which had been recently founded in that city.* Although he was silent in America, respecting his newly-acquired doctrines, and continued to profess and to preach the principles of Friends, yet, "his towering thoughts of himself," says Samuel Jennings, "rendered him a very uneasy member of any society, civil or religious." In this restless state of mind his new office became burdensome to him, and at the end of the first year he was released at his own request. In the following year he travelled as a minister in New England. Conscious of his powers in polemical discussion, he frequently, during this journey, challenged priests and professors to argue with him; "but more," observes his companion, "from vain-glory, and a desire for victory, than edification." These public disputations were often conducted with much acrimony of feeling, and were far from promoting the holy cause in which the disputants professed to be engaged.

Having wandered from the safe path of true humility, the future steppings of George Keith were marked by a gradual and increasing deviation into the mazes of error. In his early career in Pennsylvania he began by finding fault with the discipline, and, with a view to its correction, prepared an essay, which he presented to the meeting of ministers for its approval. This body, however, did not feel satisfied to sanction the document, and agreed to refer it to the consideration of the Yearly Meeting of Ministers. This meeting was similarly impressed, but proposed that it should be submitted to the Yearly Meeting of London. To this course Keith demurred, and preferred to abandon its publication, rather than risk the censorship of his English friends.† But the restraint was ill received, and instead of profiting by the circumstance, he became increasingly captious and self-willed. His conduct now began to betray a rankling bitterness of spirit, and ere long led him to an open rupture with the Society at large.

Invidiously watching his brethren for evil, it was not long before George Keith found occasion to quarrel with them. After his return from New England, he accused Thomas Fitzwater,

* Proud, vol. i. 345.   † Smith's History.

and William Stockdale, of unsoundness in doctrine, for having preached that the light of Christ was sufficient for salvation without anything else ;* choosing to infer from hence, that they excluded the outward appearance of Christ, as not necessary to salvation,—a doctrine which the accused most unhesitatingly repudiated. At the Yearly Meeting of Ministers in 1691, he also brought a charge against William Stockdale, for having said that he "preached two Christs, because he preached faith in Christ within, and Christ without us."† The expressions thus imputed to William Stockdale, were denied by him, and his denial was confirmed by some of his hearers, whilst, on the other hand, two witnesses were produced to prove the allegation. In almost all disputes some are to be found ready to countenance one party, and some the other party ; so it was in this instance. Keith had certain sympathisers, and was not lax in his efforts to gain more. "He blew the fire of this quarrel," writes Sewel, "and so obtained some adherents."‡ The discussion on this subject, owing to the turbulent behaviour of Keith and his party, was protracted through no less than six days, and at last ended in the meeting's deciding that William Stockdale was blamable in uttering the alleged expressions, and that, as George Keith had violated the gospel order, in bringing the matter before the meeting without first having communicated privately with William Stockdale, and had also used highly unbecoming expressions towards him, they could not hold him excusable.§

That George Keith, however much he endeavoured to hide it, had departed from the acknowledged views of the Society with respect to the efficacy and universality of divine grace, can scarcely be doubted.‖ At a subsequent Monthly Meeting, Fitzwater and Stockdale, who were convinced of his apostacy on this point, accused him of denying the sufficiency of divine light for salvation, in which they were supported by the testimony of several others. To the proof offered on this

* Sewel's Hist. p. 617.   † Ibid.
‡ Ibid.   § Smith's History.
‖ Vide "A Modest Account from Pennsylvania, &c.," by C. Pusey, p. 7 and p. 27.

occasion Keith objected, on the ground that the parties were prejudiced against him, and at the succeeding Monthly Meeting he and his party made a strong effort to obtain the condemnation of the accusing Friends, and an exoneration of himself; but in this they were unsuccessful.* Thus disappointed, Keith and his adherents now unworthily had recourse to stratagem. The meeting being over, and the clerk having withdrawn,† the non-contents remained behind, and, contrary to all order and decorum, agreed to adjourn the business to the following day at the school-house. At this adjournment they mustered strongly, and carried things with a high hand. Fitzwater and Stockdale, the peculiar objects of their dislike, were formally condemned, and a minute was made, requiring them to desist from the ministry until they had publicly acknowledged themselves in error, in a manner satisfactory to Keith. This artful trick raised the just indignation of Friends. An appeal to the Quarterly Meeting followed, the result of which was, that the proceedings of the irregular adjournment were declared to be null and void.

The growing discord, which thus unhappily sprang up in Pennsylvania, gave much concern to Friends in England. They knew from painful experience the withering effects of such dissensions; and, anxious that their brethren in the western world might avoid them, an earnest exhortation was addressed to them on the subject. This communication, after setting forth the value of a true union in Christ, and the importance of avoiding everything which has a tendency to weaken the bonds of love, touches on some of the points in dispute. The spiritual dispensation which had been committed to them, they distinctly declared, did, "in no wise oppose, reject, or invalidate Jesus Christ's outward coming, suffering, death, resurrection, ascension, or glorified estate in the heavens; but it brought men to partake of the remission of sins, reconciliation, and eternal redemption, which he hath obtained for us, and for all men, for whom he died, and gave himself a ransom,—which was for all men, both Jews and Gentiles, Indians, Heathens, Turks, and

---

* State of the Case, &c., by S. Jennings, p. 3.

† Elwood's Epistle, p. 26.

Pagans, without respect of persons, or people, &c. And Christ is to be fully preached unto them, according to the holy Scriptures, by them whom he sends, or may send unto them for that end; that as the benefit of his sufferings, sacrifice, and death extends to all, even to them that have not the Scriptures, or outward history thereof, they may be told who was, and is, their great and chief Friend, that gave himself a ransom for them, and hath enlightened them, yet not excluded from God's mercy or salvation by Christ them who never had, nor may have, the outward knowledge or history of him, (if they sincerely obey and live up to his light,) for his light and salvation reaches to the ends of the earth. He," continues the epistle, "is our Mediator, Intercessor, and Advocate with the Father, and ever lives to make intercession. Seeing we have the true, living, and spiritual benefit of his mediation, there is no reason for any to question or doubt of his manhood, or of his being that one Mediator between God and men, even the man Christ Jesus, whose being, as that entire, perfect, heavenly, and most glorious man, [is] ever living and endures for ever in his soul or spirit and glorious body : we having daily the spiritual advantage, comfort, and benefit of his mediation, by and through his Holy Spirit, we may suppose, that this glorious man, Christ Jesus, who is our Mediator, is and must ever be in being, and nothing proper to his being in a glorified state can be supposed to be annihilated or lost. Do not we believe our souls are immortal, and shall be preserved in their distinct and proper beings, and spiritual glorious bodies, such as shall be proper for them, as it shall please God to give, that we may be capable of our particular rewards and different degrees of glory after this life, or in the world to come, as one star differs from another star in glory and magnitude, and they that turn many to righteousness, shall shine as the stars in the firmament for ever and ever! How then can it be otherwise believed or apprehended in the truth, but that our own most blessed and elder brother, Jesus Christ, even as Mediator, is ever in being in a most glorious state, (as with his heavenly Father,) who, in the day of his flesh on earth, so deeply and unspeakably suffered for us and for all mankind, both inwardly and outwardly ; inwardly, by temptations, sorrows, and burthens, (as to his innocent soul by men's iniquities,) and outwardly, by persecutions, and the cruel death of the cross, as to his blessed body, which rose again the third day, and wherein he also ascended, according to the Scriptures. But it has not seemed proper or safe for us to be inquisitive about what manner of change his body had or met withal, after his resurrection and ascension, so as to become so glorious, heavenly, or celestial, as no doubt it is, far transcending what it was, when on earth, in a humble, low, and suffering condition. The man, Christ Jesus, was glorified as it pleased the Father ; 'tis not our concern or business to be curious to inquire or dispute, how, or after what manner was he changed, translated, or glorified, but to be content and thankful that we are spiritually united to him and his body, being partakers of Christ Jesus, by his light, life, grace, and good Spirit (in measure) revealed in us.

" None need question aforehand what manner of bodies, garments, or clothing, they shall have, after this life, in heaven ; trust God with that.   Have a care to persevere in the grace of God in Christ so as to get to heaven, and then be sure there will be no want of anything to complete your happiness and glory in such a state, wherein the body of our lowness shall be like unto Christ's glorious body, and we made equal to the angels of God in heaven, if we be faithful to the end of our days here on earth.

" Dear brethren, it would be a comfort and joy in the Lord to us, to hear of Truth's spreading, and his work prospering in those parts, and of your love, union, peace, and concord therein, as living examples for encouraging others to receive it, and not of differences and disputes among yourselves about matters of faith, doctrine, or principles, concerning Christ crucified—his body, manhood, and the resurrection—and Scriptures—tending to endanger the peace of the church.   In the fear of God, in humility, with souls bowed down before the Lord, meet together, and cease disputes and controversies, and humbly wait upon God, and come into a soul's travel, and earnest breathing to him, that he may by his power tender your hearts one towards another, unto love,

charity, and concord among yourselves, and to a right, clear understanding, that you may rather be fitted and free to give tender
advice, Christian counsel, and instruction to the weak and ignorant, than to dispute or differ among yourselves, or to receive any
that are weak into doubtful disputations, which ought not to be.
Pray keep down all heats, and passions, and aggravations, and
hard constructions of one another's words, tending to rents and
divisions.   We have largely seen the sad and ill consequences of
making parties, divisions, and separations, and making sects and
schisms, if any lust to be contentious.   We have no such custom
in the churches of Christ.   Such as be given to contention, are
foolish, heady, and self-willed, and regard not the church's peace,
nor their own, as they should do.

" We question not but you all aim at one truth, one way, and
one good end, and that you believe, profess, and preach one Lord
Jesus Christ, and not two Christs, even the very same Christ of
God, of whom the holy prophets and apostles give witness; and that
repentance and remission of sins is preached in his name, as he
told his disciples it should.   And we doubt not but you all own
him, as he is the true God, and truly man, according to the holy
Scripture testimony of him.   Why then should you differ or dis-
agree about him, or the Scriptures, you being looked upon as wise,
discreet, judicious men, possessing one and the same Spirit, Light,
and Truth!   Pray have recourse thereunto, and be conversant
therewith in yourselves, to be led and guided in meekness and
wisdom that is from above, which is pure and peaceable ; and
suffer no slight, irreverent, or undervaluing expressions to be
spoken concerning Christ, his manhood, sufferings or mediatorship
for mankind ; nor of the holy Scriptures, or reading them,
whereby to give the world, or professors thereof, occasion to reproach the blessed Truth, or stumble any.

" And, dear Friends and brethren, we conclude with the holy
apostle's counsel, If there be therefore any consolation in Christ ;
if any comfort of love ; if any fellowship of the Spirit ; if any
bowels and mercies, fulfil ye my joy, (and we may say, fulfil ye our
joy,) that you be like-minded ; having the same love, being of one
accord, of one mind ; let nothing be done through strife or vain-

glory, but in lowliness of mind, every man esteeming other better than himself."*

Conscious that much of the blame of these differences was to be attributed to George Keith, some Friends of Aberdeen who had long known him, appealed to him on the subject with much Christian kindness. After reminding him of his past services in the work of the gospel, and of the talents committed to him for " edifying, comforting, and strengthening the flocks of Christ," they say, " O George ! bear with us in love ; for we can say, it is in tender breakings of heart we utter it, and in tender breathings for thee, that if that sweet, healing, meek, self-denying spirit of lowly Jesus had been kept and abode in, your breaches thereaway would have been handled after another manner ; and such a sad occasion to amuse the world, sadden the hearts of God's children, and rejoice the enemies of Zion's peace and prosperity, had never been told in Gath, nor published in Askelon." After further brotherly advice they conclude, " So, our dear and ancient friends, [his wife being also referred to,] we earnestly desire you to receive in a right mind our innocent freedom and love ; and, in the cool of the day, go forth again with your brethren into the ancient green pastures of love, and to the healing springs of life : giving up to fire and sword, that which is for it ; so the first and the last works shall be precious together ; then righteousness and peace shall kiss each other." †

The entreaty and admonitory language of his friends in the mother country, and the forbearing spirit and kindness of his brethren in America, were all unavailing to produce any change in the disposition of this individual. He had imbibed such bitterness of spirit, and made such high pretensions, as rendered him callous to christian counsel, howsoever wisely and tenderly administered ; and from bad he proceeded to worse. His next subject of contention was relative to the time of holding

---

* Smith's History, chap. vii. in Hazard. This epistle is signed by George Whitehead, Samuel Waldenfield, John Field, Benjamin Antrobus, William Bingley, John Vaughton, Alexander Seaton, Daniel Monro, and Patrick Livingstone.

† "The Friend," [Philadelphia,] vol. vii. p. 254.

the meeting for worship in Philadelphia. He proposed some alteration, to which Friends were not disposed to accede. Insignificant as this might appear, it brought matters to a crisis. Keith and his party, no longer able to brook restraint, now manifested their contentious and dividing spirit, by setting up a separate meeting of their own, under the designation of Christian Quakers and Friends, and thus commenced this lamentable separation.

The party spirit which had developed itself by such a flagrant abuse of christian order and decorum, was immediately followed by other improprieties.   The aid of the press was sought to vindicate the disorderly proceedings—the conduct of meetings was arraigned—their active members were calumniated, and at last charges of unsoundness were preferred against the Society at large.*   At the Quarterly Meeting of Ministers, held in the First Month, 1692, Keith roundly accused them of meeting together "to cloak heresies and deceit," and maintained "that there were more damnable heresies and doctrines of devils among the Quakers, than among any profession of Protestants."†   Hitherto he had been laboured with in private, but it was now felt that these delinquencies merited a public remonstrance.   Samuel Jennings and Griffith Owen were appointed by the meeting in question to visit George Keith, and to call upon him for a condemnation of his conduct.   As might have been expected, he was in no degree disposed to listen to their counsels, and with great superciliousness he told them, that "he trampled upon the judgment of the meeting as dirt under his feet."‡   All hopes of a reconciliation being now gone, the Meeting of Ministers held in the Fourth Month, 1692, after deliberating upon the report of the committee, came to the conclusion that, for the cause of truth and for the credit and preservation of the Society, it was right to issue a declaration of disunity with him, as one who not only sought by flagrant and unjust charges to render Friends contemptible in the eyes of the world, but also to divide and scatter them as a people.   The testimony issued on the occasion was in

---

* Jennings' State of the Case, p. 18 ; see also Life of Wilson.
† Smith's Hist. in Hazard.   ‡ Ibid.

the form of an address to the Society, in which the grounds of
the proceeding are set forth.   Though long, it yet seems due to
the importance of the subject to introduce the document into this
narration.   It is as follows :—

To THE SEVERAL MONTHLY AND QUARTERLY MEETINGS IN
PENNSYLVANIA, EAST AND WEST JERSEY, AND ELSEWHERE,
AS THERE MAY BE OCCASION.

BELOVED FRIENDS,

In tender love, and with spirits bowed down before the Lord, is
this our salutation unto you, earnestly desiring your growth and
daily preservation in the ancient truth, and in the simplicity of
the gospel of our Lord Jesus Christ.   And our hope and breathings are, that no insinuations or wiles of the enemy shall prevail
to turn you aside from your stedfastness, or to cause you to
esteem lightly of the Rock and Way of God's salvation unto you ;
but that you be kept in the light and life which was and is the
just man's path, to the end of our days.   Amen.

Now, dear Friends, it is with sorrow of spirit and grief of soul,
that we signify unto you the tedious exercise and vexatious perplexity we have met with in our late friend George Keith, for
several months past.   With mourning and lamentation do we
say, How is this mighty man fallen !   How is his shield vilely
cast away, as though he had not known the oil of the holy ointment !   How shall it be told in Gath, and published in the
streets of Askelon !   Will not the daughters of the uncircum-
cised triumph, when they hear that he is fallen upon the soaring
mountains and from the high places of Israel ?   Whilst thou
walked in the counsel of God, and wert little in thy own eyes,
thy bow did abide in strength ; thy sword returned not empty
from the fat of the enemies of God ; thy bow turned not back.
His enemies were then vile unto thee, and his followers honourable in thy esteem.   Oh, how lovely wert thou in that day, when
his beauty was upon thee ; and when his comeliness covered
thee !   Why should his ornaments exalt thee, which were given
to humble thee before him ?   And how art thou fallen from thy
first love, and art become treacherous to the spouse of thy youth !

Consider where thou art fallen, and repent, and do thy first works.

But so it hath happened, Friends, lest any flesh should glory, but become silent before the Lord, that this once eminent man, and instrument of renown in the hand of the Lord, whilst he kept his first habitation, and knew the government of Truth over his own spirit, and witnessed the same to be a bridle to his tongue, was then serviceable, both in pen and speech, to the churches of Christ. But now, and of late, it is too obvious and apparent, that being degenerated from the lowly, meek, and peaceable spirit of Christ Jesus, and grown cool in charity and love towards his brethren, he is gone into a spirit of enmity, wrath, self-exaltation, contention, and janglings; and as a person without the fear of God before his eyes, and without regard to his christian brethren, and letting loose the reins to an extravagant tongue, he hath broken out into many ungodly speeches, railing accusations, and passionate threatenings toward many of his brethren and elders, and that upon slender occasions. And when some, in christian duty, have laid before him his unsavoury words and unchristian frame, he hath treated them with such vile words and abusive language, such as a person of common civility would loathe. It hath been too frequent with him, in a transport of heat and passion, to call some of his brethren in the ministry, and other elders, and that upon small provocation (if any), fools, ignorant heathens, infidels, silly souls, liars, heretics, rotten ranters, Muggletonians, and other names of that infamous strain, thereby, to our grief, foaming out his own shame. And further, his anger and envy being cruel against us, and not contenting himself with his harshness against persons, he proceeded, in bitterness of spirit, to charge our meetings with being come together to cloak heresy and deceit; and published openly several times, that there were more doctrines of devils and damnable heresies among the Quakers, than among any profession among the Protestants. He hath long objected against our discipline, even soon after his coming among us, and having prepared a draught of his own, and the same not finding the expected reception, he seemed disgusted. Since, he hath often quarrelled with us about confessions, declaring that he knew none given forth by the body of Friends to his satisfaction : and often charged most of us with being unsound in the faith.   We have offered in several meetings, for his satisfaction, and to prevent strife among us, and for preserving the peace of the church, to deliver a confession of our Christian faith, in the words of our Lord and Saviour Jesus Christ, the author of the Christian's faith, and in the words of the apostles and disciples, his faithful followers ; or we would declare our belief, in testimonies of our ancient Friends and faithful brethren, who were generally received by us ; or we would concur and agree upon a confession, and have it transmitted for the approbation of the Yearly Meeting here, or at the Yearly Meeting at London.   Yea, it was offered unto him at the same time, that a confession concerning the main matters of controversy should be given out of a book of his own ; but all was slighted as insufficient.

The Lord knows the trouble which we have had with this unruly member, and the openness of our hearts and well wishes towards him, notwithstanding his rage and violence against us ; and of the endeavours of many in this place to have gained upon him by a friendly converse, and by other means, not inconsiderable to a brotherly freedom.   But our labour hitherto seems to be as water spilt upon a rock.   And this meeting having orderly and tenderly dealt with him, for his abusive language and disorderly behaviour, he hath not only slighted all applications of gaining him to a sense of his ill-treatment and miscarriages, but in an insulting manner said to the Friends appointed by the meeting to admonish him, that he trampled the judgment of the meeting under his feet as dirt !   And hath of late set up a separate meeting here, where he hath, like an open opposer, not only reviled several Friends, by exposing their religious reputations in mixed auditories of some hundreds, endeavouring to render them, and Friends here, by the press and otherwise, a scorn to the profane, and the song of drunkards ; but he hath traduced and vilified our worthy travelling Friends, James Dickinson and Thomas Wilson, in their powerful and savoury ministry, whose service is not only here but in most meetings in England, Scotland, and Ireland, well known to have a seal in the hearts of the many thousands of the Israel of God. He hath also, within a few weeks, appeared in opposition, as it were, to the body of Friends, by putting on his hat when our well received and recommended Friend, James Dickinson, was at prayer, and that in a meeting of near a thousand Friends and others, and so going out of the meeting to the great disquiet thereof, and to the drawing some scores into the same opposition with him, by his ill example. And he thus persisting in his repeated oppositions, hard speeches, and continued separation, and labouring like an unwearied adversary to widen the breach made by him, and so abusing some of the neighbouring meetings, by being as yet under that cover of being owned by us ; we are hereby brought under a religious constraint, and to prevent other meetings from being further injured by him, to give forth this testimony, strained, as it were, from us by his many and violent provocations ; viz., that we cannot own him in such ungodly speeches and disorderly behaviour, or in his separate meetings ; and that we disown the same as proceeding from a wrong spirit, which brings into disorder inwardly, and leads into distraction and confusion outwardly. And until he condemn and decline the same, we cannot receive him in his public ministry, and would have him cease to offer his gift, as such, among us, or elsewhere among Friends, till he be reconciled to his offended brethren. And as to those few of our brethren in the gift of the ministry who are gone out with George Keith into his uncharitable and dividing spirit, (the miserable effects whereof many of us have sufficiently known in old England, and other parts), our judgment is, that whilst they continue such, they become unqualified to the work of the gospel, as degenerating from the guidance of God's blessed and peaceable Spirit in their hearts (from whence proceeds the effectual New Testament ministry), and being turned from the peaceable fruits thereof, are gone to uncharity and contention.

And now, all of you, who have walked in fellowship and communion with us, and are drawn aside, through inconsideration or otherwise, into this spirit of separation and prejudice against our meetings, orderly established, and wherein we have been mutually refreshed together, we cannot but in the fear of God, and in love to your souls, admonish you also of the insecurity of your present state, and that therein we cannot have unity with you ; and unless you return from under that spirit, dryness and barrenness from the Lord will be your reward.   And so, dear Friends, we exhort you all to behave yourselves in the spirit of meekness and peaceable truth, upon all occasions, but more especially upon any discourse or conference with any of them, who are discontented among you, or started aside from you ; and avoid all heats and contentions in matters of faith and worship, and let not the salt of the covenant be wanting in your words and actions, for thereby the savour of your conversation will reach the witness of God in them.   The grace of our Lord Jesus Christ be with you all. Amen !

Given forth by the meeting of public Friends, in Philadelphia, the twentieth of the Fourth Month, 1692.

THOMAS LLOYD,	SAMUEL JENNINGS,
JOHN WILLSFORD,	JOHN DELAVALL,
NICHOLAS WALN,	WILLIAM YARDLEY,
WILLIAM WATSON,	JOSEPH KIRKBRIDE,
GEORGE MARIS,	WALTER FAWCIT,
THOMAS DUCKETT,	HUGH ROBERTS,
JOSHUA FEARNE,	GRIFFITH OWEN,
EVAN MORRIS,	JOHN BOWN,
RICHARD WALTER,	HENRY WILLIS,
JOHN SYMCOCK,	PAUL SAUNDERS,
JOHN BLUNSTON,	ROBERT OWEN,
WILLIAM COOPER,	WILLIAM WALKER,
THOMAS THACKARY,	JOHN LYNAM,
WILLIAM BILES,	GEORGE GREY.

Before the testimony of disownment had been published, it was concluded to give George Keith, or those of his party that he might wish, a private opportunity of perusing it.   This course was adopted, in order that anything they might have to advance in opposition to it might be fully considered, and also to give him a further opportunity of reconsidering his position, and of retracing his steps. He, however, declined the offer, and not only so, but he maliciously published to the world that in the proceedings with respect to him, all gospel order and Christian kindness had been violated.* Against the judgment of the Quarterly Meeting of Ministers Keith determined to appeal to the ensuing Yearly Meeting. Previously, notwithstanding his exclamations against Friends for an alleged departure from gospel order, he grossly violated it by publishing several pamphlets containing his version of the dispute.† These publications, written with much plausibility and ingenuity, were also characterised by a departure from truthfulness. Mutilated passages from the writings of Friends, and unfair constructions upon others, were liberally resorted to, in order to substantiate the charges of unsoundness in doctrine, and to mislead the unwary. The effect of these unholy endeavours was, to a large extent, successful. Their specious pretensions drew many to unite with him and his party, and a wide and distressing schism ensued. Separate meetings were set up at Philadelphia, Burlington, Neshaminy, and other places. Families were divided, and the ties of friendship broken. Husbands and wives, professedly of the same faith, no longer worshipped in the same house, and scarcely in the history of the Society has there been a more lamentable exhibition of the devastating effects of a dividing spirit, than was manifested on this occasion.

In the course of his malevolent pamphleteering Keith had recourse to defamatory language, and, together with Thomas Budd, an active partizan, calumniated the character of Samuel Jennings as a magistrate. In his anger he had also made some severe personal reflections on Thomas Lloyd, the deputy governor. The conduct of Keith, in assailing the integrity of these and other civil officers of the province, with a view to lessen them in the estimation of the colonists, was an offence which the magistrates considered ought not to be passed over in silence, especially as it was believed that his aim was to raise a public disturbance,

* Jennings' State of the Case, &c., p. 20.

† Vide Keith's " Reasons and Causes of the Separation," &c., his " Plea of the Innocent;" and " Appeal from the Twenty-eight Judges."

and to furnish a pretext for subverting the government. In the Sixth Month, 1692, he was brought to trial, found guilty, and fined five pounds ; but the fine, it appears, was not enforced, the object being simply to vindicate and uphold the authority of the government. The excitement that prevailed was heightened by these proceedings, and Keith and his supporters endeavoured to turn this act of the judiciary to their own account, by raising the cry of persecution. The authorities anticipating that misrepresentations would be made, and their motives impugned by the guilty parties, published their reasons for the conviction. '' Now, forasmuch as we, as well as others,'' they remark, '' have borne, and still do patiently endure, the said George Keith, and his adherents, in their many personal reflections against us, and their gross revilings of our religious Society, yet we cannot, without the violation of our trust to the king and government, as also to the inhabitants of this government, pass by, or connive at, such part of the said pamphlet and speeches, that have a tendency to sedition and disturbance of the peace, as also to the subversion of the present government, or to the aspersion of the magistrates thereof. Therefore, for the undeceiving of all people, we have thought fit, by this public writing, not only to signify that our procedure against the persons now in the sheriff's custody, as well as what we intend against others concerned, (in its proper place,) respects only that part of the said printed sheet which appears to have the tendency aforesaid, *and not any part relating to differences in religion ;* but also these are to caution such, who are well affected to the security, peace, and legal administration of justice in this place, that they give no countenance to any revilers, or contemners of authority, magistrates, or magistracy ; as also to warn all other persons, that they forbear the further publishing and spreading of the said pamphlets as they will answer the contrary at their peril.''*

At the Yearly Meeting of Ministers which met at Burlington in the Seventh Month, 1692, the decision of the subordinate meeting, with respect to George Keith, was brought under review. He had given notice of his intention of appealing to this body,

* Proud, vol. i. p. 376.

but about ten days previous to the time of meeting, he printed and circulated, and even posted up in Philadelphia, the reasons which actuated him in making the appeal. When, however, the Yearly Meeting had convened, instead of proceeding in the usual course of the discipline, he and his party met separately, and, calling themselves the Yearly Meeting, sent a message to the Friends who were regularly assembled, and required that the appeal should be heard before them. As might have been expected, this disorderly requisition was not acceded to, and he was informed that at the conclusion of the usual business of the meeting they were willing to hear and determine upon his case. But this was evidently what he wished to avoid. He felt that in the regular order of the Society he had no hope of obtaining a reversal of his disownment, and consequently he resorted to the strange manœuvre. The spurious Yearly Meeting which Keith and his abettors had set up, among whom, observes Smith, were those " who made little or no profession of truth,"* now assumed an authoritative tone, and sent to require the attendance of those members of the Meeting of Ministers who had endorsed his condemnation. Finding no response to their application, they proceeded to give judgment in favour of their leader, and issued an epistle to that effect, to be read in the subordinate meetings, signed by seventy persons, " on behalf," as they state, " of ourselves and many more Friends who are one with us herein." They also published what they termed " A confession of faith in the most necessary things of Christian doctrine, faith, and practice, according to the testimony of Holy Scriptures." This " confession," was put forth to vindicate their claim to genuine Quakerism, and was drawn up with such skill, that it was difficult to distinguish it from a genuine document of the Society.

Although Keith shrank from bringing his appeal before the authorised body of Friends, yet as he had set up a separate Yearly Meeting, and was endeavouring, by all means in his power, to widen the schism he had made, Friends judged it right to give forth a testimony in condemnation of his conduct, and a paper to that purport, signed by two hundred and fourteen

* Smith's History, chap. x.

Friends, was issued, addressed "to the Monthly and Quarterly Meetings, &c., in East and West Jersey, Pennsylvania, or elsewhere, as there shall be occasion."[*]

The judgment given forth by the Yearly Meeting at Burlington, together with the public trial of Keith for impeaching the character of those in authority, rendered him still more violent and abusive. Opprobrious epithets were now coarsely and unsparingly applied to the objects of his anger. "It would be tedious," observe Friends, "to trace him in one half of his railleries, invective preachings, and loathsome printings against us, since this disorderly Yearly Meeting of his, and separation from us."[†]

This open schism was a subject which attracted the notice of Friends in other parts of America, who deeply lamented its occurrence. That precious cause which they desired to uphold and promote among men, had been grievously injured by the circumstance, and they felt called upon to declare their disunity with proceedings so utterly at variance with the religion they professed. In addition to the judgment of Pennsylvania Yearly Meeting, those for New England, Maryland, and Long Island, and other meetings, gave forth testimonies condemnatory of Keith and his adherents. He also received a severe rebuke from Friends of Barbadoes, who returned some of his controversial books which he had forwarded to them.[‡]

Finding his conduct so generally condemned by the Society in America, Keith determined to seek the judgment of the Yearly Meeting of London on his case, and in the early part of 1694, arranged with Thomas Budd, one of his most active coadjutors, to accompany him. Friends, on their behalf, appointed Samuel Jennings and Thomas Duckett to act as their respondents; and an epistle, containing an account of the separation, and the ground on which Keith had been disowned, was forwarded for the occasion. The Yearly Meeting of London in the same year commenced on the twenty-eighth of the Third Month (o. s.) On the third day of its proceedings, epistles from America relative to the schism having been read, George Keith was invited to attend,

---

[*] Smith's History, chap. x.   [†] Ibid.   [‡] Ibid.

when he presented a written defence of his case, and requested that it might be read. His request was acceded to.* From what had already been elicited, it was evident to the meeting that the case was one, which, in order to its right disposition, required much care, and a patient and full investigation, and as this would be likely to occupy no inconsiderable amount of time, it was concluded to postpone its consideration until after the usual business of the Yearly Meeting had been disposed of.

This exciting subject, it appears, had, to some extent, already claimed the attention of Friends in London; for Keith on his arrival, not having met with a cordial reception from some of them, at once preferred a complaint against them to the Six Weeks' Meeting. This meeting declined to give any judgment on the matter, and reported to the Yearly Meeting, "that upon George Keith's complaint to them of a straitness he found in some public Friends of this city towards him, and his desire that they would put those Friends upon giving the reasons of that their dissatisfaction, the Six Weeks' Meeting did thereupon inquire into it; but, finding the matter extend to the differences in America, they did not think fit to determine anything therein, but to refer it to the Yearly Meeting."† The Six Weeks' Meeting having thus been called to deliberate on the difference, the Yearly Meeting concluded that the members of that meeting should be at liberty to sit on the appeal.

The hearing of this important case commenced on the first of the Fourth Month. In those early days of the Society no precise form or rules for conducting appeals appear to have been laid down, neither, indeed, was there any settled order of the discipline which warranted Keith in thus formally appealing to the Yearly Meeting of London, against the judgment of that of Pennsylvania; and were it not that the former, as the parent Yearly Meeting, extended its care over every part of the Society, and that the case of Keith was immediately connected with a schism in the body, it is doubtful whether the Yearly Meeting of London would have entertained the appeal at all. Keith began by

---

* Minutes of London Yearly Meeting of 1694. † Ibid.

desiring that if any Friends "had any matter of offence or objection against him," it might be stated. This invitation called forth some expression of dissatisfaction, in reference to his publications, more particularly that, entitled "The Plea of the Innocent." Samuel Jennings, being present, replied to the statements of the appellant. In the afternoon sitting it was concluded that all George Keith's publications in reference to the dispute should be read in the meeting at large, including the letters and epistles forwarded by Friends in America, and also a copy of the order or proceedings of the court relating to the trial of George Keith and Thomas Budd. The reading of these, together with George Keith's oral defence, and Samuel Jennings' reply, occupied the Yearly Meeting no less than six whole days.

Having proceeded thus far, on the morning of the seventh day the meeting entered upon the consideration of the merits of the appeal. Many of the remarks made, and the opinions given on this extraordinary occasion, are recorded in the proceedings of the Yearly Meeting. The weight and simplicity of some of these are instructive, and may not be inappropriately revived. "George Keith, in discovering the weakness of some," observes one Friend, "by his printing and publishing his books, struck at the whole [body] thereby, and is contrary to truth." "As to the books and disservice of them," says William Edmundson, "need not be spoken to, it's plain—the ground of the matter [or difference] is his spirit." "These things that have happened," remarks another, "have dishonoured God, been a grief to Friends, and hath wounded George Keith's [spiritual] life, and O that that wound might be healed." The representatives from Hampshire, in giving their judgment, declare "its beginning and inroad hath been for want of true watchfulness, and keeping under the cross of Christ." "The occasion of the breach," remarks Joseph Baines, "hath been for want of true tenderness, and the honour of truth, and the prosperity of Zion ; for, had this tenderness been regarded and kept to, these things of printing, &c., had not been." "The printing of the books and the first motion to write them," says Richard Vickris of Bristol, "was wrong, and the separation was wrong, and this sense I deliver in a sense of the love of God." "The books printed by George Keith," says Richard Baker, "have been of great hurt, and I believe that the spirit that led him to print, led him to separate, and was the same." George Whitehead took a very decided view in reference to the separation : "It was unwarrantable," he said, "and not to be excused." "There is," he continues, "no precedent among the apostles or primitive Christians for it. Paul said, upon occasion of division, 'I will not know the speech of them that are puffed up, but the power ;' and some were guilty of idolatry, &c., and there were divisions and great corruptions among them, and among the seven churches, but the apostles did not go about to bring a reproach on the name of Christ, or cause separation among them."

At the afternoon sitting, George Keith was again heard in his defence. "He was sensible," he said, "of many failings, weaknesses and imperfections," but for which, he added, "he was only accountable to God." "I am not," he continued with much self-satisfaction, "under any uneasiness myself, and nothing that you can give out against me can prevail with me to condemn anything I have done, for I find peace. The Lord is with me." And concluded by telling the meeting, that he "had greater strength than they were aware of."

Some other papers having been gone through, a committee was appointed to prepare a document embodying the sense and judgment of the meeting on the case, with the special injunction, that those "that have separated be charged, in the name and power of the Lord Jesus Christ, to meet together with Friends in the love of God." The committee accordingly drew up a paper containing, as it states, "The proceedings, sense, and advice of the Yearly Meeting," in which the conduct of George Keith, in printing and publishing on the subject, is condemned as being out of "the wisdom and counsel of God," notwithstanding "that some few persons had given offence either through erroneous doctrines, unsound expressions, or weakness and want of wisdom and right understanding, the spreading of which in an aggravating manner was not consistent with the good order of the Truth ;" and it was insisted, that he ought "either to call in his books, or at least to publish something to clear the Society from the gross errors he had charged upon a few," and to "retract the bitter language in them." In reference to the separation, it distinctly states that that unhappy circumstance "lay at George Keith's door, and that he ought sincerely to use his utmost endeavours and interest with his friends concerned, to remove it, and to help forward a re-uniting and amicable composure for the holy truth's sake, and the glory of God, and peace of his people." The course adopted by the magistrates of Philadelphia towards Keith and some of his companions, did not meet the approval of the Yearly Meeting :—" It had been better they had not meddled with it, but quietly have borne it and passed it by." " There appears," continues the paper on this point, " to have been too much height of spirit on both sides, and both had need to be deeply humbled ; both provokers and provoked." The document then concludes as follows : " And lastly, this our solemn meeting, in the name and power of our Lord Jesus Christ, doth exhort and charge all them that have separated, to meet together with other Friends in the love of God, and humbly to wait for his power to repair the breach, reconcile and re-unite them in his tender love ; and earnestly supplicates the God of all our mercies, to remove all prejudices and offences out of their minds, and to effect this good end, which our souls have deeply, and in great humility and brokenness of heart, travailed for in this meeting, and are still in a travail for, that the great reproach may be removed, and God's truth exalted, and his churches' peace restored and preserved."*

The d liberate judgment of the Yearly Meeting of London, arrived at after so much patient investigation, was communicated to George Keith in one of the latter sittings on this painful business. Far, however, from manifesting that disposition of mind in which he could appreciate the tender counsel of his friends, he asserted that the advice was that of a party, and not of the Society itself ; and he began to exert himself to gain adherents to his cause, and to promote a division similar to that which he had effected in

* Minutes of London Yearly Meeting, vol. ii.

America. But in this unworthy effort he was disappointed, for, excepting "some of the old separatists," but few united with him. He also again had recourse to the aid of the press, and a sharp controversy ensued, in which he was ably met and refuted by the pens of Whitehead, Coole, Ellwood, and Claridge.

Although the appeal to London was ostensibly on Keith's account only, the Yearly Meeting was not slow to perceive that its decision also affected the position of those in America who had separated with him. In view of this, an address of Christian exhortation was soon after forwarded to them, in which they were censured for separating from and printing against the Society, and affectionately entreated to make an open confession of their fault, and to seek by an appointed meeting, a reconciliation with their injured brethren. The Quarterly Meeting of Philadelphia was not backward to forward this object, and made advances for the purpose ; but the bitterness of spirit that prevailed among the Keithians, and the hostility which they evinced towards Friends, rendered all efforts of this description unavailing.

At the next Yearly Meeting in London, the unsatisfactory conduct of George Keith was again brought under notice. Unwilling to let the opportunity pass without making another effort to sustain his wretched cause, he had prepared a written statement, which, at his own request, he was allowed to read in the meeting at large. The document contained charges against the Morning Meeting and some other Friends. He also "alleged that he was not contentious," and "that divers owned him," and concluded by offering to prove that the writings of Friends contained gross errors. On his withdrawal, the meeting, as it states, "proceeded weightily, and in the fear of God and sense of his eternal power, to give its sense of George Keith's paper and his spirit," to the following effect :—

First. "That he hath not, neither doth his said paper answer the advice given him last year, and is too directive, and filled with undue accusations against the Second-day's Morning Meeting, and many brethren that this meeting own, and are in unity with ; and they cannot receive it.

Second. "Their sense is [that] his spirit and works of division

H 2

are wrong. Therefore, the sense of Truth in this meeting is against both. And they cannot own nor receive him, nor his testimony, while he remains therein, but testify against him, and his evil works of strife and division, as such that tends not only to divide, but to unpeople us."*

On the following day Keith was admitted to hear, and, if he inclined, to reply to the decision of the meeting. On this occasion, it is recorded, that, " he broke forth into great disorder," and, after indulging in bitter and intemperate language towards Friends, he left in much anger, before the "further sense and judgment of the meeting could be given him." The Yearly Meeting, having so long forborne, now unanimously agreed no longer to recognise this turbulent man as one in religious profession with them, and to declare the same by issuing the following minute of disownment :—

"It is the sense and judgment of this meeting, that the said George Keith is gone from the blessed unity of the peaceable Spirit of our Lord Jesus Christ, and hath thereby separated himself from the holy fellowship of the Church of Christ ; and that whilst he is in an unreconciled and uncharitable state, he ought not to preach or pray in any of Friends' meetings, nor be owned or received as one of us ; until, by a public and hearty acknowledgment of the great offence he hath given, and hurt he hath done, and condemnation of himself, therefore, he gives proof of his unfeigned repentance, and does his endeavour to remove and take off the reproach he hath brought upon Truth and Friends ; which, in the love of God, we heartily desire for his soul's sake."†

Thus declared to be no longer worthy of church fellowship with a people whom he had sought to injure and divide, and many of those who at one time favoured his cause having "grown weary of him."‡ Keith now began to hold separate meetings at Turner's Hall, in London. The novelty of the circumstance, together with his bitter railing against Friends, at first attracted many to hear him. Ever delighting in polemical strife, he published a challenge to William Penn, George Whitehead, and

---

* Minutes of Yearly Meeting of 1695.　　† Ibid.　　‡ Sewel, p. 642.

others, to answer certain charges which he said he was prepared to sustain against the Society. Not feeling themselves, however, called upon to dispute with a man who had exhibited so much enmity towards Friends, and whose principles were so unfixed, the challenge was not responded to. " We know not," said they, " what religion or persuasion this wavering man is of, or what church or people he adheres to, or [who] will receive him with his speculations that led him to desert us." Keith's deviations from the principles of the Society, which in past years he so long and so powerfully advocated, gradually increased, and in 1695, he preached and published " a thanksgiving sermon." For some years he continued to employ his pen in writing against Friends ; but often were his arguments ably confuted by quotations from works of his own, published in former years.

Whilst Keith was thus endeavouring to gain adherents in England, his partizans in America had not been idle in his cause. In some parts of the country there were those who were very zealous on his behalf. In Poetquesink meeting the controversy ran so high, that the Keithians took possession of the meeting-house, and for a time, Friends were obliged to meet at a private dwelling. But symptoms of a want of unity among the separatists soon began to appear. As early, indeed, as 1694, this was apparent. " Those who have endeavoured to scatter us, and break our sweet unity and fellowship in his blessed truth," wrote Friends from Burlington, " the Lord has now suffered them to be scattered and divided into parties, to contradict and charge one another with erroneous doctrine ; they wither, and their reputation amongst the world lessens apace."*

Again in 1695, the want of unity among the followers of George Keith is more distinctly alluded to in the epistle from the Yearly Meeting held at Philadelphia. " That party that followed George Keith doth much lessen, and are much divided amongst themselves ; some of their preachers have been dipped in Delaware by a baptist preacher, and one of them having been at New York lately, was there sprinkled by an episcopal priest, and some turn to the Pietists."*

* Epistle of 1694.

At the Yearly Meeting, held at Burlington in 1696, their conduct in disturbing Friends' meetings was very disreputable ; their numbers and influence began, however, now to decline rapidly, and with diminishing numbers their dissensions appear to have increased. " Since they have ceased to give us disturbance as formerly," wrote Friends from Philadelphia in 1697, '·they are at great variance amongst themselves, biting and devouring one another—a great part of their contention is about water baptism, the supper, and oaths." " The Separatists," they write again in 1698, "grow weaker and weaker ; many of them gone to the Baptists, some to the Episcopalians, and the rest are very inconsiderable and mean, some of whom come now and then to our meetings, and some have lately brought in papers of condemnation." In the year following they had so far dwindled that " their name was scarcely heard."†

In an account of the Keithian Quakers, written by Edwards, the foregoing statements are very fully confirmed. " They soon declined," he says ; " their head deserted them, and went over to the Episcopalians. Some followed him thither ; some returned to the Penn Quakers, and some went to other societies. Nevertheless many persisted in the separation. These, by resigning themselves, as they said, to the guidance of Scripture, began to find water in the commission, Matt. xxviii. 19. Bread and Wine in the command, Matt. xxvi. 26, 30. Community of goods, love feasts, kiss of charity, right hand of fellowship, anointing the sick for recovery, and washing the disciples' feet, in other texts.—The Keithian Quakers ended in a kind of transformation into Keithian Baptists. They were called Quaker-Baptists, because they still retained the language, dress and manners, of the Quakers. But they ended in another kind of transformation into Seventh-day Baptists, though some went among the First-day Baptists, and other societies. However, these were the beginning of the Sabbatarians in this province."

For some years after his disownment, Keith continued to maintain the dress and language of a Friend ; but as he gradually progressed in a renunciation of our views, these distinguishing

* Epistle of 1695.   † Ibid. 1699.

characteristics became irksome to him   About the year 1700 he put them aside, and, courting the smiles of the Episcopal ministers, was ordained as one of them.   Bishop Burnett, referring to this circumstance, says, " he was reconciled to the church, and is now in holy orders among us, and likely to do good service, in undeceiving and reclaiming some of those misled enthusiasts." About two years after his ordination he proceeded to America as a missionary, under the auspices of the " Society for the Propagation of the Gospel in Foreign Parts." One prominent object of his mission he declared to be to " gather Quakers from Quakerism to the mother church,"* and during the two years he was thus occupied, he frequently challenged Friends to public disputations.   Whilst in New England, John Richardson ably answered him on one of these occasions.   " I spoke," he writes, "in the Lord's dreadful power, and George trembled so much as I seldom ever saw any man do : I pitied him in my heart ; yet, as Moses said once concerning Israel, ' I felt the wrath of the Lord go forth against him.' " In Maryland, Keith was anxious to engage Samuel Bownas in religious.controversy.   Bownas however intimated to him that one who " had been so very mutable in his pretences to religion " was not worthy of his notice.†   This was a stroke at Keith's pride which he could ill brook, and not long after he gratified his revenge by inciting the authorities of New York to imprison Samuel Bownas, on the vague charge of preaching against the " Church of England." After an absence of nearly two years, Keith returned to England, and made a considerable boast of his missionary labours in the New World, especially in proselyting Quakers.   But his attempt in this respect was unquestionably a failure.   His Episcopalian patrons were nevertheless on the whole pleased, and the living of Edburton, in Sussex, was the boon awarded to him for these exertions.

Keith must now have been advanced in age ; but his contentious disposition did not subside with increasing years, and frequently he became embroiled in angry disputes with his parishioners. His income was good, but in collecting the tithes he evinced an unusual degree of clerical rapacity, and descended to great

* Journal of John Richardson.   † Life of Bownas, page 57.

meanness in exacting his tenths from the most indigent, and on produce, too, of the most insignificant description.   His earthly career was, however, now drawing to a close, and in 1714, the pale messenger of death appeared at his threshold.   At this awful period, the thought that ere long he should have to stand before the judgment-seat of Him who seeth not as man seeth, raised feelings in his mind, which probably no other circumstance would have induced.   From some of his expressions we are led to conclude that, in reflecting on the latter years of his life, no small degree of remorse was his portion.   " He did believe," he remarked shortly before his close, "if God had taken him out of the world when he went among the Quakers, and in that profession, it had been well with him."   Assuredly his case presents a solemn warning to us all, and vividly reminds us of the scripture injunction, " Let him that thinketh he standeth, take heed lest he fall."

CHAPTER V.

In the previous volume, several biographical sketches have
been given of those who crossed the Atlantic, to preach the glad
tidings of the gospel. In continuing notices of this description,
our attention will be mostly confined to the settlers and colonists
in America who were called to this high and holy vocation.
Altogether, the number of these is considerable, and hence the
propriety of being brief in each individual case. Those referred
to in the present chapter, resided either in Pennsylvania or in
the Jerseys, and died prior to the year 1700, and most of them
filled the highest civil offices in the community, either as governors, councillors, representatives, judges or magistrates. The
discharge of these responsible offices was not, in their apprehension, incompatible with their allegiance to Christ, or with their
call to preach Him amongst men. The magistrate and the minister did not in their experience jar ; and, so far from the cause of
religion suffering by their engagements of this description, there
is good reason to believe, that they were often made subservient
to its promotion among their fellow-men.

In the early progress of the Society of Friends in England,
many who joined its ranks had been in the commission of the
peace ; but we do not find that, after their convincement, any of

them continued to act in this capacity. The testimony of the Society against judicial swearing, together with other acts inconsistent with the religion of Jesus, which the duties of the office involved, no doubt led our early Friends to retire from services of this character; and although in the reign of James II., partly through the court influence of William Penn, Friends were invited to accept the office of magistrate, without, it is believed, being called upon to compromise their testimony against oaths, yet it was seen by some judicious members of the body, that the time had not arrived when it would be safe for them to engage in such undertakings. But in Pennsylvania and the Jerseys, where the weight of civil affairs rested upon Friends, no objection of that nature existed, to prevent a Friend from consistently occupying posts of civil authority; a refusal to do so, therefore, under such circumstances, would have been of more than doubtful propriety, and even scarcely practicable.

RALPH WITHERS.

He lived at Bishops Cannings, in Wiltshire, and as early as 1657, appears to have identified himself with the Society of Friends. In 1660, he was imprisoned for many weeks on account of his religious principles, and again in 1678, for being married in a manner other than that directed by the liturgy.[*] He was one of the ministering Friends who issued the epistle from London Yearly Meeting in 1675, and in 1681 he attended that meeting as a representative from Wiltshire. He was one of the early emigrants to Pennsylvania, and was chosen, in 1683, as a member of the first Provincial Council;[†] his services to his brethren in the Western world were however of short duration, since in the following year his death was reported to the Yearly Meeting in London.[‡]

CUTHBERT HAYHURST.

Cuthbert Hayhurst was born in Yorkshire about the year 1632. He was among the earliest of those who professed our principles in

* Besse, vol. ii. p. 40, 45.   † Proud, vol. i. p. 235.
‡ Yearly Meeting Minutes, vol. i.

that county, and soon after attaining the age of manhood, he came forth as a minister of the gospel. As early as 1654, he suffered imprisonment in Yorkshire for preaching the truths of religion,* and in 1666, whilst on a gospel visit to some of the southern counties of England, he was taken from a meeting at Oxford and committed to gaol.† He was also at other times deprived of his liberty for the faithful maintenance of our religious principles. Cuthbert Hayhurst proceeded to Pennsylvania with William Penn in 1682, and proved an instrument, in the Divine hand, of comfort and consolation to his brethren under their new circumstances. He appears to have been a very devoted minister, and to have given up much of his time to promoting the kingdom of his Redeemer : in the minutes of London Yearly Meeting, he is referred to as "a great traveller" in the cause of truth.‡ "He was," says Nicholas Waln, who knew him well both in England and in America, "of great service to me and many others, being instrumental in bringing us near unto the Lord. I was with him," he continues, "in the time of his sickness, and beheld his meek, innocent, and lamb-like deportment, and I have great cause to believe he is one of those that died in the Lord, and is at rest with Him for ever."§ He ended his course at his residence in Bucks county, Pennsylvania, in the First Month, 1683, about the fiftieth year of his age.

FRANCIS WHITWELL.

He was one of the first settlers in Pennsylvania, prior to which no particulars of his life have been met with. He was elected to the important office of Provincial Councillor, and was one of that body chosen, in 1683, to prepare the draft of a new charter for the province. "He was," says Proud, "a preacher among the Quakers ; and every way a very useful and worthy member of society."‖ He did not however long survive, but died in the year 1684.

---

* Besse, vol. ii. p. 90.   † Ibid. vol. i. p. 571.
‡ Yearly Meeting Minutes, vol. i.   § Penn. Mem. p. 2.
                    Proud, vol i. p. 235, 237.

CHRISTOPHER TAYLOR.

Christopher Taylor is supposed to have been born near Skipton, in Yorkshire. He received a classical education, and officiated as a minister among the Puritans, until his convincement by George Fox in 1652,[*] at which time he resided at Otley, in the same county. Soon after he united with Friends, he came forth in the ministry among them, and he afterwards travelled in various parts of the kingdom. In the course of these gospel labours he passed through much persecution. In 1654, he was committed to Appleby gaol, where he was detained for about two years, under much cruel usage. On the return of the Royalists to power, he was again deprived of his personal liberty, for refusing the oath of allegiance ;[†] in the following year, we find him travelling in the ministry in the south of England, in the course of which he was taken from a meeting and sent to Aylesbury gaol.[‡] From Yorkshire he removed to Waltham Abbey, in Essex, where he opened a classical school. In those days of bigotry, the schoolmaster could not follow his profession without a licence from the bishop, and in 1670, Christopher Taylor was bound over to appear at the sessions, on the charge of violating this law.[§] About the year 1679, he removed his establishment to Edmonton, in Middlesex, in which, on his removal to America in 1682, he was succeeded by George Keith. The talents with which he was endowed were appreciated by the settlers of Pennsylvania, and he was chosen a member of the first Provincial Council ; in other respects he also proved himself, in his civil capacity, a valuable member of the community.[||] His literary qualifications were considerable, and he frequently exercised his pen in the service of the cause of truth : he had a good knowledge of Latin, Greek, and Hebrew, and in 1679, published his "Compendium Trium Linguarum" of these languages. Under date of 1686, Smith the historian has this notice of him : "In this year died Christopher Taylor of Pennsylvania. He was a diligent and faithful minister among his brethren, the Quakers.

[*] Whiting's Memoirs, p. 352.   [†] Besse, vol. ii. p. 102.
[‡] Ibid. vol. i. p. 76.   [§] Ibid. vol. i. p. 204
[||] Proud, vol. i. p. 236.

In the exercise of his gift, he was clear, solid, and lively; in prayer, solemn, reverent, and weighty; and in his general deportment, meek and humble. He was a considerable settler of Pennsylvania, and for his many services, the few years he lived there, seems to have been valued among them as one of the best men of the age in which he lived."*

Christopher Taylor

THOMAS LANGHORNE.

Prior to his settling in America, Thomas Langhorne resided in Westmoreland. The first notice that we find respecting him is under date of 1662, when he was committed to Appleby gaol, for refusing to pay a fine of five pounds for attending a Friends' meeting. For more than twenty years from this date, he underwent much persecution on account of his religious profession, during which the prison-house was often his abode, either under the stringent provisions of the Conventicle Act, or for refusing to recognise the anti-christian imposition of tithes.+ During an imprisonment in 1668, he wrote a piece entitled "The Captive's Complaint, or the Prisoner's Plea against the burdensome and contentious title of Tithes."‡ In the year 1684 he removed to Pennsylvania, and settled at Middleton, in Bucks county, for which county he was elected a representative in the Provincial Assembly.§ Proud refers to him as "an eminent preacher, of whom," he continues, "there is a very excellent and extraordinary character in manuscript, from Friends of Kendal, in Westmoreland, by way of certificate, on his removal to this country."‖ His son, Jeremiah Langhorne, after his death, filled the high office of Chief Justice of the province. John Hayton, a Friend who knew Thomas Langhorne intimately, both in England and in America, has left this testimony respecting him. "Having experienced the work of regeneration in himself, he became qualified to strengthen the brethren, and went forth in

* Smith, in Hazard.   † Besse, vol. ii. p. 10—35.
‡ Whiting's Memoirs, p. 369.   § Proud, vol. i. p. 335.
‖ Ibid. vol. i. p. 289.

the ministry and word of life, preaching the everlasting gospel of Jesus Christ ; having freely received, he freely gave, not fearing man, but obeying God, who had committed a large measure and clear manifestation of his Spirit unto him, not only for his own profit and benefit, but many others received comfort thereby ; for his doctrine dropped as the rain, and his speech distilled as the dew, to the renewing and refreshing the seed and plant of God."* He died in the Eighth Month, 1687.

JOHN SKEIN.

He was a native of Scotland, and when he first professed with Friends, resided at Aberdeen. During the greater part of 1676, and the following year, he was imprisoned under severe enactments of Scottish law for the suppression of Quakers, and in the same period, he suffered distraints for fines imposed for his refusing to give bond not to attend the meetings of his Society, to the extent of two hundred and fifty pounds.† In the year 1678, he removed from the scene of persecution to the unsectarian colony of West Jersey,‡ in which province he occupied for nearly two years the distinguished post of Governor. " He was not only a serviceable man in the Government," observes Smith the historian, " but an exemplary useful member in the religious Society of his brethren the Quakers, and had an edifying public testimony, in the exercise of which he was usually very tender."§ He died in 1687.

THOMAS ATKINSON.

This Friend was born at Newby, in the county of York, and early in life became convinced of our principles. By the testimony of his wife, we are informed, that prior to their union, which took place in 1678, he had received a gift in the ministry. In 1682 they emigrated to Pennsylvania. He is described as one " zealous for the truth, whose treasure was not in this world, and who often exhorted others to stand loose from the things which are below, and diligently to seek those things that are above." He died in 1687, giving utterance a short time before his close to many sweet and heavenly expressions.||

* Penn. Mem. p. 7. † Besse, vol. ii. p. 516. ‡ Smith's New Jersey, p. 109.
§ Smith, in Hazard. || Penn. Mem. p. 10.

JAMES HARRISON.

This individual was born near Kendal, in Westmoreland, and afterwards resided at Bolton, in Lancashire. He was one of those who very early professed with Friends in that county, and soon after appearing in the ministry, he became a powerful instrument in the hand of the Lord in turning many to righteousness. "He was," writes Whiting, "an able minister of the gospel, and a great traveller, at home and abroad, in the service of truth."* In common with many of his brethren of that period, he had to suffer severely, both by imprisonment and fines, for his faithful adherence to conscientious conviction.† On the settlement of Pennsylvania his attention was directed to the new territory, and having become a purchaser in Bucks county, to the extent of five thousand acres, he removed thither in 1682.‡ Though it is stated that "he had great concerns in this world,"§ he was, nevertheless, engaged above all to seek after heavenly things. During the early settlement of Pennsylvania, he appears to have taken an active part in its legislation. He was a member of the first Provincial Council, and one of the few chosen from that body, in 1683, to prepare the draft of a new charter. For several years he acted as William Penn's agent at Pennsbury. In 1685, he was nominated by the Council to the office of Provincial Judge, but declined to accept it.‖ "He was," says William Yardley, "bold and valiant for the truth, and his testimony was in the power of the Lord."¶ He died in much peace in the Eighth Month, 1687.

* Whiting's Memoirs, p. 368.   † Besse, vol. ii. p. 29, 69.

‡ By some MSS. papers of the Pemberton family, it appears, that the Harrison and Pemberton families, who intermarried, went over together in a vessel from Liverpool, bound for the river Delaware. By distress of weather, however, they were landed in the Patuxent river, in Maryland, from whence they proceeded on horseback to the neighbourhood of Pennsbury, "where they settled, and occupied places of distinguished trust." See Watson's Annals of Philadelphia, p. 64.

§ Penn. Mem. p. 8.   ‖ Proud, vol. i. p. 300.   ¶ Penn. Mem. p. 8.

JOHN SONGHURST.

Before his removal to America, John Songhurst resided at Coneyhurst, in Sussex. No particulars of his early life and convincement have been handed down, and the first notice which we have respecting him, is under date of 1670, when he was travelling in the ministry in London.* "He was," writes Whiting, "a brave eminent man, as well as minister, who had a very fine testimony," and "in the year 1680, he writ a very notable book, entitled 'A Testimony of Love and Goodwill unto all them who desire to come to enjoy an everlasting being with the Lord, when days in this world will have an end.'"† In 1682, he sailed with William Penn for Pennsylvania, and in the following year was elected to represent the county of Philadelphia in the Provincial Assembly, to which office he was re-elected in 1684. He died in West Jersey, but was buried at Philadelphia in the Eleventh Month, 1688.

WILLIAM PEACHY.

Before he emigrated to the western world, William Peachy lived in London. He was one of the early adventurers to the colony of West Jersey, having gone out in company with Thomas Ollive in 1677. These two, observes an early settler, "were the first among Friends in West Jersey who had a public ministry."‡ His call to the work of the gospel did not, however, prevent him from rendering services of a civil nature to his fellow-settlers, who elected him in 1682, as a representative in the Assembly of West Jersey.§ He died in the First Month, 1689, and was interred at Burlington."‖

JAMES RADCLIFF.

He appears to have lived in Lancashire. As early as the fifteenth year of his age, he was imprisoned for his religious profession, and in the course of his gospel travels in subsequent years, it is recorded, that he "underwent many hardships and

---

* Besse, vol. i. p. 408.   † Whiting's Mem. p. 387.
‡ Proud, vol. i. p. 158.   § Smith's New Jersey, p. 151.
‖ Whiting's Mem. p. 393.

imprisonments."* About 1682, he removed to America, and settled at Wrightstown in Pennsylvania, where, says Proud, he "was a noted preacher." He died in or about 1690, "being redeemed from the earth, and laying down his head in peace."†

JOHN ECKLEY.

The first notice that we find respecting this Friend occurs in 1683, when he is recorded as a representative from Herefordshire to the Yearly Meeting in London. In the following year we find him filling the high office of Provincial Judge in Pennsylvania. In 1686, he became still more distinguished, by being appointed one of the five who formed the "Commissioners of State," whose office it was to represent William Penn in the executive of the Government. The parties chosen for this responsible trust were the most eminent and influential Friends in the province. The counsel addressed to them by the proprietor on their appointment is worthy of preservation. " Be most just," he writes, " as in the sight of the all-seeing, all-searching God ; and before you let your spirits into an affair. retire to Him, that he may give you a good understanding and government of yourselves in the management thereof ; which is that which truly crowns public actions, and dignifies those that perform them."‡ As a christian legislator, the name of John Eckley is worthy of remembrance. Samuel Jennings, who knew him well, says, " I am persuaded it is a justice due to the righteous, and a duty upon us, to contribute something to perpetuate the names of such who have left a fragrancy behind them, and through faith have obtained a good report. Though their bodies sleep in the grave, and by divine appointment they die like other men, yet this signal difference hath the Lord declared : ' The memory of the just is blessed, but the name of the wicked shall rot.' The sincere affection I had for this, our dear friend, hath prevailed with me to give the following testimony concerning him. As a man he was pleasant, courteous, discreet, and grave, and in public services accompanied the foremost. The word of wisdom

* Besse, vol. i. p. 290, 318.   † Proud, vol. i. p. 217.   ‡ Ibid. 307.

was in his mouth, and he had received the tongue of the learned, to speak in due season. I might truly say much of his innocency, love, and zeal for truth, which hath left a lively impression upon the hearts of many. In his last sickness he was frequently filled with praises to God and instructions to his people."[*] He died about the year 1690.

THOMAS WYNNE.

He emigrated to Pennsylvania in 1682, in company with William Penn, having previously resided in Flintshire, North Wales, where he practised as a surgeon. He appears to have been a man of some literary attainments, and wrote several pieces in vindication of his principles as a Friend.[†] He was Speaker of the Provincial Assembly during its first and second year, and in subsequent years also formed one of that body. The historian of Pennsylvania refers to him as a "preacher among the Quakers, and a person of note and good character."[‡] He died in the First Month, 1692, and was buried in Philadelphia.

THOMAS OLLIVE.

He was of Wellingborough, in Northamptonshire, where he was convinced of our religious principles in 1655, through the ministry of William Dewsbury.[§] At what date he first appeared as a minister is not ascertained ; there is, however, reason to believe that it was soon after he joined the Society. In 1665 he suffered many weeks' imprisonment under the Conventicle Act, and in 1674, under a fresh enactment of a similar character, he had about sixty pounds worth of cloth taken from him.[||] He was one of the early adventurers to West Jersey, having proceeded thither in 1677, in the second ship which sailed for the new colony.[¶] His talents for business were considerable, and were highly appreciated by his fellow-settlers. The first Colonial Assembly appointed him its Speaker, which office he held for several

* Penn. Mem. p. 12.   † Whiting's Mem. p. 466.
‡ Proud, vol. i. p. 237.   § Whiting's Memoirs, p. 487.
|| Besse, i. p. 534, 536.   ¶ Smith's New Jersey, p. 93.

years.   In 1684, he was elected governor of the province, and in this responsible position he acted "with great circumspection and prudence."*   He was also a justice for the district of Burlington, and exercised his magisterial functions in those primitive days of the colony with patriarchal simplicity, "often doing it to good effect," says Smith, "in the seat of judgment, on the stumps in his meadows."†   "By his preaching and writing, as well as by other public and private conduct, he had gained love and esteem, which he merited to the last."   He died in the Ninth Month, 1692, and was buried in the township of Northampton, within the compass of Burlington Monthly Meeting.

WILLIAM YARDLEY.

William Yardley was born in the year 1632, and before his emigration to America, resided near Leek, in Staffordshire, where he was brought up as an agriculturist.   From early life he appears to have sought after heavenly things, and in his youthful days associated himself with a spiritually minded-people who called themselves the "Family of Love;"‡ a connection which he maintained until about the age of manhood, when he became convinced of the principles of Friends.   He first spoke as a minister about the twenty-third year of his age, and in the exercise of his gift, travelled for many years in various parts of the nation, in the course of which, he underwent much suffering by imprisonments and personal abuse.   During one of his imprisonments his only resting-place for seventeen weeks was the bare floor of his cell.§   In the year 1682, he removed to Pennsylvania, an dsettled near the falls of the Delaware, and being a man of ability and judgment, he was elected by the settlers to important offices in the province.   He represented the county of Bucks in the first Assembly, and for some years was an active member of the Pro-

---

* Smith's New Jersey, p. 209.　　　† Ibid.
‡ Penn, Mem. p. 13.　　　§ Besse, vol. i. p. 650.

vincial Council.*   "His ministry," writes his intimate friend
Thomas Janney, "was with a good understanding, not only of
what he spoke from, but also what he spoke unto ; and the things
which he testified, were what he had learned of the Lord, and
had himself seen, heard, and tasted, in the good word of life."†
He died in the Fifth Month, 1693, aged about sixty-one years,
having been a minister about thirty-eight years.

JOHN DELAVALL.

He was the son of a merchant of New York,‡ and about the
time of the settlement of Pennsylvania he was a captain in the
militia in that city, where he became convinced of our religious
views.   He became a minister soon after he had joined Friends,
and subsequently removed to New Jersey, and afterwards to
Philadelphia, where he married Hannah the daughter of Thomas
Lloyd.§   He is described as a man of an amiable and benevolent
disposition, and zealous in his ministry ; in the exercise of which
he visited other parts of America.   His literary qualifications
were not inconsiderable, and he employed his pen first in conjunction with George Keith, in defending his brethren from the
attacks of Cotton Mather, and subsequently in controversy with
Keith himself.|| He was also much engaged in the civil affairs
of the colony, and for some years was an active member of the
Provincial Council.¶   James Dickinson, who knew him intimately,
has left the following testimony respecting him :   "Although he
was one called in at the eleventh hour, yet he was faithful and
zealous for the truth, and a man of a tender, broken spirit.   The
Lord gave him a gift in the ministry, and blessed him in it, and
enabled him to get his day's work done in the day.   He was
valiant for the truth upon earth, and turned not his back to the
opposers of it, nor would spare the backsliders from it, but stood
faithful to the end.   His bow abode in strength, and in the faith

---

* Proud, vol i. p. 235, 340.   † Penn. Mem. p. 14.
‡ Whiting's Memoirs, p. 493.   § Proud, vol. i. p. 394.
|| Whiting's Memoirs, p. 493.   ¶ Proud, vol. i. 394.

of Christ he finished his testimony with a heart full of love to God and his people."* He died in the Sixth Month, 1693.

WILLIAM STOCKDALE.

William Stockdale was of Charlmount meeting in the north of Ireland. "He was convinced," says Whiting, "early, and receiving a public testimony, travelled much in the service of truth in England, Scotland, and Ireland ; and suffered much for his testimony by beatings, bruisings, &c."† He removed to Pennsylvania in the year 1687, and soon after was chosen member of the Provincial Council, which office he held until the time of his decease in 1693.‡ His remains were interred in Philadelphia.

WILLIAM WALKER.

William Walker was born in Yorkshire, and was one of the early emigrants to Pennsylvania, where he was convinced of the principles of Friends soon after his arrival. Having received a gift in the ministry, he proceeded, in 1693, on a religious visit to Friends in his native country, and after having laboured in the service in London, Wales, and some of the English counties, he was taken ill in the spring of the following year. During his illness he was favoured, in a remarkable degree, with a feeling of the divine presence and a foretaste of celestial joy. "Oh, the wonders of the Lord !" he uttered on one occasion, "what have I seen of the transcendent glory ! Though I see but little, yet it is admirable glory !" Speaking of Christ, he said, "I can see him ; his arm is open to receive me ;" and subsequently, "Oh, Lord Jesus, come ; sweet Jesus, I long for thee ; now death is pleasant—I feel the angel of thy presence to surround me !" his dying words being, "I feel the Fountain of life ; my soul's beloved is come."§ He died in the Fourth Month, 1694, and was buried in Southwark.

* Penn. Mem., p. 16. † Whiting's Memoirs, p. 493.
‡ Proud, vol. i. pp. 340, 369. § Piety Promoted.

THOMAS LLOYD.

Thomas Lloyd was born in North Wales, about the year 1649. His father was possessed of considerable wealth, and descended from an ancient family at Dolobran, in Montgomeryshire. Thomas, who was the youngest son, after receiving an education in the best schools of the day, was sent to the University of Oxford, where he is said to have made considerable proficiency in learning; and being a man endowed with good natural abilities, and much sweetness of disposition, he gained the notice and esteem of persons of the highest standing in society, and enjoyed opportunities of worldly advancement. In early life, however, his mind was richly visited by the Day Spring from on High, humbling and contriting his soul, and giving him to see the emptiness of all worldly things, in comparison of the riches of Christ his Saviour. Having heard of the people called Quakers, he went to hear them; when the divine power that pervaded the meeting, humbled and bowed his spirit before the Lord, and, clearly perceiving, that their doctrines harmonized with those of the New Testament, he took up the cross, and boldly professed them before his fellow-men. Having received a call to the ministry, he became an eminent instrument in the hand of the Lord in turning many to righteousness; and in controversy with the learned, he proved a powerful advocate for the principles he professed. In common with many others in the principality of Wales, he removed to Pennsylvania soon after its settlement as a province, where he was of great service to the state in its infant days. In 1684, he was elected President of the Council, and in 1686, was one of the five appointed by William Penn, to the responsible office of " Council of State,"—an office which he held until near the close of 1688, when he was released from its cares at his own express desire. In 1690, however, being again prevailed upon to exercise his talents in the civil affairs of the country, he presided a second time in the Council; and in 1691, when the " Council of State " was superseded by the appointment of a Deputy Governor, he was chosen for this high office, which he held for about two years, until the appointment of Fletcher by the Crown of England. Although Thomas Lloyd, from his first arrival in Pennsylvania, took an active and conspicuous part in its civil affairs, it was, nevertheless, contrary to his own natural inclination, and, so far from deriving any pecuniary advantage from devoting so much of his time and superior talents to the affairs of the colony, it is asserted, that his temporal interests suffered in consequence. " He was," records his Monthly Meeting, " an able minister of the everlasting gospel of peace and salvation, and his acquired parts were sanctified to Truth's service; his sound and effectual ministry, his godly conversation, meek and lamb-like spirit, his great patience, temperance, humility, and slowness to wrath, his love to the brethren, his godly care in the Church of Christ, that things might be kept sweet, and savoury, and in good order, his helping hand to the weak, and gentleness in admonition, we are fully satisfied, have a seal and witness in the hearts of all the faithful that knew him, both in the land of his nativity, and in these American parts ; and cannot be forgotten by them. We may in truth say, he sought not himself, nor the riches of this world, but his eye was to that which is everlasting, and he was given up to spend and be spent for the Truth, and the sake of Friends." The expressions of this eminent and devoted individual when near the close of life, evince that his foundation was laid on Christ the Rock of Ages : and he was enabled to say : " I have fought a good fight, and have kept the faith, which stands not in the wisdom of words, but in the power of God ; I have sought not for strife and contention, but for the grace of our Lord Jesus Christ, and the simplicity of the gospel. I lay down my head in peace—Friends, farewell all." He died in the Seventh Month, 1694, aged about forty-five years.*

THOMAS JANNEY.

Thomas Janney was born in Cheshire, about the year 1633. He united with Friends about the twentieth year of his age, and

* Whiting's Memoirs ; Penn. Mem.; Proud's History ; Piety Promoted ; Smith's Hist., in Hazard.

in the following year came forth as a minister of the gospel. In the exercise of his gift, he travelled extensively, both in England and in Ireland,* and he was more than once a prisoner for the truths he declared. He emigrated with his family to Pennsylvania about the year 1683, and settled near the falls of the Delaware. His station as a minister in the Society, did not preclude his engaging in the civil affairs of the country. In 1691, we find him one of the most active members of the Provincial Council ;† and in many other respects, he appears to have been serviceable to his fellow-settlers. The following testimony to his worth was borne by his Monthly Meeting : " As the Lord had bestowed on him a gift of the ministry beyond many of his fellows, so he was careful to improve it to his honour, and the comfort of his people ; not only labouring therein here, in Pennsylvania and New Jersey, but he also several times visited the churches in New England, Rhode Island, Long Island, and Maryland."‡ In 1695, he proceeded on a religious visit to his native country, where, after about eighteen months' service in the work of the Gospel, he was taken ill, and died in the Twelfth Month, 1696, in Cheshire, aged about sixty-three years, having been a minister about forty-two years.

Robert Owen.

Robert Owen emigrated to Pennsylvania in the year 1690, before which he resided in the principality of Wales. He travelled much in the work of the ministry, both in his native country, and in America. " He was," says his fellow countryman, Hugh Roberts, " a strong pillar in the Church of Christ, and his understanding was opened in those things that belong to order."§ He appears to have been endowed with many excellent qualities, and to have been of much service in various ways. He died in the Fifth Month, 1697, and was interred at Merion.||

---

* Piety Promoted.
‡ Penn. Mem. p. 26.
|| Penn. Mem. p. 29.

† Proud, vol. i. p. 217, 361.
§ Smith's Hist., in Hazard.

THOMAS FITZWATER.

Respecting the life of this Friend but very few particulars have been obtained. He came from Middlesex, and proceeded to Pennsylvania in company with William Penn in 1682, and was one of the members elected to represent the county of Bucks, in the first assembly of 1683. Seven years later we find that he was chosen a member of that body for Philadelphia. Proud remarks that he was "a valuable member of society, and a preacher among the Quakers." He died in the Eighth Month, 1699.*

* Proud, vol. l. pp. 235, 353, 422.

CHAPTER VI.

A HISTORY of the Society of Friends in America, without ample reference to the civil and political state of Pennsylvania, during the time the government was under the control of its members, would be very defective. When William Penn founded this colony, there were states on that continent, in which the non-resisting principles of Christianity were recognized ; this, as we have seen, was the case in the little colony of Rhode Island, and in the more recently established plantations of East and West

New Jersey. In political importance and general interest, however, these provinces bear no comparison to that of Pennsylvania. Its extent, its prosperity, its rapid growth in population, the entire recognition of equal rights, the democratic form of its government, together with the large proportion of Friends among the early settlers, — all contribute to render that portion of the history of the province, during which it was conducted on the christian principles of its enlightened founder, one of no ordinary moment.

In settling Pennsylvania, William Penn had a great experiment in view,—a "holy experiment," as he terms it. This was no less than to test, on a scale of considerable magnitude, the practicability of founding and governing a State on the sure principles of the Christian religion; where the executive should be sustained without arms ; where justice should be administered without oaths; and where real religion might flourish without the incubus of an hierarchical system. As a firm believer in the perfect adaptation of the precepts of the gospel to man in his corporate, as well as in his individual capacity, he had no doubt of success in the hands of a people evincing themselves, by their lives and conversation, followers of Christ ; but, if left to the hands of others, he had no confidence. Leaving, however, further remarks on this subject, we will now proceed to examine to what extent, the favoured commonwealth of Pennsylvania, realized the anticipations and hopes of its benevolent founder.

The early settlers in this province, were mostly in religious profession with William Penn. The constitution, therefore, which he had framed harmonized with their views of civil things ; and, whether in the Council, or in the Assembly, as officers of the peace, jurymen, or constables, Friends not only took their full share in serving the state, but, from the confidence reposed in them by the other colonists, the civil offices were, for a long time, mostly occupied by them. In the Council of 1683, composed of eighteen representatives, six, it appears, were ministers in our Society, and a still larger number of Friends in that station, were members of the Assembly. During his stay in the province, William Penn always presided at the Council ; and in the infant days of the colony, so largely were the practices of our religious Society recognized among the representatives, that instead of opening the proceedings of the day with formal prayer, as in the Parliament at home, and in the Assemblies of neighbouring provinces, they waited in solemn silence upon the God of the spirits of all flesh,* and inwardly craved his aid, and his blessing, in their efforts thus to serve their fellow men.

The province now known as Delaware, was also ceded to William Penn. This district had been settled by some Swedes, in the time of Gustavus Adolphus; but on the transfer, they willingly recognized the government of the new proprietor. The Swedes were an industrious and sober-minded people, and, with the German settlers of Pennsylvania, evinced great regard for Friends, and co-operated harmoniously with them in all civil matters. A few Germans and Swedes, were elected to serve, both in the Council and in the Assembly.†

In either of the representative branches of the legislature, any member was at liberty to propose whatever he thought best for the promotion of the public good. Many propositions were consequently made, and many measures concluded upon; but the chief business of the session of 1683, consisted in modifying the charter in a manner more conformable to the views of the settlers. Some of the representatives were men who had received a liberal education, and were scholars in the age in which they lived; but for the most part, the Assembly was composed of those whose literary attainments were small; yet, at the same time they were characterized by great integrity of purpose, and their manners were at once simple, hearty, and unceremonious. Writing to the Free Society of Traders in 1683, William Penn says, "Two general Assemblies have been held, and with such concord and dispatch, that they sat but three weeks, and, at least seventy laws were passed without one dissent, in any material thing—courts of justice are established in every county, with proper officers, as justices, sheriffs, clerks, constables, &c., which courts are held every two months. But to prevent law-suits, there are three

* Watson's Annals, p. 75.   † *Vide* Ferris's Delaware.

peace-makers chosen by every county court, in the nature of common arbitrators, to hear and end differences between man and man." *

The judicial proceedings of the province at this early date, present but two cases of sufficient moment to be noticed.   One was the case of a party tried in 1683, for coining, in which a greater alloy of copper was used than was lawful.   The jury having found them guilty, the principal in the fraud was sentenced to pay a fine of forty pounds, and to make full satisfaction " in good and current coin," to every person who should, within one month from the date of a proclamation to that effect, bring in any of the counterfeit money. The other case was the trial, during the same year, of a turbulent old woman for witchcraft. The charge was made by the Swedes, who, among other Scandinavian superstitions, believed in this notion, and to prevent any dissatisfaction with the issue, the jury was empannelled partly of Swedes, and partly of English.   The verdict given, was, that she had the " common fame of being a witch, but not guilty in manner and form as she stands indicted ;"† and the affair resulted simply in her friends giving security that she would keep the peace. A belief in witches, among the settlers in the New World, was far from being confined to the Swedes ; the records of New England are stained with accounts of executions arising from this superstitious notion ; ‡ and even fifty years later, civilized nations sent unoffending females to the stake on this account.§ The evidence given in the foregoing instance was like that of most others on such occasions.   One witness said, "he was told twenty years ago that the prisoner at the bar was a witch, and that several cows were bewitched by her." Another attested " that her husband took the heart of a calf that had died, as they thought by witchcraft, and boiled it, whereupon the prisoner at the bar came in and asked them what they were doing ; they said, boiling of flesh ; she said they had better to have boiled the bones, with several other unseemly expressions." Absurd and

* Proud, vol. i. p. 261.   † Colonial records, i. p. 41.
‡ Cotton Mather's Discourse, p. 10.   § Voltaire's Louis XIV.

unmeaning as were these depositions, it is doubtful whether the life of the accused would have been saved had they been given in the courts at Boston.

In Great Britain, a violation of the law by coining would, in all probability, have been attended by the capital punishment of the offender ; and with respect to witchcraft, ten years later, no less than nineteen persons were hung in Massachusetts on charges of this description. The efficacy of the milder jurisprudence of the Society of Friends was thoroughly exemplified in these instances. Henceforward no one in Pennsylvania was ever tried on the charge of witchcraft ; and, whilst in England the laws against coining were constantly outraged, the territory of William Penn was comparatively free from the offence.

Events having called William Penn to his native land, it became needful for him to make some provision for the exercise of the executive in his absence. For this purpose he authorised, in the Sixth Month, 1684, the Provincial Council to act in his stead, of which Thomas Lloyd, mentioned in the last chapter, a Friend highly qualified for the office, was president. But the power of the governor being committed to so many individuals, was attended with inconvenience, and in 1686, the commission was restricted to five persons, who were designated "Commissioners of State." The parties chosen for this responsible office, were all Friends of ability and high standing, including Thomas Lloyd, who acted as chairman. This arrangement continued until 1689, when, on the withdrawal of Thomas Lloyd from the turmoils of office, and no other colonist being found suitable to succeed him, William Penn appointed Captain John Blackwall as his deputy. Writing to the Commissioners in reference to this appointment, he says, "He is not a Friend, but a grave, sober, wise man. I have ordered him to confer in private with you, and square himself by your advice. If he do not please you he shall be laid aside."*

---

* One of the early acts of the Provincial Legislature, soon after William Penn's return to England, was the proclamation of James II. as king. The proclamation issued on the occasion was transmitted to

The administration of Blackwall disappointed the hopes of the proprietor. Unlike those over whom he ruled, he could not appreciate the Christian doctrine of non-resistance, and he attempted to raise a militia. This alone was quite sufficient to unfit him for his position, but in other respects also his actions did not harmonize with the council, and after about a year's duty, at the intimation of William Penn, he resigned and returned to England.

the Home Government, of which the following is a copy taken from the original in the *State Paper Office, Penn. B. T.,* vol. i.

Philadelphia, *the 23rd of the Third Month (May)* 1685.

PENNSYLVANIA.—The President and members of Provinciall Councill having received express advice this evening, from the Proprietary and Governor of this province and territories, and transemitted to him, from the Lords of the Councill, of the decease of our late soveraign Charles the Second, with speedy instructions to proclaim James Duke of York and Albany, and that his only brother and heir, King James the Second. In obedience whereunto, we, the President and members of the Councill, attended with the magistrates, principall officers, and inhabitants of Philadelphia, doe unanimously proclaim James Duke of York and Albany, &c., by the decease of our late soveraign Charles the Second to be now our lawfull Leige Lord and King, James the Second of England, Scotland, France, and Ireland, and among others of his dominions in America of this province of Pennsylvania and its territories, King. To whom we doe acknowledge faithfull and constant obedience with all hearty and humble affection. Beseeching God, by whom kings doe raign and princes decree justice, to bless our present soveraign King James the Second, with long, healthie, peaceable, and happy years to reign over us, and soe

GOD SAVE KING JAMES THE SECOND !

Tho: Lloyd

PRESIDENT.

No other person having been named to succeed Blackwall, the executive, according to law, devolved on the Council, and the talented but retiring Thomas Lloyd, was again induced to act as president.

Since the foundation of the colony eight years had now passed away, and during this period the population had rapidly increased, so that Pennsylvania and the territories could number twelve thousand inhabitants.* In the city new streets continued to be opened, and old ones extended; public buildings were erected, warehouses and wharfs built, and the capital of the province had already become one of the most important commercial depots of the western world. The primeval forests, which had hitherto been the abode of wild beasts, were now giving place to fruitful gardens and fields of corn; and cheerful homesteads were built where once the habitation of man consisted only of the rude wigwam of the Indian. Whether in city or country the settlers were blest with prosperity, and their civil affairs were conducted with harmony; and whilst the political liberties of neighbouring provinces were threatened by the *quo warrantos* of the infatuated James II., the court influence of William Penn protected his territory from dangers of this description.†

The concord with which the affairs of the province had been hitherto conducted was now, however, about to be seriously

---

* Bancroft's United States.

† The following letter is adduced in proof of this statement :

Windsor, *June 6th*, 1686.

MR. ATTORNEY GENERAL.

Sir,—His Majesty having, by order in council, directed you to bring writs of quo warranto against the Proprietors of Pennsylvania, Carolina, and the Bahama Islands, &c., in America, his Majesty commands me to acquaint you that he has thought fit, for some particular considerations, to suspend the proceedings against the proprietor of Pennsylvania, and accordingly, would have you forbear to do anything further in that matter till further order from him, his intention being, nevertheless, you should continue to proceed against the rest.

I am, sir, your most humble servant,

SUNDERLAND P.

Sunderland's Letter Book, vol. ii. p. 337. *State Paper Office.*

interrupted. The representatives from Pennsylvania and those from the territories were originally balanced in number ; but the growing importance of the former, had raised a jealousy in Delaware that this equality would be disturbed, to the injury of its interests. After the resignation of Blackwall, this feeling, which had been smouldering for years, was more conspicuously developed. Discontented at things taking their usual course, six members of the Council from the territories assumed the power of appointing judges without the concurrence of the board or the president ; and the disagreement did not stop here. As William Penn had no prospect of being able to return very early to the province, he gave the colonists the choice of three modes for the exercise of the executive power ; that of a deputy governor, five commissioners, or the Council. This option was given, it is believed, with a view to induce the representatives to a more united action. Pennsylvania chose the first of the three modes, while Delaware so obstinately opposed it, that, notwithstanding the efforts made to reconcile them, its members withdrew from the Council and returned home. The rupture was a source of much pain to William Penn ; but finding the discontented parties were irreconcilable, he met the difficulty by appointing Thomas Lloyd as deputy governor for Pennsylvania, and his cousin William Markham for the territories ; an arrangement which worked far better than he expected.

The want of harmony which had thus unhappily sprung up between the representatives, was soon followed by troubles of a graver description. The English and French being at war, the possessions of the former in North America were exposed to incursions from Indians subsidized by the French to ravage the frontier settlements. Alarmed at their position, the colonists of New England and New York made considerable preparations for war, in which they urgently solicited the co-operation of Pennsylvania. But Friends there, being faithful to their testimony against all wars and fightings, declined to unite in these military demonstrations. Trusting to divine protection, they had settled unarmed in the midst of warlike tribes, and they had amply experienced that this trust was not a vain one. Notwithstanding, however, the cordial friendship that existed between the colonists and the Indians of Pennsylvania, there were not a few of the more recent settlers, not professing with Friends, who were uneasy and dissatisfied at not having some means of defence. As early as the year 1688, this class were much alarmed at a report which was spread, that the natives had planned, on a given day, to massacre the whole of the settlers. Some Friends, who gave no credence to the report, endeavoured to quiet the minds of the people ; but a party employed to investigate the matter, having confirmed the rumour, the consternation became great. Five hundred Indians, it was said, were already assembled at one of the Indian towns in the vicinity, and many now believed, that ere long, the tomahawk and the scalping knife, would prove the fallacy of the Quaker doctrines of peace. The Council being at that time in session, the alarming position of the colony was brought under its notice, when Caleb Pusey, a Friend of high standing, and strong in his belief of the efficacy of gospel principles, offered to go to the place where, it was said, the warriors were assembled, provided the Council would name five others who would accompany him unarmed.*   Volunteers were not wanting, and the little band, mounted on horseback, proceeded to face the supposed array of their wonted murderers. On arriving at the Indian town, instead of meeting with five hundred warriors, they found the old king quietly reclining at his ease, the women at work in the fields, and the children at play. The rumour, in fact, turned out to be entirely unfounded.

The colonists had, however, soon to deal with something more than mere rumour. Conflicts between the natives and the settlers of New England and New York, had actually taken place, and there was good reason to suppose that Pennsylvania would be soon invaded by tribes in the pay of the French. In this time of trial, the confidence of Friends in the all-protecting arm of their God, did not fail them, and they steadfastly declined either to subscribe money, or to raise men, for the common defence. Their desire was, to live on terms of peace and friendship with the French as well as the Indians, and they boldly declared

* Proud, vol. i. p. 337.

that, if either the one or the other came against them, they would go out unarmed and tell them so.*

The calm attitude which Friends of Pennsylvania continued to maintain amidst the dangers of war, disturbed the royal authorities at Whitehall. They could not appreciate those Christian views which dictated such a course, and they knew also, that there were not a few of the settlers who were ardent to enrol themselves as soldiers for the defence of their homes.† The schism caused by George Keith, and the rupture between the province and the territories, were also circumstances that tended to lessen the confidence of the English Government in Quaker legislation ; added to which, the arrest of William Penn on the charge of treason and conspiracy, further contributed to bring about, what many of his enemies had aimed at, the transfer of his government to other hands. This was done by an order in council, dated " March 10th, 1692," by which the government of Pennsylvania was annexed to that of New York, under the administration of Colonel Fletcher.

Although a blow had been thus inflicted on the Society of Friends, and more particularly on William Penn, still the holy cause which led that great man to found a colony in the western world was not a hopeless one, and he had faith to believe, that his " holy experiment " would be triumphant. Under the great seal of England he was yet proprietor of the province, and no acts of his own, or that of the provincial power, had legally annulled or vitiated his charter. Colonel Fletcher, like most other soldiers, being unable to understand the peace doctrines of the New Testament, William Penn was fearful, lest, in attempting to carry out his military views, he might arbitrarily overrule the legislative power of the Council and Assembly. To guard, therefore, against any evil that might arise in this direction, he wrote both to Fletcher, and to the officers of the province. The former he warned, in a dignified strain, to act with caution, asserting that the king had no stronger title to the crown of England than

* Penn. Papers, Jan. 15th, 1690-91.—*State Paper Office.*

† Fletcher's Corres., "April and May."—*New York Papers. State Paper Office.*

he had to the soil and government of Pennsylvania—that the charter had not been abrogated—that he was still master of his province ; and that, as he was an Englishman, he would vindicate his right.* The officers of his government he encouraged to obey the crown when it spoke the voice of law, but in no way to surrender the rights which the charter had conferred upon them.† His advice to the colonists was a word in season. They firmly maintained their religious principles under circumstances of peculiar difficulty, and nobly resisted the attempts of arbitrary power to trample on their rights.

Early in the year 1693, Fletcher repaired to Philadelphia to assume the reins of government, and as he intended to conduct it on his principles as a soldier, he entered the Quaker city attended by a military retinue. He had previously, by letter, been urgent in his demand for supplies, but the answer being in the negative, he hastened to the province, to enforce it in person. The representatives of the province and the territories were summoned to meet him ; but in issuing the writ, both with respect to the number of delegates, and the time and form of the election, it was evident that he intended to act quite independently of the charter. As an ultra royalist, the democratic principles of Pennsylvania were anything but congenial to his political notions. The Assembly having met, the first business he introduced to it was an application from the crown, for men and money, to aid in defending the frontiers of New York from the French and Indians. The representatives felt that their rights and privileges had already been invaded, and before entertaining the requisition, they unanimously resolved that their laws were not affected by the appointment of Fletcher, and pressed him at once to give his recognition to them. " If the laws," he said, " made by virtue of Mr. Penn's charter, be of force to you, and can be brought into competition with the great seal which commands me hither, I have no business here." " The grant of King Charles," replied the speaker, " is itself under the great seal. Is that

* Penn. Papers, Dec. 5th, 1692.—*State Paper Office.*

† W. Penn's Corres., attested by Fletcher, vol. i. of Penn. Papers.—*State Paper Office.*

charter, in a lawful way, at an end?" To meet the difficulty, Fletcher proposed to re-enact the greater part of the former laws; but this was steadfastly opposed. Having firmly asserted their political rights, and at last obtained from their new governor a distinct recognition of their legislative power, the representatives passed a bill imposing a tax of one penny in the pound, to be presented to the crown, but with the understanding that, "it should not be dipped in blood." As nothing was granted for the specific purpose of war, Fletcher at first refused the bill, but finally complied. On the whole, however, he was greatly dissatisfied, and wrote to the king, setting forth the impossibility of obtaining a war vote from the Quakers of Pennsylvania, and urging the propriety of forming the colony, together with New York, the Jerseys, and Connecticut, into one province, as the only way to outvote Friends, and by this means to obtain the desired supplies.* These representations met with a cordial response from the home government, and the Privy Council proceeded so far as to direct the Attorney-general to scrutinize the patent of William Penn, in the hope that some flaw might be found in it sufficient to justify them in having it annulled.

During his administration, Fletcher was several times in the province, and in the early part of 1694, he again met the Assembly. Having found, by experience, that it was futile to look for military grants from a people who were so decidedly opposed to war, he now asked them to vote money, "to supply the Indian nations with such necessaries as might influence their continued friendship to the provinces."† Fearful in any way of compromising their religious principles, the Assembly adopted the course of the previous year, and again levied a tax of one penny in the pound. The produce of this impost was nearly eight hundred pounds, of which they stipulated that one half should be paid to William Markham and Thomas Lloyd, for their services whilst acting as deputies of the proprietary, and the remainder to the general purposes of the government. The claim of the Assembly to make specific appropriations of money, was

* New York Papers, Sept. 15th, 1693.—*State Paper Office.*
† Proud, vol. i. p. 396.

rejected as an infringement of the royal prerogative, and, after a fortnight's altercation with Fletcher, the Assembly was dissolved.

It must be admitted that, with reference to the last mentioned application of Fletcher, some of the representatives were actuated in their opposition, more with a desire to guard their political rights, than to bear a testimony against war. It is true, the majority were Friends ; but there were others, especially from Delaware, who had no fellow-feeling with them on the principles of non-resistance. Had there not existed a strong jealousy of an encroachment on their colonial privileges, the application would, probably, have been granted : William Penn himself regretted the course the Assembly took in this instance.* To feed and clothe the Indians, in order to secure their continued friendship, did not, in his view, at all compromise the testimony of Friends against war.

Whilst Fletcher and the Assembly were thus disputing, William Penn was exerting himself to recover the power of which he had been so unjustly deprived. He had been publicly acquitted before the king and council from the charge of treason—the law officers of the crown were unable to find any flaw in his charter ; neither could they discover that any of his subsequent acts could be strained into an offence to justify its forfeiture ; and his claim on the crown, for a full reinstatement of his rights and properties, being seconded by some powerful friends, his efforts at last proved successful. The patent, by which he was legally re-invested with his former power and functions, was dated " August," 1694.

Previously to his restoration, William Penn had conferences with the Government in reference to the course he was willing to take, in defending the province as an integral part of the British dominions. By an order in council it is stated, that he did not object to supply a contingent of money or men for the defence of the frontiers. † The records of the Committee of Trade and Plantations, speak less definitely, and go no further than to state that he would transmit to the Council and Assembly, " all orders that the crown might issue for the safety and security

* Proud, vol. i. p. 397.

† Privy Council Registers, W. R. III. p. 455.—*Privy Council Office.*

of the province ;"* whilst in the patent itself, by which the administration was restored to him, no distinct provision is made on the subject. This document is, indeed, good evidence, that in negotiating for his reinstatement, William Penn did not compromise the principles of the Society on war. His position was, undoubtedly, an extremely delicate one ; for, whilst satisfied that so long as his fellow-members were chosen as the representatives of the people, no military supplies of any description would be voted, yet, as there was already no inconsiderable number of persons in the province who were ready to bear arms, and as this class was daily augmenting by immigration, it was impossible for him to say what, in future years, might be the voice of the colony on the subject ; and he believed it right to leave the decision in their hands. It has been stated by more than one historian, that William Penn, on being reinstated in his government, agreed to provide means for its defence ; but this is manifestly an error. On a careful investigation of all the facts of the case, taken in connexion with the course which he afterwards pursued, it is evident that he could not have committed himself to any distinct or implied promise to this effect.

Circumstances having prevented the proprietary from returning at once to his province, his cousin Markham was invested, in 1694, with the executive power. Excepting in the very early part of his administration, he appears to have given satisfaction to the colonists, and to have discharged his functions with vigour and success. With the peace of Ryswick, the war between France and England was brought to a close ; and during the five years that Markham ruled in Pennsylvania, it was blessed with almost uninterrupted peace and harmony.

Towards the close of 1699, after an absence of fifteen years, William Penn arrived a second time in Pennsylvania, with the intention of remaining there for life, to govern in person the commonwealth which he had founded, and on which his hopes had been so long and anxiously set. During the winter, he attended many meetings of the Council, and in the Eleventh

* State Paper Office, B. T., Penn. vol. ii. p. 51.   † Ibid. vol. i. B. A. p. 19.

Month he also met the Assembly. For some years past, complaints had been transmitted to the home government, that piracy, and illicit trading, were not sufficiently suppressed in the colony. After advocating and watching the passing of certain acts to check these evils, he dissolved the Assembly.

Since 1683, that body, without consulting the proprietary, had introduced several important changes in the constitution, and a strong desire was now prevalent for a new one. In the kindness of his heart, he did not reproach them for their stretch of authority, or complain of their wish for further modifications. Early in 1700, he again met the Assembly. In his address to them on this occasion, he began by reminding them that, though the colony was but nineteen years old, it was already equal in population to neighbouring ones of twice and thrice that standing. He admitted that their laws, though good, were open to improvement. " If, in the constitution by charter," he said, " there be anything that jars, alter it. If you want a law for this or that, prepare it ;" adding the caution, " [But] I advise you not to trifle with government : I wish there were no need of any ; but since crimes prevail, government is made necessary by man's degeneracy."* In the following year a fresh code of laws was passed, and the benevolent governor conceded to the settlers, all the political privileges they desired.

About this time William Penn received a letter from the home government, requiring the sum of three hundred and fifty pounds from the province, towards erecting forts on the frontiers of New York. As the circumstance was one of considerable moment to Friends, he immediately convened the Assembly, and in laying the letter before them, he stated that it was impossible for him to answer the application without having their decision in reference to it. As might have been expected, they declined to accede to the demand. The money was for a warlike purpose, and as such, repugnant to their religious views. They did not, however, distinctly state this as the ground of their non-compliance, but rested it rather on their alleged poverty in the infant

* Penn. Hist. Soc., vol. ii. part ii. p. 187.

state of the province, desiring the governor, nevertheless, to assure the king "of their readiness to comply with his commands, as far as their religious persuasions would permit."* The representatives from the territories, who differed from Friends on the subject of military preparations, chose to return a separate answer. They, however, also declined, but not from any objection to the character of the requisition. They pleaded their own defenceless condition, and desired to be excused from "contributing to forts abroad, while they were unable to build any for their own defence at home."

It was not long after the royal requisition had been discussed in Pennsylvania, that the startling intelligence arrived, that a bill had been introduced into the House of Lords, for annexing to the crown all the proprietary governments of North America. The dispute on the Spanish succession had led to a rupture between the courts of Great Britain and France, and North America once more became the scene of hostilities. The opportunity was seized by the enemies of William Penn ; and, under disguised pretences of public good, they thus sought a second time to deprive him of his property and his political power. The representatives were again convened, and, alarmed at their position, solicited William Penn to return at once to London to defend their common rights.† Reluctant as he was to leave his adopted country, yet as its interests were thus endangered, he decided to go, and having, with the full concurrence of the Assembly, appointed Colonel Hamilton as deputy-governor, and James Logan as his secretary, towards the close of 1701, he sailed for England.

The unhappy want of concord, which had so long existed between the province and the territories, had become in no way lessened by the lapse of time. During his last visit the proprietary had tried in vain to reconcile them. Foreseeing that this dispute might, in the end, lead to a separation, he introduced a provision to meet such an emergency in the new charter which he granted, by which he allowed that each should separately "enjoy all the liberties, privileges, and benefits, granted jointly to them."‡ The administration of Governor Hamilton was but

* Proud, i. p. 426.   † Hazard, xii. p. 363.   ‡ Proud, i. p. 450.

of short duration. About one year after his appointment he was taken off by death. He spent, however, much of this limited period in endeavouring to bring about a union in legislation between the contending parties. But his efforts were unavailing, and in the year 1703, they agreed to separate and form distinct representative assemblies.

On the death of Hamilton, the executive authority devolved on the Council, until the appointment of Governor John Evans, in the Twelfth Month, 1703.

In appointing deputy-governors for his province, subsequently to the restoration of his charter, William Penn, it appears, invariably sought the approval of the crown for the person of his choice. Although the charter of renewal makes no reference to such submission, there was undoubtedly some understanding to that effect.*

Evans commenced his official career with efforts to restore the union between the province and the territories. The representatives of the latter were willing to accede to the proposal, but those of the province unhesitatingly declined. The refractory conduct of the members from Delaware, and the disorders to which it had given rise, were still fresh in their remembrance, and they were not disposed to place themselves in a position which might again subject them to similar annoyance.

Notwithstanding Evans's good offices in endeavouring to effect a union between these parties, his appointment as deputy-governor appears to have been an unhappy one. At the time of his arrival, the war was still raging between France and England, and, having no sympathy with Quaker views on the doctrine of peace, he

---

* The following order in council confirms this view:—

"At the Court at Hampton Court, the 30th day of July, 1703.

Present—

"The Queen's Most Excellent Majesty in Councill.

"Her Majesty in Council, is pleased to declare hereby, her royall approbation of the said Evans to be Deputy Governor of Pennsylvania, without limitation of time, and of ye 3 Lower Counties on Delaware Riv^r during her Maj^{ties} pleasure only."

State Paper Office. Propr. B. T. vol. vii. L. 47.

attempted, like his predecessor, to organize a militia. He treated, indeed, the conscientious scruple of Friends against bearing arms with absolute contempt, and, entertaining the notion that, if fully tested, they would abandon their professions, he unwisely determined to prove it by raising a false alarm. Having planned his scheme, in the early part of 1706, a messenger, in great haste, arrived at Philadelphia from Newcastle, on the Delaware, with the information that the French were coming up the river. Evans, assuming the greatest alarm, rode through the city with his sword drawn, calling upon the inhabitants to arm themselves and follow him.* The consternation was great. Some burned their goods, many fled into the woods, and others, to the number of three hundred, seized arms and placed themselves under the command of the deputy-governor. Notwithstanding the terror which prevailed among many of the citizens, the design of Evans with respect to Friends did not succeed. Instead of flying to arms in the supposed emergency, they exemplified the steadfastness of their faith, by calmness and fortitude of mind ; and, it being the regular meeting-day, they met as usual. " There was not a Friend of any note," observes Isaac Norris, in reference to this occasion, " but behaved as becomes our profession." † Proud states that four persons only, " who had any pretence to be accounted Friends, appeared under arms."‡ The manœuvre was, in fact, a complete failure.

The unfitness of Evans to govern Pennsylvania, was soon after manifested in another case. Having prevailed upon the territories to erect a fort at Newcastle, he also induced them to pass a law for its maintenance, by levying a tax upon all inward-bound vessels passing the fort, whilst all vessels passing down the Delaware, were, under certain penalties, to drop anchor and to ask permission to pass. This was held by the Pennsylvanians to be a direct violation of the charter ; but, despite their strong remonstrances, the illegal exaction was still pressed. The matter being too serious to rest here, it was determined to withstand the imposition in another way. Three Friends of Philadelphia,

* Proud, vol. i. p. 469.   † Janney's Life of Penn, p. 505.
‡ Proud, vol. i. p. 471.

Richard Hill, Isaac Norris, and Samuel Preston, "men," says Proud, "of the first rank and esteem," were owners of a vessel then about to sail for Barbadoes, and having acquainted Evans of their intention, they went on board and proceeded down the river. The governor, with a view to enforce the obnoxious impost, hastened to Newcastle, and ordered a watch to be kept for the vessel. On nearing the fort she anchored, when Samuel Preston and Isaac Norris landed, and, informing the commandant of the fort that she was regularly cleared, demanded their right to pass without interruption. This was distinctly refused. Richard Hill now took the helm, and, undaunted by the cannon of the fort, proceeded to pass it. Whilst within range of the guns the firing was kept up, but, excepting a shot through the mainsail, the vessel received no injury. Unwilling to be foiled in his purpose, the commandant now pursued the vessel in an armed boat. As he came alongside, instead of opposing him with force, the crew assisted him to board, but afterwards, immediately cut the boat's rope, which caused it to fall astern. The commandant thus became the easy prisoner of Richard Hill, who proceeded on his way. Evans, who had watched the proceedings, being exasperated, commenced a pursuit in another boat as far as Salem, in New Jersey, where Richard Hill landed and presented his prisoner to Lord Cornbury, the governor of that state. Cornbury, who claimed to be Vice-admiral of the river, was incensed at his conduct, but after severely reprimanding him, and receiving a promise to act differently for the future, he dismissed him, and never afterwards was "powder money," attempted to be exacted from vessels trading to Philadelphia.

It was about this time that Friends of Pennsylvania were much annoyed by the machinations of one Colonel Quarry and his party. Quarry was an Admiralty officer, and a bigoted Episcopalian. He had an inveterate dislike to all democratic forms of government ; and, regarding the passing events of the colony through a prejudiced medium, he was constantly forwarding evil reports of its state and prospects to the Board of Trade, and busied himself, in various ways, to undermine the authority of the proprietary. Not content also, to see those professing with the

Anglican church, on a level with others in regard to religious liberty, he intrigued for sectarian domination. The early settlers were nearly all Friends, and even after the large influx of those of other persuasions, they far outnumbered any other religious sect, and at this period were equal to all the rest in the province. Neither at first, nor at any other time, however, did Friends in Pennsylvania ever attempt to force their religious views on others, nor did they in any way assume the character of a colonial church. The entire recognition of liberty of conscience had attracted men of all shades of religious opinion ; but notwithstanding this diversity of profession, no heart-burnings for ecclesiastical pre-eminence had been exhibited, until the Episcopalians, prompted by their party in England, and by the renegade Keith, their missionary, fruitlessly attempted to procure special and exclusive privileges. One point of Quarry's attack on Friends was relative to oaths ; and by his misrepresentations, he succeeded in obtaining, from the home government, an order for their enforcement on all who did not conscientiously object to them. The effect of this, which no doubt Quarry foresaw, was to disable Friends from acting as magistrates, as they felt restrained from asking others to do that which they themselves believed to be wrong. William Penn blamed Friends for not resisting the order, opposed, as it manifestly was, to their chartered rights and privileges. At length, the Board of Trade was convinced that Quarry's interference proceeded from malicious motives, and they sent him a remonstrance which quieted him.

Besides Evans's attempt to raise a militia, his false alarm, and the affair of the fort at Newcastle, he, in many other respects, did not please the colonists. This was a source of grief to William Penn, who rebuked him severely for his mal-administration. The admonition had a salutary effect, and he began to adopt a policy more in harmony with the pacific views of those over whom he was placed. But his altered conduct came too late. He had lost the confidence of the settlers : in 1707 the Assembly memorialized the proprietary for his removal, and in 1709, he was superseded by Gookin.

Speaking of Gookin, William Penn says, " I have sent a new

governor, of years and experience ; of a quiet, easy temper ;—
the queen very graciously approved of him at first offer."
Gookin had been a military man, but he had left the occupation
of a soldier, and possessed many qualifications for the distinguished post to which he was appointed.

The new governor had not long entered upon the duties of his
responsible office, before he received from the Crown orders to
provide one hundred and fifty men, together with officers, to aid
in an expedition which England had fitted out for the conquest
of Canada.   Anticipating the objection of the Assembly to all
provisions of a military character, Gookin, with a view to meet
it, proposed that four thousand pounds should be voted instead ;
that being the sum needful to raise the force required.   As on
all former applications of the same sort, this also was met by the
Assembly with a decided negative.   " Were it not," said they in
their answer, " that the raising of money to hire men to fight
or kill one another, was matter of conscience to them, and against
their religious principles, they should not be wanting, according
to their abilities, to contribute to those designs."   After some
expressions of loyalty and attachment to the queen, they concluded by saying, that they had resolved to vote a present to her
of five hundred pounds for the general purposes of government,
and not as a military supply.   Gookin, dissatisfied with the
answer, pressed the Assembly to reconsider their decision, and
several messages and answers passed between them.   But
the representatives adhered to their former resolution, and
declared that " they would not agree to the proposal of raising
money, either directly or indirectly, for the expedition to
Canada."†   The governor was vexed at the result and refused
to proceed to any other business ; the Assembly, however, satisfied with having thus borne their religious testimony against war,
quietly adjourned.

At their next meeting the governor renewed his application
with greater urgency ; especially as the danger of incursions was
alarming.   But his entreaties were of no avail.   The Quaker
legislators of Pennsylvania were inflexible.   Their abhorrence of

* Proud, vol. ii. p. 26.   † Ibid. vol. ii. p. 29.

war was founded on its utter repugnance to the spirit and precepts of Christ their Saviour, and they admitted no grounds of mere expediency, as an excuse for violating their conscientious convictions on a matter of so much moment. Excepting an additional sum of three hundred pounds for the Queen, and two hundred for the governor, the Assembly repeated their refusal.

It was about the time of Gookin's appointment, that an unhappy dispute arose between the Council and the Assembly. The origin of the difference may, in great measure, be traced to the turbulent spirit of David Lloyd, a man of considerable ability, a lawyer by profession, and an influential member of the Assembly. Assuming to be the guardian of colonial rights, he ingratiated himself in the favour of the people. But his factious opposition to the government, together with his implacable and ungrateful conduct to William Penn, rendered him undeserving of favourable distinction. James Logan, a leading member of the Council, had been for some years David Lloyd's most powerful opponent; and against him the displeasure of himself and his party was most directed, till at last, articles of impeachment, for an alleged endeavour to deprive the people of their political rights, were preferred against Logan. These charges were ultimately transmitted to England, and Logan having followed, was, after a full hearing, entirely acquitted, "both by Friends and the civil authorities."* He was a man of sterling integrity, of much ability and great learning. Fully appreciating the exalted views and benevolent disposition of William Penn, he was warmly devoted to his interest; in fact his efforts, as secretary, to collect the quit-rents and other proprietary dues, rendered him unpopular among the less scrupulous portion of the colonists; and of this David Lloyd and his associates took advantage, and turned it to their own dishonourable party purpose.

Hitherto Pennsylvania, so far from rendering any pecuniary advantage to its founder, had, on the contrary, entailed upon him a very considerable loss. The dissension caused by David Lloyd and his party, and their endeavours in all possible ways to injure the proprietary rights, was consequently the more keenly felt by

* Proprietary Corresp. in Phil. Friend, vol. xix. p. 210.

William Penn. It evinced a degree of ingratitude, if not of absolute injustice, which he little expected from those whose interests he had sincerely studied ; and at last, in 1710, it called from him a calm and dignified remonstrance. "I cannot but think it hard measure, that while that has proved a land of freedom and flourishing, it should become to me, by whose means it was principally made a country, the cause of grief, trouble, and poverty." "The attacks on my reputation," he continues, "the many indignities put upon me in papers sent over hither, into the hands of those who could not be expected to make the most discreet and charitable use of them ; the secret insinuations against my justice, besides the attempt made upon my estate ; resolves passed in the assemblies for turning my quit-rents, never sold by me, to the support of the government ; my lands entered upon without any regular method ; my manors invaded (under pretence I had not duly surveyed them), and both these by persons principally concerned in these attempts against me here ; a right to my overplus land unjustly claimed by the possessors of the tracts in which they are found ; my private estate continually exhausting for the support of that government both here and there, and no provision made for it by that country ; to all which I cannot but add, the violence that has been particularly shown to my secretary ; of which (though I shall by no means protect him in anything he can be justly charged with, but suffer him to stand or fall by his own actions), I cannot but thus far take notice, that, from all the charges I have seen or heard of against him, I have cause to believe, that had he been as much in opposition to me, as he has been understood to stand for me, he might have met with a milder treatment from his prosecutors ; and to think that any man should be the more exposed there on my account, and, instead of finding favour, meet with enmity for his being engaged in my service, is a melancholy consideration."

In his attacks on Logan, and in his incessant clamours for the interests of the colonists at the expense of the proprietary, David Lloyd veiled the maliciousness of his motives under the plea of promoting the public good ; and he and his party thus artfully obtained many supporters, and indeed, for a short time, they had a majority in the Assembly. "Most of these sticklers in the Assembly," writes Isaac Norris, "are either Keithians, or such as stand loose from Friends, who have other ends than what is penetrated into by some pretty honest, but not knowing men."* But the injustice of their conduct at last became apparent, and before the expostulatory letter of William Penn had reached the province, his friends were thoroughly aroused. Many, whose quiet and retired habits of life led them to avoid political contests, entered warmly into the question at issue. They felt that the honour and integrity of Pennsylvania had been compromised, and at the election of 1710, they flocked to the hustings to redeem its character. "I cannot but take notice," writes Isaac Norris to James Logan, "how universally and resolutely Friends were spirited about this election ; nay, some, from whose cautious or careful temper so much could hardly be expected." The result of the contest was remarkable. Not a single member of the previous Assembly was elected ; the whole were friends of the proprietary ; and instead of bickerings and contention, all was now harmony and peace.

In 1711, Gookin again received a requisition from England, for aid in prosecuting the war in Canada ; and, as before, applied to the Assembly for a war vote. The subject was an unpleasant one to the representatives, and some delay in its consideration took place. Adhering, however, to their principles of peace, they went no further than to grant the sum of two thousand pounds for the Queen's use. "We did not see it," says Isaac Norris, "to be inconsistent with our principles, to give the Queen money, notwithstanding any use she might put it to ; *that* not being our part, but hers." The influence of Friends being predominant in the Assembly, an act was passed in 1712, "to prevent the importation of negroes and Indians into the province."† The object of this humane movement proved unavailing. The home government, more disposed to promote unrighteous gain than to hearken

* Letter of Isaac Norris to Joseph Pike, 18th of Twelfth Month, 1709-10.

† Colonial Records, ii. p. 578.

L

to the cry of the oppressed, negatived the law. In a future chapter this subject will be treated more at large.

Another cause of disturbance in Pennsylvania arose in 1716, through Governor Gookin's perverse policy in reference to affirmations. Some years previously, an act had been passed, which allowed affirmations to be taken by all persons who were scrupulous of taking oaths. This act was superseded by another in 1715, recognising the same principle ; and to this the Governor had given his sanction. Under the plea, that the enactment was adverse to the laws of England, he subsequently undertook to negative it. The consequence was, that Friends were excluded from filling civil offices ; many of them who were judges and magistrates were dismissed, and the whole judicial system became greatly disorganized. These difficulties were increased by Gookin's disagreement with the Council, and by his charges against James Logan, and the Speaker of the Assembly, of disaffection to the Crown — charges which he refused to sustain by any proof. His conduct altogether was, indeed, so unaccountable, that some thought him partially deranged. The result was, that both the Council and Assembly requested his recall ; and in 1717, he was superseded by the appointment of Sir William Keith.

OLD ASSEMBLY HOUSE AND MARKET STREET, PHILADELPHIA.

For some years past the health of William Penn had been gradually declining, and in the summer of 1717, his strength was so greatly reduced, that he could scarcely walk without assistance. In the early part of the following year, his decline was more rapid ; and on the 30th of the Fifth Month, 1718, being then in his seventy-fourth year, he breathed his last.

At the decease of William Penn, the European population of his province is estimated to have numbered not less than 40,000, of whom one-fourth were inhabitants of the city of Philadelphia. The remaining portion of the population were engaged in the cultivation of the soil, and occupied the country for about one hundred miles along the banks of the Delaware, and from twenty to thirty miles west of that river. About one half of the community were Friends;[*] the other religious bodies being chiefly Presbyterians, Lutherans, and Episcopalians. But the differences in religious belief did not interfere with the concord of society, and, without distinction of sect, the colonists appeared to delight in being reciprocally kind and helpful to each other. Throughout they were characterized by a frank and generous hospitality. The tone of moral feeling which prevailed was high, and must have cheered the lovers of truth. The first day of the week was religiously observed ; and, indeed, all who laboured on that day were liable to fines. There were no theatres or dancing-schools ; no pawnbrokers or beggars. Lotteries were forbidden ; and so much regard was paid to integrity and uprightness in trading, that when a colonist failed, which was of rare occurrence, it occasioned much sensation ; " it was a cause of general and deep regret, and every man who met his neighbour, spoke of his chagrin." [†] In the absence of military parade, the martial spirit found no fostering influences ; and so remarkably did the spirit of peace reign throughout Pennsylvania, that during the lifetime of its founder a duel had not disgraced the community.[‡] Profane swearing and drunkenness were punishable by law, and horse-racing and brutal sports were also similarly suppressed. The only

---

[*] Proud, vol. ii. p. 102.　　　　[†] Watson, p. 163.
[‡] Ibid. p. 280.

instrument of authority in the province was the constable's staff; and yet, "never," says Clarkson, "was a government maintained with less internal disturbance, or more decorum and order." * The "holy experiment" of William Penn had, indeed, been successful; and he realized the truth, that the regulation of a state on Christian principles, is eminently conducive to the general happiness of the people.

* Clarkson's Life of Penn.

CHAPTER VII.

CONDUCT OF FRIENDS IN THE GOVERNMENT OF PENNSYLVANIA AND THE JERSEYS.

William Penn's successors—Negotiations with the Crown—Administration of Keith—Act on Affirmations—Keith superseded by Patrick Gordon—Governor Thomas—Causes of the progress of the Colony—Religious equality—Episcopalians aim at Ecclesiastical power—Their success in other Colonies—Friends in England assist in opposing their designs—Efforts of Governor Thomas for warlike measures—London Friends active in opposing his views—Opinion of the Law Officers of the Crown—The power with the Provincial Assembly—Rapid increase of population—Relative position of Friends—England and France at war—Corporation of Philadelphia petitions the Crown for military defences—Franklin raises a Militia—John Churchman's interview with the Assembly—English soldiers arrive at Pennsylvania under Braddock—His disastrous defeat by the French and Indians—Consternation of the Colonists—A war cry is raised—Friends outvoted at the election of 1756—The Government passes from their control—Effects of military scenes and habits on the morals of the people—Remarks on the government of Friends—Government of New Jersey —Life and character of William Penn.

On the decease of William Penn, in 1718, the government of Pennsylvania was claimed by his eldest son William, the issue of his first marriage ; and after the death of this son, in 1720, by his next son, Springett. This was contrary to his will ; for, as the eldest son was amply provided for by a settlement of his mother's, William Penn devised the whole of his property in Pennsylvania, with the exception of 20,000 acres of land, to the children of his wife Hannah Penn, whom he had appointed his sole executrix. In the codicil to his will, he thus expresses himself on the subject :—" As a further testimony of my love to my dear wife, I, of my own mind, give unto her, out of the rents of America, viz., Pennsylvania, three hundred pounds a year, for her natural life, and for her care and charge over my children, in their education, of which she knows my mind ; as also, that I desire they may settle, at least in good part, in America, where I leave them so good an interest, to be for their inheritance from generation to generation, which the Lord preserve and prosper. Amen." * By a decision in Chancery, the will was confirmed ; and the government of Pennsylvania was, consequently, vested in the widow and other trustees, for the benefit of her children ; and thus John, Thomas, and Richard Penn, subsequently became proprietors.

For some years before his decease, William Penn had been in negotiation with the Crown, for the sale of his political power as Governor of Pennsylvania. His pecuniary embarrassments, arising from the unjust claim of his steward, together with the difficulties which he had experienced in administering the affairs of the province, partly from the factious proceedings of David Lloyd and others, and partly from the desire of the home government for the adoption of a military policy, were the chief motives which induced this negotiation. The unfitness of his eldest son to succeed him in the responsibilities of office was, probably, another reason. William Penn was not without strong conflicts of mind in reference to this question. He had founded Pennsylvania on the broad basis of entire liberty of conscience—as a " free colony for all mankind ;" and he had realized the idea, that a state could not only be governed on the principles of the gospel of peace, but that this was, above all others, a policy most conducive to the prosperity and happiness of the people. In his negotiations with the government, he was so anxious to secure the equal religious and political privileges which were enjoyed in his province, that it was several years before the form of contract was concluded upon. In the summer of 1712, he thus writes to some of his friends in America, on the subject :—" Now know, that though I have not actually sold my government to our truly good Queen, yet her able Lord Treasurer and I have agreed to it. But I have taken effectual care that all the laws and privileges I have granted you, shall be

* Proud, vol. ii, p. 116.

observed by the Queen's governors, &c. ; and that we who are Friends, shall be in a more particular manner regarded and treated by the Queen. So that you will not, I hope and believe, have a less interest in the government ; being humble and discreet in your conduct." * At this stage of the business William Penn was seized with paralysis ; and although he had received an instalment of one thousand pounds of the purchase-money, yet as his mind was much affected, the crown lawyers gave it as their opinion, that he was incompetent to complete the surrender ; and consequently the sale was not confirmed.

The administration of Governor Keith commenced auspiciously. He harmonized both with the Council and with the Assembly, and many excellent laws were passed, among which was one for imposing a duty on the importation of negroes ; and another to prevent the sale of rum to the Indians. The former was not enacted for the purpose of revenue, but solely to discourage a sinful traffic, which, but for the veto of the home government, would have been abolished altogether.

During Keith's governorship, an important act was passed, reviving those privileges in reference to affirmations, which had been in 1705, to some extent interfered with, because the penalty for falsely affirming was greater than that imposed by the laws of England for false swearing ; and this, the then Attorney-general, held to be unconstitutional.† Attempts had, on several occasions, been made to meet the difficulty, but without success, until 1725, when an act passed by the Assembly, prescribing the respective forms of a declaration of fidelity, abjuration, and affirmation, obtained the sanction of the crown, and became law.‡ The Meeting for Sufferings in London, at the request of Friends in Pennsylvania, made considerable exertion to procure the royal assent to this measure, and a deputation from the meeting after-

---

* Letter to S. Carpenter, Ed. Shippen, R. Hill, and others, 24th of Fifth Month, 1712.

† Proud, vol. ii. p. 190—State Paper Office. Propr. Board of Trade, Oct. 12, 1704, to Nov. 6, 1706.

‡ Proud, vol. ii. p. 191.

wards waited upon the king to "thank him for the favour."*
The Yearly Meeting of Philadelphia also in the same year forwarded an address to the king, expressive of their gratitude for
his royal confirmation of the act.

Towards the close of 1724, the concord with which the affairs
of the province had been conducted, was again unhappily interrupted. This arose from an attempt on the part of Keith, to
pass laws without the sanction of the Council, contrary to the
terms of his appointment. In this injudicious course he was
supported by the factious David Lloyd, who enlisted the sympathies of the Assembly in the dispute, by persuading them that,
according to their chartered privileges, the Council formed no
part of the legislature. In this opinion Lloyd was probably correct; but as Keith, on taking office, had agreed to consult the
Council before giving his assent to any bill, James Logan, on
the part of the Council and proprietary, insisted on its fulfilment. The governor, however, was obstinate and refused to yield,
and the affair was at length terminated by his being superseded
in his office, by the appointment, in 1726, of Patrick Gordon.

The policy of Governor Gordon was distinguished by much
wisdom and prudence, and during the ten years he held the
important office, the affairs of the province were conducted with
great harmony. On his death in 1736, the executive devolved
on the Council, of which James Logan was president, until the
appointment of Governor George Thomas in 1738.

It was about this time that Andrew Hamilton, on retiring,
by reason of age, as Speaker of the Assembly, made a memorable
speech on the causes of the prosperity of Pennsylvania. "It is
not," he said, "to the fertility of our soil, and the commodious-
ness of our rivers, that we ought chiefly to attribute the great
progress this province has made, within so small a compass of
years, in improvements, wealth, trade, and navigation, and in the
extraordinary increase of the people, who have been drawn hither
from almost every country in Europe;—a progress, which much

* Minutes of the Meeting for Sufferings, Ninth Month, 1724, and
Second Month, 1725. Proud, vol. ii. p. 193.

more ancient settlements on the main of America, cannot, at present, boast of: no, it is principally and almost wholly owing to the excellency of our constitution ; under which we enjoy a greater share both of civil and religious liberty than any of our neighbours." After adverting to their civil and political privileges, he touches on the complete religious toleration recognised by the laws and foundation of the colony ; "Nor are we," he continues, "less happy in the enjoyment of a perfect freedom, as to religion. By many years experience we find, that an equality among religious societies, without distinguishing any one sect with greater privileges than another, is the most effectual method to discourage hypocrisy, promote the practice of the moral virtues, and prevent the plagues and mischiefs that always attend religious squabbling."*

The entire civil equality of all religious denominations in Pennsylvania, which had so much conduced to the happiness of the community, was far from congenial to the hierarchy of England. For many years they had been exerting their power and influence with both the local and home governments, to obtain an ecclesiastical ascendency in the colonies of North America, similar to that which they enjoyed at home. This power they had secured in Virginia from its foundation, and tithes were there regularly imposed ; from which Friends suffered "great havoc" of their goods.†

In 1693, they obtained ecclesiastical authority and power in the colony of New York, where the Assembly in that year passed an act "for settling and maintaining a ministry."‡ So domineering and arbitrary, indeed, had they become in this once tolerant portion of the New World, that a few years later, when Samuel Bownas visited those parts on a gospel mission, he was imprisoned for a whole year on the vague charge of "speaking against the Church of England as by law established."§

In 1700, they induced the once free and catholic province of Maryland, to pass an Act "for the service of Almighty God, and

* Proud's Hist. vol. ii. p. 218.
† MSS. Epistle from Virginia Yearly Meeting, 1727.
‡ Holmes's Annals.   § Life and Travels of Samuel Bownas, p. 70.

establishment of religion according to the Church of England," *
and in 1706, Friends remark in their epistle, "Here the priests'
hire lies hard upon us."† Following up their success, four years
later, the Anglican Church obtained, by an act of the local legislature, a similar ascendency in Carolina.‡ By this time also, they
had erected places of worship in the cities of Philadelphia and
Burlington, and in 1716, the officiating priest of the former,
nothing daunted by the isolation of his position, or by the number
of those around him who were firmly and conscientiously opposed
to all sectarian domination, actually petitioned the Crown to
provide for his maintenance, by directing that a certain amount
be paid him out of the customs on tobacco.§ Having succeeded
in establishing their power in most of the other colonies of
America, they were not easy without assuming a similar dicta-
torial attitude in Pennsylvania, and for this purpose they left no
means untried to undermine the religious and even political
privileges recognised in the province. One of their favourite
objects for this end was, the annexation of the colony to the Crown.
They complained that their clergy had not the same rank and the
same rights as in England. In a land of equals they wished to
be superior, and claimed immunities which the provincial laws
denied them. ||

In 1737, the clergy of Maryland, who were now in the enjoyment of ecclesiastical authority, thought it advisable that another
attempt should be made to extend their power over Pennsylvania.
They therefore addressed the king, and "prayed that a regular
clergy might be encouraged, under royal protection, to reside not
only on the borders, but also in the whole province of Pennsylvania."¶ Friends in England, on behalf of their brethren in
Pennsylvania, closely watched these prelatical attempts, and a

---

* "Annals of America," by Abiel Holmes, vol. i. p. 467—*Vide* also
Trott's Laws Brit. Plant. *art.* Maryland.

† Maryland Epistle.   ‡ Holmes' Annals, vol i. p. 489.

§ State Paper Office. Jenney's Petition, Aug. 31, 1716, Am. and W.
Ind. V. 388.

|| Proprietary Correspondence in Phil. Friend, vols. xviii. and xix. ;
Dixon's Life of Penn.

¶ Min. of the Meeting for Sufferings in London, vol. 26, pp. 366, 460.

Committee of the Meeting for Sufferings in London, was heard before the "Committee of Council," on the injustice and absolute illegality of the request. The result was, that the petition met with no encouragement from the authorities at home ; * and Pennsylvania has remained to this day, one of those favoured spots on earth, unsullied by sectarian domination, and untrammelled by hierarchical oppression.

Governor Thomas is represented as a man of ability, and for some years his administration gave much satisfaction ; but he never appreciated the views of Friends on the subject of peace ; and after the breaking out of the Spanish and French war in 1739, he raised much discontent by pressing for military supplies, and by enlisting indented servants as soldiers.

Not only, however, did the efforts of Governor Thomas for the introduction of warlike measures, meet with the decided opposition of Friends in Pennsylvania, but their brethren in England actively co-operated with them. As early as 1741, the Meeting for Sufferings in London were, at their request, allowed to be heard before the Lords Commissioners for Trade and Plantations upon this subject ; and afterwards, at the suggestion of the latter, they presented a petition to the king in council.† In the course of the same year they were heard a second time before the Board of Trade, &c. ; and in 1743, no less than from thirty to forty of their members appeared before "the Committee of Council," when a petition, "from divers merchants and others, inhabitants of Pennsylvania,"—one from the Meeting for Sufferings on behalf of Friends of Pennsylvania, and one from the agent to the Assembly, were severally presented, and each party was allowed to plead the respective merits of his cause.‡ Though the result of these persevering exertions was favourable to Friends, yet the governor still urged the authorities at home, to take some decided steps to place the province "in a state of defence." The Board of Trade, however, beginning to entertain doubts as to the power of the government to enforce such a proposition, wisely submitted

* Minutes of the Meeting for Sufferings in London, vol. xxvi. p. 460.
† Ibid, vol. xxvii. p. 41.
‡ Ibid, vol. xxvii. p. 333.

the case for the opinion of the legal advisers of the Crown, and in the Eighth Month, 1744, the Attorney-general and Solicitor-general, gave the following joint opinion : "That they have no doubt but that, in point of prudence for their own immediate safety, they are obliged to do everything that is necessary to put that province in a good state of defence, by making such laws as may enable the governor to erect forts and raise soldiers, sufficient to answer that end. But as their Assembly is constituted, and makes part of the legislature there, they are the only immediate judges for themselves of the methods to be taken for that purpose. And they do not see how they can be compelled to do more towards it, than they shall think fit; unless by the force of an Act of Parliament here, which can alone prescribe certain rules for their conduct."*

This important opinion settled the question ; and henceforward, neither Governor Thomas nor his successors attempted to overrule the decisions of the local legislature of Pennsylvania on the subject of war.

Governor Thomas resigned in 1747, and was succeeded by James Hamilton, a man of considerable wealth, who was much esteemed by the colonists.

The population of Pennsylvania by natural increase, but more particularly by immigration, had, during the last thirty years, or since the decease of its founder, nearly trebled. Anderson, in alluding to its rapid growth, states that it contained in 1731, more white inhabitants than all Virginia, Maryland, and both the Carolinas ;† and ten years later, Oldmixon estimates the population at one hundred thousand.‡ In 1729, no less than six thousand two hundred fresh settlers landed at Philadelphia. This rapid influx alarmed the authorities, and in order to discourage it, a tax of five shillings per head was imposed on all "new comers."§ But they soon discovered that such a regulation

* MSS. of the Meeting for Sufferings in London.—Book of Cases, vol. iii. p. 12, and Minutes of ditto, vol. xxvii. p. 472.
† Origin of Commerce, by Adam Anderson, vol. iii. p. 171.
‡ British Empire in America, by Oldmixon, vol. i. p. 304.
§ Ibid. vol. i. pp. 318, 321.

was an unwise one, and after it had existed two years the law was repealed.

The rapid increase of population in the province, did not, however, extend in the same ratio to Friends, and consequently they gradually became as a body relatively less, and at the time of Hamilton's appointment in 1747, they could not have formed more than one third of the population. The anxiety of many of the other settlers, especially in times of apprehended danger, for the establishment of a military force, has already been noticed. On the breaking out of the war in 1739, this feeling was greatly increased, more particularly in Philadelphia, in the corporation of which Friends were in the minority. The Common Council, in fact, in 1744, went so far in direct opposition to the provincial legislature on this subject, as to petition the Crown for a military establishment ; one of their chief arguments being, that the prevalence of Quaker principles "denied them that security which is the main end of society."* By the exertions of English Friends at Whitehall, who were in constant communication with their American brethren on the subject, the efforts of the war party, in this direction, were neutralized. "We think it may not be improper," remark Philadelphia Friends to those in London, on this question, "to inform you that this Council is not composed of the representatives of the citizens."† It was, in fact, a self-elected body, at first composed mostly of Friends, but, "either by carelessness, or negligence in making the choice," many opposed to them in sentiment on military matters were introduced : eventually this class obtained a majority, and took care to maintain it. Yet, though in the majority, they were aware it would be somewhat difficult to succeed in the petition they had prepared. They knew that the lovers of peace had the confidence and esteem of the colonists, both in the city and in the country. But, bent on their purpose, the war party had recourse to unworthy means, and, departing from the usual candid and open manner of conducting the business of the Council, they resorted to secret and underhand dealing. "It is not to be

* Watson's Annals, p. 276.
† MS. Epistle of Philadelphia Quarterly Meeting, 1744.

wondered at," say Philadelphia Friends on this point, "that anything of this kind should be readily agreed to, especially when
the occasion of their meeting was kept secret from those of
different sentiments, of whom there is a considerable number."*

Recruiting for soldiers for foreign service had been privately pursued in Philadelphia for some years, and in 1744, it was actively
renewed for the West India Islands. During the same year also the
citizens for the first time witnessed privateering outfits. These
were things which the provincial legislature, as a dependency of
Great Britain, had no power to restrain. In 1747, great consternation prevailed in Philadelphia, from a rumour that French
privateers intended to attack and sack the city. A meeting of the
citizens was called, and means of defence were resolved upon. To
forward the movement, a Presbyterian minister preached a sermon
on the lawfulness of war, and in favour of the association for defence.
To this Friends published a rejoinder; and, observes Watson, "On
the whole it was a moving and busy time of deep excitement."†
The ingenious Franklin was at this time a citizen of Philadelphia,
and to his perseverance and contrivances, may be attributed the
permanent establishment of a military force. Availing himself of
the lax state of morals, as compared with the earlier times of the
colony, he had recourse to lotteries for raising the needful supplies.
By these means he was enabled to commence the erection of two
batteries on the river; and he "found a way," says James Logan,
"to put the country on raising above one hundred and twenty
companies of militia."‡ Through Franklin's ingenuity a martial
spirit was kindled in the province ; and Governor Hamilton,
hoping that the Assembly would sympathize in the general movement, called upon them to grant money for stationing a vessel
of war at the Capes of Delaware, and to assist in the erection of
the batteries which had been begun. It was at this eventful
period that John Churchman was engaged in visiting the families
of Friends in Philadelphia. He was deeply affected at the state
of things, and felt himself religiously bound to go to the Assembly,

---

* MS. Epistle of Philadelphia Quarterly Meeting, 1744.
† Annals of Phil. p. 274.   ‡ Logan's MSS. in Bancroft.

to warn its members not to depart "from trusting in that Divine arm of power, which had hitherto protected the inhabitants of the land in peace and safety."* Although there was no precedent for the admission of an individual under such circumstances, John Churchman was admitted without hesitation. He began by reminding them of the scripture declaration, that "the powers that be are ordained of God," and that if those who were placed in authority sought to Him for wisdom and counsel, such would be a blessing to their country. But that if, on the other hand, through fear or persuasion, they turned from the Divine counsel, and enacted laws for defence by carnal weapons, the Lord in his anger, by the withdrawal of his protecting arm, might cause those evils which they feared to come suddenly upon them. After alluding to the remarkable manner in which the province had, from its rise, been preserved in peace—that no foreign enemy had invaded it—that their treaties with the Indians had been preserved inviolate, he exhorted the Assembly to trust in the arm of God's power, as their surest defence and safety.† Several members were anxious to adopt the recommendation of the governor; but the majority were Friends, and, true to their gospel principles, they negatived the proposal. Peace having been restored by the treaty of Aix-la-Chapelle, in 1748, the fears of the colonists subsided, and the Quaker legislature of Pennsylvania quietly pursued its non-resisting policy.

Notwithstanding the establishment of peace, considerable jealousy continued still to exist between the Courts of Great Britain and France, in reference to their respective territories in North America. Anxious to extend and fortify their limits, the French colonists in Canada were not unfrequently led into collision with the English, in their exertions for this object; and numerous incidents in America, prognosticated another rupture between the two nations. In 1754, things were still worse, and both countries began to make preparations for a contest. One of the measures adopted by the English was, to order the governors of the several North American colonies to form a political

* Churchman's Journal, p. 96.   † Ibid, p. 96.

confederacy for their mutual defence. In the following year, the contemplated rupture broke out, and the English landed a considerable force in Virginia, under the command of General Braddock, to repel the advances of the French on the frontiers of Pennsylvania.* "The first foreign military," observes Watson, "that ever reached our peaceful city of Brotherly Love, were those arriving and preparing for Braddock's expedition to the west." †

The citizens of Philadelphia had now become somewhat familiar with military parade, and its pomp and splendour had allured many of their young men into its ranks. Their standards were stirring and exciting. "*Deus adjuvat fortes*," or, "God helps the brave," was the motto chosen for one of them; another was, "In God we trust,"—a motto more appropriate, certainly, for the adoption of a people without arms. The proprietaries, Thomas and Richard Penn, also, were not backward to encourage these proceedings. As a proof of their warlike zeal, they presented a considerable number of cannon for the new batteries, which now mounted more than fifty guns.

But amidst all the military fervour that prevailed, Friends still retained their ascendency in the Assembly. The confidence reposed in them by a large number of the settlers who differed from them in religious belief, particularly the Germans, who formed nearly one-third of the community, was unabated; "notwithstanding the greatest industry often used to induce them to the contrary." ‡ It was evident, however, that in this state of things, with a diminishing proportion of numbers, the Society of Friends could not much longer retain their control in the legislature; and among other things which hastened their being overruled was, the abandonment of the non-resisting principle by some of their own body; who were afterwards distinguished by the name of Free Quakers. In 1755, Braddock's disastrous defeat in the west, near the spot where Pittsburg now stands, took place. The degree of excitement which it caused in Pennsylvania, was most intense. It was the first time that the territory of William Penn

---

* Hume and Smollett. † Annals of Phil.
‡ Watson's Annals, p. 492.

had been stained by the blood of the battle-field ; and now that the desolations of war had actually entered the province, the cry for means of defence became loud and overwhelming. Quaker principles were denounced as visionary and absurd ; and, taking advantage of this state of things, the war party, at the election which followed in 1756, carried twenty-four out of the thirty-six representatives which composed the Assembly. * From this date Pennsylvania ceased to be governed in accordance with the principles of the Society of Friends. It was now no longer the Arcadia of peace. The murderous conflicts of Fort Pitt and Bushy Run soon followed ; and within twenty-five years from this time, it had also to record the sanguinary battles of Trenton, Germantown, and Brandywine, and the occupation of the fair city of Philadelphia by troops of British soldiery. But the altered state of things did not stop here. The whole social system of this once favoured community seemed affected by the change. With the presence of armies, its high tone of morality rapidly declined. Theatres were built, and lotteries were encouraged ; duelling was not unfrequent, and brutalizing sports were patronised ; whilst gaming, and cursing, and swearing, became lamentably prevalent.

Turning again to the political state of the province whilst under the rule of Friends, it must be admitted, that notwithstanding the difficulties which occasionally arose, and which, under the best regulated system are ever likely to arise, it was confessedly a triumph of Christian principle. The period from 1682, to 1754, has been called the golden age of Pennsylvania " During the seventy years," writes Clarkson, " while William Penn's principles prevailed, or the Quakers had the principal share in the government, there was no spot on the globe where, number for number, there was so much virtue, or so much true

---

* In the early part of 1756, the bodies of several who had been slain by the Indians on the frontiers, were carried through the streets of Philadelphia, " with an intent," writes John Churchman, " as was supposed, to animate the people to unite in preparations of war. Many people followed, cursing the Indians and also the Quakers."—*Churchman's Journal*, p. 239.

M

happiness, as among the inhabitants of Pennsylvania."* As an example of Christian principles applied in the government of a country, it unquestionably stands without parallel in the history of mankind. While in England the law of triennial parliaments was overruled at the caprice of the sovereign, and while both papists and dissenters were persecuted and disfranchised, in Pennsylvania the inherent rights of the settlers were recognised and protected. Even the enemies of William Penn have unwillingly admitted that his laws were in harmony with, and based on, enlightened reason. "Of all the colonies that ever existed," says professor Ebeling, "none was ever founded on so philanthropic a plan, none was so deeply impressed with the character of its founder, none practised in a greater degree the principles of toleration, liberty and peace, and none rose and flourished more rapidly."† The language of the eloquent Duponceau on this subject is still more striking, and we cannot better close this portion of the history than by introducing it. "Let it not be imagined," he says, "that the annals of Pennsylvania are not sufficiently interesting to call forth the talents of an eloquent historian. It is true, that they exhibit none of those striking events which the vulgar mass of mankind consider as alone worthy of being transmitted to posterity. No ambitious rival warriors occupy the stage, nor are strong emotions excited by the frequent description of scenes of blood, murder and devastation. But what country on earth ever presented such a spectacle as this fortunate commonwealth held out to view for the space of near one hundred years; realizing all that fable ever invented, or poetry ever sang of an imaginary golden age? Happy country! whose unparalleled innocence already communicates to thy history the interest of romance! Should Pennsylvanians hereafter degenerate, they will not need, like the Greeks, a fabulous Arcadia to relieve the mind from the prospect of their crimes and follies, and to redeem their own vices by the fancied virtues of their forefathers. Pennsylvania once realized what never existed before, except in fabled story. Not that her citizens were entirely free

---

* Clarkson's Life of W. Penn, vol. ii. p. 485.
† Hazard's Register, vol. i. p. 340.

from the passions of human nature, for they were men and not angels ; but it is certain that no country on earth ever exhibited such a scene of happiness, innocence, and peace, as was witnessed here during the first century of our social existence."*

As stated in the previous volume, East and West Jersey were colonised under the auspices of Friends, and therefore, some further notice of their political history seems called for. Though by purchase, East Jersey came within the control of Friends, it never, like its sister province of West Jersey, attracted many members of our Society to its soil. The circumstance of Pennsylvania having been founded about the period of its purchase was, probably, one cause of this. At the date of its transfer, East Jersey numbered about five thousand inhabitants. These were mostly Puritans, and for many years after, the new settlers consisted chiefly of Presbyterians from Scotland. In 1682, there were but three small meetings of Friends in the whole of the province, and twenty years later there appears to have been no increase to the number. " The line that divides East and West Jersey," says an eminent writer, " is the line where the influence of the humane Society of Friends is merged in that of Puritanism."†

In West Jersey, Friends constituted the larger portion of the settlers, and for some years they maintained this position. They formed the majority in the Assembly, and the early governors and Council, together with the justices and other civil officers of the province, were mostly chosen from among them; Samuel Jennings, Thomas Ollive, and John Skein, Friends in the station of ministers, were successively its governors. The arbitrary colonial policy of James II. in 1688, threw things into confusion, and under his despotic measures, East Jersey, in common with other English colonies in North America, Pennsylvania only excepted, was, in 1688, deprived of its political power, and by a *quo warranto,* annexed to the province of New York, under the government of Andross.   The freemen of West Jersey were not, however,

---

* Duponceau's Discourse before the American Philo. Soc. 1821.
† Bancroft's Hist. of the United States.

inclined to submit to this unconditional invasion of their privileges, and all that was effected in their case was, a surrender by a council of the proprietaries, not by the people, of " all records relating to government." The Lords of trade held that the domains of the proprietaries might be bought and sold, but disputed their right to exercise the executive power, and for about twelve years from this date, West Jersey was in a state of great unsettlement, during which the government was conducted under proprietary jurisdiction. The Lords of trade, however, still claimed West Jersey as a royal province, and the proprietaries being at last threatened with the interference of Parliament, relinquished the unequal contest, and resigned their pretensions to Queen Anne, in 1702.

On the surrender of the "pretended rights," East and West Jersey were consolidated into one province, and placed under the administration of Lord Cornbury; but no charter was afterwards obtained. The royal commission and instructions to Lord Cornbury constituted its form of government. To the governor appointed by the Crown, with consent of the royal Council, and the representatives of the people, belonged the power of the local legislature. The franchise was a freehold or property qualification. The people had no power as formerly in electing the judiciary; and liberty of conscience was granted to all but papists; but the hierarchy of England, watchful of every opportunity for extending their influence in the New World, seized the occasion, and obtained ecclesiastical power and privileges; the Bishop of London was invested with diocesan control, and, without his sanction, no minister could be preferred to any benefice in the territory. But the restrictive character of the new order of things did not stop here. By the influence of bigotry, the liberty of the press was curtailed, and under the royal instructions, " no book, pamphlet, or other matter whatsoever,"* was allowed to be printed without a license; and worse than this, to please and pander to the cupidity of the African Company, the sinful and debasing traffic in slaves was encouraged, that the province, as stated in

* Smith's Hist. of New Jersey, p. 259.

Cornbury's instructions, "may have a constant and sufficient supply of merchantable negroes."* Provisions of great severity were also made for maintaining a militia, under which, those who had a conscientious scruple against bearing arms, were great sufferers. In truth, a dark day had come over the once free province of New Jersey, and the freemen were not insensible to the unhappy change. The aristocratic policy of the mother country had overtaken them across the wide Atlantic, and instead of enjoying absolute religious freedom, they had now merely toleration ; and to make things worse, Cornbury proved not only an inefficient, but also a self-willed and intolerant governor. In 1688, this province had a population of about ten thousand, and at the date of its transfer to the crown in 1702, it had increased to fifteen thousand. At this period Pennsylvania had a population of about twenty thousand,† but, whilst in the next sixty years New Jersey had advanced to fifty-five thousand, the former province had increased to nearly four-fold that number. But it can excite no surprise that, under its altered circumstances, New Jersey should have lost its attraction as a home, to those who sought the far-famed freedom of the Western World.

That such a character as William Penn should have had many biographers can excite no surprise. His fame may be said to be world-wide, and men of far different sentiments have inscribed his name on the pages of history, as one of the most illustrious of his age—an age, it should be remembered, of stirring events, and conspicuous for men of brilliant attainments. It may, therefore, be superfluous to occupy much space in the present volume, in relating the incidents of a life so well known ; but we shall hardly be doing justice to a history of Friends in America, without including a brief outline of the life of one who was so conspicuously connected with them.

He was the son of Vice-Admiral Sir William Penn, a distinguished commander in the British navy, and was born in London in the Eighth Month, 1644. His father, who cherished

---

* Smith's Hist. of New Jersey, p. 254.   † Holmes's Annals.

the hope of advancing him in the world, gave him a liberal education. While very young he evinced promising talents, and at fifteen, he had made such progress in learning as induced his father to send him to Oxford,* where he "matriculated as a gentleman commoner at Christ Church," and advanced rapidly in his studies. As early as eleven years of age, he experienced, in a remarkable degree, the inshinings of divine light upon his soul, by which he was made inwardly sensible of the "being of a God, and that the soul of man was capable of enjoying communion with him."† He was often drawn, amidst the buoyancy of youth, to a contemplation of divine things, and by the crook of the Heavenly Shepherd, was preserved from the dissipation and wickedness which surrounded him. When about sixteen, he attended a Friends' meeting at Oxford, appointed by Thomas Loe. The living and powerful ministry of this devoted servant of the Lord, made a deep and lasting impression on the mind of William Penn, and excited in him more earnest desires after an experimental knowledge of vital religion. He was now given to see the lifelessness and emptiness of those forms and ceremonies in religion, which so generally prevailed, and, together with some of his fellow-students who were similarly impressed, he withdrew from the established worship of the university, and assembled with them for divine worship. The heads of the college took great offence at this procedure, and the absentees were fined for their non-conformity. These were means not at all calculated to effect a change in the purposes of William Penn. They tended rather to increase his zeal for the principles he had adopted, and continuing to meet with his associates, he was finally expelled the university.‡

The expulsion of William Penn was a severe blow to his father, and when he came home he met with a very cool reception. The society of the fashionable and the gay had now no attractions for him, for his eye had been opened to see the beauty of holiness. The Admiral was not long in perceiving the change that had

---

* Besse, vol. i. p. 1. † Clarkson, vol. i. p. 7
‡ Pepys' Diary, Nov. 2nd, 1662.

taken place, and fearing that the prospects of worldly greatness which he had fondly pictured for his son, would all be blasted if he persisted in the course he had chosen, he endeavoured, by persuasion and entreaty, to alter his purpose. All, however, was in vain, and, unable to appreciate the pure and heavenly motives which influenced his son, he resorted to severity, and drove him from his house.

The harsh measures pursued by the Admiral soon caused him uncomfortable reflections. Though hasty in temper, and accustomed to receive implicit obedience to all his commands, he was, nevertheless, a man of a kind disposition ; he began to relent, and, influenced also by the entreaties of his wife, he soon forgave his son. But the hope of producing a change in the mind of his favourite child was not abandoned, and seeing that sternness failed to effect it, he determined to adopt another expedient. Change of scene and connexions, together with the gaiety of Parisian society, he thought might dissipate the growing seriousness of his mind, and, acting on the idea, he sent him, in 1662, to the continent. After spending some time in brilliant and fashionable society in the French capital, he proceeded to Saumur. Here he studied ecclesiastical literature, and the languages, under Moses Amyrault, one of the most learned and distinguished men in the reformed churches of France. He sequently visited Turin, and returned, after an absence of about two years, to superintend his father's affairs whilst he was at sea.

During his residence abroad William Penn had insensibly acquired a politeness of demeanour : " A most modish person," says Pepys, " grown quite a fine gentleman." His father was delighted at the change, and now spared no pains to introduce him to the drawing-rooms of the great, and the fascinating circles of royalty. It was about this time also that he entered Lincoln's Inn, to acquire a knowledge of the laws of his country. His legal studies occupied him about one year, or until 1665, when he left London on the breaking out of the great plague.

The fashionable appearance and altered air of William Penn, was, however, no true index of the state of his mind. Religious things frequently engaged his attention ; and at times he passed through much spiritual conflict. There is no doubt that the awful visitation of the great plague had a powerful effect on his contemplative mind,* and tended to revive the religious impressions of his earlier years. But whatever the inciting cause may have been, he again sought the company of the grave and the serious. His father, on returning from sea, observed the change with much uneasiness, and again exerted himself to dissipate his religious impressions. He now concluded to send him to the Vice-regal Court of the Duke of Ormond, at Dublin. The scheme proved a failure. His love for the transcendent truths of the gospel had too strong a hold upon him to be shaken by courtly splendours.

Whilst William Penn was in Ireland his father came into possession of Shangarry Castle, and he was sent to take charge of the property. On one of his visits to Cork, he happened to hear that Thomas Loe was there, and intended to hold a meeting. The effect of his ministry at Oxford was still fresh in his remembrance, and he determined to attend the meeting. It was a memorable occasion. Thomas Loe rose with the words, " There is a faith which overcomes the world, and there is a faith which is overcome by the world." On these words he enlarged with great force and clearness ; contrasting the efficacy of that living, purifying faith, which works by love, and enables the Christian to overcome the world and all its allurements, with that formal, dead faith, which consists in a literal knowledge only of divine truths ; and which has ever failed to be proof against the temptations of evil. William Penn was deeply affected. The inward conflicts arising from the strife of natural inclinations with the attractions of heavenly love were alluded to, and, in touching language, the invitation was given to a renunciation of worldly glory, for the more substantial and enduring joys of heaven. No cross, no crown, was, indeed, livingly set before him ; and, bending humbly to the call of his Saviour, he meekly, and yet boldly, declared himself a Quaker.†

There are but few incidents in the history of Friends more

* Journey in Holland, &c.   † Besse, vol. i. p. 3.

interesting than the convincement of William Penn. It took place in 1667, in the twenty-third year of his age, and in a period one of the most remarkable of later times. During the Commonwealth the Society had been persecuted under various pretexts; but it was not until after the Restoration that acts were passed specifically directed against them : the first of these was in 1661, enforcing, under heavy penalties, the oath of allegiance; and soon after this followed the cruel and oppressive Conventicle Act, than which there has rarely been a greater invasion of the rights of conscience, and the true liberties of Englishmen. By these enactments, and the revival of old laws originally designed for the suppression of popery, such a torrent of persecution burst on the Society as has scarcely been known in the history of this nation. At the time William Penn joined Friends, thousands of them were lying in the loathsome, pestilential gaols of the kingdom ;* in which the lives of hundreds of this people had already fallen a sacrifice to Episcopalian reaction and intolerance. At this juncture, Friends were not only a greatly persecuted people, but a greatly despised one also. How great then must have been the sacrifices of William Penn, in the very morning of life, to turn from the dazzling prospects of wealth and honour, and worldly greatness, so alluringly spread before him ; and, in the sure prospect of suffering, to unite himself with a people who were regarded but as a despicable remnant of those fanatics that arose in the days of Puritan power. But he had " seen the King, the Lord of Hosts"—he had seen the beauty of holiness ; and in holy magnanimity of soul he pressed forward, counting nothing too dear to part with, so that he might win Christ.

Imprisonment was very early the experience which the new convert had to realize in the path he had chosen, and that before he left Ireland. By the aid of influential friends, however, he soon obtained a release and returned to England. But here a trial even more severe awaited him. His father, disappointed and incensed at his conduct, expelled him from his home, and turned him away, pennyless, an outcast on the world. In his ex-

* Whiting's Catalogue. p. 171.

tremity he found, as all others have found who have rightly trusted in the Lord, that refuge did not fail him. The Most High by his good Spirit was near to uphold him ; and in the faith and patience of the saints he journeyed forward. In the year following that of his convincement, he came forth in the ministry ; and, richly qualified for the work, he soon became a powerful labourer in the heavenly vineyard. He also became eminent as a writer. His first work was "Truth Exalted ;" written to show the spiritual nature of true religion. Next followed his "Guide Mistaken ;" and then "The Sandy Foundation Shaken ;" both controversial pieces. The latter gave great offence to the dignitaries of the church ; and, at the instance of the Bishop of London, he was arrested and sent to the Tower, under the charge of blasphemy—a charge under which George Fox and others of his contemporaries were not unfrequently incarcerated. William Penn remained nearly nine months * in the Tower. The Bishop of London, indeed, declared that he should either publicly recant or die a prisoner,—a resolve which that intolerant prelate would, doubtless, have carried into effect, had he possessed the power. But the Bishop was ignorant of the character of his prisoner : "My prison," said William Penn, "shall be my grave, before I will budge a jot. They are mistaken in me : I value not their threats. I will weary out their malice. In me they shall all behold a resolution above fear. Neither great nor good things are ever attained without loss and hardship. He that would reap and not labour, must faint with the wind and perish in disappointments."† This was the indomitable language of the youthful prisoner. He soon after wrote his "Innocency with her Open Face," which was issued with a view to correct some misapprehensions as to his religious belief, which had arisen by the publication of his "Sandy Foundation Shaken."

It was whilst he was in the Tower, that William Penn wrote his memorable work, "No Cross, No Crown." This is a composition exhibiting great erudition and research ; and sets forth in a lucid and impressive manner, the necessity of taking up the daily cross

* Penn. Hist. Soc. Mem. vol. iii. part ii. p. 239.
† Besse, vol. i. p. 6.

to the corrupt inclinations of the heart, if we would be partakers of the crown of eternal life. His release from imprisonment took place towards the end of 1669 ; and being now reconciled to his father, he again proceeded to Ireland on his behalf.

The sufferings of Friends in England about this time, were exceedingly severe, arising from a renewal of the Conventicle Act ; the former having expired by efflux of time. This act aimed at the suppression of all religious meetings not conducted " according to the liturgy and practice of the Church of England." William Penn exerted himself to obtain a mitigation of the sufferings of his friends ; but it was not long before he became himself a victim to this persecuting enactment. With William Mead and many others, he was arrested at Gracechurch Street Meeting, and taken by soldiery to Newgate. His memorable trial at the Old Bailey soon followed—a trial which did much for religious liberty in England. William Penn, well read in the history and laws of his country, took an unexpected ground of defence. He boldly declared that the Conventicle Act, though passed by Parliament and sanctioned by the crown, possessed no force, inasmuch as it was opposed to the fundamental rights of the nation, secured under Magna Charta. In the grounds of the argument he was more than a match for the magistrates ; while on the plea in question, he appealed to and was acquitted by the jury, and that too in the face of the most unblushing attempts of the bench to overrule their verdict. The trial was afterwards published by William Penn, under the title of " The People's Ancient and Just Liberties Asserted," &c. ; and is well worthy the perusal of every one interested in the great question of the rights of conscience.

Whilst William Penn was pleading the cause of religious liberty at the Old Bailey, his father was lying on his death-bed. The Admiral had now become fully reconciled to his son ; and not only so, but even commended the principles he had adopted. " Son William," he said, " if you and your friends keep to your plain way of preaching, and also to your plain way of living, you will make an end of the priests to the end of the world." Like many others, this naval hero, when near the confines of eternity, saw things in their true proportions, and felt how infinitely above all worldly considerations was a well grounded hope of salvation : one of his dying exhortations to his son was, " to let nothing in this world tempt him to wrong his conscience." *

On the decease of his father, William Penn came into the possession of large property, and his liberal aid to objects of a charitable nature, evinced how strong was his desire to be a good steward of the trust. The popularity of his memorable trial at the Old Bailey increased the displeasure of the city magistrates, and it was not long ere these persecutors found an opportunity of gratifying their revenge. He was again arrested at a meeting ; but, fearing to proceed against him on the questionable validity of the Conventicle Act, the magistrates took the more sure method of securing his committal by tendering him the oath of allegiance. As they had foreseen, he refused to take the oath, and an incarceration in Newgate followed. During the six months of his imprisonment in this miserable abode, he wrote no less than four important treatises ; these were, " The Great Case of Liberty of Conscience," " Truth rescued from Imposture," " A Postscript to Truth Exalted," and " An Apology for the Quakers."† His " Caveat against Popery," he had published a short time before. Soon after his release, being then in the twenty-eighth year of his age, he was united in marriage with Gulielma Maria, daughter of Sir William Springett.

During the next ten years, or until the settlement of Pennsylvania, he travelled in the work of the gospel in many parts of England, and twice into Holland and Germany : his pen was also frequently engaged in the service of religion. His chief publications during this period were, " The Christian Quaker," " A Treatise on Oaths," " England's Present Interest Considered," " The Cry of the Oppressed," &c., and " An Address to Protestants." He was frequently engaged in controversial disputes, and in interceding with local authorities and the government for his suffering brethren, on whose behalf he was twice heard before a committee of the House of Commons.

* No Cross No Crown.
† Whiting's Catalogue, p. 116.

Soon after his return from Pennsylvania in 1684, he again visited the Continent of Europe on a gospel mission. His influence with James II. was great, and during his reign he was frequently at court, to plead the cause of the suffering non-conformists. It was mainly in consequence of his exertions that a general pardon was at length obtained, liberating a very large number of conscientious sufferers from the gaols of the kingdom, among whom were no less than thirteen hundred Friends. To William Penn's influence with the king is also to be attributed the "Declaration of Indulgence," which was issued by James II. in 1687. Alluding in after years to these services, he says, "I acknowledge I was an instrument to break the jaws of persecution."* Between this period and that of his second visit to Pennsylvania in 1699, it pleased the Most High, in many ways, to prove the faith of this devoted Christian. In 1690, he was arrested on the charge of holding treasonable intercourse with the exiled James II. On this charge he was, at his own desire, heard before King William and the Council, by whom he was honourably acquitted. In a short time, however, through the perjured evidence of a wretched informer, he was again arrested on the same charge. In the year following he was subjected to the crushing disappointment of being deprived of the government of Pennsylvania. Then followed domestic affliction in the loss of his beloved wife, and for a short time, the censure of some of his brethren under misapprehensions relative to his political conduct.† Amidst these accumulated afflictions, William Penn was sustained in firm confidence in God, and realised that his Name was a strong tower, and a shelter from all the storms and tempests of time. "Under and over it all," he writes, "the Ancient Rock has been my shelter and comfort: 'This world passeth away, and the form and beauty of it fadeth;' but there are eternal habitations for the faithful; among whom I pray that my lot may be, rather than among the princes of the earth."‡ These severe trials he was permitted to surmount and to outlive.

* Letter to Friends.   † Clarkson, vol. ii. p. 74.
‡ Letter to T. Lloyd.

It was during these years of trial that he wrote several valuable pieces, among which may be enumerated his " Key " concerning the doctrines of Friends, " Maxims and Reflections," " Rise and Progress of Friends," and " Primitive Christianity ;" all of which have passed through numerous editions in English, and have also been printed in other languages."*

Soon after William Penn's return from his second visit to Pennsylvania, he was brought into much trouble and perplexity by the treacherous conduct of his steward ; who, on an unjust demand of a large amount, had him arrested and imprisoned. The affairs of his province occupied much of his time until 1712, when he was seized with paralysis, which so greatly weakened his constitution, and impaired his memory, as entirely to unfit him for business during the remainder of his life. He lingered for some years in great sweetness and cheerfulness of mind, until 1718 ; when he died, being in the seventy-fourth year of his age.

That William Penn was a man of extraordinary powers of mind, no one acquainted with his writings can doubt, and his whole life proves how strong was his desire for the promotion of righteousness among men. Much, indeed, might be written in his praise. " He abounded," says his intimate friend Thomas Story, " in wisdom, discretion, prudence, love, and tenderness of affection, with all sincerity, above most in this generation ; and, indeed, I never knew his equal."† The present notice of this great and good man may be closed by the beautiful and touching description of his character contained in the testimony issued respecting him by his Monthly Meeting. " He was a man of great abilities ; of an excellent sweetness of disposition ; quick of thought and ready of utterance ; full of the qualifications of true discipleship, even love without dissimulation ; as extensive in charity as comprehensive in knowledge, and to whom malice

* His " Key " has been printed in French, Danish, and Welsh—his " Maxims and Reflections " in French, Dutch, and Danish—his " Rise and Progress " in French, German, Danish, and Welsh, and his " No Cross no Crown " in all of them.

† Story's Journal.

and ingratitude were utter strangers—ready to forgive enemies, and the ungrateful were not excepted.—In fine he was learned without vanity; apt without forwardness; facetious in conversation, yet weighty and serious; of an extraordinary greatness of mind, yet void of the stain of ambition; as free from rigid gravity as he was clear of unseemly levity; a man—a scholar—a friend; a minister surpassing in speculative endowments, whose memorial will be valued by the wise, and blessed with the just."

CHAPTER VIII.

FEW, if any, of the social evils that have afflicted mankind,
are more terrible, or more affecting, than the evil of slavery. In
its most comprehensive meaning, slavery may be simply defined
to be, the absolute and unconditional subjection of one human
being to the will of another, in which state he is recognised in
law as a mere chattel, to be bought and sold as an implement, or
as a beast of the field. That it was ever consistent with the holy
and beneficent designs of his Creator, for man to be reduced to

such a state of degradation, no one, having a just sense of the attributes of the Most High, can suppose. God created man "a living soul." He recognised no distinction in our race; but, as the inspired penman tells us, "made of one blood all nations of men, for to dwell on all the face of the earth." The origin of slavery, like that of its somewhat kindred evil, war, can only be traced to human depravity, violating the laws of God's immutable righteousness. What, but an evil influence, could possibly have prompted the strong, to such an absolute tyranny over the weak? What, but sinful usurpation, could thus dare to outrage and suppress the dearest rights of man's existence?

Like war, slavery also seems to have pervaded every nation of antiquity. In the time of Moses the demoralising practice was almost universal; the whole Israelitish nation, we know, were held in the most cruel and abject bondage. As in the case of other evils which had become interwoven in the social systems of men, the laws of Moses did not aim at once entirely to abolish slavery, so much as to mitigate and restrain the evil, and thus gradually to prepare the way for the introduction of that better day, when, under the light of the glorious gospel of Christ, these enormities would find no place among the children of men.

On the institution of the Christian, as on the institution of the Mosaic dispensation, slavery was equally common, and formed a part of the civil constitution of most countries. It existed, in fact, not only in barbarous nations, but throughout the extensive regions of the Roman Empire; and in the slave-markets of Rome were to be found persons of every complexion and every clime, from the Celtic and Sclavonic, to the Mongolian and Ethiopian races of men.

This was a state of things essentially opposed to the benign nature and scope of the religion of Christ. The New Testament, it is true, does not specifically condemn slavery, but the spirit which it breathes is utterly opposed to oppression, and, in opposition to previous habits of thinking, the Christian religion tended to diffuse ideas and feelings which were entirely subversive of such relations of society, and which would, if allowed to operate, have led to their ultimate and entire extinction. "It does not

N

follow," says Paley, the great moralist, in reference to this sub-ject, "from the silence of Scripture concerning them, that all civil institutions which then prevailed were right; or that the bad should not be exchanged for the better."*

Among the early converts of the church were many who were held in bondage, and respecting whom Polycarp, in writing to the Bishop of Smyrna, says, "Let them not be anxious to be redeemed at the expense of the church, lest they be found slaves of their own lusts."† Great exertions were, nevertheless, made by the early Christians for the release of their brethren held in bondage. "Both religion and humanity," says Cyprian, "make it a duty for us to work for the deliverance of the captive. They are sanctuaries of Jesus Christ, who have fallen into the hands of the infidel.‡" The early Christian emperors, though they did not directly interfere with the institution of slavery, did much to ame-liorate the condition of the slave. This was very strikingly the case among the Saxons in England, soon after they had embraced Christianity. Ina, king of the West Saxons, enacted in 693, that if a slave were compelled to work on a "Sunday," he should become a freeman. About the same period, Withred, king of Kent, decreed that if a master gave freedom to his slave at the altar, his family also should be free; and at a general Synod in 816, it was provided that, at the death of a bishop, every English-man of his, who had been made a slave during his episcopate, should be set at liberty, and that every prelate and abbot should liberate three slaves.§ The renowned Alfred advanced still

* Paley's Moral and Political Philosophy, book iii. chap. iii.
† Neander's Church Hist. vol. i p. 372.
‡ St. Cyprian, to the Bishops of Numidia.
§ The practice of manumitting slaves in the church, appears to have existed from the early part of the fourth century. In the African code of canons, confirmed at a full synod at Carthage in the year 418–19, from which many of the *Excerptions of Egbert* are transcribed, is the following, " No. 64 : And that the manumission of slaves be published in churches, if our fellow-priests in Italy be found to have this practice among them ; and that to this purpose a legate be sent to do all that can be done, for the good of souls and of the Church." "It is certain," says Johnson, in reference to this translation, "that in Italy, and some

further in the good work, and enacted that some particular days should be granted to all slaves, for their own enjoyment and benefit; and, in order to suppress the sinful practice of man-stealing and theft, he made a statute strictly forbidding "the purchase of a man, a horse, or an ox, without a voucher to war-

other parts of the empire, slaves were solemnly set at liberty by their masters in the church and presence of the bishop, from the time of Constantine."

In a copy of the four gospels, in the vulgate version, formerly belonging to the church of "St. Petroc," in Bodmin, in the county of Cornwall, but now deposited in the British Museum, (No. 9381), and which is supposed to be of the ninth century, and by some critics, of a yet earlier date, are records of the manumission of slaves. Some of the entries are written in Anglo-Saxon; but the greater part are in Latin, with a copious intermixture of Saxon letters. The entries (forty-six in number,) seem to be contemporaneous with the manumissions which they record; viz., between the years 940 and 1020. The translation of some of these are as follows :—

No. 1.—These are the names of those persons, Huna and his sister Dolo, whom Byrhtflœd freed for the redemption of his soul, on the altar of St. Petroc, before these witnesses: Leofrie, presbyter; Budda, presbyter; Morhaytho, presbyter; Deni, presbyter; Hresmen, deacon; Custentin, layman; Hurlowen, layman; that they may have their freedom, with their seed for ever; and may he be accursed who shall infringe this liberty.

3.—Budic, Glowmœth, two (whom ?) Uulfsie, the Bishop, freed on the altar of St. Petroc.

12.—These are the names of the men whom the clerks of St. Petroc freed, Sulleisoc, Ousdwythal, for the soul of Eadgar King, on the altar of St Petroc, on the feast of St. Michael, before these witnesses: Byrhsie, presbyter; Osian, presbyter; Austinus, reader; Siol, deacon.

20.—This is the name of that woman, Aelfgyth, Æthaelflœd freed for his soul, and for the soul of his lord Aethelwerd, the duke, on the (cimbalum ?) of St Petroc, in the town which is called Lyscerruyt, [Liskeard] before these witnesses seeing it.

27.—Here be it known in this book, that Aelsig bought a woman named Ongynethel, and her son Gythiecail, from Thurcilde, for half-a-pound, at the church doors, in Bodmin, and gave four-pence, as toll, to Aelsige, the portreve, and to Maccosse, the hundreds' man; then went Aelsig to them that were bought, and took them, and freed them upon Petroc's altar, ever to remain sackless, on the testimony of these good men, [then follow the names of several "mass-priests,"] and whoever rant the sale." * Athelstan, one of the ablest of our Saxon kings, was imbued with sentiments which made a very near approach to the condemnation of slavery. He decreed that, on certain occasions, "some one should be set at liberty, who, for his crimes, had been condemned to slavery ;" and this was to be done, "for the mercies of Christ." "It is necessary," observes the same statute, "that every master be compassionate and condescending to his servants, in the most indulgent manner that is possible. The slave and the freeman are equally dear to the Lord, who bought them, and bought them all with the same price : we are all, of necessity, servants of God, and he will judge us in the same manner, in which we on earth judged them over whom we had a judicial power."† The feelings which prompted our Saxon ancestors thus to mitigate the condition of the slave, led them also by degrees to the increased manumission of those who were held in a state of semi-slavery, as serfs or villeins ; a state which had long existed among the people inhabiting the north of Europe.‡

The progress which anti-slavery feeling made under Saxon rule, in no wise lessened under Norman authority. William the Conqueror enacted, that the residence of a slave for "a year and a day, in any city, burgh, walled town, or castle," without being

this freedom breaks, let the point be settled in common between him and Christ. Amen.

43.—These are the men whom Hulfsige, the bishop, freed for (the benefit of) King Eadgar, and of himself, at Petroc's altar : Leuhelec, Helet, Unwalt, Beli, Josep, Dengel, Proswetel, Tancwuestel, and these are the witnesses [then follow the names, &c].

45.—These are the names of the sons of Hurcon, Aethan, Indhend, Henweothu, Gunuaret, whose sons and grandsons, and all their descendants, defended themselves by an oath, by permission of king Edgar, because their fathers were said, on the accusation of an evil one, to have been villeins (coloni ?) of the King ; Gomoere, bishop [with others] being witness."—*Vide The Bodmin Register, and Gilbert's History of Cornwall.*

* London Encyclo. *art.* Slavery.—*Vide* also Wilkins's Coll. of Laws from Ethelbert to Henry III.

† Ibid.

‡ Hist. of the Anglo-Saxons by Sharon Turner, vol. iv. p. 142.

claimed, should entitle him to liberty. Nor did his legislation for the enslaved stop here. He gave them legal rights, and rescued them from arbitrary bondage. The serfs were not to be deprived of their land, so long as they did the proper service for it, and they were not to be called upon to do any other work than their due service. It was also expressly forbidden for any man to be sold out of the country.*

Notwithstanding the efforts that had been made to suppress trading in the persons of men, it was carried on in some places to a large extent. The cities of Lyons, Hamburg, and Rome, on the continent, and of Bristol in our own island, were notorious for this traffic, particularly the last named, where the citizens sold large numbers whom they had kidnapped, and even their own children, to the Irish people.† Widely as the Christian church had apostatized from its ancient simplicity and purity, it did not allow this sinful practice to pass unnoticed or unreproved. In an ecclesiastical council held in London, in the year 1102, one of the canons thus condemns this violation of the rights of man :—
" Let no one from henceforth presume to carry on that wicked traffic, by which men in England have been hitherto sold like brute animals."‡ Half a century later, we find the church taking, in the person of Pope Alexander III., a yet more decided attitude on this subject, and making the enlightened and important declaration, that " nature having made no slaves, all men have an equal right to liberty ;" and so largely had this opinion been accepted, that at a national synod, convened at Armagh, by the clergy of Ireland, in 1172, it was unanimously agreed, not only to put an end to the nefarious traffic in English slaves, but to emancipate all that were held in bondage throughout the nation.§ The example of the Irish nation was soon followed by that of France. In 1315, Louis X. passed a law enfranchising all serfs belonging to the crown. " Slavery," he declared, " was contrary to nature, which intended that all men

---

* Sharon Turner's History of England, from the Norman Conquest, &c., vol. i. p. 104. *Vide* also Leg. W. Conq. p. 229.

† Ency. Metropolitana, *art.* Slavery.   ‡ Wilkins's Concilia, i. p. 383.

§ Moore's Hist. of Ireland.

by birth should be free and equal."*   These are noble instances of conscientious action, which, contrasted with much that was gloomy and vicious in that age, shine forth with peculiar lustre.

Wycliffe, who has been justly called the morning star of the Reformation, was not behind the ecclesiastical authorities of his day in declaring his abhorrence of slavery.   This great and good man, with other enlightened views, declared that it was contrary to the principles of the Christian religion that any one should be a slave.

The wars that took place between the professors of Christianity and the followers of Mahomet operated unhappily for mankind and for the cause of true religion ; since to the frenzied zeal of Peter the Hermit, may be mainly traced the African bondage of the present day.   But for the Crusades, there is, in fact, great reason to believe that before the discovery of the western world, the benign spirit of the Christian religion would have led, at least, to the entire abolition of slavery in Christendom.   Already had its principal slave-markets been broken up, and the voice of enlightened reason was fast demanding the emancipation of the serfs ; but bigotry, alike impervious to reason and to justice, intervened, and circumscribed the bounds of humanity.   Mahommedanism, whilst it pandered to the sensuality of human nature, denounced the enslavement of the faithful, and no Mussulman dared to hold a Mussulman in bondage ; but the enslavement of the heretic was deemed right and just.   With the Saracen, therefore, the captive Christian had no alternative but servitude, or the profession of the Koran ; and, in retaliation, Christians enslaved the Turks.   The number of Saracens sold into Christian bondage, is said to have exceeded the number of all the Christians ever sold by the pirates of Barbary.   The clergy, who had pleaded successfully for the Christian slave, were deaf to the cries of the unbeliever.   The final victory of the Spaniards over the Moors of Granada, — an event contemporary with the discovery of America, drove the Moors, after dreadful sufferings, to the coasts of northern Africa, where each mercantile depôt became a nest of pirates, and every Christian the wonted booty of the corsair.

* Koch's Revolutions of Europe, chap. v.

Bondage thus befel the European in northern Africa, and an indiscriminate retaliation without remorse doomed the sons of Africa to bondage ; and hence the origin of negro slavery among Christians.

For centuries before, the Moors had trafficked in gold dust and slaves with central Africa; but to Antonio Gonzalez, a Portuguese, belongs the unenviable notoriety of being the first to introduce the negro race to European bondage.   Having, in a predatory excursion on the coast of Africa, in 1440, captured some Moorish persons, he was commanded to restore them.   He did so, and received in exchange ten " black Moors," with curled hair.* Mercantile cupidity and avarice was not slow to perceive that the negro race might become an object of profitable commerce.   Spain soon followed her neighbour in the odious trade, and years before Columbus sailed on his western expedition, the merchants of Seville and Portugal imported gold dust and slaves from the western coast of Africa.

The profit which resulted to the Peninsular adventurers by their kidnapping expeditions to the coasts of Africa, led the early discoverers of America to follow their example, and hence the atrocities of Cortereal, Soto, and others, in capturing the Indians. Columbus himself sent no less than five hundred of them to be publicly sold at Seville.†   But the Indians, though strong and robust, and hardy in the chase, did not thrive under domestic slavery, and disappeared rapidly before the oppressions of the white man. The negroes, however, were better fitted for labour in a tropical climate ; it was said that one negro could do the work of four Indians, and in 1503, considerable numbers of them were sent to the mines of Hispaniola.   The scheme appears to have been a profitable one, and the enslavement of the negro race extended rapidly.   In 1511, a royal ordinance of Ferdinand V. of Spain, encouraged a direct traffic in slaves between Guinea and Hispaniola ; and in 1517, the Emperor Charles V. granted a patent for the exclusive supply of no less than four thousand annually for the West Indies, to be employed chiefly in agriculture.

* Ency. Brit. *art.* Slavery.   † Irving's Columbus.

The rapid development of this atrocious system, under the fostering influences of Spanish and Portuguese avarice and cruelty, did not pass without strong and decided censure. It was emphatically denounced by the highest authorities in the church, and at times by the most powerful men in the state. Pope Leo X. declared against it in a very early stage of its existence, and he did so under somewhat extraordinary circumstances. The Dominicans, who witnessed the horrors of this cruel bondage, held that it was utterly repugnant to the gospel, and pleaded for its entire abolition. The Franciscans, another order of the Romish church, took a different view, and eventually an appeal was made by the contending parties, to the pope, as head of the church. This was in 1513. His reply was a memorable one. " Not only the Christian religion, but nature herself, cries out against a state of slavery."* Leo X. was one of the most learned of the popes, and, doubtless, was fully aware that, mainly by the voice of the church, slavery had been extinguished in western Europe. It is true his life was a voluptuous one, and his unceasing attempts to promote ecclesiastical power might have deadened his feelings of humanity; but he was not so entirely lost to the requisitions of Christian duty as to sanction negro slavery. Yet, strong as was the opinion of Pope Leo X., the opinion of Paul III., about twenty years later, was still stronger. In two separate briefs he imprecated a curse on any Europeans who should enslave the Indians or any other class of men.† The slave-trade between Africa and America was never, it is believed, expressly sanctioned by the see of Rome.

These noble sentiments of the church dignitaries at Rome, met with a hearty response from Francis Ximenes de Cisneros, a Spanish Cardinal of great learning and eminence. On the death of Ferdinand he was appointed Regent until Charles V. became of age. He had, in the lifetime of Ferdinand, strenuously endeavoured to check the progress of slavery; and, during his regency, his efforts to this purpose were still more earnest. When

---

* Clarkson's Hist. of the Abolition of the Slave-trade, vol. i. p. 39.
† *Vide* the Brief in Remesal. Hist. de Chiappa, quoted in Bancroft's United States.

Las Casas, a missionary in America, and bishop of Chiappa, applied, in 1516, for liberty to establish a regular trade in African negroes, in order to relieve the Indians, who were fast disappearing under the oppression of their conquerors, Cisneros, true to his enlightened principles, refused the request. Not only did he do much to restrain this evil, but he also spent a large portion of his enormous income in ransoming captives from Africa, and he may be justly regarded as the earliest man of eminence who sought the extinction of negro slavery.

On the death of Cisneros, in 1517, Charles V., Emperor of Germany and Sovereign of the Netherlands, ascended the Spanish throne. He was then only in his eighteenth year, and it was at this period that, in order to gratify one of his Flemish favourites, he granted the exclusive right of supplying his West India possessions with four thousand slaves annually. Charles V. was altogether an extraordinary monarch, and though he devoted himself closely to the affairs of his extensive dominions, yet he visited Spain but six times during his reign, and when the patent in question was granted, he was, doubtless, ignorant of the cruelties of this nefarious traffic. As time passed on, however, he became better acquainted with its true character, and embraced more enlightened views on the subject; and at length, in 1542, he astounded his avaricious courtiers, by at once suppressing the African slave-trade, and by manumitting all the slaves in his western dominions, sending Pedro de la Gasca to enforce the order. His health having become much impaired, Charles V. in 1556 resigned his crown to his son Philip, and retired to a monastery. Gasca, the minister of his mercy, soon after returned to Spain, when the tyrant authorities of the west, unchecked probably, by Philip, resumed their former cruelties, and again reduced the African to bondage.

The immediate and unconditional emancipation of all the slaves in the Spanish dominions was a circumstance of no ordinary character. For nearly forty years the traffic in slaves had been steadily progressing, and at the time of the humane edict, their number must have been very considerable. It is probable that the declarations of Pope Leo X. in 1513, and of

Paul III., only five years before the decree was issued by Charles V., together with the Christian example of Cardinal Cisneros, did much to strengthen the good resolutions of the Spanish monarch ; but, whether strengthened in this direction, or by his own growing conviction of the sinfulness of the system, we cannot question that in thus, at one stroke, annihilating a lucrative traffic, and also a large property which the law recognised in the persons of men, he must have had no inconsiderable amount of opposition to encounter.   This transaction of Charles V., and the analogous one of the Irish nation in 1172, are among the most striking instances of humanity in the history of the world.

For the first hundred years after Spain had engaged in negro slavery, she was at the height of her national greatness, and her powerful fleets made her mistress of the seas.   By the close of the sixteenth century, however, the Dutch and English nations had greatly progressed in naval power, and it was no uncommon thing for some of their bold adventurers to roam the ocean in quest of new discoveries and fresh sources of gain.   One of these was Sir John Hawkins, whose youth was spent in trading to Spain and Portugal.   The wealth amassed by the African slave-trade, had then become notorious, and kindled in his daring mind a desire to share in the guilty enterprise.   Having procured the assistance of some London merchants, in 1562, he fitted out a small squadron, and kidnapped, on the coast of Guinea, three hundred negroes, whom he sold to the planters of Hispaniola. Queen Elizabeth, though anxious to extend her maritime trade, at first revolted at the idea of her people being engaged in this traffic, and on the return of Hawkins she sent for him, and expressed her fear lest any of the negroes had been carried off without their free consent, declaring that, " It would be detestable, and call down the vengeance of heaven upon the undertakers."* But Hawkins deceived the Queen, and notwithstanding her injunctions, he himself relates that, on one occasion, he set fire to a city having eight thousand inhabitants, and that he suc-ceeded in capturing two hundred and fifty of them.†   These

---

* Clarkson, vol. i. p. 40.   † Hakluyt, vol. iii. p. 618.

adventures were the first instance of Englishmen engaging in the inhuman system of the African slave-trade, a trade which Europe now stigmatizes as piracy. It is somewhat remarkable that the crest granted to this violator of the laws of God and man, was the expressive one of "a demi-moor in his proper colour, bound with a cord."*

The first permanent settlement of the English in America took place nearly fifty years after Hawkins commenced his wicked career. This was the colony of Virginia, founded in 1607. But so slowly did the colony advance, that in 1660, it numbered no more than ten thousand inhabitants, of whom not more than three hundred and fifty were blacks. The commerce of the plantation was at first monopolized by the company who founded it ; but in 1620, it was declared open to free competition. At this period the Dutch also had sullied their national character by a participation in the African slave-trade; and on the adoption of the free-trade principle by the Virginians, a Dutch man-of-war entered James's River, and offered twenty negroes for sale. The demand for labourers in the colony was pressing, and already had the planters become familiar with a sort of semi-slavery, by receiving indented servants from England, who, on their arrival, were sold to the highest bidder. The Dutch speculation was, unhappily, a successful one ; and thus commenced the gigantic evil of negro slavery in North America.

The year in which Virginia became a market for Africans, was the year of Puritan settlement in Massachusetts, and to the praise of those zealous reformers it must be recorded, that they at once bore a decided and uncompromising testimony against slavery. They enacted that, except in the case of prisoners of war, "no man should buy or sell any slaves ; nor any person be subject to slavery, villeinage, or captivity." The Pilgrim Fathers were successful colonists, and Boston, their capital, took the lead among the commercial entrepots of the western world. In 1645, two of its citizens, allured by the lucrative character of the trade, then mostly in the hands of the Dutch, sailed "for Guinea to

* Life of Hawkins, in Penny Encyclo.

trade for negroes." * As soon as the speculation became known, it produced an excitement throughout Massachusetts. The two traders were denounced by the people as malefactors and murderers. The authorities characterized it as " expressly contrary to the law of God and the law of the country," and the guilty men were committed for the crime. † Of so much importance was this matter considered, that the representatives of the people were convened ; who, after a consultation with the elders of the church, bore a further "witness against the crime of man-stealing," by ordering the negroes to be restored at the public charge "to their native country, with a letter expressing the indignation of the General Court " at their wrongs. ‡ To prevent a recurrence of this crime, the slave-trade was forbidden by the Puritan authorities, under penalty of death. §

The next European settlement in America was New Netherlands, (now New York,) founded by the Dutch in 1625. In the very next year, the merchants of Amsterdam landed negroes on Manhattan, and New Amsterdam became a slave mart ; for the prosperity of which, Dutch cupidity instructed Stuyvesant the governor, to use every effort.|| Maryland was settled a few years after, and, like Virginia, was also polluted with slaves ; but not so much at first with negroes as with whites under sentence. In the same year the enlightened Roger Williams founded Rhode Island ; and, perceiving a disposition in some of the settlers "to buy negroes " and " hold them as slaves for ever," he subsequently enacted that "no black mankind" should be held in perpetual bondage, but that " at the end of ten years the master should set them free, as the manner is with English servants." The liberties of blacks and whites were equally dear to Roger Williams. Carolina was settled by charter in 1667 ; and Locke, in framing its "constitutions," gave the freeman absolute power and authority over his negro slave." A portion of this territory had been

* Winthrop, vol. ii. p. 243.

† Colonial Records, iii. 45, in Bancroft.   ‡ Ibid. c. xii.

§ The words of the law are, " If any man stealeth a man, or mankind he shall be put to death."

|| Albany Records, iv. 371.

previously occupied by Sir John Yeamans, a needy baronet and Barbadoes planter, who brought over a number of Africans with him.   From its commencement, therefore, Carolina appears not to have been exempt from the crime of slavery.   On its conquest by the English in 1664, New Netherlands was dismembered.   James, Duke of York, obtained the larger portion, whilst the country afterwards called New Jersey was assigned to Berkeley and Carteret. The Duke of York was then President of the African Company, and, as such, a patron of the slave-trade : Berkeley and Carteret, as Carolinean proprietors, and already conversant with the system, promoted it in their new domains, and offered a bounty of seventy-five acres for the importation of every able-bodied slave.   New Hampshire and Connecticut, being colonized by emigrants from Massachusetts, bore a noble testimony against African bondage ; whilst Delaware, under Dutch auspices, maintained opposite views.

At the time, therefore, when William Penn founded Pennsylvania, the negro race were held in bondage in every colony south of Rhode Island, though not in large numbers.   In Virginia, where they were most numerous, they did not, even thirty years after their introduction, form more than one in thirty of the inhabitants : it is questionable, indeed, whether the negroes at that time were more numerous than the whites who were held in bondage for crime, or under covenant for a term of years to defray the cost of emigration.   In England, the evil of negro slavery, before the rise of our religious Society, seems to have attracted but little attention ; and down to the close of the seventeenth century, very few, excepting Friends, had raised their voices against its atrocities.   Godwyn, a clergyman who had been an eye-witness of its cruelties in Barbadoes ; Bishop Sanderson ; Baxter, the noted nonconformist ; and our great poet, Milton ; were the most conspicuous on the anti-slavery side.

The first time that George Fox witnessed men in slavery, was during his visit to Barbadoes, in 1671.   On that island, as well as in some other parts of the West Indies, many who had been brought up in the practice of holding slaves, joined our religious Society ; and it does not appear that at first their views on the subject underwent much change.   George Fox, however,

boldly proclaimed to them the sinfulness of a traffic in men; "Consider with yourselves," he says; "if you were in the same condition as the poor Africans are—who come strangers to you, and were sold to you as slaves. I say, if this should be the condition of you or yours, you would think it a hard measure; yea, and very great bondage and cruelty." Alluding, in his journal, to the counsel which he gave Friends in Barbadoes, he says, "I desired also, that they would cause their overseers to deal mildly and gently with their negroes, and not to use cruelty towards them, as the manner of some had been; and that after certain years of servitude, they should make them free." During his stay on the island he had many meetings with the negroes. This was obnoxious to the ruling planters, some of whom maliciously raised an outcry that he was "endeavouring to make the negroes rebel," which, he promptly observed, was a "wretched slander." *
William Edmundson accompanied George Fox to Barbadoes; and he, too, reprobated slavery. On a subsequent visit to the island, in 1675, he mentions having "negroes' meetings in families," and that "several meetings were settled on such accounts." For these gospel labours he was brought before the governor on a charge of "making the negroes Christians, and [that he] would make them rebel." † It appears to have been during this second visit to the western world, that he addressed an epistle to Friends of Maryland, Virginia, and other parts of America, containing some strong remarks on the wickedness of the system. "Truth," he writes, "must regulate all wrongs and wrong dealings."

The evil of slavery, it is evident, was seen by some of the most eminent of our early Friends; and it appears, by a provision which William Penn made with the "Free Society of Traders," that he participated in the feeling, and, like George Fox and William Edmundson, would, after the lapse of a few years, have set the bondmen free. "If the Society should receive blacks for servants," it was agreed "that they shall make them free at fourteen years, and upon condition that they will give unto the Society's warehouse two-thirds of what they are capable of pro-

* Journal of George Fox.   † Journal of W. Edmundson.

ducing on such a parcel of land as shall be allotted to them by the Society, with a stock and necessary tools."* During the early progress of Pennsylvania and the Jerseys, many of the settlers had lands, but were not supplied with labourers, as in the mother country; and in many instances, families were without servants. By English law, the African Company had the monopoly, and also the right, of importing slaves into the North American colonies, and no power, as hereafter will be shown, rested with William Penn, or the legislature of his province, to prevent it. The colonists were also in great ignorance of the cruelties employed in procuring the negroes; and, with other humane and pious persons, Friends in America fell into the practice of keeping slaves.

But although, under their peculiar circumstances, the Society of Friends in America were thus drawn to sanction the system of slavery, their conduct towards the negro differed widely from the general practice. Not only were their slaves treated with much care and kindness, but great pains were also taken for their moral and religious culture. No flogging-houses, no branding nor spiked collars, were allowed by them—no harrowing severance of husband and wife, and of parents from children. They at least sanctioned no law to keep them in ignorance of divine things; no unholy daring prompted them to interpose between God and the souls of men; and far less did they inflict punishment on the poor slave for "the sin of praying!" † So different, indeed, was the conduct of Friends from that of most others towards their slaves, that in the West India islands it excited alarm and jealousy among the planters, and gave rise to persecution. Recognising the negroes as equal objects of our heavenly Father's regard with

* Watson's Annals, 480.

† In most of the slave states, laws are enacted to prevent slaves from being taught to read; and Bible Societies do not distribute the Scriptures among them, because it is prohibited, and because slaves are generally unable to read. "We have, as far as possible," said one of the members of the House of Delegates of Virginia, "closed every avenue by which light might enter their minds. If we could extinguish the capacity to see the light, our work would be completed; they would then be on a level with the beasts of the field, and we should be safe! I am not certain that we should not do it, if we could find out the process, and that on the plea of necessity."—*Goodell's American Slave Code*, p. 301.

themselves, Friends were anxious to bring them to a knowledge of that glorious redemption which is in Christ Jesus our Lord, and invited them to their religious assemblies. But so opposed were the authorities to this attempt to impart religious truth to these poor oppressed people, that in Barbadoes they actually passed an Act, in 1676, "to prevent the people called Quakers from bringing negroes to their meetings," &c.* It was under this Act that Ralph Fretwell and Richard Sutton—the former of whom had been one of the chief judges in the island†—were severally fined in the sum of eight hundred pounds and three hundred pounds, for having negro meetings at their houses.‡ In 1680, the Governor of Barbadoes interdicted Friends' meetings altogether; but his edict, not being founded on any act or statute, was extra-judicial, and of no force. In Nevis, Friends were, after a time, prohibited from coming on shore; and negroes were placed in irons for attending their meetings. In 1671, William Edmundson and Thomas Briggs were both prevented from landing there; § and in 1677, masters of vessels who brought them were subjected to heavy penalties. Similar proceedings were also adopted in Antigua; "and the poor slave," remarks Clarkson, "who saw nothing but misery in his temporal prospects, was deprived of the only balm which could have soothed his sorrow—the comfort of religion." ‖

But even in the primitive days of Pennsylvania, and with slavery under its mildest form, some of its citizens were favoured with clear views on this important subject. The most prominent of these were Friends of Germantown, emigrants from Kreisheim, in Germany. These unsophisticated vine-dressers and corn-growers from the Palatinate of the Upper Rhine, the converts of the devoted William Ames, revolted at the idea of good men buying and selling human beings, heirs with themselves of immortality. Faithful to their convictions, they at once bore an uncompromising testimony against the evil, and, as early as the year 1688, prepared an address to their Monthly Meeting on the subject. Their reasoning was strong and cogent, and evinced

* Besse's Sufferings, vol. ii. p. 308.   † Ibid, vol. ii. 291.
‡ Ibid, vol. ii. 309 and 311.   § Journal of W. Edmundson.
‖ Clarkson, vol. i. p. 135.

not only a clear appreciation of the inalienable rights of man, but also of the humanizing tendency of the religion of Christ. The Monthly Meeting appears to have been impressed with the truths laid before it ; but the subject being new to many of the members, and containing as it did, an unqualified condemnation of man holding a property in man, in which so many of their brethren in other parts were involved. it was agreed to refer it to the attention of the Quarterly Meeting. But this meeting also hesitated to pronounce an opinion. The subject, they said, was of " too great weight for them to determine," and it was sent on to the Yearly Meeting. To this meeting the subject was equally new, and, without disputing the important and decided position taken by Friends of Germantown, it came at that time to no specific judgment on the matter. The following was the record made on the occasion :—" A paper was presented by some German Friends concerning the lawfulness and unlawfulness of buying and keeping negroes ; it was adjudged not to be so proper for this meeting to give a positive judgment in the case, it having so general a relation to many other parts, and therefore at present they forbear it."*

* The German Friends arrived at Philadelphia in the Sixth Month, 1683. They settled near together, and, in 1686, were joined by a number from different parts of Holland and Germany. Some few years since, it was supposed that the address of these Friends to their Monthly Meeting above alluded to was lost ; but in 1844 it was discovered, and printed in the *Philadelphia Friend* for that year, from which it is here copied entire.

This is to the Monthly Meeting held at Richard Worrell's.

These are the reasons why we are against the traffic in the bodies of men, as followeth :—Is there any that would be done or handled in this manner [themselves] ? viz., to be sold or made a slave for all the time of his life ? How fearful and faint-hearted are many on the sea when they see a strange vessel, being afraid it should be a Turk, and they should be taken, and sold for slaves into Turkey. Now what is this better than Turks do ? Yea, rather is it worse for them, which say they are Christians ; for we hear that the most part of such negroes are brought hither against their will and consent, and that many of them are stolen. Now, though they are black, we cannot conceive there is

The discussion of the views enunciated by Friends of Germantown, was not without effect : in a few years we find Friends in
other parts of Pennsylvania expressing similar sentiments.   " I
have seen," says Watson, " among the earliest pamphlets extant

more liberty to have them slaves, than it is to have other white ones.
There is a saying, that we should do to all men, like as we would be done
[unto] ourselves ; making no difference of what generation, descent, or
colour they are.   And those who steal and rob men, and those who buy
or purchase them, are they not all alike ? There is liberty of conscience
here, which is right and reasonable ; and there ought to be likewise
liberty of the body, except of evil doers, which is another case.   But to
bring men hither, or to rob and sell them against their will, we stand
against.   In Europe there are many oppressed for conscience sake ; and
here there are those oppressed which are of a black colour.   And we
who know that men must not commit adultery—(some do commit
adultery *in* others, separating wives from their husbands and giving
them to others ; and some sell the children of these poor creatures to
other men).   Ah ! do consider well this thing, you who do it, if you
would be done [unto] in this manner ? and if it is done according to
Christianity ? You surpass Holland and Germany in this thing.   This
makes an ill report in all those countries of Europe, where they hear
of it, that the Quakers do here handle men as they handle there the
cattle.   And for that reason some have no mind or inclination to come
hither.   And who shall maintain this your cause, or plead for it ? Truly
we cannot do so, except you shall inform us better hereof, viz., that
Christians have liberty to practise these things.   Pray, what thing in
the world can be done worse towards us, than if men should rob or steal
us away, and sell us for slaves to strange countries ; separating husbands
from their wives and children.   Now this is not done in the manner we
would be done by, therefore we contradict and are against this traffic
in the bodies of men.   And we who profess that it is not lawful to steal,
must, likewise, avoid purchasing such things as are stolen, but rather
help to stop this robbing and stealing, if possible.   And such men ought
to be delivered out of the hands of the robbers, and set free, as in
Europe.*   Then would Pennsylvania have a good report ; instead
[whereof] it hath now a bad one for this sake in other countries.
Especially as the Europeans are desirous to know in what manner the
Quakers do rule in their province ; and most of them do look upon us
with an envious eye.   But if this is done well, what shall we say is done
evil ?
    If once these slaves (which they say are so wicked and stubborn)

_____

    * Alluding probably to the abolition of the old feudal system.

of Philadelphia publication, one from the Friends' Meeting of Philadelphia of the 13th of Eighth Month, 1693, giving 'exhortation and caution to Friends concerning buying and keeping negroes.' The sum of the counsel was, that none should attempt 'to buy except to set free.' "* Three years later the

should join themselves [together], fight for their freedom, and handle their masters and mistresses as they did handle them before ; will these masters and mistresses take the sword and war against these poor slaves, like, we are able to believe, some will not refuse to do ? Or have these negroes not as much right to fight for their freedom, as you have to keep them slaves ?

Now consider well this thing, if it is good or bad ? And in case you find it to be good to handle these blacks in that manner, we desire and require you hereby lovingly, that you may inform us herein, which at this time never was done, viz., that Christians have such a liberty to do so. To the end we may be satisfied on this point, and satisfy likewise our good friends and acquaintances in our native country, to whom it is a terror, or fearful thing, that men should be handled so in Pennsylvania.

This is from our meeting at Germantown, held the 18th of the Second Month, 1688, to be delivered to the Monthly Meeting at Richard Worrell's.

GARRETT HENDERICK.
DERICK UP DE-GRAEFF.
FRANCIS DANIEL PASTORIUS.
ABRAHAM JR. DEN GRAEF.

At our Monthly Meeting at Dublin, the 30th of Second Month, 1688, ·we having inspected the matter above mentioned, and considered of it, we find it so weighty that we think it not expedient for us to meddle with it here, but do rather commit it to the consideration of the Quarterly Meeting ; the tenor of it being nearly related to the truth.

Signed on behalf of the Monthly Meeting,

Jo. HART.

This, above mentioned, was read in our Quarterly Meeting, at Philadelphia, the 4th of the Fourth Month, 1688, and was from thence recommended to the Yearly Meeting ; and the abovesaid Derick, and the others mentioned therein, to present the same to the above said Meeting, it being a thing of too great a weight for this Meeting to determine.

Signed by order of the Meeting,

ANTHONY MORRIS.

* Watson's Annals, p. 480.

subject had made so much progress, that at the Yearly Meeting of 1696, it was again brought under consideration, when it was agreed to issue the following advice : " Whereas, several papers have been read relating to the keeping and bringing in of negroes ; which being duly considered, it is the advice of this meeting that Friends be careful not to encourage the bringing in of any more negroes ; and that such that have negroes, be careful of them, bring them to meetings, have meetings with them in their families, and restrain them from loose and lewd living as much as in them lies, and from rambling abroad on First-days or other times."

William Penn deeply lamented the state of degradation to which the African race had been reduced by the wrongs and cruelties of their bondage, and was anxious to raise them in the scale of society, and in no more effectual way did he consider this could be accomplished, than by bringing them under the influence of religion. In the First Month of 1700, during his second visit to America, he brought the subject before the Monthly Meeting of Philadelphia. " His mind," he said, " had long been engaged for the benefit and welfare of the negroes,"* and he exhorted and pressed his brethren, to a full discharge of their duty in every way regarding them, more especially in reference to their mental and religious improvement. The Monthly Meeting was not backward in responding to the humane feelings of the governor, and it was concluded, once in every month to hold a meeting for worship specially for the negro race. The following was the minute made on the occasion : " Our dear friend and governor, having laid before this meeting a concern, that hath laid upon his mind for some time, concerning the negroes and Indians, that Friends ought to be very careful in discharging a good conscience towards them in all respects, but more especially for the good of their souls ; and that they might, as frequent as may be, come to meetings upon First-days ; upon consideration whereof, this meeting concludes to appoint a meeting for the negroes, to be kept once a month, &c., and that

* Proud, vol. i. p. 423.

their masters give notice thereof in their own families, and be present with them at the said meetings as frequent as may be."*

The attention of William Penn was next directed to an improvement in their social condition, and for this purpose, with the full sanction of the Colonial Council, he introduced into the Assembly two bills. The first provided for a better regulation of the morals and marriages of the negroes, and the second, for the modes of their trial and punishment in cases of offence. There existed at that time, a considerable degree of jealousy on the subject, and the first was rejected.† But it was evident that a feeling adverse to slavery, was gradually gaining ground among the legislators of Pennsylvania, and efforts for its suppression were reiterated in the Assembly. A practice had existed of Carolinians bringing Indian slaves to the province. This was entirely prohibited by an act passed in 1705 ; and, in order also to lessen the number of blacks, in the same year a duty on their importation was imposed, which was renewed in 1710. In the following year a more important and decided movement took place, which promised to go far to meet this great evil. The Assembly, chosen at the memorable election of 1710, and consisting almost wholly of Friends, now passed an act absolutely prohibiting the importation of negroes for the future, under any condition‡—an act which gave great satisfaction to William Penn.§

But whilst in Pennsylvania the anti-slavery feeling was thus making progress, England was becoming more and more involved in the crime. Some years before, it had formally declared in the statute book, that the trade in slaves was highly beneficial to the country and the colonies,‖ and in the very same year that the legislature of Pennsylvania sought thus to suppress the iniquity, a committee of the House of Commons was devising means to facilitate the capture of Africans, in order that their value might be reduced in the slave markets of the plantations.¶ No wonder,

---

* Rise and Progress of the Testimony of Friends against Slavery, p. 9.
† Watson's Annals, p. 481.   ‡ Ibid, p. 481.
§ Dixon's Life of W. Penn, p. 428.
‖ *Vide* 8 and 10. Will. III. c. 26.
¶ Dixon's Life of W. Penn, p. 429.

then, that the Crown peremptorily cancelled the humane Quaker law. The Privy Council, indeed, was indignant at the provincial legislature for proposing such a measure for confirmation, and at once quashed the act.* But the subject had taken so deep a hold on the Assembly, that, undaunted by the repulse of the parent state, they endeavoured, in 1712, upon petition " signed by many hands," to accomplish their object by imposing a duty of twenty pounds a head on all slaves imported. The same adverse policy of the home government again interposed, and its recognition as law was refused.† In the same year a petition was also presented to the Assembly " for the total abolition of slavery in Pennsylvania."‡

Whilst the provincial legislature was thus endeavouring to use its power and influence for the suppression of slavery, Friends in several localities were becoming still more abhorrent of this infraction of human rights. In the Sixth Month, 1711, the Monthly Meeting of Chester brought the subject under discussion in its Quarterly Meeting, then comprising most of the meetings south of Philadelphia. This meeting sympathized in the views of its subordinate meeting, and concluded, as its records state, to express to the next Yearly Meeting its " dissatisfaction with Friends buying and encouraging the bringing in of negroes." The Yearly Meeting, too, responded to the declaration of the Quarterly Meeting, and a record was made, calling the attention of its members to the minute of 1696, advising also " that all merchants and factors write to their correspondents to discourage them from sending any more negroes." §

So strong a hold had the subject now taken on the minds of Friends in Pennsylvania and the Jerseys, that it was introduced again in their next Yearly Meeting. A desire evidently prevailed to effect something more towards the uprooting of this unrighteous system. Conscious, however, that the Society in other parts had insensibly gone with the tide in the recognition of negro slavery,

* Proprietary Papers, vol. ix.—State Paper Office.
† Philadelphia Epistle to London Y. M. 1714.
‡ Watson's Annals, p. 481.
§ Rise and Progress of the Testimony of Friends against Slavery, p. 10.

a fear pervaded the meeting, of coming hastily to a judgment condemnatory of their brethren so circumstanced ; and it was agreed to take counsel with the Yearly Meeting of London.   In thus bringing the subject under the serious notice of their English Friends, after alluding to the advice already issued, they remark : "As our settlements increased, so other traders flocked in amongst us, over whom we had no gospel authority ; and such have increased and multiplied negroes amongst us, to the grief of divers Friends, whom we are willing to ease, if the way might open clear to the general." *

The delicacy in giving an opinion affecting so many Friends in America and the West India Islands, was felt also by the Yearly Meeting of London ; and the fact that they had not been appealed to on the matter by any other Meeting, increased their difficulty. In returning an answer, therefore, they did it in the following cautious language :—" You had better first have advised with other plantations, and so have stated the case conjunctly ; for want whereof we shall say the less, until such time as it is more generally represented.   Only this we think meet to impart unto you, as the sense of the Yearly Meeting,—that the importing them from their native country by Friends, is not a commendable nor allowed practice ; and we hope Friends have been careful to avoid the same, remembering the command of our blessed Lord, ' Whatsoever ye would that men should do to you, do ye even so to them.' "†   In reply to this, the Epistle of 1714 from Philadelphia, after stating that none of their members had " any hand or concern in bringing negroes out of their own country," and that " the practice is not commendable nor allowable amongst Friends," contains a request that Friends in England would " consult or advise with Friends in other plantations, where negroes are more numerous ; because," they add, " they hold a correspondence with you, but not with us, and your meeting may better prevail with them, and your advice prove more effectual."   Excepting the full declaration by London Yearly Meeting,—" that to be any ways

---

* Epistles received 1712—London Y. M. Records.
† Epistles sent 1713—London Y. M. Records.

concerned in bringing negroes from their native country, and selling them for slaves, is a trade not fit for one professing truth to be concerned in " *—nothing further appears to have transpired at that time between the two bodies on the subject.

The more deliberately the system of slavery was contrasted with the requisitions of Christianity, the more clearly was it seen to be incompatible with the benign character and object of that holy religion ; and hence these frequent discussions were productive of good.   Jonathan Dickinson, a merchant and Friend of Phila-delphia, in writing to his correspondents in Jamaica, in 1715, says, " I must entreat you to send me no more negroes for sale ; for our people don't care to buy.   They are generally against any coming into the country.   Few people care to buy them, except for those who live in other provinces."†   But the progress of the cause did not lessen the ardour of Friends.   In 1715, the zealous members of Chester Monthly Meeting again raised their voice against the system, and forwarded a minute to the Quarterly Meeting, expressive of their " great concern," not only at Friends "being concerned in importing," but also at their "buying of negroes ;" and Newark Monthly Meeting, belonging to the same Quarterly Meeting, echoed the sentiment.   The result of this movement was the adoption of a minute, (though certainly not coming up to the wish of Chester and Newark Friends,) to be forwarded to the Yearly Meeting, stating its " unanimous sense and judgment, that Friends should not be concerned in importing and bringing of negro slaves for the future."   The object ap-parently was, to obtain the sanction of the Yearly Meeting to some disciplinary proceedings, in the event of a member acting contrary to such a decision—an object which, to a considerable extent was obtained.   The minute of the Yearly Meeting was as follows :—" If any Friends are concerned in the importation of negroes, let them be dealt with, and advised to avoid that practice, according to the sense of former meetings in that behalf ; and that all Friends who have or keep negroes, do use and treat

* Epistles sent 1715—London Y. M. Records.
† Logan MSS. quoted in Watson, p. 482.

them with humanity, and with a Christian spirit: and that all do forbear judging or reflecting on one another, either in public or private, concerning the detaining or keeping them as servants."*

As the Yearly Meeting had not yet committed itself to a condemnation of the purchase of negroes, but only of their importation, the Friends of Chester Quarterly Meeting in 1716, renewed their solicitations on the subject. They urged, that " the buying and selling gave great encouragement for the bringing of them in, and that no Friends be found in the practice of buying any that shall be imported hereafter."† The Yearly Meeting was not, however, disposed to move quite so fast. It could not then see " any better conclusion," than its judgment of the previous year, " yet in condescension," so runs the minute, " to such Friends as are straitened in their minds against the holding them, it is desired, that Friends generally do, as much as may be, avoid buying such negroes as shall hereafter be brought in, rather than offend any Friends who are against it ; yet this is only caution, not censure."‡

Whilst Friends of Pennsylvania and the Jerseys were thus gradually progressing in their opposition to slavery, the other colonies of America, and the West India Islands, under English patronage, had made rapid strides in the gigantic evil. From 1680 to 1700, the English took from Africa about three hundred

* Rise and Progress, &c., p. 12.
Isaac Norris, a Friend of Philadelphia, writing about this time, thus refers to the discussion. His expressions elucidate the question as it then stood in the minds of Friends. " Our meeting was large and comfortable, and our business would have been very well, were it not for the warm pushing by some Friends of Chester, chiefly in the business of negroes. The aim was to obtain a minute that none should buy them for the future. This was opposed, as of dangerous consequence to the peace of the church; for, since they could not tell how to dispose of those we have, and that many members must still possess them, and then it might fall to their lot in duty to deal with future offenders, which, as it could not in itself be equitable, such must do it with an ill grace, and at best it would be a foundation for prejudice, and evil speaking one o another.— *Watson's Annals*, p. 481.
† Rise and Progress, &c., p. 12.   ‡ Ibid, p. 13.

thousand negroes, or about fifteen thousand annually, and in the following half-century, the number is calculated to have been not less than one million and a half, of whom one-eighth perished in the Atlantic, victims to the cruelties of the middle passage.* This enormous increase of the traffic, partly resulted from England having, at the treaty of Utrecht in 1713, gained the Assiento, or monopoly to supply the Spanish dominions with not less than four thousand eight hundred Africans yearly, for thirty years, at a given rate, and as many more as they pleased, at a lower rate; a treaty which both the French and Portuguese nations had previously made with Spain. † The supply of Africans for the English colonies, had been monopolized by the Royal African Company; but in the time of William and Mary, "for the better supply of the plantations," it was proposed to lay open the trade, which the statute book in 1695, declared to be "highly beneficial and advantageous to the kingdom and colonies."‡ In 1708, a Committee of the House of Commons reported that the trade was "important, and ought to be free;" and again, in 1711, that "the plantations ought to be supplied with negroes at reasonable rates." Queen Anne, who, in 1710, quashed the act passed by the legislature of Pennsylvania, forbidding the importation of slaves, three years later congratulated Parliament in having secured for the nation, by the Assiento, a new market for slaves in the Spanish dominions. So great was, in fact, the importance attached by the mother country to this sinful commerce, that in 1745, a British merchant published a political treatise, entitled "The African Slave Trade the great pillar and support of the British Plantation Trade in America." The humane Oglethorpe, in 1732, obtained of the Crown, a charter for the colony of Georgia. His object was, to provide for the persecuted Protestants on the Continent a region where they might grow the vine and rear the silkworm, and where also they

---

* Bancroft's United States.

† Assiento Treaty; in Spanish, *El Assiento de los Negros;* and, *El Pacto del Assiento;* that is, the compact for the farming or supply of negroes.

‡ 8 and 10 Will. III. c. 26.

might be free from the arm of ecclesiastical oppression and cruelty. It was one of those schemes of mercy which found general acceptance, and many promoted it with religious zeal. Parliament, responding to the prevalent feeling, granted ten thousand a year to encourage it—sermons were preached in aid of the undertaking, and John and Charles Wesley, enthusiastic in the cause,'spent years in America in promoting its interest. It was, indeed, regarded as a "religious colony," and among the early immigrants were numerous Moravians from Germany. Some of the laws of Georgia were extraordinary, and, perhaps the most so, those which related to slavery ; for, despite the onward course of the African slave-trade, and the pro-slavery feeling of the government, one law emphatically forbade the introduction of slaves ;—" Slavery," said Oglethorpe, "is against the gospel, as well as the fundamental law of England. We refused, as trustees, to make a law permitting such a horrid crime." Such was the happy beginning of Georgia. But mark its change. Only two years after its foundation, some of the inhabitants of Savannah petitioned "for the use of negroes ;"* and Whitfield, though he exerted himself to improve the condition of the negro, in a blind belief that slavery would terminate for the advantage of the Africans, pleaded in favour of the slave-trade as essential to the prosperity of the colony.† The Moravians, who at first saw in it a sinful oppression, strangely abandoning these enlightened views, "agreed, that if the negroes are treated in a Christian manner, their change of country would prove to them a benefit,"—a conclusion which their brethren in Germany sanctioned. "If you take slaves in faith," they wrote in 1751, "and with the intent of conducting them to Christ, the action will not be a sin, but may prove a benediction." Thus did specious reasoning and covetousness silence conscientious conviction, and convert the territory of Georgia into a land of slaves. The baneful system, pressed on by the cupidity of man, had even found its way into Massachusetts, whilst Rhode Island had also so far degenerated, as to become both a place of import, and a mart for human beings.‡ In 1705, the white population

---

* Tailfer, 23, quoted by Bancroft.   † Uurlsperger, iii. 482 in do.
‡ Clarkson, vol. i. p. 160.

of South Carolina was about six thousand ; in less than twenty
years more it had no less than three times that number of slaves,
and in 1765, they amounted to ninety thousand, or double the
number of whites.   At the same date, Virginia possessed one
hundred thousand slaves to seventy thousand whites.*

These facts strikingly evince the growing contamination of
negro slavery, and show also, how even those, who at one time
revolted at this atrocious and daring violation of human rights,
allowed their feelings to be gradually blunted by sophistry and
selfish reasoning, and at length recognised its existence with
an easy and an unconcerned conscience.   It seemed, indeed, as
though the Christian world, in its unhallowed attempts after gain,
was fast settling down under the delusive idea that slavery was
an institution of Heaven.   At one time, from New England to
Carolina, it was generally held that " being baptized is inconsistent with a state of slavery ;" and down to 1729, or until the
Crown lawyers gave a contrary opinion, all negroes brought to
England, who could manage to get baptized with water, obtained
their freedom ;✝ but this feeling, too, gradually wore away, and, in
1727, we find the Bishop of London lending his aid to bind the
fetters of the enslaved African, and declaring that " Christianity
and the embracing of the gospel does not make the least alteration
in civil property."   It surely then, would have been no marvel
if, under the prevailing influence of things around them, the
Society of Friends had also retrograded in their views on this
subject.   But, for the blessing of mankind, such was not the case.
They were not only preserved steadfast in the degree of advance
they had attained, but, through the enlightening influences of
Christ their Saviour, they made further progress in the relinquishment and condemnation of a system essentially opposed to his
reign and government in the earth.

After the decision of the Yearly Meeting of Pennsylvania in
1716, no further notice of the subject appears on its minutes for
the space of ten years.   But during this period the conviction of
the sin of slavery had deepened.   The Monthly Meeting of
Chester, acting under this impression, revived the subject in 1729,
and submitted to the Quarterly Meeting, " that inasmuch as we

* Holmes's Annals.   ✝ Clarkson, vol. i. p. 65.

are restricted by a rule of discipline, from being concerned in fetching or importing negro slaves from their own country, whether it is not as reasonable we should be restricted from buying of them when imported ; and if so, and the Quarterly Meeting see meet, that it may be laid before the Yearly Meeting for their approbation and concurrence." The Quarterly Meeting adopted this suggestion, and forwarded a minute to that effect to the Yearly Meeting, which concluded to defer the consideration for one year, when the subject was fully discussed, and resulted in the issue of the following advice to its members :   "The Friends of this meeting resuming the consideration of the proposition of Chester Meeting, relating to the purchasing of such negroes as may hereafter be imported ; and having reviewed and considered the former minutes relating thereto, and having maturely delibe-rated thereon, are now of opinion, that Friends ought to be very cautious of making any such purchases for the future, it being disagreeable to the sense of this meeting.   And this meeting recommends it to the care of the several Monthly Meetings, to see that such who may be, or are likely to be, found in that practice, may be admonished and cautioned how they offend herein."

For nearly every year until 1743, the foregoing advice was substantially repeated, and the subordinate meetings reported annually their care in reference to the subject.   Much labour appears to have been bestowed to induce those who were in the practice of buying or selling negroes, no longer to engage in such transactions ; nor were these labours ineffectual.   The next step taken by the Yearly Meeting for the discouragement of slave-holding, was to frame a special query on the subject, to be regularly answered by the respective subordinate meetings.   This took place in 1743.   The query adopted was as follows :—" Do Friends observe the advice of our Yearly Meeting not to encourage the importation of negroes ; nor to buy them after imported ?" In 1755 the query was enlarged to the following form :—" Are Friends clear of importing or buying negroes ; and do they use those well which they are possessed of by inheritance or otherwise ; endeavouring to train them up in the principles of the Christian religion ?"

Whilst the Society, in its collective capacity, was thus progressing in the great and good cause, the enlightened views and zealous advocacy of some individual Friends were fast preparing the body for the condemnation of slavery itself. Ralph Sandiford, a merchant of Philadelphia, was one of these. He was born in Liverpool in 1693, and in his youth removed to Philadelphia, where he soon united in religious fellowship with Friends.* His commercial pursuits took him occasionally to the West India islands, and here he witnessed the revolting cruelties of African slavery. His benevolent and susceptible mind was much affected by what he saw, and he was soon brought to the conclusion, "that the holding of negroes in slavery, is inconsistent with the rights of man, and contrary to the precepts of the Author of Christianity."† He was earnest in urging on his brethren the duty of emancipating their slaves, and, in 1729, he published a forcible treatise on the subject. Next came the eccentric Benjamin Lay of Abington. He had for some years, like his coadjutor Ralph Sandiford, been a witness to the cruelties of African bondage in the West Indies, and they made a deep and abiding impression upon him. His feelings were at times much excited on this matter, and his mind became almost unhinged in dwelling upon the sufferings of the slave. In 1737, he published a treatise on this subject, which he took much pains to circulate, especially among the young.‡ But by far the most energetic and

* Life of, by Roberts Vaux.
† Mystery of Iniquity, &c., by R. Sandiford.
‡ Benjamin Lay, though not in membership with Friends, professed with them, and as such, a few particulars of his life may not be out of place in this history. He was born at Colchester in England, in 1681,* of parents who were consistent members of our religious Society. On reaching manhood he followed the life of a sailor, in which employment he visited various parts of the globe. On his marriage in 1710, he changed his occupation, and settled in his native town. Lay was a man of an active and energetic mind, and one who took a more than ordinary interest in the public matters of the day, of which ecclesiastical imposition appears to have been one. On this subject he presented to

* Colchester Register of Births of the Society of Friends.

influential in this cause, were John Woolman and Anthony Benezet. John Woolman was born at Northampton, in West Jersey, in the year 1720, and settled at an early age at Mount

George I. and George II., a copy of Milton's essay, entitled "Considerations touching the likeliest means to remove Hirelings out of the Church," and on the last occasion, obtained a private audience of the royal family, a favour which was certainly remarkable for a man whose station, a few years before, had been only that of a sailor. It is believed that the part which he took in public and exciting subjects gave uneasiness to Friends, and was the cause of his being disunited from them in 1717. In the following year he settled in Barbadoes as a merchant, where his sensitive mind was greatly shocked at the cruelties he saw inflicted on the enslaved Africans, and, with his natural independence of character, he inveighed loudly against such atrocities. His fearless philanthropy on the subject drew upon him the displeasure of the slave-holders, and, after a residence of thirteen years on the island, he determined to remove to Philadelphia. Here he proclaimed so vigorously against slavery, although existing under its mildest form, as to elicit considerable opposition from those whose views were less warm and enlightened ; and, disappointed at his reception, he resolved to retire to the country, where he adopted habits of the most rigid temperance and self-denial. In his rural retreat, however, he did not relax his exertions on behalf of the negro. He visited the governors of the adjacent provinces and pleaded with them, and with other influential individuals, on the subject ; but with none more unceasingly and zealously than with Friends, whose principles he still professed. In the decline of life he removed to Abington, and boarded in a Friend's family, soon after which he was deprived by death of his wife, who was an intelligent woman, and a valuable minister in our religious Society. But his feelings on the subject of slavery did not slacken with the advance of age ; and, without regard to religious distinction, he visited all places of public worship to declare against the evil, in pursuance of which he became at times greatly excited, and conducted himself with much eccentricity. But his motives were truly good, and he was highly esteemed and respected. He was intimately acquainted with Ralph Sandiford, Dr. Franklin, and many other distinguished persons. A short time previous to his death, which took place in 1759, a Friend called upon him to inform him that the Society had resolved to disown such of their members as persisted in holding slaves, on hearing which he ejaculated, "Thanksgiving and praise be rendered unto the Lord God !" adding, after a short pause, "I can now die in peace !"*

---

* Life of B. Lay, by Roberts Vaux.

Holly in that province. When quite a young man he became a minister of the gospel, in the service of which he afterwards travelled very extensively. Soon after reaching manhood, he had a clear sense that "the practice of slave-keeping was inconsistent with the Christian religion,"* and during the remainder of his active and useful life, he bore an uncompromising testimony against it, and pleaded unremittingly with his brethren on the subject. Whilst on a religious visit to the southern colonies in 1746, his mind was deeply and sorrowfully impressed with what he witnessed of this system. "I saw," he writes, "in these provinces, so many vices and corruptions increased by this trade, and this way of life, that it appeared to me as a gloom over the land." A few years after he visited the south again, on which occasion he remarked that "some of our Society, and some of the society called new-lights, use some endeavours to instruct their negroes in reading; but in common this is not only neglected but disapproved. These are the people by whose labour the other inhabitants are in a great measure supported, and many of them in the luxuries of life. These are the people who have made no agreement to serve us, and who have not forfeited their liberty that we know of. These are the souls for whom Christ died; and for our conduct towards them, we must answer before Him who is no respecter of persons. They who know the only true God, and Jesus Christ whom He hath sent, and are thus acquainted with the merciful, benevolent, gospel spirit, will therein perceive that the indignation of God is kindled against oppression and cruelty; and in beholding the great distress of so numerous a people will find cause for mourning." Writing at this time to Friends in North Carolina, he says, " I have been informed that there is a large number of Friends in your parts, who have no slaves; and in tender and most affectionate love, I beseech you to keep clear from purchasing any. In 1754, he published his "Considerations" on the keeping of negroes, which, being widely circulated among Friends, tended to increase their zeal against the evil. In subsequent years he published several other pieces

* Journal of John Woolman.

on the same subject. It is questionable indeed, whether any one individual has done more to promote the abolition of slavery than John Woolman. Some further particulars of the life of this devoted and self-denying Christian will be given in a subsequent chapter.

Anthony Benezet was born at (Saint) Quentin, in France, in the year 1713. His father, who was wealthy, had associated himself with the Huguenots, and his estate having been confiscated on the revocation of the edict of Nantes, he fled from his native country, and settled in London in 1715. Anthony received a liberal education, and was placed in a mercantile house. In very early life his mind became religiously impressed, and at the early age of fourteen, he was received as a member of our religious Society.* From conscientious motives he declined to engage in commerce, and placed himself with a cooper. But this occupation proved to be too laborious for his naturally delicate frame.. In 1731, at the age of eighteen, he removed with his parents to Philadelphia. Here, his three brothers were highly successful in business, and he might have shared in their prosperity, had he not felt himself restrained from engaging in trade. He was favoured to see how unimportant was the acquisition of wealth, in comparison with heavenly riches ; and, making worldly concerns subservient to higher duties, he chose the humbler path of a teacher in a school. He followed this occupation for twelve years, after which he attended, as a private tutor, some of the most affluent families in Philadelphia. He was deeply interested in the education of youth, and wrote several works in furtherance of that important object. About the year 1750, the degraded condition of the African race attracted his attention, and his feelings became painfully affected at the atrocities of the slave-trade. The interest which these subjects excited in him, drew him from private life, to plead before the world the wrongs of Africa. One of his first steps in this benevolent cause, was, the establishment of an evening school for negroes, which he taught gratuitously himself. His efforts were next directed to the publication of pieces in almanacks and newspapers, on the unlawful.

* Life of Anthony Benezet, by Roberts Vaux

ness of slavery; and in 1762, he issued a work, entitled "An account of that part of Africa inhabited by the Negroes." This was soon followed by, "A caution and warning to Great Britain and her colonies, on the calamitous state of the enslaved negroes." His third was, "An historical account of Guinea, with an enquiry into the rise and progress of the slave-trade, its nature and calamitous effects." The last of these, says Clarkson, "became instrumental, beyond any other book ever before published, in disseminating a proper knowledge and detestation of this trade."* Anthony Benezet was untiring in his efforts for the benefit of the oppressed slave. His correspondence on the subject was very extensive, and his pathetic addresses to his brethren did much to awaken them to a just sense of the iniquity of slavery. In 1770, he was appointed to the station of elder in our religious Society; and his remarkably useful and self-denying career terminated in 1784, at the age of seventy-one.†

Anthony Benezet

Returning to the proceedings of the Society at large in Pennsylvania, we find that, in 1754, the Yearly Meeting issued an epistle to its members on this subject, which is supposed to have emanated from the pen of Anthony Benezet. It was a document of much force, and calculated, as the following extract shows, clearly to set forth the inconsistency of slavery with the religion of Christ. "Now, dear Friends, if we continually bear in mind the royal law of 'doing to others as we would be done by,' we should never think of bereaving our fellow-creatures of that valuable blessing, liberty; nor endure to grow rich by their bondage. To live in ease and plenty, by the toil of those whom violence and cruelty have put in our power, is neither consistent with Christianity nor common justice; and, we have good reason to believe, draws down the displeasure of Heaven; it being a melancholy, but true reflection, that where slave-keeping prevails, pure religion and sobriety decline; as it

---

* Clarkson, vol. i. p. 169.   † Life, by Vaux.

evidently tends to harden the heart, and render the soul less susceptible of that holy spirit of love, meekness, and charity, which
is the peculiar character of a true Christian. How then can we,
who have been concerned to publish the gospel of universal love
and peace among mankind, be so inconsistent with ourselves, as
to purchase such who are prisoners of war, and thereby encourage
this anti-christian practice : and more especially as many of
those poor creatures are stolen away, parents from children, and
children from parents ; and others, who were in good circumstances in their native country, inhumanly torn from what they
esteemed a happy situation, and compelled to toil in a state of
slavery, too often extremely cruel. What dreadful scenes of murder and cruelty those barbarous ravages must occasion, in the
country of those unhappy people, are too obvious to mention.
Let us make their case our own, and consider what we should
think, and how we should feel, were we in their circumstances.
Remember our blessed Redeemer's positive command ; ' to do
unto others as we would have them to do unto us ; ' and that
with what measure we mete it shall be measured to us again.
And we entreat all to examine, whether the purchasing of a
negro, either born here, or imported, doth not contribute to a
further importation, and consequently to the upholding of all the
evils above mentioned, and the promoting of man-stealing—the
only theft which by the Mosaic law was punished with death.
' He that stealeth a man and selleth him, or if he be found in
his hands, he shall surely be put to death.' "—Exod. xxi. 16.
After alluding with feelings of satisfaction to those Friends who
had liberated their slaves, it concludes thus : " Finally, brethren,
we intreat you in the bowels of gospel love, seriously to
weigh the cause of detaining them in bondage. If it be for
your own private gain, or any other motive than their good, it is
much to be feared, that the love of God and the influence of the
Holy Spirit, is not the prevailing principle in you, and that your
hearts are not sufficiently redeemed from the world ; which, that
you, with ourselves, may more and more come to witness, through
the cleansing virtue of the Holy Spirit of Jesus Christ, is our
earnest desire."

Hitherto the discipline of the Society had enforced no stronger repressive measure with reference to slave-holding, than the extension of advice. In 1755, however, the Yearly Meeting of Pennsylvania expressed its " sense and judgment," that Friends who were concerned in importing or buying slaves ought " speedily" to be reported to their Monthly Meeting and dealt with on the matter. Three years later the rule of the Society was made still more stringent. It was then agreed that, after the sense and judgment of the meeting " now given against every branch of this practice," any who imported, bought, sold or held slaves, should not be allowed to take part in the affairs of the church. The principle " to do unto others as we would they should do unto us," records the Yearly Meeting of 1758, as it " appears to this meeting, would induce Friends who have any slaves, to set them at liberty,—making Christian provision for them, according to their ages, &c. And in order," continues the minute, " that Friends may be generally excited to the prac- tice of this advice, some Friends here have now signified to the meeting, their being so fully devoted to endeavour to render it effectual, that they are willing to visit and treat with all such Friends who have any slaves ; the meeting therefore approves of John Woolman, John Scarborough, John Sykes, and Daniel Stanton, undertaking that service ; and desires some elders, or other faithful Friends, in each quarter to accompany and assist them therein ; that they may proceed in the wisdom of Truth, and thereby be qualified to administer such advice as may be suitable to the circumstances of those they visit, and most effec- tual towards obtaining that purity, which it is evidently our duty to press after."

For nearly twenty years from the date of the foregoing appointment, the records of Pennsylvania Yearly Meeting show that the subject claimed its close and increasing attention, and exhortations were repeated to the subordinate meetings, to labour in Christian love and meekness with delinquents. From 1767, accounts of labours of this description, and of the success that attended them, were forwarded regularly to the Yearly Meeting. But very few were disowned for purchasing or selling slaves.

The mild, yet decided and earnest course pursued, produced a happier result. A considerable number of Friends had already manumitted their slaves, and by the year 1774, the Yearly Meeting of Pennsylvania and the Jerseys appears to have been free from the sin of trafficking in men.*

The holding of slaves had not yet been held to be a disownable offence, nor was a Friend brought under church censure for transferring or accepting a slave without pecuniary consideration. With this degree of leniency some of the Quarterly Meetings became dissatisfied, and, on a proposition from two of them, a committee of thirty-four Friends was appointed, in 1774, to consider with respect to the regulations on this matter, " what additions or amendments are seasonable and necessary." The propositions were favourably entertained, and the committee made the following report :—" That such professors among us who are, or shall be, concerned in importing, selling or purchasing ; or that shall give away, or transfer, any negro or other slave, with or without any other consideration than to clear their estate of any future incumbrance, or in such manner as that their bondage is continued beyond the time limited by law or custom for white persons ; and such member who accepts of such gift or assignment, ought to be speedily treated with, in the spirit of true love and wisdom, and the iniquity of their conduct laid before them. And if, after this Christian labour, they cannot be brought to such a sense of their injustice as to do every thing which the Monthly Meeting shall judge to be reasonable and necessary for the restoring such slave to his or her natural and just right to liberty, and [do not] condemn their deviation from the law of righteousness and equity, to the satisfaction of the said Meeting, that such member be testified against, as other transgressors are, by the rules of our discipline, for other immoral, unjust, and reproachful conduct." It was also added, that Friends " should be advised and admonished against being accessory to the promotion of this unrighteous traffic," by " hiring slaves on

* Rise and Progress of the Testimony of Friends against Slavery, p. 24—Several of the foregoing extracts of minutes have been taken from this interesting pamphlet.

wages." In 1776, the same Yearly Meeting evinced its earnestness in the cause by adopting a minute directing Monthly Meetings to proceed to disownment in cases where their labours had proved unavailing. The query also on the subject was modified as follows :—" Are Friends clear of importing, purchasing, disposing of, or holding mankind as slaves ? And do they use those well, who are set free, and necessarily under their care, and not in circumstances through nonage, or incapacity, to minister to their own necessities ? And are they careful to educate and encourage them in a religious and virtuous life ?"

On receipt of the minute of 1776, the subordinate meetings appointed committees to carry out the views of the Yearly Meeting, respecting such of their members as had not yet complied with these recommendations of the Society. By the reports forwarded from the Quarterly Meetings, it is both cheering and instructive to observe how generally the call of the body at large was responded to, and how effective are the labours of concerned brethren, when undertaken in a spirit of love and solicitude for their fellow-members.

PHILADELPHIA reports, in 1776, " A considerable number of the slaves heretofore belonging to members of this meeting have been set at liberty." In 1778 seven members were disowned for holding slaves ; and a few years later, the meeting reported that " there were no slaves owned by its members."

HADDONFIELD, in 1781, reported that " there had been a general releasement from bondage of the Africans among us."

CHESTER, in 1777, states, " A considerable number of slaves have been manumitted—but there are some members that still hold them ;" and such members, they remark, " may be safely reported to their Monthly Meetings."

BURLINGTON, in the same year, says, " Most of those who were in a state of slavery among Friends, have been manumitted since last year ;" and in 1781, it reports being " clear of all cases of this kind then known."

THE WESTERN, which stretches into Maryland, thus answers the query, in 1777 : " Clear of importing and disposing of mankind as slaves, also of purchasing, in all our meetings, except one, from which a doubt is hinted in one case. Some within the compass of the meeting yet continue to hold slaves; though many have been manumitted since last year."

BUCKS, in the same year, says, " some have complied, so far as to give those they had in bondage their liberty, by instruments of writing, given under their hands and seals ; but there are others who still persist in holding them as slaves."

The latest record of the Yearly Meeting of Pennsylvania which notices slaves being held by some of its members, is in the year 1781 ; and it is believed, that before the occurrence of another Yearly Meeting, this large section of our religious Society in America was free from the guilt of holding their fellow-men in bondage. But the exertions of Friends did not end here. They viewed the emancipated negro as an injured fellow-being, for whom the law of righteousness claimed a reparation. " We are united in judgment," reports a committee, in 1779, " that the state of the oppressed people who have been held by any of us, or our predecessors, in captivity and slavery, calls for a deep inquiry and close examination, how far we are clear of withholding from them, what, under such an exercise, may open to view as their just right," &c. The philanthropic appeal was not in vain, and the respective meetings answered heartily to the call. Religious meetings were frequently held with the negroes—the families of large numbers of them were visited—funds were raised for the education of their children, and in some instances pecuniary compensation was made, varying according to the duration of their bondage.

The religious exercise into which the Society had been introduced on the subject of the slave-trade and slavery, led the members of this large Yearly Meeting, into a deep and earnest solicitude for the suppression of the African slave-trade, " as grossly unchristian and reproachful to humanity," and also for the utter extinction of slavery in their own land ; and from this time forward, memorials and remonstrances on these questions, were repeatedly laid before persons in power and the public at large. " Let no opportunity be lost," wrote the Yearly Meeting in 1787, " of discouraging the unrighteous business, and manifesting to the world, the religious ground of our Christian testimony against this public wickedness." As early, indeed, as 1773, Friends of East and West Jersey petitioned their local legislature on this subject.   In this effort they were joined by many not in religious profession with them, and altogether the petition was signed by no less than three thousand persons.   It was presented by a deputation ; and William Dillwyn, being one of them, was heard at the bar of the Assembly in support of the general manumission of the slaves.*   Nor were these more public efforts of the Society on this great question unavailing.   Their enlightened views and Christian advocacy, had awakened among their fellow-citizens of Pennsylvania, a strong sense of the injustice of slavery ; and in 1780, they had the satisfaction to witness the local legislature responding to this altered tone of feeling, by passing an act for the extinction of the evil within its borders. The language of this enactment is remarkable, and deserves to be handed down to succeeding generations.   It was passed in the Third Month, 1780, and contains the following passage, " It is not for us to enquire why, in the creation of mankind, the inhabitants of the several parts of the earth were distinguished by a difference in feature or complexion.   It is sufficient to know, that all are the work of an Almighty hand.   We find in the distribution of the human species, that the most fertile as well as the most barren parts of the earth are inhabited by men of complexion different from ours, and from each other ; from whence we may reasonably as well as religiously infer, that He who placed them in their various situations, hath extended equally his care and protection to all, and that it becometh not us to counteract his mercies—Be it enacted, that no child born hereafter shall be a slave—that negro and mulatto children shall be servants only till twenty-eight years of age—that all slaves shall be registered before the first of November next—that negroes, &c., shall be tried like other inhabitants—that none shall be deemed slaves but those registered—that no negroes or mulattos, other than infants, shall be bound longer than seven years."†

* Clarkson, vol. i. pp. 187, 198.

† Gordon's Hist. of the Rise, &c., of the Independence of the United States, vol. iii. p. 377.

The effect of this law was, gradually to redeem the state from the pollution of this crime, and to make it, what it now is, in the broad and plain sense, a Free State. In 1790, it possessed 3,737 slaves : ten years later they were two thousand less : in 1810 the number was reduced to 795, and in 1820 to only 211, in a population of more than a million.

This act may be justly deemed the crowning one of Pennsylvania, and contrasts strikingly with the revolting laws of the slave-system prevailing in other States of the Union. Indeed, but for its federal connexion with these, there is even reason to believe that Pennsylvania would ere this have attained that noble position which England assumed in 1772, by declaring personal freedom inherent to the British soil, and which the poor fugitive now realizes in an ecstacy of joy, as he passes the line that divides the great slave-holding republic from the Canadian frontier.

In the year 1783, a year memorable in the history of the United States, as that in which their independence was recognised by Great Britain, and most of the other European powers, the Yearly Meeting of Pennsylvania addressed Congress on the iniquity of the slave-trade. The address was presented by a special deputation, who were admitted to the assembled Representatives of the Republic. It was signed in the meeting at large, and by more than five hundred members, and it earnestly solicited the interposition of the Federal Government, for the suppression of this atrocity.*

In 1774, William Dillwyn visited England. He had already become distinguished as the energetic friend of the negro, and, through Anthony Benezet, he was introduced to Granville Sharpe, a man of kindred feelings on this great question, through whose untiring efforts had been obtained, only two years before, the memorable decision of law, that slaves could not be recognised in Britain. William Dillwyn went back in the following year to America ; but on his return to England to settle, he formed a Committee of influential Friends for the suppression of slavery. It was soon after this that Thomas Clarkson's attention was first

* Gordon's Hist, of the Rise, &c. vol. iii. p. 377.

directed to the subject, and in a somewhat remarkable manner. He was then studying at Cambridge University, and had distinguished himself in 1784, by gaining the highest prize for the Latin essay. In the year following, Dr. Peckard, Vice-chancellor of the University, an enlightened man, especially on the subject of slavery, proposed for the prize essay of that year, this subject : " *Anne liceat invitos in Servitudem dare ?*" or, " Is it right to make slaves of men against their will ?" As Clarkson had gained considerable reputation by his previous success, it was of some importance to him to maintain his advanced position by gaining the prize in the present instance. But he was wholly unacquainted with the subject of negro slavery. It had not been, nor was it then, a popular theme, or one to which men of literary taste and acquirements had given their attention. He saw that the question was a large one—that it involved important considerations ; but as for materials he neither had any, nor knew he where to obtain them, and but a few weeks only were allowed for the composition. What was he to do ? His situation was peculiar. But he was soon relieved ; and herein we may clearly mark the finger of Providence. Happening casually to take up a newspaper, his eye caught an advertisement of Anthony Benezet's " Historical Account of Guinea, &c." " In this precious book," he says, "I found all I wanted. I obtained, by means of it, a knowledge of, and gained access to, the great authorities of Adamson, Moore, Barbot and others." He wrote the essay and gained the prize. University honours were, however, of small moment compared with the subsequent results of this college exercise. Clarkson, so far from deriving his wonted pleasure from this effort for literary fame, was deeply affected by the painful details which were brought before him. " It was," he writes, " but one gloomy subject from morning to night. In the day-time I was uneasy. In the night I had little rest. I sometimes never closed my eyelids for grief. It became now not so much a trial for academical reputation, as for the production of a work which might be useful to injured Africa." But we must not in this work follow Clarkson further, except to say, that henceforth the whole energies of his powerful mind were given to the subject. His acquaintance was soon sought by Dillwyn, Phillips, and other Friends, who had taken up the cause of African freedom ; and in 1787, he united in Committee with eleven others, nine of whom were Friends, in forming the Society for the Abolition of the Slave-trade, a society whose labours were crowned with remarkable success, in inducing the British nation to suppress within its territories this violation of law * and equity.

From these few facts we may perceive what a powerful influence for good on the world at large, was excited or largely promoted through the faithfulness of Friends of Pennsylvania and the Jerseys on the subject of slavery ; for it is evident that their brethren in England were induced to act in this matter, mainly through their example. The first minute of London Yearly Meeting on the slave-trade, was in 1727, and stated that "the practice was not a commendable nor allowed one ;"† an opinion which Pennsylvania Yearly Meeting had pronounced thirty years before. And whilst in the latter Yearly Meeting the subject was almost annually discussed, in the former no further notice of it appears on the minutes until the year 1758, when urgent advice was issued to its members, not to be in any way engaged in the slave-trade, which, forty years before was in Pennsylvania, an offence followed by disciplinary proceedings. In 1761, London Yearly Meeting, under an apprehension that many of its members were engaged in the African slave-trade, then made it a disownable offence.‡ John Woolman, when in England in 1772, was deeply pained at what he saw among Friends, in reference to negro slavery. "I have felt," he writes, "great distress of mind, since I came on this island, on account of the members of our Society being mixed with the world in various sorts of traffic, carried on in impure channels. Great is the trade to Africa for slaves ! and for the loading of these ships, a great number of people are employed in their factories ; among whom are many of our Society."§ His faithfulness had, doubtless, much weight with his brethren ; and in the same

---

* Amidst all its national guiltiness in this matter, Great Britain never recognised negro slavery as legal.

† Rules of Discipline—" Slave-trade and Slavery."   ‡ Ibid.

§ Woolman's Journal.

year, some information on the subject having been transmitted from America, induced the Yearly Meeting of London to notice it in its printed Epistle. In 1783, for the first time, the Society in England petitioned Parliament against the slave-trade.

Of the thirteen States of the Union, at the period of American independence, all appear to have been slave-holding, and all to have regarded it as legal. In 1780, Massachusetts, in framing its constitution, adopted words analogous to these memorable ones, contained in the Declaration of Independence:—" We hold these truths to be self-evident:—that men are created equal; that they are endowed by their Creator with certain unalienable rights; that among these are life, liberty, and the pursuit of happiness." The introduction into their constitution of the great principle here enunciated, was not intended as a declaration antagonistic to negro slavery. But the judiciary of Massachusetts, contrary to the views of the Federal Government, as honest men, accepted them literally, and in the first case that came before them, decided that, by virtue of such a declaration, slavery no longer existed in their state. The early emancipation of Massachusetts, therefore, from this evil, may be regarded rather as an accidental circumstance, than as a designed object.

The noble course adopted in 1780, by Pennsylvania, in declaring itself a free state, incited the citizens of the Republic to a deeper consideration of the subject; and in a few years its example was followed by other states of the Union. Rhode Island and Connecticut were the first to move; and their initiation as free states, took place in 1784; New Jersey in 1804; and New York in 1817. New Hampshire seems never to have possessed many slaves: in 1808, there were only eight in the province. Seven of the thirteen original states have, therefore, by ostensible acts of their legislatures, pronounced an emphatic condemnation of the system of slavery. The remaining six, viz., Delaware, Maryland, Virginia, North Carolina, South Carolina, and Georgia, together with the slave-holding states which have since been founded, continue, with unmitigated severity, to sanction and encourage this outrage on humanity and religion;—an outrage, it should be remembered, rendered now doubly sinful, perpetrated as it is, under a degree of light on the subject, to which the early settlers in America were strangers.

Had the poor Quaker emigrants from Germany—had Sandiford and Lay, and Benezet and Woolman, allowed their convictions to have been silenced by the prevailing public opinion, or even by the views of their brethren in religious profession, it is doubtful whether at this day a Free State would be found throughout the widely extended limits of the great American republic. But the labours of Friends, in this great work, though so effective, have been conducted throughout with much circumspection, forbearance, and kindness. In pleading with their fellow-christians, no boisterous manifestations, no violation of order, no impetuous zeal, have marked their steps. They have not sought to excite the passions of men, or to raise feelings of angry recrimination between one section of the community and another; but, in promoting this Christian work, prayerfully seeking, as they have been wont to do, for that wisdom which is profitable to direct, they have been made instrumental in the hand of the Lord, in the propagation of those truths which have tended to restrain the wickedness and the tyranny of man. " The weapons of their warfare were not carnal, but mighty, through God, to the pulling down of strongholds."

222

CHAPTER IX.

IN the year 1699, Sarah Clemens from London, whom John Richardson mentions as one that "lived near the kingdom," visited America. No particulars of her gospel mission appear to be preserved, further than that it was to the "good satisfaction" of Friends.

During the year 1700, five gospel messengers from England crossed the Atlantic; these were John Salkeld, Thomas Thompson, Josiah Langdale, John Richardson, and John Estaugh, of whom the last four came in the same ship. John Salkeld was from Westmoreland. "He had," says Smith, "a great gift in the ministry, and passed through these and other provinces with good success." * He subsequently settled in Pennsylvania. Thomas Thompson was from Saffron Walden, in Essex. He came forth in the ministry at an early age, and travelled

* Smith's Hist. chap. xv.

extensively in the work of the gospel.   In a letter written from
America in 1703, he says, "we have had some glorious meetings
in Maryland, Pennsylvania, and East and West Jersey,"*   In
1705, he gave to London Yearly Meeting an account of his
visit, and, referring to Friends of Pennsylvania and the Jerseys,
he says, "they thrive in the Truth, and in the love thereof."†
He visited America again in 1715.   Thomas Thompson died in
1727, and witnessed in his last moments the triumphs of religion
in a remarkable degree.   "Oh, glory, glory, to thy divine name
and power, thou Infinite Fountain of light and immortality.
My soul blesses thee, and my spirit magnifies thy name, in the
sense of that eternal Word and Wisdom that was in thy bosom
from eternity; that light which shone everlastingly, and will be
a glory and crown to all them that believe and walk therein :
and in the faith of that I live and die."   And shortly before his
close he added, "The rays of his beauty shine upon me ; I am
filled with the power of his love; glory be to his name for
ever."‡

Josiah Langdale was from Bridlington, in Yorkshire.   He
appears to have travelled with Thomas Thompson, and at the
Yearly Meeting in London in 1705, he also gave a brief outline
of his movements.   "The Lord," he remarked, "is enlarging his
tents in those wilderness countries—many are convinced, and a
great openness is among the people ; and he believed a great
people will be gathered."§   In 1714, Josiah Langdale visited
America again, and in 1723, embarked with his family with the
intention of settling there.   He was, however, taken ill, and died
on the passage, his end being full of peace.‖

Respecting John Richardson's visit, his journal supplies us
with many interesting details.   He was at that time in the
thirty-fourth year of his age, and he also came from Bridlington,
in Yorkshire, where about this time so many young Friends

* Life, &c. of W. and A. Ellis, p. 202.
† London Y. M. Mins. vol. iii. p. 199.
‡ Piety Promoted, part ix.
§ Mins. of London Y. M. vol. iii. p. 199.
‖ Life, &c. of W. and A. Ellis, p. 203.

came forth in the ministry, that it became, he says, a proverb that "Bridlington was become a school of prophets."* He visited most of the meetings in Pennsylvania Yearly Meeting, where, he says, "I had good service for the Lord,—the Lord helping me by his mighty power through all my trials, as my heart and mind was devoted and resigned to answer his requirings." At North Wales Meeting, which he states "had not long been planted, there was a fine, tender people, with whom he had a good meeting," Truth being over all. They were Welsh people, and Rowland Ellis interpreted on the occasion. Whilst in Pennsylvania, John Richardson also had gospel labours among the Indians.

John Estaugh came from Dunmow, in Essex, and subsequently settled at Haddonfield, in New Jersey. He joined Friends at the early age of seventeen, and came forth in the ministry in the year following. As a gospel minister, he travelled extensively both in Great Britain and America, and died in 1742, at the age of sixty-six, whilst on a religious visit in Tortola, one of the West India islands. He is described by his Monthly Meeting, "as a humble minded, exemplary Friend, solid and grave in his deportment, well becoming a minister of Christ; zealous for pressing good order in the church, and maintaining love and unity, that badge of true discipleship; remarkably careful in his conversation among men, his words being few and savoury."†

FRIENDS' MEETING-HOUSE, HADDONFIELD, NEW JERSEY.

* J. Richardson's Journal.   † Penn. Memorials, p. 14.

In the year 1703, Samuel Bownas arrived in Pennsylvania on a gospel visit.   He had already been more than a year in America, but during most of that time he was imprisoned on Long Island, on an alleged charge of "speaking against the Church of England:" of this persecution, George Keith appears to have been the instigator.   Samuel Bownas came from Westmoreland, and was then only in the twenty-seventh year of his age.   In the Jerseys he was at most of the meetings, also at "some fresh places where he found the truth growing."   He then proceeded to the Falls, in Pennsylvania, passed down through the Welsh towns to Philadelphia, and from thence to the south of the province.   "There is," he says, "a noble and numerous people in Pennsylvania, and in all the places that I have yet been in, I was never at greater country meetings. Many young people, both men and women, come forth in a public testimony for Truth."*

In the following year, Friends in America were visited by four of their brethren from England: These were Thomas Turner, whose previous visit has already been noticed ; Joseph Glaister of Cumberland, Mary Banister of London, and Mary Ellerton of York.   Their religious labours "were well received, and some of them" are said to have been "of eminent service."†   "In West Jersey," remarks Thomas Turner, "a great many people come in ; and some that formerly turned from Friends to George Keith are returned."‡   Joseph Glaister some years after settled in North Carolina.   Mary Ellerton came forth in the ministry at a very early age, and her communications were powerful and edifying.§   She travelled largely on gospel missions, and died about 1736, at an advanced age.   Respecting the visit of Mary Banister the following record appears on the minutes of Devonshire House Monthly Meeting: "Our friend, Mary Banister, being, through the goodness of God, returned from her travelling in the ministry in sundry provinces on the main land of

* Mins. of London Y. M. vol. iii. p. 331.
† Smith's Hist. chap. xv.
‡ Mins. of London, Y. M., vol. iii. p. 200.
§ Coll. of Test., p. 95.

America, brought with her certificates from Friends in several of these countries, which were read in this meeting expressing the good unity they had with her, both as to conversation and ministry."

The next gospel labourers from England were John Fothergill, and William Armistead, two young men from Yorkshire; the former about thirty, and the latter about twenty-four years of age. "Though but young," writes William Ellis to one of his American friends, "they are well approved of, and zealous both in doctrine and discipline; men that I look for a great deal of good service out of, if they live; and if they come, you may receive them as such."* They landed on the banks of the Patuxent, in Maryland, in the early part of 1706, and arrived at Philadelphia in time to attend the Yearly Meeting. Most of the summer they were occupied in visiting the meetings in Pennsylvania and the Jerseys, which, writes John Fothergill, "very much spent my bodily strength, and, so far, that I think I never recovered it. But the Lord added a blessing to our labours in these parts; some were convinced and gathered to the Truth."† "We had," he said on another occasion, "a laborious time in those provinces, in endeavouring to weigh down what would do hurt, and to search out the obstructions of the love and life of the Lord Jesus Christ our Saviour and our Head, and to strengthen and comfort the travailer in spirit, and gather back, and hedge in, some such as were like to wander away."‡ These youthful messengers of the gospel "left a sweet savour behind them," and they are, writes the observing James Logan, "of good sense every way."§

In the year 1707, Patrick Henderson and Samuel Wilkinson, both from the north of Ireland, travelled on a gospel mission throughout the limits of Pennsylvania Yearly Meeting. They also were but young in years, yet eminent ministers, and their labours were appreciated by their brethren. "Patrick Henderson,"

* Life, &c., of W. and A. Ellis, p. 208.
† Journal of J. Fothergill, p. 49.
‡ Mins. of London Y. M., vol. iii. p. 396.
§ Logan Corresp.

writes James Logan to William Penn, "is I think Scotch by birth, and is a most extraordinary young man as ever visited these parts. Of such as these," alluding also to his companion, "the more always the better."*

It was in the early part of 1709, that the newly appointed Governor Gookin arrived in Pennsylvania, by whom William Penn sent an epistle to his brethren in the province, introducing him to their notice. The epistle also contained some religious counsel, which is too valuable to be omitted in these pages. It is as follows :—

"London, 28th of Seventh Month, 1708.

"DEAR FRIENDS AND BRETHREN,—My ancient love, if you can believe it, reacheth to you as in times past, and years that are gone, even in the divine root and principle of love and life, that made us near to one another above all worldly considerations ; where our life, I hope, is hid with Christ in God our Father, so that when he appears, we shall also appear with him in glory, and in the mean time through us to those that love and wait for his appearance, as the desire of nations ; that we may glorify God, his and our Everlasting Father, in our bodies, souls, and spirits ; in temporal and eternal affairs, being indeed none of our own, for so much as we are our own, we are none of the Lord's : a great mystery, but a great truth, and of absolute necessity to witness, to be of the number of the chosen nation, the peculiar people and royal priesthood of Christ and his glorious kingdom.

"Oh, my dear friends ! let all below this keep on the left hand, and wait to feel those blessed things to inherit the right hand, and in faith and courage cry aloud to the Lord for his renewing and refreshing power, that may revive and reform his work upon our hearts and minds, and our humility, meekness, patience, self-denial, and charity, with a blameless walking, may plainly appear, and manifest the work of God upon our hearts to those that are without ; which is not only the way to bring up the loiterers and gather in the careless ones to their duty, but

* Logan Corresp.

Q 2

fetch home and bring in the strangers, and the very enemies of the blessed truth, to confess and acknowledge that God is in you, and for you of a truth.

" In the first love I leave you, committing you and yours, and all the Lord's people amongst you, my own family and affairs, to the merciful providence and orderings of our great and gracious God, that welcomed us in poor America, with his excellent love and precious light, and will, I hope once more ; and remain your loving and faithful friend,

" WILLIAM PENN."

" Herewith comes your school charter."

William Baldwin of Lancashire, appears to have been the next from the mother country, who visited the churches in America. He landed in Virginia in the Third Month 1709, and went direct to Philadelphia. In giving an account of this religious engagement to London Yearly Meeting in 1711, he remarked that " he found Friends a people of a generous spirit, and an openness in their hearts and houses." He afterwards settled in Pennsylvania, and died there in 1721. He had an eminent, deep, and reaching ministry, was in great esteem among his friends, and well beloved by his neighbours.[*]

Towards the close of 1713, Thomas Wilson and James Dickinson proceeded again to America, this being the second visit of the former and the third of the latter. They landed on this occasion in Virginia, and, taking the meetings in that and the adjoining province of Maryland, they passed through Delaware to the Jerseys in time to attend the Yearly Meeting of Salem, where, says Thomas Wilson, " the truth was largely opened to the people."[†] They then visited the meetings in the Jerseys and Pennsylvania, " some of which," writes James Dickinson, " were the largest I had ever been at : people flocked so to them that several hundreds were forced to stand without doors, the meeting-house not being large enough to contain them. At Burlington Yearly Meeting," he continues, " the Lord owned us with his

---

[*] Smith's Hist. chap. xviii.
[†] Journal of T. Wilson.

living presence, and we had a glorious season together. The meeting held five days ; and there was such a concourse of people that we had two meetings at once, one in the Court House, and the other at the Meeting House." After this they visited, he says, "the out corners of Pennsylvania."*

During the year 1715, three gospel labourers came over from England. These were Thomas Thompson, Josiah Langdale, and Benjamin Holme. A visit from the first-named two Friends, about fourteen years previously, has already been noticed ; no account of the present service appears to be preserved, further than that it was " an acceptable religious visit." Benjamin Holme was from the city of York. He was born at Penrith, in Cumberland, in 1682 ; he spoke as a minister when but fourteen years of age, and, only three years later, travelled to distant parts in this holy calling. He was now in his thirty-fourth year, and had already visited most parts of England, Wales, and Scotland, and also some parts of Holland. In America he was largely engaged for about four years in the work of his Divine Master ; and it is recorded " that divers meetings were settled by him." Before leaving the country he addressed a farewell epistle to his brethren. " It was," say Friends of his Monthly Meeting, " as his daily food to be found doing the will of God ; and a divine ardour and zeal remained on him to the last."† He died in 1749, aged sixty-seven years.

William Armstrong, of Cumberland, and James Graham, appear to be the next who crossed the Atlantic in this good work. They arrived in America in 1717 ; but little, however, is known of their services during this engagement. James Graham died in the course of the visit, at Burlington : " his loss," says Smith, " was regretted by many, who had the opportunity of his acquaintance during his small stay in this country." ‡ William Armstrong joined the Society about the year 1690. He travelled extensively as a minister of the gospel in England, Ireland, and Scotland, as well as in the western world. About three years

* Journal of J. Dickinson.
† Life of B. Holme, p. 5.
‡ Smith's Hist. chap. xvi.

after the visit in question, being in the fifty-eighth year of his age, he was taken ill and died, having been "much weakened by hard exercises and travels in America."* The power of religion on the mind was strikingly exemplified during the illness of this devoted Christian. "Jacob's God is my God," he said, "He forgets me not in this time of trial—I am inwardly refreshed and comforted."† After commemorating the Lord's goodness to all them that seek him, he concluded, it is said, with "a spiritual song."‡

* MS. Test. vol. i. p. 313.   † Piety Promoted, p. 6.

‡ The gospel labours of several of those whom we have recently noticed, are alluded to in a memorandum penned by one of the early settlers in Pennsylvania. The brevity and simplicity of the remarks, combined with a fulness and evident truthfulness of expression, render them interesting, notwithstanding the quaintness of the style ; and, as historical data, they are here inserted :—

"*A short account of some Ministers of Christ, who, within these seventeen years came from England and the other islands, &c. to visit Friends and brethren here in Pennsylvania.*

"*First.*—William Ellis and Aaron Atkinson, whereof William was an authoritable minister of the gospel, and Aaron a mighty tender man, and his testimony very prevailing and powerful, so that their service is not yet forgotten by many honest Friends hereaway.

"*Secondly.*—Roger Gill, and Thomas Story. The power of the Lord was with him, the said Roger, so that his testimony was with authority, and the truth was raised by it in others. When he was gone to visit Friends in New England, and there heard of the hand of God being upon the people of Philadelphia, of which Friends had their share, he was so in love with them that he came hither, and prayed to the Lord that he would be pleased to take his life as a sacrifice for theirs in that day of great calamity ; that he was ready to lay it down ; and accordingly the Lord took him to himself, and there was health among the people from that time.*

"*Thirdly.*—Thomas Thompson, and Josiah Langdale. Thomas informed us that when he was binding sheaves in his native land, he became impressed with a duty to visit us, and the Lord had been with him by sea and land—he was a sound preacher. His companion, Josiah, was also a fine tender man, earnestly pressing people to fear the Lord ;

* The yellow fever of 1699, before-mentioned.

During the early part of this century, several ministers from other parts of America visited the meetings in Pennsylvania and the Jerseys.   Among these may be noticed George Skeffington

saying, if he could but gain one soul, or turn but one to Truth in all his travels, he would be well satisfied.

" *Fourthly.*—John Salkeld, a notable man to proclaim the gospel ; he had great openings in the scriptures, which was a mighty help and comfort to many tender Friends.

" *Fifthly.*—Thomas Turner, an ancient Friend, whose testimony was, that the enemies should be scattered, and the truth come into dominion. He had meetings with the Indians in their places of abode, and was very loving, and the Indians had great regard and kindness for him.

" *Sixthly.*—John Richardson, the bent of whose testimony was much to press people to honesty and uprightness.

" *Seventhly.*—John Estaugh, a mild man, desiring people to be true to what was made known to them.

" *Eighthly.*—Mary Ellerton, and Mary Banister, both valiant, faithful women, endeavouring to persuade to the true and continual fear of the Lord, and proclaiming woe to them that were covered with a covering, but not of God's Spirit.

" *Ninthly.*—John Fothergill, and William Armistead, who were also very tender, honest Friends. Their testimony was fervent, and powerful to all sorts, to fear God.   Oh ! the good frame of spirit, and how the power of the truth was with John Fothergill !

" *Tenthly.*—Samuel Bownas, a mighty valiant minister to open the mystery of Babylon.

" *Eleventhly.*—Samuel Wilkinson, and Patrick Henderson, whereof Samuel was a plain man, had a fine testimony for truth, and an excellent gift to open the Revelations and other parts of scripture for the edification and comfort of Friends.   And his companion was a wise man, or learned : large in his testimony, and of singular parts : may he keep to the Root that bore him.

" *Twelfthly.*—John Turner, a good and sound old man ; his testimony was much against wrath and contention, sometimes between neighbours, sometimes between near friends, and sometimes between man and wife ; and, oh ! he said, how busy the enemy is to plague poor men and women. He warned the people to depart from their wickedness, and turn to the Lord Jesus Christ.

" *Thirteenthly.*—Thomas Wilson, and James Dickinson : these were both very noted men.   They were men for God, and he had given them power to preach the gospel with boldness.   They had an open door among all sorts, and reached the hearts of many people.

of Newfoundland, in 1700. Gabriel Newby of North Carolina, in 1701, and again in 1715, with Matthew Pritchard, also of North Carolina. Esther Palmer of Long Island, and Susannah Freeborne from New England, in 1704 : some years before, the latter had visited these parts in company with Jannah Mott of New England. In 1705, Esther Palmer came twice on a visit to these provinces ; she held meetings in several localities where there had been none before, and many, it is said, were brought to a knowledge of the truth through her ministrations.*   John Oxley of Barbadoes, also visited this part in 1711, and again in 1719 ; and Lydia Norton from New England, in 1718.

The Yearly Meeting for Pennsylvania and the Jerseys appears to have been on many occasions divinely favoured, tending largely to strengthen its members in the Lord, and in love and unity one with another. The sittings were in general very numerously attended, and became larger as years passed on. In addressing, in 1701, their brethren assembled in London, they thus speak of their meeting : " We have cause to bless the name of the Lord, that we have the good tidings to send you of his more than common appearance and presence with us in this our Yearly Meeting, where his divine life and love, hath flowed in an extraordinary manner amongst us, so that the hearts of Friends have been deeply humbled and affected with his goodness to them ; travelling Friends, and such of those whom the Lord hath concerned and engaged in the work of the ministry,

" *Fourteenthly.*—William Armstrong, and James Graham : their testimony was precious. Oh ! the good frame of spirit they were in, entreating people to walk humbly, and serve the Lord fully. James Graham having finished the service God required of him in these American parts, he took him to himself in the Seventh Month, 1717.

" May we praise and magnify the Lord of the great harvest, in that he was pleased to send so faithful servants amongst us to proclaim his truth, and pray that he may send more like true labourers, that knowledge and faithfulness be increased upon earth, to the exalting and glorifying of his great and worthy name for ever.   Amen." *

* Smith's Hist. chap. xv.

being mightily enlarged in his power and wisdom, to divide his holy word and mind aright to the people. Truth prospers amongst us, and meetings are generally large in town and country." They write again in 1705, "We have had a very large and heavenly Yearly Meeting; the glorious presence of God crowned our assemblies; it was a time of brokenness of heart, and of great refreshment and edification to the heritage of God in these parts; and we hope shall not be forgotten by us." In 1713, their language was equally encouraging: they had "a very precious, large, and heavenly meeting, overshadowed with his tendering love, power, and presence, so that the rain and dew of heaven descended in a plentiful manner, and Friends in a general way were tendered and overcome with it, and brought to the valley of humility, where we hope it will lay long upon our branches, and cause us to bring forth savoury and acceptable fruit to our God."

The sense of encouragement was not confined to the heavenly and heart-tendering opportunities experienced by Friends at their annual assemblies. The state of the church throughout their borders, notwithstanding some causes of uneasiness, presented much that was calculated to cheer and animate them in their Christian course. In 1705, alluding to their state they say, "The Truth prevails and prospers, and great openness in many places, and many flocking to hear the testimonies of it, and some are convinced, and some that are young coming forth in a testimony; and good discipline increases amongst the churches." In 1711, the same cheering description was reiterated. "By the particular returns and accounts from our several Quarterly Meetings, it appears that truth in a general way continues to prevail and prosper in this part of the world; the churches everywhere moving and pressing forwards towards a perfect standard in all the holy discipline and order." The willingness manifested by the people generally to listen to the public ministrations of Friends,—the convincements which, in "many places," followed this disposition,—the new meetings that were established, where, to use their own expression in 1712 "the sound of the gospel hath not long been uttered," were circumstances also of no small comfort to them. " A visitation," says William Penn, " both inwardly and outwardly is come to America."

Up to the date of the foregoing, many excellent advices relative to the conduct and conversation of Friends, and regulations for the right conducting of the discipline of the Society, had been issued. In 1703, the disciplinary regulations were written out for the use of the respective meetings ; a work which was repeated in 1720. In 1709, written reports of the state of the Society within their respective limits, were first directed to be sent up by the Quarterly Meetings ; a regulation which was superseded in 1755, by the adoption of queries to be answered by the subordinate meetings.

The Yearly Meeting of Pennsylvania and the Jerseys, soon after its establishment, had occasionally corresponded with some other Yearly Meetings in America, and generally with that of London. During the early part of the eighteenth century, the interchange of these tokens of love had become more frequent, and about the year 1720, a correspondence appears to have been pretty regularly maintained with most, if not all, the Yearly Meetings.

Returning to the gospel visits of Friends from Europe, we find that in the year 1718, no less than five ministers left England on this service ; these were John Danson, Isaac Hadwin, Elizabeth Rawlinson, Lydia Lancaster, and Rebecca Turner. They all sailed in the same ship direct from London to Philadelphia, in company with Thomas Chalkley of Pennsylvania, and John Oxley of Barbadoes, both returning from a religious visit to Great Britain.* John Danson was from Swarthmore Monthly Meeting, and Isaac Hadwin was also from the same county : but no particulars of their gospel labours have been met with. Isaac Hadwin having, some years after, visited America on business, died at Chester, in Pennsylvania. Lydia Lancaster was from Westmoreland, and was then but about thirty-five years of age.† She travelled with Elizabeth Rawlinson, who came from Lancaster ; and they visited most of the meetings

* Chalkley's Journal.   † Piety Pro. part viii.

on the American continent. Elizabeth Rawlinson came forth in the ministry at the early age of seventeen, and lived to the advanced period of eighty ; her companion attained the age of seventy-seven, having been a minister fifty-three years. Both of these aged handmaidens of the Lord experienced, in their dying moments, a remarkable degree of the joyful realities of the religion of Christ their Saviour, and an assurance of a blessed resurrection in Him, " A glorious crown, and everlasting song is before me, " said Lydia Lancaster, "and if the foretaste be so joyous, what are the riches of the saints' inheritance beyond the grave ?"*   " My heart," said Elizabeth Rawlinson, " is full of the joy of God's salvation ; yea, full of the comforts of the Holy Ghost.   Oh ! the height, and length, and breadth, of the comfort and joy that flows in my soul ; my tongue is too short, and my lips are too narrow, to set forth one half of the goodness of my God."†

In the year following, Elizabeth Whartnaby arrived in Pennsylvania.   She appears to have united in gospel labour with Rebecca Turner, and their visit is mentioned as having been " acceptable to their brethren."   Both were from England, but no account of their lives has been met with.

In 1720, John Appleton of Lincolnshire proceeded to America. He visited the meetings throughout this Yearly Meeting, and had, he remarks, " many fresh, living meetings," where " some were convinced."   In the First Month of 1721, " I was," he states, " at a great meeting at North Wales ; I was made to say, the Lord would pour forth of his Spirit upon them, and that many of them should have a public testimony, both men and women, if they were faithfully resigned in heart to the Lord ; and before the Tenth Month following, there were nine men and women came forth in a testimony, and some of them were likely to be of good service."‡   In the early part of 1723, he visited the families of Friends in Philadelphia, and soon after returned

---

* Piety Pro. part viii.
† MS. Test. of Ministers, vol. i. p. 325.
‡ Mins. of London Y. M. vol. vi. p. 227.

to England. He travelled much as a gospel minister in Great Britain and Ireland, and died in 1741.

In the year 1721, four English Friends visited their brethren in America, viz., Margaret (wife of Josiah) Langdale, who afterwards married Samuel Preston, of Philadelphia, and who was, says Smith, "long an eminent preacher in that city;"[*] Margaret Payne, respecting whom we have no particulars, and John Fothergill, and Laurence King. This was the second visit of John Fothergill. They landed in York River, Virginia, in the Fifth Month, 1721, and reached Pennsylvania in the Tenth Month. John Fothergill was engaged about three years in America on this occasion. Reaching London in time for the Yearly Meeting of 1724, he made the following statement respecting Pennsylvania : " We found in that province, an enquiring openness in divers parts among people of several professions ; some were convinced of, and, we hope, received the Truth in the love of it. There is a large body of religiously-minded people among Friends, who are growing up in a true care for the honour of Truth ; though these are mixed with many earthly-minded, and some loose, libertine people, who occasion much exercise to the right-minded : yet the Lord's goodness and care is near and over that country, and his Truth prospers in it."[†] Laurence King was from Salterforth, in Yorkshire, and died soon after his return from America.[‡]

In the next year, 1722, Benjamin Kidd visited Pennsylvania ; and, in company with Thomas Lightfoot, also held meetings in " some remote places in the Jerseys."[§]   He came from Settle, in Yorkshire, and was then about thirty years of age.   Like many others who crossed the Atlantic, he appeared as a minister when only about twenty-one. He is described as one " eminently qualified for great and singular services in the church, not only in discipline, in which he was excellent, exerting himself in great wisdom ; but, through the lively and powerful influences of Divine

* Smith's Hist. chap. xviii.
† Life and Travels of John Fothergill, p. 188.
‡ Life, &c. W. and A. Ellis, p. 189.
§ Mins. of London Y. M. vol. vi. p. 304.

grace, conspicuously arrayed with beauty and brightness in his ministry." He died in 1751, at the age of fifty-nine, having been a minister thirty-eight years.*

The epistle of 1725, from Pennsylvania, notices the attendance of Abigail Bowles from Ireland, who, the year following, united in religious service with Jane Hoskens, of Pennsylvania, " in which journey," says the latter, " we travelled about one thousand seven hundred miles "†—a much more laborious undertaking then, than in the present day. In the year following, William Piggott and Joshua Fielding, both of London, proceeded to America, and also Samuel Bownas, on his second visit. Joshua Fielding landed at Charlestown, and visited the meetings generally within the limits of Pennsylvania Yearly Meeting. He stated to London Yearly Meeting in 1729, that during the visit he had travelled twenty-one thousand miles, to four hundred and eighty meetings, in nine hundred and fifty-two days.‡ In passing to South Carolina, he journeyed for five hundred miles through the forests, with only a pocket compass to direct him.§ William Piggott landed at Philadelphia, and visited his brethren throughout these provinces, in which he remarks, are " a very great body of Friends, and many concerned to maintain Truth's testimonies in all its branches."||

Samuel Bownas arrived in Virginia in the Second Month, 1727, and reached Pennsylvania a few months later. " He preached," says Besse, " with such a divine authority and majestic innocence, as commanded the attention of his hearers." His visit to Pennsylvania was looked forward to with considerable interest, and on his way to Philadelphia a large number of Friends came out to meet him, which, he observes, " gave me great uneasiness, fearing I should never be able to answer the expectations that were raised by such conduct." He had previously attended many meetings west of that city, some of

* MS. Test. vol. i. p. 350.
† Life of Jane Hoskens.
‡ Mins. of London Y. M. vol. vii. p. 81.
§ Life of Bownas, p. 139.
|| Mins. of London Y. M. vol. vi. p. 554.

which were very large, amounting, he says, "to fifteen hundred, and some more." "But very few," he adds, "of the elders, that twenty years before were serviceable, zealous men, were now living ; and many of the rising youth did come up in the form, more than in the power and life that their predecessors were in ; nevertheless, there was a fine living people amongst them, and they were in a thriving good way, sundry young ministers being very hopeful, both men and women." "I was," he continues, "at three meetings in Philadelphia, exceeding large, more like Yearly Meetings than common First-day Meetings."* After visiting New England, he attended most of the meetings in Pennsylvania and the Jerseys. He alludes to Burlington Quarterly Meeting, as a remarkable occasion, in which he says, "I was divinely opened with fresh matter, setting forth the service of a divine, spiritual ministry, which was free from all contrivance and forecast of the creature, in preparing itself, either with former openings, or beautiful collections of texts, or sayings from books or writings, all which gatherings would bring death, and could be no other in the best and most favourable construction, though well looked on by some, than the ministry of the letter, under pretence of the ministry of the Spirit, which is a deception of the highest nature."†

Samuel Bownas was occupied about two years on this gospel mission. He was a man of an intelligent, quick, and observing mind ; and his remarks on the state of our religious Society in that land, at the period of his visit, are entitled to more than ordinary attention. "As I had been out of that country," he remarks, " somewhat more than twenty-one years, and found so great an increase of the professors of truth, I had a curiosity to examine a little into it,—finding most of the old meeting-houses very much enlarged, some to hold double, and some treble, and some four times the people that the old ones would, in my first going thither ; and even now some wanted to be enlarged, or new ones to be built at proper distances ; besides the account of new houses, built in that time, in places where none were, nor meetings but in private

* Life of Bownas, p. 141.   † Ibid. 159.

houses, which grew so numerous that necessity put them upon erecting houses to accommodate themselves. In New England and Rhode Island are twelve ; in the government of New York are six ; in both East and West Jersey are nine ; in Pennsylvania, thirteen ; in Maryland, four ; in Virginia, nine ; and in North Carolina, three. In all, there have been fifty-six new meeting-houses built within these two or three and twenty years past ; and in these provinces there are about ten places more that want, where they have none; and many old ones want to be enlarged, not having room for half the people. Now the extraordinary increase of Friends, is much to be attributed to the youth retaining the profession of their parents, and marrying such: for, indeed, most of the people in Pennsylvania are of this profession, as well as in the Jerseys and Rhode Island ; so that young people are not under the temptation to marry such as are of different judgments in religion, as in some parts." *

During the year 1728, Rowland Wilson, and Joseph Taylor, crossed the Atlantic on a religious mission ; but no account of their travels or history has been met with. The next gospel labourer from England, was Henry Frankland, of Yorkshire, whom John Richardson describes as an "innocent good man." He arrived in the colonies in the year 1731, and held meetings with many not in profession with Friends. Speaking of Pennsylvania, he says, he "found very large meetings throughout that province, where, although the church has its exercises, yet some of their youth are hopeful, and some of them are become living ministers, to the great strength of the brethren."† He died in 1739, having been a minister twenty years.

Very soon after, John Richardson proceeded to America on his second visit ; and meeting with Henry Frankland at the Yearly Meeting of Philadelphia, in 1731, they visited the colonies in the south. It was about thirty years since John Richardson's former visit to this country ; and he also was struck with the great increase among Friends in the interim. He relates that he had "very large meetings," and that there was in many, great attention to hear the testimony of truth, and an open door

* Life of S. Bownas, p. 172.   † MSS. of London Y. M.

of utterance."* He was then about sixty-five years of age, and was absent from home about two years. He was one of those who were called to the work of the ministry at a very early age, and he was much devoted, and travelled extensively in the service of his Divine Master. He died in 1753, at the advanced age of eighty-seven, having been a minister sixty-seven years. His Journal, numerous editions of which have been printed, is replete with instructive and interesting details.

In 1732, no less than six Friends crossed the Atlantic in gospel love to their American brethren. These were Mungo Bewley, Paul Johnson, and Samuel Stephens, from Ireland; Alice Alderson, and Hannah Dent, of Yorkshire, and Margaret Copeland, from Westmoreland. No particulars of their services on this occasion appear to be preserved. Mungo Bewley, besides the visit in question, which occupied him about two years, travelled as a minister in England, Wales, Scotland, and in Holland. He is represented as a man of superior qualifications, of a noble mind, and a discerning spirit, and a living, powerful minister of the gospel of Christ. He died in 1747, in the seventieth year of his age, having been a minister about forty years.† Alice Alderson, respecting whom a testimony is preserved, though far from possessing much human learning, was frequently copious in expressions well adapted to her subject, as well as deep and weighty in spirit. She lived to the age of eighty-eight, having been a minister sixty years; and her closing moments were remarkable for the divine serenity and sweetness which attended her therein.‡ Margaret Copeland came forth in the ministry at the age of twenty-two. She died in 1759, at the age of seventy-six.§

In the year 1734, John Burton, William Backhouse, and Joseph Gill, visited America. John Burton was from Sedbergh Monthly Meeting, in Yorkshire. He was an unlearned man, but endued with a large and powerful gift in the ministry, and strong

* Journal of J. Richardson.
† Rutty's His. of Fr. in Ireland, p. 340.
‡ Piety Pro. part. viii.
§ MS. Test. vol. ii. p. 57.

were his desires " that the Church of Christ might flourish, and Zion keep her garments unspotted from the world." He died in 1769, aged eighty-seven years, " being filled with light, and divine consolation and peace.* William Backhouse was of Yealand, in Lancashire. He was first engaged in the ministry at the age of twenty-six, and was thirty-nine at the time of the visit in question. He died at the age of sixty-six, rejoicing, at that awful period, that, through Divine grace, he had been more concerned for God's honour and the good of souls, than for any other considerations.† Joseph Gill was from Ireland ; he arrived at Philadelphia in time to attend the Yearly Meeting of 1734, after which he travelled to some of the "remote back settlements of the province." He was highly gifted in the administration of the discipline, and his ministry was attended with Divine life and power. He died in 1741, aged sixty-seven years; a minister about thirty years.‡

The devoted John Fothergill was the next that proceeded to the Western world, this being his third visit to his brethren in that land. He sailed in 1736, direct for Philadelphia, and visited most of the meetings in Pennsylvania and the Jerseys. In his ministry he is described as " awful and weighty, being endued with true wisdom—strong and immoveably bent against all unrighteousness—quick in discerning, and powerful in detecting the mysteries of antichrist. As a flame of fire to the rebellious and stubborn, but refreshing as the dew of Hermon to the honest traveller—zealous and wise in the support of the discipline." The mighty God, who visited him in his youth with the discovery of his saving power, and sanctified him to Himself a chosen vessel, was near him in the decline of life, and became his evening song.§ He died in 1744, at the age of sixty-nine ; a minister fifty years.

Soon after the last-mentioned visit, John Tylee, from near Bristol, Ruth Courtney, and Susanna Hudson, of Ireland, and, in 1738, John Hunt of London, visited Friends in America ; but no

* Piety Pro., part viii.   † Ibid.   ‡ Rutty's Hist. p. 333.
§ Life of John Fothergill, p. 336.

account of their visit, or of their history has been found.   Thomas Gawthorp, of Westmoreland, was the next.   He went over in 1739, being then in the thirtieth year of his age.   About six years after he paid a second visit to his transatlantic brethren, a third in 1754, and a fourth in 1766.   No memoranda of his religious engagements during these gospel missions appear to exist, excepting that on his third visit he was particularly interested on behalf of the negro population.   Thomas Gawthorp was a deep and able minister of the gospel, not in the wisdom of man, nor with eloquence of words, but in the power and demonstration of the Spirit, by which it is recorded, " he reached the witness in the hearts of many." He died in 1781, aged seventy-one, having been a minister forty-seven years.*

The Yearly Meeting of Pennsylvania and the Jerseys was mostly attended by some Friends in the ministry from England, and continued to be a time of much spiritual refreshment and comfort.   The epistle to London Yearly Meeting, in 1738, thus refers to the Divine favour which marked that occasion.

" This our annual meeting hath been large and solid, tending to build up the true believers in the faith and righteousness of Christ Jesus our Lord, the fountain of love, truth, and abundant grace, both in things spiritual and temporal, whereof we are partakers in his name, and are thereby excited to perseverance and constancy in the way of our duty and true interest (that is) in the love and service of God and of one another, as brethren and fellow-members of the one holy body of Christ, redeemed with his blood, instructed by his blessed Spirit, who ever remains to make intercession for the saints.   Divers testimonies have been borne amongst us with energy and demonstration, for a general gathering and settlement on this self-evident and permanent foundation of piety and sound morality, confirmed by scripture authority, which was the basis and fundamental principle of our ancient worthy Friends, and of all truly Christian reformers in every age, whereby they obtained a good report, and, amidst manifold conflicts, had the strongest assurances of future and eternal happiness."

* Piety Pro., part viii.

In the year 1741, Samuel Hopwood, of Austle, in Cornwall, proceeded to America. He landed at Boston, and went without much delay to the Jerseys, and Pennsylvania, visiting the meetings, it is said, " to satisfaction." He died in 1760, aged eighty-six ; a minister sixty-one years.

Edmund Peckover of Norfolk, and John Haslam of Yorkshire, crossed over in 1742. The former reached Burlington in time for the Yearly Meeting. At this date many Friends of Pennsylvania had removed to inland parts, and settled in a wilderness country, rarely visited by Friends from England. To this class the attention of Edmund Peckover was directed ; and during his travels, " the back-settlers on the Susquehanna" were not forgotten. " Here," he says, " I found, in about thirty miles riding, more than one hundred who go to meetings ; and this was the most general visit they had had since they settled there. It may be observed," he continues, " that but very few of these back-settlers (who in a general way removed from Pennsylvania) from Opeckon all along to Susquehanna, were of much note amongst Friends ; but since their leaving that province, they seem, as I apprehend, more near to a growth in the best sense, and I hope the Lord will bless them every way. In Lancaster County, in the province of Pennsylvania, several Friends from Ireland dwell, and there are three or four meetings; though Friends are but thin here to what they are in other parts of the province. In the three lower counties [Delaware], viz., Newcastle, Kent, and Surrey, there are not many meetings, and [they] lay a great distance from each other ; and, in a general way, Friends are weak and feeble in these parts." Returning from a visit to New England, he again visited this part, and went to the back-settlements " beyond the Jerseys and Pennsylvania," to a place called " Mendon Creek, and the Forest, where," he says, " are many Friends settled who came from Ireland; there are six or seven meeting-houses that have been built that way of late years."*

Edmund Peckover entered on the work of the ministry as early

* Mins. of London Y. M., vol. ix. p. 322.

as the fifteenth year of his age, and only three years later visited several parts of England in that service. In his ministry " he was frequently enlarged in divine counsel, and as a cloud filled with celestial rain to the reviving and refreshment of the living heritage of God." In his dying moments he was favoured with a foretaste of the glorious immortality and endless felicity prepared for the righteous, and he " passed away as with a heavenly song of divine praise in his mouth." He died in 1767, aged seventy-two years.

Of John Haslam's religious services we have no account. He also once visited the continent of Europe, and twice the nation of Ireland. He is mentioned " as being exemplary in a deep inward exercise of spirit and patient waiting for the arising of the divine life, as a necessary qualification for service, either in the ministry or in discipline." He died in 1773, aged eighty-three, having been a minister fifty-seven years.*

Christopher Wilson of Cumberland, and Eliezer Sheldon of Ireland, also visited Pennsylvania about the same time ; no record, however, of their labours appears to be extant, excepting the following minute of London Yearly Meeting in 1745 : " Our dear and well esteemed friends, Samuel Hopwood of Cornwall, John Haslam of Yorkshire, Edmund Peckover of Norfolk, Christopher Wilson of Cumberland, and Eliezer Sheldon of Dublin, being, through the merciful providence of Almighty God, returned safe from their visit to Friends in America, gave this meeting a very comfortable and satisfactory verbal account of their said visit."

In the year 1747, Samuel Nottingham visited America. He first appeared as a minister when about twenty-three. After his gospel mission to America he resided for some years first in Tortola, and then in Long Island until 1779, when he returned to England. His ministry is described " as not in the enticing words of man's wisdom, but in the fresh openings and flowings of light and life and love." He died at Bristol in 1787, at the age of seventy-one.†

During the year 1750, Josiah Thompson, James Thornton, and

* Piety Pro. part ix.   † MS. Test. vol. iii. p. 330.

Mary Weston, all from England, visited, in the love of the gospel, their brethren in the American plantations.

The gospel labours of many devoted ministers of Christ, to which allusion has been thus briefly made, together with those of other zealous servants of the Lord in the Yearly Meeting of Pennsylvania and the Jerseys, were eminently blessed to the church in that land.   Their powerful and lively addresses, delivered in the authority, and in dependence on the immediate influence of Him who is both tongue and utterance to those whom He sends forth, tended not only to comfort and confirm the fainting and the feeble-minded on their heavenly way, but also to arouse those who were resting too much in the mere profession of religion, to the momentous concerns of eternity, and to alarm the careless ones to the dangers of their situation.   It is, indeed, questionable, whether in the history of the Society, there have been any portions of the Church more highly favoured with the labours of faithful ministers, than were the early settlers in these provinces.   It is true, and it may be noted as one of the remarkable features in the history of Friends, that most of those who crossed the Atlantic in the work of the Lord, were, during the period in question, but young in years ; yet were they also strong and valiant in Him, deeply experienced in the mystery of godliness, and zealously affected in his holy cause. Nor were the religious services of these, as we have seen, confined to Friends.   They were called forth largely in public ministrations to others,—ministrations which, as in the earlier days of the Society in England, were attended with a convincing effect on the hearers, and followed by considerable additions of members. So that in consequence of the natural increase of population in these newly-settled countries, the immigration of Friends from Europe, and the numerous convincements which took place, the members of the Society in this Yearly Meeting had, from the year 1700 to 1750, more than doubled ; whilst the number of meetings for worship had also increased from about forty-three to one hundred, comprehending, it is believed, about thirty thousand members.

Previously to the year 1680, the district included in this Yearly Meeting numbered but four meetings for worship, and those were situate in the Jerseys. In the following ten years, during which so many Friends emigrated to Pennsylvania, the new meetings established amounted to no less than twenty-seven. From 1690 to 1699, the increase was twelve, and successively for similar periods, ten, nine, thirteen, twelve, and thirteen, which brings us to the year 1750. Up to the year 1700, the meetings most distant from Philadelphia were Gwynned and Buckingham in the north, and Concord and Middletown in the west, the latter two not being more than fifteen miles from the banks of the Delaware. In the following twenty years, however, settlements of Friends had extended considerably westward. Of the nineteen established during this time, four were in the Jerseys, three in the northern parts of Maryland, and eight in Chester Quarterly Meeting, reaching westward as far as Caln and London Grove, and to East and West Nottingham on the borders of Maryland. During the ten years following, five were settled in the Jerseys, one at Cold Spring or Monaquassy in Maryland, one as far north as Plumstead in Bucks Quarterly Meeting, and the rest mostly in the western parts of Chester Quarterly Meeting as far as Sadsbury. From the year 1730 to 1750 the movement inland was still more apparent. Friends had now settled and established meetings west of the Susquehanna, and over the Blue Mountains in the remote parts of Virginia, at least one hundred and fifty miles in a direct line from Philadelphia. Of the additional meetings during these twenty years, ten were in the Jerseys, three in the distant settlements of Virginia, four west of the Susquehanna, three in the northern parts of Maryland, and the others mostly in the western parts of Chester Quarterly Meeting.

As yet there were no Europeans resident west of the Alleghany Mountains, except a few traders who wandered from tribe to tribe, and dwelt among the Indians, neither cultivating nor occupying land. The first movement towards the formation of settlements over the Alleghanies did not take place until after this date ; the earliest treaty with the Indians for the cession of lands on the basin of the Ohio was in 1744,* and this was in Virginia.   In 1752 a treaty for land was held with the Indians on the right bank of the Ohio in Pennsylvania, but the war with the French, and the conflicts which followed with them in this direction, checked the stream of emigration westward, and five-and-twenty years later, even the now populous Pittsburg did not exceed thirty houses.

MEETINGS IN THE YEARLY MEETING OF PENNSYLVANIA AND THE JERSEYS IN 1750.			
	When Esta-blished.	House when Built.	Remarks.
PHILADELPHIA QUARTERLY MEETING.	1682		
Philadelphia Monthly Meeting . .	1682	..	The first meeting was held at Shackamaxon.
Philadelphia (Centre). . .	1681	1684	
Ditto (Bank) . . .	1685	1685	
Ditto (High Street) .	1695	1695	
Abington Monthly Meeting . . .	1684	..	Byberry (called at first Postquessing) was settled in 1682 by Friends from England, whose dwellings at first were small rough log-houses. One family lived in a wigwam which they built under the instruction of the Indians, until they erected a small log-house. The Meeting-house was rebuilt in 1714, and was 50 feet by 30, with galleries. Frankfort, (called at first Tookany,) and Byberry, were constituted a Monthly Meeting under the following minute of Philadelphia Quarterly Meeting of Fifth Month, 1683 : " It was agreed and concluded, that there be established a First-day Meeting of Friends at Tookany and Poetquessing, and that these two make one Monthly Meeting of men and women, for the ordering of the affairs of the church." Germantown was settled by Friends from Germany, who bought 6,000 acres of land.
Abington	1682	..	
Byberry	1683	1694	
Frankfort	1683	..	
Cheltenham	1683	..	
Germantown	1683	early	
Fairhill	early	..	
Horsham	1716	early	
Haverford Monthly Meeting . .			These Meetings were settled by Friends from Wales, who bought of W. Penn 40,000 acres of land in this part
Haverford	1683	..	
Radnor	1683	..	
Merion	1683	1695	
Gwynned Monthly Meeting . .	1714	..	It previously formed a part of Haverford Monthly Meeting.
Gwynned or North Wales . .	1698	1700	A larger house built in 1712, and a still larger one in 1823. Most of the Friends of this Meeting were convinced Welsh settlers.

* Day's Pam. p. 70.

	When Established.	House when Built.	Remarks.
Plymouth	1685	early	This meeting was at first composed of Friends from Plymouth in Devonshire. They met at the house of James Fox. "But being most of them tradesmen and citizens, and not used to a country life, they removed to Philadelphia," and thus the meeting was discontinued for a time.
BUCKS QUARTERLY MEETING . .	1684	..	In 1690, there were many settlements of Indians in the townships of this district, who were "kind neighbours."
The Falls Monthly Meeting . . .	1683	..	These two Monthly Meetings established Bucks Quarterly Meeting by direction of the Yearly Meeting of 1684.
The Falls	1680	1690	
Bristol	1680	1710	
Neshaminy Monthly Meeting . .	1683	..	
Neshaminy	1682	1690	
Southampton	1683	..	
Buckingham Monthly Meeting.			
Wrightstown	1686	1721	House built on land given by John Chapman's family.
Buckingham	1700	1706	Rebuilt in 1729, and a larger one subsequently.
Plumstead	1727	1750	
Richland Monthly Meeting . .	1742	..	This meeting belonged previously to Gwynned Monthly Meeting.
Richland	1710	..	
CHESTER QUARTERLY MEETING .	1683	..	The first minute of the Monthly Meeting runs thus: "10th of Eleventh Month, 1681. A Monthly Meeting of Friends belonging to Marcus Hook, alias Chester and Upland, held at the house of Robert Wades."

The meetings at first all belonged to Chester Monthly Meeting, but in 1721 it was agreed to divide them into two Monthly Meetings. A General or Yearly Meeting for worship was set up at Goshen in 1726.

Uwchland was settled principally by Welsh Friends. |
Chester Monthly Meeting . . .	1681	..	
Chester	1681	..	
Springfield	1696	..	
Providence	1696	..	
Middletown	1696	..	
Goshen Monthly Meeting . . .	1721	..	
Goshen	1703	..	
Newton	1720	..	
Uwchland	1720	..	
Exeter	1745	..	
Nantmeal	1750	..	
Concord Monthly Meeting . .	1684	..	
Chichester	1683	..	
Concord	1684	1697	
Birmingham	1718	1718	
Darby Monthly Meeting . . .	1684	..	Before 1684, it formed a part of Chester Monthly Meeting.
Darby	1682	soon	Many of the early settlers were from Derbyshire in England.
Newark Monthly Meeting . .	1686	..	
Newark	1682	1688	
Centre	1687	1707	
Kennett	1707	1710	House enlarged in 1719 and again in 1731.

	When Established.	House when Built.	Remarks.
George's Creek	1703	..	{ Settled by consent of Newark Monthly Meeting.
Hockesson	. 1737	1738	House enlarged in 1745.
Wilmington Monthly Meeting .	1750	..	
Newcastle	1684	1705	{ Previous to 1750, these meetings formed a part of Newark Monthly Meeting.
Wilmington	1738	1748	
New Garden Monthly Meeting.			
New Garden	1712	1715	A larger house built in 1743.
London Grove	1714	..	
East Nottingham Monthly Meeting .	1730	..	{ John Churchman was one of the early settlers here.
East Nottingham	1704	..	{ Meeting held in a log-house until 1721. Previous to 1730, these meetings formed part of New Garden Monthly Meeting.
West Nottingham . . .	1719	1727	
Bush River, or Deer Creek . .	1736	..	
Little Britain	1749	..	
Bradford Monthly Meeting.			
Caln	1716	1716	
Bradford	1722	1727	
Sadsbury Monthly Meeting . .	1737	..	
Sadsbury	1724	1725	
Leacock	1732	..	
Duck Creek Monthly Meeting .	1706	..	{ A Half-year's Meeting was established at Duck Creek in 1715.
Duck Creek	1704	..	{ Previous to 1706 this meeting belonged to Newark Monthly Meeting.
Mush Mullion Creek . . .	1707	..	
Little Creek	1714	..	
Lewistown	1720	..	
Warrington Monthly Meeting . .	1747	..	{ This Monthly Meeting previously formed a part of Sadsbury Monthly Meeting; the particular meetings are all on the west of the Susquehanna.
Warrington	1745	..	
Newbury	1745	..	
Minallon	1748	..	
Huntingdon	1750	..	
Hopewell Monthly Meeting . .	1744	..	{ In 1732, some Friends of Pennsylvania and Elk River in Maryland, obtained a grant of 100,000 acres of land on Opeckon Creek, and settled there.
Hopewell or Opeckon (Virginia) .	1732	soon	
Providence or Tuscarara (ditto) .	1733	..	
Fairfax Monthly Meeting . .	1744	..	In 1733, some Friends from Bucks County settled at Fairfax, about forty miles south of Hopewell.
Fairfax (Virginia)	1733	1741	
Coldspring, or Monaquassy, in Maryland . . . }	1720	1736	In 1736, these meetings were, by consent of Chester Quarterly Meeting, constituted a Monthly Meeting. In 1744, Friends being much increased, it was divided.
BURLINGTON QUARTERLY MEETING .	1682	..	{ Women Friends' meetings for discipline were set up here in 1681.
Burlington Monthly Meeting . .	1678	..	{ Meetings here were first held in tents.

	When Esta-blished.	House when Built.	Remarks.
Burlington	1677	1685	{ A new house built in 1716, on ground given by Thos. Wetherill.
Rancocas	early	1703	{ House built on ground given by John Wills; at first the meetings were held at the house of Thomas Olive.
Old Springfield	1690	1698	{ House built on ground given by Richard Ridgway.
Mount Holly	1718	1718	Ditto, Nathaniel Crips.
Upper Springfield	1728	1728	
Mansfield	1731	1731	
Woodwards	1742	1742	{ House built on ground given by Joseph Arney.
Chesterfield Monthly Meeting.			
Chesterfield	1677	1680	
Crosswicks	1699	..	
Stoney Brook	..	1726	{ House built on ground given by Benjamin Clark; meetings were held in Friends' houses here many years before.
Trenton	1731	1740	
Allentown . . . . ,	1727	..	
Bordentown	1740	1740	{ House built on ground given by Joseph Borden.
Bethlehem Monthly Meeting .	1744	..	
Bethlehem	1731	1746	Burnt down and rebuilt in 1752.
Great Meadows	1740	1751	
Little Egg Harbour Monthly Meeting	1715	..	
Little Egg Harbour . . .	1704	1709	{ This meeting was established through the gospel labours of Ed. Andrews. A Yearly Meeting for worship was established here in 1729.
Barngat	1746	..	
SALEM QUARTERLY MEETING			
Gloucester Monthly Meeting . .	1682	..	
Newtown	1682	1687	{ Settled by Friends from Ireland in the Spring of 1682, before the arrival of William Penn.
Evesham	1694	1698	
Woodbury	1696	early	
Haddonfield	1721	1721	{ Built on ground given by John Estaugh.
Chester	1721	1721	
Salem Monthly Meeting . . .	1676	..	
Salem	1675	early	{ A Yearly Meeting chiefly for worship, was established here in 1686.
Greenwich	..	..	
Alloways Creek	..	..	
Glass House	..	..	
Egg Harbour Monthly Meeting . .	1702	early	
Great Egg Harbour . . .	1702	..	{ Two meeting-houses were afterwards built here.
Cape May	1750	..	

	When Esta-blished.	House when Built.	Remarks.
SHREWSBURY QUARTERLY MEETING.			
Shrewsbury Monthly Meeting . .	1670	..	
Shrewsbury	1670	1672	A new house built in 1719. Meetings were held here occasionally a few years previous.
Manasquan	1700	1730	
Middletown	early	..	
Upper Freehold	1740	1740	A meeting was held at Freehold in 1683, but given up in 1698, as most of its members went off with George Keith.
Rahway Monthly Meeting . . .	1686	..	
Rahway	early	..	
Woodbridge or Amboy . .	1680	1709	
Plainfield	1721	1731	House built on land given by John Laing.

ABINGTON MEETING HOUSE.

CHAPTER X.

Memorials of deceased Ministers, from 1700 to 1750, viz. : Hugh Roberts, John Simcock, Eleanor Smith, Samuel Jenings, Richard Gove, John Lowdon, Edward Andrews, John Smith, Griffith Owen, Ellis Pugh, Vincent Caldwall, Anthony Morris, Thomas Lightfoot, Aaron Coppock, Hannah Hill, Hannah Carpenter, Rowland Ellis, Joseph Booth, Richard Townsend, Joseph Kirkbride, John Salkeld, Christopher Wilson, Thomas Chalkley, Esther Clare, Robert Jordan, John Cadwallader, Margaret Preston, Cadwallader Evans, Evan Evans, Jacob Holdcombe, William Trotter, Elizabeth Wyatt ; and some other public characters among Friends in Pennsylvania, viz. : Samuel Carpenter, Jonathan Dickinson, Caleb Pusey, Richard Hill, Isaac Norris, Samuel Preston, James Logan.

In the preceding chapter but little allusion has been made to the gospel labours of those Friends, of whom there were not a few in Pennsylvania and the Jerseys, who travelled in the work of the ministry in other colonies of America, or in Europe. The following memorials will, to a large extent, supply this information, but it must not be understood that all who were called to the work of the ministry are here noticed : they are presented to the reader in the order in which the decease occurred.

HUGH ROBERTS.

Hugh Roberts emigrated from Wales in 1684. He is represented as "a man fitted and qualified by God's power to be a serviceable minister to the church of Christ. His doctrine in meetings," continues the account, " dropped as dew, and his speech as small rain upon the tender plants ; for in the openings of life, things new and old came forth of the treasury of wisdom." He travelled in the work of the gospel in Maryland, Long Island, and New England, where, it is said, " his services were effectual to the people." He died in 1702, and was buried at Merion.*

JOHN SIMCOCK.

John Simcock removed to Pennsylvania from England about 1682, and settled in Chester county. He was one of William Penn's first Council, and one of his commissioners of property, and subsequently also a member and speaker of the Assembly. These civil services were not, however, permitted to interfere with his call as a minister of the gospel, in which he travelled extensively. He was, says one who knew him well, " a nursing father in Israel—his ministry was sound and edifying, and he was endued with a spirit of discerning and wisdom beyond many in spiritual things." During his illness he was favoured with a sweet and heavenly serenity of mind. " The Keeper of Israel," he remarked, " is near to all them that wait upon and truly put their trust in Him." The day preceding his dissolution he bore a living testimony to the necessity of dwelling in love. " It is," he said, " the desire and earnest prayer of my soul, that the heavenly spring of true love and stream of divine life, may ever be known to spring and run amongst those who would be accounted children of God, and followers of Christ Jesus our blessed Lord and eternal Saviour, who laid down his life to be a ransom for fallen man, and to be an atonement for all them that would come to God by him, who is the living Word, and promised Seed of the covenant." He died in 1703, aged about seventy-three years.†

ELEANOR SMITH.

Eleanor Smith was a native of Leicestershire, in England, and joined in religious profession with Friends about 1666, when but thirteen years of age. On emigrating to America she became a member of Darby Monthly Meeting ; and some years prior to her decease was called by her Divine Master to declare

* Piety Promoted, part iii.   † Col .of Memorial, p. 63.

to others the good things of his everlasting kingdom. This handmaiden of the Lord, was one of those who, in their dying moments, have realised the triumphs of religion : " I can praise thy name, O Lord," she said, " in the midst of affliction ; for surely thou art worthy of all praise, honour, and glory, and that for evermore ; for thou neither leavest nor forsakest those that put their trust in thee ;" adding, " the presence of the Lord I feel flowing as a river into my soul." She died in 1708, aged fifty-five years.*

SAMUEL JENINGS.

Samuel Jenings emigrated to New Jersey, from Coleshill in Buckinghamshire, in 1680. He was at that period in the station of a minister. His signature appears among others to the epistle issued by London Yearly Meeting in 1677. On his arrival in New Jersey, Byllinge, the proprietary governor, appointed him his deputy, in which capacity he acted until 1683, when he was chosen governor for one year by the Assembly ; and up to the time of his removal to Philadelphia in 1692, we find him occupy-ing the highest offices in the province. His abilities were highly appreciated by the executive of Pennsylvania, and soon after, he was nominated to the commission of the peace. About this time the controversy with George Keith arose, in which Samuel Jenings was much engaged on behalf of the Society ; and in the early part of 1694, he sailed for London and as respondent on the appeal of Keith to that Yearly Meeting, he ably vindicated the cause of his American brethren from the aspersions of their detractor. Soon after his return from England he removed to Burlington, the place of his former residence ; and in 1702, the Crown, to which the government of New Jersey had been transferred by the proprietaries, appointed him one of the Provincial Council ; and in 1707, the year preceding his death, he filled the office of Speaker of the Assembly, in which station he distinguished himself by a bold and fearless opposition to the arbitrary misrule of the bigoted Lord Cornbury.† As a labourer in the work of the gospel, he appears to have been

---

* Coll. of Mem. p. 37.   † Smith's New Jersey, p. 231, 294.

highly valued by his brethren. "He was," says the historian Proud, "of worthy memory, endued with both spiritual and temporal wisdom. He was a suppressor of vice, and an encourager of virtue ; sharp towards evil-doers, but tender and loving to them that did well ; giving good counsel, and wholesome advice to friends and neighbours ; an able minister of the gospel, and laboured much therein to the comfort and edification of many people, both in this province and other places."[*] Samuel Jenings was one of those rare individuals, in whom was concentrated a variety of qualifications and mental endowments, by which, under the sanctifying power of Truth, he was made eminently useful to his fellow-men, both in his ministerial and civil capacity. He died at Burlington in 1708, leaving three daughters, who all intermarried with three brothers named Stephenson.[†]

RICHARD GOVE.

This Friend emigrated from Plymouth, in Devonshire, in 1685, and, with several other Friends of that place, settled on a spot in Pennsylvania, which they called Plymouth. He afterwards resided in Philadelphia, and was much engaged, both at home and abroad, in the service of his divine Master. In 1702, he visited New England ; in 1704, the Carolinas ; and in the same year, in company with John Estaugh, the West India Islands. Whilst on this voyage, they were taken by a French privateer, and carried into Martinique, where they were detained as prisoners about two months, during which period they had much religious service with the inhabitants. In 1707, he visited the West Indies a second time, in company with Thomas Chalkley. They had service in Barbadoes, Jamaica, Antigua, Nevis, Christophers, Anguilla, and Montserrat. From the West Indies they sailed for

[*] M.S. in Proud, vol. i. p. 159.   [†] Smith's New Jersey, p. 354.

England, and during the voyage were twice chased by French privateers. In the first instance they escaped, by the privateer's masts having broken down ; and in the second, by running on the coast of Ireland, the captain preferring rather to lose his vessel and rich cargo in this way, than to fall into the hands of his pursuers, who, observing this, gave up the chase ; and the captain casting anchor in time, saved his vessel. After visiting Friends in Ireland, Scotland, and England, for nearly three years, Richard Gove died at Uxbridge, in 1709, at the age of fifty-eight.* He is described by Thomas Chalkley, as an "inoffensive, loving Friend, whose testimony was sound, serviceable, and convincing, and who left a good savour and report behind him, wherever he travelled in the world."†

JOHN LOWDON.

This Friend emigrated from Ireland in 1711, and settled at New Garden, in Chester County ; soon after which, he was engaged in different parts in gospel labours. In 1714, he was occupied in this service on Long Island, in New England, and in the counties of Bucks and Philadelphia, but was taken ill in the same year, and died at Abington. "He was," says Proud, "an eminent preacher among the Quakers, travelled much in that service, and was much esteemed and beloved."

EDWARD ANDREWS.

He was the son of Samuel and Mary Andrews, of Mansfield, in New Jersey. His mother's maiden name was Mary Wright ; who, when very young, went to Boston to remonstrate with the rulers on their cruelty to Friends. Edward, in his youth, wandered from the paths of true peace, and brought much sorrow on his parents, who were deeply solicitous for the best welfare of their children. "As I grew in years," he remarks, "vanity increased upon me, and I took great delight in music and mirth, and by this means would strive to stifle the witness of God in

---

* London Registers.   † T. Chalkley's Journal.

my heart." As years passed on he deviated more widely, and at last left off attending meetings, " to take," as he said " my swing in the world." But the Lord visited him with his judgments ; " crosses, losses, with great afflictions," were the means employed in heavenly love to bring him home to the true sheepfold ; and, " so the Lord followed me," he says, " until my music became a burden to me, and I grew weary of my sin." About this time also, he appears to have been " mightily reached " through the ministry of Thomas Chalkley, at a meeting held under the trees at Crosswicks, and to which Thomas Chalkley particularly refers in his journal. But turning again a deaf ear to the voice of the good Shepherd, he slighted these mercies of God, and again turned to evil. He now removed to Egg Harbour, prompted by the idea, that in the wilds of that remote district, he might pursue his wickedness unrestrained by human observation. But the Lord followed him, and by his good Spirit pleaded mightily with him. " I saw my sins," he writes, " which made me abhor myself, and I cried out, Lord, be merciful to me ! Oh ! the bitter days and nights I had, in weeping and mourning, and there was no man nor woman that knew my condition. I soon became a gazing stock to the people ; for I had no comfort in anything, but weeping alone and crying to the Lord for strength to please him." " After some time," he writes, " I felt the favour of God unto me : and the Lord shewed me his people ; and my heart was filled with love to all mankind." This appears to have been about 1704, when in the twenty-seventh year of his age. He was soon required to prove his love and allegiance to God by a call to the ministry, and being faithful therein, was instrumental to the gathering of many to the fold of Christ ; and to the establishment of a meeting at Egg Harbour. His removal from time was in the meridian of life. In the Tenth Month, 1716, he was seized with the small-pox, and died after an illness of thirteen days, but was throughout sweetly attended with the presence of the Lord.*

* Philadelphia Friend, vol. xix. p. 55.

JOHN SMITH.

He was a member of Darby Monthly Meeting, having been an early emigrant from Leicestershire in England. When but fourteen years of age he joined our Society from religious conviction, and some time after came forth as minister, but of his labours in this character no particulars appear to be preserved. Shortly before his close he said, " I feel the fresh remembrance or renewings of the love of God, flowing into my heart, which is of much more comfort to my soul than all transitory things ; now I feel that God's living, divine presence, is with me, which bears up my spirit over that which flesh and blood would or could not be able to bear." At another time he said, " he was full of pain, yet he could sing of the mercy and goodness of God to his soul in the midst of affliction ;" adding, soon after ; " do not mourn for me, but be still and quiet, and let me pass away quietly, that so my soul may enter into God's everlasting rest ;" and nearly his last words were, " Come Lord Jesus, receive my soul ; thy servant is ready, come quickly." He died in 1714, aged about sixty-nine years.*

GRIFFITH OWEN.

Griffith Owen resided in Philadelphia ; the following brief notice is given respecting him. " He came over among the early settlers of Pennsylvania, and was of eminent service among them in divers capacities. As a minister among Friends, he had a sensible, pathetic, and lively testimony. As a member of that religious community, he was active, exemplary, and useful. In civil society, his merit raised him to several public stations, wherein he acted with judgment and a becoming integrity. But his practice as a physician, in which he was very knowing and eminent, rendered him of great additional value in the place where he lived. With these qualities he preserved the sincerity and meekness of a Christian, was ready to every good office, and died greatly beloved and lamented by a large acquaintance of

* Coll. of Mem. p. 39.

people of different ranks and persuasions."* For some years he was an active member of the legislative council,† and in 1709, he went on a gospel mission to New England.

Griffith Owen

ELLIS PUGH.

He was born at Dolgelly, in Merionethshire, in the year 1656. At the age of eighteen he was convinced of the principles of Friends through the ministry of John-Ap-John, and six years afterwards spoke as a minister of the gospel. He removed to Pennsylvania in 1687, and with several of his countrymen settled at Gwynned, where his gospel services appear to have been much blessed to his friends. "His pious labours," they remark, "have been profitable in directing and edifying us in the way of truth ; for by the tenderness and influence which came as dew upon our souls, while we sat under his ministry, we believed his doctrine was of God. He was," they add, "of a meek and quiet spirit, considerate and solid in his judgment, of few words, honest and careful in his calling, honourable among his Friends, and of good report among people generally."‡ In 1706, he went on a gospel visit to Great Britain, which occupied him about two years, and a short time previous to his decease he wrote his "Salutation to Britons," a piece which has been widely circulated, and shows him to have been largely experienced in divine things. He died in 1718, at the age of sixty-two.

VINCENT CALDWELL.

Vincent Caldwell resided at Marlborough in Chester county, Pennsylvania. He had emigrated about the year 1699, from Derbyshire, his native country, where he was brought to unite with Friends when about seventeen years of age, through the

---

* Smith's Hist. chap. xviii.   † Proud, vol. ii. p. 100.
‡ Coll. of Mem. p. 46.

ministry of John Gratton.   He travelled much on the continent of America in the work of the ministry, particularly in the more southern provinces ; and in 1718, visited several of the West India islands, where he was instrumental to the gathering of many to Friends.   He was a man of but little learning, yet eminent as a gospel minister, his communications being convincing, and affecting the hearts of the hearers.*   His end was bright and peaceful.   "Give me a little water," he said just before his close, "and I think I shall not want any more, till I drink at that fountain which springs up into eternal life."   He died in 1720, in the forty-sixth year of his age, and was interred at Kennet.†

ANTHONY MORRIS.

Anthony Morris emigrated to New Jersey in 1680, and after residing for some years at Burlington, he settled in Philadelphia. He first appeared as a minister in 1701, being then in the forty-seventh year of his age, and soon after circumscribed his worldly affairs, that he might devote himself more entirely to the promotion of righteousness among men.   He travelled in the work of the gospel in most of the colonies of North America, and in 1715 he visited Great Britain.   Towards his close, he was favoured with that peace which passeth all understanding, and impressed upon his friends, "that his hope for eternal salvation was alone in the mercy of God through his Son Christ Jesus, the only Saviour and Mediator.   Remember," he said, "my dear love to Friends in general ; tell them I am going, and that all is well."‡   He died in 1727, aged sixty-seven years.

Antho: Morris

THOMAS LIGHTFOOT.

He resided at New Garden, in Chester county, Pennsylvania, having emigrated from Ireland, in 1716.   In the year 1724,

---

* Proud, vol. ii. p. 126.   † Coll. of Mem. p. 56.   ‡ Ibid. p. 58.

being then nearly eighty years of age, he accompanied his young
friend Benjamin Kidd from England, on a religious visit to
Friends in New England. " He was," says his intimate friend
Thomas Chalkley, " greatly beloved for his piety and virtue, his
sweet disposition and lively ministry : the Lord was with him in
his life and death, and with us at his burial."* His decease
took place in the year 1725.

AARON COPPOCK.

Aaron Coppock was born in the year 1662, and united with
Friends when but a young man, and soon after he removed to
Pennsylvania. For some years he was an elder in Nottingham
Monthly Meeting, but during the latter period of his life occupied the station of minister, in which he manifested a deep
concern that his friends might live a life of self-denial, watchfulness and prayer. He died in 1725, at the age of sixty-seven, in
a sure hope of an entrance into everlasting life.†

HANNAH HILL.

Hannah Hill was the wife of Richard Hill of Philadelphia,
and relict of John Delavall, her first husband. She was the
daughter of Governor Thomas Lloyd, and was born in Wales, at
Dolobran, the family seat, in the year 1666. Her natural
accomplishments were many, and she was conspicuous for her
Christian virtues. It pleased the Lord to call her in her younger
years to bear a public testimony to his truth, and though her
communications were not long, yet " her doctrine dropped as the
dew, and distilled as the small rain." She travelled in the
service of the gospel in New England, and other parts of North
America, and for some years filled the office of Clerk to the
Women's Yearly Meeting. " She was," say her friends, " a true
servant of the church, and in the sense of the Apostle's expressions ' One that washed the saints' feet,' receiving with joy into
her house, the ministers and messengers of the gospel, for whom
her love was great." During the latter years of her life, much
bodily weakness attended her, but under this she experienced the

* T. Chalkley's Journal.　　　　† Coll. of Mem. p. 60.

Everlasting Arm to be near her, comforting and sustaining her in the eventide of life. She died in 1726, in the sixty-first year of her age.*

HANNAH CARPENTER.

Hannah Carpenter was born at Haverfordwest, in South Wales, where she was convinced of the principles of Friends, and where, it is said, "she became very serviceable to those who were in bonds for Christ's sake." After her settlement in Pennsylvania, she was united in marriage to Samuel Carpenter of Philadelphia, a Friend of considerable influence in the province. Her gospel ministry was attended with much divine sweetness, and was truly acceptable and edifying. She was a tender nursing mother in the church, and a bright example of Christian meekness. Her decease took place in 1728, at the advanced age of eighty-two years.

ROWLAND ELLIS.

Rowland Ellis was born in Merionethshire in the year 1650; where, it is said, "he was a man of note." He united with Friends about the twenty-second year of his age, and for several years suffered imprisonment for his religion; and, in 1697, settled with his family within the compass of Gwynned Monthly Meeting, in Pennsylvania. His communications in the ministry were not frequent, but sound and edifying. "He was," says Proud, "an acceptable man in every station, his services both in the Church and the State being considerable." The members of his meeting being Welsh people, his ministry was in that language, and he was also useful as the interpreter of others.† He died in 1729, in the eightieth year of his age, and was buried at Plymouth.‡

Rowland Ellis

---

* J. Richardson's Journal.   † Coll. of Mem. p. 85.
‡ Coll. of Mem. p. 65.

JOSEPH BOOTH.

Joseph Booth was born at Scituate, in New England, and was brought up as an Independent. When a young man he removed to Delaware, where for many years he filled the station of a magistrate, and was also chosen as a member of the Assembly for Sussex, the county in which he resided. He was convinced of the principles of Friends in 1699, through the ministry of Thomas Story, who, in alluding to him, remarks, "that he was the most sober and knowing person in those parts. Continuing faithful to the divine manifestations, it pleased the Lord to call him to declare to others what had been done for his own soul, and his communications were solemn and awful, delivered in the power of Truth." It was through his instrumentality, that the meetings at Motherkill, in Delaware, and Cold Spring, in Maryland, were settled. He died about the year 1732.*

RICHARD TOWNSEND.

He was a member of Philadelphia Monthly Meeting, which meeting issued the following brief testimony concerning him : " He was a meek and humble man, sincerely concerned for the promotion of piety and virtue ; his ministry, being sound, living, and tending to edification, was well accepted. He visited Friends in the service of truth in Great Britain, continued faithful to the end of his days, and departed this life in 1737."†

JOSEPH KIRKBRIDE.

He emigrated when but a boy, in one of the three ships that left England in 1681 for Pennsylvania, "and is an instance," says Proud, "among many others that might be given, in the early times of this country, of advancement from low beginnings, to rank of eminence and esteem." For many years he filled the responsible office of magistrate in Bucks county, and was frequently chosen to represent that county in the Assembly.‡ He is referred to as a " sound and serviceable " minister of the gospel, of an exemplary life, and zealous in the cause of truth. In the

---

* Coll. of Mem. p. 85.   † Ibid. p. 95.   ‡ Proud, vol. i. p. 193.

year 1699, he crossed the Atlantic on a gospel mission to his brethren in England ; and in after years was similarly engaged in some of the northern provinces of America. " He finished his course in the unity of his brethren, in which he had lived near fifty years."* He died in 1737.

JOHN SALKELD.

John Salkeld visited America in the year 1700, on a gospel mission, his home being then in Westmoreland. Some years after he emigrated to Pennsylvania, and settled at Chester. He is thus described by Smith : " He was long and fervently engaged for truth's prosperity and the promotion of righteousness in the earth. To this purpose he travelled several times through most of this continent ; often to many of the meetings in these and the neighbouring provinces, and about the year 1712, visited his native country of England ; also Scotland and Ireland. He was naturally of a cheerful disposition, and in conversation found it necessary to keep a constant guard. He had a clear, distinct, intelligible method and utterance in his ministry, which being often attended with great life and authority, generally had an uncommon reach upon his auditory, and was sometimes crowned with great success."† He died in 1739, at the age of sixty-eight years.

THOMAS CHALKLEY.

This able and devoted minister of Christ was born a member of our religious Society, in the borough of Southwark, in the year 1675. " My parents," he says, " were careful of me, and brought me up in the fear of the Lord." In very early life he was sensible of the extendings of heavenly goodness to his soul, awakening conviction, and preserving him from the snares which surrounded him. At the age of ten years the fear of the Lord

* Smith's Hist. chap. xviii.   † Ibid. chap. xix.

wrought so powerfully on his mind that " he could not forbear," he writes, " to reprove those lads who took the Lord's name in vain."* As he advanced in years, he grew in religious experience, and being brought more fully to see the beauty and the excellency of true religion, the Lord was pleased to visit his soul abundantly with his enriching presence, and to call him to the ministry when about twenty-one years of age. In the year following he proceeded on a religious visit to Scotland, and in the succeeding one to America. Soon after his marriage in 1699, believing it to be his religious duty to settle in America, he bought a lot of ground near the Delaware, where he pursued the business of an agriculturist. Pennsylvania was his home during the remainder of his life, though many of his latter years were spent on the ocean as the master of a vessel. Few characters present instances of greater devotedness in the work of their Divine Master than Thomas Chalkley. In addition to his gospel labours in Great Britain and Ireland, he once visited Holland and Germany, and repeatedly most of the North American colonies and the West India islands ; his religious labours being blessed to many, both Friends and others. He wrote several instructive essays on divine things, one of which, entitled " God's great love to mankind through Jesus Christ," has been very extensively circulated. In his temporal affairs, through losses by fire and at sea, many were the trials and discouragements which were permitted to attend him ; but through all, his faith was unwavering in the ever-watchful care of the unslumbering Shepherd of Israel, and he was enabled to exemplify to those around him, a remarkable degree of resignation to these proving dispensations. He was a man greatly beloved and esteemed by his brethren. His virtues are said to have been many, his faults few ; and he evidenced to the world in many countries, and on some closely trying occasions, a bright example of a meek and quiet spirit. His ministry was " informing, edifying, and tender," and was accompanied with an evident sense in the hearers, that he felt what he said. His manner also was marked by an inviting sweetness.† He died at Tortola in 1741, whilst on a gospel mission to those parts,

---

* T. Chalkley's Journal.   † Smith's Hist.

and this passage of Scripture, so peculiarly applicable to himself, comprised the last words which he uttered as a minister: "I have fought a good fight, I have finished my course, I have kept the faith: henceforth there is laid up for me a crown of righteousness."*

ESTHER CLARE.

Of Esther Clare's life and gospel labours, but few particulars have been preserved. In 1722, she crossed the Atlantic, on a religious visit to Great Britain and Ireland; and in Philadelphia Monthly Meeting, of which she was a member, it appears she was often largely engaged in the ministry. She is represented as one " well qualified for the publication of the doctrines of the gospel ;" and her ministrations were often attended with evidences of Divine help. She died in 1742, in the sixty-eighth year of her age.†

ROBERT JORDAN.

Robert Jordan was born in Nancemund county, Virginia, in the year 1693, of parents who were members of our religious Society, and received a call to the ministry at the age of twenty-five. He was unwearied in the exercise of his gift, and paid repeated religious visits to Friends in the several colonies of America. He was an unusual instance in that country, of suffering severely for his testimony against war and tithes, and was once imprisoned for the non-payment of the latter. In 1728, he came to Europe, on a religious visit to Friends in Great Britain and Ireland, and in one of his visits to the southern colonies, proceeded as far south as Georgia. He afterwards removed to Philadelphia, where he resided the remainder of his life. " His ministry," say Friends of his meeting, " was convincing and consolatory ; his delivery graceful but unaffected ; in prayer he was solemn and reverent ; he delighted in

‡ T. Chalkley's Journal.   † Coll. of Mem. p. 102.

meditation, recommending, by example, religious retirement in his familiar visits among his friends. In his sentiments he was generous and charitable, yet a firm opposer of obstinate libertines in principles or practice, demonstrating his love to the cause of religion and righteousness above all other considerations." It pleased the Most High to remove this devoted minister from his labours, when in the meridian of his day. He died of a fit of apoplexy, in 1742, in the forty-ninth year of his age.*

JOHN CADWALLADER.

John Cadwallader lived at Horsham, in Pennsylvania, and became convinced of our principles in early life. He travelled extensively as a minister, and twice visited Europe in that capacity. In 1742, he proceeded, in company with John Estaugh, on a religious visit to Tortola, and, whilst on that island, was taken ill and died.† He was then about sixty-six years of age, and his end was unclouded and peaceful. "He had a lively testimony, and was in great esteem among his brethren everywhere."‡

MARGARET PRESTON.

She was formerly the wife of Josiah Langdale of Yorkshire, and went to America in 1721, on a religious visit ; and in 1723, left England, to settle in Pennsylvania with her husband, who died on the passage. She afterwards married Samuel Preston of Philadelphia. She travelled much in the work of the ministry on the continent of North America ; her communications being "lively, sound, and edifying." She died in 1742, in the fifty-eighth year of her age.

CADWALLADER EVANS.

He was one of the Welsh emigrants who settled at Gwynned in 1698, and who soon after became convinced of our principles. His offerings in the ministry, though short, were "instructive, lively, and manifestly attended with a divine sweetness ;" and his meek, affable manners, combined with a marked gravity of mind, greatly endeared him to his friends.   In his later moments, it is

* Coll. of Mem. p. 110.   † Ibid. p. 111.   ‡ Smith's Hist.

recorded, that "his soul overflowed with love to God and man," and he was favoured with "a blessed hope and confidence that he was going to that place which God had prepared for those that love him ; and he had a happy exit from time to eternity, in 1745, aged eighty-one years."*

EVAN EVANS.

Evan Evans was born in Merionethshire, in 1684, and in 1698 emigrated with his parents to Gwynned. He had an excellent gift in the ministry, which he exercised in much fear and reverence of soul, visiting most of the colonies of North America, and the meetings in his own province. His service in the ministry, his friends remark, "was rendered more effectual, by the distinguishing marks which he bore of 'an Israelite indeed, in whom was no guile ;' a plainness and simplicity of manner in word and deed, with a zeal seasoned with divine love ; and as he had large experience in the work of regeneration, and the mysteries of the heavenly kingdom, as well as the snares of the world, he was thereby well qualified to administer to the states of the people." His conduct and conversation in life adorned the doctrine he preached ; and the God of his youth, who had raised him up as an instrument in his hand, and on whom he relied all his life, continued to be his shield and support in the evening of his days.† He died in 1747.

JACOB HOLCOMBE.

He resided at Buckingham, in Pennsylvania, having been born at Tiverton, in Devonshire, of parents who were members of our religious Society. He was of a naturally quick and cheerful disposition, and endowed with strong mental powers. His early days were devoted to vanity and folly ; but the Lord mercifully followed him with the visitations of his good Spirit, and wrought a willingness in him to take up the daily cross, and to bow to his redeeming judgments. He was diligent in the exercise of his gift in the ministry, and zealously concerned to commemorate the goodness of the Lord, by declaring to others what he had done for his soul.

* Coll. of Mem. p. 122.   † Ibid, p. 128.

His last illness was a short one, but the prospect before him was unclouded. "He was thankful," he said, "that he had known his Redeemer to live, and redeem him from all iniquity, and that he was well assured he should see a happy eternity." He died in 1748, a minister upwards of eighteen years.*

WILLIAM TROTTER.

William Trotter was educated in our religious principles, and resided at Plymouth, in Pennsylvania. He early chose the Lord for his portion, and about the twenty-first year of his age received a gift in the ministry. "His preaching," it is said, "was sound and savoury, attended with a good degree of that life and power by which the dead are raised, and without which all preaching is vain. In his life and conversation he was grave, yet innocently cheerful, and was a lover and promoter of peace, unity, and brotherly love among Friends." He died in 1749, aged about fifty-three years, in the good hope of an entrance into that kingdom "where the wicked cease from troubling, and the weary are at rest."†

ELIZABETH WYATT.

She was the wife of Bartholomew Wyatt, and during the latter period of her life resided within the limits of Salem Monthly Meeting in New Jersey, having previously been a member of Haddonfield and Philadelphia Meetings. She was one who possessed mental qualifications of a superior order, and, submitting to the baptizing, sanctifying power of Truth, she became a dignified servant of the Lord. Her gift in the ministry was large and edifying, and she was sound in word and doctrine. To the humble-minded she was comforting, but to the backslider and unfaithful, as a sharp threshing instrument in the hand of the Lord. It pleased the Good Husbandman to send her forth in his service in many parts of his vineyard, and her labours were extended to nearly all the colonies in North America. Her life was, however, cut short in righteousness; she died in 1794, at the age of forty three.

* Coll. of Mem. p. 131.   † Ibid, p. 137.

Hitherto these biographical notices have been confined to those who were called to preach the glad tidings of the gospel of Christ, and to declare to others what God had done for their own souls. There were, in the provinces of North America, more especially in those of Pennsylvania and the Jerseys, many Friends not called thus publicly to labour in word and doctrine, who were eminent for their Christian virtues, and who, by the grace bestowed upon them, were enabled to contribute much to advance the cause of righteousness among men. Some of these were hidden characters, whose deeds and whose prayers for the eternal welfare of their fellow-men are never likely to be chronicled by the pen of the historian. Concerning a few others of this class, memorials exist, which it is due to posterity and the cause of truth to notice ; for, occupying as some of these did, distinguished positions in the community, their light was placed as on a candlestick, and their faithful occupation of the gifts committed to their trust, tended to the glory of Him whose bounteous hand had dispensed them.

SAMUEL CARPENTER.

Samuel Carpenter emigrated to Pennsylvania a few years after its settlement. He had previously resided in Barbadoes, where in 1673, and again in 1685, he suffered considerably in distraints for his faithful testimony against bearing arms.* Next to William Penn, he was considered as the most wealthy person in the province ; for, besides large mills at Bristol, Darby, and Chester, and dwelling houses, warehouses, and wharfs, in Philadelphia, he also held nearly twenty thousand acres of land in different parts of the province,† and was largely engaged as a merchant. In 1693, he became member of the Assembly, and a few years later one of the Council ; and ultimately the Treasurer of the province. "Through a great variety of business," says Proud, " he preserved the love and esteem of a large and extensive acquaintance. His great abilities, activity and benevolent disposition in divers capacities, but more particularly among his friends the Quakers,

---

* Besse, vol. ii.   † Watson's Annals, p. 503.

are said to have distinguished him as a very useful and valuable member, not only of that religious Society, but also of the community in general."*   He died in the year 1713.

Sam. Carpenter

JONATHAN DICKINSON.

He emigrated with his family from Jamaica, in 1696, and was shipwrecked on the voyage in the gulf of Florida.   His remarkable preservation on that occasion, especially among the Indians, is commemorated in an interesting and well-known narrative, which he wrote and published, entitled "God's protecting providence man's surest help and defence." He became an influential merchant at Philadelphia.   For some years he filled the office of Speaker in the Assembly, and was also Chief Justice of the province.   He was a Friend much and universally beloved; and died in the year 1722.

CALEB PUSEY.

Caleb Pusey was born in Berkshire, in England, about 1650, and at an early age united in religious profession with Friends. He subsequently resided in London, from whence he emigrated in 1682, to Pennsylvania, and settled near Chester.   He was long one of the Provincial Council, and was also on several occasions elected to the Assembly. It was Caleb Pusey who, in 1688, when the alarming report was spread that the natives were coming to massacre the colonists, offered to go out and meet them unarmed, provided five others accompanied him.   New Garden Monthly Meeting thus recorded its testimony respecting him : " He was a worthy elder of the church, being endowed with a good natural capacity, sound in judgment, and zealous in maintaining the cause of truth against contrary and contending spirits.   His

* Proud, vol. ii. p. 60.

constancy in attending meetings for worship and discipline was remarkable, and worthy of imitation. Much might be said of his zeal, and integrity for truth, which he retained to the last ; but, for brevity's sake let it suffice, that he was a just man, therefore, let him be had in remembrance." He died in 1726, aged about seventy-six years, and was interred in Friends' burying-ground at London Grove.*

Caleb Pusey

RICHARD HILL.

Richard Hill was born in Maryland, and was brought up to the sea. As early as 1703, he was a member of the Provincial Council in Pennsylvania. He possessed considerable ability and influence among the settlers, and became additionally popular by the bold and decisive course he adopted in resisting the enforcement of "powder-money" by the fort at Newcastle, as mentioned in a preceding chapter. In 1703, he was united in marriage to Hannah, the widow of John Delavall, and daughter of Thomas Lloyd, who was a valuable minister and of whom a notice has been given. Richard Hill was twenty-five years a member of the Council ; many times Speaker of the Assembly ; for years First Commissioner of Property, and, during the last ten years of his life, one of the provincial judges. He was an active member of our religious Society, his services being much appreciated by his brethren. "He had," says the historian of Pennsylvania, "by nature and acquisition, such a constant firmness, as furnished him with undaunted resolution to execute whatever he undertook. His sound judgment, his great esteem for the English constitution and laws, his tenderness for the liberty of the subject, and his zeal for preserving the reputable order established in his own religious community, with his great generosity to proper objects, qualified him for the greatest services, in every station in

* Penn. Mem. p. 65.

which he was engaged, and rendered him of very great and uncommon value, in the place where he lived. He died in Philadelphia, in 1729."*

ISAAC NORRIS.

He emigrated from Jamaica, where he had been a merchant of respectable standing.† In 1701, we find him one of the Assembly of Pennsylvania, and during the remainder of his life he held many public offices with "great reputation and honour." He was endowed with good natural abilities, which, from conscientious conviction, "he improved and applied to the benefit of mankind." His services among Friends were many and highly esteemed by them. "His character," says Proud, "in most respects was so honourable among men in general, and his services so universally beneficial, more particularly to his brethren in religious profession, that he has been justly called an ornament to his country and religious profession."* He died in 1735, being at that time Chief Justice of Pennsylvania.

SAMUEL PRESTON.

Samuel Preston was born in Maryland, and, after the settlement of Pennsylvania, resided in Sussex county, Delaware, which he represented in the Assembly in 1701. He subsequently became a member of Philadelphia Monthly Meeting, and filled some of the highest stations in the government of the province, having been for a long time one of the Council, and Treasurer of the province. His first wife was Rachel, the daughter of Thomas Lloyd, and his second, Margaret, the widow of Josiah Langdale. He is described as a man of great benevolence, of sound judgment, and much presence of mind, whose life was

* Proud, vol. i. p. 473. † Watson's Annals, p. 501.
‡ Ibid.

instructive to others, "and his practice a continued series of good offices." In a testimony issued by his Monthly Meeting, he is thus spoken of: "He was an Elder circumspect in his conduct, and carefully concerned for the good of the Church ; active and serviceable in the maintenance of our Christian discipline, and by his attention to the dictates of Divine grace, he became well qualified for this service."* He died in great resignation of mind, in 1743, in the seventy-ninth year of his age.

JAMES LOGAN.

James Logan was descended of an ancient family of high standing in Scotland, but was born at Lurgan, in Ireland, about 1674, to which country his father had removed. He early evinced an aptitude for learning, and before he was thirteen years of age had learnt not only the Latin and Greek languages, but, to some extent, the Hebrew also ; and in a few years more he made himself master of French and Italian. In the year 1698, he commenced business in Bristol ; but at the solicitation of William Penn, he accompanied him in the spring of the following year to America, where he acted confidentially and faithfully as his secretary. Being a man of powerful intellect, he filled with great ability and integrity the offices of Commissioner of Property, Chief Justice, and for nearly two years, that of Governor of the province. He was deeply skilled in mathematics, in natural and moral philosophy, and was the author of several works in Latin and English. His learning led him into an extensive correspondence with the literati of Europe. To the citizens of Philadelphia he bequeathed a choice library of three thousand volumes, with a sum of thirty-five pounds a year for

* Coll. of Mem. p. 118.

its maintenance.   It is still known there as the famous Loganian Library.   Except on the subject of defensive war, to which it is remarkable that he seems to have had no very decided objection,* James Logan was a consistent Friend.   He was a man of sterling integrity and worth, and preserved through life a character marked by piety and uprightness.   He died in 1751, at the age of seventy-six years.†

J Logan

* Vide Logan Correspondence in the Philadelphia Friend.
† Memoirs of James Logan, by Wilson Armistead.

CHAPTER XI.

IN the year 1753, Mary Peisley, afterwards Mary Neale, and
Catherine Payton, afterwards Catherine Phillips, visited the
colonies of North America. They were then young and unmarried, the former about thirty-six and the latter about twenty-
six years of age. Landing at Charlestown in the Twelfth Month,
they attended nearly all the meetings of Friends within the
compass of Pennsylvania Yearly Meeting, including some of the
most remote. Of the state of the Society in Bucks county,
Catherine Payton remarks, " There is in this county a weighty,
living number of Friends, unto whom my spirit was closely united
in the covenant of life ; but there are many dwellers at ease.
Some of the youth appear promising, and the divine visitation
was largely extended to many."* During their travels in Pennsylvania the people were greatly excited by the incursions and
devastations of the Indians on the frontiers in the pay of the
French ; and it was a time of close trial to Friends. " I was
concerned," writes Catherine Payton, " to testify against that

* Memoirs of C. Phillips.

spirit, which, from human considerations, was for war ; and to strengthen the minds of Friends against leaning thereto.   Divers times during those troubles, I was concerned publicly to assert the consistency of our peace principles with the gospel dispensation."   Catherine Payton was from home about three years on this visit, and travelled in America nearly nine thousand miles. For further particulars of this journey the reader may be referred to her published journal.   She died in 1794, in the sixty-eighth year of her age, and forty-sixth of her ministry.   Mary Peisley returned with her companion.   She was a very eminent minister, and had "extraordinary service" in America.   Her death took place in 1757, a few months after her return, at the age of thirty-nine.*   A memoir of her life has been published.

Samuel Fothergill of Warrington, and Joshua Dixon of Durham, appear to have been the next ministers that visited Friends in America.   Of the religious labours of the latter we have no account, but the two Friends reached America, and returned nearly at the same time, but not together.   Samuel Fothergill was then in the fortieth year of his age, and was a very powerful, baptizing minister of the Gospel.   He landed at Wilmington in Delaware, in the Eighth Month, 1754, and proceeded from thence to Philadelphia, where he remarks, "the meetings are exceedingly large, all sorts and ranks of people flock to them, and the mighty name is deservedly exalted."   Of the state of the Society in Delaware, and some parts of Maryland, he speaks discouragingly : "their numbers being small, but their care and zeal for the truth in general less than their numbers." He extended his visit to the meetings in the remote parts of Pennsylvania, Maryland, and Virginia, "and along the Blue Mountains ;" going also to a settlement of Friends "beyond those mountains, who were then," he writes, "in great quiet, but have since all removed through fear of the Indians, and left their plantations and dwellings desolate."   Speaking of the incursions of the Indians, he says, "Many thousand pounds of the province's money have, by the Assembly's committee, been laid out in erecting forts upon the frontiers, and placing men in them ; a

* Life of Mary Neale.

step as prudent, and likely to be attended with as much success, as an attempt to hedge out birds or the deer. The distress of this province is great—its commotions violent—all the desolations of a cruel Indian war impendent, and the legislature in a great degree infatuated; it seems like a judicial desertion of all their counsels, and every step they take increases their perplexity. Friends have interposed for the restoration of peace, and borne their testimony faithfully."* Samuel Fothergill was about two years in America, and came back in the same vessel with Catherine Payton and Mary Peisley. He brought returning certificates from most of the provinces to this effect: "His public labours amongst us, both in the ministry and the discipline, have been fervent, deep, and lively; to the edification and building up of the Church, the information of strangers, and to the great satisfaction of such as wish well to Zion's cause."† "His ministry at times went forth as a flame, often piercing into the inmost recesses of darkness and obduracy; yet descended like dew upon the tender plants of our Heavenly Father's planting. . . . He proposed to the people no cunningly devised fables, but, full of charity, he skilfully divided the word aright, speaking whereof he knew, and what his own hands had handled, of the good word of life."‡ He died in the Sixth Month, 1772, in the faith and hope of the gospel he had preached, having a foretaste of that ever-lasting rest and joy into which he was about to enter. He was in the fifty-seventh year of his age, and the thirty-sixth of his ministry.

The ravages of the Indians, under French influence, on the frontier settlements of Pennsylvania, caused a great degree of alarm among the colonists, and increased their outcry against Friends, as legislators and lovers of peace. So strong, indeed, had this feeling become, and so great the dread of these incur-

* Memoirs of S. Fothergill, p. 255.   † Ibid. 264.
‡ Testimony concerning S. Fothergill.

sions, that loud complaints were transmitted to England. The authorities at Whitehall began also to entertain the notion that, unless some decided steps were taken to quash Quaker rule in Pennsylvania, the province would fall into the hands of the French; and in 1756, they actually prepared a Bill, making the taking of an oath imperative on every member of the Assembly; the effect of which they knew would be, to exclude Friends from that body.

The misrepresentations to which the members of our Society were subjected at this period, rendered their position a painful one; and at the Quarterly Meeting of Philadelphia, in the Fifth Month, 1755, it was concluded again to seek the aid of their brethren in England. The application was heartily responded to, and the Meeting for Sufferings in London exerted its influence with the government on behalf of their calumniated brethren. The result of the labours of this body was, to obtain the withdrawal of the Bill instituting oaths as a test. But this was not effected without considerable difficulty, and on condition only, that Friends "would give a reasonable hope of their not allowing themselves to be elected" as members of the Assembly; accompanied with a strong recommendation, that Friends in England should send a deputation to Pennsylvania, to promote this course. In their epistle to Friends of Philadelphia, the Meeting for Sufferings in London thus describes the state of feeling in England on the subject:—

"You are not, we believe, unacquainted, that great pains have been taken to represent the conduct of the Assembly, and Friends in general in Pennsylvania, in such a manner as to create a belief here, that the calamities, which the country hath of late sustained, proceed from the principles and behaviour of the Society, and this we apprehend with a view to subject us to public odium and resentment, as the majority of representatives is known to consist of persons under our profession.

"These charges have been laid with so much industry and success, and our known sentiments respecting war so speciously alleged in support of them, as to excite a general and strong prepossession against us; insomuch, that not only the lower and less discerning, but even those in the administration, have been so far influenced by these charges, as to think that Friends in Pennsylvania, merely to preserve their power, have procured a majority of their persuasion to be elected into the Assembly; though they knew their religious principles would restrain them from providing for the security of the province, then exposed to the incursions of a cruel and barbarous enemy.

" The government was likewise induced to believe, that the dangers which threatened this flourishing colony, could not be so easily averted, as by excluding those from its legislation who professed such principles ; and as they saw that this might speedily be done by imposing an oath as a test, a Bill was ordered, and actually prepared, for excluding all those from having seats in any legislative Assembly in America, who refused to take and subscribe the oaths directed as a qualification.

" Though we were early apprised that some steps were taking for this purpose, and were not wanting in a timely and diligent application on your behalf, yet our utmost endeavours would undoubtedly have been ineffectual, had not some persons in high stations, from a steady regard to the Society, greatly assisted in preventing any further proceedings relative thereto, this sessions of Parliament. And which we esteem a favourable interposition of Providence.

" This short suspension has not been obtained without considerable difficulty, and our engaging to use our utmost endeavours with you to decline being chosen into the Assembly during the present situation of affairs in America."*

In pursuance of the recommendation of the British Government, it was concluded to send a deputation to Pennsylvania, and John Hunt of London, and Christopher Wilson of Cumberland, were appointed to the important service. These Friends had, some years before, crossed the Atlantic on a gospel mission, and were well known, and highly esteemed, by their brethren in America. They arrived at Philadelphia in the Tenth Month, 1756, and were warmly welcomed. A conference was soon had

---

* Minutes of Meeting for Sufferings, vol. xxix. p. 524.

with Friends of the city : there was, however, but little for the deputation to do, for already had the advice from London, of which they were the bearers, been anticipated and acted upon. Six of the representatives in the Assembly who were Friends, had vacated their seats, and at the close of the session for that year, other members of the Society declined to offer themselves as candidates. -From this date it was the constant care of Friends, to discourage their members from being candidates for office, and but few of our members of any religious standing ever after formed part of the local legislature of Pennsylvania. "Upon the whole," write Friends of Philadelphia to their brethren in London in 1759, " you may observe somewhat of our present circumstances, and that our connections with the powers of the earth are reduced to small bounds, which we fervently desire may have the proper effect to establish the Church in righteousness, and fix our trust in the Lord alone for protection and deliverance."

The incursions of the Indians on the western frontiers were attended with very calamitous results.   A number of the settlers fell victims to the tomahawk and the scalping knife, and many settlements were entirely destroyed, causing great distress to the inhabitants, who, to avoid further danger removed to the interior. For the relief of these a subscription was entered into, towards which a large amount was contributed by Friends.   At Pennsylvania Yearly Meeting in 1756, it was agreed to raise a thousand pounds for this object.   Very early also after these Indian outrages, Friends exerted themselves to obtain a reconciliation with them.   They used their endeavours to induce the local government to take steps for this purpose, but all their efforts proved unavailing.   The public mind was too highly excited on the subject to listen to pleadings for forbearance and peace, and the rulers, under similar feelings, fostered a spirit of revenge.   To increase the excitement, the mangled bodies of some of the settlers who had been massacred, were purposely brought to Philadelphia, and paraded through the streets ; "many people," says John Churchman, "following, cursing the Indians, and also the Quakers, because they would not join in war for their destruction. The sight of the dead bodies, and the outcry of the people, were very afflicting and shocking."* In the Assembly too the conflict ran high, between those who took different views on the subject; but the war party prevailed, armaments were prepared, and many of the Indians were destroyed.†

Seeing no prospect of obtaining assistance from the government towards a peaceful termination of hostilities with the natives, in the Eleventh Month, 1756, an association was formed, consisting chiefly of Friends, "for gaining and preserving peace with the Indians by pacific measures." This association continued its exertions until the time of the definitive treaty in 1764, during which period, by their private and individual subscriptions, several thousand pounds were raised to enable them to carry out their designs.‡ The money thus raised was expended, chiefly in presents to the Indians, in order to conciliate them; and sometimes to induce them to seek out and release the settlers whom they had taken prisoners. These exertions appear to have had a most salutary effect, and, indeed, they were mainly instrumental in restoring the peace of the province.§ But benevolent and disinterested as their designs were, Friends were still reproached by many, and even the government, in some instances, repelled their proffered services to preserve peace.‖ During the war, several treaties were held with the Indians at Easton, Lancaster, &c. On these occasions Friends believed it to be their duty to attend, notwithstanding the governor's dislike to their presence; and they were instrumental in assisting on these occasions to a peaceable settlement of the questions at issue.

The war cry throughout the province, entailed other difficulties on Friends. In Delaware, or the three lower counties, a militia bill was passed, and passed, too, without the slightest regard to the known conscientious scruples of the Society, but rather, with

---

* Journal of J. Churchman.   † Watson's Annals, p. 450.

‡ The total amount raised was £4004 1s. 6d. £430 of which was contributed by the Menonists. In addition to this sum a German sect called Swingfielders, raised £236 14s. to be applied for the redemption of the captives among the Indians.

§ Friends and the Indians, p. 91.   ‖ Watson's Annals, p. 450.

the aim to bring suffering upon them. A memorial on this subject was presented to Thomas and Richard Penn, the proprietaries, but without producing any effectual relief. Friends were also involved in difficulty by the imposition of a tax in Pennsylvania, to defray the expenses of the war.

It was during these troubles, that steps were taken to form a representative body, to act on behalf of the Society in the interval of the Yearly Meetings. During 1755, conferences of Friends were held in Philadelphia, which addressed the Assembly, and also issued, on the emergency, an epistle of advice to the members of the Society under their altered circumstances. These conferences not-being regularly constituted meetings, at the Yearly Meeting in 1756, it was concluded to establish a Meeting for Sufferings, to be composed of four representatives from each Quarterly Meeting, together with twelve others appointed by the Yearly Meeting. This was the first meeting of this description established in America, and it has continued to be held, down to the present time, with much advantage to the body. The Meeting for Sufferings in London, had been established as early as the year 1675, or within a very few years after the Yearly Meetings were held in that city ; its object being, chiefly to obtain relief for Friends under suffering in support of their various christian testimonies. The objects of the Meeting for Sufferings of Philadelphia were defined as follows :—

" To hear and consider the cases of any Friends under sufferings, and to administer relief as necessity is found to require, or to apply to the government, or persons in power, on their behalf.

" To correspond with the Meeting for Sufferings or the Yearly Meeting in London, and to represent the state of Friends here, and in general to represent this (the Yearly) Meeting, and appear in all cases where the reputation and interest of truth and our religious Society are concerned, but not to interfere in matters of faith or discipline, which are not already determined by the Yearly Meeting.

" To consider the uses and manner of application of charitable legacies and donations, and to advise respecting the titles of any land, or other estate belonging to the several meetings, &c.

" To receive an account from the several particular meetings, of any sufferings to which Friends may be subjected for the testimony of truth.

" And that fair minutes of all their proceedings' should be kept, and laid before the Yearly Meeting from time to time."

Some years after, the revisal of all manuscripts intended for publication by any member, having reference to Friends, was transferred from the Meeting of Ministers and Elders, to the Meeting for Sufferings ; and any proposal for reprinting a work was also committed to its care.

The massacres that had taken place during the late war, had raised in the minds of most of the settlers on the frontiers, a strong feeling of hatred toward the Indians, and also towards those who were supposed to be advocates of Indian rights, or friendly towards them, more especially Friends. In no part was this feeling more conspicuous than in Lancaster county, where also some pulpit discourses of a sect of zealots, chiefly Presbyterians from the North of Ireland, added religious fanaticism to the already excited passions of the people. At Conestogoe, in this county, there resided a small remnant of an Indian tribe who had welcomed William Penn on his first visit to Pennsylvania. They had always preserved an inviolate friendship with the settlers, and had lived in harmony and good-will with those in their own immediate neighbourhood. Their numbers had, however, gradually dwindled, and in 1763, their community consisted of but twenty individuals. In the Twelfth Month of this year, a band of cruel fanatics came to their village, with the avowed intention of destroying them, to avenge the whites slain on the frontier, and to extirpate, as they declared, the heathen from the land, that the saints might inherit the earth.* The ruffians were all armed, and, surrounding the Indian huts, they fell upon the defenceless inmates, and murdered in cold blood, three men, two women, and a boy, being all that happened to be then at home. After the massacre, the murderers set fire to the huts.

The news of this dreadful act produced great sensation in the province, and a proclamation was issued, calling upon the officers

* Watson's Annals, p. 45?.

both civil and military, to exert themselves in bringing the perpetrators to justice. No inconsiderable number of the inhabitants of the county of Lancaster abetted this wicked proceeding, and with this encouragement, in about two weeks after, a similar band of ruffians actually rode into the town of Lancaster, and in full day, broke open the workhouse where the remaining fourteen Indians were placed for protection, and deliberately put them all to death. But the wickedness of these lawless destroyers did not stop here ; they even attempted to murder all the Indians within their reach, and, understanding that some of them had fled to Philadelphia for protection, they determined to march on to the city to carry out their dreadful designs. Their numbers were formidable, amounting to between two and three hundred, and they advanced as far as Germantown, threatening death, not only to the officers of the government, but also to some prominent members of the Society of Friends. On the emergency, the governor called a public meeting ; a large number of the citizens enrolled themselves for the common defence ; cannon were planted to command the principal streets ; and the ferries on the Schuylkill were put in a state of defence. This was a time of peculiar trial to Friends, for they were deeply concerned not only for the preservation of the poor Indians, but for the lives of their beloved brethren.

The determination of the citizens of Philadelphia to resist these wretched men by force of arms, caused them to hesitate in this mad career, and, on reaching Germantown, they contented themselves by forwarding to the governor a detail of their alleged grievances ; Friends being thus specifically alluded to : "The hands that were closely shut, nor would grant his Majesty's General a single farthing against a savage foe, have been liberally opened, and the public money basely prostituted, to hire, at an exorbitant rate, a mercenary guard to protect his Majesty's worst of enemies, those falsely pretended Indian friends ; while at the same time, hundreds of poor, distressed families of his Majesty's subjects [have been] obliged to abandon their possessions, and fly for their lives at least, or left, except a small relief at first, in the most distressing circumstances, to starve neglected, save

what the friendly hand of private donations has contributed to
their support, wherein they who are most profuse towards savages,
have carefully avoided having any part."* in about a week
after, they presented a second paper to the governor; in which
among the grievances set forth, Friends are again referred to:
"We complain," say they, "that a certain society of people in
this province, in the late Indian war and at several treaties held
by the king's representatives, openly loaded the Indians with
presents, and that Israel Pemberton, a leader of the said society,
in defiance of all government, not only abetted our Indian
enemies, but kept up a private intelligence with them, and
publicly received from them a belt of wampum, as if he had been
our governor, or authorised by the king to treat with his enemies.
By this means the Indians have been taught to despise us as a
weak and disunited people, and from this fatal source have arisen
many of our calamities under which we groan."†

The return of the rioters to their homes, was followed by the
issue of a number of bitter and abusive publications against
Friends. These were promptly and fearlessly answered. The
malevolent feeling thus exhibited, although fostered by many
Presbyterians of Philadelphia, drew down on the authors and
abettors of such unworthy attacks the contempt of the community
at large. During this time of excitement, the Meeting for
Sufferings was not inactive. They published, in the form of an
address to the governor, an answer to the charges contained in
the two papers just referred to. The document is too long for
insertion in these pages. Alluding to the government of the
province under the auspices of Friends, they thus remark:
"From the first settling of the province, till within a few years
past, both the framing and administration ·of the laws were
committed chiefly to men of our religious principles, under whom
tranquillity and peace were preserved among the inhabitants, and
with the natives. The land rejoiced, and people of every denomination were protected in person and property, and in the full
enjoyment of religious and civil liberty. But with grief and

* "The Friend," Philadelphia Journal, vol. xx. p. 13.
† Ibid. p. 14.

sorrow, for some years past, we have observed the circumstances of the province to be much changed, and that intestine animosities and the desolating calamities of war have taken the place of tranquillity and peace :" in addressing the Meeting for Sufferings of London, about the same time, they observe, " During these tumults, a few members of our Society were hurried, under the apprehension of immediate danger, to appear in arms, contrary to our Christian profession and principles, whose example was followed by some of our youth ; which hath been, and is, a real concern to those who experienced in this time of trial, the calming influences of that Spirit, which preserves in a steady dependence on the alone protection of Divine Providence. We hope endeavours will be extended in the meekness of true wisdom for the help and restoration of such that have thus erred. When we consider the ferments which were then excited and prevailed, and the numbers suddenly brought together from different places in this state of mind, we have abundant cause with deep and reverent thankfulness to acknowledge and remember the merciful interposition of favour extended toward us, that through the commotion no lives were lost, nor personal injury done to any, that we have heard of, and that the mischiefs which seemed for some time inevitable, are for the present arrested."*

The original laws of Pennsylvania, framed under the influence of Friends, did not allow exhibitions of a theatrical character, "as tending to looseness and immorality;" and hence, for a period of nearly seventy years from the settlement of the province, no attempt to introduce them took place. The first appearance of entertainments of this description, in Philadelphia, was in the year 1749 ; but, at the instance of the Common Council, they were speedily suppressed as illegal, and the actors bound over " to their good behaviour."† Six years later, a similar effort was made, when the Common Council, not then under the control of Friends, gave the actors licence " to act a few plays," provided "nothing indecent or immoral was offered." But the more

* London Yearly Meeting Records.—Philadelphia Epistles, vol. i.
† Watson's Annals, p. 408.

religious portion of the citizens, who witnessed with sorrow the opening of this floodgate of vice, endeavoured to counteract the evil by the distribution of tracts, setting forth the demoralizing tendency of all such exhibitions. Their efforts appear to have been successful; for after two months only, the performers ceased to act in Philadelphia; and no further movement of this sort took place until 1759, when a theatre was opened a little southward of the city bounds, in order to be out of the reach of civic control.

It may be remarked, that the progress of theatrical entertainments in Philadelphia nearly kept pace with the gradual increase of military display; and the "pomp and circumstance of war," seems to have been especially congenial to the growth of this potent instrument of vice and irreligion. The dancer in the theatre first established in the province, was a military character; and whilst the English army occupied Philadelphia, plays were frequently acted; the officers themselves being the principal performers.*

In 1766, the city authorities had so far relaxed in their views on this subject, as to allow these entertainments within their limits. Friends were much distressed at the circumstance; and with a view to induce the Governor, John Penn, to suppress them, they addressed him on the occasion. It was, however, unavailing. The actors had already obtained his consent; and, so far from sympathising with Friends on the matter, he openly expressed his approval of such exhibitions. The exertions having thus failed of success, an epistle of caution was addressed to the younger members of the Society on the temptations placed before them. In the following year, the Governor was again memorialised on the subject, and also the Assembly; but, as in the former instance, the "remonstrances were ineffectual to induce a suppression of these seductive scenes."

As a natural consequence of the deplorable change that had taken place, through setting aside the original laws of the province, in reference to theatrical and other vain amusements,

* Watson's Annals, p. 410.

vice and immorality made rapid strides in the once quiet and orderly city of Philadelphia. The attention of the Meeting for Sufferings was closely directed to the subject ; and it was concluded, in 1770, once more to plead with the Governor respecting it. A promise that he would use his authority in suppressing booths on the race grounds, appears to have been, in this instance, the only favourable result. A few months afterwards, the same Meeting memorialized the proprietaries, Thomas and Richard Penn ; they being resident in England, the memorial was forwarded to Friends of London for presentation, accompanied by a letter, in which occurs the following passage :—" Whether our endeavours may succeed or not to prevent the torrent of corruption overspreading the city and country, we think it our duty to bear our testimony against it ; desiring, by every means in our power, to perpetuate the happiness we have heretofore enjoyed, and that our successors may have such proofs of our concern for their welfare, as we have of the virtue of our predecessors."*

Returning to the gospel labours of Friends from England, we find that William Reckitt of Lincolnshire landed at Philadelphia in the Ninth Month, 1757. He had in the previous year sailed from London for this purpose ; but the vessel being taken by a privateer, he was carried as a prisoner to France. William Reckitt's gospel mission in America occupied him about two years ; during which he visited nearly all the meetings within the limits of this large Yearly Meeting, including those in the remote parts of Virginia and Maryland. He refers to the meeting at Shrewsbury, in New Jersey, as a memorable time, and very large, people of all ranks being present. " I had," he writes, " to declare of the Lord's mercy and goodness towards the children of men, and to invite them to come and see for themselves, what great things the Lord will do for them that trust in Him."† Salem Yearly Meeting, which held three days, for worship and discipline, was, he remarks, " an edifying time, things being conducted in a degree of the pure wisdom ; and the over-

* " The Friend " of Phil., vol. xx. p. 133.
† Life of William Reckitt, p. 73.

shadowing of divine power was witnessed by many."* Bucks
Quarterly Meeting he mentions, as consisting of several hundreds,
mostly a young generation.   He "was glad he was here, and his
spirit rejoiced in the Lord." Many of the meetings in Pennsylvania,
he speaks of, as consisting of a large body of Friends; "the
sight of whom," he says, "in many places, and the sense of
divine favour still extended towards them, was cause of humble
thankfulness."† In the year 1764, he made a second visit to the
provinces in North America, "and passed through most of them;"
but his return home was hastened in the early part of 1766, by
the decease of his wife.   No particulars of this visit are extant.
William Reckitt came forth in the ministry about the thirty-sixth
year of his age.   "He was," record Friends of his own meeting,
"deep in the ministry, and powerful in prayer."   He died, after
a very short illness, in 1769, at the age of sixty-three.

Samuel Spavold of Hertfordshire, and Mary Kirby of Norfolk,
went on a gospel errand to their brethren in America, in 1757;
but no record of their services on the occasion has been preserved.   Samuel Spavold first spoke in the ministry when very
young, and travelled extensively therein in Great Britain and
Ireland, as well as in America.   Although he was at times largely
engaged in gospel labours, yet he was a lover of silent waiting
upon God.   "Oh, how I love this silent waiting," he said, "and
to feel my mind humbled before that great Power!   We want to
be more inward; the Lord's people are an inward people."‡   He
died in great peace and assurance of acceptance with God his
Saviour, in the First Month, 1795, aged eighty-seven years.

In the year 1760, four ministers crossed the Atlantic to North
America.   These were John Storer of Nottingham, Jane
Crosfield of Westmoreland, George Mason of Yorkshire, and
Susannah Hatton, formerly Susannah Hudson, and afterwards
Susannah Lightfoot.   No particulars of their religious engage-
ments during the visit have been met with, nor of five others who
went over in the following year, viz., Robert Proud, John
Stephenson, Hannah Harris, Elizabeth Wilkinson, and Alice

* Life of W. Reckitt, p. 104.   † Ibid. p. 142.   ‡ Piety Pro. part ix.

Hall, the last of whom died at Philadelphia in the following year.[*]

We come now to notice the services of John Griffith of Essex, but who had previously resided in Pennsylvania. He landed at Philadelphia in the Ninth Month, 1765, and visited most of the meetings throughout America; first attending the "great meeting," in Philadelphia, where, on First-day, "nearly if not quite fifteen hundred Friends" were present. He then proceeded to the Jerseys. John Griffith's gospel labours in America occupied him about a year. "In ministry he was sound, powerful, and clear; and in discipline, diligent and judicious." He died in 1776, at the age of sixty-three, having been a minister about forty-two years.[†] A journal of his life and travels has been published, containing many instructive incidents.

In the same year 1765, Abigail Pike visited America on a like gospel mission, and was followed in 1768, by Rachel Wilson of Kendal; and two years later, by Joseph Oxley of Norwich, and Samuel Neale of Ireland. Of the religious labours of the first two no account is extant, excepting that it is recorded of Rachel Wilson, that her ministry was "remarkably interesting and eloquent," and that she "was much admired by people of all classes."[‡] Of the movements of Joseph Oxley and Samuel Neale, our biographical publications supply some interesting details.

Samuel Neale landed at Newcastle in Delaware in the Tenth Month, 1770, and proceeded at once to Philadelphia. In the early part of the following year, he visited many of the meetings in the remote parts of the province and in Maryland. "I have rode," he remarks in the Third Month, 1771, "already upwards of seventeen hundred miles, and have lain out five nights in the woods; I have breakfasted, dined, and supped in the woods, as contented as if I were in a palace, and though I have had to partake of fare that in Ireland would go hardly down with any servants, yet the contentedness of the mind made it a feast."[§]

---

[*] Piety Pro. part xi.   [†] Journal of John Griffith.
[‡] Phil. Friend, vol. xx. p. 108.   [§] Life of S. Neale, p. 48.

His religious labours in America occupied him about two years, and extended to most of the meetings in that land. "There are," he says, "a great body of Friends on this continent, beyond what I expected ; many of them deep and valuable in the church, and many of them too deeply settled in earth and earthly things ; and though they are not in much pomp as to worldly splendour, the root and leaven of that spirit which dissipates and renders useless, very much hurts and weakens as to coming forward in the brightness of Truth, and in service in the church."* Samuel Neale died in 1792, aged sixty-two years, having been a minister forty years.

Joseph Oxley landed at New York in the Ninth Month, 1770, and reached Philadelphia during the sitting of the Yearly Meeting in the same month. Respecting this meeting he made the following entry in his journal : "It was a very large, awful, and solemn gathering, *such as I had not seen before ;* so consistent in appearance of dress and uniformity throughout, agreeable to our holy profession, as greatly affected my mind ; and my tongue was loosened to speak of the love I was made comfortably to partake of, in this the latter part of their feast, which they acknowledged had been throughout to mutual comfort and edification. The meeting continued two days after my coming, and concluded in solemn prayer, thanksgiving, and praise, to Him that opened his hand, and filled with his blessing ; who is ever worthy !"† He travelled largely in the provinces of America for about a year and a half, going over about seven thousand miles in that time, and nearly fourteen thousand during his absence from home. Alluding to the visit of this devoted Friend, John Pemberton says, "he has stepped along wisely, and has gained the love of Friends, and, indeed, it is a great blessing and mercy to be so preserved, so that I expect he will leave us much united to him."‡ Joseph Oxley died in 1775, in the sixty-first year of his age, and thirty-fourth of his ministry.

In 1773, or soon after the return of the two last mentioned Friends, Robert Walker and Elizabeth Robinson of Yorkshire, and Mary Leaver of Nottingham, visited America. The two

* Life of S. Neale, p. 171.   † Journal of J. Oxley, p. 317.
‡ John Pemberton's Letter to Mary Oxley.

women Friends were companions in their gospel labours, in the course of which they visited the families of Friends in Phila-delphia. It was from the ministry of Elizabeth Robinson that Thomas Scattergood dates his awakening, and he ever after re-garded her as his mother in the Truth. Robert Walker was largely engaged in the love of the gospel among his American brethren. He was given to see the approaching troubles of the revolution, and ardently desired that Friends might find a hiding-place in Him who is the only sure refuge from the storms and tempests of time. "He was wise in his counsels, prudent in his cautions, and prophetic in his warnings;—the humble were encouraged by his ministry, and the faithful were strengthened."* He finished his religious labours among Friends in America in the early part of 1775, and, with Elizabeth Robinson and Mary Leaver, went on board a vessel to return to England. There was, however, one religious requirement from which he had shrunk, and that was to have a meeting with the Congress, then sitting in Phila-delphia. The wind being adverse, the captain did not think it prudent to set sail with the first tide, and told his passengers that they might go on shore again. Robert Walker now saw that he must embrace this opportunity to give up to the call of his Divine Master, and seek an interview with Congress, and through the influence of some of his brethren this was granted him. Excepting Matlack, the secretary, they all heard him attentively and patiently. In the evening Robert Walker went on board again, and the ship immediately put to sea. No record exists of the character of his communication to the Congress ; but whether from any doubt of what he said, or from sheer malicious-ness on the part of Matlack, before the following morning, the house where Robert Walker had been lodging was surrounded by a body of soldiers, sent at the instigation of Matlack to arrest him. Finding he had sailed, a cutter was forthwith sent after him. It soon neared the object of its pursuit, and its prey seemed almost within grasp, when, unexpectedly, a thick cloud enveloped them, putting an end to the chase, and thus by a

* T. Scattergood and his Times.

marked interposition of Providence, Robert Walker escaped the hands of his enemies.   He died in a sweet and heavenly state of mind, whilst on a visit to London in the year 1785, aged about sixty-nine years, a minister about thirty-four years.*

FRIENDS' MEETING-HOUSE, MEDFORD, NEW JERSEY.

* Piety Promoted, part ix.

CHAPTER XII.

SCARCELY had peace with the Indians been restored to Pennsylvania, and hostilities between England and France suspended
by the treaty of Fontainbleau, in 1762, ere troubles of another
description arose in North America, and proved the incipient
cause of the War of Independence. Hitherto, Great Britain had
not attempted to increase its revenue by taxing its American colonies, and when, for the first time, it entertained the idea of doing
so, the colonies boldly disputed the point. They contended that
the mother country possessed no such right over their properties ;

but, despite their remonstrances, the memorable and impolitic Stamp Act was passed in 1765. This attempt roused the indignation of the Americans, and from New England to Georgia, the whole community was in a state of fervid excitement. The Assembly of Virginia at once declared the act invalid, and recorded its resolution "that the colony alone had the right of taxing its inhabitants."—Massachusetts proposed a Congress of Representatives from each of the provinces, to deliberate on the alleged infraction of their rights ; whilst at Philadelphia, when the vessel bearing the stamped paper arrived, the general feeling was demonstrated by a public mourning—the bells were muffled —the shipping hoisted colours half-mast high, and, on the day when the act was to take effect, the newspapers of the city were issued in mourning. These demonstrations in Philadelphia were soon followed by others more grave, for in a very short time, no less than four hundred traders of the city bound themselves neither to buy nor to sell British exports, so long as the obnoxious enactment continued in force.

Although some Friends united in this compact, the Society was generally preserved in much calmness ; and they remark in 1766, " Under the violent ferment reigning at this time in the colonies, the observation, that the people of Pennsylvania and West Jersey have hitherto kept more free from tumults and riots than their neighbours, gives us cause to believe, that the conduct and conversation of Friends, hath in some measure tended to promote this good effect."* In the Second Month, an epistle of caution was issued by the Meeting for Sufferings of Philadelphia to the members of that Yearly Meeting.

The attitude assumed by the colonies alarmed the Home Government, and during the session of 1766, the Stamp Act was repealed. Parliament, however, unwilling to concede the point for which the Americans contended, formally declared its right to tax the colonies. Acting upon this resolution, in the following year a bill was passed, imposing a duty of three-pence per pound on tea imported from England, with taxes on some other

* Epistle to London Meeting for Sufferings.

articles. The colonists were again roused, and a "non-importation agreement" was entered into, extending now throughout the colonies. The opposition succeeded, and, for some years, but little tea was imported from England, the colonists being supplied mainly from Holland. The East India Company soon felt the effect of this. Their warehouses becoming overstocked with the article, they began to complain, and in 1773, the duty was repealed. Thus a second time, by a peaceful yet firm and unbending course among themselves, the American people defeated the designs of the Imperial Parliament. The British Government, however, still unwilling to yield the point, now adopted a somewhat ingenious course to maintain it. It was enacted, that the duty charged on tea exported by the East India Company should be repealed, but that the Company should pay a small duty on all teas landed by them in the American colonies. The Americans were still dissatisfied, for though tea was thus rendered to them at a lower rate, the principle of raising a revenue from them without their consent was retained, and they determined to resist. At Boston, and in South Carolina, cargoes of tea brought over by the East India Company were seized and thrown into the sea, and in Philadelphia, also, it was resolved to oppose the landing.

The destruction of property which thus took place, was clearly inconsistent with the acknowledged views of our Society, and Friends were urged not to engage in any political movement which might compromise their Christian principles. In the following year the aspect of things grew worse, and the Meeting for Sufferings, anxious for the religious welfare of its members amidst the general excitement, was closely engaged in deliberating on the subject. At the Meeting in the Sixth Month, 1774, this record occurs: "A considerable time was spent in this meeting, in a weighty consideration of the fluctuating state of people's minds. In the situation of public affairs, it appeared to be the sense of the meeting, that it would be the safest, and most consistent for us, as a religious Society, to keep as much as possible from mixing with the people in their human policy and contrivances, and to forbear meeting in their public consultations. Snares and dangers may arise from meetings of that kind, however well disposed individuals may be to mitigate and soften the violent disposition too prevalent ; it being a season in which it is abundantly needful to seek best Wisdom, to guide and preserve in safety and in consistency of conduct with our religious profession."

In the Ninth Month of the same year, a Congress of Representatives from the colonies assembled in Philadelphia, and determined, as in the previous instances, on resisting by a non-importation compact, the designs of Parliament ; agreeing to meet again in the spring of the following year. During this first sitting of the American Congress, the Yearly Meeting was also held in Philadelphia. Amid the commotions of that excited period, Friends were mercifully preserved in much quietness, and were enabled to put their trust in Him who is a sure refuge at all times to those who truly seek him. In a feeling of deep solicitude for the best interests of the members generally, an epistle of advice was issued to Friends throughout the whole of the North American provinces. In this address they thus urge the example of our early Friends : " Our forefathers and predecessors, were raised to be a people in a time of great commotions, contests, and wars, begun and carried on for the vindication of religious and civil liberty, in which many of them were zealously engaged, when they received the knowledge of the truth ; but through the influences of the love of Christ in their minds, they ceased from conferring with flesh and blood, and became obedient to the heavenly vision, in which they clearly saw that all wars and fightings proceeded from the spirit of this world, which is enmity with God, and that they must manifest themselves to be the followers of the Prince of Peace, by meekness, humility, and patient sufferings."

After the termination of the war between England and France by the treaty of 1762, Friends in Pennsylvania did not feel the same objection as before to serve as Representatives in the Assembly, and during the struggle for independence, some of them were members of that branch of the local legislature. The resolutions passed by the Congress having been introduced to the

Assembly of Pennsylvania, received its sanction, and hence a fear pervaded the minds of Friends, that there was still a danger· of their members who were of that body, compromising our religious testimony against war, and a Committee of the Meeting for Sufferings was appointed to confer with them respecting it.

In so large a religious community as that of Friends in Pennsylvania and the Jerseys, it was likely that there should be some who differed from the body at large in reference to these civil commotions, and whose conduct was more or less cause of anxiety to their brethren. This circumstance led the Meeting for Sufferings, in the First Month, 1775, to issue an exhortation to Friends, to recur in that period of confusion and excitement, "to the doctrines and precepts of our Lord Jesus Christ, who expressly declared, ' My kingdom is not of this world :' " and also to reflect on the sufferings which their forefathers endured, in the maintenance of their religious testimonies in times of great difficulty. This address thus proceeds : " As divers members of our religious Society, some of them without their consent or knowledge, have been lately nominated to attend on and engage in some public affairs, which they cannot undertake without deviating from these our religious principles ; we therefore earnestly beseech and advise them, and all others, to consider the end and purpose of every measure to which they are desired to become parties, and with great circumspection and care, to guard against joining in any, for the asserting and maintaining our rights and liberties, which, on mature deliberation, appear not to be dictated by that " wisdom which is from above ; which is pure, peaceable, gentle, full of mercy and good fruits."

About the same time, the Meeting for Sufferings also addressed an epistle to the several Monthly and Quarterly Meetings, in which elders and overseers, and all others who had the real prosperity of our religious Society at heart, were earnestly exhorted "to unite in their respective Monthly Meetings in the fervency of brotherly love," to labour with all their members who might have been concerned in promoting the hostile attitude taken by the Colonists towards Great Britain; special reference being made to the minute of the Yearly Meeting of 1710 on this subject.* Addressing their brethren in London, the Meeting for Sufferings of Philadelphia, in the Third Month, 1775, remarks: " On the late return of two Friends, members of this Meeting, who have been on a visit to many of the meetings in those provinces, we are informed, that there is a number of Friends there, careful to avoid joining with the people in their public consultations, and the commotions prevailing, who, we hope, will be instrumental to advise and caution the weak and unwary, in order that such a conduct may be observed, as will contribute to their own peace, and the maintaining the testimony of Truth among them." The epistle concludes: " That the exigencies of the present time of probation may have the happy effect to excite all more closely and more earnestly to seek after and know the munition of rocks,—the quiet habitation, where alone is safety, is the sincere concern of many among us."

Having counselled their brethren in religious profession, the Meeting for Sufferings next thought it right to address the inhabitants at large, and the following, expressive of the views of the Society on the existing state of things, was accordingly issued :—

" THE TESTIMONY OF THE PEOPLE CALLED QUAKERS, GIVEN FORTH BY A MEETING OF THE REPRESENTATIVES OF SAID PEOPLE, IN PENNSYLVANIA AND NEW JERSEY, HELD AT PHILADELPHIA THE 24TH DAY OF THE FIRST MONTH, 1775.

" Having considered, with real sorrow, the unhappy contest between the legislature of Great Britain and the people of these colonies, and the animosities consequent thereon ; we have, by repeated public advices and private admonitions, used our en-

---

* The minute is as follows :—" As to matters of government, we advise that all Friends concerned therein, whether in legislation or administration, may be very careful to act therein according to Truth, and the testimony of it in all things, and not to think to excuse a contrary practice by any temporal station, or evade the due censure of Truth, on pretence of any conjunction with such as may take liberty to act such things as consist not with our holy communion, profession and discipline ; for notwithstanding any such station, where any offend, the judgment of Truth must go out against them.

deavours to dissuade the members of our religious Society from joining with the public resolutions promoted and entered into by some of the people, which, as we apprehended, so we now find, have increased contention, and produced great discord and confusion.

" The divine principle of grace and truth which we profess, leads all who attend to its dictates, to demean themselves as peaceable subjects, and to discountenance and avoid every measure tending to excite disaffection to the king, as supreme magistrate, or to the legal authority of his government; to which purpose many of the late political writings and addresses to the people appearing to be calculated, we are led by a sense of duty to declare our entire disapprobation of them—their spirit and temper being not only contrary to the nature and precepts of the gospel, but destructive of the peace and harmony of civil society, disqualify men in these times of difficulty, for the wise and judicious consideration and promoting of such measures as would be most effectual for reconciling differences, or obtaining the redress of grievances.

" From our past experience of the clemency of the king and his royal ancestors, we have grounds to hope and believe, that decent and respectful addresses from those who are vested with legal authority, representing the prevailing dissatisfactions and the cause of them, would avail towards obtaining relief, ascertaining and establishing the just rights of the people, and restoring the public tranquillity ; and we deeply lament that contrary modes of proceeding have been pursued, which have involved the colonies in confusion, appear likely to produce violence and bloodshed, and threaten the subversion of the constitutional government, and of that liberty of conscience, for the enjoyment of which, our ancestors were induced to encounter the manifold dangers and difficulties of crossing the seas, and of settling in the wilderness.

" We are, therefore, incited by a sincere concern for the peace and welfare of our country, publicly to declare against every usurpation of power and authority, in opposition to the laws and government, and against all combinations, insurrections, conspiracies, and illegal assemblies : and as we are restrained from them by the conscientious discharge of our duty to Almighty God, "by whom kings reign, and princes decree justice," we hope through His assistance and favour, to be enabled to maintain our testimony against any requisitions which may be made of us, inconsistent with our religious principles, and the fidelity we owe to the king and his government, as by law established ; earnestly desiring the restoration of that harmony and concord which have heretofore united the people of these provinces, and been attended by the divine blessing on their labours.

"Signed in and on behalf of the said meeting,

"JAMES PEMBERTON, *Clerk at this time.*

It has been seen in the course of this history, that the welfare of our religious Society in America was always dear to Friends in England ; and that the latter were ever ready, when circumstances appeared to call for it, to exert themselves on behalf of their distant brethren, whether in pleading for them with the authorities of the state, in defending them more generally from unjust imputations of designing men, or in conveying to them brotherly advice in times of difficulty. The peculiar situation of Friends on the American continent, in the political contest then prevailing, did not fail, therefore, to obtain the lively sympathy of Friends in the mother country ; under a feeling of which, and of ardent solicitude for their preservation, amid the many dangers and temptations with which they were surrounded, the Yearly Meeting of London in 1775, addressed to them the following epistle :—

"FROM OUR YEARLY MEETING HELD IN LONDON BY ADJOURNMENTS, FROM THE 5TH OF SIXTH MONTH, 1775, TO THE 10TH OF THE SAME INCLUSIVE."

"TO OUR FRIENDS AND BRETHREN IN AMERICA."

"DEAR FRIENDS.—Our minds have been awfully bowed in this our annual assembly, before the God and Father of all our mercies ; and we have been brought in deep humility, to sympathize with you our brethren in this time of outward trial and affliction, under a sense whereof we affectionately salute you.

" Our hearts being tenderly affected with the consideration of the difficulties to which you are exposed, and filled with earnest desire for your preservation amidst the present confusions, we feel ourselves engaged to recommend you to attend to the seasonable advices communicated to you from hence, as well as those from our concerned brethren on your continent ; but we exhort you above all things, to keep near to the pure principle of Truth, not only in your meetings and in your families, but throughout your whole conversation and conduct, as the alone sure and safe guide to peace and rest. It will be a comforter in adversity, and a guard against dangers that may attend in times of prosperity.

" Great indeed, and exercising in divers respects, may be the trials which now attend many ; and how long or how far they may prevail, is known only to the Lord, who, though he afflicts not willingly, sees meet at times to suffer his judgments to be in the earth, that its inhabitants may learn righteousness.

" The wise in heart will enquire, if there be not a cause, and if proper returns have been made for the innumerable mercies you have so long enjoyed. We tenderly advise one and all, diligently to examine themselves, and profit by the instruction that may in mercy be conveyed by these calamities.

" It will add much to your safety in every respect, to dwell alone, to suffer your minds to be agitated as little as possible by the present commotions, to keep out of the spirit of parties, and to cherish in your hearts the principle of peace and good-will to all.

" This will help those who live under its influence, to walk wisely as in the day, will enable them to comfort the afflicted, add strength to the weak, restrain the hasty and inexperienced from rushing into dangers of which they are not aware, and may be the means, through divine favour, of preserving the Church, and its members, holy and acceptable unto God

" And dear Friends, we earnestly entreat you, live in unity, the unity of the spirit, the bond of peace. Let nothing arise to scatter and divide you ; wait, one and all, to feel that amongst you, which would root out contention ; so will you be preserved a comfort one to another, and a stay to the minds of many who may be tossed with the waves of affliction, and know not where to seek for a quiet habitation.

"Dwell under a sense of the power and presence of God, all-sufficient and merciful, so will ye be preserved in peace and innocency amidst all the various exercises ye may meet with ; and if afflictions, such as neither we nor our fathers have felt, are permitted to come upon you, you will be enabled to bear a part in the general calamity, with a patience and resignation that a sense of the Lord's presence only can inspire.

"Finally, dear Friends, may you in humble confidence be enabled, from a degree of living experience, to say with the prophet formerly, 'Thou wilt keep him in perfect peace, whose mind is stayed on Thee, because he trusteth in Thee. Trust ye in the Lord for ever, for in the Lord Jehovah is everlasting strength.'

"We salute you in much love, and are

"Your friends and brethren.

Signed in and on behalf of the said Meeting, by

JOSEPH DOCWRA,
Clerk to the Meeting this Year."

The violent course adopted by the citizens of Boston in destroying the cargoes of tea in their port, greatly incensed the government at home, and a bill was quickly passed, imposing on that city a penalty, to the full value of the property destroyed, and closing it as a port during the pleasure of the Crown. These measures brought on the colonists of Massachusetts much distress, from which Friends were not exempt. Their trials did not escape the notice of Friends in Philadelphia ; but in the early stage of these portentous proceedings, so anxious were they not to appear in any way to sanction the belligerent course pursued by their countrymen, that they felt restrained from aiding their brethren in New England, lest such an act should be construed into an approval of their conduct. Towards the close of the year 1775, however, after warlike measures had been taken by Great Britain,

to enforce its arbitrary policy, and Lexington and Bunker's Hill
had already become the scene of bloodshed, Friends of Pennsylvania and New Jersey no longer hesitated to act for the relief
of their suffering brethren and others in those parts. An epistle,
representing the distress to which the inhabitants of New England
were exposed, and inviting Friends to contribute for their assistance, was addressed to the several meetings of the two provinces.
The appeal was liberally responded to, a large sum was raised,
and, under the feeling which prompted the benevolent design,
two Friends visited New England to assist in the distribution of
two thousand pounds, of which they were the bearers, accompanied by an epistle of affectionate sympathy. Up to the Ninth
Month 1776, the amount collected for the sufferers from the war
amounted to three thousand nine hundred pounds, of which the
greater part had been sent to the Meeting for Sufferings in
New England, and distributed, according to accounts received,
to about seven thousand persons under suffering.* A further
relation of the trials of Friends in New England at this period
will be given in a subsequent division of the history.

The agitation of the colonies became greatly increased by the
conflicts of Lexington and Bunker's Hill, and war, not with the
Indians, but with British forces, was the fearful prospect that
now awaited the Americans. The inhabitants of Pennsylvania,
impetuous in the quarrel, petitioned their Assembly for the
adoption of warlike measures in defence, and there appeared to
be a danger that Friends might be involved in much difficulty
and trial in consequence. The Meeting for Sufferings was fully
alive to this critical situation of things, and in the Tenth Month
1775, prepared an address to the Assembly, which was presented
by a deputation of ten Friends. After alluding to the popular
cry for an appeal to arms,—to their own well-known principles
against all wars and fightings—to the settlement of the province
in unison with those principles, and to its prosperity under them,
they refer to that part of the charter of Pennsylvania, wherein
it is expressly provided that Friends should not be obliged " to

* Gough's MSS.

do or suffer any act or thing contrary to their religious persuasion;" concluding with the expression of a fervent desire, that "the most conciliatory measures" may be pursued, "and that all such may be avoided, as are likely to widen or perpetuate the breach with the parent state, or tend to introduce persecution and sufferings among them."

The opening of the year 1776, was inauspicious for peace. A petition from Congress to the British Parliament, styled by the Americans, "The Olive Branch,"* and presented at the Bar of the House of Commons by Richard Penn, one of the proprietaries of Pennsylvania, had been rejected ; and, under the idea of possessing superior force, a disposition to refuse all further attempts to promote an amicable arrangement of the dispute, prevailed in the councils of George III. In the First Month of this year, therefore, the Meeting for Sufferings of Philadelphia, in order to make the conscientious views of the Society in reference to this distressing state of affairs more widely known, determined on an extensive circulation of a paper entitled "The ancient Testimony and Principles of the people called Quakers, renewed with respect to the King and Government, and touching the commotions now prevailing in these and other parts of America, addressed to the people in general." It commences with an expression of religious interest for all classes of the community, and a desire that all may "in the most solemn manner," carefully examine, in reference to the present troubles, "whether they are acting in the fear of God and in conformity to the precepts and doctrines of our Lord Jesus Christ." It then refers to the blessings of peace with which the provinces had been signally favoured, and urges the enquiry how far these blessings had been met with corresponding dedication of heart to the Lord. After setting forth the peaceable nature of the religion of Christ, and quoting from an early declaration of the Society on civil government, and on the duty of Friends " to live a peaceable and quiet life, in all godliness and honesty, under the government which God is pleased to set

---

* Hume and Smollett's Hist. of England.

over us ;" it concludes by desiring that nothing may be done " to break off the happy connection heretofore enjoyed with the King of Great Britain."

The gloomy aspect of things at this period, and the difficulties which appeared to be hastening on Friends in the respective colonies of America, induced the appointment of representatives from New England, Virginia, and North Carolina, to attend Philadelphia Yearly Meeting of 1776, to consult on their trying circumstances—a course which was adopted during the greater part of the revolutionary war.

A circumstance which at this period distressed Friends, was the defection of a number of their members who were but ill-grounded in their attachment to the principles of the Society, from its acknowledged testimony against war. Associations having been formed to learn military exercise, the individuals in question evinced their declension by joining in the movement. The Church was not backward in labouring with such, but unsuccessfully as regarded many of them, who afterwards formed themselves into a distinct Society, under the name of "Free Quakers." The number of these was not however large. In and near Philadelphia they amounted to about one hundred, but, except within the limits of two country meetings, there were very few besides.*

Friends were, also, brought into much trial and perplexity, with respect to the issue of paper notes of credit, for the purpose of carrying on the war. Many felt themselves religiously restrained from countenancing this plan devised expressly for warlike ends, and refused to receive the notes as money. It does not appear, however, that the Society in its collective capacity enforced such a course, or that those who took a contrary view in this particular were censured.† Some members were also severe sufferers through distraints for military purposes. A demand having been made on the city of Philadelphia for a supply of blankets for the American army, many families had all they possessed of these articles forcibly taken from them, and were obliged to pass the winter without them. Others had their

* Gough's MSS. † *Vide* Journals of John Woolman and Job Scott.

x 2

houses stripped of the lead for the use of the army. The habitations also of many were wantonly attacked by the rabble, for opening their shops on a day appointed by Congress for a general fast; whilst others, for refusing to act in military service, were committed to prison; and some for declining to accept public offices to which they had been nominated were fined twenty pounds each, and distrained upon for the same to much larger amounts. Israel Morris, whilst travelling in New Jersey, was imprisoned for refusing to take the declaration of allegiance required by a recent law, and, after a trial at Trenton, was fined seventy-five pounds, to be levied on his estate. John Cowgill of Duck Creek, for refusing to take the paper currency, was arrested and taken before a body called a Committee of Inspection; and having declined to give assurances that he would alter his course, was advertised in the newspapers, as an enemy to his country, all persons being warned against having any dealings with him. The effect was, that some millers refused to grind his corn, whilst the schoolmaster who taught his children, sent them home. On one occasion as he was going with his family to a week-day meeting, he was seized by a number of armed men, who told him that the Committee had sent for him. These men, having fixed a paper on his back inscribed, " On the circulation of the Continental currency depends the fate of America," conveyed him in a cart to a neighbouring town, and in this manner paraded him through it.

The foregoing are a few of the cases selected from many recorded by the Meeting for Sufferings of Philadelphia. They are, however, sufficient to illustrate the feeling entertained towards Friends by their excited neighbours, in their determined resistance to British authority. But notwithstanding these trials of faith and patience in the spoil of their goods, in the imprisonment of their persons, and in the aspersion of their characters, Friends were in general preserved in much union and harmony of spirit, and experienced Him who is the all-sufficient helper and strength of his people, to be their safe hiding-place in the day of trouble. Under this feeling the following epistle was indited, which was printed and widely circulated among Friends.

To some of the revolutionists it seems to have given great umbrage, and Mark Millar of Woodbury, and Thomas Redman of Haddonfield, in New Jersey, were imprisoned eight weeks for reading it in their religious assemblies.

"To our Friends and Brethren in religious profession, in these and the adjacent Provinces.

"Dearly beloved Friends and Brethren,—Our minds being renewedly impressed with a fervent religious concern for your spiritual welfare, and preservation in the love and fellowship of the Gospel of our Lord Jesus Christ, the Prince of Peace, by the constrainings of his love, we are engaged to salute you in this time of deep exercise, affliction, and difficulty ; earnestly desiring that we may, by steady circumspection and care, in every part of our conduct and conversation, evidence, that under the close trials which are and may be permitted to attend us, our faith and reliance is fixed on Him alone for protection and deliverance ; remembering his gracious promise to his faithful followers, ' Lo, I am with you alway, even unto the end of the world.' And as 'it became Him for whom are all things, and by whom are all things, in bringing many sons unto glory, to make the Captain of their salvation perfect through suffering,' let us not be dismayed, if we are led into the same path. As we keep in the Lord's power and peaceable Truth, which is over all, and therein seek the good of all, neither sufferings, persecutions, nor any outward thing that is below, will hinder or break our heavenly fellowship in the light and spirit of Christ.

"Thus we may, with Christian firmness and fortitude, withstand and refuse to submit to the arbitrary injunctions and ordinances of men, who assume to themselves the power of compelling others, either in person or by other assistance, to join in carrying on war, and of prescribing modes of determining concerning our religious principles, by imposing tests not warranted by the precepts of Christ, or the laws of the happy constitution, under which we and others enjoyed tranquillity and peace.

"We therefore, in the aboundings of that love which wisheth the spiritual and temporal prosperity of all men, exhort, admonish, and caution all who make religious profession with us, and especially our beloved youth, to stand fast in that liberty, wherewith, through the manifold sufferings of our predecessors, we have been favoured, and steadily to bear our testimony against every attempt to deprive us of it.

"And, dear Friends, you who have known the truth, and the powerful operations thereof in your minds, adhere faithfully thereto, and by your good example and stability, labour to strengthen the weak, confirm the wavering, and warn and caution the unwary against being beguiled by the snares of the adversaries of truth and righteousness. Let not the fear of suffering, either in person or in property, prevail on any to join with or promote any work or preparations for war.

"Our profession and principles are founded on that spirit, which is contrary, and will in time put an end to all wars and bring in everlasting righteousness ; and by our constantly abiding under the direction and instruction of that spirit, we may be endued with that 'wisdom from above, which is first pure, then peaceable, gentle and easy to be entreated, full of mercy and good fruits, without partiality, and without hypocrisy.' That this may be our happy experience is our fervent desire and prayer.

"Signed in and on behalf of the Meeting for Sufferings held in Philadelphia, for Pennsylvania and New Jersey, the 20th day of the Twelfth Month, 1776.

"JOHN PEMBERTON, *Clerk.*"

In the course of the year 1777, many Friends suffered imprisonment, and others were distrained upon to some thousands of pounds in the aggregate, for bearing a faithful testimony against war. From the members of one meeting alone, goods to the value of near twelve hundred pounds were taken for their refusal to enrol in the militia.* Some Friends residing near Hopewell in the western parts of Virginia were, under the militia laws, forcibly taken from their homes to the army ; and continuing steadfast in their refusal to bear arms, they were at last forced to move from place to place in military order, and some of

* Records of Philadelphia Meeting for Sufferings.

them even had muskets tied to their persons. Critical as was the state of things in the American army at this period, these were acts which did not meet the approval of General Washington, and soon after arriving at his camp the Friends were discharged.*

Severe as were some of the foregoing cases of suffering, a much heavier trial befel some others. Ever since the war with the Indians and French, in 1755, a strong prejudice had been entertained towards the Society of Friends, arising mainly from their opposition to the warlike course pursued by the Assembly. They still possessed large influence in Pennsylvania; and this fact, in connection with their general withdrawal from official stations, placed them in a somewhat isolated situation, and contrasted strikingly with their former position as rulers of the province. Throughout their history, Friends, as a people, have leaned in politics to the popular and democratic view of things. Their conduct throughout America, and more especially the laws and government which they were instrumental in establishing in Pennsylvania, support this assertion; and none have been more bold and unflinching in the maintenance of the inherent rights of the subject, and in passive resistance to oppression and tyranny in government. But whilst this has been, and still is, a characteristic of Friends, yet an utter abhorrence of violence and war, as opposed to the plainest commands of Christ and the very spirit of his holy religion, and a belief that it is the duty of Christians to "live a peaceable and quiet life, in all godliness and honesty, under the government which God is pleased to set over them,"† are characteristics of the body not less prominent. Friends in America, though professing and sustaining the principles of peace, have been intrepid and fearless defenders of their natural and political rights. As early as 1679, when the Duke of York, who claimed the sovereignty over New Jersey, attempted to tax the settlers, they made a bold remonstrance against it. They declared that taxation without representation was untenable, being opposed to the fundamental laws of the British constitution, and that the King of England cannot take

---

* Exiles in Virginia, p. 181.
† Ancient Testimony, 1696. Sewel's Hist.

the goods of his subjects without their consent.* The firmness of their opposition carried the point ; and thus, without a resort to arms, the Friends of New Jersey successfully resisted an imposition which, as we have seen, was followed by others, and at length gave rise to the American Declaration of Independence. The successful resistance of Friends to the exactions levied on vessels by the fort at Newcastle, is another instance of what a peace policy can effect ; and the extent to which this policy succeeded with the aboriginal tribes of North America, is of historical notoriety.

At the commencement of the disputes with the mother country on the subject of the Stamp Act, Friends united with others of their countrymen, in remonstrating against its injustice ; and the non-importation agreement of 1765, was signed by no less than fifty of our members, nine of whom were afterwards objects of the persecution we are about to detail, in consequence of their condemning a warlike course, which, though taken in maintenance of civil rights, they believed to be contrary to the spirit of the gospel.

The various epistles and advices which had been issued by the Society in Pennsylvania, cautioning its members against participating in any movement that compromised their religious principles on the subject of war, together with the disownment of those who had joined the republican army, were regarded by many of their fellow-citizens as demonstrations adverse to the American cause. But though Friends, disapproving of warlike measures, reprobated the hostile progress of the revolution, yet this was the natural result of their principles, and did not arise from any favourable leaning towards the pretensions of England. It was their religion alone which caused them to differ from others of their countrymen, who had no conscientious objection to seek redress for colonial grievances by an appeal to arms.

Notwithstanding their endeavours to explain their objections to war, Friends were viewed by the republican party through a prejudiced medium, and with an unkind and jealous eye. A feeling, in fact, of great suspicion and dislike to them,

* Smith's New Jersey, p. 120 ; and Proud's Penn. vol. i. p. 151.

prevailed among those who called themselves patriots. About the Eighth Month, 1777, this feeling seemed to have reached its height; when the notorious Spanktown forgery appeared, and led to the banishment of a number of Friends to the remote parts of Virginia. The circumstances of this affair are now to be related.

During the second year of the war of Independence, the English army, which had been landed at New York, proceeded by sea to the head of Chesapeake Bay, and after the battle of Brandywine, in the Ninth Month, 1777, they took possession of Philadelphia. New Jersey was then held by the American army; and so anxious were they to prevent their movements from being known to the British, that it was death for any person to pass their lines into Pennsylvania, without having first obtained a pass. A few weeks before the entry of the British into Philadelphia, General Sullivan succeeded on the 22nd of the Eighth Month, in capturing on Staten Island the baggage of an English officer. Amongst the papers found in this baggage, one was stated to be from "the Yearly Meeting of Spanktown," held a few days previously to the capture; and a copy of this document Sullivan forthwith sent to Congress, then sitting at Philadelphia. Writing on the 25th, he says, "Among baggage taken on Staten Island, the 22nd instant, I find a number of important papers. A copy of three I enclose, for the perusal of Congress. The one of the Yearly Meeting of Spanktown, held the 19th instant, I think worthy the notice of Congress." This is the paper:—

"*Information from Jersey, 19th August*, 1777.

" It is said General Howe landed near the head of Chesapeake Bay ; but cannot learn the particular spot, or when.

" Washington lays in Pennsylvania, about twelve miles from Coryell's Ferry.

"Sullivan lays about six miles north of Morristown, with about two thousand men.

" SPANKTOWN YEARLY MEETING."*

* Exiles in Virginia, p. 62.

Spanktown was a nickname for Rahway in East Jersey, at which place no Yearly Meeting of Friends had ever been held. The letter, also dated in East Jersey on the 19th, spoke of the actual landing of the British army in Chesapeake Bay ; but this did not take place until the 22nd, and was known in Philadelphia on the day following ; and on the 25th, it was recorded on the minutes of Congress. The forgery was, in fact, a clumsy performance ; and that its true character was not immediately detected is to be attributed to the general agitation which then prevailed. It may here be remarked that, on the approach of the British army, Congress, a few days before the receipt of Sullivan's despatch had resolved " That the executive officers of the states of Pennsylvania and Delaware, be requested to cause all persons within the respective states, *notoriously disaffected*, forthwith to be disarmed and secured, until such time as they may be released without injury to the common cause."* It was under this order that several Friends of high standing in Philadelphia were arrested ; and as they refused to sanction the measures of the revolutionary party, the Supreme Executive Council declared " the Friends to be notoriously disaffected to the cause of American freedom,"† and as such they were reported to Congress, most of its members being, it is believed, ignorant of their real principles and the cause of their conduct. It was at this juncture that Congress received the Spanktown paper, the reading of which caused an apparent panic among the members ; who at once drew the inference that the religious meetings of the Society of Friends were intimately connected with politics, and that they were promoting the interests of the enemy. The following is the record made by Congress on the occasion :—

" Thursday, *August* 28*th*, 1777.

" A letter of the 25th, from General Sullivan, at Hanover, with several papers enclosed, also another from him without date, were read.

" *Ordered*, That the letter of the 25th, with the papers enclosed,

* Exiles in Virginia, p. 35.   † *Ibid.* p. 36.

be referred to a committee of three. The members chosen, Mr. J. Adams, Mr. Duer, and Mr. R. H. Lee.

" The Committee to whom the letter of General Sullivan, with the papers enclosed, was referred, report :—

" That the several testimonies which have been published since the commencement of the present contest between Great Britain and America, and the uniform tenor of the conduct and conversation of a number of persons of considerable wealth, who profess themselves to belong to the society of people commonly called Quakers, render it certain and notorious that those persons are with much rancour and bitterness disaffected to the American cause. That as these persons will have it in their power, so there is no doubt it will be their inclination, to communicate intelligence to the enemy, and in various other ways to injure the counsels and arms of America.

" That when the enemy in the month of December, 1776, were bending their progress towards the city of Philadelphia, a certain seditious publication addressed ' To our friends and brethren in religious profession in these and the adjacent provinces ; signed John Pemberton, in and on behalf of the Meeting for Sufferings, held at Philadelphia, for Pennsylvania and New Jersey, the 20th of Twelfth Month, 1776,' was published, and as your committee is credibly informed, circulated amongst many members of the Society called Quakers through the different States.

" That as the seditious paper aforesaid originated in the city of Philadelphia, and as the persons whose names are undermentioned have uniformly manifested a disposition highly inimical to the cause of America, therefore

" *Resolved*, That it be earnestly recommended to the Supreme Executive Council of the State of Philadelphia, forthwith to apprehend and secure the persons of Joshua Fisher, Abel James, James Pemberton, Henry Drinker, Israel Pemberton, John Pemberton, John James, Samuel Pleasants, Thomas Wharton, sen., Thomas Fisher (son of Joshua), and Samuel R. Fisher (son of Joshua), together with all such papers in their possession as may be of a political nature.

" And whereas there is strong reason to apprehend that these

persons maintain a correspondence and connexion highly prejudicial to the public safety, not only in this state, but in the
several States of America.

"*Resolved,* That it be recommended to the executive powers
of the respective States, forthwith to apprehend and secure all
persons, as well among the people called Quakers as others, who
have in their general conduct and conversation evidenced a disposition inimical to the cause of America ; and that the persons
so seized be confined in such places and treated in such manner
as shall be consistent with their respective characters and the
security of their persons.

" That the records and papers of the Meeting of Sufferings in
the respective States, be forthwith secured and carefully examined,
and that such parts of them as may be of a political nature be
forthwith transmitted to Congress."

" The said report being read, and the several paragraphs considered and debated, and the question put severally thereon, the
same was agreed to."

For some weeks a report had been current, that lists of a great
number of the citizens of Philadelphia were made out, with a
view to their arrest.   But as it was supposed that these reports
originated only from personal animosity, they were generally
discredited.   It is clear, however, that a design of this nature
had been entertained for some time ; and there is no doubt that
the Spanktown forgery was one of the means devised for its
accomplishment.   The day on which Congress recorded the
foregoing, the Supreme Executive Council, losing no time, issued
a warrant for the apprehension of a considerable number of
Friends, in which one of the instructions was, that "early
attention should be paid to John Hunt, who lives on the Germantown road, about five miles from the city, and to John Pemberton,
Samuel Emlen, and other leaders in the Society of Quakers,
concerning books and papers."*   The parties named in the
warrant were called upon to subscribe to a declaration, promising
not to depart from their dwellings, " and to be ready to appear

* Exiles of Virginia.

on demand of the President and Council of the State of Pennsylvania, and to engage to refrain from doing anything injurious to the United States of North America, by speaking, writing, or otherwise, and from giving intelligence to the commander of the British forces, or any person whatever, concerning public affairs." Conscious of their innocence with reference to the charges insinuated by the declaration, and valuing their liberty as free citizens, and disdaining also to recognise the imputation that they had forfeited this liberty by crime, they at once rejected the proposal ; immediately on which, arrests took place in the following order : —

1777, *Ninth Month 2nd.*—William Drewit Smith, Thomas Affleck, Thomas Gilpin, William Lennox, Alexander Stedman, Charles Stedman, Samuel Rowland Fisher, William Inlay, James Pemberton, Miers Fisher, Thomas Fisher, Thomas Wharton, Edward Pennington, John Pemberton, Owen Jones, jun., Charles Eddy, Joseph Fox, Thomas Combe, jun., William Smith, broker.

Ninth Month 3rd.—Henry Drinker, Charles Jervis, John Galloway, William Hollingshead, E. Ayres, Phineas Bond, Thomas Pike.

Ninth Month 4th.—John Hunt, Israel Pemberton, Samuel Pleasants.

Ninth Month 5th.—Elijah Brown.

The seizure of these citizens in an arbitrary and illegal manner, on a declaration of Congress and on orders issued by the Executive Council, without any specific charge of offence, and without an opportunity of being heard in their own defence, was one of the extraordinary incidents of the revolution, and one, certainly, which leaves a stain on the characters of the members of the Executive Council, who were the chief actors in the affair. The parties arrested immediately remonstrated against the injustice of the proceeding. Israel Pemberton, John Hunt, and Samuel Pleasants presented, on the day of their arrest, a strong document to the Council. " We claim," they said, " our undoubted right as freemen, having a just sense of the inestimable value of religious and civil liberty, to be heard before we are confined in the manner directed by the order ; and we have the more urgent cause for insisting on this our right, as several of our fellow-citizens have been some days and now are confined by your order, and no opportunity is offered them to be heard ; and we have been informed that it is your purpose to send them and us into a distant part of the country, even beyond the limit of the jurisdiction you claim, and where the recourse we are justly entitled to, of being heard or clearing ourselves from any charge or suspicions you may entertain against us, will be impracticable.'' On the same day, another address of a similar character, signed by twenty of the prisoners, was drawn up. The day following, they addressed Congress ; and their address seems to have opened the eyes of that body to the injustice of the act, for on the 6th of the Ninth Month, they passed this resolution :—

"That it be recommended to the Supreme Executive Council of the State of Pennsylvania, to hear what the said remonstrants can allege, to remove the suspicions of their being disaffected or dangerous to the United States."*

The ruling men in the Council, however, had evidently made up their minds to punish Friends ; and despite the recommendation of Congress, and setting at nought the common principles of justice, they resolved as follows :—

"That the President do write to Congress, to let them know that the Council has not time to attend to that business in the present alarming crisis, and that they were, agreeably to the recommendation of Congress, at the moment the resolve was brought into Council, disposing of everything for the departure of the prisoners."

Other remonstrances followed ; but the Council were unmoved in their resolution to send the prisoners into exile, unless they would sign a test, which, on the grounds of their previous refusal, they again unanimously declined, addressing the Council to that effect. " Having thus," they conclude, "remarked on your proposal, protesting our innocence, we again repeat our pressing demand, to be informed of the cause of our commitment, and to have a hearing in the face of our country, before whom we

---

* Exiles of Virginia, p. 39.

shall either stand acquitted or condemned."* A remonstrance stigmatizing the proceedings as "an alarming violation of the civil and religious rights of the community," was also presented to the Council, signed by one hundred and thirteen Friends.

In order to give colour to these proceedings, and to quiet the public mind, the epistles of advice issued at different times by the Meeting for Sufferings, of which several of the prisoners were members, were, by order of Congress, published in the newspapers of the day ; care being taken also to subjoin the Spanktown paper.

On the 9th of the Ninth Month the Council resolved, that twenty-two of their prisoners should without delay be removed to Staunton, in Virginia. Having failed by remonstrances to gain a hearing before the tribunals of their country, the Friends concluded to offer a solemn protest on the subject. " As we consider this," they said in an address to the inhabitants at large, " to be the highest act of tyranny that has been exercised in any age or country where the shadow of liberty was left, we have in the following manner entered our protest against these proceedings :"—

PROTEST.

9th of Ninth Month, 1777.
" TO THE PRESIDENT AND COUNCIL OF PENNSYLVANIA.

" The remonstrance and protest of the subscribers, sheweth :

" That your resolve of this day was this afternoon delivered to us ; which is the more unexpected, as last evening your secretary informed us you had referred our business to Congress, to whom we were about further to apply.

" In this resolve, contrary to the inherent rights of mankind, you condemn us to banishment *unheard*.

" You determine matters concerning us, which *we could have disproved*, had our right to a hearing been granted.

"The charge against us, of refusing ' to promise to *refrain* from corresponding with the enemy,' insinuates that we have already held such correspondence, *which we utterly and solemnly deny.*

* Exiles of Virginia, p. 110.

"The tests you proposed, we were by no law bound to subscribe, and notwithstanding our refusing them, we are still justly and lawfully entitled to all the rights of citizenship, of which you are attempting to deprive us.

"We have never been suffered to come before you to evince our innocence, and to remove suspicions, which you have laboured to instil into the minds of others, and at the same time knew to be groundless; although Congress recommended you to give us a hearing, and your President this morning assured two of our friends we should have it.

[After then making a declaration that they had held no correspondence with the "contending parties," it proceeds:]

"Upon the whole, your proceedings have been so arbitrary, that words are wanting to express our sense of them. We do therefore, as the last office we expect you will now suffer us to perform for the benefit of our country, in behalf of ourselves and those free-men of Pennsylvania who have any regard for liberty, *solemnly remonstrate and protest* against your whole conduct in this unreasonable excess of power exercised by you.

"That the evil and destructive spirit of pride, ambition, and arbitrary power, with which you have been actuated, may cease and be no more; 'and that peace on earth and goodwill to men,' may happily take the place thereof, in your and all men's minds, is the sincere desire of your oppressed and injured fellow-citizens,

ISRAEL PEMBERTON	OWEN JONES, JUN.
JOHN HUNT	THOMAS GILPIN
JAMES PEMBERTON	CHARLES JERVIS
JOHN PEMBERTON	PHINEAS BOND
THOMAS WHARTON	THOMAS AFFLECK
EDWARD PENNINGTON	WILLIAM DREWIT SMITH
THOMAS COOMBE	THOMAS PIKE
HENRY DRINKER	WILLIAM SMITH (broker)
THOMAS FISHER	ELIJAH BROWN
SAMUEL PLEASANTS	CHARLES EDDY
SAMUEL R. FISHER	MIERS FISHER."

On the 11th of the Ninth Month, the prisoners were all sent off from Philadelphia, in carriages provided by the Executive and guarded by soldiers. To witness their departure, a motley crowd of spectators had assembled, who appeared, however, generally affected with sorrow at this extraordinary instance of cruelty towards some of their most esteemed and valued fellow-citizens. Through the influence of some kindly disposed individuals, the place of their exile was finally fixed to be at Winchester, a place in the back settlements of Virginia, about three hundred miles from Philadelphia. The journey to their destination was a tedious one and occupied no less than twenty days.

On the seizure of the papers and minutes of the Meeting for Sufferings, by order of Congress, a committee of that meeting was appointed, to enquire into the circumstances of such an extraordinary and unlooked-for event ; and for the purpose, also, of recovering possession of their documents. All of these were returned, excepting three, which it was understood Congress intended to hold. The three thus retained were copies of epistles issued by the Meeting for Sufferings in 1775 and 1776.

With a view to obtain further evidence against the Society, the minutes of several Monthly and Quarterly Meetings were also seized, under the powers of the same warrant. On the minutes of the Executive Council is recorded the report, of "the gentlemen appointed and authorized to arrest" Friends. In fourteen of the arrests their language is, "*no papers ;*" of four, "*no papers found of a public nature;*" of Samuel Emlen, Jun., "*confined to his bed ; we broke open his desk, but found no papers of a public nature;*" of Henry Drinker, "*a number of papers found of a public nature, belonging to the Monthly Meeting;*" of John Pemberton, "*a number of papers in a brown bag;*" of William Lenox, Jun., "*had a pocket-book and some papers;*" of William Smith, (broker), "*his chamber is locked up for the inspection of his papers, the key in the possession of Captain Smith;*" Samuel Jackson, "*out of town ; no search has been made for papers as yet.*"

Several writers on the American War of Independence have censured the Society of Friends for their expressions of attachment to the British Government, and for the advice to its members contained in the epistles issued at that period. By minute of " September 28," 1777, Congress itself, mainly from the character of these epistles, declared of Friends that it is evident " they are, with much rancour and bitterness, disaffected to the American cause," and the epistle of Twelfth Month 20th, 1776, inserted in a previous page, is expressly referred to as a "seditious publication." It is singular that the Christian addresses of a religious Society, which conscientiously believed all war to be wrong, exhorting its members to act consistently with those views, should have been so construed. There must have been men in Congress, who were fully aware that such were the religious principles of Friends in this matter, and that in warning their members at such an excited period not to compromise them, they were only performing a consistent duty. With respect to their attachment to the powers that be, it is notorious that even Congress itself surpassed them in the strength of its language on this head ; and at dates too, subsequent to the issue of the epistles of which they complain. In illustration of this statement the following may be referred to, for comparison of the language of both :—

Epistle of Philadelphia Meeting for Sufferings, First Month 5, 1775.

"Should any now so far deviate from their example, and the practice of faithful Friends at all times since, as to manifest a disposition to contend for liberty, by any methods or agreements contrary to the peaceable spirit and temper of the gospel, which ever breathes peace on earth and good will to all men ; as it is the duty, we desire it may be the care of Friends, in every meeting where there are any such, speedily to treat with them, agreeable to our Christian discipline, and endeavour to convince them of their error."

Declaration of Congress to the People, July 6th, 1775.

"Our forefathers, inhabitants of Great Britain, left their native land to seek on these shores a residence for civil and religious freedom, at the expense of their blood, at the hazard of their fortunes, without the least charge to the country from whence they removed.

"Lest this declaration should disquiet the minds of our friends and fellow-subjects in any part of the empire, we assure them that we mean not to dissolve that union, which has so long and so happily subsisted between us, and which we sincerely wish to see restored."

Testimony of Philadelphia Meeting for Sufferings, First Month 24, 1775.

" We are, therefore, excited by a sincere concern for the peace and welfare of our country, publicly to declare against every usurpation of power, in opposition to the laws and government ; and against all combinations, insurrections, conspiracies, and illegal assemblies ; and as we are restrained from them by a conscientious discharge of our duties to Almighty God, by whom " kings reign, and princes decree justice," we hope, through his assistance and favour, to be able to maintain our testimony against any requisitions which may be made of us, inconsistent with our religious principles, and the fidelity we owe to the king and his government as by law established ; earnestly desiring the restoration of that harmony and concord, which have hitherto united the people of these provinces, and been attended by the divine blessing on their labours."

Address of Congress to the King, July 8th, 1775.

"Attached as we are to your Majesty's person and government, with all the devotion that principle and affection can inspire ; connected with Great Britain by the strongest ties which can unite societies ; and deploring every event that tends in any degree to weaken them ; we solemnly assure your Majesty, that we not only most ardently desire that the former happiness between her and these colonies may be restored, but that a concord may be established between them upon so firm a basis, as to perpetuate its blessings, uninterrupted by any future dissensions, to succeeding generations in both countries, and to transmit your Majesty's name to posterity, adorned with that signal and lasting glory, that hath attended the memory of those illustrious personages, whose virtues and abilities have extricated states from dangerous convulsions, and by securing happiness to others, have added the most noble and durable monuments to their own fame."

The Yearly Meeting of Philadelphia, sitting in usual course in the Tenth Month, felt constrained to issue an address to the inhabitants at large, relative to the banishment of their friends. This paper sets forth the peaceable principles of the Society, controverts the charge against Friends of favouring the cause of England, and denies " in general terms all charges and insinuations which in any degree clash with their profession." It also "solemnly denies" the Spanktown letter, asserts that the "banished Friends had done nothing to forfeit their just right to liberty," and calls upon the authorities to restore them to their families and friends.

A few days after the arrival of the prisoners at Winchester, feeling their lives insecure, they once more addressed Congress on the injustice of their arrest, and of their banishment without a hearing. "If you are determined," they conclude, "to support the Council in the unjust and illegal steps they have taken, to carry your first recommendation into execution, by continuing us in a country so dangerous to our personal safety, we shall commit ourselves to the protection of an all-wise overruling power, in whose sight we trust we shall stand in this matter acquitted, and who, if any of us should lose our lives, will require our blood at your hands."

On the day following, they forwarded an address "to the Governor and Council of Virginia," representing their situation, and soliciting "that protection which the claims of hospitality and the common right of mankind entitle us to, in a country where we are strangers. The firm manner," they add, "in which we have demanded our rights, and the reluctance we have shown in parting with our liberty, will, we hope, be forcible evidence in our favour, and suspend the opinions of all candid persons until the charge, founded on our 'general conduct and conversation,' is properly inquired into." Towards the close of the Twelfth Month, they drew up a memorial "to the Congress and to the Executive Council," remarking therein, "As our banishment was the act of both your bodies, we think it most proper to address you jointly."

An opinion was now rapidly gaining ground, that the exile of these Friends was unjustifiable, and some of the more considerate both of the Executive Council and of Congress, condemned it as such. "As things have turned out," wrote the Secretary of the Executive, "the original arrest was thought by many not to have answered any good purpose, and detaining them in confinement not serviceable to the public cause."* On receiving the last memorial, Congress appointed three of its members to meet Isaac

---

* Exiles in Virginia, p. 198.

Zane and some other Friends, who presented it; after an interview with whom, the Committee candidly avowed, writes James Pemberton, "that they had no other accusation against us, than the several epistles of advice which had been published."* The Committee having urged on Congress the propriety of either hearing the prisoners in their defence, or of discharging them from custody, that body on the 29th of First Month, 1778, passed a resolution for their discharge, on their taking an affirmation of allegiance to the State of Pennsylvania, as a free and independent State; but, as in the former instance, Friends declined to accept their liberty on such a condition.

During this banishment, no provision whatever was made by the authorities for their support. "You will dispose of them," was the direction of the War-office to its agent, "in a manner suitable to their respective characters and stations, and suffer them to be supplied with every necessary they may want, *at their own expense.*"† They boarded with some of the inhabitants of Winchester, but were at times exposed to inconveniences and hardships to which some of them had hitherto been strangers. Towards the latter end of the Second Month, 1778, Thomas Gilpin, one of their number, was taken ill with fever, the consequence of a severe cold, which he had caught by exposure about two weeks before; and on the 2nd of the Third Month, he died. Within the same month, John Hunt, another of the exiles, being an aged minister, was also taken off by death. About the same time, several others of their number, suffered severely from indisposition.‡

There is no doubt but that the death of the two Friends, and the illness of others, hastened the release of their companions. The public sympathy was increasingly awakened, as it was considered that these circumstances were attributable to causes connected with their banishment. Almost as soon as the news of the decease of Thomas Gilpin reached Lancaster, where Congress was then sitting, it resolved on liberating the prisoners. This was

---

* Diary of James Pemberton during his exile.
† Exiles of Virginia.   ‡ Diary of James Pemberton.

done by a resolution on the 16th of Third Month, placing them at the disposal of the Council of Pennsylvania. The latter body, however, were not disposed to hasten in the matter, and nothing was done by them until the decease of the second Friend was made known to them. This event, together probably with the growing discontent of the people on the subject, appears to have quickened them ; and on the 8th of the Fourth Month, they decided to set the prisoners free, adding, however, this unjust proviso : " That the whole expense of arresting and confining the prisoners sent to Virginia, the expenses of their journey, and all other incidental charges, be paid by the said prisoners."

By virtue of the foregoing resolution, the remaining prisoners, who had now been in exile more than seven months, were brought to Lancaster on the 27th of the Fourth Month ; from whence they were forwarded to Pottsgrove, in the county of Philadelphia, and discharged. Thus ended this extraordinary affair. It is much to be regretted that the American people, whilst struggling for political rights, against the oppression of the parent state, should have so far compromised their consistency in the professed love of freedom, as to have thus unconstitutionally and unwisely exiled, unheard, a number of their best citizens—men who were confessedly ornaments to the country in which they lived.

As the deaths of Thomas Gilpin and John Hunt have been mentioned, it seems due to their memories, before passing on to other subjects, to refer to a few facts on record respecting them. Thomas Gilpin was a man of a mild and amiable disposition, and possessed good mental abilities. He bore his trials with much resignation, and throughout his illness was favoured with great composure. " I am going the way of all flesh," he remarked, a short time before his close, adding, " and I hope it is in mercy." —" There are many religions in the world, and a variety of forms, which have occasioned great persecutions and the loss of many lives ; each contending that they are right ; but there is but one true religion, arising from faith in God, and in his Son, Jesus Christ, and hope in his mercy. A monitor is placed in every mind, which if we attend to, we cannot err." He was buried at Friends' burial-ground at Hopewell, on the 3rd of Third Month,

1778. His fellow-prisoner, Israel Pemberton, has left this testimony respecting him: "I had but little acquaintance with him before our being confined together; but his conduct recommended him much to my esteem. He was steady in maintaining his own sentiments, but with due care to give no cause of offence to others. His principles were liberal, free from bigotry to any party: thus he could discover that which was laudable or culpable in either. He supported his opinion, but without severity, and never expressed one murmur or complaint on our unjust suffering during his illness."

John Hunt was formerly of London. He came to America in 1756, with Christopher Wilson, as a deputation from the Society in England, to assist Friends during the difficulties of that period. After going back to Europe, he returned and settled in Philadelphia. Towards the close of the Second Month, 1778, whilst an exile at Winchester, he was taken ill; and being confined to his bed, he was suddenly seized with pain in his leg; mortification followed, and amputation became necessary. He was enabled to bear the operation with great patience and resignation. His health, however, continued to give way, and an attack of paralysis having come on, his speech faltered, and he gradually grew weaker until the 31st of Third Month, when the vital spark fled. James Pemberton, in a diary which he kept at Winchester, recorded the following of his deceased fellow-sufferer, after the funeral: "Thus the last act of respect and love was solemnly paid to the remains of a dignified minister of the gospel, whose gift was eminent—and he had laboured in it forty years. His delivery was clear and intelligible, and his doctrine sound and edifying. He was often favoured with great power and demonstration, singularly manifested in meetings for worship [which] we had during the time of our exile at Winchester. He expressed himself much concerned that the inhabitants should come to a knowledge of the truth and a due feeling for their own eternal welfare; and although but few of them knew us, yet they were desirous to attend our meetings. Being a man possessing a clear judgment and strong natural abilities, improved by long religious experience, he was a useful member of our religious

Society, careful for the support of our discipline, and spoke often pertinently to matters under consideration. He was in the sixty-seventh year of his age ; of a strong constitution ; low in stature ; but favoured through life with general good health."*

In almost all revolutions there have been some who have adopted a course opposed to the popular will. This was the case during the American war of Independence ; and among these were a few members of the Society of Friends, who, contrary to the example of their brethren, and to the principles of the Society, became partisans in the struggle. John Roberts and Abraham Carlisle were of this number. John Roberts resided at Merion, near Philadelphia, and was much respected for his hospitality and benevolence. He appears to have been a man of a warm and zealous temperament ; and on hearing of the arbitrary acts of the revolutionary party in banishing Friends, he became greatly excited, and began to devise plans for the rescue of his brethren. He hastened to the English army, then approaching Philadelphia, gave them information of the arrest of his friends, and proposed that a troop of horsemen should be sent to intercept the guard who were on their way with the exiles to Reading. Abraham Carlisle was a citizen of Philadelphia, of good moral conduct, and esteemed by his neighbours, though inconsistent as a Friend. The city of Philadelphia was occupied by the English for about nine months, and during that time its outlets were guarded by soldiers, no one being allowed to pass without an order. The office for granting these orders to persons with produce for sale, or on visits to their friends, was accepted by Abraham Carlisle, who was known to be much attached to the British Government. He was strongly remonstrated with by his friends on the subject, as acting in direct opposition to the advice of the Yearly Meeting, and as compromising his principles as a Friend. He, however, unwisely pleaded that he was engaged in a good and benevolent work, and declined to accede to the solicitations of his brethren. In the Sixth Month, 1778, the Americans retook Philadelphia, and very soon after Roberts and

* Diary of James Pemberton, 2nd of Fourth Month, 1778.

Carlisle were arrested as traitors to their country, and tried on the charge of high treason. The violence of popular feeling against all who sympathised with the British, was at that time very strong, and the prejudice against Friends was but little if at all diminished; and disappointed, as many of the revolutionists were, in not being able to sustain a case against the exiles to Winchester, every effort was now made to procure the conviction of the accused, in a spirit of revenge on the Society to which they belonged. The prosecution was conducted with rigour, and notwithstanding the evidence adduced was contradictory, and much of it was evidently prompted by private revenge and party feeling, they were found guilty. There is no doubt that their attachment to the Crown had been imprudently manifested; but some of their friends who attended the trial, and were acquainted with all the facts of the case, have left a record to show that they were neither guilty of high treason, nor had had a fair hearing. After the condemnation, many persons not members of our Society exerted themselves to obtain a pardon for the prisoners. All, however, was unavailing. Their death had evidently been determined upon by the leading men of the Executive Council, and these were deaf to all solicitations and reasoning on the subject. As a body, Friends made no effort for the condemned. Had they done so, not only would it have been ineffectual, but their motives might have been misconstrued and misrepresented. The result was that both Roberts and Carlisle were hung. Whilst in prison they were visited by many Friends, and were brought to see their error in deviating from the Christian counsel of their brethren. They were favoured to meet their solemn change with resignation, and with hope in the unmerited mercies of God, expressing their forgiveness of those who had sought their destruction.* It is singular that the public records of these trials cannot be discovered, having been either secreted or destroyed. To conceal the authentic evidences of the slender ground on which the conviction rested, is probably the cause of their being thus withheld from the scrutinizing eye of the public, and from the condemnation of the proceedings by posterity.

* T. Scattergood and his times.

CHAPTER XIII.

DURING the occupation of Philadelphia by the British army, the
members of our religious Society, in common with others of the
citizens, suffered considerably by the wanton excesses and plunder
of the soldiery. A committee of Friends had an interview with
General Howe on this subject.* In the country, over most parts
of which the Americans still held control, the sufferings of
Friends were even more severe. Many were subjected to heavy
fines, imprisonments, and other oppressions, for conscientiously
refusing to join in warlike demonstrations ; and it is not a little
singular, that in Pennsylvania and New Jersey,—provinces
founded under the especial auspices of members of our Society,—
their trials in this respect were greater than in other parts of the
Union. The Meeting for Sufferings of Philadelphia, having
received information of the imprisonment of many on this account,
in several localities, presented an address, in the Eighth Month,
1778, to the Assembly of Pennsylvania on the subject. " They
respectfully represent, that the government of the consciences of
men is the prerogative of Almighty God, who will not give His
glory to another ; that every encroachment on this his prerogative,

* Gough's MSS.

is offensive in his sight, and that he will not hold them guiltless who invade it, but will sooner or later manifest his displeasure to all who persist therein. These truths," they say, "will, we doubt not, obtain the assent of every considerate mind. The immediate occasion of our now applying to you, is [that] we have received accounts from different places, that a number of our friends are and have been imprisoned, some for refusing to pay the fines imposed in lieu of personal services in the present war, and others for refusing to take the test prescribed by some laws lately made. The ground of our refusal is a religious scruple in our minds against such compliance, not from obstinacy, or any other motive than a desire of keeping a conscience void of offence towards God, which we cannot, without a steady adherence to our peaceable principles and testimony against wars and fightings, founded on the precepts and example of our Lord Jesus Christ, the Prince of Peace ; by a conformity to which we are bound to live a peaceable and quiet life, and restrained from making any declaration or entering into any engagements as parties in the present unsettled state of public affairs." After alluding to the manner in which civil and religious liberty had been secured to the inhabitants of Pennsylvania under the charter of its enlightened founder, they express a desire that "the laws which have a tendency to oppress tender consciences may be repealed," and that provision may be made for the release of those who are in "bonds for the testimony of a good conscience, and which may prevent others hereafter from suffering in like manner."

The year 1779, brought no mitigation of the sufferings of Friends. Fines and imprisonments for refusing to bear arms, were rigorously enforced, and not only so, but many were now subjected to heavy exactions for refusing to become collectors of the taxes imposed for maintaining the war ; an office which the Revolutionists seemed determined to urge on their more peaceable neighbours. Strong remonstrances on this grievance were made to those in power ; but amidst the excitement and tumults of war, very little disposition existed to lend an ear to conscientious pleadings for the Christian principles of peace. The distraints upon Friends on these various accounts, in five of the Quarterly

Meetings, in Pennsylvania Yearly Meeting, as returned to the Meeting for Sufferings, amounted during this year to upwards of nine thousand five hundred pounds,* three of the Quarterly Meetings having omitted to make a return ; and even this large sum did not include many cases of spoil, the value of which had not been returned.

About this time sufferings of another kind arose, in consequence of a recent law rendering the execution of the test acts more rigorous, and incapacitating all persons refusing to take them from conducting schools or engaging in certain other employments. This was a grievance that closely affected Friends ; and in truth, any law, by which a religious body is prevented from educating its youth according to its own principles, is a serious infraction of the inalienable rights of conscience, and utterly inconsistent with the American professed zeal for liberty. The Meeting for Sufferings at once decided to remonstrate with their rulers on the injustice of this oppressive measure, and in the Eleventh Month, 1779, a forcible appeal against it was presented to the Assembly of Pennsylvania. On the subject of education they observe :—

"Our predecessors, on their early settlement in this part of America, being piously concerned for the prosperity of the colony, and the real welfare of their posterity, among other salutary institutions, promoted at their own expense the establishment of schools for the instruction of their youth in useful and necessary learning, and for their education in piety and virtue, the practice of which forms the most sure basis for perpetuating the enjoyment of Christian liberty and essential happiness. By the voluntary contributions of the members of our religious Society schools were set up, in which their children were taught ; and careful attention hath been given to the instruction of the children of the poor, not of our Society only, but our liberality hath been extended to poor children of other religious denominations generally, great numbers of whom have partaken thereof ; and these schools have been in like manner continued and maintained for a long course of years."

* Records of Philadelphia Meeting for Sufferings.

On the subject of conscience they remark, " Duty to Almighty
God made known in the consciences of men, and confirmed by the
Holy Scriptures, is an invariable rule, which should govern their
judgment and actions. He is the only Lord and sovereign of
conscience, and to Him we are accountable for our conduct, as by
Him all men are to be finally judged.—By conscience we mean,
the apprehension and persuasion a man has of his duty to God ;
and the liberty of conscience we plead for, is a free open profession
and unmolested exercise of that duty—such a conscience as,
under the influence of Divine Grace, keeps within the bounds of
morality in all the affairs of human life, and teacheth to live
soberly, righteously, and godly in the world."

After alluding to the grounds of their objection to war and
oaths, to the sufferings of many of their members on these accounts,
and to the " groundless reports and misrepresentations " respecting Friends, they conclude thus :—" The matters we have now
freely laid before you are serious and important, which we wish
you to consider wisely as men, and religiously as Christians ;
manifesting yourselves friends to true liberty, and enemies to
persecution, by repealing the several penal laws affecting tender
consciences, and restoring to us our equitable rights, that the
means of education and instruction of our youth, which we conceive to be our reasonable and religious duty, may not be
obstructed, and that the oppressed may be relieved. In your
consideration whereof we sincerely desire that you may seek for,
and be directed by that supreme " wisdom, which is pure, peaceable, gentle, and easy to be entreated, full of mercy and good fruits."

In presenting the address, the Committee accompanied it with
a selection of cases of oppression arising from the laws in question. All the documents were referred by the Assembly to the
Committee of Grievances, who, in the Fourth Month, 1780, took
the extraordinary and inquisitorial course of proposing a series of
questions to the Society to be answered in writing. These related
chiefly to an acknowledgment of the American Government—
to the validity of its laws—to the paper money, and concluded
with the following singular request : " As you are specially
associated together, though not incorporated in law, and issue

public letters and recommendations, and promulgate opinions not only on religious, but political subjects, or at least uniting them together, you are requested to communicate the letters and testimonies which have been published from time to time for seven years past, and signed by the clerks of your General or Quarterly Meetings of this city, to be sent to other meetings, or to persons of your Society."

The questions proposed had the close and serious consideration of the Friends appointed on the subject, who did not think proper to submit so far to this categorical and despotic proceeding, as to return specific answers to the several questions; but concluded again to invite those in power to a calm and impartial examination for themselves, of the principles of Friends set forth in their address, as furnishing a sufficient explanation for their not uniting in the present contest with Great Britain. The reply commenced as follows :—

"To the Committee of Grievances,

"Your paper directed to Isaac Zane and others, propounding divers questions to our religious Society, hath been considered, and, agreeable to the advice of an eminent Apostle to his Christian brethren, it becomes us 'to be always ready to give an answer to every man that asketh a reason of the hope that is in us with meekness and fear,' so also we think it necessary, according to their practice, after the example of their Lord and Master, to adapt the answer to the nature and tendency of the question proposed.

"On reviewing the Memorial presented to the Assembly, and our address to you, they appear to us to contain matter of such importance, and so clearly point out the sentiments and practice of our religious Society, in the various changes and revolutions which have occurred in civil government since we were distinguished from other Christian professions, that a weighty, impartial attention to them, and a willingness to remove the cause of oppression complained of, would, we apprehend, sufficiently enable you to represent to the House, the justice and expediency of relief, on the principles of Christian and civil liberty.

"Our religious meetings were instituted for the laudable intention of inculcating in our fellow-members, worship to Almighty God, benevolence to mankind, and to encourage one another in a steadfast, upright conduct, according to the pure principles of the Gospel ; and have been continued for those Christian purposes for more than a century past ; nor hath the original design of their institution been perverted to the purpose of political disquisitions, or any thing prejudicial to the public safety : we therefore conceive the queries you have proposed to us in a religious capacity, are improper, and a mode of redressing grievances new and unprecedented, and such an inquisition made on a religious Society, as we have not known nor heard of in America ; nevertheless, we may briefly repeat what has been already declared on behalf of our religious Society, to revive the important subject of the Memorial in your view ; which we think is still worthy of a very serious and unbiassed consideration.

"Our Friends have always considered Government to be a divine ordinance, instituted for the suppressing vice and immorality, the promotion of virtue, and protection of the innocent from oppression and tyranny. And they esteem those legislators and magistrates, who make the fear and honour of God the rule of their conduct, to be worthy of respect and obedience. And that it is our duty to live a godly, peaceable, and quiet life. It is also our firm belief that conscience ought not to be subject to the control of men, or the injunctions of human laws ; and every attempt to restrain or enforce it, is an invasion of the prerogative of the Supreme Lord and Lawgiver."

After referring to their reasons for objecting to all war, it proceeds thus : "As our Christian principle leads into a life of sobriety and peace, so it restrains us from taking an active part in the present contest, or joining with any measures which tend to create or promote disturbance or commotions in the government under which we are placed ; and many of our brethren, from a conviction that war is so opposite to the nature and spirit of the Gospel, apprehend it their duty to refrain in any degree voluntarily contributing to its support; some of whom, for a considerable number of years past on former occasions, have not actively complied with the payment of taxes raised for military services ; and divers, from conscientious motives, have now avoided circulating the currency which hath been emitted for the immediate purpose of carrying on war ; although on these accounts, they have been, and still are, subjected to great inconvenience, losses, and sufferings. It hath been the uniform practice of our religious Society, after the example of other Christian churches in every age, to issue epistles of counsel and admonition to their members as occasion required ; those and the testimonies you allude to, contain seasonable exhortations to observe a godly conduct, consistent with the peaceable principles of our Christian profession ; and the papers and records of some of our meetings were seized and detained in the Ninth Month, 1777, and, after undergoing a scrutiny and examination, nothing seditious or prejudicial to the public good being found in them, they were returned.

" In whatever mistaken or unfavourable light our religious Society may be held, by those who are unacquainted with us and our principles, or prejudiced against us, we hope to manifest by our conduct, that we are true friends to all men, and sincerely desirous to promote and inculcate such a temper of mind in our fellow-professors in general, as to enable us to forgive them who evilly entreat us, and pray for them who persecute us.

" Signed on behalf of the Committee of the people called Quakers, who waited on the Assembly of Pennsylvania, with a memorial and address, in the Eleventh Month, 1779.

" ISAAC ZANE."

So greatly and singularly was the original feeling of the public towards Friends in Pennsylvania now reversed, that their efforts for a mitigation of their sufferings appear to have produced but little effect. The Meeting for Sufferings in Philadelphia, addressing their brethren in London in 1781, thus allude to their situation : " Various are the trials and sufferings of Friends on this continent, and in many instances very grievous ; men actuated by the spirit of war, prejudiced and blinded by party heats and animosities, are unwilling to understand our peaceable Christian testimony, as anything more than a political enmity against them ; and thus precluding themselves from the candid exercise of their own reason as men, they treat Friends in some cases with great rigour and inhumanity." During the same year, the subject is thus referred to by the Yearly Meeting, in their epistle to London Yearly Meeting. " The sufferings of Friends in these parts have much increased, and continue increasing, in a manner which, to outward prospect, looks ruinous. . . . . Our two brethren who have been long imprisoned in Lancaster jail, are still under confinement there, although their innocence of any crime is acknowledged by those who detain them."

Not only was severity used towards the Society of Friends during the American war by laws of an oppressive character, expressly directed against them, but they were also at times exposed to great havoc and spoil of their goods, and to much personal suffering, by both civil and military officers, without any legal sanction or authority whatever. The imprisonment of the two Friends at Lancaster, referred to in the preceding extract, was a case of this description, and strikingly illustrates the excited and vindictive feeling entertained towards members of our religious Society, by the Revolutionists, during their struggle for political independence. The Friends in question were Moses Roberts and Job Hughes, residents at a new settlement composed mostly of Friends at Catawissa in the present county of Columbia, and at that time on the northern frontiers of Pennsylvania. The ravages from Indians in the employ of the British had, for some years, been great in this part of the country and many of the inhabitants had fled to the interior for safety. But, confiding in Him who has the hearts of all men at his disposal, these Friends did not feel it right to remove, and no harm, it appears, befel them from the dreaded inroads of the red man. In the Fourth Month, 1780, however, they were attacked from a quarter least expected. One First-day morning, as Moses Roberts, who was a valued minister among Friends, was preparing to set out for meeting, he was arrested by a company of armed men, and, together with Job Hughes and some others, taken before a military officer, who, without alleging any offence, sent them forthwith to Sunbury jail, to be placed in irons. In a few days they were brought before a "private Court of Sessions," where also no accusation of any breach of the laws was preferred against them ; and they were astonished to find, that their liberation was only to be obtained, on their giving bail in the enormous sum of ten thousand pounds each, that they would not appear in that part of the province during the war.   The bail of course was not given, and, fettered with irons, the two Friends were passed down the Susquehanna in a canoe to Lancaster, where, notwithstanding the intercessions of Friends of Philadelphia with the President and other heads of the government, they were imprisoned for the space of more than eleven months without the opportunity of a trial, and without a single specific charge of offence.   A suspicion, it appears, that the two Friends had held intercourse with the Indians who had made devastating inroads in the north, was the sole ground of these illegal proceedings.   But their unjust imprisonment was not all.   About two months after their arrest, a body of armed men proceeded to their farms, and forcibly ejected their wives and children, nine in number, who, destitute of all means of support, were thus driven from their homes, to seek shelter where they best might find it, and to depend on the bounty of the humane ; their property, which was large, being all seized by their jealous and unprincipled oppressors, to the entire ruin of the two families.

LOG FARM HOUSE, ON THE FRONTIERS OF PENNSYLVANIA.

Within a few days after the arrest at Catawissa, two other families of Friends, consisting of fourteen persons, and residing on the northern frontiers of Pennsylvania, within forty miles of that place, were suddenly seized and carried off by a company of Indians in the interest of the British. This was the memorable captivity of Benjamin Gilbert and family, a brief notice of which is here introduced.

Benjamin Gilbert was born at Byberry, in 1711, and resided there until the year 1775, when he removed with his family to a farm on Mahoning Creek, near the township of the present Mauch Chunk, in Carbon County. He soon provided himself with a good log dwelling-house, barn, and saw and grist mill, and for five years had pursued his course quietly and prosperously, little expecting the affliction that awaited him, or that, from the pure pleasures of domestic life, he should so soon be a captive with a wandering and warlike band of Iroquois Indians.

Early on the morning of the 25th of the Fourth Month, 1780, the family, consisting of twelve individuals, were surprised by a party of eleven Indians, by whom they were all seized as prisoners of war, any attempt at escape being death.* The Indians then proceeded about half-a-mile to the dwelling of Benjamin Peart, whom they captured, together with his wife, and their child nine months old. Having bound their prisoners with cords, the captors next proceeded to plunder and fire the dwellings; and the last look that Benjamin Gilbert and his family had of their once happy and peaceful homes, was to behold them wrapt in flames. They were then led by a toilsome path over the hills of Mauch Chunk to Mahoning mountain, on which, tied to large poles and stakes after the manner of the Indians, they passed the first night of their captivity.

* Their names were Benjamin Gilbert, aged 69 years; Elizabeth his wife, 55; with their children—Joseph, aged 41; Jesse, 19; Rebecca, 16; Abner, 14; Elizabeth, 12; and Sarah, wife of Jesse, 19; Thomas Peart, son of Benjamin Gilbert's wife, 23; Benjamin Gilbert, son of John Gilbert of Philadelphia, 11; Andrew Harrigar, a servant of Benjamin Gilbert, 26; and Abigail Dodson, 14, a daughter of Samuel Dodson, who lived on a farm about one mile from Gilbert's mill.

For the space of two months was this forlorn band dragged over the wild and rugged region of northern Pennsylvania, and through the swamps and rivers of the Genessee country, to Fort Niagara on lake Ontario. Often from fatigue and hunger were they ready to faint by the way, but the threat of immediate death from their ferocious captors urged them again to the march. At times their provisions were nearly exhausted, and on one occasion they were reduced to feed on "a little hominey and a hedge-hog;" at another on soup made of wild onions and turnip-tops; and more than once on wild potato roots : "days of bitter sorrow and wearisome nights," were truly the experience of these unhappy sufferers. The aged Benjamin Gilbert's health began at last to give way, which the Indians observing, painted him black, as a prelude to death by their own hands, and which they would have carried into execution, had not his wife's intercession prevailed. When he afterwards remarked to the Indian chief on their having brought them alive through the country, the chief replied, "It was not I, but the great God, who brought you through ; for we were determined to kill you, but were prevented."

On the fifty-fourth day of their captivity, entering an Indian town not far distant from Fort Niagara, they had to encounter the fearful ordeal of the gauntlet. On these occasions, the Indians, men, women, and children, with clubs and stones, assemble to vent on the unhappy prisoners their revenge for relatives who have been slain, until they are weary of the cruel sport. There is no escape ; and the blows, however cruel, must be borne without complaint. The sufferings of the devoted family on this occasion, were excessive. But a severer trial even than this awaited them. Being entirely at the disposal of their captors, they were soon separated from each other. Some were given to Indians to be adopted into their tribe, others were hired out by their Indian owners to service in white families ; and others were handed over to the British, and sent down the (St.) Lawrence to Montreal as prisoners of war. Among the latter was the aged Benjamin Gilbert. Accustomed to the comforts of civilized life, he sank under his accumulated sufferings, and in about two months from the date of his seizure, death relieved him from all earthly sorrows. His end was marked by much patience and holy resignation of mind ; and his remains were interred at the foot of an oak on the (St.) Lawrence, below Ogdensburgh.* Andrew Harrigar, had made his escape on the eleventh day of his captivity, and was the first to give an authentic account of the rest of the family, who were all eventually redeemed from the Indians and collected at Montreal in the Eighth Month, 1782, whence they returned to Byberry, after a captivity of two years and five months.†

In the Tenth Month, 1781, the British forces under Lord Cornwallis, in Virginia, surrendered themselves to the American army under General Washington. The event was cause of great exultation to the Revolutionists, and an illumination was determined upon. But the Society of Friends, acting in accordance with their ancient testimony, declined to exhibit any such marks of rejoicing. Their conduct was, as before, attributed to a disposition inimical to the American cause, and " outrages and violences " were committed on their property and persons, by " companies of licentious people who paraded the streets of Philadelphia." Doors and windows were destroyed, and houses broken into and plundered, to the great loss and injury of Friends of that city. Notwithstanding the repeated addresses of the Society to those in power, the Meeting for Sufferings of Philadelphia concluded it right once more to place before them and the inhabitants generally, the real grounds of their declining to take any part in the existing struggle with the mother country, and also of their refusal to unite with their fellow-citizens in exhibitions of public rejoicing. A document to this effect was consequently prepared, addressed " To the President and Executive Council, and General Assembly of Pennsylvania, and others whom it may concern." After alluding to the dawn and commencement of the Reformation—to the breaking forth of a

* Day's Historical Coll. of Pennsylvania, p. 191.
† A Narrative of the Captivity, &c., of B. Gilbert and his Family,

greater degree of light on the minds of men which succeeded, and to the rise of our religious Society from individuals thus enlightened—to their condemnation of war as opposed to the doctrines and precepts of Christ—to their testimony against all "public fasts, feasts, and thanksgivings," as only of human authority—to the continued profession of these views by the Society, and to that "full and free enjoyment of liberty of conscience" secured to the early settlers in Pennsylvania by its founder, they conclude as follows :—

"We are not incited by party views or vindicative motives in this representation, but to awaken your cool and dispassionate attention to our multiplied sufferings, and the abuses we have received ; knowing that magistracy is intended for a terror to evil-doers, and an encouragement to the virtuous ; but where the necessary care and exertions are not used for the prevention and suppression of profanity, tumults, and outrage, and a virtuous part of the community are oppressed and insulted, the true end of government is neglected, and anarchy, confusion, contempt of authority, and insecurity to persons and property will succeed ; and although public fasts may be proclaimed, and days under the name of humiliation recommended and appointed, and confession of sin and transgression verbally made, yet unless there be a true and sincere fasting from ambition, strife, ill-will, animosities, infidelity, fraud, luxury, revelling, drunkenness, oppression, and all manner of evil, it cannot be a fast, or acceptable day to the Lord, nor can we have a well-grounded hope, that the scourge with which the inhabitants have been visited will be removed, and days of peace and tranquillity restored.

"The dispensation of war, bloodshed, and calamity, which hath been permitted to prevail on this continent, is very solemn and awful, demanding the most serious and heartfelt attention of all ranks and denominations among the people, individually to consider and examine how far we are each of us really and sincerely engaged to bring forth fruits of true repentance and amendment of life, agreeable to the spirit and doctrine of the Gospel. And although we have been exposed to great abuse and unchristian treatment, we wish to be enabled, through the assistance of

Divine Grace, to cherish in ourselves, and inculcate in others with whom we have an influence, that disposition of forgiveness of injuries, enjoined by the precepts and example of Christ our holy lawgiver ; and to manifest our desires and endeavours to promote the real good of our country."

In addition to the trials already mentioned, the Society, towards the close of the war, was troubled by those who had been disowned during that period, for various departures from our acknowledged principles. Taking advantage of the general pre-- judice against Friends at that critical juncture, these individuals made a combined effort to obtain a part of the property of the Society in Pennsylvania. For this purpose they petitioned the State Legislature to interfere and enforce their claim. "Your petitioners," they said, " are not only by birth, but some of us also by subscription to the common stock, and by subscription for particular purchases, &c., justly entitled to the common use and possession of the estates so held by the said people." After stating that many had been disowned " by the leading men of the Society,"—some for holding offices in the government,—some for bearing arms "in defence of their invaded country," and some for paying taxes, and that such had been refused the use of Friends' burial-grounds for their friends, &c., they close by pray- ing for a bill "recognizing the right of persons disowned by the people called Quakers, to hold in common with others of that Society, the meeting-houses, school-houses, burying-grounds, lots of land, and other the estates held by that people as a religious Society ; and to recognize their right to search, examine, and take copies of the records, books and papers of the said Society."* The petition was signed by Timothy Matlack, who was noto- riously malicious towards Friends, and by about sixty other com- plainants.

This mean attempt, although annoying, was not difficult to be met with sound and common sense argument, and a counter petition was forthwith prepared by the Meeting for Sufferings. " The religious liberty of a person," they observe, " consists not

* " The Friend," Phil. pub., vol. xxi. p. 53.

in a power to impose himself upon any religious society against
the rules of its communion, but in a freedom to join himself to
one whose rules, doctrines and worship, are conformable to his
conscience." The right of the Society to disunite from membership those who violate its doctrines and rules was asserted as
consistent with the laws of the land, and as having been publicly established by high legal authority. After stating the fact
that many of the complainants were so disunited, it was added
" the causes, for their sakes, we do not choose to revive,
unless they should make it unavoidable. There are also in the
number such who were never acknowledged members amongst
us." After distinctly denying that any had been disowned for
the payment of taxes to support government, the petition proceeds to say, " the petitioners do not agree with us on the
fundamentals of our faith, and what has been the uniform practice from our first becoming a united Society."

It was evident that the legislature did not sympathize with the
discontented applicants, and was not disposed to accede to their
wishes. They were, however, pressing and in earnest, and in a
few months made a second appeal " for leave to bring in a Bill."
This petition was referred by the Assembly to a Committee,
before whom the complainants were allowed to produce evidence
in support of their cause. Matlack, and a few of his associates in
the business attended; whilst several members of the Meeting for
Sufferings appeared on behalf of the Society. The occasion was
one of no small interest. The talented and acute Nicholas
Waln, who was by profession a lawyer, and at that time
a man in the vigour of life, watched the proceedings closely.
The evidence adduced by the petitioners related, for the most
part, to cases of individuals disowned by the Society. By the
time they had gone fairly through their case, he had determined
on his course of action. Quick-sighted as he was, he saw
that the leaders in the attempt were careful not to bring into
view their own individual cases; and he knew their reasons.
Addressing the Committee, he freely admitted that a number
of those present who complained against Friends, had been disowned by them, and that on various accounts. Then turning

suddenly round to one who had been disunited for cock-fighting, and fixing upon him his penetrating eye, he said, "What wast thou disowned for?" The question was so unexpected, and the true answer to it so damaging to his character and to the cause he was espousing, that he was completely confounded. He durst not answer; and his confusion told its own tale. Nicholas Waln having rested his eye on the man, until the full effect of such an unlooked-for exposure had been produced on the Committee, then turned with a like enquiry to a second and a third—each having been disowned for something disreputable. The unworthy design was completely baffled. The Committee could not fail to see that its promoters had been disowned for no love of country, or devotion to its cause. Their application was negatived.*

The cessation of hostilities between Great Britain and the United States, in 1782, and the recognition of the political independence of the latter in the year following, greatly relieved the sufferings and the difficulties of Friends. The old confederation of the States being superseded in 1789 by the federal constitution of a President, Senate, and House of Representatives, and George Washington being first elected to the high office of President, it was thought by the Society to be a fitting occasion to testify their adhesion to the ruling powers, by addressing him on the occasion. When the form of Government in the United States became settled and established, and especially when it was recognised by Great Britain, the Society of Friends in America cheerfully acknowledged the new Government, as that of the "powers that be," and declared their resolution to yield to it submission and allegiance. The sufferings and difficulties to which they had been subjected during the eventful period of excitement and conflict, were naturally to be expected from the circumstances of such a period. Many of them were the immediate consequence of their firm adherence to the doctrines of peace and their unqualified advocacy of them; and to similar sufferings the Society of Friends have been exposed at different periods and in various countries, on this account. But in other respects, the situation of Friends in

* Scattergood and his Times.

America during the revolutionary war was extremely perplexing and difficult.   By Friends, as a religious body, obedience to government, and a rendering " unto Cæsar the things that are Cæsar's," have always been inculcated ; and all combinations of a hostile nature, in opposition to those who, in the order of Providence, are placed in secular authority, have been uniformly condemned.   On the formation, therefore, of the American Confederation, for the express purpose of resisting by force of arms, the laws and ordinances of Great Britain, Friends could not, as they apprehended, consistently with these views, acknowledge either such a combination or the object attempted, as legitimate ; while, on the other hand, their principle against war precluded their being in any way partizans in favour of the British, vindicating their cause, as they then were, with violence and bloodshed, and by fleets and armies.   Throughout this contest by arms, Friends invariably declined to make any formal declaration renouncing their allegiance to England ; and hence, together with their Christian testimony against war, arose the sufferings they underwent, and the antipathy they encountered from the people.   With the return of the blessings of peace, they regained also the inestimable blessings of liberty of conscience and protection, which have ever since been happily enjoyed, together with the regard and confidence of their fellow-citizens.

This chapter may be closed with the address to President Washington, already referred to, together with his answer.

To the President of the United States.

The Address of the Religious Society called Quakers, from their Yearly Meeting for Pennsylvania, New-Jersey, Delaware, and the Western parts of Maryland and Virginia.

" Being met in this our annual assembly, for the well ordering the affairs of our religious Society, and the promotion of universal righteousness, our minds have been drawn to consider, that the Almighty, who ruleth in heaven, and in the kingdoms of men, has permitted a great revolution to take place in the government of this country ; we are fervently concerned, that the rulers of the people may be favoured with the counsel of God, the only sure means of enabling them to fulfil the important trust committed to their charge ; and, in an especial manner, that divine wisdom and grace, vouchsafed from above, may qualify thee to fill up the duties of the exalted station to which thou art appointed.

" We are sensible thou hast obtained great place in the esteem and affections of people of all denominations over whom thou presidest ; and many eminent talents being committed to thy trust, we much desire they may be fully devoted to the Lord's honour and service—that thus thou mayst be a happy instrument in his hand, for the suppression of vice, infidelity, and irreligion, and every species of oppression on the persons or consciences of men, so that righteousness and peace, which truly exalt a nation, may prevail throughout the land, as the only solid foundation that can be laid for the prosperity and happiness of this or any country.

" The free toleration which the citizens of these States enjoy, in the public worship of the Almighty, agreeable to the dictates of their consciences, we esteem among the choicest of blessings ; and as we desire to be filled with fervent charity for those who differ from us in matters of faith and practice, believing that the general assembly of saints is composed of the sincere and upright-hearted of all nations, kingdoms, and people ; so, we trust, we may justly claim it from others : and in a full persuasion that the divine principle we profess, leads unto harmony and concord, we can take no part in carrying on war on any occasion, or under any power, but are bound in conscience to lead quiet and peaceable lives, in godliness and honesty among men, contributing freely our proportion to the indigencies of the poor, and to the necessary support of civil government, acknowledging those that rule well to be worthy of double honour ; and if any professing with us are, or have been, of a contrary disposition and conduct, we own them not therein ; having never been chargeable from our first establishment as a religious Society, with fomenting or countenancing tumults or conspiracies, or disrespect to those who are placed in authority over us.

"We wish not improperly to intrude on thy time or patience, nor is it our practice to offer adulation to any; but as we are a people whose principles and conduct have been misrepresented and traduced, we take the liberty to assure thee, that we feel our hearts affectionately drawn towards thee, and those in authority over us, with prayers, that thy presidency may, under the blessing of Heaven, be happy to thyself and to the people; that through the increase of morality and true religion, Divine Providence may condescend to look down upon our land with a propitious eye, and bless the inhabitants with the continuance of peace, the dew of Heaven, and the fatness of the earth, and enable us gratefully to acknowledge his manifold mercies: and it is our earnest concern, that He may be pleased to grant thee every necessary qualification to fill thy weighty and important station to his glory; and, that finally, when all terrestrial honours shall fail and pass away, thou and thy respectable consort may be found worthy to receive a crown of unfading righteousness in the mansions of peace and joy for ever.

"Signed in and on behalf of the said meeting, held in Philadelphia by adjournments, from the 28th of the Ninth Month, to the 3rd of the Tenth Month inclusive, 1789."

"NICHOLAS WALN, *Clerk.*"

THE ANSWER OF THE PRESIDENT OF THE UNITED STATES, TO THE ADDRESS OF THE RELIGIOUS SOCIETY CALLED QUAKERS, FROM THEIR YEARLY MEETING FOR PENNSYLVANIA, NEW-JERSEY, DELAWARE, AND THE WESTERN PARTS OF MARYLAND AND VIRGINIA.

GENTLEMEN,—I receive with pleasure your affectionate address, and thank you for the friendly sentiments and good wishes which you express for the success of my administration, and for my personal happiness.

"We have reason to rejoice for the prospect, that the national government, which, by the favour of Divine Providence, was formed by the common councils, and peaceably established with the common consent of the people, will prove a blessing to every denomination of them; to render it such, my best endeavours shall not be wanting. Government being among other purposes instituted to protect the persons and consciences of men from oppression, it certainly is the duty of rulers, not only to abstain from it themselves, but according to their stations to prevent it in others.

"The liberty enjoyed by the people of these States of worshipping Almighty God agreeably to their consciences, is not only among the choicest of their blessings, but also of their rights; while men perform their social duties faithfully, they do all that society or the state can with propriety expect or demand, and remain responsible only to their Maker for the religion or mode of faith which they may prefer or profess.

"Your principles and conduct are well known to me; and it is doing the people called Quakers no more than justice to say, that (except their declining to share with others, the burthen of the common defence) there is no denomination among us who are more exemplary and useful citizens. I assure you very explicitly, that in my opinion, the conscientious scruples of all men should be treated with great delicacy and tenderness; and it is my wish and desire, that the laws may always be as extensively accommodated to them, as a due regard to the protection and essential interests of the nation may justify and permit.

(Signed)   "GEORGE WASHINGTON."

CHAPTER XIV.

THE gradual extension of European settlements into the interior of the North American continent, caused the aborigines repeatedly to retire farther westward, and their associations with Friends became consequently, less frequent. But the solicitude of the Society for this interesting people, did not lessen by distance, and, under a sense of religious duty, we find our members and ministers occasionally labouring among them. John Woolman in 1763, and Zebulon Heston in 1773, were thus engaged ; the latter visiting the Indian settlements as far west as one hundred and twenty miles beyond the river Ohio. The former exertions of the Society were not forgotten by the Indians, and for several years they had repeatedly solicited Friends of Philadelphia to send some well-qualified persons to settle among them for their religious instruction. On the occasion of the visit of Zebulon Heston, accompanied by John Parish, the Meeting for Sufferings of Philadelphia addressed an epistle to the Indians, in which their desire for religious instructors is alluded to with approbation and encouragement. To this they replied, " We are poor and weak, and not able to judge for ourselves, and when we think of our poor children, it makes us sorry ; we hope you will instruct us in the right way, both in things of this life, as well as the world to come."*

Though the Indians were so far removed, yet they had occasionally business to transact with the government, which brought some of their chiefs to Philadelphia. It was the practice of Friends at such times to notice them with friendly regard, to endeavour to inculcate on their minds a peaceable disposition, and to cultivate that mutual feeling of cordiality which had always subsisted. In 1791, two such occurrences took place, and a similar one in the year following. On one of these occasions, a request was made by a Seneca chief, that Friends would undertake the instruction of his son and some other Indian boys. For such a purpose, he remarked, " We have too little wisdom among us, we cannot teach our children what we perceive their situation requires them to know, and we therefore ask you to instruct some of them ; we wish them to be instructed to read and to write, and such other things as you teach your own children ; and especially to teach them to love peace." The request was readily acceded to. A few years later other interviews of this character took place, with tribes more remote.

In 1792, the Indians were again involved in war with the United States. Impressed with the belief that they had been unjustly deprived of the land of their fathers, they were vainly

---

* Friends and the Indians, p. 98.

endeavouring to redress their wrongs by physical force. The circumstance excited the sympathy of Friends, and the Yearly Meeting of Philadelphia, with a view to promote the termination of these hostilities, appointed a large Committee to unite with the Meeting for Sufferings. A memorial was presented to the President and Congress on the subject, and in the Second Month, 1793, at the request of the Indians, a few Friends were deputed to attend a treaty to be held at Sandusky in Ohio. In their report on this mission, the deputation say : " Notwithstanding the desirable object of peace was not obtained, we have not a doubt of the rectitude of our submitting to go on the arduous and exercising journey ; we believe it tended to renew the ancient friendship with the Indian natives ; and although we were not admitted to see them in full council, yet we have reason to believe they were all made acquainted with our motives and friendly sentiments towards them, through divers of their chiefs."*
William Savery, one of the Friends on this appointment, has left in his journal some interesting memoranda of the interview.

In 1793, a visit was paid by two Friends to the Delaware Indians, who were then located near Muskingham, in Ohio. The desire which they had expressed in former years for religious teaching, was still prevalent ; " when we think of our poor children," they said, " our hearts are affected with sorrow—we hope you will send us teachers."†

In 1794, another Indian treaty was held at Canandaigua, in the State of New York, to which the attendance of Friends was particularly solicited by the natives. Four members of the Meeting for Sufferings offered themselves for the service, of whom the benevolent and sympathizing William Savery was one. There were assembled on this occasion no less than sixteen hundred Indians, by whom the friendly offices of the deputation were much appreciated. The Indians, they remark in their report, " still retain a lively remembrance of the just and friendly treatment their forefathers experienced from the first founder of Pennsylvania, continue to distinguish him by the name of Onas, and

---

* Friends and the Indians, p. 105.   † Ibid. p. 106.

consider Friends as his descendants, expressing that if we deceive them they can no more place any confidence in mankind. We continued with them about seven weeks. Many are the difficulties and sufferings to which the Indians are subject, and their present situation appears loudly to claim the sympathy and attention of the members of our religious Society, and others, who have grown opulent on the former inheritance of these poor declining people. We cannot but believe some mode may be fallen upon of rendering them more essential service than has yet been adopted.''

The war between the Indians and the Federal Government being happily terminated in 1794 (to effect which Friends had unremittingly laboured) the way was again open for promoting the good of the natives. At the Yearly Meeting of 1795, the subject obtained much consideration, and issued in the appointment of a committee, '' to promote,'' as the report states, ''among the Indians, the principles of the Christian religion, as well as to turn their attention to school learning, agricultural and useful mechanical employments.'' The Committee, by circular letters, soon communicated to the Indian tribes the solicitude of Friends for their welfare. Many of them received the intelligence with joy; and the Oneida Indians and a portion of the Stockbridge and Tuscarora tribes, who were settled on their reservations in the State of New York, expressed their anxiety to avail themselves of the assistance of Friends. They were not kept long in suspense ; and in the summer of 1796, three Friends settled among them. Unaccustomed as these sons of the forest had been, to any settled habits of labour, the difficulty of inducing them to abandon the chase for the more profitable cultivation of the soil, was very great. Much, however, was effected by the persevering efforts of Friends. By first proceeding to improve a piece of land, they soon strikingly exhibited to the Indians the fruits of steady industry. In a few years, many of these roving tribes were to be seen industriously occupied on their little allotments of land, or in the handicraft trades of the blacksmith and the carpenter; whilst the women and girls were busily engaged with the spinning-wheel and the needle. A school for the instruction of the children was also opened among them, and an educated Indian employed, at a salary, as their teacher.   In addition to this assistance, several of the young Indian women and girls were received into the families of Friends in Philadelphia, where they were instructed in reading, and writing, and such other things as might be beneficial to themselves and their community.

The amount expended by Friends in these benevolent objects, in the supply of tools, farming implements, the erection of grist-mills, and saw-mills, and houses, and barns, was considerable. The Indians, who had too much cause to be suspicious of the motives of their white neighbours, began to imbibe the notion, that Friends, like some others, must have a sinister object in rendering them so much aid : a fear, in fact, possessed them, that their land would be claimed as a compensation for the outlay. To convince the natives that no such ulterior view was enter-tained, it was deemed advisable, in 1799, for the resident Friends to return.

The advantage which had resulted to the Oneida Indians by these efforts, did not escape the notice of other tribes ; and in 1798, the Seneca nation solicited similar aid.   Their request was promptly acceded to ; and three Friends proceeded to their towns, on the Alleghany river, for the purpose.   To learn to plough, and to do what was proposed, appeared to the poor Senecas almost impossible, seeing, as they said, "they had no horses or oxen, and were poor, living in cabins covered with bark." In one of their councils on this subject, a chief, touched with a sense of the love and interest manifested towards them, said, in addressing the Friends who were present, "Brothers, we can't say a word against you.   It is the best way to call Quakers brothers.   You never wished any part of our lands ; therefore, we are determined to try to learn your ways."

An ancient Indian village called Genesanghota, in the State of New York, but near the boundary line of Pennsylvania, was fixed upon for the residence of the Friends, being about the centre of the settlements on the Alleghany.   Here, as among the Oneidas, the progress of civilization was striking.   In a very few years, their bark cabins had been replaced by substantial log dwellings; fencing had been erected, and roads made; whilst gloomy forests had given place to pasture lands and fields of yellow corn. But the improvements of these poor people did not stop here. Their moral condition also underwent a change. School learning had been afforded; and the use of spirituous liquors, so much the besetment of the Indian, had been greatly discouraged. Although the establishment of Friends was at Genesanghota, their labours extended to other villages of the Senecas. Occasionally, some of the Committee visited the settlements, and handed them Christian counsel. In 1803, Friends removed their Indian establishment about two miles from the former place, to Tunesassah, where it has continued, down to the present time; and reports of its progress are annually made to the Yearly Meeting.

The successful efforts of Friends of Philadelphia Yearly Meeting in this good work, excited a deep interest in the minds of their brethren in England, and a very prevalent desire existed to encourage their endeavours, by rendering some substantial assistance. In 1806, the subject was discussed in the Yearly Meeting of London, and a liberal subscription was raised, amounting to above seven thousand pounds sterling, equal to nearly twelve thousand pounds in American currency. Of this amount about two-fifths were transmitted to Philadelphia, and the remainder to New York and Maryland, where similar exertions for the improvement of the natives had been made.

The labours of Friends of Philadelphia on behalf of the Indians, some years later, appeared likely to be much frustrated by an attempt which was made to induce those on the Alleghany reservation to remove to the uncultivated wilds of the far West. In 1817, the Committee of Friends on Indian affairs memorialized the President on the subject, stating that upwards of forty thousand dollars had been expended by the Society, for the purpose of promoting among them the principles of the Christian religion and the arts of civilized life; and urging the President to use his influence in preventing the unjust measures contemplated, and also in promoting among this remnant of the aboriginal inhabitants, a separate ownership of land, in order that the

2 A 2

power of transferring their reservations as a whole, might no longer exist. In 1819, the Meeting for Sufferings of Philadelphia addressed Congress on this subject. "With deep concern," says the memorial, "we have observed a disposition spreading in the United States, to consider the Indians as an incumbrance to the community, and their residence within our borders as an obstruction to the progressive improvements and opulence of the nation." In 1818, a school was opened for the Indians at Cattaraugus ; and in 1820, the school at Tunesassah, under the tuition of a Friend, was regularly attended by about twenty-five boys, in a building erected for the purpose.

Throughout their history, the Society of Friends in America have been the steady and uncompromising friends of the Indian population. But the gradual removal of most of the tribes from the land of their fathers to the wilds of the far West, by unjust and oppressive measures on the part of the Federal Government, has largely interfered with opportunities for benefiting them. Like most others of the uncivilized races, they have been marked victims of the avarice and cunning of the more enlightened sections of mankind, and in the guilt of this conduct, it must be confessed, that the professors of the Christian name are deeply implicated.

The distress in which numerous families of Friends in America were involved during the revolutionary war, excited the sympathy and the liberality of their brethren in the mother country, and many thousands of pounds were raised for their relief. During the time of active hostilities, the sums applied were mostly on behalf of Friends in New England and the Carolinas.* Several years after the conclusion of the war, Friends in England raised sums also for their brethren who had been sufferers by it in Pennsylvania and the Jerseys, several thousand pounds having been remitted for this purpose, from 1789 to 1797. The amount was distributed chiefly to about seventy families, who in most cases

---

* Epistles of Philadelphia Meeting for Sufferings, and Gough's MSS.

had been reduced to great trial and difficulty by either one or other, or by both of the contending parties.*

The views of the Society of Friends on Christian benevolence, and on the support and maintenance of their poor and distressed, form a distinguishing trait in their character. " As mercy, com-

* Records of Philadelphia Meeting for Sufferings.

The following, selected from the list of recipients, will convey an idea of the general character of the whole :—

	£	s.	d.
To — of Abington, who suffered much loss and damage by the two contending armies	20	0	0
„ — of Abington who was plundered of nearly all his property by the contending armies . . .	30	0	0
„ The Widow and Children of Moses Roberts, who were driven from Catawissa	50	0	0
„ — who, with his family, was driven by the Indians from their dwelling in Northampton County . . .	37	10	0
„ — with six young Children, a like case in Northampton County	37	10	0
„ — of Mount Holly, New Jersey, whose house was plundered by the British army, and he with his wife and eight children obliged to flee and shelter themselves in a neighbouring county	50	0	0
„ — of Philadelphia, whose house and shop were broken into and robbed by the British army of a variety of valuable goods, on the sale of which he depended for the support of his family	100	0	0
„ — of New Jersey, who had a wife and eleven children, and was frequently much stripped of his property by the contending armies and militia	75	0	0
„ — of Shrewsbury, New Jersey, who was grievously stripped during the war ; the whole of his stock taken away	15	0	0
„ — of Horsham, Pennsylvania, whose house was forcibly entered and plundered	25	0	0
„ — of Abington, who suffered greatly by the ravages of the British army, which made a barrack of his house, burned his fences, and laid waste his farm . .	70	0	0
„ — of Pennsylvania, who suffered considerably by the American army ; the camp being near his farm. He was also taken prisoner and carried to the camp on suspicion of being disaffected to the American cause	50	0	0

passion, and charity, are eminently required in this new covenant
dispensation we are under," observe their rules,—" so, respecting
the poor and indigent amongst us, we must see that there be no
beggar in Israel." The rules of the Society, from a very early
date, have clearly set forth, that for such, " nothing was to be
wanting for their necessary supply ; " and equally explicit have
they been that " none were to be sent to the township for relief."*
The feelings of Christian love which led Friends thus to care
for their brethren in distress, as well as to adopt rules and regulations for carrying the same into practice in our several Monthly
Meetings, have at times taken an extensive range, as was the case
in reference to the sufferers by the American war. Within four
years after, a similar illustration of this Christian virtue was
exhibited in a reciprocal benevolent exertion. In the beginning
of the present century, many Friends and others in England,
were distressed by the long-continued high prices of food ; arising
partly from the Continental wars, and partly from a failure of the
crops. To relieve this distress, Friends in America in 1801, transmitted no less than £5691. To this circumstance they thus allude
in their epistle of that year : " In the course of the sittings of this
Yearly Meeting, the situation of things amongst you, and the
various distresses known on your side the water, from the scarcity
and high price of bread, have excited our fellow-feeling, and our
minds have been impressed with humble thankfulness, in the
remembrance of the many favours we enjoy from the all-bountiful
hand, under which sensations, a disposition became prevalent to
share with you a portion of the abundance with which we have

	£	s.	d.
To — who, during the battle of Brandywine, lost most of his property	37	10	0
„ — of Philadelphia, who, in consequence of the war, sustained a loss of £1500.	100	0	0
„ — of Concord, widow, who suffered greatly by the distresses which ensued after the battle of Brandywine, being plundered of her live stock and produce . .	25	0	0
„ — of Chester County, who sustained so much loss by fines, &c., as to break him up from farming . .	37	10	0

* Philadelphia Rules of Discipline, first ed. p. 106.

been blessed." How greatly would the sum of human happiness be increased, were the professors of Christianity more generally disposed to similar acts of liberality and brotherly kindness!

At a very early period, the Yearly Meeting of Pennsylvania and the Jerseys, following the example of the Society in England, printed and circulated books and writings illustrative of our doctrines. This also was one of the subjects to which the attention of the Meeting for Sufferings of Philadelphia was early and specially directed. In furtherance of this object, that Meeting, about the year 1771, issued directions to the several Quarterly and Monthly Meetings, more particularly those in remote and distant parts, to institute an inquiry, " in order," as it is expressed, " to learn how the poorer families of Friends are furnished with Bibles and Friends' books, and where it is necessary, that they be supplied therewith, as also to excite their members in general to be conversant therein."* Nor were the efforts of the Meeting for Sufferings limited to its own Yearly Meeting. Other Yearly Meetings in America were encouraged to do the same; and in 1772, an epistle was addressed to Friends of New York and New England on this subject; "We are desirous," they say, " that a like brotherly care may be promoted in your several meetings as your settlements increase, that every family of Friends may be encouraged and expected to put the writings of Friends in the hands of their children, servants and others, who may thus at times be induced to peruse them to their profit. As there is a great increase of vain books, that amuse the thoughtless youth, and lead such who love to read them from the simplicity of the Truth, we are the more concerned to urge this religious care, which we desire may increase among us, that all may be done that is in our power towards the preservation of our youth, and their growth in piety and virtue.

" On this occasion, we use the brotherly freedom of mentioning to you, that it appears to have been the early care of Friends of our Yearly Meeting to provide a stock for the divers necessary purposes, which did and might arise for the general service of

* Epistle of Philadelphia Meeting for Sufferings, 1771.

Friends. A part of this has been frequently applied for printing and dispersing books and other writings of our Friends. We believe a provision of the like sort may be useful among you, as it may be an easy means for the poor and sober inquirers within the compass of your meetings, to be the more generally furnished with the means of instruction, and in many other occurring cases may be found necessary and of service."

To this epistle was appended a list of Friends' books which had been printed by direction of Philadelphia Yearly Meeting, and could be furnished at very low prices.*

A similar care was extended to Friends in the southern states, and in 1785, the epistle of the Meeting for Sufferings of Philadelphia to that in London, notices the supply of school books to Friends in the western parts of North Carolina. In 1798, no fewer than nine hundred copies of Gough's history of Friends were subscribed for through this meeting.

It was about the year 1785, that some Friends who had settled in Nova Scotia, obtained the care and attention of Philadelphia Meeting· for Sufferings.† In 1787, some of its members united with John Townsend of London, then on a religious mission to America, in a visit to these settlers. There were, it appears by their report, " a considerable number in different places who made profession with Friends." At Beaver Harbour, in the neighbourhood of which they chiefly resided, there were forty in membership, and a large number " professing, but not in membership." Many of these being reported to be in very straitened circumstances, a Committee of the Meeting for Sufferings was appointed to render them some pecuniary aid ; and out of the money raised in England for Friends in America, five hundred pounds were allotted for their relief.

The attention of Philadelphia Yearly Meeting to those in distant settlements, was next directed to Friends in Upper Canada, to which several families from Pennsylvania had removed about the year 1792. The emigration of our members to this

* Philadelphia Friend, vol. xx. p. 204.   † Epistle to London, MS.

region continued to increase, being induced mainly by the inviting terms offered by the British Government to settlers, among whom were some from New Jersey. In 1797, the subject obtained the attention of the Yearly Meeting, and as no meetings had yet been settled in Upper Canada, a committee was appointed to render such assistance as might be needed ; the Committee visited some of them in the same year. Their number consisted at that time of twelve families and parts of families, who resided on Black Creek, and Short Hills, near the river Niagara.*

A similar visit was made in 1799, when a Monthly Meeting was established to be held at Pelham and Black Creek; to which Friends of Yonge Street, about a hundred miles northward, near Lake Simcoe, were afterwards united. As there was no Quarterly Meeting to which Friends in Upper Canada could be conveniently associated, Pelham Monthly Meeting for a few years, forwarded answers to the queries to Philadelphia Yearly Meeting. In 1805, there were regularly settled meetings for worship at Pelham, Black Creek, and Yonge Street ; and in the following year, another Monthly Meeting was set up at Yonge Street. About this time some difficulty arose to the members of these meetings on the question of oaths, in connexion with the patents under which their lands were held ; and by refusing to take the oaths the legal tenure of their estates was endangered. On this subject, the Meeting for Sufferings of Philadelphia memorialized the Government and Legislature of Upper Canada, for an "abrogation or explanation of the exceptionable clauses" in the patents, "so as to prevent any future molestation on these accounts." Referring to this matter some years later, the Meeting for Sufferings remark, that "from the kind disposition of the Government towards them, there is reason to believe they have not suffered much inconvenience."†

Settlements in Upper Canada had also been formed by Friends from the State of New York. These were in the vicinity of Kingston, near Lake Ontario ; and a care had been extended to them by the Yearly Meeting of New York. In 1809, the

* Jacob Lindley's Journal.   † Epistle of Meeting for Sufferings, 1807.

meetings in Canada were formed into a Quarterly Meeting, under the sanction of the Yearly Meetings of Philadelphia and New York, and with the latter it was soon after incorporated. Subsequently a Half-year's Meeting was established for Friends in Upper Canada, composed, in 1820, of four Monthly, and seventeen particular Meetings.

Until a comparatively recent period of the history of Friends, it had been the practice of the Monthly and Quarterly Meetings, to preserve in manuscript the various minutes and advices issued from one time to another by the Yearly Meetings for the right conducting of the discipline of the Society. It was found, however, that in many instances, sufficient care was not taken in this respect. To meet the difficulty, the Yearly Meeting of London, in 1781, concluded to arrange its minutes and advices under suitable heads in one volume, and so to print them, that each meeting, as it states, " may be furnished with a complete and correct collection, and that being thus more generally made known, may be more uniformly put in practice, that order, unity, peace and harmony may be preserved throughout the churches."* This example was soon followed by the Yearly Meeting of New England ; in 1797 by that of Philadelphia, and subsequently, by other 'American Yearly Meetings.

In issuing its " Rules of Discipline and Christian Advices," for the use of the subordinate meetings, Philadelphia Yearly Meeting accompanied them with the following observations :—

" In the early times of Christianity it was found necessary for the apostles, disciples, and believers, to meet often together for the consolation and strengthening one of another ; when, pursuant to the very nature and design of the gospel, which brought peace on earth, and good-will to men, a care arose for the establishment and edification of the church, and their labour was, that all should be of one mind, and become as one family.

" And, as it hath pleased the Lord in these latter days to call a people to freedom, and from under that unwarrantable yoke of

* Preface to the London Rules of Discipline.

bondage [set up in the apostacy], so he hath been pleased to raise in the hearts of his servants, that primitive love and good-will which eminently distinguish his disciples; wherein they have been persuaded and directed by his wisdom and power, to have meetings established for like good purposes as in the primitive times; therein to worship him, and have oversight, care, and compassion, one over another, and to endeavour that all may walk humbly, decently, and honestly, and be of one mind, as becomes the servants and followers of our holy Lord.

" This is called our Discipline, in the exercise whereof, persuasion and gentle dealing is, and ought to be our practice; and when any, after all our Christian endeavours, cannot be reclaimed, the extent of our judgment is censure, or disowning such to be of our religious communion.   And as this authority and practice is Christian, so it is laudable and reasonable in Society; for the good and reputation of the whole body ought to claim our greatest regard, subordinately including that of every member.   Hence arises a care and concern for decency and comely order in all our meetings for worship and discipline, as well as honesty, plainness, and orderly walking, in all the members of our religious Society, that others seeing our good works may be induced to glorify our Father, who is the author of them, and thereby be brought into that faith which works by love to the purifying of the heart."

For many years, the Book of Discipline of Philadelphia Yearly Meeting was kept in the different meeting houses of the Society, under the special charge of the overseers and clerks, and however much any other individual member of the meeting might be interested in its contents, the volume was, for the most part, inaccessible to them."*   In 1825, however, Friends of that meeting determined on a wider circulation of the volume. " What is good in itself," they remark on this occasion, " cannot be too widely diffused, or too extensively known.   We believe that the rules of our discipline have this tendency; and so believing, we have taken the usual means of making them public;

* Preface to Rules of Philadelphia Y. M., ed. 1825.

and we earnestly hope, that all our good intentions may be realised."*

In addition to the printing of its Rules of Discipline, Philadelphia Yearly Meeting published, in 1808, a small volume of "Christian Advices," consisting of extracts from its records, having reference to the support of our several Christian testimonies, and to our conduct and conversation among men ; compiled, as its introduction states, "for the benefit of the members of our Yearly Meeting ; that observing the travail of the Church under various concerns, which in divine wisdom have been communicated for its weighty attention, they may be drawn to the principle of life and light manifested in the mind, which points out the path of duty, and can alone preserve therein."

* Preface to Philadelphia Rules, ed. 1825.

The following are the heads of arrangement as printed in the edition of 1825 :—

Appeals.
Arbitrations.
Births and Burials.
Books.
Certificates and Removals.
Charity and Unity.
Civil Government.
Conduct and Conversation.
Convinced Persons.
Days and Times.
Defamation and Detraction.
Discipline and Meetings for Discipline.
Donations and Subscriptions.
Family Visits.
Gaming and Diversions.
Law.
Marriages.
Meeting Houses.
Meeting for Sufferings.
Meetings for Worship.
Memorials [of Ministers & Elders.]

Ministers and Elders, and Meetings of Ministers and Elders.
Moderation and Temperance.
Negroes or Slaves.
Oaths.
Overseers.
Parents and Children.
Plainness.
Poor.
Queries.
Schools.
Scriptures.
Stock [Collections].
Taverns.
Testimonies of Denial and Acknowledgments.
Trade.
War.
Wills.
Women's Meetings.
Yearly Meetings.

From an early period, the subject of a guarded religious and literary education of their offspring engaged the serious attention of Philadelphia Yearly Meeting. In 1746, Friends of the "several Monthly Meetings were encouraged to assist each other in the settlement and support of schools for the instruction of their children, and to employ such masters and mistresses as are concerned, not only to instruct their children in learning, but are likewise careful to bring them to the knowledge of their duty to God, and one to another."*

Various plans had been proposed for more effectually ensuring this object, and an effort was made in 1769, to found a boarding-school for the accommodation of a number of boys not exceeding thirty. For the purchase of a farm and for the erection of the necessary buildings, it was proposed that funds should be raised in shares of twenty pounds each, the proprietors of which, with others under appointment, were to exercise a supervision of the establishment. The remuneration of the master and teachers was to depend on the payments of the children. The instruction was to include "reading, writing, arithmetic, navigation, survey-ing, gauging, and such other learning as is usually taught, and the parents may direct ; and likewise the Latin, Greek, and French languages." The annual charge for each pupil was to be twenty pounds ; and about three pounds on entering for buying household linen, &c. Whether on account of the troubles which arose out of the dispute between England and her American colonies, or from other obstacles, the proposal did not at that time succeed, and for several years little appears to have been effected by united efforts.

In the year 1778, the subject of education was revived with increasing earnestness, and an address and observations, principally from the pen of Anthony Benezet, who took a deep interest in the matter, were issued by the Yearly Meeting. It was recom-mended that "the former advice of collecting a fund for the establishment and support of schools, under the care of a standing committee appointed by the several Monthly or Particular Meet-

* Rules of Discipline, first ed., p. 114.

ings, should generally take place.—That within the compass of each meeting, where the settlement of a school is necessary, a lot of ground be provided, sufficient for a garden, orchard, grass for a cow, &c. ; and that a suitable house, stable, &c., be erected thereon. There are few meetings," continues the address, "which may not, in labour, in materials or money, raise so much as would answer this charge. Such a provision would be an encouragement for a staid person with a family, who will be likely to remain a considerable time, perhaps his whole life, to engage therein. The benefit of the youth, and the means of a comfortable living for the master, may be increased, by the conveniency which might be made for boarding some children, under his care, whose distant situation might otherwise impede their instruction."*

The effect of this address was encouraging. Subscriptions were raised, amounting to many thousands of dollars. School-houses were built in most localities where there were Friends sufficient to form a school, and in some places for the accommodation also of teachers ; committees for superintending them also were appointed in Monthly or Preparative Meetings; and with these lay the choice of the master. In some places these schools still exist ; but the subsequent establishment of the large boarding-school at West-town, together with the district or State school system, has broken up several.

Although the attempt, in 1769, to found a boarding-school in Pennsylvania had failed, yet it did not cease to find earnest advocates and supporters. About the same time the idea was a favourite one with Friends in England, and in 1779, the experiment of a school, under the care of London Yearly Meeting, was made at Ackworth. The success of this institution probably quickened the zeal of our American brethren ; at any rate, in 1792, the Quarterly Meeting of Philadelphia proposed to its Yearly Meeting the founding of a similar institution. A committeee to consider the subject was appointed, who reported favourably, and in 1794, an appointment was made to carry out the design. Within two years more a sum of twelve thousand

* Rules of Discipline, pp. 116, 117.

pounds was raised, and an estate at West-town in the county of Chester, about forty miles from Philadelphia, containing about six hundred acres, was bought for the purpose. The cost of the original purchase was about six thousand pounds, and the outlay in the requisite buildings involved about three thousand three hundred pounds more. The accommodations were for two hundred and fifty children of both sexes. The following were some of the regulations laid down for its government :—

"That this institution, being intended for the benefit of the children of Friends generally, shall continue under the care and superintendence of a standing committee of the Yearly Meeting.

"That spelling, reading, writing, arithmetic and book-keeping, shall be taught in the different schools ; and such other useful branches of learning as the circumstances of the pupils may require, and the state of the institution shall permit.

"That the boarding and lodging of the children shall be plain and frugal, without distinction, except in cases of sickness.

"That no children shall be taken in under the age of eight years, or entered for less than one year.

"That whenever there shall be more applications than can be received, a preference be given to the members of our own Yearly Meeting."

The school was opened in 1799, and up to the present time no less than ten thousand children have been educated therein for longer or shorter periods of time. For some years past the Latin and Greek languages have also been taught.

The exertions of Friends of Pennsylvania and New Jersey had, as we have seen in a former chapter, accomplished much on the subject of slavery ; their Christian endeavours to uproot this monstrous evil, did not, however, stop there. In writing to their brethren in England in 1785, they remark : " The silence of Congress on the subject-matter of our Yearly Meeting's address in 1783, relating to the slave-trade, engaged us to revive that important affair in their view by a letter to the President." In 1789, they memorialized Congress a second time on the subject. The noble example set in 1780, by the inhabitants of Pennsylvania, in declaring theirs a free state, had not as yet been followed by New Jersey ; and in 1792, the Meeting for Sufferings of Philadelphia, addressed the legislature of that State on the question of negro rights. In the same year they also presented a " Memorial of Congratulation," to the Senate and House of Representatives of Pennsylvania, for having refused the petition of sundry persons from the French West India Islands, praying that their domestic negroes may be exempted from the operation of the law, passed in this Commonwealth for the abolition of slavery."*

Steadily pursuing the great work of negro emancipation, Philadelphia Meeting for Sufferings, in 1799, prepared and issued an address " To their fellow-citizens of the United States of North America, and others whom it may concern." The enormity of the evils of slavery was boldly asserted ; " Whether people will hear, or forbear," they observe, " we believe ourselves authorised to say, that it is the mind and will of the Most High, that slavery should be abolished." The address also included a general exhortation to piety. In 1802, the same Meeting, united with Friends of Maryland, in memorializing the legislature of that state on behalf of the " poor blacks."

In the year 1804, the Meeting for Sufferings, as the representative body of Friends in Philadelphia Yearly Meeting, again pleaded with Congress on behalf of the injured African. By a deputation of four Friends, a memorial was presented, containing a bold remonstrance on the wickedness of slavery. The following is an extract :—

" We believe the testimony against slavery is advancing, and will in time overcome all opposition. We pray the Almighty Sovereign of the universe, to carry on, bless, and prosper this good work, and that legislatures, as well as individuals, may co-operate with the benign spirit of the gospel, in dispelling the dark clouds which hang over this country, by doing justly to all men—the work of righteousness being peace, and the effect thereof quietness and assurance for ever.

* Epistle to London Meeting for Sufferings.

" Can it be supposed that the Almighty Creator, who made of one blood all nations of the earth, beholds with indifference one part of his rational creatures, equally the objects of his love and mercy, held under oppression by another part ?   And is it not just and reasonable to fear, if the gentle language of his Spirit—'let this people go '—is not attended to, that he will by terrible things in righteousness evince his sovereignty, and sustain the character of a God of justice, who is no respecter of persons."

" The temporal sufferings of this people will, by the course of nature, terminate in a few years : but what will be the lot of their oppressors ?   We wish the attention of all to the awful consequence of neglecting in time to hear the cries of the poor. We are sensible that we have to encounter the prejudices of interested men, and may subject ourselves to the obloquy and reproach of such ; but a sense of duty and the noble cause we espouse is our firm support : to God we leave the event, who knows that in this regard our hearts are upright before him."

The unceasing efforts of Friends of America, in this righteous cause, were not without good results ; and in 1807, they were cheered in their work by the passing of an Act of Congress, prohibiting the African slave-trade. In this national act of justice, the United States preceded Great Britain. The abolition of the foreign slave-trade took place, in fact, as early as the constitution gave the Federal Government the power to effect it.   Over the internal slave-trade it possessed no control.   The exertions made by Friends in England, with their Government, on this question, had, for twenty years past, been very considerable ; but it was not until the United States of North America had taken the initiative, that the legislature of Great Britain declared the African slave-trade to be illegal—this was in 1808.   Would that the Americans had not slackened in their onward progress in the vindication of human rights ! but that they had preceded England in not merely declaring to the civilized world, that " all men are created equal ;—that they are endowed by their Creator with certain unalienable rights ;—that among these are life, liberty, and the pursuit of happiness ;" but that they had followed up the declaration of these great truths by a consistent course of action.

Had this been the case, how powerful would have been their example! and how far would it have gone in removing the foul stain of slavery from among the nations of men. And until this great and rising commonwealth shall have ceased its iniquitous inconsistency, and emancipated the negro race, so long, we feel assured, will the Society of Friends, in faithfulness to its principles, continue to lift up its voice against an evil, destructive alike of the temporal and the eternal interests of mankind.

Delaware, like New Jersey, had been slow to recognise the rights of the negro; and in 1812, the Meeting for Sufferings of Philadelphia addressed the legislature of that State on the subject. In 1816, they also presented a memorial to Congress against the Fugitive Slave Law of 1793, by which many free blacks were kidnapped and taken back into slavery; and two years later, they appeared again before this body, to remonstrate on the same unrighteous enactment.

Before turning from the subject of slavery, it seems only right to notice the civil disabilities to which persons of colour in North America are subjected, and the strong prejudice which is generally entertained against them. In some of the States of the Union, coloured persons, when they obtain their freedom, are obliged forthwith to leave the State. In Georgia, not only is one free negro prohibited from teaching another, but a white man is liable to a fine of five hundred dollars, for teaching him to read and write.* In Louisiana it is gravely set forth, by express statute, that "free people of colour ought never to insult or strike white people, nor presume to conceive themselves equal to the whites."† In other states, whatever may be his attainments or his standing, a coloured man, in the eye of the law, is rendered incapable of preaching the gospel. Their civil rights and liberties are also greatly curtailed in some of the professedly free states. Until recently, a law existed in Ohio, excluding blacks from the benefit of the public schools. This law has been lately repealed, but in New York and some other northern cities of the Union,

---

* Goodell's American Slave Code, p. 337.
† Martin's Digest, p. 640 in Goodell.

coloured persons are still denied licences to drive carts, and to pursue other common avocations for a livelihood. In the free State of Indiana, the testimony of free negroes and mulattoes is not received against a white man, and the constitutions and statutes of most of the free States debar the coloured citizen from eligibility to office, and from equal access to the ballot box. Of this oppressive legislation of the northern states, it has been justly observed, that "the negro pew, and the corresponding treatment of negroes in seminaries of learning controlled by the church, are the principal supports."* The social customs are in strict keeping with this state of things, and access within the pale of refined society is denied to coloured people.

The origin of this systematic persecution of free Africans is to be found simply in the desire to perpetuate slavery. Freedom for whites, but slavery for the blacks, is an all-important article of the American slave-holder's creed ; the foundation stone, indeed, of his wretched system. The line of distinction which, with unrighteous assumption, he has thus dared to draw between the children of the One Great and Universal Parent of mankind, he knows would be rendered less definite, and less clear, by the presence of free blacks among slaves, and hence his endeavours to prevent the mingling of the two. That the northern states should have pandered to such wicked policy, and lent themselves to this indirect mode of maintaining slavery, is truly to be deplored.

This invidious distinction in reference to coloured people being thus generally entertained in America, it is not at all surprising that Friends should have partaken in some degree of the prejudice ; and that, as in other Christian communities, a question should have been raised on the propriety of admitting them as members of the Society. Up to the year 1785, only one instance of an application of this description appears to have occurred, but the subject had excited much attention.† No rule seems

* Goodell, p. 348.

† Letter of James Pemberton to James Philips of London, 18th of Eleventh Month, 1785, in S. Dimsdale's Collection.

to have existed, excluding any of the negro race from church fellowship ; and in 1796, on the question being submitted by one of the Quarterly Meetings to the Yearly Meeting of Philadelphia, that meeting adopted this just and Christian judgment: "Where Monthly Meetings are united in believing that the applicants are clearly convinced of our religious principles, and in a good degree subject to the Divine witness in their own hearts, manifested by a circumspect life and conduct, said meetings are at liberty to receive such into membership, without respect to nation or colour."* Paul Cuffé, a free negro of Massachusetts, was not only admitted a member, but became also a minister in the Society of Friends.†

Friends in Pennsylvania and the Jerseys remonstrated occasionally with their rulers on other subjects of importance. The proposal, in 1790, for establishing a general militia throughout the United States, was one of these. On this occasion the Yearly Meeting addressed the American Congress, plainly setting forth the grounds of our testimony against all war. The Meeting for Sufferings memorialized Congress on a similar occasion in 1796, referring with much emphasis to the rights of conscience. "By conscience," they observe, "we mean that apprehension and persuasion a man has impressed on his mind of his duty to God— and the liberty of conscience we plead for, is a free and open profession, and unmolested exercise of that duty ; such a conscience as keeps men within the bounds of morality in all the affairs of human life, and requires us to live soberly, righteously, and godly in the world, on which depend the peace, safety, and happiness of every government." The relief sought for by these representations, was not, however, obtained, and some young men were imprisoned for not complying with the militia laws. These sufferings called forth, in 1808, another remonstrance to the legislature, which was repeated in 1813. The United States being at that time involved in war with Great Britain, the Meeting for Sufferings of Philadelphia, in the following year, also addressed Congress on the subject.

* Memorials of Rebecca Jones, p. 232.
† Memoir of Paul Cuffé, by Wilson Armistead, p. 34.

The last previous notice of Friends from England who visited America in the work of the gospel, was under date of 1775. In that year the American war of Independence commenced, and for ten years after, no Friend from the mother country appears to have crossed the Atlantic on service of this description. The difficulty of performing a religious visit during most of this period, is the simple explanation of the circumstance. Very soon after its conclusion, by the recognition of American independence, gospel messengers from England again sought the shores of the new world. In 1785 three arrived in Pennsylvania; these were John Storer on a second visit; John Townsend of London, and Thomas Colley of Sheffield. Four years later, Mary Ridgway, and Jane Watson of Ireland, proceeded on a similar errand. Of their gospel labours on this occasion very little is on record; it appears, however, that the mission occupied some of them for several years.

In 1793, Deborah Darby and Rebecca Young, from Shropshire, crossed the Atlantic. Their gospel visit occupied them about four years. John Wigham of Scotland, and Martha Routh from Staffordshire, were the next. They passed over in 1794; Samuel Emlen, who was then returning from a similar visit to his brethren in England, being their fellow-passenger.* The two last-mentioned ministers visited Friends generally throughout America. They were the first gospel messengers from Great Britain to the meetings settled west of the Alleghany mountains. Although not associated during their travels on the western continent, they completed their visits about the same time, and returned together to their native land.† John Wigham states that he travelled 10,979 miles in America, and " in all, by sea and land 22,752 miles." Martha Routh says, "I was three years, three weeks, and three days on the continent, and travelled about 11,000 miles." In 1801 Martha Routh proceeded on a second visit to that country, but she has left very few memoranda respecting it.

In 1797, Jervis Johnson of Ireland paid a religious visit to America, but no account of it appears to be on record. Mary

---

* Memoirs of J. Wigham, p. 19.   † Life &c., of Martha Routh, p. 269.

Pryor of Hertford was the next: she crossed over in 1798. During about twelve months spent in America, her "fervent labours" in the service of her Lord, and the sweetness and humility of her deportment, greatly endeared her to her friends in that land.* In 1799, John Hall from Cumberland visited North America. His gospel mission occupied him about three years, and is recorded as being acceptable to his transatlantic brethren.† Sarah Stephenson from Wiltshire crossed over in 1801. She landed at New York, and for several months was occupied among Friends of that state. Thence she proceeded to Philadelphia, where, after a short illness she died, in the Fourth Month, 1802. Following her was Ann Alexander of York, in 1803, whose visit occupied about two years, during which she visited most of the meetings of Friends in the United States, and held many with those not of our religious Society.‡

Several years now elapsed without a visit from any Friend of the United Kingdom; in 1810, however, Susanna Horne, afterwards Susanna Bigg, was led in this direction. She was absent about three years, "labouring diligently in the different parts of that continent where Friends were settled, to their cordial acceptance and the strengthening of their faith." § Mary Naftel, from Essex, was the next. She was engaged in America about two years. Referring to this visit, she writes, "Oh! how often is my mind bound up with some there in the ever-blessed covenant of love and life." || The last visit of this description that will be noticed in the present volume, is that of William Rickman, of Kent, who left England in 1818, in company with Hannah Field, who was returning from a gospel visit to England. William Rickman paid a very general visit to the meetings of Friends in America.

From the time when Mary Fisher and Ann Austin sailed on their gospel mission to New England in 1656, down to the date of William Rickman's visit, Friends in Great Britain and Ireland had undertaken no less than a hundred-and-eighty-three gospel

---

* Piety Pro., part xi. p. 207.   † Ibid., p. 24.
‡ MS. Testimony.   § Ibid. || Piety Pro., part xi. p. 230.

missions to America. Within the same period, but not commencing till 1693, there had been a hundred and ten visits paid
by our transatlantic brethren to the mother country. With
reference, however, to these missions, there are two circumstances which deserve particular notice, viz., the gradually de-
creasing number of gospel messengers from the United Kingdom,
and the increasing number of those from America. Dividing the
one hundred and sixty-four years, the whole time comprehended
in these visits, into four equal periods, we find, that during the
first period no less than seventy-three Friends went on religious
visits to America ; in the second, fifty-seven ; in the third,
thirty-five ; whilst in the last they decreased to eighteen. From
America in the first period there were only four ; in the second,
twenty-nine ; in the third, thirty-eight, and in the last, thirty-
nine. This altered state of things is, however, what might be
reasonably expected, seeing that the Society has so largely increased in the western world, and by emigration and other means
has diminished in Great Britain.

The increase of the Society, and the establishment of new
meetings within the limits of the Yearly Meeting of Pennsylvania
and New Jersey, have already been noticed down to the year 1750.
At that date no settlements of Friends had been formed west of
the Alleghany mountains, or further north than the meeting at
Plumstead in Pennsylvania. The war, which broke out between
England and France soon after, and the conflicts which ensued
between the colonists and the French in Canada, and the Indians
in their pay, checked the extension of settlements in Pennsylvania. Scarcely had these troubles subsided, ere the War of
American Independence began ; throughout which, but little
desire, and probably less opportunity, existed for extending cultivation into the interior.

Soon after the restoration of peace between Great Britain and
the United States, many fresh settlements of Friends were formed
in the northern and southern parts of Pennsylvania. In the
northern, meetings were established about 1790, on branches
of the Susquehanna at Catawissa, Muncy, and Elklands, and
some years after at Stroudsburg, near the Delaware. These, with

the exception of a small meeting at Friendsville, lying still further north, but now extinct,* were the only meetings in the northern parts of Pennsylvania. About 1793, a considerable number of Friends settled about Martinsburgh, a mountainous district in Bedford county.† In the south, the increase of Friends was much more considerable ; and as new meetings were set up and old ones became larger, additional Monthly and Quarterly Meetings were formed. Thus the Quarterly Meeting of Philadelphia, which in 1750, included but four Monthly Meetings was, in 1785, divided into the Quarterly Meetings of Philadelphia and Abington, embracing in 1820, at least twelve Monthly Meetings. In the Quarterly Meeting of Chester, the increase was yet more apparent. In 1758, this Meeting was divided into that of Concord and the Western ; from the latter of which, in 1800, the Quarterly Meeting of Caln was set off. The meetings west of the Susquehanna had also increased ; and the Monthly Meetings of Warrington, Hopewell, and Fairfax were, in 1775, erected into a Quarterly Meeting, and this, in eight years after, was divided into two Quarterly Meetings. In the Jerseys there had also been an increase ; and in 1794, the Quarterly Meeting of Haddonfield was divided off from that of Salem.

Large, therefore, as was the Yearly Meeting of Philadelphia in 1750, it increased considerably during the next half-century, and its maximum of members could not have been much, if at all, under forty thousand.‡ As a Yearly Meeting, its importance, from 1769 to 1788, was yet further increased by the Friends of Maryland forming a constituent part of it. During this period, representatives regularly attended from that State ; and, in common with the other members of the Yearly Meeting,

---

* Day's Collection, p. 622.   † Ibid. p. 12.

‡ In the year 1766, Franklin, in his evidence before the British Legislature, stated the population of Pennsylvania at 160,000 whites, of whom, he said, one-third were Quakers. But this estimate is, as regards Friends, much over-rated. In Hazard's Register, vol. v., page 339, the population of the province is set down, in 1757, at 200,000 ; of whom, it is stated, Friends formed one-eighth. The population of New

they were appointed on disciplinary services. On some alterations which took place in 1789, this arrangement ceased.*

Jersey, in 1745, is stated at 61,403, and the number of Friends, 6079. In 1765, the number of places of worship were stated as follows :—

Presbyterians	55	Dutch Reformed	12
Quakers	39	Dutch Calvinists	10
Episcopalians	21	Lutherans	8
Baptists	20	Other Sects	5

—Vide Smith's Hist. of New Jersey.

* Friends' Library [Philadelphia] vol i. p. 120.

The following statistics of the meetings of Friends in North America, is taken from a MS. account, forwarded by Mary Elliott of Philadelphia, to Rachel Wilson of Kendal, in the year 1768, previously to the embarkation of the latter on a gospel visit to that country :—

RHODE ISLAND YEARLY MEETING.

	Quarterly Meetings.	Monthly Meetings.	Meetings for Worship.
Newport	8		28
Sandwich		2	7
Salem		4	13
	14		48

and seven General Meetings for worship held once a-year.

FLUSHING YEARLY MEETING.

	Quarterly Meetings.	Monthly Meetings.	Meetings for Worship.
Flushing		2	9
Purchase		2	11
	4		20

and four General Meetings.

PENNSYLVANIA YEARLY MEETING.

	Quarterly Meetings.	Monthly Meetings.	Meetings for Worship.
Shrewsbury		2	6
Burlington		4	15
Gloucester and Salem	4		11
Bucks		4	7
Philadelphia		6	21
Concord		5	14
Western		10	37
	35		111

and eleven General Meetings.

MARYLAND YEARLY MEETING.

	Quarterly Meetings.	Monthly Meetings.	Meetings for Worship.
Gunpowder		2	11
Chopthank		2	9
	4		20

and two General Meetings.

VIRGINIA YEARLY MEETING.

	Quarterly Meetings.	Monthly Meetings.	Meetings for Worship.
Cedar Creek		3	15
Blackwater		2	11
	5		26

NORTH CAROLINA YEARLY MEETING.

Perquimons and Pasquotank	...5 (6 in pt.)
New Garden and Crane Creek	2 11

TOTAL IN 1768 :—

18 Quarterly Meetings,
69 Monthly Meetings,
242 Meetings for Worship (not quite complete).

No sooner had the political horizon cleared, and peace again beamed on the Anglo-American population of the western world, by the recognition of their independence, than a desire arose to form settlements in the interior, and more especially on the rich alluvial soil extending westward from the great chain of the Alleghany mountains. Before the outbreak of actual hostilities, some Friends from Virginia, in 1769, had founded Union Town, on a tributary of the Monongahela :* and when Zebulon Heston, and John Parish, were returning from a mission to the Indians in Ohio in 1773, they had some religious service with Friends in that newly-settled district.† Warrington and Fairfax Quarterly Meeting, to which these belonged, reported to the Yearly Meeting, in 1776, that eighteen families of Friends were then residing west of the Alleghanies, about Redstone, Union Town, and Brownsville.

About the same date, other inhabitants from Virginia, and also from Maryland, who were not Friends, removed to the banks of the Ohio, westward of the boundary line of Pennsylvania. These took their slaves with them, under the impression that the locality was within the limits of the slave-state of Virginia. As soon as they discovered their mistake, many of them descended the river to Kentucky, as being a district more secure for the possession of their human " chattels." It was on this occasion that some Friends from New Jersey, and from Chester county in Pennsylvania, purchased the property of these slave-holders and settled on their farms. ‡

The first meeting for worship established west of the Alleghany Mountains was Westland. Thomas Scattergood, who visited these

---

In the district embraced by the above Yearly Meetings, there were in 1850,

> 44 Quarterly Meetings,
> 145 Monthly Meetings,
> 348 Meetings for Worship,

and these do not include the Yearly Meetings of Ohio and Indiana, which contain as many members as in all other parts of America.

* Day's Collection, p. 340.   † MS. Epistle of Philadelphia M.S., 1774.
‡ Day's Collection, p. 343.

parts in 1787, mentions his attendance of four particular meetings, which appear to have composed one Monthly Meeting, called Redstone.* From this date there was a rapid increase. When Martha Routh visited the district in 1795, it had two Monthly Meetings, and at least eight particular meetings. Ten years later, it was computed that no less than eight hundred families of Friends had emigrated into the State of Ohio alone,† and in the year 1820, not less than twenty thousand of our members were settled westward of the Alleghany range.

Although a considerable number of the Friends in the new settlements of the west, had removed from other Yearly Meetings in America, and some also from the British Islands, yet a very large proportion of them appear to have come from the Yearly Meeting of Pennsylvania and New Jersey, and of course the number of members of that Meeting was correspondingly diminished. "On a beautifully shady knoll, a little apart from the dust and din of the village of Catawissa," says Day, "stands, the venerable Quaker meeting-house; a perishable monument of a race of early settlers that have nearly all passed away. 'And where are they gone?' we inquired of an aged Friend, sitting with one or two sisters on the bench, under the shade of the tall trees that overhang the meeting-house. 'Ah,' said he, ' some are dead, but many are gone to Ohio, and still further west : once there was a large meeting here, but now there are but few of us to sit together."‡ It does not appear, however, that many meetings were closed on account of this western migration, although some suffered much diminution.

Another circumstance by which Philadelphia Yearly Meeting was reduced in numbers, was the transfer, in 1789, of the two Quarterly Meetings of Warrington and Fairfax to Maryland Yearly Meeting, which then included all the meetings west of the Susquehanna, and in the western parts of Maryland and Virginia ; Maryland Yearly Meeting transferring in exchange the small Quarterly Meeting on its eastern shore. By these altera-

---

* Memoirs of T. Scattergood, p. 28.
† Sutcliff's Travels in America, p. 235.
‡ Day's Collection, p. 244.

tions, together with the great movement westward, the Yearly Meeting of Philadelphia, though still very large, had in 1820, probably not less, than thirty thousand members, of whom about five thousand were in the city of Philadelphia.*

FRIENDS' LOG MEETING-HOUSE, CATAWISSA, PENNSYLVANIA.

The middle of the last century was a very low period with the Christian church under various names and in most countries. Of the state and condition of the Society in Pennsylvania and the Jerseys, during the period from 1750 to 1820, it may be more difficult to speak with precision. In many parts much weakness existed, particularly in the period preceding the revolutionary war. Prosperous in the things of time, too many were forgetful of those pertaining to eternity. John Smith of Marlborough, in Pennsylvania, an aged minister, who had witnessed, as he believed, considerable declension among his brethren, expressed himself on this subject in 1764, in a meeting of ministers and elders to the following purport :—" That he had been a member of our Society upwards of sixty years, and he well remembered that in those early times [about 1700], Friends were a plain, lowly-minded people ; and that there was much tenderness and contrition in their meetings. That at twenty years from that

* In 1828, the numbers as given on evidence in the case of Shotwell v. Hendrickson and Decow, are stated at about twenty-seven thousand. —*Vide Foster's Report,* vol. ii. p. 461, 495.

time, the Society increasing in wealth, and in some degree conforming to the fashions of the world, true humility was less
apparent, and their meetings in general were not so lively and
edifying. That at the end of forty years, many of them were
grown very rich ; and many of the Society made a specious
appearance in the world ; that marks of outward wealth and
greatness appeared on some in our meetings of ministers and
elders ; and as such things became more prevalent, so the powerful
overshadowings of the Holy Ghost were less manifest in the
Society. That there had been a continued increase of such ways
of life, even until the present time, and that the weakness which
hath now overspread the Society, and the barrenness manifest
among us, is matter of much sorrow."* The answers to the
queries bore out the conclusions of John Smith. " By the
accounts from our several Quarterly Meetings," records Philadelphia Yearly Meeting in 1768, " there are sundry sorrowful
remarks of deficiencies."

The trials and sufferings, to which Friends were subjected
during the War of Independence, caused many of their nominal
and superficial professors—the traditional Quakers—through the
fear of penalties, to relinquish their connection with the Society ;
whilst others during that period were drawn off by the influence
of the martial spirit. On the other hand, the troubles of that
day unquestionably drove many others to a nearer acquaintance
with Him who is the only sure and unfailing refuge, and to a
firmer establishment in the Christian principles they had professed. Many, during this memorable period, were refined in the
furnace of affliction, and at the conclusion of the war, the Society
was in a more healthy and vigorous state than it had been for
many years previously. The numbers added to the Society on
the ground of convincement, were again cheering, and in 1788,
they could announce to their brethren in England, " in most of
our Monthly Meetings, divers sober persons have, on their application been admitted into membership."†

---

* Journal of John Woolman.
† Epistle to London Yearly Meeting, 1788.

The Yearly Meetings of Philadelphia continued to be very largely attended. In the early part of the present century there were usually present on these occasions not less than two thousand of each sex.* "In this our large and solemn gathering," they write, in 1803, "we have the acceptable company of brethren from all the Yearly Meetings on this continent but one, and an evident increase of weight in our deliberations has from time to time been experienced, inducing a hope and belief that many are concerned to dig deeper and deeper, in order to an establishment upon the true foundation, where, in quietude and stillness of mind the voice of truth is heard, and our several duties are discerned."

The present chapter may be closed with an extract from their epistle to London Yearly Meeting in 1807 :—

"In the rise of our religious Society, many of its members were exposed to trials and difficulties; by their dedication and faithfulness to divine requirings, and not despising the day of small things, they arrested the attention of the serious, and the cause was advanced; the spirit of opposition was subdued by patient suffering, and the way has been opened before us to the inheritance of many important privileges. We are now at liberty to meet together, and attend to the discharge of conscientious duty unmolested; we may educate our offspring, we may cultivate their understanding, and bestow upon them every advantage which human learning can furnish.—If those natural means were made subservient to the best of purposes, if they were all sanctified by the power of truth, what an interesting band would our Society be !"

* Sutcliff's Travels in America, pp. 85, 230.

CHAPTER XV.

A FEW biographical notices are again introduced, commencing with some members of the Pemberton family.

ISRAEL PEMBERTON.

He was born in Bucks county, Pennsylvania, in 1684. His father, Phineas Pemberton, emigrated in 1682 from Lancashire, and having bought three hundred acres of land, he settled on them by the Delaware, near Bristol. He was an active, useful member of the Society, and for some years occupied the important office of clerk to the Yearly Meeting. He also filled, with reputation, several civil offices in the province. In 1697, he was a member of the Council, and Speaker of the Assembly. He died in 1702, aged about fifty years.*

Israel served his apprenticeship in Philadelphia, where he resided during the remainder of his life. Being a man of a calm, even, and cheerful disposition, and whose daily walk was in the fear of the Lord, his whole life afforded an instructive example of the Christian virtues. He was one of·the most considerable merchants of Philadelphia, and was, for nineteen years succes-

---

* Memoirs, &c. of Samuel Fothergill, p. 160.

sively, a representative of that city in the General Assembly.* Friends of his Monthly Meeting say in a testimony concerning him, " He was a member of this meeting near fifty years, and being well grounded in the principles of truth, of sound judgment and understanding, he approved himself a faithful elder ; adorning our holy profession with a life of meekness, humility and circumspection. He had a disinterested regard to the honour of truth ; and was of great use in the exercise of our discipline, being a lover of peace and unity in the church, careful to promote and maintain it ; constant in the attendance of meetings, and his deportment therein grave, solid, and reverent ;—a true sympathizer with those who were honestly concerned in the ministry ; a conspicuous example of moderation and plainness ; extensive in his charity, and of great benevolence. In conversation cheerful, attended with a peculiar sweetness of disposition, which rendered his company both agreeable and instructive."† He died suddenly in 1754, being then in the sixty-ninth year of his age.

Israel Pemberton

ISRAEL, JAMES, AND JOHN PEMBERTON, were the sons of Israel, just referred to. Israel Pemberton had ten children, of whom only these three survived : they inherited a considerable estate, received a liberal education, and were brought up with great parental care for their spiritual welfare. They became influential men in Pennsylvania, and were among those who were banished to Virginia in 1776, by the American revolutionists.

ISRAEL Pemberton, the eldest, though not so active as his brothers, in the concerns of our religious Society, was strongly attached to its principles : as a man he was upright ; feared as well as beloved—as a citizen he was useful and respected. He filled many public appointments with dignity, and discharged the duties attached to them with propriety and faithfulness.‡ He

* Memoirs, &c. of Samuel Fothergill, p. 161.
† Penn. Memorials, 145.
‡ Scattergood and his Times.

was also extensively engaged in commerce and in benevolent pursuits. He died in 1779, at the age of sixty-four.

JAMES PEMBERTON, the second son, was a man of a mild disposition, and from early years he manifested great steadiness of conduct. His intellectual powers were great, and highly cultivated. Possessed of ample pecuniary means, endowed with a sound judgment, and influenced by enlarged benevolence, he cheerfully devoted his powers, his time, and his substance, to promote the good of his fellow-creatures. To the various benevolent institutions of Philadelphia, he was a liberal benefactor, and in their management he took an active share. With his brother Israel, he was the steady friend and advocate of the oppressed African race, and of the Indian tribes. They were both at one period members of the State legislature, and possessed considerable influence, which they often exerted on behalf of the Indians.* He was an approved Elder among his brethren, acted for many years as Clerk of the Meeting for Sufferings, and filled with ability many other offices in our religious Society. He died in 1809, at the advanced age of eighty-five years.† His close was peace. Trusting to the mercy of the Lord Jesus Christ, he looked forward with joy to an entrance into those mansions, of which the Lord had said there were many in his Father's kingdom. "What a blessed company," he exclaimed, "are already gone there before me! I feel the time of my own departure draw nigh." Then, full of love to his friends, and in unity of feeling with all who loved the Lord Jesus, he sweetly and in great humility put off the shackles of mortality.‡

* Memoirs, &c. of S. Fothergill, p. 162.   † Watson's Annals, p. 564.
‡ T. Scattergood and his Times.

JOHN PEMBERTON was a young man of an amiable and tender disposition, and one who early sought the Lord for his portion. Being of a delicate constitution, he was induced, in 1750, for the sake of his health, and also on account of business, to take a voyage to Europe. He had for companions, John Churchman and William Brown, who were both going on a religious visit to England. After their arrival, he accompanied John Churchman for a time, and while with him first spoke as a minister. He returned to Philadelphia in 1754, and soon after, with his two brothers and other Friends, formed the "Friendly Association," for preserving peace with the Indians. During the labours of this association, he had, on several occasions, some of the Indian chiefs for his guests. The three brothers appear to have possessed great influence with the natives. John Pemberton was also much engaged in endeavouring to suppress theatrical exhibitions in Philadelphia, and with a few others had interviews with the governor on the subject. As a gospel minister he visited Friends in most parts of North America, and in 1783, proceeded on a second voyage to Europe. This gospel mission occupied him about six years, during which time he visited most parts of Great Britain and Ireland. In 1794, he again crossed the Atlantic, on a religious visit to Holland and Germany, and after labouring about six months in those countries, he was taken ill at Pyrmont, in Germany, and died in about a month, being then in his sixty-eighth year. Throughout this trying season, he was preserved in great patience; his mind being anchored on Christ the rock of ages. A few hours before his close, he said triumphantly, "I am departing for heaven; from you all, to the kingdom of God and of Christ." His last words which could be distinctly understood were, "I can sing the songs of Zion, and of Israel." The Friends of Pyrmont, with whom he spent much time, have given this testimony respecting him as a minister. "It was his principal concern to turn people from darkness to light, and from the power of Satan to God; endeavouring to show that God has given a measure of his Spirit, light or grace, to all men, as a talent which he has placed in their hearts. His ministry was in plainness of speech, and attended with divine authority; for his words, whether they contained exhortation, comfort, or reproof, reached the inward states of those concerned.—The solemn reverence of his waiting spirit appeared so manifest in his countenance, that others who beheld him, were thereby invited to stillness; and such as had a desire of hearing words were taught by his example to turn their minds inward, to the measure of grace in themselves; showing that it is infinitely better to keep silent before the Lord, than to utter words that are not accompanied with the life-giving and baptizing power of the Spirit."* John Pemberton left a valuable journal of his life.

Rarely have three brothers been so eminent and useful in civil and religious society, as were Israel, James, and John Pemberton.†

MICHAEL LIGHTFOOT.

Michael Lightfoot emigrated from Ireland to Pennsylvania in 1712. He came forth as a minister about the forty-second year of his age, and travelled extensively in the exercise of his gift both in America and in Great Britain and Ireland. "His ministry was deep and penetrating, attended with the demonstration of the spirit and power; under the influence whereof he was frequently led to unfold the mysteries of the kingdom, and eminently qualified to set forth the excellencies of the gospel dispensation, with the benefit and advantage of inward and spiritual worship; recommending diligent attendance on the Spirit of Truth, for instruction and assistance therein. His delivery was clear, distinct, and intelligible, and in supplication humble and reverent."‡ He died in 1754, after a short illness, being in the seventy-first year of his age, and twenty-ninth of his ministry.

---

* Life of J. Pemberton.   † Scattergood and his Times.
‡ Penn. Mem. p. 149.

Susanna Morris.

The following is extracted from a testimony issued by Richland Monthly Meeting in Pennsylvania, concerning this devoted handmaiden of the Lord,—"She was the wife of Morris Morris, and was a member of our Monthly Meeting near fifteen years of the latter part of her time. Her memory still lives, and yields a precious savour to those who are measurably sharers of that divine love and life, with which she in an eminent degree was endowed. She was frequently made an instrument to others, by a living and powerful ministry; in which she faithfully laboured with unwearied diligence both at home and abroad, for the space of forty years and upwards, having travelled much in the service of the gospel, both in America and Europe, made three voyages over the seas to visit the Meetings of Friends in Great Britain, and twice through Ireland and Holland. In which voyages and travels the gracious arm of Divine Providence was evidently manifested, in preserving and supporting her through divers remarkable perils and dangers, which she ever reverently remembered and gratefully acknowledged.

"Her life and conversation were innocent and agreeable, seasoned with Christian gravity; she was a bright example of plainness, temperance, and self-denial; devoted to the service of truth, and the propagating of religion and piety amongst mankind. In which ardent love and zeal she continued, until it pleased her great Lord and Master, in his wisdom, to put a period to her pious labours, and to take her to himself, as a shock of corn gathered in due season." After a short illness of nine days, during which she lay in a calm and quiet state of mind, she died in the Fourth Month, 1755, in the seventy-third year of her age.

Abraham Farrington.

He was born in Bucks county, Pennsylvania, of parents in profession with Friends. In early life he was exposed to many temptations and snares. Referring to this period, he says, "Yet I took delight in my Bible, and believe the good hand was with me that inclined me thereto. Though I followed lying vanities

before his close, " is in Christ—soon, my little strength may be dissolved, and if it so happen, I shall be gathered to my everlasting rest." " My dependence," he said on another occasion, " is on the Lord Jesus, who I trust will forgive my sins, which is all I hope for." He died in the Tenth Month, 1772, being then in the fifty-third year of his age. The life of John Woolman presents a striking instance of self-denial and dedication of heart to the Lord. " He was a man endued with a large natural capacity" —" His ministry was sound, very deep and penetrating," and " often flowed through him with great sweetness and purity, as a refreshing stream to the weary travellers towards the city of God." His abundant labours in the cause of negro emancipation have already been referred to in the chapter relating to that subject, and need not be repeated here. His journal is one of deep instruction, and has had a wide circulation among members of our religious Society.

WOOLMAN HOUSE, NEAR MOUNT HOLLY, NEW JERSEY.

The above is a representation of " Woolman Place," situated a little out of the village of Mount Holly, on the road to Springfield. The house represented was built according to the particular directions of John Woolman, in which his wife and daughter resided after his decease.

John Woolman

DANIEL STANTON.

He was born in Philadelphia in the year 1708. He was left an orphan when but a child, and in early life passed through many hardships. Under the visitations of divine love, he was early given to see the exceeding sinfulness of sin, and to seek the paths of piety and virtue. Referring to this period of life, he remarks, " Great was the goodness of the Almighty, in giving me a sense of many things appertaining to godliness in the time of this tender visitation ; and I found by the Divine witness in myself, that if I would be a disciple of Christ, I must take up my cross daily to that which displeaseth God ; he being greatly to be feared and obeyed, and worthy of the deepest reverence that my soul, body, and strength, could ascribe to his all-powerful name." * The first meeting of Friends that Daniel Stanton attended was to him a memorable occasion. John Estaugh was present, under whose ministry he was greatly contrited and baptized : " it was," he says " a joyful day of good tidings to my poor seeking soul." He now delighted much in retirement, and often walked alone to pour out his heart before the All-seeing eye ; the language of his soul being, " Create in me a clean heart, O God, and renew a right spirit within me." He first spoke as a minister when about twenty years of age, and in his twenty-third year he went on a gospel mission to New England. From this period to the year of his decease in 1770, he was diligently engaged in this divine calling. He visited most of the provinces of North America, and some of them several times, and also the West India Islands, Great Britain, and Ireland. Within a short time previous to his decease he penned these concluding lines of his journal :—" In the course of my religious labours and travels a number have been reached by conviction, and several convinced of the blessed truth, as I have understood, some of whom remained serviceable among Friends, which I just mention as the Lord's blessing upon his own work ; who is worthy of all praise, glory, and honour for ever ! I have endeavoured to serve him in fear and trembling, and frequently have been bowed under a sense of my great

* Journal of D. Stanton, p. 4.

unworthiness; but great have been his mercy and power, extended towards me, a poor tribulated sufferer in spirit for the blessed seed's sake; magnified be his eminent name! He hath hitherto been my rock, fortress, and deliverer, and through his great kindness, I have a fixed hope in my mind of his salvation, through Christ Jesus, my dear Redeemer, whose glorious name let it be magnified and adored for evermore!"* He died at the house of Israel Pemberton, at Germantown, after a very short illness, in the Sixth Month, 1770, being the sixty-second year of his age.

JOHN CHURCHMAN.

He was born at Nottingham, in Chester county, Pennsylvania, in the year 1705. His parents, who were members of our religious Society, brought him up in the fear of the Lord; and at an early age he was sensible of the touches of a Saviour's love. When only eight years old, he says, " as I sat in a small meeting, the Lord, by the reaching of his heavenly love and goodness, overcame and tendered my heart—Oh! the stream of love which filled my heart with solid joy at that time, and lasted for many days, is beyond all expression."† The happy and circumspect state of mind into which he was brought, was, through unwatchfulness, lost before he was twelve years of age; and, for a long time after, in consequence of disobedience, he passed through much sorrow. About his twentieth year it pleased the Lord again to visit his soul in a powerful manner; " my heart," he writes, " was made exceedingly tender; I wept much, and an evidence was given me that the Lord heard my cry, and in mercy looked down on me from his holy habitation." Continuing to follow on to know the Lord he grew in religious experience, and at the age of twenty-five was appointed to the station of an elder; three years after which he came forth in the ministry of the gospel. In this service he travelled largely, both in his own land, and in Great Britain, Ireland, and the continent of Europe. He was an able minister of the word. " We think," write Friends of his Monthly Meeting, " it may be truly said, his doctrine dropped as the dew; being lively and edifying to the

* Journal of D. Stanton, p. 172.   † Journal of J. Churchman, p. 2.

honest-hearted, though close and searching to the careless professors." * The closing moments of this dedicated servant of the Lord were deeply instructive. " I feel," he said, " that which lives beyond death and the grave, which is now an inexpressible comfort to me." Divine refreshment and joy passed through him like a flowing stream. " I may tell you of it," he said, to those around him, " but you cannot feel it as I do." He died in the year 1775, aged nearly seventy years, and was buried at East Nottingham. He left a very interesting and instructive journal of his life, experiences, and labours.

J^{n̄}^o Churchman

SARAH MORRIS.

Sarah Morris was born in Philadelphia about the year 1703. Her parents were careful to train her up in the fear of the Lord and in an early acquaintance with the Holy Scriptures,—privileges to which she often referred in after-life, as having been blessed to herself, and to others also. " But what was far beyond all outward blessings," she remarks, " the Lord in his mercy was pleased to make very early impressions of religion on my soul, by his immediate grace and good Spirit." Having through illness been brought as on the verge of eternity, her mind was awfully impressed with the prospect. " O ! then," she said, " the emptiness and vanity of all the world ; the pleasures and friendships of it appeared in a clear and strong light ; nothing then but the hope of an entrance into the kingdom of heaven seemed of any value, and that hope the Lord was at that time pleased in some degree to afford me."† She first spoke as a minister in the forty-first year of her age, and, increasing in divine knowledge and experience, she became an able gospel minister, being sound in doctrine, pertinent in exhortation, clear and audible in utterance, and careful to adorn the doctrine she preached by a pious exemplary life and conversation. Her gospel labours were abundant in the colonies of North America, and

* Penn. Memorials, p. 302.   † Penn. Memorials, p. 313.

extended also to Friends in Great Britain. She died in much peace in the year 1775, and her funeral was attended by many of her fellow-citizens.

JOSEPH WHITE.

Joseph White was born at the Falls in Pennsylvania, in the year 1712. He early felt the extendings of heavenly regard ; and being faithful to the teachings of divine grace, he was preserved from the follies incident to youth. In the twentieth year of his age he was called to the ministry, in which service he was eminently gifted, and travelled extensively, both in America and in Europe. The latter moments of this devoted Christian were signally favoured, and he was given in no ordinary degree to have a foretaste of celestial joy. A few days before his close, which took place in 1777, he broke forth in these expressions : " The door is open ; I see an innumerable company of saints, of angels, and of the spirits of just men, and long to be unembodied to be with them, but not my will, but Thy will be done, O Lord ! I cannot utter, nor my tongue express, what I feel of that light, life, and love that attends me, which the world cannot give, neither can it take away. My sins are washed away by the blood of the Lamb that was slain from the foundation of the world ; all rags and filthiness are taken away, and in room thereof love and good-will for all mankind. I am near to enter that harmony with Moses and the Lamb, where they cry holy ! holy ! holy ! I cannot express the joy I feel. My heart (if it were possible) would break for joy. If any inquire after me, after my end, let them know all is well with me. I have never seen my end till now, and now I see it is near, and the holy angels enclose me around, waiting to receive me."

SUSANNAH LIGHTFOOT.

She was a native of Ireland, having been born at Grange in the year 1720. When she was young her father died in very low circumstances, and she was obliged to follow the humble occupation of a domestic servant. But though poor as to the things of this life, the Lord enriched her with the treasures of his heavenly kingdom, and in the seventeenth year of her age dignified her with a gift in the ministry. In the same year she went on a religious visit to Friends in America, being, it is believed, the youngest minister in our religious Society who crossed the Atlantic on a gospel mission. In 1740, she visited England and Wales, and twenty years after proceeded on a second visit to America, in which she was engaged for about two years. In 1764, she removed with her husband Thomas Lightfoot, from Ireland, and settled within the compass of Uwchlan Monthly Meeting in Pennsylvania. Before the breaking out of the American war, she had in a very awful manner to speak of an impending calamity, which would shake the foundations of the formal professors in our Society, "Having passed through the deep waters of affliction herself, her eye was not unused to drop a tear for and with others in distress, either in body or mind, and she rejoiced in comforting and doing them good. She was a living and powerful minister of the Word, careful not to break silence in meetings, until favoured with a fresh anointing from the Holy One ; whereby she was preserved clear in her openings, awful and weighty in prayer, her voice being solemn and awakening under the baptizing power of truth."* Her expressions, during a lingering illness which preceded her dissolution in 1781, were remarkably instructive and weighty, and an unclouded prospect of an entrance into the heavenly kingdom was vouchsafed to her. " One evening, after a solemn silence, she broke forth in a sweet melody, saying, 'I have had a prospect this evening, of joining the heavenly host, in singing praises to Zion's King : for which favour, my soul, and all that is sensible within me, magnifies that arm which hath been with me from my infant days, and cast up a way where there was no way, both by sea and land.' On another occasion she said, 'Oh, dearest Lord ! take me to Thyself, even into Thy heavenly kingdom ; for I long to be with Thee there.' "†

THOMAS ROSS

Thomas Ross was a native of Ireland. His parents, who were Episcopalians, and occupied a respectable position in life, brought

---

* Penn. Memorials, p. 375.   † Ibid. p. 379.

him up with much care in the principles of their religion. About
the twentieth year of his age he emigrated to Pennsylvania, where
he became convinced of the principles of Friends, and was received
into membership by Buckingham Monthly Meeting. He soon
afterwards came forth in the ministry, in which he laboured in
several provinces of North America, and also in Great Britain.
In 1786, whilst on a visit to England, he was taken ill at York,
and died in a few days, being then in the seventy-eighth year of
his age. His ministry, it is recorded, "was attended with living
virtue and deep instruction ; not in the words which man's
wisdom teacheth, but in godly simplicity, and with a zeal according to true knowledge." During his illness he was greatly
favoured with the divine presence, his mind was remarkably filled
with love to his brethren, and he was much impressed with the
preciousness of true Christian unity : " O ! the harmony there is
in the Lord's family !" he said, " Ephraim shall not envy Judah,
nor Judah vex Ephraim ; nothing shall hurt or destroy in all thy
holy mountain." On another occasion he said, " Dear friends,
what a people should we be, did we dig deep enough ; our lights
would shine before men ; and we should be as the salt of the earth."
Shortly before his close he broke forth in these words, " O joy !
joy ! joy !" again, " O death ! where is thy sting ? O Grave !
where is thy victory ? the sting of death is sin : I see no cloud
in my way, I die in peace with all men."*

Isaac Zane.

He was born in New Jersey, in 1710, and about his fourteenth
year removed to Philadelphia. Though not a minister, he was
much concerned for the advancement of truth, and, both by
example and precept, adorned the doctrine of God his Saviour.
He manifested great regard for the Indians, and endeavoured in
various ways to promote their temporal and eternal interests. As
one of the members of the " Friendly Association" for regaining
peace with the Indians, he was particularly active. He died in
1794, in the eighty-fourth year of his age. Divine support and

* Penn. Memorials, p. 20.

consolation were richly vouchsafed to this faithful servant in his dying moments,. " I have seen," said he, " the arms of everlasting mercy open to receive me, and have a full assurance, that I shall be permitted to join the heavenly host, in singing hallelujah, and enabled with the seraphims to say, ' Holy, holy is the Lord of Hosts; the whole earth is full of his glory.' "*

SAMUEL EMLEN.

Samuel Emlen was born in Philadelphia in the Fourth Month, 1730. His parents who were members of our religious Society were very watchful over him, and in his tender years, endeavoured to inculcate the necessity of obedience to the restraints and convictions of the Spirit of Truth. In very early life, he experienced the attractions of heavenly love, out of the vanities of time, into the paths of peace, and communion with God. His natural endowments were considerable, and he evinced great aptitude for the acquisition of learning. He spoke several of the European languages, and was also acquainted with Latin and Greek. His apprenticeship was passed in the counting-house of James Pemberton, where he acquired a knowledge of mercantile business, in which, however, he never embarked, being possessed of a competent patrimonial estate. His mind was early devoted to the cause of Truth, and the welfare of our Zion occupied his deep consideration. The ministry of Samuel Fothergill, it appears, was much blessed to him : in after life he was much attached to this Friend, and held frequent correspondence with him. Soon after reaching manhood, he travelled as companion with Michael Lightfoot, on a religious visit to some of the southern provinces, and in 1756, with Abraham Farrington, to the meetings of Friends in Great Britain and Ireland. It was during the latter visit that he first spoke as a minister. Possessed of great powers of mind, and a peculiar readiness of expression, he became, under the baptizing power of Truth, an able and a valiant minister of Christ. In this capacity, he travelled much on the American continent, and visited his brethren in Great Britain no

* Penn. Mem. and Scattergood and his Times.

less than six times. He also visited once the island of Barbadoes, and travelled extensively in Ireland, and on the continent of Europe. On one occasion, during his gospel labours, he addressed a learned audience in Latin, and whilst in Europe his French and German were frequently called into exercise. His last visit to England was in the year 1796, and after his return home in the following year his health became much impaired. His constitution was naturally weak and infirm, and from this period he gradually declined. His mental energy, however, seemed in no way to slacken, and his labours in the work of his Divine Master, were unabated. He had, he said, the assurance, that he must shortly put off this earthly tabernacle, and he desired to be found at his post of duty, with his loins girded, and his light burning.* In the summer of 1799, he had a slight attack of paralysis. In the Twelfth Month following, whilst at his own meeting in Philadelphia, and towards the conclusion of an earnest and fervent gospel exhortation, he was taken suddenly very ill. Leaning for support on the rail of the gallery, he pathetically uttered these lines of Addison :—

> " My life, if thou preservest my life,
>   Thy sacrifice shall be ;
> And death, if death should be my doom,
>   Shall join my soul to thee."

On the following day, he was sufficiently recovered to attend the meeting of ministers and elders, and the day after, his usual week-day meeting. At the latter, he was enabled, in the authority and power of the gospel, to set forth the excellency of that faith which is the saints' victory, and which overcometh the world. This was the last occasion on which he publicly advocated the cause of his Divine Master. His weakness rapidly increased, and he was subjected to much bodily suffering ; but under all he was preserved in calmness and cheerfulness of mind. The consolations of that religion which, for the space of more than forty years, this devoted Friend had preached to others, were, in this trying season, his own rich experience ; and in melodious

* Scattergood and his Times.

tones, he uttered forth the goodness and faithfulness of his God. "Their sins and their iniquities will I remember no more." "I will cast all their sins behind my back." "Ye shall have a song, as in the night when a holy solemnity is kept; and gladness of heart, as when one goeth with a pipe to come into the mountain of the Lord." "Oh, the tears of holy joy, which flow down my cheeks! Sing praises, high praises, to my God! I feel nothing in my way. Although my conduct through life has not been in every respect as guarded as it might have been, yet the main bent of my mind has been to serve thee, O God, who art glorious in holiness and fearful in praises! I am sure I have loved godliness and hated iniquity." A few hours before his close, he said, "All I want is heaven. Lord, receive my spirit." "My pain is great. My God, grant me patience, humble, depending patience." "Call upon me in the day of trouble: I will deliver thee, and thou shalt glorify me." "Oh how precious a thing it is, to feel the Spirit itself bearing witness with our spirits, that we are his!" "Oh! this soul is an awful thing! I feel it so. You that hear me, mind, it is an awful thing to die: the invisible world, how awful!" Believing that the time of his departure was near, he desired not to be disturbed, except at his own request, "that my mind may not be diverted — that my whole mind may be centred in aspirations to the throne of Grace." At three o'clock in the morning, he enquired the hour, and then said, "The conflict will be over before five." He soon added, "Almighty Father, come quickly, if it be thy holy will, and receive my spirit." After lying for some time in great quietness, he was heard in a faint whisper to say, "I thought I was gone." "Christ Jesus, receive my spirit." He expired at half-past four in the morning, on the 30th of Twelfth Month, 1799, aged about seventy years.* No journal of this Friend, remarkable as a man and a minister, has ever been published.

Saml Emlen

---

* Scattergood and his Times. Memoirs of S. Fothergill, p. 266.

WILLIAM SAVERY.

He was born in Philadelphia, in 1750, and was brought up in the principles of our religious Society. His natural disposition was lively and social. In early life he associated with the votaries of folly and vanity, and, by degrees, became much estranged from the voice of the Heavenly Shepherd. Whilst he was thus turning aside from the paths of purity and peace, it pleased the Most High, through the powerful convictions of his Holy Spirit, to arrest the downward progress of his erring child. This was about the twenty-eighth year of his age, and having felt the terrors of the Lord for sin, he was enabled to enter into covenant with a covenant-keeping God. He first spoke as a minister in the year following; " and, dwelling inward with those gifts and qualifications with which he was favoured, he became an able advocate for the cause in which he had embarked; and by faithful attention thereto, his labours were blessed to the benefit of numbers, especially amongst the youth, to many of whom he was an eminent instrument of good." * He travelled much in the service of the gospel in America, and also, from 1796, to 1798, in Great Britain and Ireland, and on the continent of Europe. It pleased the Lord to remove this devoted Friend from time to eternity, in the meridian of his day. He died in 1804, at the age of fifty-four years, leaving an interesting narrative of his spiritual life and labours. With a firm and unshaken belief in the divinity of our Lord and Saviour Jesus Christ, in his propitiatory sacrifice for the sins of the world, and in all his glorious offices for the salvation of mankind: he was often fervently engaged in setting forth these blessed gospel doctrines, and enforcing them on his hearers; and in the solemn moments of disease and death, his reverent dependence and hope in his Saviour did not fail, but proved as an anchor to his soul. A short time before his death, under the feeling of heavenly peace and joy, he exclaimed, " Glory to God !" and continued in great

* Testimony of Friends of Philadelphia.

composure of mind, until he calmly resigned his spirit into the hands of Him who gave it. *

W^m — Savery

NICHOLAS WALN.

Nicholas Waln was the son of Nicholas and Mary Waln, of Fairhill, a few miles from Philadelphia, and was born in 1742. Being deprived of his father's care when about eight years of age, he was brought up with much tenderness by his affectionate mother, and placed at the school under the management of Friends, founded under the charter of William Penn. Here he not only acquired a good classical education, but, what was far more important, was brought up in the nurture and admonition of the Lord, and in a love for those principles which distinguish Friends from others of the Christian name. On leaving this establishment, and whilst but a lad, he commenced the study of the law, devoting also a part of his time to the German language. His habits, at this early period of life, were marked by great industry, and although he was naturally vivacious and witty, and fond of gaiety and merriment, he suffered nothing to interfere with his studies. In his profession he made great progress, and while yet a minor, was admitted to practice in the courts. During one term in 1763, he was employed on no less than eight cases, though not then twenty-one years of age. With a view to enlarge his knowledge of the law, he embarked for London, and entered himself there as a student in the Temple. During a year spent in London, he was much preserved from the dissipations of a great city, and it appears also to have been a time of divine visitation to his soul, in which he was enabled to enter into covenant with his God, and to resolve on a life of holy dedication. On returning to Philadelphia he followed his profession with great success, and, in addition to his city business, had an extensive and lucrative

---

* Journal, &c., of William Savery, p. 316.

practice in the county courts.   He was now making rapid strides
to wealth ; yet during this time of prosperity and legal fame, he
was again and again powerfully visited from on high, and called
to a closer walk with God.   About the twenty-ninth year of his
age, and one year after his marriage, He, who is " a consuming
fire," wrought so powerfully on his mind that he became entirely
indisposed for business, or for seeing or conversing with persons
respecting it.   It was at this period, that in a youth's meeting
for worship he was engaged in a very remarkable manner in supplication ; which circumstance, heightened by his public reputation, deeply affected most present.   The prayer seems to have
alluded to his own state of mind, being nearly as follows:—

" Oh Lord God ! arise, and let thine enemies be scattered !
Baptize me—dip me yet deeper in Jordan.   Wash me in the
laver of regeneration.   Thou hast done much for me, and hast a
right to expect much ; therefore, in the presence of this congregation, I resign myself and all that I have, to thee, oh Lord !—
it is thine ! And I pray thee, oh Lord, to give me grace to enable
me to continue firm in this resolution ! Wherever thou leadest
me, oh Lord ! I will follow thee ; if through persecution, or
even to martyrdom.   If my life is required, I will freely sacrifice
it.—Now I know that my Redeemer liveth, and the mountains of
difficulty are removed.   Hallelujah ! Teach me to despise the
shame, and the opinions of the people of the world. Thou knowest,
oh Lord ! my deep baptisms.   I acknowledge my manifold sins
and transgressions.   I know my unworthiness of the many
favours I have received ; and I thank thee, oh Father ! that
thou hast hid thy mysteries from the wise and prudent, and
revealed them to babes and sucklings.   Amen."

He now gave up his practice as a lawyer, and for several
years led a very retired life.   He was, however, diligent in his
attendance of meetings ; in which his deportment was solid and
reverential.   During this period, his communications as a minister
were but infrequent and short, though weighty.   His religious
services were pretty much confined to Philadelphia, until the
year 1783, when he proceeded on a gospel visit to Friends in
England.   In 1796, he crossed the Atlantic on a similar service

to Ireland. The character of the gift in the ministry of this extraordinary man, seems to have been different at different periods of his life. From 1780 to 1796, he was often largely engaged on doctrinal subjects, and many who were not in membership with Friends were drawn to hear him. Replete with gospel truths, and delivered in strains of persuasive eloquence and christian fervour, his ministry made a deep and lasting impression on his hearers. From about 1796, his communications were brief but weighty, and addressed more particularly to individual states. An instance of the powerful and heart-tendering character of his ministry occurred at a meeting held at Abington. With a heart overflowing with gospel love, he preached for about an hour in a striking, persuasive manner ; after which, on the bended knee, he lifted up the voice of solemn prayer and praise to the Father of all our mercies. So baptizing was the season, and so great the solemnity, that when Friends in the gallery shook hands to separate, no one would rise ! After a pause, Nicholas Waln rose and said, " Under the solemn covering we are favoured with, perhaps Friends had better separate." A few young men near the door, rose ; but observing no one to follow them, they resumed their seats, and the meeting continued for a time in sweet and reverential silence. Richard Jordan then rose, and broke forth with the song of triumph which greeted the Saviour's entrance into Jerusalem :—" Hosannah ! Blessed is he that cometh in the name of the Lord ;"—adding a few words on the blessedness of such seasons of divine favour. The meeting soon after broke up. But solemnity and silence still prevailed, as Friend separated from Friend. Many such descriptions of his meetings, it is said, might be given. Though thus divinely favoured and acceptable to his brethren, Nicholas Waln was remarkable for his humility. "As a great man, as a wise man, as a learned man, and as a rich man," said one who knew him well, " I know of none possessed of as much childlike humility and simplicity as Nicholas Waln."

For some years he acted as clerk to the Yearly Meeting and the Meeting for Sufferings, and his services in the discipline of the church were highly appreciated. In 1812, his health became much enfeebled, but he continued to attend meetings for worship until near his end. In the summer of 1813, his remaining strength declined rapidly. Towards the close he passed through a season of deep conflict of mind, wherein his faith in the all-sufficient help of God his Saviour was closely proved. He died in the Ninth Month, 1813, aged seventy-one years; his last words, uttered with much emphasis, being, " To die is gain."*

THOMAS SCATTERGOOD.

He was born at Burlington in New Jersey, in 1748, of parents who were members of our religious Society. His father died whilst he was young, and he was placed as an apprentice in Philadelphia: when, by following his own corrupt inclinations, he was led to deviate from the paths of true peace. He was, however, richly visited by divine grace, brought under a deep sense of his estrangement from God, and made willing to bear the yoke and cross of Christ his Saviour. For several years he was under a sense of a call to the ministry, and by not yielding to the work was brought into deep and distressing conflicts of mind. About the thirty-fourth year of his age he gave up to the requirement, by the expression, at times, of a few sentences only. But keeping faithful to his Divine Master's leadings, he grew in his gift, and became prepared for extensive service in the church. In this work he visited most of the States of North America, and was also occupied for about seven years among Friends of Great Britain and Ireland. In a testimony given forth by his Monthly Meeting in Philadelphia respecting him, his services as a minister are thus alluded to: " He was much devoted to the promotion of the cause of truth and righteousness, and through the efficacy of heavenly love, was at times enabled to say, it was more to him than his necessary food; but, being sensible of his various infirmities, he was frequent in inward retirement, and hence his mind became strengthened in watchfulness against those things which interrupt the aspiration of the soul towards the Fountain of everlasting life. Being thereby made quick in the fear of the Lord, he increased in solid experience, and gradually advanced in the way and work of salvation. His example in silent waiting

* Scattergood and his Times.

in our religious meetings was instructive, and in the exercise of his gift it was evident that he had been careful to feel the putting forth of the Divine hand, being at times eminently endued with a clear discernment of the states of meetings and individuals, and, in the power of the gospel, was made instrumental to baptize many into deep contrition, through a heartfelt sense of their own state. Thus, as a scribe well instructed unto the kingdom, he brought forth out of the treasury things new and old, to the edification of the body, and to the praise of its ever adorable Head."* He died in the year 1814, in the sixty-sixth year of his age, in a peaceful assurance of an entrance into the kingdom of everlasting rest.†

T Scattergood

REBECCA JONES.

She was born in Philadelphia in the year 1739. Her father was a mariner, and died while absent from home during her childhood. " My mother," she observes, " by hard labour, keeping a school, brought us up reputably, gave us sufficient learning, and educated us in the way of the Church of England." At a very early age she had a strong inclination to attend the meetings of Friends, " though I knew not," she says, " why I went, for I liked not their way of preaching, but was always best pleased with silent meetings ;" and she further remarks on reference to this period, " I loved even the sight of an honest Friend." About the sixteenth year of her age, she was brought under deep religious convictions, and opened her mind to Catherine Peyton, then on a visit to America, who was made an instrument of good to her seeking soul. She first spoke as a minister when about nineteen, and as such she travelled much in her own land, and also in Great Britain and Ireland. She died in 1817, at the age of seventy-eight years ; a minister fifty-nine years. In view of the solemn prospect of her final change, she said a few hours before her close, " Not by works of righteousness which I have done, but according

* Testimony of the Northern District Monthly Meeting of Philadelphia.
† Memoirs of Thomas Scattergood.

to His mercy he saveth us, by the washing of regeneration, and the renewing of the Holy Ghost! After having done all, we are but unprofitable servants."* Interesting memoirs of the life of this experienced and dignified minister have been recently published, and the volume, with many others of a similar kind, will well repay a serious perusal.

George Dillwyn.

George Dillwyn was born in Philadelphia in the year 1738, of parents who were members of our religious Society. In early life he appears to have had a strong inclination to the vanities of dress and youthful amusements. But his mind was often brought under the contriting humbling power of truth, and outward afflictions tended to his further refinement. About the twenty-eighth year of his age he came forth as a minister. His character and labours in this capacity are thus referred to by his Monthly Meeting:— "Endowed with a comprehensive and penetrating mind, which was sanctified by the great Head of the church, he was made eminently useful in promulgating the glad tidings of the gospel of peace on this continent; and being earnestly engaged to keep his eye single to the pointings of his Divine Master, who had called him to the work, he felt drawn to pay a religious visit to parts of Great Britain, Ireland, Holland, Germany, and the south of France." This visit to Europe occupied him from the year 1784 to 1791; and in 1793, under a feeling of religious duty, he removed with his wife to reside in England, but returned to Burlington in 1802. In his private life he was a bright example; daily evincing a concern to live near the spring of divine grace; and in social intercourse with his friends, he was remarkable for the sweetness of his spirit and conversation. He lived to the advanced age of eighty-two years, his declining ones being passed in much retirement. For some months previous to his decease, he endured much bodily suffering, but through all he was sweetly and divinely supported. "I find," he said, "there is a comfort over which disease has no power." In a full persuasion that there was a mansion prepared for him in his Heavenly Father's house,

* Memorials of Rebecca Jones, p. 355.

he died in the Sixth Month, 1820. Some of the aphorisms of this dear Friend have been published, but no memoirs of his remarkable services as a minister of the gospel.

The present chapter concludes a history of the Yearly Meeting of Friends in Pennsylvania and the Jerseys, from its origin in 1681, down to the year 1820. That the Society of Friends, as a Christian community, was raised up in the counsels of divine wisdom, but few among us will be disposed to question. It has pleased the Most High to call them to uphold many important testimonies to the purity of Divine truth; in the faithful maintenance of which, they have become prominently distinguished among others of the Christian name. But though thus distinguished, they have had no new doctrines to teach; their principles, they conscientiously believe are, all of them, founded on the declarations of Holy Writ, as being in entire accordance with those which were preached and enforced by our Holy Redeemer and his apostles, and practised in the primitive ages of Christianity. It has not been, then, the enunciation of new views which has caused them to differ from other religious professors, but simply their dissent from those practices in the Church, which, as they conceive, originated in the apostacy, and were but partially renounced under the Reformation.

In the history of this people, many circumstances have tended, in no small degree, to disseminate their views on some important points of Christian doctrine. Thus in Great Britain and Ireland, their conscientious, firm, and passive opposition, under aggravated sufferings, to the enforcement of oaths, and to the payment of tithes, caused their testimony against these things, as anti-christian impositions, to be known throughout the land; whilst the barbarities which they endured in Puritan New England, proclaimed throughout Christendom their principles in relation to worship, and the freedom of gospel ministry. But in no country did circumstances tend so conspicuously to exhibit the Christian principles of Friends as in the province of Pennsylvania, where, whilst the government was under their control, the efficacy and excellency of the gospel principles of peace were practically exemplified to a slowly believing and distrustful world. It was here that, by the original constitution, the inalienable rights of conscience were scrupulously respected, and protected by law ; and as a consequence, all ecclesiastical domination and priestly assumption were utterly condemned. It was here that the just rights of the aboriginal though uncivilized inhabitants of the land were, on Christian grounds, fully recognized by William Penn. Here also it was that the testimony of Friends against the enslavement of their fellow-men took root and flourished ; setting a noble example, and calling up, it is not too much to say, the anti-slavery movements of the past and the present age. Had nothing further been effected through the instrumentality of the Society of Friends, than the promulgation and faithful maintenance of these Christian views, they would suffice to show that its existence as a distinct religious community has not been in vain. To what extent our christian principles, in their practical application to man, in his corporate as well as his individual capacity, as set forth in the present volume, have influenced, and may yet influence mankind, is beyond our power to determine. Evidences, however, are not wanting to show, that already their effect has been great and beneficial ; the sense of which should incite us to greater zeal, consistency, and faithfulness.

We close this volume in the language of Philadelphia Yearly Meeting : " As a religious Society, we have often had undoubted persuasion, that, in unerring wisdom, we have been raised up and called to bear testimony to the purity and excellency of the Gospel dispensation ; not for any inherent worth or righteousness in us, but that, through faithful dedication manifest in our humble walking, others may come more availingly to see the emptiness of shadows and ceremonies, and be made partakers of that substantial bread which nourisheth the soul unto eternal life. How awful then is our situation ; and how obligatory our duty ! that, loving the Lord above all, we may have light upon our path, and discern the dangers that are on the right hand, and on the left ; thus, being kept by his power through faith, we may be built up a spiritual house, an holy priesthood, a peculiar people."*

* Epistle to London Yearly Meeting, 1816.

LONDON :
RICHARD BARRETT, PRINTER, 13, MARK LANE.

Religion in America
Series II

An Arno Press Collection

Adler, Felix. **Creed and Deed:** A Series of Discourses. New York, 1877.

Alexander, Archibald. **Evidences of the Authenticity, Inspiration, and Canonical Authority of the Holy Scriptures.** Philadelphia, 1836.

Allen, Joseph Henry. **Our Liberal Movement in Theology:** Chiefly as Shown in Recollections of the History of Unitarianism in New England. 3rd edition. Boston, 1892.

American Temperance Society. **Permanent Temperance Documents of the American Temperance Society.** Boston, 1835.

American Tract Society. **The American Tract Society Documents,** 1824-1925. New York, 1972.

Bacon, Leonard. **The Genesis of the New England Churches.** New York, 1874.

Bartlett, S[amuel] C. **Historical Sketches of the Missions of the American Board.** New York, 1972.

Beecher, Lyman. **Lyman Beecher and the Reform of Society:** Four Sermons, 1804-1828. New York, 1972.

[Bishop, Isabella Lucy Bird.] **The Aspects of Religion in the United States of America.** London, 1859.

Bowden, James. **The History of the Society of Friends in America.** London, 1850, 1854. Two volumes in one.

Briggs, Charles Augustus. **Inaugural Address and Defense,** 1891-1893. New York, 1972.

Colwell, Stephen. **The Position of Christianity in the United States,** in Its Relations with Our Political Institutions, and Specially with Reference to Religious Instruction in the Public Schools. Philadelphia, 1854.

Dalcho, Frederick. **An Historical Account of the Protestant Episcopal Church, in South-Carolina,** from the First Settlement of the Province, to the War of the Revolution. Charleston, 1820.

Elliott, Walter. **The Life of Father Hecker.** New York, 1891.

Gibbons, James Cardinal. **A Retrospect of Fifty Years.** Baltimore, 1916. Two volumes in one.

Hammond, L[ily] H[ardy]. **Race and the South:** Two Studies, 1914-1922. New York, 1972.

Hayden, A[mos] S. **Early History of the Disciples in the Western Reserve, Ohio;** With Biographical Sketches of the Principal Agents in their Religious Movement. Cincinnati, 1875.

Hinke, William J., editor. **Life and Letters of the Rev. John Philip Boehm:** Founder of the Reformed Church in Pennsylvania, 1683-1749. Philadelphia, 1916.

Hopkins, Samuel. **A Treatise on the Millennium.** Boston, 1793.

Kallen, Horace M. **Judaism at Bay:** Essays Toward the Adjustment of Judaism to Modernity. New York, 1932.

Kreider, Harry Julius. **Lutheranism in Colonial New York.** New York, 1942.

Loughborough, J. N. **The Great Second Advent Movement:** Its Rise and Progress. Washington, 1905.

M'Clure, David and Elijah Parish. **Memoirs of the Rev. Eleazar Wheelock, D.D.** Newburyport, 1811.

McKinney, Richard I. **Religion in Higher Education Among Negroes.** New Haven, 1945.

Mayhew, Jonathan. **Observations on the Charter and Conduct of the Society for the Propagation of the Gospel in Foreign Parts;** Designed to Shew Their Non-conformity to Each Other. Boston, 1763.

Mott, John R. **The Evangelization of the World in this Generation.** New York, 1900.

Payne, Bishop Daniel A. **Sermons and Addresses,** 1853-1891. New York, 1972.

Phillips, C[harles] H. **The History of the Colored Methodist Episcopal Church in America:** Comprising Its Organization, Subsequent Development, and Present Status. Jackson, Tenn., 1898.

Reverend Elhanan Winchester: Biography and Letters. New York, 1972.

Riggs, Stephen R. **Tah-Koo Wah-Kan; Or, the Gospel Among the Dakotas.** Boston, 1869.

Rogers, Elder John. **The Biography of Eld. Barton Warren Stone, Written by Himself:** With Additions and Reflections. Cincinnati, 1847.

Booth-Tucker, Frederick. **The Salvation Army in America:** Selected Reports, 1899-1903. New York, 1972.

Satolli, Francis Archbishop. **Loyalty to Church and State.** Baltimore, 1895.

Schaff, Philip. **Church and State in the United States** or the American Idea of Religious Liberty and its Practical Effects with Official Documents. New York and London, 1888. (Reprinted from *Papers of the American Historical Association,* Vol. II, No. 4.)

Smith, Horace Wemyss. **Life and Correspondence of the Rev. William Smith, D.D.** Philadelphia, 1879, 1880. Two volumes in one.

Spalding, M[artin] J. **Sketches of the Early Catholic Missions of Kentucky;** From Their Commencement in 1787 to the Jubilee of 1826-7. Louisville, 1844.

Steiner, Bernard C., editor. **Rev. Thomas Bray:** His Life and Selected Works Relating to Maryland. Baltimore, 1901. (Reprinted from *Maryland Historical Society Fund Publication,* No. 37.)

To Win the West: Missionary Viewpoints, 1814-1815. New York, 1972.

Wayland, Francis and H. L. Wayland. **A Memoir of the Life and Labors of Francis Wayland, D.D., LL.D.** New York, 1867. Two volumes in one.

Willard, Frances E. **Woman and Temperance:** Or, the Work and Workers of the Woman's Christian Temperance Union. Hartford, 1883.